# Islamic Perspectives on God and (Other) Monotheism(s)



*Edited by*

Wahid M. Amin
Aaron W. Hughes
Sajjad H. Rizvi

AMI PRESS

AMI Press is a deparment of the Al-Mahdi Institute. It furthers the Institute's objective of excellence in research, scholarship and education by publishing worldwide.

Published in the United Kingdom by AMI Press, 60 Weoley Park Road, Selly Oak, Birmingham, B29 6RB.



ISBN 978-1-915550-05-7 (hardback)
ISBN 978-1-915550-06-4 (paperback)



A catalogue record for this book is available from the British Library.

Typesetting and design by Wahid M. Amin

## Table of Contents


List of Contributors i
Introduction 1

**Part 1: Contesting Monotheisms: A Judeo-Christian-Muslim Encounter**

1. Religious Others and the Shaping of Orthodoxy in the Early Islamic Period 19
   *Aaron W. Hughes*

2. The Influence of Christian Theology on the Development of *Tawḥīd* in Early *Kalām* 38
   *Romain Louge*

3. On Religion: Ṣadrian Metaphysics as 'Islam's Argument' (*Ḥujjat al-Islām*) against Henry Martyn 60
   *Sajjad H. Rizvi*

**Part 2: Sunnī Theological Perspectives on God and Monotheism**

4. The *Tawḥīd*s of Ibn Taymiyya 89
   *Jon Hoover*

5. The Qurʾanic Argument for Monotheism: Controversies between al-Taftāzānī (d. 792/1390) and His Contemporaries 111
   *Syamsuddin Arif*

**Part 3: Shīʿī Theological Perspectives on God and Monotheism**

6. Visions of *Tawḥīd*: Reconciling a Statement in the Twenty-Eighth Supplication of *al-Ṣaḥīfa al-Sajjādiyya* 137
   *Zoheir Esmail*

7. Apophatic *Tawḥīd*: A Philosophical Account of Shīʿī Ismāʿīlī Theology 154
   *Khalil Andani*

**Part 4: Philosophical Perspectives on God and Monotheism**

8. Mullā Ṣadrā and His Commentators on Ibn Kammūna's Argument Against Divine Unity 193
   *Wahid M. Amin*

9. Logico-linguistic Analysis of the *Kalimat al-Tawḥīd*: al-Rāzī vs al-Kūrānī 245
   *Yusuf Daşdemir*

**Part 5: Contemporary Perspectives on God and Monotheism**

10. Divine Names for Interreligious Engagement 275
    *Celene Ibrahim*

11. God as a Moral Agent: An Inquiry into the Nature of Divine Agency 297
    *Abolghasem Fanaei*

12. Friendly (A)theism: A Philosophical-Theological Defence 327
    *S. Yaser Mirdamadi*

13. Towards a Grammatical Approach to Monotheism: Unpacking Ṭabāṭabā'ī's Theological Perspective 355
    *Javad Taheri*

## List of Contributors

**Wahid M. Amin** is Lecturer in Islamic Philosophy at the Al-Mahdi Institute and Head of Publishing for AMI Press. He is an Associate Lecturer at the University of Birmingham and has held visiting lectureships at the University of Oxford. He holds a BSc (hons) degree in Physics from Imperial College, London and obtained his Masters and DPhil degrees from the University of Oxford specialising in Islamic philosophy.

**Khalil Andani** serves as an Assistant Professor of Religion at Augustana College. He holds a Ph.D. and MA in Islamic Studies and a Master of Theological Studies (MTS) from Harvard University. His scholarship focuses on Quranic studies, Islamic intellectual history, Sufism, Ismailism, and the Philosophy of Religion. Khalil's current book project is an analytical study of revelation in early and classical Islam. His most recent publications appear in Zygon, the European Journal of Analytic Philosophy and Global Intellectual History.

**Syamsuddin Arif** is Associate Professor at Darussalam University (UNIDA) Gontor Ponorogo Indonesia. He received his M.A. (1999) and Ph.D. (2004) from the International Institute of Islamic Thought and Civilization (ISTAC) Kuala Lumpur. His research focuses on Islamic philosophy and theology in both historical and contemporary settings. Prior to joining Gontor Darussalam University, he was Assistant Professor at the International Islamic University Malaysia (2007–2012) and later served as Associate Professor at the UTM Center for Advanced Studies on Islam, Science and Civilisation (2012–2015). He was Executive Director of INSISTS Jakarta from 2015 to 2017 and held a Visiting Research Fellowship at the Oxford Centre for Islamic Studies, UK from 2017 to 2018.

**Yusuf Daşdemir** is a research fellow at the University of Jyväskylä, Finland. He completed his Ph.D. (2016) on Avicenna's modal logic in Turkey. In addition to several articles, he has authored a book on Avicenna's modal logic (in Turkish) and co-edited a volume on Ottoman tradition of logic and dialectics. He has also translated into Turkish Khaled El-Rouayheb's *The Development of Arabic Logic 1200-1800*. His current studies focus on Arabic logic, philosophical theology, Sufism, and Ottoman philosophy and logic.

**Zoheir Ali Esmail** began his Islamic education studying Arabic at the University of Damascus while studying introductory hawza studies. He then continued his education in London and also gained an MA in the Islamic sciences from Middlesex University. He then moved to Iran to pursue further studies where he obtained an MA in Islamic Mysticism from the hawza of Imam al-Khumayni in Qom. He was awarded a doctorate in Islamic philosophy from the University of Exeter in 2016.

**Abolghasem Fanaei** is Professor of Islamic Legal Theory at Al-Mahdi Institute in Birmingham, UK and head of the Department of Philosophy at Mofid University in Qom, Iran. He specialises in moral philosophy, epistemology, philosophy of law, Qur'ānic Hermeneutics and Islamic legal theory. He has authored several books and articles on the relationship between religion and morality, religious epistemology, foundations of Islamic Jurisprudence, Islamic theology, religion and environmental ethics, and sacred spirituality.

**Jon Hoover** is Associate Professor of Islamic Studies at the University of Nottingham. He specialises in Islamic intellectual history, medieval Islamic theology and philosophy, Christian–Muslim relations, and the thought of Ibn Taymiyya. He is the author of *Ibn Taymiyya's Theodicy of Perpetual Optimism*, and numerous articles and book chapters on Ibn Taymiyya's theology and ethics.

**Aaron W. Hughes** is the Dean's Professor of the Humanities and the Philip S. Bernstein Professor of Religious Studies at the University of Rochester. He has held visiting positions at the Hebrew University of Jerusalem, McMaster University, the University of Oxford, and the Aga Khan University. His research has been supported by the Social Sciences Research Council of Canada (SSHRC), the Lady Davis Fellowship Trust (Jerusalem), the Killam Foundation, the National Endowment of the Humanities (NEH), and Fulbright Canada.

**Celene Ibrahim** is the author of *Women and Gender in the Qur'an* (Oxford University Press, winner of the Association of Middle East Women's Studies Book Award, 2021) and *Islam and Monotheism* (Cambridge University Press, 2022). She is the editor of *One Nation, Indivisible: Seeking Liberty and Justice from the Pulpit to the Streets* (Wipf & Stock Publishers, 2019).

**Fr. Romain Louge** is a French priest from the diocese of Marseille in France and currently the parish priest of Saint Eugene d'Endoume. He is a Ph.D. candidate at the Catholic University of Lyon in the Theology Department. He graduated from the Pontifical Institute of Arabic and Islamic Studies (PISAI) in Rome and holds a master's degree in Arabic and Islamic Studies. His area of research is the theological works in Arabic at the time of the beginning of Islam, either Christian or Muslim and their interactions.

**S. Yaser Mirdamadi** has previously served as a Visiting Teaching Fellow in Muslim Ethics at Maktoum College, Dundee. He joined the Institute of Isma'ili Studies in 2016 as a researcher in Muslim bio-medical ethics. He is the first recipient of The Muhammad Arkoun doctoral scholarship. In addition to his seminary background (from Hawza 'Ilmiyya of Mashhad), he received his Ph.D. in Islamic Studies from the University of

Edinburgh. His research fields are philosophical and political theology, philosophy of religion, modern Islam, and Muslim ethics. One of his recent publications is "Why I Am Muslim," in The Rowman & Littlefield Handbook of Philosophy and Religion, edited by Mark Lamport, London, 2022.

**Sajjad H. Rizvi** is Professor of Islamic Intellectual History and Islamic Studies at the University of Exeter, where he is also involved in the Centre for the Study of Islam. His research interests include the intellectual history of the Safavid-Mughal period, as well as Qur'anic exegesis and textual hermeneutics. His publications include *The Spirit and the Letter: Approaches to the Esoteric Interpretation of the Qur'an* (2016, ed. with Annabel Keeler), *Mulla Sadra and the Later Islamic Philosophical Tradition* (2010), *An Anthology of Qur'anic Commentaries Volume I: On the Nature of the Divine* (2008, ed. with Feras Hamza and Farhana Mayer), and *Mulla Sadra Shirazi: His Life, Works and Sources for Safavid Philosophy* (2007). He received his B.A. and M.A. degrees from Oxford and his Ph.D. from Cambridge.

**Javad Taheri** has a Ph.D. in comparative philosophy of religion from the University of Groningen, the Netherlands. His areas of specialisation include philosophy of religion, Islamic philosophy and theology, and comparative philosophical theology (with a particular emphasis on ʿAllāma Ṭabāṭabāʾī and David B. Burrell). Among his latest works are 'Traditions-Oriented Approach in the Comparative Philosophy of Religion' (2022) and 'Semantics of Divine Names: Ṭabāṭabāʾī's Principle of 'Focal Meaning' and Burrell's Grammar of God-Talk' (forthcoming).

# Introduction

*Monotheisms*

Despite the famous (and much misunderstood) contention of Friedrich Nietzsche that god is dead, there is little doubt that we live in a world full of God(s); beliefs in a deity or deities that constitute the ground of existence as well as the pleroma of what is and might be persists. Devotion, ritual, and worship oriented to such entities permeate daily lives across cultures, even in supposedly 'secularised' spaces.[1] Social scientists remain concerned with the inability of humans to rid themselves of the infantility of clinging to a belief and hope in the existence of a caring supernatural being that will ultimately save us—a concern with the perpetuity of this belief is accentuated because of its implications for how we act; surely, humans will have progressed beyond this need?[2] But as an old piece in *The Atlantic* from 1912 by the American theologian George Hodges (1856–1919) shows, people have been assessing the history and the persistence of religion across modernity and for long before.[3] This prevalence of belief—in the intangible or the unseen (*al-ghayb*) as the Qur'an would put it —means that we live in a somewhat polarised world: on the one hand, the survival of belief has led to a highly creative (analytic and otherwise) philosophy of religion that retains popular interest in questions such as the reality of religious experience of the noumenal, and on the other, a tracing of atheism or the rejection of gods as an ancient, philosophical, and scientifically correct human maturity that lays out the absurdity of beliefs in gods including those of the Jewish, Christian, and Islamic traditions.[4] This polarisation lies between the enchanted and the disenchanted (to index Weber); still we ought to recognise that disenchantment in modernity is somewhat exaggerated and notions such as tradition and religions and their others are increasingly defined in terms of what we thought had

---

1 The famous quotation (with its variants) occurs a few times in the 1882 *The Gay Science*, trans. Walter Kaufmann (New York: Vintage Books, 1974), 167, and in the following years, *Thus Spake Zarathustra*, trans. Thomas Common (New York: The Modern Library, 1917), 83.

2 This is partly predicated upon the faith in modernity and progress which is critiqued: Amy Allen, *The End of Progress* (New York: Columbia University Press, 2016).

3 https://www.theatlantic.com/magazine/archive/1912/03/the-persistence-of-religion/644691/# accessed 15 September 2024.

4 On the former, one thinks of the many works of Graham Oppy (*Ontological Arguments and Belief in God* [Cambridge: Cambridge University Press, 1995]; *Arguing about Gods* [Cambridge: Cambridge University Press, 2006]; as well as the critical debate between Kenneth Pearce and Graham Oppy, *Is there a God? A Debate* [London: Routledge, 2021]) and three more popularly oriented volumes, David Bentley Hart, *The Experience of God: Being, Consciousness, Bliss* (New Haven: Yale University Press, 2013), Joshua Rasmussen, *How Reason can Lead to God: A Philosopher's Bridge to Faith* (Downers Grove, IL: Inter-Varsity Press, 2018), and Jack Symes (ed), *Philosophers on God: Talking About Existence* (London: Bloomsbury Publishing, 2024). On the latter, we also have Graham Oppy's *The Argument against God* (Basingstoke: Palgrave Macmillan, 2013) and two more historical works on the antiquity of atheism and the absurdity of belief in a deity, Tim Whitmarsh, *Battling the Gods: Atheism in the Ancient World* (London: Faber and Faber, 2016), and Francesca Stavrakopoulou, *God: An Anatomy* (London: Pan Macmillan, 2021).

passed.[5] Psychological approaches do not necessarily take the metaphysical claims of monotheists seriously.[6] What is also striking is how the impact of 'new atheism' has been to revive older culturalist arguments for beliefs that are growing among the avowedly 'secular' non-believers.[7] Belief in monotheism seems to be encroaching even there, just as the death of god led to a revived theology in Protestant circles since the 1970s and then through atheology and anatheism in the continental tradition more recently.[8] Or at least it reflects the persistence of the need for cultural identity rooted in the manifestations of the notion of religious belief.

Monotheism itself, a term famously coined in the 17th century by the Cambridge Platonist Henry More (1614–1687), is nowadays associated with the notion of 'classical theism' and with a focus on metaphysics.[9] It can be defined as the belief that 'reality's ultimate principle is God—an omnipotent, omniscient, goodness that is the creative ground of everything other than itself. Monotheism is the view that there is only one such God'.[10] This contention, historically, has led to two types of critiques. The first came from the direction of the 'pagans', thus constructed by the new religious movements of Judaism and Christianity in late antiquity, especially in response to Christian monotheism's insistence upon the trinity, the incarnation, and the need for a personal god who acts voluntarily. The 2nd century Greek philosopher, Celsus (d. c. 177), famously critiqued the unoriginality of monotheistic doctrine—indicating how pagan monotheisms and henotheisms were dominant in late antiquity—and its irrationality and weakness compared to 'true Greek doctrine'.[11] Similarly, the Neoplatonist philosopher Porphyry (d. c. 305) in his attack on Christians maintained the weakness of Christian monotheism (based on what he saw as

---

5 Jason Ānanda Josephson-Storm, *The Invention of Religion in Japan* (Chicago: University of Chicago Press, 2012) and *The Myth of Disenchantment: Magic, Modernity, and the Birth of the Human Sciences* (Chicago: University of Chicago Press, 2017).

6 See, for example, Neil van Leeuwen, *Religion as Make-Believe: A Theory of Belief, Imagination, and Group Identity* (Cambridge, MA: Harvard University Press, 2023).

7 Christopher Hitchens, Richard Dawkins, Sam Harris, and Daniel Dennett, *The Four Horsemen: The Conversation that Sparked an Atheist Revolution* (New York: Penguin Random House, 2019). On the revival, see Justin Brierley, *The Surprising Rebirth of Belief in God* (Carol Stream, IL: Tyndale House Publishers, 2023).

8 For example, Paul Tillich, *The Courage to Be* (New Haven, CT: Yale University Press, 1952). On continental atheologies and anatheism, see Richard Kearney, *Anatheism: Returning to God after God* (New York: Columbia University Press, 2011), and Slavoj Žižek, *Christian Atheism: How to be a Real Materialist* (London: Bloomsbury Publishing, 2024).

9 Best defended in the classic work of Richard Swinburne, *The Coherence of Theism* (revised edition, Oxford: Clarendon Press, 2016), and on which there is much recent work. For example, Jonathan Fuqua and Robert C. Koons (eds), *Classical Theism: New Essays on the Metaphysics of God* (London: Routledge, 2023).

10 William Wainwright, 'Monotheism', *The Stanford Encyclopedia of Philosophy* (Winter 2021 Edition), Edward N. Zalta (ed.), URL = <https://plato.stanford.edu/archives/win2021/entries/monotheism/>.

11 John Marenbon, *Pagans and Philosophers* (Princeton: Princeton University Press, 2015), 1–22; Celsus, *On the True Doctrine*, trans. R. Joseph Hoffmann (New York: Oxford University Press, 1987), 55–115, the text is extant in the Christian Origen's *Contra Celsum*. On the prevalence of pagan monotheisms and henotheisms in late antiquity, see Polymnia Athanassiadi and Michael Frede (eds), *Pagan Monotheism in Late Antiquity* (Oxford: Oxford University Press, 2002).

a false homology with monarchy) with respect to Greek tradition, arguing that for a god to be supreme he would need to be supreme over other gods just as a king would be supreme over other humans—a nod towards henotheism.[12] Perhaps the best known of these attacks is the 4th century Roman Emperor Julian the Apostate (d. 363) and his *Against the Galileans* in which he critiques the scripturalist approach and rejection of the rationality of a natural theology by Christians and prefers Plato to the exclusivism of Moses and Jesus.[13]

The second critique came from theists who rejected the exclusivity of monotheism usually from the perspective of dualism—the *thanawiyya* of the Arabic doxographies. This was a particular issue in early Islam as dualists—sometimes anathemised as *zanādiqa* or *malāḥida*—were astonished by the insistence upon a good and omnipotent God who was responsible for evil and yet expected humans to be morally repulsed by it.[14] They also fundamentally disagreed on their moral cosmology. Zoroastrian critiques of Islam focused on the irrationality of the story of creation and the first humans, were perplexed by Muslim cosmology, failed to understand how a sole God would solve the problem of evil, and ridiculed the analogy that we have already seen between monarchy and monotheism, for example in the *Škand Gumānīg-Wizār*.[15] How could one account for evil if God is sole creator while also being essentially good? Early Muslim theologians clearly understood both the ontological and moral challenge of dualism and attempted to respond accordingly with their own metaphysical principles and sense of ridicule for the creation myths of dualists.[16] The problem of evil, of course, remains a salient challenge to monotheism.[17]

12 Porphyry, *Against the Christians*, trans. R. Joseph Hoffmann (rpt. Amherst, NJ: Prometheus Books, 1994), 83–90. This text is also a reconstruction from Christian responses; see this study: Robert M. Berchman, *Porphyry Against the Christians* (Leiden: Brill, 2005).

13 Julian, *Against the Galileans* (in Volume III), trans. Emily Wilmer Cave Wright (Loeb Library, Cambridge, MA: Harvard University Press, 1923).

14 For a summary of the challenge of dualism (which does tend to assume a rather austere, even Salafī, notion of monotheism as normative), see Patricia Crone, *The Nativist Prophets of Early Islamic Iran: Rural Revolt and Local Zoroastrianism* (Cambridge: Cambridge University Press, 2012), 453–460.

15 *The Definitive Zoroastrian Critique of Islam.* Chapters 11-12 of the *Škand Gumānīg-Wazīr* by Mardānfarrox son of Ohrmazddād, trans. Christian C. Sahner (Liverpool: Liverpool University Press, 2024), 119–147.

16 For example, the Muʿtazilī theologian ʿAbd al-Jabbār (d. 1025), *al-Mughnī fī abwāb al-tawḥīd wa-l-ʿadl*, ed. Maḥmūd Muḥammad al-Khuḍayrī (Cairo: al-Hay'a al-Miṣrīya al-ʿĀmma Li'l-Kitāb, 1958), V, 22–79.

17 Michael L. Peterson, *Monotheism, Suffering, and Evil* (Cambridge: Cambridge University Press, 2022), and for a more classic account, Eleonore Stump, 'The problem of evil', *Faith and Philosophy* 2.4 (1985): 392–423. For some recent Islamic responses to the problem of evil in monotheism, see Nasrin Rouzati, 'Evil and suffering in Islamic thought—towards a mystical theology', *Religions* 9 (2018) https://doi.org/10.3390/rel9020047; Safaruk Chowdhury, *Islamic Theology and the Problem of Evil* (Cairo: The American University in Cairo Press, 2021); and Qudratullāh Qurbānī, 'Mas'alah-yi sharr u ufuq-hā-yi pīshravī-yi khudābāvarī-yi tawḥīdī', *Faṣlnāmah-yi andīshah-yi falsafī* 2, no. 3 (1401Sh/2022): 192–207.

What these critiques do indicate is how the contention was not about (mono)theism as such but how the notion of a principle and the idea of creation itself was understood.[18] Monotheism is a point of convergence as well as divergence within traditions and across them. Not all theisms and indeed monotheisms were equal or understood equally. Aristotle's notion of the principle later known as the unmoved mover (*ho ou kinoúmenon kineî* or *primum movens* in Aquinas' 'first way' of the *quinque viæ*) was influential especially because of its description in book *lambda* of the *Metaphysics* as 'beautiful' (the 'Good' of the Neoplatonists which became *al-khayr al-maḥḍ* in the Arabic reception), indivisible and simplex (hence the 'doctrine of divine simplicity' or God as *basīṭ al-ḥaqīqa* whose very essence and reality was to exist—*innīyatuhu māhīyatuhu* in Avicenna's terminology), and perfectly (self-)intellecting (leading to the notion of the identity thesis that was highly influential in later epistemology or what the Islamic traditions called *ittiḥād al-ʿāqil waʾ-l-maʿqūl*).[19] The Arabic Aristotle, as indicated in the famous doxography of Shahrastānī (d. 548/1153), professes belief in the unmoved mover who is also singular, perfectly self-intellecting, immutable, and from him only one thing emanates (the so-called Rule of One).[20] The Platonists disputed the meaning of such a principle; was it a singular, efficient (and final) cause of the cosmos that manipulated the stuff of metaphysics (as held by Simplicius and Ammonius) and did not create *ex nihilo* (hence was neither the formal cause nor the material cause since it was itself immaterial) or could it be assimilated to the god of scriptures? Plato's model of creation in the *Timaeus* was also highly influential in Christian, Jewish, and Islamic conceptions later; the demiurge was just, good, and wise and it was his rational order of the cosmos and its understanding to which philosophers aspired to attain through 'godlikeness'.[21] This latter notion—*taʾalluh* or *al-tashabbuh biʾl-Bāriʾ* in Arabic—was especially current in later philosophical, Sufi and more mystical contemplations of monotheism and the quest for wisdom in Islam.[22] The Arabic Plato posits a god who is necessary in its very essence (using the terminology of Avicenna), whose comprehensive knowledge eternally resides in the Forms of all things

18 Lloyd Gerson, *God and Greek Philosophy* (New York: Routledge, 1990), and David Sedley, *Creationism and its Critics in Antiquity* (Berkeley: University of California Press, 2007).

19 Enrico Berti, 'Unmoved mover(s) as efficient cause(s) in *Metaphysics* λ 6', in Michael Frede and David Charles (eds), *Aristotle's Metaphysics Lambda* (Oxford: Oxford University Press, 2000), 181–206.

20 Muḥammad b. ʿAbd al-Karīm al-Shahrastānī, *al-Milal wa-l-niḥal*, ed. Muḥammad Sayyid Kaylānī (rpt., Beirut: Dār al-Maʿrifa, 1984), 2:119–124. On the Avicennian rule of One (*al-wāḥid lā yuṣdiruhu illā l-wāḥid*, *ex uno non fit nisi unum*), see Wahid M. Amin, 'From the One, only one proceeds: The post-classical reception of a key principle of Avicenna's metaphysics', *Oriens* 48 (2020): 123–155, and Davlat Dadikhuda, 'Rule of One: Avicenna, Bahmanyār and al-Rāzī on the argument from the Mubāḥathāt', *Nazariyyat* 6, no. 2 (2020): 69–97.

21 Gretchen J. Reydams-Schils (ed), *Plato's Timaeus as Cultural Icon* (Notre Dame, IN: Notre Dame University Press, 2003), and Francesco Celia and Angela Ulacco (eds), *Il Timeo. Esegesi greche, arabe, latine* (Pisa: Pisa University Press, 2015).

22 One of the best known versions that correctly maps upon the rational order ascribed to the cosmos by the demiurge that one finds in the Timaeus is Mullā Ṣadrā Shīrāzī (d. 1636), *al-Ḥikmat al-mutaʿāliya fī l-asfār al-ʿaqlīya al-arbaʿa*, eds. F. Ummīd et al (rpt., Beirut: Dār Iḥyāʾ al-Turāth al-ʿArabī, 1981), 1:20.

and who creates through the mediation of the universal intellect and the universal soul from which form and matter ensue.[23] The *Timaeus*' creation myth and metaphysics in rather diluted form was present in the paraphrastic translation of Galen's epitome, in some citations in the *Uthūlūjiyā*, and a few rare fragments cited in later texts such as al-Bīrūnī's study of the philosophies and religions of India (*al-Taḥqīq mā li'l-Hind*).[24]

Monotheism within Islamic contexts was further contested along two axes. On the vertical, one encounters many positions on the relative role of the transcendence of the One and its immanence in the cosmos, most aptly reflected through the many exegeses of Qur'an 42:11: 'there is nothing that is like him and he is all-hearing, all-seeing' (*laysa ka-mithlihi shayʾ wa-huwa l-samīʿu l-baṣīr*). Is God a personal deity to whom one supplicates and prays and expects responses to petitions and intervention in the cosmos (which raises problems associated with foreknowledge and possibility)?[25] Is God analogous to us and how should we understand the anthropomorphisms of the Qur'an and the scriptural traditions?[26] On the horizontal, there was a tendency towards monism—or rather what one might more appropriately call non-duality, the postulation that only God is true being expressed in the term *waḥdat al-wujūd* that was popular in the many manifestations of the school of Ibn ʿArabī. It was precisely that tradition that was less concerned with retaining an ontological difference between God and creation on the basis of the reality of that duality and more concerned with safeguarding the aseity of the divine in one sense and the possibility and desire of God for its theophanies on the other. Both of these axes did, however, tend towards determinism of different types. As ever, the scope and sense of what we mean by *tawḥīd* in Islam, even whether we translate it as the transcendent unity of God or making God one or monotheism—and how that might apply to other traditions—remains a point of contention that was the very dynamic at the heart of Islamic theologies, past and present, as this collection of studies will show.

### *Provenance of the Volume*

This volume consists of a selection of papers delivered at the 'Islamic Perspectives on God and (other) Monotheism(s)' conference which took place at Al-Mahdi Institute, Birmingham, on 20-21 February 2023. This two-day event brought together scholars and

---

23 al-Shahrastānī, *al-Milal wa-l-niḥal*, 2: 88–89.

24 Rüdiger Arnzen, 'Plato's *Timaeus* in the Arabic tradition', in Celia and Ulacco (eds), *Il Timeo. Esegesi greche, arabe, latine*, 220–257.

25 On the philosophical problem, see Scott Davison, *Petitionary Prayer: A Philosophical Investigation* (New York: Oxford University Press, 2017), and for the extension of this in a sense to the Islamic context, posed in more moral terms, Amir Saemi, *Morality and Revelation in Islam and Beyond: A New Problem of Evil* (New York: Oxford University Press, 2024) as well as Özgür Koca, *Islam, Causality, and Freedom* (Cambridge: Cambridge University Press, 2020).

26 This remains a raging debate and there is a rather vast literature on this. One recent intervention that insists that Qur'anic theology is faithful to other earlier Near Eastern theologies (as we saw with the Stavrakopoulou book cited above) in positing a rather material and corporeal god is Nicolai Sinai, *Key Terms of the Qur'an: A Critical Dictionary* (Princeton: Princeton University Press, 2023).

academics specialising in various fields within Islamic Studies, allowing them to present their research on the concept of God and monotheism in Islam and in other religious traditions. The range of topics covered included theological, historical, philosophical, mystical and contemporary perspectives, each engaging with the theme of divine unity (*tawḥīd*) and how it has been approached within and beyond Islamic discourse. The diverse backgrounds and scholarly expertise of the contributors enriched the discussions, resulting in a multifaceted examination of one of the core tenets of the Islamic faith.

As such, this volume is the first of three planned edited collections, each corresponding to a series of conferences that explore the central doctrines of Islamic belief; namely, divine unity (*tawḥīd*), prophecy and revelation, and belief in an afterlife. These three elements constitute the foundation of Islamic theology, and this series seeks to explore their historical development, theological implications, and contemporary relevance. By delving into the interpretations and debates surrounding these doctrines, the volumes aim to offer a comprehensive and nuanced understanding of Islamic beliefs, both for scholars within the field and for those interested in interreligious dialogue.

*Tawḥīd*, the belief in the oneness of God, is the most fundamental tenet of the Islamic faith.[27] All Muslims, regardless of sectarian affiliation, are required to uphold the doctrine of divine unity, which forms the basis of Islamic theology and underpins the Islamic worldview. However, despite its centrality, interpretations of what *tawḥīd* entails and its implications have been the subject of extensive debate across different schools of thought throughout Islamic history. Far from being a monolithic concept, *tawḥīd* has been understood in various ways, from the early forumulation of it as a requirement of belief (*iʿtiqād*) in the legal and theological frameworks of the jurists (*fuqahāʾ*) and *mutakallimūn*, to the later metaphysical expositions of the philosophers (*falāsifa*) and the mystical experiences of Sufis. The doctrine of *tawḥīd*, while envisioned as a unifying belief for Muslims, has historically been the focus of intense theological and philosophical discussions. In some instances, it has acted as a rallying point for Muslim unity, emphasising the shared belief in the oneness of God as a common ground between different Islamic traditions and other faiths.[28] At other times, however, it has been a source of division, as scholars and theologians have accused one another of violating the principles of *tawḥīd*.[29] This

---

27 For a brief overview of the concept of *tawḥīd* in Islam, see Asma Asfaruddin, 'Monotheism in Islam', in *Monotheism and Its Complexities: Christian and Muslim Perspectives*, eds. Lucinda Mosher and David Marshall (Washington, DC: Georgetown University Press, 2018), 33–44.

28 For a nunaced perspective of the category 'monotheism' as a site for interfaith dialogue, see the collection of essays in Lucinda Mosher and David Marshall (eds.), *Monotheism and Its Complexities: Christian and Muslim Perspectives*.

29 In the modern context, this is most noticeable in contemporary Salafi puritanism. But perhaps the most famous historical example of intolerance and persecution within Muslim communities is the infamous '*miḥna*' initiated by the Abbasid caliph al-Maʾmūn (r. 813–883), in which the Muʿtazilī doctrine of the Qurʾan's createdness was enforced across the Islamic empire on the theological premise that it contradicted the correct understanding of *tawḥīd*. The claim was rejected by many traditionalist scholars including, most famously, Aḥmad b. Ḥanbal (d. 241/855).

is particularly evident in the polemical engagements between Sunnī and Shīʿī theologians, as well as in the debates between different sects such as the Muʿtazila, Ashʿariyya, Imāmiyya, Ismāʿīliyya and Ḥanābila, to name but a few. These intra-faith debates often centre around the interpretation of God's attributes, His relation to creation, and the nature of divine will and human agency.

Additionally, *tawḥīd* has not only been a point of internal contestation but has also featured prominently in interfaith debates since the inception of Islam as a religious movement in seventh-century Arabia. Given the shared monotheistic heritage of Muslims, Jews and Christians, discussions about divine unity have frequently engaged with the theological claims of other Abrahamic religions.[30] While early Muslims often positioned *tawḥīd* in opposition to what they perceived as the trinitarian doctrine of Christianity and the over-ritualised legalistic emphasis in Judaism—attitudes which, it could be argued, are expressed in the Qur'an itself—the engagement with these traditions was not always adversarial. In fact, there were moments of intellectual exchange and ecumenical understanding, particularly in the Abbasid period (mid-8th–13th centuries) when Islamic scholars engaged with their (Arabic) Jewish and Christian counterparts in the shared pursuit of understanding the nature of God and His creation. However, the polemical tone that sometimes characterised these exchanges underscored the challenges of reconciling differing interpretations of divine unity across the Abrahamic faiths.

This volume aims to showcase both the internal and external debates surrounding *tawḥīd*, emphasising that the doctrine of divine unity has functioned both as a site for interfaith and intra-faith cohesion and as a point of contestation. Within Islam, *tawḥīd* serves as the bedrock of the faith, yet the diversity of approaches to understanding this doctrine reveals the richness of Islamic thought. Scholars of different theological persuasions, as well as philosophers and mystics, have all debated how to properly conceptualise God's unity, the extent to which God's attributes can be understood by human reason, and how divine action operates within the created world. These discussions have often led to accusations of heresy or doctrinal deviation, with certain scholars accusing others of compromising *tawḥīd* by anthropomorphising God or by adhering to philosophical interpretations that appeared to undermine the transcendence of the divine.[31]

---

30 As an example of this early interfaith exchange on the issue of God's unity specifically, see Sara Leila Husseini, *Early Christian-Muslim Debate on the Unity of God: Three Christian Scholars and Their Engagement with Islamic Thought (9th Century C.E.)* (Leiden: Brill, 2014).

31 One brings to mind the famous legal edict of Abū Ḥamid al-Ghazālī (d. 505/1111) condemning the Neoplatonising philosophers Avicenna and al-Fārābī, which he issued at the end of his *Tahāfut al-falāsifa*. On this document, see Frank Griffel, *Apostasie und Toleranz im Islam: Die Entwicklung zu al-Ġazālīs Urteil gegen die Philosophie und die Reaktionen der Philosophen* (Leiden: Brill, 2000). For accusations of unbelief (*kufr*) against philosophers and others more generally, see Camilla Adang, Hassan Ansari, Maribel Fierro and Sabine Schmidtke (eds.), *Accusations of Unbelief in Islam: A Dichronic Perspective on Takfīr* (Leiden: Brill, 2016).

The volume also addresses how *tawḥīd* has been a focal point of dialogue between Muslims and adherents of other monotheistic faiths. Throughout history, Islamic thinkers have engaged with Jewish and Christian ideas of God, often critically assessing their doctrines in light of Islamic theology. However, such interactions have not always been hostile; there have been periods of intellectual exchange in which Muslim, Jewish, and Christian scholars shared insights and collaborated in their efforts to understand the divine. This volume seeks to reflect this dual nature of *tawḥīd*—as both a point of interfaith commonality and a source of theological divergence. One of the primary aims of this volume is to highlight the diverse perspectives on divine unity in Islam. By incorporating contributions from scholars specialising in different fields, the volume presents an overview of how *tawḥīd* has been understood and interpreted across time and space. Theological, philosophical, and contemporary approaches to *tawḥīd* are all represented, offering readers a broad and nuanced understanding of the doctrine.

Theologically, discussions of *tawḥīd* have centered on the nature of God's attributes and the relationship between God and creation. Classical Islamic theology (*kalām*) grappled with the question of how God's oneness could be reconciled with the multiplicity of divine attributes, and how human beings could come to know God through these attributes. The Muʿtazila, for example, emphasised the absolute unity of God and denied the real existence of (separate) divine attributes, while the Ashʿarīs argued for a more nuanced understanding of attributes as inherent in the divine essence. These theological debates continue to inform Islamic thought today. Philosophically, Islamic thinkers such as Avicenna (Ibn Sīnā) and Mulla Ṣadrā developed sophisticated metaphysical systems that explored the nature of divine unity. Avicenna's conception of God as the Necessary Being (*wājib al-wujūd*) became a cornerstone of Islamic philosophy, while Mulla Ṣadrā's theory of the unity and modulated nature of being (*waḥdat al-wujūd al-tashkīkiyya*) integrated philosophical and mystical insights into a holistic vision of the divine. This volume explores how these philosophical approaches to *tawḥīd* have influenced Islamic thought and continue to shape contemporary discussions of metaphysics and theology. Mystically, the doctrine of *tawḥīd* has been central to the teachings of Sufi masters, who have sought to experience divine unity directly through spiritual practice. Sufism's emphasis on the immanence of God and the possibility of union with the divine has sometimes led to tensions with more orthodox theological perspectives, which stress the transcendence of God. This mystical understanding of *tawḥīd*, particularly as articulated by figures such as Ibn al-ʿArabī, adds another layer of complexity to the debates over the nature of divine unity. Finally, the volume addresses contemporary perspectives on *tawḥīd*, examining how modern Muslim thinkers have engaged with the doctrine of God's uniqueness in light of new intellectual and social challenges. In a globalised world marked by pluralism and secularism, the concept of divine unity remains a vital part of Islamic identity, yet its meaning and relevance are continually being reinterpreted. The contributors to this volume engage with these modern debates, offering insights into how *tawḥīd* continues to evolve in contemporary Islamic thought.

By presenting a range of scholarly perspectives, the papers collected in this volume seeks to demonstrate both the diversity of interpretations of divine unity within Islam and the ongoing significance of this doctrine in interfaith and intra-faith discussions. Whether approached through theology, philosophy, mysticism, or contemporary thought, *tawḥīd* remains the defining tenet of Islamic belief, a doctrine that has both united and divided Muslim scholars over the centuries, and one that continues to inspire debate and reflection today.

### *Contents*

The chapters that follow can be broken down into what we are calling five different perspectives: 1) Contesting Monotheisms; 2) Sunnī Theology; 3) Shīʿī Theology; 4) Philosophy; and 5) Contemporary Issues. The first section, subtitled 'A Judeo-Christian-Muslim Encounter', begins with the earliest period in Islam as the tradition emerged on the scene of world history in conversation with other religious traditions and ends in the nineteenth century with Muslim-Christian polemics in the Qajar period. Where there is conversation, it should perhaps go without saying, there is inevitably debate and contestation, and the present section seeks to showcase this. In chapter one, 'Religious Others and the Shaping of Orthodoxy in the Early Islamic Period', Aaron W. Hughes examines how the early framers of Islam struggled with religious others, both external and internal, and how this struggle was ultimately responsible for the creation of what would emerge as (Sunnī) orthodoxy.

In a similar vein, in the second chapter, 'The Influence of Christian Theology on the Development of *Tawḥīd* in Early Kalām', Romain Louge explores how Christian theological speculation on the Trinity and, particularly, on the Christ-figure in the first theological Christian writings in Arabic played an important role on the development of *kalām*, especially the concept of *tawḥīd*, and that this led slowly to negative theology and to the concept of the falsification of the Scriptures of *ahl al-kitāb*.

The third chapter, by contrast, stays with the theme of debate and contestation, but now takes us into the more modern period. In 'On Religion: Ṣadrian Metaphysics as "Islam's Argument" (*Ḥujjat al-Islām*) against Henry Martyn', Sajjad Rizvi focusses on Muslim-Christian polemics on the nature of beliefs, doctrines, and practices in the Qajar period, and especially the reactions to the work of the Anglican missionary Henry Martyn (1781–1812). After a brief contextualisation of Muslim-Christian polemics on the nature of monotheism in this period and the development of the study of Ṣadrian metaphysics, he turns to an examination of one text that deploys Ṣadrian thought and principles to provide rational responses to Martyn: *Ḥujjat al-Islām aw Burhān al-milla*, the work of the philosopher and occultist ʿAlī Nūrī (d. 1831).

The second section, 'Sunnī Theological Perspectives on God and Monotheism', draws our attention to the later Sunnī theological tradition. John Hoover, in chapter four, 'The *Tawḥīds* of Ibn Taymiyya' examines how this important eighth/fourteenth thinker distinguishes between two *tawḥīds*: *tawḥīd al-ulūhiyya*, which demonstrates God's exclusive divinity (*ulūhiyya*); and *tawḥīd al-rubūbiyya* that confesses the exclusivity of God's lordship (*rubūbiyya*) by acknowledging God as the sole creator of all things and as the only real source of help. Hoover does this by arguing that Ibn Taymiyya (d. 728/1328) invokes a post-classical division of Arabic sentences into two types: *khabar* and *inshāʾ*. The term *khabar* refers to informational statements or assertions that, as Ibn Taymiyya himself notes, may be affirmed as true or denied as false. *Inshāʾ* covers all other types of sentences, including imperatives, requests, wishes, exclamations, and promises.

In chapter five, Syamsuddin Arif's 'The Qurʾanic Argument for Monotheism: Controversies between al-Taftāzānī (d. 792/1390) and His Contemporaries' begins with a question: If cosmic order implies the unity of God, does the corrosion of heaven and earth imply the plurality of gods? Although many would readily give an affirmative answer to this question, the Māturīdī theologian Saʿd al-Dīn al- Taftāzānī's (d. 792/1390) explanation of the concept using Qur'an 21: 22 ('If there were other gods [in heaven and earth] besides Allāh, they would both dissolve into chaos') sparked considerable and often heated debate among fellow Sunnī thinkers and continued to trigger controversy in later scholarship down to Maḥmūd al- Ālūsī (d. 1270/1854) and Jamāl al-Dīn al-Qāsimī (d. 1332/1914). Arif examines this issue of the *burhān al-tamānuʿ* and explores this debate and the controversies it engendered by exploring the meaning of the counterfactual conditional statement used by the Qur'an.

The third section—'Shīʿī Theological Perspectives on God and Monotheism'—is also comprised of two chapters. In chapter six, 'Visions of *Tawḥīd*: Reconciling a Statement in the Twenty-Eighth Supplication of *al-Ṣaḥīfa al-Sajjādiyya*', Zoheir Esmail examines Sayyid ʿAbdullāh Shubbar's (d. 1241/1775) investigation of the statement 'You have, my Lord, numerical oneness', specifically his attempts to reconcile the statement's outward commitment to a numerical conception of *tawḥīd* with an agreement amongst Shīʿī scholars that *tawḥīd* is not numerical. In his *Maṣābīḥ al-anwār fī ḥall mushkilāt al-akhbār*, a book dedicated to reconciling difficult *aḥādith*, Sayyid Shubbar summarises and evaluates different opinions produced by Shīʿī scholars who have attempted to explain this statement. His evaluation, Esmail argues, gives us a window through which we can observe different conceptions of how numerical oneness can be reconciled with the visions of *tawḥīd* held by the ʿulamāʾ beyond numerical oneness.

Chapter seven, 'Apophatic *Tawḥīd*: A Philosophical Account of Shīʿī Ismāʿīlī Theology', has Khalil Andani examine the famous Ismāʿīlī doctrine that advocates for an apophatic theology concerning the nature of God in which all names, descriptions and real predications to describe God are negated. This doctrine, he suggests, allows human souls to achieve perfection by submitting to the infallible guidance of the Imām of the time, whose pure soul receives continuous emanation and light from the Universal Intellect. This process of 'integration', by which the human soul assimilates into its spiritual origin (*aṣl*), he argues, involves the act of *tawḥīḍ*, where the soul must divest and isolate every rank of God's creation from divinity and thereby recognise the absolute unity of God.

The fourth part—'Philosophical Perspectives on God and Monotheism'—also consists of two chapters. Chapter eight, Wahid Amin's 'Mullā Ṣadrā and His Commentators on Ibn Kammūna's Argument Against Divine Unity' explores the doctrine of divine unity and its attendant problems in Islamic philosophical texts composed between the twelfth and twentieth centuries. He explains the philosophical challenges faced by post-classical Muslim philosophers and theologians in their attempts at proving divine unity after a so-called 'doubt' (*shubha*) mistakenly attributed to Ibn Kammūna (d. 683/1284) thwarted the standard Avicennian proof of God's unity. The severity of the challenge that the *shubhat al-tawḥīd* posed was so immense that influential Muslim figures such as Ibn Taymiyya relied on it to dismiss any proof of divine unity within the writings of the *falāsifa*. Following this, Amin demonstrates how Shīʿī philosophers grappled with the problem of divine unity and the challenges that were raised because of *shubhat Ibn Kammūna*. This leads him to conclude that later Shīʿī philosophy is intricately woven with philosophical speculation on the traditions of the Imams, and that rather than there being a tension between philosophy and scripture, the two in fact come together for true *ḥikma*.

In the ninth chapter, 'Logico-linguistic Analysis of the *Kalimat al-Tawḥīd*: al-Rāzī vs al-Kūrānī', Yusuf Daşdemir examines *Kalimat al-tawḥīd*, namely, 'there is no deity but God' and the *basmala*, the first verse of the Qurʾan, which functions as the commonest prayer of a Muslim's daily life. Daşdemir examines the philosophical, logical, and linguistic treatment of the *Kalimat al-tawḥīd* by Fakhr al-Dīn al-Rāzī (d. 606/1210) and Ibrāhīm al-Kūrānī (d. 1101/1690), who represent two main strands of philosophy in the post-classical era, namely, philosophical *kalām* and Akbarian Sufism, respectively.

In the fifth and final section—'Contemporary Perspectives on God and Monotheism'—we see how many of the themes and concepts explored in previous sections play out in modern and contemporary Islamic discourses. In chapter 10, 'Divine Names for Interreligious Engagement', Celene Ibrahim explores the significance of 'the most beautiful names' (*al-asmāʾ al-ḥusnā*) from an interreligious and comparative perspective. She suggests that particular names, and the concept of divine names more broadly, have the potential to resonate with those who seek paradigms for conceptual enrichment, moral introspection, and spiritual development across metaphysical paradigms.

In the eleventh chapter, 'God as a Moral Agent: An Inquiry into the Nature of Divine Agency', Abolghasem Fanaei begins by stating that the nature of God and His attributes are two of the most fundamental questions and major points of dispute in mysticism, theology, and philosophy of religion. How we answer these questions, he suggests, have profound practical significance for both private and public aspects of life, to say nothing of both their theoretical implications for our worldview and their practical consequences on our understanding of politics and morality. To get at some of these tensions, Fanaei reflects upon a particular conception of God, 'God as a moral agent', and elaborates on the practical implications of seeing God in this way for the life of religious people.

The twelfth chapter, 'Friendly (A)theism: A Philosophical-Theological Defence', sees S. Yaser Mirdamadi examine the root cause of intolerance among (1) theists on theological issues such as *tawḥīd*; and (2) between theists and atheists, particularly on their mutual accusation of irrationality. He begins his chapter developing an epistemological model called 'friendly (a)theism', initially suggested by William Rowe (1931–2015), that enables both theists and atheists, under certain circumstances, to consider the other side of the debate as reasonable without taking a relativist approach or compromising their own (a)theistic position. He next asks if such a philosophical model is theologically viable. He concludes that it is and that the friendly theism model is also theologically defensible by defending an Islamic concept of faith. This thesis lies at the core of the Islamic concept of faith; that *īmān* and *kufr* are mainly moral categories rather than doxastic ones. Such aphilosophical-theological approach to rationality, he suggests, paves the way for inter(a) faith dialogue among Muslims and non-Muslims (theist or atheist) in the contemporary multicultural context.

In the final chapter, 'Towards a Grammatical Approach to Monotheism: Unpacking Ṭabāṭabāʾī's Theological Perspective', Javad Taheri discusses how the 'principle of focal meaning' proposed by Ṭabāṭabāʾī may be rethought in light of the findings presented in David B. Burrell's Grammatical Thomism. He does this by demonstrating how Ṭabāṭabāʾī's *tanzīh fī l-tashbīh* (dissimilation-within-assimilation) strategy might be used to realise a term's focal meaning. He then suggests how a type of univocity Ṭabāṭabāʾī associated with the focal meaning must be reinterpreted in accordance with the Wittgensteinian concept of family resemblance, in a manner similar to Burrell's interpretation of the way of analogy in a discussion of the concept of God as both transcendent and related to the world. Taheri next argues that this interpretation of Ṭabāṭabāʾī's concept of focal meaning offers a novel approach to comprehending the Shīʿī doctrine of *tawḥīd* that will be argued to be more accurate.

Taken together, these diverse chapters, provide a good sense and overview of the diversity of Islamic perspectives on God and monotheisms from the earliest period into the present.

## Bibliography

Adang, Camilla, Hassan Ansari, Maribel Fierro, and Sabine Schmidtke, eds. *Accusations of Unbelief in Islam: A Dichronic Perspective on Takfīr*. Leiden: Brill, 2016.

Allen, Amy. *The End of Progress*. New York: Columbia University Press, 2016.

Amin, Wahid M. 'From the One, Only One Proceeds: The Post-Classical Reception of a Key Principle of Avicenna's Metaphysics.' *Oriens* 48 (2020): 123–155.

Arnzen, Rüdiger. 'Plato's *Timaeus* in the Arabic Tradition.' In *Il Timeo. Esegesi greche, arabe, latine*, edited by Francesco Celia and Angela Ulacco, 220–257. Pisa: Pisa University Press, 2015.

Asfaruddin, Asma. 'Monotheism in Islam.' In *Monotheism and Its Complexities: Christian and Muslim Perspectives*, edited by Lucinda Mosher and David Marshall, 33–44. Washington, DC: Georgetown University Press, 2018.

Athanassiadi, Polymnia, and Michael Frede, eds. *Pagan Monotheism in Late Antiquity*. Oxford: Oxford University Press, 2002.

Berchman, Robert M. *Porphyry Against the Christians*. Leiden: Brill, 2005.

Berti, Enrico. 'Unmoved Mover(s) as Efficient Cause(s) in Metaphysics λ 6.' In *Aristotle's Metaphysics Lambda*, edited by Michael Frede and David Charles, 181–206. Oxford: Oxford University Press, 2000.

Brierley, Justin. *The Surprising Rebirth of Belief in God*. Carol Stream, IL: Tyndale House Publishers, 2023.

Celia, Francesco, and Angela Ulacco, eds. *Il Timeo. Esegesi greche, arabe, latine*. Pisa: Pisa University Press, 2015.

Celsus. *On the True Doctrine*. Translated by R. Joseph Hoffmann. New York: Oxford University Press, 1987.

Chowdhury, Safaruk. *Islamic Theology and the Problem of Evil*. Cairo: The American University in Cairo Press, 2021.

Crone, Patricia. *The Nativist Prophets of Early Islamic Iran: Rural Revolt and Local Zoroastrianism*. Cambridge: Cambridge University Press, 2012.

Dadikhuda, Davlat. 'Rule of One: Avicenna, Bahmanyār and al-Rāzī on the Argument From the Mubāḥathāt.' *Nazariyyat* 6, no. 2 (2020): 69–97.

Davison, Scott. *Petitionary Prayer: A Philosophical Investigation*. New York: Oxford University Press, 2017.

Fuqua, Jonathan, and Robert C. Koons, eds. *Classical Theism: New Essays on the Metaphysics of God*. London: Routledge, 2023.

Gerson, Lloyd. *God and Greek Philosophy*. New York: Routledge, 1990.

Griffel, Frank. *Apostasie und Toleranz im Islam: Die Entwicklung zu al-Ġazālīs Urteil gegen die Philosophie und die Reaktionen der Philosophen*. Leiden: Brill, 2000.

Hart, David Bentley. *The Experience of God: Being, Consciousness, Bliss*. New Haven: Yale University Press, 2013.

Hitchens, Christopher, Richard Dawkins, Sam Harris, and Daniel Dennett. *The Four Horsemen: The Conversation that Sparked an Atheist Revolution*. New York: Penguin Random House, 2019.

Hodges, George. 'The Persistence of Religion.' *The Atlantic*, 1912. https://www.theatlantic.com/magazine/archive/1912/03/the-persistence-of-religion/644691/. Accessed September 15, 2024.

Husseini, Sara Leila. *Early Christian-Muslim Debate on the Unity of God: Three Christian Scholars and Their Engagement with Islamic Thought (9th Century C.E.)*. Leiden: Brill, 2014.

Jabbār, ʿAbd al-. *al-Mughnī fī abwāb al-tawḥīd wa-l-ʿadl*. Edited by Maḥmūd Muḥammad al-Khuḍayrī. Cairo: al-Hayʾa al-Miṣrīya al-ʿĀmma Liʾl-Kitāb, 1958.

Josephson-Storm, Jason Ānanda. *The Invention of Religion in Japan*. Chicago: University of Chicago Press, 2012.

———. *The Myth of Disenchantment: Magic, Modernity, and the Birth of the Human Sciences*. Chicago: University of Chicago Press, 2017.

Julian. *Against the Galileans*. Translated by Emily Wilmer Cave Wright. Loeb Library. Cambridge, MA: Harvard University Press, 1923.

Kearney, Richard. *Anatheism: Returning to God after God*. New York: Columbia University Press, 2011.

Koca, Özgür. *Islam, Causality, and Freedom*. Cambridge: Cambridge University Press, 2020.

Leeuwen, Neil van. *Religion as Make-Believe: A Theory of Belief, Imagination, and Group Identity*. Cambridge, MA: Harvard University Press, 2023.

Marenbon, John. *Pagans and Philosophers*. Princeton: Princeton University Press, 2015.

Nietzsche, Friedrich. *The Gay Science*. Translated by Walter Kaufmann. New York: Vintage Books, 1974.

———. *Thus Spake Zarathustra*. Translated by Thomas Common. New York: The Modern Library, 1917.

Oppy, Graham. *Arguing about Gods*. Cambridge: Cambridge University Press, 2006.

———. *Ontological Arguments and Belief in God*. Cambridge: Cambridge University Press, 1995.

———. *The Argument against God*. Basingstoke: Palgrave Macmillan, 2013.

Pearce, Kenneth, and Graham Oppy. *Is There a God? A Debate*. London: Routledge, 2021.

Peterson, Michael L. *Monotheism, Suffering, and Evil*. Cambridge: Cambridge University Press, 2022.

Porphyry. *Against the Christians*. Translated by R. Joseph Hoffmann. Reprint. Amherst, NJ: Prometheus Books, 1994.

Qurbānī, Qudratullāh. 'Masʾalah-yi sharr u ufuq-hā-yi pīshravī-yi khudābāvarī-yi tawḥīdī.' *Faṣlnāmah-yi andīshah-yi falsafī* 2, no. 3 (1401Sh/2022): 192–207.

Rasmussen, Joshua. *How Reason Can Lead to God: A Philosopher's Bridge to Faith*. Downers

Grove, IL: Inter-Varsity Press, 2018.
Reydams-Schils, Gretchen J., ed. *Plato's Timaeus as Cultural Icon.* Notre Dame, IN: Notre Dame University Press, 2003.
Rouzati, Nasrin. 'Evil and Suffering in Islamic Thought—Towards a Mystical Theology.' *Religions* 9, no. 2:47 (2018).
Sadrā Shīrāzī, Mullā. *al-Ḥikmat al-mutaʿāliya fī l-asfār al-ʿaqlīya al-arbaʿa.* Edited by F. Ummīd et al. Reprint. Beirut: Dār Iḥyāʾ al-Turāth al-ʿArabī, 1981.
Saemi, Amir. *Morality and Revelation in Islam and Beyond: A New Problem of Evil.* New York: Oxford University Press, 2024.
Sahner, Christian C., trans. *The Definitive Zoroastrian Critique of Islam. Chapters 11-12 of the Škand Gumānīg-Wazīr by Mardānfarrox son of Ohrmazddād.* Liverpool: Liverpool University Press, 2024.
Sedley, David. *Creationism and Its Critics in Antiquity.* Berkeley: University of California Press, 2007.
Shahrastānī, Muḥammad b. ʿAbd al-Karīm al-. *al-Milal wa-l-niḥal.* Edited by Muḥammad Sayyid Kaylānī. Reprint. Beirut: Dār al-Maʿrifa, 1984.
Sinai, Nicolai. *Key Terms of the Qur'an: A Critical Dictionary.* Princeton: Princeton University Press, 2023.
Stavrakopoulou, Francesca. *God: An Anatomy.* London: Pan Macmillan, 2021.
Stump, Eleonore. 'The Problem of Evil.' *Faith and Philosophy* 2, no. 4 (1985): 392–423.
Swinburne, Richard. *The Coherence of Theism.* Revised edition. Oxford: Clarendon Press, 2016.
Symes, Jack, ed. *Philosophers on God: Talking About Existence.* London: Bloomsbury Publishing, 2024.
Tillich, Paul. *The Courage to Be.* New Haven, CT: Yale University Press, 1952.
Wainwright, William. 'Monotheism.' In *The Stanford Encyclopedia of Philosophy* (Winter 2021 Edition), edited by Edward N. Zalta. https://plato.stanford.edu/archives/win2021/entries/monotheism/.
Whitmarsh, Tim. *Battling the Gods: Atheism in the Ancient World.* London: Faber and Faber, 2016.
Žižek, Slavoj. *Christian Atheism: How to Be a Real Materialist.* London: Bloomsbury Publishing, 2024.

# PART 1

## *Contesting Monotheisms: A Judeo-Christian-Muslim Encounter*

# Religious Others and the Shaping of Orthodoxy in the Early Islamic Period

*Aaron W. Hughes*

The Qur'an is a text that is relentlessly self-conscious of the fact that it exists in a world occupied by earlier but now rival monotheisms.[1] We see this, for example, in its constant acknowledgement that it is intimately connected to the two earlier monotheisms in the area, namely, Judaism and Christianity. Perhaps not surprisingly, most of the verses in the Qur'an that refer to these other religions are frequently ambiguous. They offer words of acknowledgement and praise, on the one hand, yet, on the other, are often highly critical of them, trying to offer a road map of just how and why they went astray. Anyone working in or even familiar with the earliest period of Islam, which spans from the death of the Prophet in 632 CE to the early Abbasid period (roughly 800 CE), realises that this is among the most difficult to document. The dense and multifaceted thicket of early Arabic literature's version of this history makes the search for tidy answers next to impossible.[2] To avoid some of these historical problems, this article focuses on, what are for all intents and purposes, a set of literary tropes. Such tropes, as any good novelist might tell us, sometimes allow us to get closer to truth—howsoever one wishes to define this term—by allowing us access to areas otherwise cordoned off. Here I take a cue from the late John Wansbrough, who once remarked that 'if what we know of the seventh-century Hijaz [i.e. Mecca and Medina] is the product of intense literary activity, then that record has got to be interpreted in accordance with what we know of literary criticism'.[3]

The Jews and Christians I want to focus on here, then, are not real individuals or groups; rather, they appear as textual foils that can be orchestrated to facilitate Muslim self-definition and thus used in the further articulation of Islamic monotheism. Now if we situate Islam as a continuation of the late antique period, a practice that is becoming

1 Parts of this article draw upon my *An Anxious Inheritance: Religious Others and the Shaping of Sunnī Orthodoxy* (New York and Oxford: Oxford University Press, 2022).

2 Here I could cite the usual sources from John E. Wansbrough, *The Sectarian Milieu: Content and Composition of Islamic Salvation History* (Oxford: Oxford University Press, 1977) and Patricia Crone and Michael Cook, *Hagarism: The Making of the Islamic World* (Cambridge: Cambridge University Press, 1979) to more recent iterations such as Peter Webb, *Imagining the Arabs: Arab Identity and the Rise of Islam* (Edinburgh: Edinburgh University Press, 2016), Stephen J. Shoemaker, *The Apocalypse of Empire: Imperial Eschatology in Late Antiquity and Early Islam* (Philadelphia: University of Pennsylvania Press, 2018), and Sean W. Anthony, *Muhammad and the Empires of Faith: The Making of the Prophet of Islam* (Berkeley: University of California Press, 2020).

3 John E. Wansbrough, *Res Ipsa Loquitur: History and Mimesis* (Jerusalem: Israel Academy of Sciences and Humanities, 1987), 14–15.

increasingly common,[4] this means that its early framers inherited a social world that had been largely defined by previous empires in the region (i.e. Roman, Byzantine, Sasanian). Of especial significance was *The Theodosian Code*, commissioned by the emperor Theodosius and compiled between 429 and 438, which represented a compilation of all the laws of the Roman Empire under Christian emperors since 312.[5] In its sixteenth and final book, dealing specifically with the matter of religion, we witness the increased political necessity of defining and establishing one orthodoxy at the expense of what could now, at least through back-projection, be defined as a variety of heterodoxies and heresies all to do with what consisted of proper monotheistic belief. In so doing, the *Code* further reinforces the notion that orthodoxy and heterodoxy are intimately connected in the religious imagination.[6] They feed off one another, with each requiring the perceived negative traits of the other for its existence and sustenance. The definition of one is necessarily contingent upon the definition and subsequent elucidation of the other.

Since Islam entered a world that was in large part defined by the *Code*'s desire to create communal divisions based on religion, the new religion, perhaps not surprisingly, took religion for granted as it imagined social differences between communities.[7] As the conquering armies made their way into places like Iraq, Syria, and Egypt, everywhere Muslims looked, they would have encountered the spiritual and physical traces of these other religions.[8] As a new religion lacking such an ancient pedigree, inevitable questions arose: what were those responsible for articulating Islam to do with these other religious traditions? How, for example, could older religions be situated within a much broader

4 See Garth Fowden, *Before and after Muhammad: The First Millennium Refocused* (Princeton, NJ: Princeton University Press, 2014), 1–17; most recently, see the impressive study in Jack Tannous, *The Making of the Medieval Middle East: Religion, Society, and Simple Believers* (Princeton, NJ: Princeton University Press, 2018).

5 For relevant context, see Jill Harries and Ian Wood, eds., *The Theodosian Code: Studies in the Imperial Law of Late Antiquity* (Ithaca, NY: Cornell University Press, 1993); John F. Matthews, *Laying Down the Law: A Study of the Theodosian Code* (New Haven, CT: Yale University Press, 2000); Fergus Millar, *A Greek Roman Empire: Power and Belief under Theodosius II (408–450)* (Berkeley: University of California Press, 2006).

6 See, for example, Judith McClure, 'Handbooks against Heresy in the West from the Late Fourth to the Late Sixth Centuries', *Journal of Theological Studies* 30 (1979): 186–97; Averil Cameron, 'How to Read Heresiology', *Journal of Medieval and Early Modern Studies* 33 (2003): 471–92; Richard Flower, '"The Insanity of Heretics Must Be Restrained": Heresiology in the *Theodosian Code*', in *Theodosius II: Rethinking the Roman Empire in Late Antiquity*, ed. Christopher Kelly (Cambridge: Cambridge University Press, 2013), 172–94.

7 Ahmet Karamustafa, for example, has argued that one of the Qur'an's main concerns is with *ummāt* (sing. *umma*, to wit, 'religious communities') than it is with other descriptors, such as *shuʿūb* ('race/ethnicity'). See his 'Community', in *Key Themes for the Study of Islam*, ed. Jamal J. Elias (Oxford: Oneworld, 2010), 95–97. See also Frederick Matthewson Denny, 'Community and Society in the Qur'ān', in *Encyclopaedia of the Qurʾān*, ed. Jane McAuliffe (Leiden: Brill, 2005), 1:372–73.

8 For the complexities of this rapid spread, see Robert G. Hoyland, *In God's Path: The Arab Conquests and the Creation of an Islamic Empire* (New York and Oxford: Oxford University Press, 2014). For an account of some of the various Christian responses to it, see Michael Philip Penn, *When Christians First Met Muslims: A Sourcebook of the Earliest Syriac Writings on Islam* (Berkeley: University of California Press, 2015); more generally, see his *Envisioning Islam: Syriac Christians in the Early Muslim World* (Philadelphia: University of Pennsylvania Press, 2015), 102–40. See also Sidney Griffith, *The Church in the Shadow of the Mosque: Christians and Muslims in the World of Islam* (Princeton, NJ: Princeton University Press, 2010), 23–44.

monotheistic narrative landscape that naturally culminated in Islam's rise and florescence? The interpretive acts used to address Islam's relationship to these other religious traditions were necessarily fraught with tensions as a set of deep-rooted connections between the old and the new that needed to be mined and ascertained with the aim of using the former to make sense of the latter. While the early framers of Islam (e.g. Qur'anic redactors, *ḥadīth* collectors, early legists, doxographers, *mutakallimūn* (rational theologians), and popular preachers, among others)[9] could tap into these previous narratives, whether positively or negatively, the last thing they could do was ignore them since religious others were, especially in the early period, quite literally everywhere.[10] Not to mention the basic fact that the majority of early Muslims in these areas would have come from the ranks of earlier monotheisms.

One of the central themes of late antiquity is how various social groups creatively used the past, both their own and that of others. For example, Eusebius of Caesarea referred to Constantine as the new Moses, a role that conveniently combined the latter's Christian bona fides with his role as emperor of Rome.[11] It was the Christian past, in other words, that provided Constantine with the legitimacy to extend Roman might and power beyond anything that previous pagan emperors had imagined. He did this, moreover, by incorporating bishops into the traditional Roman governing elite, thereby displacing the traditional polytheistic hierarchy. This use of select features associated with the Roman past combined with a reworking of a monotheistic heritage in the service of rapid political transformation is certainly not unique to Rome's imperial aspirations. Imagining histories of social groups—one's own and those of one's rivals—functioned as an intricate part of the late antique world to which Islam was heir.

The use and creative deployment of others' pasts in the service of communal self-definition, however, had the potential to produce disconnection from those pasts and ultimately one's claim to them. This was especially the case since others, one's political or religious rivals, might very well have possessed or been perceived to possess better claims. Not infrequently this resulted in the production of alternative 'histories' of others with the ultimate aim of ascertaining one's own divine legitimacy, as, for example, in the early Christian disparagement of the Pharisees for misunderstanding their own tradition. The desire to create an imperial orthodoxy frequently coincided, then, with a set of internal tensions. The question for early Muslims, therefore, became, how to shape

9 On the social, political, and historical settings of these types of individuals who sought to understand their past, the historical record, and how they differed from other genres of contemporaneous Arabic literature, see Chase F. Robinson, *Islamic Historiography* (Cambridge: Cambridge University Press, 2002), 3–17.

10 A particularly good example of an interpretive grid that situates this process is David S. Powers, *Muhammad Is Not the Father of Any of Your Men: The Making of the Last Prophet* (Philadelphia: University of Pennsylvania Press, 2009), 3–31. See also Tannous, *The Making of the Medieval Middle East*.

11 Philip Wood, 'Introduction', in *History and Identity in the Late Antique Near East*, ed. Philip Wood (Oxford: Oxford University Press, 2013), xi.

selectively the past or the pasts of other monotheists in a way that included some but that simultaneously excluded others.

In the time afforded me here I want to examine some of these tensions as they manifested themselves in early Islam. More specifically, I want to explore how the early framers of that tradition struggled with religious others, mainly external ones, and how this struggle was ultimately responsible for the creation of what would emerge as Sunnī orthodoxy and its articulation of monotheism. While the latter would appear as the natural outgrowth of Muḥammad's preaching to those doing the framing, it was ultimately little more than a subsequent development accompanied by a retroactive projection onto the earliest period. Non-Muslims (among them Christians, Jews, and Zoroastrians) and the 'wrong' kinds of Muslims (e.g. Shīʿa) became integral—by virtue of their perceived stubbornness, infidelity, heresy, or the like—to understand what true religion was not and, just as importantly, what it should be.

Such groups, or even individuals, were—as I have already suggested—rarely real, however. They were instead literary characters. They may have been called 'Jews' or 'Christians' in name, but they rarely resembled real flesh-and-blood historical Jewish or Christian actors. Instead, they became a series of imagined tropes and other fictions to define what proper Islam was or ought to become. They were often encapsulated in personifications, taking the form, for instance, of the 'good' Jew (e.g. Kaʿb al-Aḥbār) or the 'good' Christian (e.g. Baḥīra) or alternatively the 'bad' Jew (e.g. ʿAbdullāh b. Sabaʾ) or the 'bad' Christian (e.g. Paul), all to be discussed presently.

What was it about such literary creations, expanded to the level of generalised sociological characteristics, that appealed to Muslim thinkers? I want to suggest that the self-perceived newness of Islam in the earliest centuries, including the necessity of establishing its doctrinal and theological intent, compounded with Muslim encounters with ancient and now rival religious competitors and their monotheisms, inevitably and inexorably created a set of inherent tensions. Islamic monotheism had to be imagined, but such an activity could only be done in counterpoint with the conception of the monotheisms of rival religions, all of which had to be shown to be wrong at certain stages in their own doctrinal development. Islam, perhaps more than other religions, tended to be thought about and constructed comparatively from its very beginning. The early framers of Islam needed to denigrate other religions, or at least give them alternative histories than the ones they told themselves, while simultaneously defining Islam as either their obverse or what they were supposed to be but had failed to become on account of perfidy and tampering (*taḥrīf*). The subsequent articulation of orthodoxy was thus continuously contingent upon working out the differences with these other religions.[12]

12 On the problems of these term in early and medieval Islam, see Alexander Knysh, 'Orthodoxy and Heresy in Medieval Islam', *Muslim World* 83, no. 1 (1993): 48–67. And more recently, see the study found in John P. Turner, *Inquisition in Early Islam: The Competition for Political and Religious Authority in the Abbasid*

Here it might be worth recalling that the mischaracterisation of the religious beliefs and practices is unique to Islam. As John B. Henderson argued several decades ago, there exists a set of common strategies used to distinguish orthodox 'truth' from heretical 'errors' that we witness across numerous religious traditions. Buddhists thinkers, for example, have no problem misrepresenting Advaita Vedanta, just as thinkers associated with the latter tradition certainly mischaracterise Buddhist views with the aim of articulating their own first principles; the same, of course, could be said for Catholics and Protestants, and Christians and Jews. In this case, then, we should not expect Islamic views of the other to be more neutral or objective, given the fact that religious polemic by virtue of what it is always strategically distorts the other.[13]

While clear to the early framers of Islam that their tradition was in conversation with previous monotheisms, it was equally clear that the new needed to be differentiated from the old, and in such a manner that the latter had to be made to attest to the former. This enabled early Muslims to show how all previous species of unbelief differed significantly from what was actively being constructed as proper Muslim belief.

One of the main ways that Islamic thinkers dealt with religious others was to argue that, at the moments of their revelation, these other religions were essentially Islam in the sense that they exhibited a pure monotheism and that they were in possession of their own versions of the Qur'an. At their moments of historical rupture, in other words, these other religious communities were, for all intents and purposes, Islam or at the very least the 'Islams' of their days. Over time, according to the later narrative, these other religions became so corrupted by human desire and ideology that they forfeited connections to divine truth, all but rendering themselves useless.

If the Muslim theological tradition regarded earlier religions as corrupt and Islam as pure, why not simply bypass earlier religions and forgo their narratives? This was not such an easy process, however, given the fact that Islam only made sense if and when it was situated against the much larger backdrop of the rise and fall of previous monotheisms. Since these monotheisms were associated with the imperial remains of grandiose civilisations into which Muslims entered, tales of the former's rise and fall had to be written. And since the Qur'an referred so frequently to them, other religions had to be mapped, contextualised, and 'historicised' in a manner that made sense to Muslims. Positive characteristics were neatly differentiated from negative ones, and in such a manner that the former found their fullest expression in Islam.

One way to do this was for later Muslim theologians, following the Qur'an's lead, to differentiate between what rival monotheisms—to wit, Christianity or Judaism—were

---

*Empire* (London: I.B. Tauris, 2013), 23–32. More comparatively, see John B. Henderson, *The Construction of Orthodoxy and Heterodoxy: New-Confucian, Islamic, Jewish, and Early Christian Patterns* (Albany: State University of New York Press, 1998).

13 Henderson, *The Construction of Orthodoxy and Heterodoxy*, 39–84.

at their beginnings and that into which they had currently devolved. Islam, on this reading of other religions' so-called histories, could now emerge on the scene to correct the excesses of previous monotheisms. The framers of Islam now constructed the tradition as paring away such accumulations and agglutinations and offering a return to that which previous monotheisms had originally been. Within this narrative, present-day forms of earlier monotheisms were no longer seen to be authentic versions of what they had initially been.

A second and related way to deal with other monotheisms was to understand Islam as their correct and original versions. Other monotheisms, on this reading, were essentially 'Islamic' at earlier stages of their development and their messages were subsequently corrupted and tampered with by priests, bishops, rabbis, and so on. Regardless of the paradigm, common to both—and this is a theme we see throughout the history of religions—is the notion that the new transcends the old by reclaiming that which was originally good about the latter while simultaneously discarding all those elements subsequently deemed as irrelevant or even dangerous. Either way, imagined religious others continued to function as the prime foils by which Islam could articulate itself and clarify its doctrines and practices in the process.

## 1. Judaism

Moving from these general theoretical and introductory comments I now want to explore how this works using a literary dialectic common in early Islamic literature, that between the 'good' religious other and the 'bad' religious other. In particular, between the 'bad' Jewish convert, to wit, ʿAbdullāh b. Saba', and the 'good' Jewish convert, to wit, for example, ʿAbdullāh b. Salām or Kaʿb al-Aḥbār; following that I want to compare and contrast this with the 'good' Christian (e.g. Baḥīra) vis-à-vis the 'bad' Christian (e.g. Paul).

Perhaps the most famous Jew in all Islamic literature is ʿAbdullāh b. Saba', believed to have been a Jew from Yemen who converted to Islam after the death of Muḥammad.[14] His date of conversion is perhaps significant from a literary point of view since it meant that he never actually met the Prophet in person, implying that this might well be the reason for the lack of respect for his message. According to al-Ṭabarī, Ibn Saba' was a Jew from Ṣanʿā', and his mother was a black woman—thus functioning as both a religious and an ethnic other. In al-Ṭabarī's own words,

14 For relevant secondary literature, see Israel Friedländer, "ʿAbd Allāh ibn Sabā, der Begründer der Sīʿa, und seine jüdischer Ursprung', *Zeitschrift für Assyriologie* 23 (1909): 296–327 and 24 (1910): 1–46. Most recently, see Sean W. Anthony, *The Caliph and the Heretic: Ibn Saba' and the Origins of Shīʿism* (Leiden: Brill, 2012). Though not important to my argument here, it is perhaps worth pointing out that his Jewish bona fides have been questioned by some. Most notable is Marshall G. S. Hodgson, "ʿAbd Allāh ibn Saba'", *EI2*, 1:51; Marshall G. S. Hodgson, 'How Did the Early Shīʿa Become Sectarian?', *Journal of the American Oriental Society* 75 (1955): 1–12. For other sources see the footnotes immediately following.

> He converted to Islam in the time of ʿUthmān, then roamed around about the lands of the Muslims attempting to lead them into error. He began in the Ḥijāz, and then [worked] successively in Basra, Kufa, and Syria. He was unable to work his will upon a single one of the Syrians, they drove him out and he came to Egypt. He settled among the Egyptians, saying to them, among other things, 'How strange is it that some people claim that Jesus will return, while denying that Muhammad will return. As Almighty God has said, "He who ordained the Qur'ān for thee will surely restore thee to a place of return [Q. 28:85]". Now surely Muhammad is more worthy that Jesus to return.'[15]

Here Ibn Saba' is credited with trying to trick early believers into thinking that Muḥammad would return after his death. Just as the Jews had convinced Jesus's followers to worship him as God, here the Jew Ibn Saba' attempts to do the same to the early Muslim community.

Ibn Saba' functions as one of the first instantiations of the tendency in Islamic sources to attribute subversive and extremist doctrines to Jewish origin and malfeasance. Indeed, as Sean Anthony has shown, Ibn Saba' is presented in the earliest Islamic historiographical and heresiographical tradition as the nemesis of the early community's caliphs, those recognised as the so-called *rāshidūn* ('rightly guided').[16] He is made to be the first to recognise ʿAlī as the true successor to Muḥammad, of ascribing esoteric knowledge to him, and of cursing the three caliphs prior to him (i.e. Abū Bakr, ʿUmar, and ʿUthmān) as illegitimate. Such heretical behaviour, signified as somehow Jewish, is subsequently responsible for the creation of the Shīʿa, often imagined as *the* arch-heresy within the Islamic tradition, at least according to subsequent Sunnī sources. But even later Shīʿī sources accuse him of introducing extremism that late *ghulāt* picked up on.[17]

One of the earliest treatments of Ibn Saba' appears in the work of the second/ninth-century Kufan historian Sayf b. ʿUmar al-Tamīmī (d. ca. 180/796).[18] For Sayf, as indeed for the later heresiographical tradition more generally, Ibn Saba' is the one responsible for the first *fitna* ('civil strife' or 'sedition') in Islam:

15 al-Ṭabarī, *Ta'rīkh al-rusul wa-l-mulūk*, ed. M. J. de Goeje, 3 vols. (Leiden: Brill, 1879–1901), 1:2942; English translation in *The History of al-Ṭabarī*, vol. 15, *The Crisis of the Early Caliphate*, trans. R. Stephen Humphreys (Albany: State University of New York Press, 1985), 145–46.

16 Anthony, *The Caliph and the Heretic*, 3.

17 See Heinz Halm, *Das islamische Gnosis: Die extreme Schia und ʿAlawiten* (Zürich: Artemis and Winkler, 1982), 33–42; Josef van Ess, *Das Kitāb an-Nakṯ des Naẓẓām und seine Rezeption im Kitāb al-Futyā des Ǧāḥiz; eine Sammlung der Fragmente mit Übersetzung und Kommentar* (Göttingen: Vandenhoeck & Ruprecht, 1972), 50–57; see also Mushegh Asatryan, *Controversies in Formative Shīʿī Islam: The Ghulat Muslims and Their Beliefs* (London: I.B. Tauris, 2017).

18 For a survey of al-Tamīmī's place in the Islamic literary tradition, see Anthony, *The Caliph and the Heretic*, 9–18.

> Not a year had passed from the rule of ʿUthmān when men from the Quraysh appropriated properties in the garrison cities, and the people attached themselves to them. They were steadfast in doing this for seven years, while other groups desired that their leader should rule. Then Ibn Sawdāʾ [i.e. Ibn Sabaʾ] converted to Islam and began to speculate in religious matters [*aslama wa-takallama*]. The world passed into chaos, and by his hands harmful innovations [*aḥdāth*] arose. People then felt that ʿUthmān's years were too long.[19]

Here Ibn Sabaʾ is held up as the one responsible for the introduction of innovations into Muslim belief and practice, which led directly to the subsequent problems that plagued ʿUthmān's caliphate. These included, but were certainly not limited to, his preaching of Muḥammad's imminent return. Again, according to Sayf, Ibn Sabaʾ

> would say, 'What a marvel it is that some believe that Jesus will return while disbelieving that Muhammad will return!' God Almighty has said, 'Indeed, He who has ordained the Qur'ān for you will bring you back to place of return' [*inna alladhī faraḍa ʿalayka al-qurʾāna la-rādduka ilā maʿād*] (Q. 28:85). For Muhammad is more deserving of returning than Jesus! That was accepted from [Ibn Sabaʾ by his followers]. And he fabricated for them [the doctrine of return; *al-rajʿa*], and they began to speculate over it.[20]

If 'the Jew' can be a villain needed to carve out space for proper belief, there must also exist Jews who function in the opposite capacity. The 'good' Jew is also necessary because, again as a textual trope if not an actual historical individual, he symbolises the conduit between the old revelation and the new. If the 'bad' Jew sought to undermine Muḥammad's message, the 'good' Jew legitimates it. The latter individual, familiar with ancient Jewish lore and traditions, can be made to prophesy the coming of Muḥammad as predicted, for example, in the original and untampered version of the Torah. In the later Islamic literary tradition, the 'good' Jew also becomes the person who seeks to protect the Prophet from the intrigues of his erstwhile co-religionists. These 'good' Jews are also multi-purpose. They predict; they warn; and they protect. In so doing, they become, like their doppelgangers, literary characters who further aid in the articulation of the new message.

One such individual comes to us by way of ʿAbdullāh b. Salām (d. 43/663). According to tradition, he was born in Medina within the tribe Banū Qaynuqāʿ and originally had the

19 Sayf b. ʿUmar al-Tamīmī, *Kitāb al-ridda wa-l-futūḥ wa-K. al-jamal wa-masīr ʿĀʾisha wa-ʿAlī: A Critical Edition of the Fragments Preserved in the University Library of Imām Muhammad ibn Saʿud Islamic University in Riyadh, Saudi Arabia*, ed. Qasim al-Samarrai, 2 vols. (Leiden: Brill, 1995), 1, 122. Quoted in Anthony, *The Caliph and the Heretic*, 23.

20 Quoted in Anthony, *The Caliph and the Heretic*, 77.

name Ḥusayn.[21] When he converted to the new message, shortly after Muḥammad's arrival in the town, the Prophet gave him the name ʿAbdullāh, that is, 'the servant of God'. Note that, unlike Ibn Sabaʾ, he was born at the time of and actually met and interacted with the Prophet. According to al-Ṭabarī, he was also with ʿUmar in Jerusalem and subsequently supported ʿUthmān against his critics. Also, according to him, when anti-government rebels were set to attack ʿUthmān in his home, to quote al-Ṭabarī,

> ʿAbdallāh b. Salām came forth and stood at the door of the house, forbidding them to kill [ʿUthmān]. 'O my people', he said, 'do not unsheathe God's sword against yourselves. By God, if you draw it, you will not put it back in its scabbard. Woe to you! Your government today is based on the whip, and if you kill him it will rest only on the sword. Woe to you! Your city is surrounded by God's angels. By God, if you kill him they will surely forsake it'. 'What is this to you, son of a Jewess?', they said and he withdrew.[22]

ʿAbdullāh b. Salām here, as the voice of reason, functions as the prescient one who issues a warning to the rebels that any violence committed against the third caliph will only reverberate throughout the generations. Here the 'good' Jew undoes what the 'bad' Jew had set in motion. Such violence would lead, in other words, to a host of other problems revolving around succession and inevitably draw in the larger community. However, the rebels refuse to listen to his warnings because, at least in the words al-Ṭabarī ascribes to them, he is the 'son of a Jewess'.

ʿAbdullāh b. Salām becomes the righteous non-Arab who could both predict and accept the message of Muḥammad. In his description of Medina as 'surrounded by God's angels' and his warning of the fate that met other rebellious cities, the historian Tayeb El-Hibri sees in him a biblical model of the rise and fall of nations.[23] This has the advantage, as we have seen, of linking Islam's new history with the ancient history of the Israelites. Figures such as ʿAbdullāh b. Salām, I would suggest, provide an important, even necessary, link between the two traditions that certain framers so desired.

Kaʿb al-Aḥbār, a seventh-century Yemenite Jew who converted to Islam, according to al-Ṭabarī, in the first year of ʿUmar's reign (13/634), also plays a significant role in the fledgling community's growing self-awareness. According to the third/ninth-century biographer Ibn Saʿd, when asked why he waited until after the death of the Prophet to convert, Kaʿb responded, and I quote from his account:

21 Though, according to Uri Rubin, and without any proof, ʿAbdullāh b. Salām seems to have been closer to a *ḥanīf* than a Jew. See Uri Rubin, 'Ḥanīfiyya and Kaʿba: An Inquiry in the Arabian Pre-Islamic Background of the *Dīn Ibrāhīm*', *Jerusalem Studies in Arabic and Islam* 13 (1990): 109.

22 al-Ṭabarī, *Taʾrīkh*, 1:3017 (Humphreys, *The Crisis of the Early Caliphate*, 215).

23 Tayeb El-Hibri, *Parable and Politics in Early Islamic History* (New York: Columbia University Press, 2010), 14.

> My father wrote out a book for me from the Torah and gave it to me. [My father] said, 'Act according to this'. Then he sealed the rest of his books and took from me the right of a father from his son that I would not break the seal. When the time came and I saw that Islam had emerged and I did not see any harm in it, I said to myself, 'Perhaps my father has concealed some knowledge from me. I should read It'. I opened the seal and read it, and in it I found the description of Muhammad and his community. So now I come as a Muslim.[24]

Here Kaʿb, as the embodiment of both religious and filial piety, is described as someone who was—unlike his former co-religionists—able to witness the truth and validity of the new religion. Even his father, who had written a book for him based on the Torah, predicted the coming of the new prophet. Kaʿb serves as a link to the past. Kaʿb functions as a '*the* good Jew', someone who, as originally belonging to Judaism, can see and attest to the truth of Muḥammad's message based on his understanding of the truths of Judaism. Not only does he agree to join the new *umma* but also helps to give it form by providing it with an ancient patina.

Kaʿb is the wise person, knowledgeable in the Torah,[25] and, as such, someone who offers council to caliphs based on his ancient wisdom. When ʿUmar wants to begin his administrative survey of the burgeoning empire, he asks Kaʿb for advice. The latter asks the caliph: 'Where would you like to make a start, Commander of the Faithful?' ʿUmar replied, 'Iraq.' Kaʿb said, 'Do not do that. Evil and good both consist of ten parts. But whereas the one part that is good lies in the East and nine in the West, the one part that is evil lies in the West while the nine other evil parts lie in the East. The devil and every severe disease are linked with Iraq.'[26] This cryptic expression reveals Kaʿb as a figure who, based on his knowledge of Jewish lore, can see into the future. When ʿUmar arrives in Jerusalem, for example, Kaʿb informs him, 'O Commander of the Faithful, five hundred years ago a prophet predicted what you have done today.'

## 2. Christianity

Let me now put this Jewish example in counterpoint with a Christian one. The new, if the history of religions tells us anything, must understand itself in light of that which came before, especially when the former taps into the frameworks of the latter. The new religion, in other words, must be imagined to provide a better and more spiritually refined worldview than its predecessors. This often involves a complex negotiation that shows

24 See Ibn Saʿd, *Kitāb al-ṭabaqāt al-kabīr* (Beirut, 1957); English translation in *The Men of Madina*, trans. Aisha Bewley (London: Ta-Ha Publishers, 1997), 1:277.
25 See Ibn Saʿd, *Kitāb al-ṭabaqāt al-kabīr* (Bewley, *The Men of Madina*, 1:68).
26 al-Ṭabarī, *Taʾrīkh*, 1:2514; English translation in *The History of al-Ṭabarī*, vol. 13, *The Conquest of Iraq, Southwestern Persia, and Egypt*, trans. G. H. A. Juynboll (Albany: State University of New York Press, 1985), 95.

just when, where, why, and how the old went astray and what of value might be inherited and transformed. The manner whereby Christian thinkers imagined their religion as emerging from the ashes of Second Temple Judaism is perhaps most apposite here. To make theological sense of the new message embodied in the persona of Jesus, Christian theologians, as early as Paul, had accused Jews of misreading and misunderstanding their own scriptures.[27] The history of religions also informs us that those points where similarities are most acute and differences most pronounced involve the expenditure of significant intellectual labour to account for difference while simultaneously nuancing similarity. This not infrequently involves accusations of stubbornness, excess, and infelicity on the part of the old. No religion, in other words, can risk appearing fully de novo or contextless. On the contrary, the new must portray itself as providing a reformation, a perfection, or the like of that which pre-existed it. Yet, figuring out the dynamics between new and old is a potentially fraught activity and must therefore be carefully choreographed.

If we fast-forward to the other end of late antiquity, to the emergence of Islam, we should not be surprised to find that of paramount importance on the part of its earliest framers was the desire to work out, often in painstaking detail, the new tradition's relationship to its predecessors. The Qur'an certainly provided an initial framework to undertake this endeavour; it was, after all, full of—often contradictory, to be sure—references to Jews, Christians, and others. This early account, however, subsequently needed to be amplified, supplemented, and further articulated, and often done so in such a manner that later concerns and anxieties could be back-projected onto the earliest period. The process was delicate, to be sure, since the Qur'an and other early Islamic literature constructed Islam's prophet using familiar Near Eastern paradigms and presented him as following in the path of earlier prophets whose message his was largely seen to agree with. Yet, if in agreement, this gave rise to the inevitable question: if the same or similar, then how was it different?

In the case of Christianity, this means that the old had to be confronted head-on, showing where, when, and by whom it went astray. This largely involved the need to create an Islamically infused 'history' for Christianity that could subsequently be used for Muslim self-understanding. Christianity was not to be understood on its own terms, in other words, but only in an idealised and essentialised fashion that would further aid in the articulation of Islam and a Muslim worldview. As a result, Christianity was provided

27 I certainly have no intention of saying that they did, only that it was theologically necessary to do so. Relevant secondary literature includes Wayne A. Meeks, *The First Urban Christian: The Social World of the Apostle Paul*, 2nd ed. (New Haven, CT: Yale University Press, 2003). See also Paula Fredriksen, *Augustine and the Jews: A Christian Defense of Jews and Judaism* (New York: Doubleday, 2008). I certainly have no intention of wading into the debates prominent in this field. However, I have found the essays collected in the following volume to be helpful: Adam H. Becker and Annette Yoshiko Reed, eds., *The Ways That Never Parted: Jews and Christians in Late Antiquity and the Early Middle Ages* (Minneapolis: Fortress, 2007).

with a narrative of devolution: a pristine and pure antiquity wherein the religion initially resembled Islam to its present bastardised form.

Not unlike the 'good Jew'/'bad Jew', which I shall discuss in just a moment, we see a similar construction when it comes to the 'good Christian'/'bad Christian'. And, once again, the prototype for this is spelled out in the Qur'an. As already mentioned, its attitude towards them constellates between praise and disparagement. This ambiguity would seem to stem from the fact that, while necessary, Christianity—not unlike Judaism—posed fundamental problems for the young community. Not infrequently, the Qur'an, to signal its own originality and to distinguish itself from its rivals, presented alternative events in the lives of earlier prophets. Perhaps most famously in the account of the crucifixion of Jesus found in Q. 4:157–58:

> And for their saying, 'Surely we killed the Messiah, Jesus son of Mary, the Messenger of God'—yet, they did not kill him, nor did they crucify him, but it [only] seemed like that to them. Surely those who differ about him are indeed in doubt about him. They have no knowledge about him, only the following of conjecture. Certainly, they did not kill him. No! God raised him to Himself. God is mighty, wise.

Implicit in verses such as these is that the original message of the New Testament has been tampered with (the technical Arabic term for this is *taḥrīf*).[28] The real story of Jesus's crucifixion is not what Christians have traditionally thought it to be, in other words, and it is certainly not the account presented in their New Testament.[29] On the contrary, the true version is the one that Islam has archived in its own foundational text. It is the Qur'an and not the New Testament, then, that reveals the religious truths of Christianity, and what those who practise that religion are supposed to believe.

Another way that the Qur'an undermines other religions is by providing alternative renditions of prophetic sayings that were imagined to be lost. In Q. 19:30, for example, the infant Jesus speaks from the cradle, informing his audience that he is both a servant of God (*ʿabd Allāh*) and a prophet (*nabī*), that is, he is not the son of God, and that he has been given a scripture (*al-kitāb*). In Q. 61:6, we read the following: 'And remember when Jesus, son of Mary, said, "Sons of Israel! Surely I am the Messenger of God [*rasūl Allāh*] to you, confirming what was before me of the Torah [*al-tawra*], and bringing good news of a messenger [*rasūl*] who will come after me, whose name will be Aḥmad."' The

28 See Jane Dammen McAuliffe, *Qurʾanic Christians: An Analysis of Classical and Modern Exegesis* (Cambridge: Cambridge University Press, 1991), 258–59.

29 On the role of Jesus in the Qur'an more generally, see Geoffrey Parrinder, *Jesus in the Qurʾān* (Oxford: Oneworld, 1965); Todd Lawson, *The Crucifixion and the Qurʾan: A Study in the History of Muslim Thought* (Oxford: Oneworld, 2009); Tarif Khalidi, *The Muslim Jesus: Sayings and Stories in Islamic Literature* (Cambridge, MA: Harvard University Press, 2003); Gabriel Said Reynolds, *The Qurʾān and the Bible: Text and Commentary* (New Haven, CT: Yale University Press, 2018).

Qurʾan here implies that Jesus, as both a human and a *rasūl*, predicted the coming of Muḥammad, who is here given the variant name of 'Aḥmad'. The implication is that such verses were excised from the book that would eventually become the New Testament. The accounts of Jesus's life found in Christian scriptures are here used to offer further proof that Christianity is corrupt.

The basic Muslim narrative maintains that at the time of Muḥammad, there existed very few Christians who possessed the true and uncorrupted Gospel of Jesus. Those who did and who practised the religion as Jesus had intended are the ones who are, perhaps not surprisingly, most amenable to Muḥammad and his message. Since Christianity's original message—not unlike that of Judaism—was Islam, those who understood it properly and in its uncorrupted form would have no problem either recognising or accepting the new religion.

The appropriation of other pasts into the Muslim historical imagination helped to establish a relevant pre-Islamic history, both for Islam and for the other monotheisms it encountered. The latter were now understood solely from the perspective of Islam, either as leading up to or as falling away from it.[30] Not only did this allow Muslims to create a past and an identity for themselves, but also it enabled them to situate that past and identity into the narrative frameworks supplied by others. According to al-Ṭabarī, for example:

> After Jesus, kings distorted the Torah and the Gospel. The kings summoned people to choose between death and relinquishing their reading of their books, except what had been distorted. A group of them chose to live on pillars, others to roam about, eating what beasts eat, others built monasteries in the deserts, digging wells and growing herbs. Each group was imitated by others, but they [eventually] became polytheists. When Muhammad came, only a few of them remained. Then the hermits descended from their cells, the monks came out of their convents, and the roaming monks came back from their wandering. All of them believed in him and gave credence to him. These are the ones that have a twofold recompense (Q. 57:28).[31]

Al-Ṭabarī here explains that it is these hermetic Christians, maintaining secretly the pure tradition and in danger of persecution, who recognised Muḥammad as a prophet and messenger of God. One of the most famous of these is Baḥīra. According to the biography of the Prophet, both the future prophet and his uncle Abū Ṭālib meet a monk by the name of Baḥīra in the desert, who is described as 'being well-versed in the knowledge of Christians'—but interestingly not in that of the Jews—and in possession of a book that had

30 See, for example, Harry Munt, 'The Prophet's City before the Prophet: Ibn Zabāla (d. after 199/814) on Pre-Islamic Medina', in *History and Identity in the Late Antique Near East*, 103–21.

31 al-Ṭabarī, *Jāmiʿ al-bayān ʿan taʾwīl āy al-Qurʾān*, ed. Aḥmad Saʿīd ʿAlī et al. (Cairo: Muṣṭafā al-Bābī al-Ḥalabī, 1954–68), Q. 57:27.

been handed down to him 'from generation to generation' (*kābir ʿan kibr*).[32] When Baḥīra looks at the young Muḥammad's back he sees 'the seal of prophecy [*khātam al-nubuwwa*] between his shoulders in the very place described in his book'.[33] Baḥīra then informs Abū Ṭālib, 'Take your nephew back to his country and guard him carefully against the Jews [*al-yahūd*], for by Allah! If they see him and know about him what I know, they will do him evil: a great future lies before this nephew of yours, so take him home quickly.'[34] Baḥīra thus functions as a monotheist who is able to legitimate Muḥammad's prophecy as he simultaneously differentiates Muḥammad from 'the Jews'.[35] Baḥīra, thus, secretly preserved a pure and untampered version of Christianity that was quantitatively and qualitatively different from that produced by the churches of the Roman and Persian empires. In so doing, he functions as textual ciphers that, in his case, provided Muslims access to earlier iterations of their own religion. Islam was not a new religion, in other words, but had always existed wherever righteous individuals were present.

But, if we find *the* 'good' Christian, we should also expect to find his nemesis, the 'bad' Christian. Much anti-Christian polemical literature produced by Muslims is interested in ascertaining at what point Christianity went from being a religion that resembled, if not actually was, Islam to a bastardised and corrupt version thereof. Most seem to locate the blame squarely at the feet of 'the accursed' (*al-laʿīn*) Paul. The latter character, this literature charges, was the one responsible for adapting the original and authentic message of Jesus to, among other things, Roman tastes. According to the tenth-century ʿAbd al-Jabbār, for example, 'Paul was an evil, disgusting Jew, pursuing wickedness and intent upon vicious acts, an inciter of seditions, a seeker of leadership and governance for which he strove in every way.'[36] And, according to another tenth-century thinker, Ibn Ḥazm, subsequent to this various priests and bishops built upon the innovations of Paul until 'there was not a thing in the Gospel that determined the text of the creed without which faith [*īmān*], according to them, is not complete, except the mentioning together of the father, the son, and the holy spirit. Whatever else is in it is merely the imitation [*taqlīd*] of their early generation of bishops.'[37]

---

32 ʿAbd al-Malik Ibn Hishām, *Kitāb sīrat rasūl Allāh*, ed. Ferdinand Wüstenfeld (Göttingen, 1858–60), 1:115; English translation in *The Life of Muhammad: A Translation of Ibn Ishaq's Sirat Rasul Allah*, trans. A. Guillaume (Oxford: Oxford University Press, 1955), 79.

33 Ibn Hishām, *Sīrat rasūl Allāh*, 1:116 (Guillaume, *Life of Muhammad*, 80).

34 Ibn Hishām, *Sīrat rasūl Allāh*, 1:116–17 (Guillaume, *Life of Muhammad*, 80).

35 The story is repeated in al-Ṭabarī, *Taʾrīkh*, 1:1123–26; English translation in *The History of al-Ṭabarī, vol. 6, Muḥammad at Mecca*, trans. W. Montgomery Watt and M. V. McDonald (Albany: State University of New York Press, 1985), 44–46.

36 ʿAbd al-Jabbār, *Tathbīt dalāʾil al-nubuwwa*, ed. ʿAbd al-Karīm ʿUthmān, 2 vols. (Beirut: Dār al-ʿArabiyya, 1966), 2:156.

37 Ibn Ḥazm, *Kitāb al-fiṣal fī al-milal wa-l-ahwāʾ wa-l-niḥal*, 5 vols. (Baghdaad: Maktabat al-Muthannā, n.d.), 1:56.

## 3. Conclusions

The anxiety afforded by religious competition is why so many of the literary genres that emerge out of the early period seem to be so conscious of religious difference and alterity. Islam, to return to a point I made in the introduction, is always thought about comparatively. It is, as we have seen time and again, actively constructed by being put in counterpoint with others. I have tried to make the case that this was because the seminal work of Islam, the Qur'an, was born into a late antique environment that was highly cognisant of religious differences. Islam's framers—Qur'an redactors, *ḥadīth* collectors, legists, poets, theologians, and heresiologists, among others—were thus fully attuned to such alterity and expended great energy to differentiate the new from the old. They did this by, among other things, creating a grand narrative that was biblical in proportion to other religions and that charted their rise, florescence, sin, and ultimate fall from divine favour. This not only fitted Islam into these other religions but also showed how Islam represented their perfection and functioned as a warning to Muslims lest the same fate befall them.

My concern has been to show how orthodoxy is extracted out of a complex set of comparative procedures, and not infrequently in times of political and social turmoil. Religions—and Islam is certainly no different—do not, Athena-like, emerge completely formed from the heads of divine beings. Nor do their origins appear, to invoke Renan's famous—or better infamous—formulation of Islam, 'in the full light of history'. Rather, religions emerge slowly and through working out a complex set of doctrinal, liturgical, and related issues that not infrequently revolve around highly political binaries of orthodox/heterodox and us/not-us.

Orthodoxy, both in sum and in substance, is a political process and not a natural one. It is perhaps for this reason that it was primarily at those points at which Islam and religious others intersected with one another—at least in the idealised textual worlds of our sources—that we witness a real anxiety when it comes to thinking about and through alterity. No one can doubt, for example, that Islam is related to other monotheisms, yet it was clear to its early framers—as it is to modern scholars—that the new religion could not be reducible to them. This means that Jews, for example, had to be assigned a set of essentialised character traits, emerging from the Qur'anic narrative and subsequently expanded upon, that make them perfidious or appear as tricksters. In like manner, Christians, again based on the Qur'an's initial description of them, are often reduced to their inability to understand their own Christology properly, something that was further assumed to be based on Jewish perfidy. Time and again, we witness other religions—often stripped down, essentialised, and personified as a set of stock literary characters—interact with Muḥammad and the early Muslim community, and in such a manner that they permit their authors to bring Muslim dogma and practice into clearer focus.

Despite such negative characteristics, it was clear to the early framers of Islam that their own religion everywhere referred to these other religions. Since there was no way to escape such references, and given the fact that for the first century Islam was a minority religion surrounded by non-Muslim religions, religious others played a central role in the construction of Islamic identity. Islam, situated within the larger constellation of religions, needed a genealogy; yet, at the same time, if Islam appeared as too similar to its precursors, it risked the accusation that it was little more than a pale imitation of them and thereby meeting the same fate that they did. The result is that these points of contact had to be carefully mined and choreographed so that Islam represented either their corrective or their natural fulfilment.

## Bibliography

ʿAbd al-Jabbār. *Tathbīt dalāʾil al-nubuwwa*. Edited by ʿAbd al-Karīm ʿUthmān. 2 vols. Beirut: Dār al-ʿArabiyya, 1966.

Anthony, Sean W. *The Caliph and the Heretic: Ibn Saba' and the Origins of Shiʿism*. Leiden: Brill, 2012.

———. *Muhammad and the Empires of Faith: The Making of the Prophet of Islam*. Berkeley: University of California Press, 2020.

Asatryan, Mushegh. *Controversies in Formative Shiʿi Islam: The Ghulat Muslims and Their Beliefs*. London: I.B. Tauris, 2017.

Becker, Adam H., and Annette Yoshiko Reed, eds. *The Ways That Never Parted: Jews and Christians in Late Antiquity and the Early Middle Ages*. Minneapolis: Fortress, 2007.

Bewley, Aisha, trans. *The Men of Madina*. London: Ta-Ha Publishers, 1997.

Cameron, Averil. 'How to Read Heresiology'. *Journal of Medieval and Early Modern Studies* 33 (2003): 471–92.

Crone, Patricia, and Michael Cook. *Hagarism: The Making of the Islamic World*. Cambridge: Cambridge University Press, 1979.

Denny, Frederick Matthewson. 'Community and Society in the Qurʾān'. In *Encyclopaedia of the Qurʾān*, edited by Jane McAuliffe, 1:367–86. Leiden: Brill, 2005.

El-Hibri, Tayeb. *Parable and Politics in Early Islamic History*. New York: Columbia University Press, 2010.

van Ess, Josef. *Das Kitāb an-Nakṯ des Naẓẓām und seine Rezeption im Kitāb al-Futyā des Ǧāhiz; eine Sammlung der Fragmente mit Übersetzung und Kommentar*. Göttingen: Vandenhoeck & Ruprecht, 1972.

Flower, Richard. '"The Insanity of Heretics Must Be Restrained": Heresiology in the *Theodosian Code*'. In *Theodosius II: Rethinking the Roman Empire in Late Antiquity*, edited by Christopher Kelly, 172–94. Cambridge: Cambridge University Press, 2013.

Fowden, Garth. *Before and after Muhammad: The First Millennium Refocused*. Princeton, NJ: Princeton University Press, 2014.

Fredriksen, Paula. *Augustine and the Jews: A Christian Defense of Jews and Judaism*. New

York: Doubleday, 2008.

Friedländer, Israel. "ʿAbd Allāh ibn Sabā, der Begründer der Sīʿa, und seine jüdischer Ursprung'. *Zeitschrift für Assyriologie* 23 (1909): 296–327 and 24 (1910): 1–46.

Griffith, Sidney. *The Church in the Shadow of the Mosque: Christians and Muslims in the World of Islam.* Princeton, NJ: Princeton University Press, 2010.

Guillaume, A., trans. *The Life of Muhammad: A Translation of Ibn Ishaq's Sirat Rasul Allah.* Oxford: Oxford University Press, 1955.

Halm, Heinz. *Das islamische Gnosis: Die extreme Schia und ʿAlawiten.* Zürich: Artemis and Winkler, 1982.

Harries, Jill, and Ian Wood, eds. *The Theodosian Code: Studies in the Imperial Law of Late Antiquity.* Ithaca, NY: Cornell University Press, 1993.

Henderson, John B. *The Construction of Orthodoxy and Heterodoxy: New-Confucian, Islamic, Jewish, and Early Christian Patterns.* Albany: State University of New York Press, 1998.

Hodgson, Marshall G. S. 'How Did the Early Shīʿa Become Sectarian?'. *Journal of the American Oriental Society* 75 (1955): 1–12.

Hoyland, Robert G. *In God's Path: The Arab Conquests and the Creation of an Islamic Empire.* New York and Oxford: Oxford University Press, 2014.

Hughes, Aaron W. *An Anxious Inheritance: Religious Others and the Shaping of Sunnī Orthodoxy.* New York and Oxford: Oxford University Press, 2022.

Humphreys, R. Stephen, trans. *The Crisis of the Early Caliphate.* Vol. 15 of *The History of al-Ṭabarī.* Albany: State University of New York Press, 1985.

Ibn Ḥazm. *Kitāb al-fiṣal fī al-milal wa-l-ahwāʾ wa-l-niḥal.* 5 vols. Baghdad: Maktabat al-Muthannā, n.d.

Ibn Hishām, ʿAbd al-Malik. *Kitāb sīrat rasūl Allāh.* Edited by Ferdinand Wüstenfeld. Göttingen, 1858–60.

Ibn Saʿd. *Kitāb al-ṭabaqāt al-kabīr.* Beirut, 1957.

Juynboll, G. H. A., trans. *The Conquest of Iraq, Southwestern Persia, and Egypt.* Vol. 13 of *The History of al-Ṭabarī.* Albany: State University of New York Press, 1985.

Karamustafa, Ahmet. 'Community'. In *Key Themes for the Study of Islam*, edited by Jamal J. Elias, 93–103. Oxford: Oneworld, 2010.

Khalidi, Tarif. *The Muslim Jesus: Sayings and Stories in Islamic Literature.* Cambridge, MA: Harvard University Press, 2003.

Knysh, Alexander. 'Orthodoxy and Heresy in Medieval Islam'. *Muslim World* 83, no. 1 (1993): 48–67.

Lawson, Todd. *The Crucifixion and the Qurʾan: A Study in the History of Muslim Thought.* Oxford: Oneworld, 2009.

Matthews, John F. *Laying Down the Law: A Study of the Theodosian Code.* New Haven, CT: Yale University Press, 2000.

McAuliffe, Jane Dammen. *Qurʾanic Christians: An Analysis of Classical and Modern Exe-*

*gesis*. Cambridge: Cambridge University Press, 1991.

McClure, Judith. 'Handbooks against Heresy in the West from the Late Fourth to the Late Sixth Centuries'. *Journal of Theological Studies* 30 (1979): 186–97.

Meeks, Wayne A. *The First Urban Christian: The Social World of the Apostle Paul*. 2nd ed. New Haven, CT: Yale University Press, 2003.

Millar, Fergus. *A Greek Roman Empire: Power and Belief under Theodosius II (408–450)*. Berkeley: University of California Press, 2006.

Munt, Harry. 'The Prophet's City before the Prophet: Ibn Zabāla (d. after 199/814) on Pre-Islamic Medina'. In *History and Identity in the Late Antique Near East*, edited by Philip Wood, 103–21. Oxford: Oxford University Press, 2013.

Parrinder, Geoffrey. *Jesus in the Qurʾān*. Oxford: Oneworld, 1965.

Penn, Michael Philip. *Envisioning Islam: Syriac Christians in the Early Muslim World*. Philadelphia: University of Pennsylvania Press, 2015.

———. *When Christians First Met Muslims: A Sourcebook of the Earliest Syriac Writings on Islam*. Berkeley: University of California Press, 2015.

Powers, David S. *Muhammad Is Not the Father of Any of Your Men: The Making of the Last Prophet*. Philadelphia: University of Pennsylvania Press, 2009.

Reynolds, Gabriel Said. *The Qurʾān and the Bible: Text and Commentary*. New Haven, CT: Yale University Press, 2018.

Robinson, Chase F. *Islamic Historiography*. Cambridge: Cambridge University Press, 2002.

Rubin, Uri. 'Ḥanīfiyya and Kaʿba: An Inquiry in the Arabian Pre-Islamic Background of the *Dīn Ibrāhīm*'. *Jerusalem Studies in Arabic and Islam* 13 (1990): 85–112.

Shoemaker, Stephen J. *The Apocalypse of Empire: Imperial Eschatology in Late Antiquity and Early Islam*. Philadelphia: University of Pennsylvania Press, 2018.

al-Ṭabarī. *Jāmiʿ al-bayān ʿan taʾwīl āy al-Qurʾān*. Edited by Aḥmad Saʿīd ʿAlī et al. Cairo: Muṣṭafā al-Bābī al-Ḥalabī, 1954–68.

———. *Taʾrīkh al-rusul wa-l-mulūk*. Edited by M. J. de Goeje. 3 vols. Leiden: Brill, 1879–1901.

al-Tamīmī, Sayf b. ʿUmar. *Kitāb al-ridda wa-l-futūḥ wa-K. al-jamal wa-masīr ʿAʾisha wa-ʿAlī: A Critical Edition of the Fragments Preserved in the University Library of Imām Muhammad ibn Saʿud Islamic University in Riyadh, Saudi Arabia*. Edited by Qasim al-Samarrai. 2 vols. Leiden: Brill, 1995.

Tannous, Jack. *The Making of the Medieval Middle East: Religion, Society, and Simple Believers*. Princeton, NJ: Princeton University Press, 2018.

Turner, John P. *Inquisition in Early Islam: The Competition for Political and Religious Authority in the Abbasid Empire*. London: I.B. Tauris, 2013.

Wansbrough, John E. *Res Ipsa Loquitur: History and Mimesis*. Jerusalem: Israel Academy of Sciences and Humanities, 1987.

———. *The Sectarian Milieu: Content and Composition of Islamic Salvation History*. Oxford: Oxford University Press, 1977.

Watt, W. Montgomery, and M. V. McDonald, trans. *Muḥammad at Mecca*. Vol. 6 of *The History of al-Ṭabarī*. Albany: State University of New York Press, 1985.

Webb, Peter. *Imagining the Arabs: Arab Identity and the Rise of Islam*. Edinburgh: Edinburgh University Press, 2016.

Wood, Philip. 'Introduction'. In *History and Identity in the Late Antique Near East*, edited by Philip Wood, xi–xxii. Oxford: Oxford University Press, 2013.

# The Influence of Christian Theology on the Development of *Tawḥīd* in Early *Kalām*

*Romain Louge*

## 1. Introduction

In the seventh century, a new religious paradigm is setting place in the Arabic Peninsula. With the rise of Muḥammad and his followers, a new way of believing in God spreads fast. This new way finds its roots in the Qur'an, the holy scriptures of the Muslims written in Arabic. This language sets a new word to talk about God: *Allāh*, which literally means 'the divinity', the one and only. From this moment on, Arabic is gaining power as the new official language and Christian thinkers who used to work on Greek start to do theology in this language. The goal of this paper is to study the beginnings of this Christian theology in Arabic which is intimately linked to the new beliefs supported by Islam, focusing particularly on the methodology used by the first Arabic theologian and its link to the new way of talking about God or *kalām*.

To that end, I will develop first the context in which Islam appears and its relationship with Christianity and the impact it had on the Christian intellectual milieu and the theological work, creating a new methodology in a new language to defend their doctrine, especially of the unity of God in a Trinity, switching then to the development of *ʿilm al-kalām* and its development in the Islamic milieu, inspired by this methodology to defend the new doctrine of the absolute unicity of God or *tawḥīd*.

## 2. Context

To begin with, we must consider the context in which the idea of God starts to be a real question in the Arabic language. In fact, before the eighth century, it is not a problem, even though there are already Arabic-speaking Christian communities in the Arabic Peninsula or Ḥijāz in Arabic, especially in Yemen. Even though we do not have actual proof of Arabic manuscripts before the eighth century, there are numerous accounts of witnesses of Arabic tribes that adopted Christianity as their religion.[1] The beginning

1 The first signs of a Christian presence are in the letter of Paul to the Galatians (Galatians 1:15–17) where Paul explains he went to Arabia to announce the good news. Then Eusebius of Caesarea, in his *Ecclesiastical History*, shows several testimonies of Arab Christian presence, such as Philip the Arab emperor. Irfan Shahîd is a great contributor to this proof also: in some of his works he shows how Arab Christianity was present in the Ḥijāz. See Irfan Shahîd, *Rome and the Arabs: A Prolegomenon to the Study of Byzantium and the Arabs* (Washington, DC: Dumbarton Oaks Research Library and Collection, 1984) and *Byzantium and the Arabs in the Sixth Century* (Washington, DC: Dumbarton Oaks Research Library and Collection, 1995).

of theological writings in Arabic is then linked to the rise of Islam among the empire of Constantinople, and to the rapid Arabisation and Islamisation of the Middle East. And this process is fast: in 632, Muḥammad dies. At that time, the conquest has already begun in the Ḥijaz, specially in Mecca. The year after, in 633, all the Ḥijāz is conquered and the Muslim troops are already looking north. In 635, the army enters Damascus; in 637, the Patriarch of Jerusalem, Sophronius (550–638), surrenders the key of Jerusalem to the caliph ʿUmar (584–644) and the Muslim troops also enter Antioch; and in 641, Alexandria falls.[2] In ten years, all Middle East is conquered, and the new regime sets up. The process of Arabisation begins at that time even though the new power seeks to keep the former administration in place to run the country and keep the taxes flowing to fund the new conquests. It is in that context that Manṣūr b. Sarjūn (675–749), also known as John of Damascus, was born and educated, his father being one of the senior officers in the administration in Damascus. He was a native Arabic-speaker, even though we do not have any text from him in any other language but Greek. Yet, Greek tends to disappear rapidly from the intellectual work, being replaced by Arabic. John of Damascus is important because he is the one to introduce in his theological works the rising of Islam and the questions raised by this new religious paradigm. He criticises different aspects of Islam in *De Haeresibus* and specially the accusation made by Muslims that Christians are associating God and humanity as they themselves call him Word: 'You say that Christ is Word and Spirit of God, why did you insult us as associators?[3] Word and Spirit are inseparable things from the one whom they are in naturally. Then if he Is in God as Word of God, then he is also obviously God.'[4] Or in another text, also a controversy between a Christian and a Muslim, he writes about Jesus as Word and Spirit:

> Say to him: according to your scripture, are the Spirit of God and the Word told uncreated or created? If he tells you uncreated, tell him: you agree with me, for that which is not created by somebody, but creates, is God. But if he dares to tell you without doubt they are created, tell him: who created the Spirit and the Word of God? And if he tells, embarrassed, that God created them, tell him … Before creating the Spirit and the Word, was God without Spirit and without Word? He will flee you, for he has no answer.[5]

John is emphasising two important words that would later be at the heart of the Islamo-Christian controversy: Word and Spirit, *kalima* and *rūḥ*, which are central to the

2 Françoise Micheau, *Le début de l'Islam. Jalons pour une nouvelle histoire*, L'islam en débats (Paris: Téraèdre, 2012), 137.

3 He uses the term ἑταιριαστάς, which derives from the word ἑταιρίζω 'to make society'.

4 Jean Damascène, *Ecrits sur l'Islam*, Sources Chrétiennes 383 (Paris: Cerf, 2019), 219. All translations are mine.

5 Ibid., 239–41.

Christian doctrine of Trinity (one God in three persons) and Christology (Jesus is the son of God and the son of man).

## 3. First Theological Writings in Arabic and Its Methodology

At the end of the life of John of Damascus, the first theological works in Arabic are being written. Let us study the first of them that is known. This work is a theological apology written on a manuscript that was found at the end of the nineteenth century in the library of the monastery of Saint Catherine in Mount Sinai by Margaret Dunlop (1843–1920), one of the most pre-eminent scholars in Arabic and Islamic science at the time. This manuscript is very old, written in Kufic, and bears a colophon, dating it to 746. Although the actual date is debated, what is clear is that it cannot date after 780. Moreover, it is from Melkite tradition, and emanates from Mar Sabbas Monastery near Jerusalem.

Notably, this manuscript does not use the traditional vocabulary, main ideas, and theological descriptions of the Trinity and of Christology. Even though all these notions are in place in the theological culture, the author of the manuscript, who is unknown, makes the deliberate choice to take a different path for his apologetical proof. Indeed, the discourse suggests a new goal. The new political and religious paradigm that changed the face of the Middle East demands a new way of expressing faith. Therefore, the author never writes about the Greek philosophical categories, but makes the deliberate choice to place analogy and scriptural proof at the heart of his argumentation. And then, talking about the Trinity is always talking about 'God, his Word, and his Spirit' (*Allāh wa-kalimatuhu wa-rūḥuhu*).[6] Despite the opening sentence of the treatise, 'In the name of the Father and of the Son and of the Holy Spirit, the One God' (*bi-ism al-abb wa-l-ibn wa-l-rūḥ al-qudus Ilāh wāḥid*),[7] there is no other sign of Father and Son, only God and his Word. And, on his apologetic path, the author has two goals in mind: speaking to the Christians of his time and showing them by simple reasoning that the Christian faith is not unreasonable, or impossible to believe in; and speaking to Muslims, showing them the same thing. He therefore uses indistinctly the Bible and the Qur'an to make his proof clear and show that we find traces of the Trinity in the Qur'an as well as in the Bible.

For example:

> Therefore, as no one can reach the things coming from the power of God, nobody can reach the Word of God and his Spirit. Moreover, God said in the Torah: 'Let us make man to our image and our resemblance.'[8] And God, blessed be his name,

6 Margaret Dunlop Gibson, ed., *An Arabic Version of the Acts of the Apostles and the Seven Catholic Epistles: From an Eighth or Ninth Century Ms. in the Convent of St. Catherine on Mount Sinai*, Cambridge Library Collection (Cambridge: Cambridge University Press, 1899), 75.

7 Ibid., 74.

8 Genesis 1:26.

> did not say: 'I created man.' He said so: 'We created man.' To teach man that God, by his Word and his Spirit, created all things, gave life to all things, and that he's the creator by excellence. And you will find this in the Qur'an as well: 'We created man in distress' (*laqad khalaqnā al-insān fī kabad*).[9] And 'We opened the floodgates of heaven with water pouring down' (*fa-fataḥnā abwāb al-samāʾ bi-māʾ munhamir*).[10] And 'You have come to us individually, just as we created you the first time' (*taʾtūnā*[11] *furādā kamā khalaqnākum awwala marra*).[12] And believe in God and in his Word, and also in his Holy Spirit because 'the Holy Spirit has brought it down from your Lord [...] as grace and guidance' (*nazzalahu rūḥ al-qudus min rabbika* [...] *raḥmatan wa-hudan*)[13].[14]

As we can observe, the author uses both scriptures, the Bible and Qur'an, to help with his proof. This is one of the points of method used that is important to us.

The other two important points follow the two parts of the apologetical work: the Christological and Trinitarian proofs. For the Trinitarian proof, the author uses seven analogies to describe how the unity of God can be described in a trinity.

The first is the analogy of the sun: 'This is like the disc of the sun which is in heaven, and the rays which issue from the sun, and the heat which comes from the sun, each from the other. We do not say that these are three suns, but one sun, and these are three names not to be separated from one another.'[15] The second is the analogy of the eye, the pupil, and light: 'Also like the eye, and the pupil of the eye, and the light which is the eye; we do not say that there are three eyes, but one eye with three names in it.'[16] The third is the analogy of man: 'Also like the soul and the body and the spirit; we do not separate them from one another; we do not say there are three men but one man and three names in one person.'[17] And so on with the four others—the tree, the water, the mouth, and the man:

> Also like the root of the tree, and the branches of the tree, and the fruit of the tree; we do note say that these are three trees, but one tree, one part of it from another part. And when it begins to appear to men in its season, we know that all this is in the tree when it appears and before it appears. Also like the fount of the water,

9 Q. 90:4.

10 Q. 54:11.

11 We can observe an error of transmission: *taʾtūnā* whereas in the *muṣḥaf* it is *jiʾtumūnā*.

12 Q. 6:94.

13 Q. 16:102, but with further errors of transmission: the verse has been condensed, *wa-bushrā* has been replaced with *raḥmatan*, and *wa-hudan* has been moved to the end.

14 Gibson, *An Arabic Version*, 77.

15 Ibid., 4.

16 Ibid.

17 Ibid.

> which springs up from the source and a river flows from it, and some of the water of the river collects and becomes a lake. You cannot distinguish one apart from another; and though its names are different, we do not say that it is three waters but one water in the source and the river and the lake. Man and his intellect and the word which is generated from his intellect, one from the other, and the spirit which is in the intellect, and the word from the intellect, one from the other; we cannot distinguish between them, and each one has its beginning from the others and is known from it. Also like the mouth and the tongue that is in the mouth and the word which issue from the tongue; so is our saying about the Father and the Son and the Holy Spirit. By it the prophets prophesied, and said, the mouth of the Lord has spoken.[18]

In the Arabic corpus, these analogies are the only ones used all together and all after the others, which proves that they play a central role in the argument of the manuscript.

As for the Christological proof, the author uses the scriptural argument along with prophecy and achievement. He seeks to show that every event in the life of Christ finds its source in what was announced by the patriarchs and the prophets in the scriptures of the Jews. In this part, he does not use the Qur'an, but only biblical references, to emphasise an announced truth that was established: Christ is the son of man and son of God.

This new way of forming theology in response to Islam will have a rapid answer in the Islamic milieu. Indeed, *kalām* will not wait for 300 years to develop itself as it did for Christian theology before the Council of Nicaea. The rapid rise of Islam is also a time when intellectual works will be gaining in power. The opening of the *buyūt al-ḥikma*, the houses of wisdom, is a wonderful opportunity to gain knowledge from different traditions, and to build an Arabic repository of all kinds of sciences: medicine, astronomy, mathematics, music, but foremost philosophy and more specifically the philosophy of Aristotle and Plato. In this upsurge of intellectual works, controversy starts to strike the theological milieu.

## 4. *ʿIlm al-Kalām* and Its Development

After having studied the first Christian theological writing in Arabic, its origins, as well as posterity, and highlighted the two great pillars of theological proof as thought by the anonymous author of the manuscript Sinai Arabic 154 by analogical theology and the importance of scriptural proof, it seems significant to question the reception in the Muslim world of this innovative methodology in the theological world. There are then two elements to consider: the theological work and the theology in comparison.

18 Ibid.

Indeed, theology or *ʿilm al-kalām* is the intellectual and rational work carried out by Muslim scholastic theologians (*mutakallimūn*), which takes its roots from the revealed scripture of the Qur'an, as well as from the corpus of *ḥadīths*, to organise the Muslim thought around a profession of faith and a praxis, and therefore a law. It thus develops in two different ways: by talking about Islam or by comparing it with other religious traditions in order to specify the dogmatic statements that are emerging in this new religious paradigm. Thus *ʿilm al-kalām*, or more commonly, *kalām*, is a science which seeks to answer questions about divine life (theodicy, eschatology, etc.) and human life (anthropology, soteriology, free will, etc.). Traditionally, the founding of *kalām* is traced back to Abū Ḥasan al-Ashʿarī (873–935) in the response he offers to the Muʿtazilīs. This is why it is necessary to distinguish two things: *kalām* in the sense of theological reflection and *kalām* in the sense of the theological methodology proposed by al-Ashʿarī who uses a form of dialectics derived from the Greek tradition.[19] It is a question here of focusing more particularly on reasoning in the broad sense rather than reflection on a particular method.

The second element is the question of the comparison with other religions, and particularly here, Christianity. Indeed, Islam was born following a religious history marked by Judaism and Christianity and the comparison is then one of the pillars of the theological method to show the differences and the stumbling blocks between distinct religious traditions.

The goal pursued by this reasoning is to deepen the study of the nascent *kalām* in order to propose, after a brief history of Islamic–Christian theological relations on the Muslim side, a study on a work by a Muslim author showing how the theological methodology of the author of the Christian apology previously studied had a singular impact on Islamic theological methodology. This, in turn, led to the laying of fundamental dogmatic bases on the nature of certain aspects of Christianity in Islamic doxa and had an influence on *kalām*.

*Kalām* as a religious science is rather difficult to date precisely; indeed, it is difficult to determine when it becomes an autonomous science. However, we traditionally notice certain names at the origin of discussions on important subjects of Islam. The most important of them is Abū Ḥanīfa (699–767), the eponymous founder of what will later be called the Ḥanafī legal school. Abū Ḥanīfa is known to have introduced an early notion of right in the face of questions posed about moral life. Indeed, there are quite precise prescriptions in the Qur'an, but what to do in a case where there is no determined answer in the corpus of the Qur'anic text? This is one of the questions that Abū Ḥanīfa tries to answer by leaving room for personal judgement or *qiyās*.[20] It is the notion of *fiqh* that appears which will then be translated as 'law' in its legal dimension. Howev-

19 William Montgomery Watt, 'al-Ash'arī, Abu'l-Ḥasan', *Encyclopaedia of Islam* [henceforth: *EI*] (Leiden: Brill, 1960), 1:695.

20 Louis Gardet, *L'islam: religion et communauté*, 3rd ed. (Paris: Desclée de Brouwer, 1982), 190.

er, before being thought of as law in a systematic way, *fiqh* was rather conceived of as 'speculative meditation, thus distinct from *ʿilm* in the sense of traditional knowledge'.[21] Thus, as Louis Gardet (1904–86) develops in his article on *kalam*,[22] it was after the Battle of Ṣiffīn between ʿAlī and Muʿawīya concerning the caliphal succession of Muḥammad that we can see the first debates emerging on the content of the faith and in particular on the question of the Imāmate and on the status of the believer that the Imām must possess.[23] This status then presupposes that one defines what one believes in order to postulate the conditions of salvation and the responsibility for acts. Then, from these moral considerations, a development is made on the question of the legitimacy of what leads to consider these questions and therefore on the nature of the Qurʾan. And finally, on the nature of the one who is at the origin of the Qurʾan, and more specifically on the subject of his attributes and therefore of divine uniqueness or *tawḥīd*. This systematic questioning leads to a methodology which, through the concrete questioning of the first believers and the nascent community, tries to evolve and make the movements essential for a systematisation of the question of faith and thus express what it is to be a believer in submission to God. These questions quickly give rise to theological tensions reflecting political ones over the succession of Muḥammad between the partisans of the hereditary and therefore dynastic dimension of this succession, which will give birth to the great family of the Shīʿa, and the partisans of the succession of the charism and therefore of the consensus on the name of a successor or caliph who will give birth to the great family of the Sunnīs. Obviously, this split has repercussions on the way of seeing this succession and therefore of the Imāmate. In his article on the Imāmate, Wilferd Madelung retraces this original epic and thus shows how the internal dissensions of the early days of Islam are at the origin of the first reflections on Islam.[24] In a first part on the early developments, Madelung shows that the central point is the designation of Abū Bakr as *khalīfat rasūl Allāh*, successor of the Messenger of God, thus ensuring the continuity of the unity of the Muslim community headed by a single person. He indicates that there is not too much discussion at that time on this question of inheritance, but voices began to rise under the caliphate of ʿUthmān. Indeed, some will qualify the caliph as just and others as unjust, thus making a moral judgement on his action and inheritance quality: is he therefore a successor or not because of the morality or immorality of his actions? The Shīʿa proclaim the injustice of the actions of ʿUthmān and the difficulty of recognising him as successor and therefore propose an alternative to this moral difficulty, namely, a succession of blood and hereditary or dynastic in the person of ʿAlī, the cousin of Muḥammad. There is a conflict that arises between the Shīʿa in

21 Louis Gardet, 'ʿIlm al-kalām', *EI*, 3:1141.
22 Ibid.
23 Wilferd Madelung, 'Imāma', *EI*, 3:1163–64.
24 Ibid.

favour of heredity and its representative, ʿAlī, and the Sunnīs in favour of designation around consensus and its representative, Muʿāwiya (602–80). At the Battle of Ṣiffīn in 657, an arbitration was reached and Muʿāwiya founded the Umayyad caliphate in 661 following the assassination of ʿAlī by a group of Shīʿa dissidents who did not accept the arbitration carried out following the Battle of Ṣiffīn and call themselves the Khawārij. It is in this context that the reflection around the morality of acts grows with the focal questions: what makes an act moral or immoral? How does on qualify the morality of an act? What criteria allow this qualification?

It is therefore the question of revelation that arises here and of its legitimacy. What ultimately allows one to define this morality, since the Word of God is announced by Muḥammad and transmitted orally? Why are these words authoritative and not others? Many questions colour the nascent intellectual life around this new religious paradigm that seeks to express itself and to reflect on itself. However, very quickly, another parameter comes into play in this expression of faith, namely, the different religious expressions of this new religious paradigm which come to confront this emerging reality. Indeed, during the early expansion of Muslims north and west, they arrived in places where the populations were predominantly Christian, with traces of Judaism and other primitive religions. The relationship with these populations will therefore be fundamental to establish a certain authority but also in the dialogue around religious questions.

This questioning around the different religious realities is particularly evident in the Qurʾan itself where we find biblical characters such as Adam and Eve, Noah, Abraham and his descendants, prophets, or even Mary and Jesus. This is how the focus on the biblical universe allows for an opening unto the Jewish and Christian worlds. However, it is true that in a predominantly Christian world at the time and in these places, it is the question of the Muslim relationship with Christians that is important and for Christians of the relationship with these believers of a new kind. In order to observe these relationships, the first thematic question to study therefore is how Christians and Christianity are seen in the first theological writings.

Following the writing, collection, and fixation of the Qurʾan, the first commentators of the verses in the sixth and eighth centuries were numerous, but their writings are mostly lost though cited in later works. The first theological writings take the form of commentaries on the Qurʾan which also focus on talking about the different extra-Islamic realities, but which are found in the narrative, especially on the question of Christians, their faith, their origin, and so on. One of the very important early commentators is al-Ṭabarī (839–923), known for his *Jāmiʿ al-bayān fī tafsīr al-Qurʾān*, also called *Tafsīr al-Ṭabarī*, a highly significant work of verse-by-verse commentary. It is in such works that we see references to authors who preceded them and who are authoritative by the chains of transmission cited and thus guarantee the authenticity of the reported message. Thus, one of the keys to understanding how Christians and Christianity are perceived in the first Qur'anic writings lies in a statement of Ibn ʿAbbās (619–87) reported by al-Ṭabarī. Ibn ʿAbbās was a cousin of Muḥammad and he is known as one of the first commentators on the Qur'an and a collector of *ḥadīth*. He was close to ʿAlī and therefore to the nascent Shīʿa world. His authority is, however, recognised in all Muslim denominations. He writes about Christians:

> After Jesus, the kings changed the Torah and the Gospel. Among them were believers who read the Torah and the Gospel. It was said to their king: 'Nothing is more painful to us than the insults hurled at us by these people.' They recite: "Those who do not judge according to what God has revealed are infidels" (Q. 5:44). They recite verses and in doing so they dishonour us. Summon them, then, that they read the same texts as ours and believe like us!' The king summoned them, gathered them together, and gave them the choice between death and giving up reading the Torah and the Gospel, except what changed. They replied, 'How can you ask us that! Let us go!'[25]

And then, from the commentary of Q. 57:27:

> We then sent our other prophets in their footsteps, whom we had followed by Jesus, son of Mary, to whom we gave the Gospel. And we kindled in the hearts of those who followed him kindness and compassion. As for the monasticism that they established themselves, we did not impose it on them. They themselves were impelled to it by their own desire to please God, without observing it as they should have done. We gave their reward to those who believed among them, but many of them were perverts.

This *sūra* is called *al-ḥadīd*, iron, because this term is used in verse 25. It is constructed as a sort of exhortation to the glorification of God in various ways and this can be understood in the first sentence after the *basmala* which expresses '*sabbaḥa li-Lāh mā fī al-samāwāt wa-l-arḍ*' or 'What is in the heavens and on earth glorify God'. The *sūra* is therefore built around this idea of glorifying divine omnipotence, then around various exhortations to believe in God, followed by an explanation of the penalties inflicted on men and therefore the sending of messengers and scriptures before a final exhortation to faith. At the heart of this *sūra*, verse 27 shows two realities: that willed by God (kindness and compassion) and that which is not willed by God (monasticism and its way of life). Ibn ʿAbbās therefore commenting on this part, quoted by al-Ṭabarī, affirms that the kings changed the Torah and the Gospel. The term used is *baddalū*, which means to alter, or to change something by another. Here appears a fundamental concept in the Islamic

25 Claude Gilliot, 'Exégèse et sémantique institutionnelle dans le commentaire de Tabari', *Studia Islamica* 77 (1993): 73–74.

vision of Christianity and Christians called the falsification of the scriptures or *taḥrīf*. There is therefore a difference in treatment between Christianity and Christians. Those whom Ibn ʿAbbās attacks are the Christians who modified, or altered, the Torah and the Gospel, and modified and altered religious practice by inventing monasticism, which is not the will of God, as opposed to Christianity itself, which in its original version carried the message of God. Moreover, for him, after Jesus was taken up to heaven, his disciples were divided into four groups. The first is what is called the religion of the emperor, *dīn al-malik*, which sees Jesus as one of three gods along with God and Mary. The second group, the Jacobites, assert that God was in their midst as long as he wanted, until he ascended into heaven. The third group, the Nestorians, profess that the son of God was in their midst as long as God willed him, and God raised him up to heaven. These latter two groups grew and took precedence over the last group, the Muslims who remained in the background until the coming of Muḥammad.[26]

These first testimonies on the Christian faith in Muslim theological writings show that Christianity is not condemned or attacked because Christians are above all the disciples of Jesus, considered a prophet by Muslims, but Christians are the origin of a falsification of the scriptures, of a change of doctrine in relation to the message that Jesus had been able to bring from God. It is therefore in this perspective that the first Muslim authors will approach the question of Christianity in their writings.

In this dynamic and upsurge of theological works and nascent relationship between Islam and Christianity, there exists a direct response to the first Christian apology. At the beginning of the ninth century, the Muslim author al-Qāsim al-Rassī (785–860) writes his *al-Radd ʿalā al-Naṣārā* (Refutation of the Christians).[27]

## 5. Biographical Elements on al-Rassī

Al-Qāsim b. Ibrāhīm b. Ismāʿīl al-Rassī was a religious leader of the ninth century. He is from the family of al-Ḥasan (625–70), the second Imām, descendant of ʿAlī, Muḥammad's son-in-law. He is more precisely the great-grandson of Ibrāhīm al-Shibh, grandson of al-Ḥasan.[28] He therefore grew up in Medina, the city of the Prophet, where his family taught him the Zaydī doctrine, the *ḥadīth*s, the reading of the Qurʾan, as well as Arabic.[29] In 815, it is attested that he was in Egypt around al-Fusṭāṭ, a city founded during the conquest

26 Claude Gilliot, 'Christians and Christianity in Islamic Exegesis', in *Christian–Muslim Relations: A Bibliographical History, Volume 1 (600–900)*, ed. David Thomas and Barbara Roggema, The History of Christian–Muslim Relations 11 (Leiden: Brill, 2009), 43–44.

27 al-Qāsim al-Rassī, *al-Radd ʿalā al-Naṣārā*, ed. Imām Ḥanafī ʿAbd Allāh (Cairo: Dār al-Āfāq al-ʿArabiyya, 2000).

28 A. B. D. R. Eagle, 'Al-Hādī Yaḥyā b. al-Ḥusayn b. al-Qāsim (245–98/859–911): A Biographical Introduction and the Background and Significance of the Imamate', *New Arabian Studies* 2 (1994): 103.

29 'al-Rassi', *EI*, 8:453.

on a Byzantine fortress, and which became the capital of the province, located in Old Cairo today. He may have been sent to this city by his brother Muḥammad, recognised as an Imām by the Zaydīs.[30] There he studied Christian and Jewish scriptures, as well as Christian theology and philosophy, a source of debate between Muslims and non-Muslims.[31] It was there that he composed two of his greatest works, namely, his refutation of the Manichaeans and his refutation of the Christians. It is under this influence of writings and Christian theology that he develops his arguments on the divine attributes and on free will. He was suspected of seditious activities by the city authorities and left Egypt to return to Medina in 826.[32] He settled in al-Rass where he wrote and ended his days by welcoming passing Zaydīs to his home.

Opinions about his political activities differ. Madelung suggests he lived rather quietly, without causing any problems.[33] However, in the Muslim tradition, we see him more as a revolutionary who tackled the Sunnī problem head-on and sought to have the Zaydī thesis triumph over the Imāmate. This would be because his brother Muḥammad, himself considered an Imām, was assassinated and defended what he was fighting for.[34] However, he did it in a discreet way, refusing to be proclaimed Imām in public, and also refusing to call for revolt following the disappointments suffered by his brother in trying to move the political lines and his failure in the revolt that ended with his assassination.[35] According to Imām Ḥanafī ʿAbd Allāh, editor of *al-Radd*, al-Rassī was very successful in Medina and went to Egypt to escape the fate that might have been in store for him following the death of his brother. Then, after this ten-year exile, returning to Medina and going to Yemen, he regained success before settling and disappearing in the countryside to avoid repression by the army.[36] He is also at the beginning of a second Zaydī movement after the Kūfa movement, a movement that was born in Tabaristan, on the shores of the Caspian Sea, which was then called the Caspian movement. Following the theological teachings of al-Rassī, particularly on the absolute dissociation of God from evil and the absolute dissimilarity of God from all created things, this movement was born around 860 with a strong desire for rebellion.[37] This desire was realised in 864 and led to the creation of a Zaydī state with Amul as its capital in Tabaristan. This city saw the passage of al-Rassī before he settled in al-Rass where he lived a secret life to write and teach people passing through.[38]

---

30 Ibid.

31 Ibn-Ibrāhīm ar-Rassī Qāsim, *La lotta tra l'islām e il manicheismo: un libro di Ibn al-Muqaffaʿ contro il Corano*, trans. Michelangelo Guidi (Rome: Roma Accademia Nazioale dei Lincei, 1927), 15.

32 'al-Rassi', 453.

33 Ibid.

34 al-Rassī, *al-Radd*, 15.

35 Eagle, 'A Biographical Introduction', 109.

36 al-Rassī, *al-Radd*, 15.

37 Wilferd Madelung, 'Zaydiyya', *EI*, 11:478.

38 al-Rassī, *al-Radd*, 15.

A good part of his works have come down to us, such as *The Great Eulogy* (*al-Madīḥ al-kabīr*) and *The Little Eulogy* (*al-Madīḥ al-ṣaghīr*), his refutation of the Manichaeans and his refutation of the Christians, two opuses on the Imāmate, *The Imāmate* (*al-Imāma*) and *The Installation of the Imāmate* (*Tathbīt al-imāma*), *The Five Sources*, *The Duties*, *The Policy of the Soul*, *Justice and Unification* (*al-ʿAdl wa-l-tawḥīd*), *The Abrogating and the Abrogated* (*al-Nāsikh wa-l-mansūkh*), *The Great Proof* (*al-Dalīl al-kabīr*) and *The Small Proof* (*al-Dalīl al-ṣaghīr*), and *Killing and Fighting* (*al-Qatl wa-l-qitāl*).

After having presented the life of al-Rassī, the framework of this study imposes a particular judgement on his work which is related to Christianity, *al-Radd ʿalā al-Naṣārā* or *The Refutation of Christians*. Indeed, the author chooses an original method to carry out his argument, which is to go through what Christians have already been able to write, writings that he has already studied during his stay in Egypt. However, before discussing the work itself, it is important to present the theological context in which the author operates, and which allows him to carry out his thesis.

## 6. Theological Context

As seen earlier, al-Rassī is not only interested in studying Christian scriptures and opuses, but also Jewish scriptures and theological works. And the focal point is the person of Christ, who is at the centre of the theological problem. Indeed, for Muslims, the Jews received Christ wrongly, not accepting his prophetic mission, just as they distorted the message of the prophets of God who came before him. Consequently, the relationship between Jews and Christians remained tense and not peaceful throughout their history until the seventh century. This is due to several reasons, the most telling of which is the rejection of Christ as a prophet by the Jews, but also a rejection of his words although Christ preached around the Torah and the Word of God. However, the upheaval that Judaism experienced in the face of nascent Christianity did not allow Jews to accept faith in Jesus, son of Mary, and thus to submit to his words. On the contrary, they have reached the point of denying it existence to be able to preserve the characteristics of the Jewish religion: 'a priestly religion which has its own rituals, incantations, masters and scholars'.[39] So, they denied him his lineage and they denied his prophecy.

Similarly, however, in Muslim culture, Christians who saw Jesus flouted and denied his existence have wished to exalt him to the point of making him like God. Thus, shortly after the death of Christ, some of his disciples made gospels to tell of their conceptions of Jesus. They each offer a different one, which casts doubt on the authenticity of what is told and therefore of the message supposedly delivered by these writings. It is necessary to wait for the arrival of the Qur'an as the main, unique, and truthful source of testimony

39 Ibid., 5.

of the life of Jesus, son of Mary, to re-establish the reality of what he really is: a prophet and not the son of God.

Finally, there are three conceptions of Christ that will balance in the story. The first denies him completely and seeks to erase his existence and all traces thereof. The second sanctifies him insofar as he is considered a divinity. The third is brought by a man, a messenger, 'who brought the gifts of heaven to earth and rejected the material of the Jews, and again led the flock of the lost children of Israel to the fold of the faith, so that they return to the Mosaic law, to respect among those who followed him, those who distorted the words it brought'.[40] The latter hid much of what was happening to them, and construed some of the law 'according to their whims' and according to their interests.

These three conceptions are then like three ways: (1) the *via minima*, where the figure of Christ is set aside, as if forgotten and denied his existence; (2) the *via maxima*, where the figure of Christ is exalted, sanctified, and deified—these two ways being exaggerated, each in its own manner, either under the aspect of slander against Jesus, or under the aspect of divine presumption against the uniqueness of God; or (3) a *via media* that recognises Christ for what he really is, a man who bears no divine particularity, but carries prophetic dignity. Islam thus positions itself in front of Judaism and Christianity as the way of moderation, reason, and realism which befits divine revelation and seeks to bring consideration to the prophecy and to the messages announced by the prophets. Al-Rassī thus places both religions in the category of exaggeration in their welcoming of the person of Christ.

Through this way of seeing the person of Christ, we can detect a double will. The first is to place Islam as a true religion because it is reasonable. The second is to introduce through its exaggerated link to Jesus, the link to Muḥammad, which will be just as exaggerated.

So, the Jews, just as they denied the message of Jesus, also denied the message of Muḥammad. And the Christians, in the same way that they distorted the reality of the man Jesus, twisted the reality of monotheism into a trinity, and perverted the reality of Muḥammad. Using important artifices to think the unthinkable, and passing through ancient philosophy which further complicates the debate when Muḥammad came to announce a clear and simple truth: there is only one unique God. Christians, by not recognising Muḥammad as a prophet, by distorting what he is, are authors of a narrative imposed on the truth itself: monotheism against the Trinity, prophecy against the saviour.

We can therefore see that the emerging theological context of how Islam looks at Christianity goes hand in hand with its view of Judaism and that the emphasis is increasingly placed on confrontation. Moreover, the subjects at the heart of this confrontation and which join those at the heart of the first Christian apologies clearly emerge: the question of the uniqueness of God, and the question of Christ.

---

40 Ibid.

After discussing this general theological context, let us now consider how al-Rassī positions himself in his work.

## 7. Al-Rassī's Method

Al-Rassī, in this theological context, therefore, also seeks in his *al-Radd* to place the person of Christ at the centre of his argument by recalling the impossibility for God to be father or son because of his absolute dissimilarity to the created world. Indeed, the son bears the characteristics and traits of his father, and his father also bears the characteristics of his son. So, there is a physical similarity that follows. What physical similarity between Jesus and God would be possible? The divinity of Jesus would amount to denying parenthood. Moreover, al-Rassī is astonished at those who adore him without considering his mother, Mary, since she is associated in the same way by her offspring, with the plan of God. He argues that Christians testify against the divinity of Jesus by showing that he suffered and rejoiced with human beings, and that he ate like human beings. This invalidates, for him, the Christian claim to divinity.

Even if the Christians worshipped Jesus, al-Rassī trivialises the matter by asserting that they worshipped him as others worshipped the stars and the planets, and thus accuses them of polytheism. However, for al-Rassī, there is something in the divinity which refuses all similarity, and even if one must speak of attributes associated with God, they are there to represent divine unity. Thus, the birth of Jesus, his resemblance, and his connivance with other human beings can only be a proof of his humanity because he ultimately has no resemblance to the creator. Moreover, the creator cannot have begotten nor have been begotten, no one is equal to him, he is neither father nor son, and has no partner.

In order to engage with this dynamic, al-Rassī considers it necessary that whoever does justice to an adversary in his dispute with him must show him honour before offering an eloquent response, by first presenting his adversary's arguments, such that whoever hears them deems them rational and well-founded.

Al-Rassī thus presents the different schools of Christianity and their opinions on who Jesus is to show that differences of opinion cannot be a source of unity and unification. The differences between Nestorians, Jacobites, and Melkites on the mechanics of unity and union of the divine hypostases lead these confessions to uphold the Trinity in the face of monotheism and that amid this confusion, there is a need to abandon this theory to rely on the word of the prophets which alone leads to a word of truth. Al-Rassī, however, seeks to make himself understood by all, and to carry out his testimony he invites readers to understand this confusion by the interpretation of five fundamental testimonies: the testimony of God, the testimony of the angels of God, the testimony of the Verb of God, Jesus, the testimony of the people and of his mother, and the testimony of the apostles.

Thus al-Rassī establishes a method to organise the proof to challenge his opponents, one of the pillars of which is the Bible testifying that Jesus is the son of David. Also, he shows that Jesus tells his disciples that they are sons of the Lord and elsewhere he calls them his brothers or his mother. In another place, he testifies that he is the son of Joseph. In short, he takes as witness the Christian scriptures of which he faithfully transmits long passages, in particular the Sermon on the Mount, and methodically comparing them with passages from the Qur'an, seeks to show that the supposed divinity of Jesus is rather the work of Satan. Moreover, it is not a question of the divinity of Jesus, but of his quality of prophethood.

## 8. *Al-Radd ʿalā l-Naṣārā*

Among the polemical works of Muslims against Christians, this opus is one of the oldest known. One of its remarkable aspects is its style in rhymed prose, imitating the method that some Christian authors adopted for the same kind of work. He thus presents a way of giving rise to controversy in these early times when Muslim doctrine begins to reflect and express itself, in the light of other doctrinal realities coming from different religious traditions with which Islam interacted in its primitive expansion. This opus is written in a simple way, without artifice or emphasis, but with the desire to go to the core of the argument. It thus constitutes an important document in the history of the Islamic–Christian controversy, at the intersection of a new genre.

In a pure and elegant style, the language is very understandable in the proper genius of the Arabic tongue. The 2000 edition is edited by Imām Ḥanafī ʿAbd Allāh at the Dār al-Āfāq al-ʿArabiyya. It is edited from a microfilm of the House of Egyptian Books from a manuscript kept at the library of the Great Mosque of Sanaa in Yemen.[41] Another edition was produced in 1922 by an Italian author from five manuscripts, four from the library of the Ambrosian University of Milan and another from the Royal Library of Berlin.[42]

The main objective of *al-Radd* is to refute the two realities, which, in the eyes of the author, are fundamental to the Christian faith, namely, the Trinity and the divinity of Jesus. It is by the argument of the principle of generation according to nature and exclusively in this mode that the author excludes the divine generation of the Word and therefore its consequences, particularly the need for a divine generation by a divine mother. Thus, the divinity of Jesus is totally denied, and he is truly considered as a servant of God, and therefore a man with needs, pains, and other aspects which make him only a prophetic messenger like the others. Al-Rassī rejects all multiplicity in God and demonstrates divine unity. He thus refutes the Christian doctrine of the Trinity based on comparisons which

41 Ibid., 13.

42 Ignazio Di Matteo, 'Confutazione contro i cristiani dello Zaydita al-Qāsim b. Ibrāhīm', *Rivista degli Studi Orientali* 9, no. 3 (1922): 303.

he asserts that Christians use: that of the sun, rays, and heat and that of man, body, soul, and word. These comparisons are based on analogies already used and al-Rassī refutes them according to the total difference between the natural order and the divine order.

What is striking is the levelling up of the theological knowledge. Indeed, as the title says, the author is trying to refute Christian beliefs, and he does so in the same manner as the author of the Christian apology. He moves from the theology of analogy to negative theology: all the analogies one can choose to somehow show a part of God's reality are false, because they are taken from the created world and cannot be applied to the divine reality. God is greater than analogies and so we can say what he is not, but not what he is. For example, al-Rassī describes the analogy of the sun used by the Christian apology: God is like the sun, the Word is like the rays emitting from the sun, and the Spirit is like the heat emanating from the sun; then there is only one sun with its rays and its heat. He refutes that analogy via two arguments: (1) rays and heat are not the sun and therefore are not part of the sun and are two distinct entities, and (2) God is not the sun.[43]

Al-Rassī begins his letter by firstly speaking of God, exalting his transcendence, and the impossibility for him to engender or be engendered, because of his nature being different from any created nature. The son bearing the characteristics and attributes of his father bears a likeness, a likeness that anyone who comes from a father receives as a son. We therefore only deny the divine filiation of Jesus since he cannot bear the attributes of God given that he has a human body. If there is a divine filiation, it must only come from the mother of Jesus, who herself would be of a divine nature, which is impossible because it introduces a paradox into the uniqueness of God. Jesus therefore cannot share the divinity, but only the quality of a prophet.

Prophets are human beings like everyone else: they eat, they drink, they bear witness, they suffer. And according to the testimony of Christians, Jesus experienced these same things. He is therefore identical to all other men and the claim of his divinity is not fair in the eyes of what he has experienced.

For al-Rassī, Christians adore Jesus, as others adored the stars, introducing intermediaries between God and them. These intermediaries are, however, part of the created world, and this is indicative of polytheism and disbelief, since God created creatures, whether they are men or stars, arranges them as he wishes, and causes death.

The birth of Jesus and his resemblance to human beings can only be a proof of his humanity, and despite his extraordinary character, by the miracles he can perform, whereby he may appear like God because of that power, his similarity to God's creatures prevents him from being similar to the divine as the text of the Qurʾan proclaims.

Thus, all the proofs testify that the creator is one, he did not beget, nor is he not begotten, no one can be his equal; he cannot be a father or a son because it would be a

43 al-Rassī, *al-Radd*, 33–34.

proof of deficiency, of need, and therefore of a created character because the claim of paternity and filiation contradicts the sense of eternity and introduces temporality. This proves that Christ cannot be a son of God, but a faithful servant with his individuality, his unity, but who does not interfere in the divine unity.

Al-Rassī then shows that this analogical theology is the source of separation between the Christians. For him, taking these examples to talk about God is the main source of confusion that the Christians had. Al-Rassī is also aware of all the differences the Christians have among themselves, which, for him, is yet another proof that there is a problem in the veracity of this religion. He accurately describes these differences as follows:

> The Rum, the Melkites, say: 'The divine person, that has always been present, before centuries, engendered from the Father, descended upon the Virgin Mary, and took from her a nature, without person, and he was from her nature, subsistent by her nature that he took from her.'[44]

And he does the same thing for the Jacobites and the Nestorians:[45]

> The Jacobites say: 'The Son that did not descend before descended, from heaven on earth, goodness to it, as mercy for man, goodness from him to mankind by good will. He took a body from the Virgin Mary, became flesh from this body, and they became one.'[46]

> The Nestorians say: 'The Son that did not descend by love before descended by goodness and good will, and he became flesh from Mary at his descent in a full and perfect body, in a nature and a hypostasis from humanity and Adam, and the Messiah had two natures and two perfect hypostasis, after his incarnation in the body.'[47]

His conclusion is then that if the analogy is the source of confusion and separation, it cannot be used and it cannot tell a truth. Analogy must therefore give way to apophatic theology, which states the absolute diverseness of God from all created things and then his uniqueness in nature.

Al-Rassī moves on to a third part where he cites the scriptures, but in a unique way using more Bible than Qur'an. He finds different passages from the scriptures and specially from the Gospels and proves that the latter say different than what the Christians say. For example: 'Here is how was born Jesus, son of David. This is the testimony, that

44 Ibid., 36.
45 Ibid., 36–39.
46 Ibid., 36.
47 Ibid.

he was among the Apostles, and that the father of the Messiah is David, and that the Messiah is his son, and he is begotten from here.'[48]

## 9. *Tawḥīd* and *Taḥrīf*

We can see that the methodology used by the author of the Christian apology and al-Rassī are very similar. First, they use either analogy or apophatic theology, which permits a discussion of the intellectual work on God. Then they make use of the scriptures, the Bible or Qur'an, to help each in his own way, making a proof by their respective understanding of prophecy. The goal is essentially to prove the falseness of the other's assumption, but never in a bad spirit. This introduction to an Arabic *kalām*, Christian or Muslim, will lead afterwards to the reckoning of two separate ways and the source of the theological absoluteness of *tawḥid*, and observing the scriptures of the Christians, to the declaration of the falsification of the scriptures by later theologians.

The goal of each theologian is to prove the veracity of what he believes in. Both are trying to prove the unicity of God in their own belief, and they use every means available to make themselves clear to the other, without any concession on doctrine, but with a kind of openness to the other that can challenge us.

Either the author of the apology or al-Rassī are using both scriptures, the Bible and Qur'an, to prove their point. This is interesting because, as we understand it today, they should not be linked this way. Christians do not cite the Qur'an for their proof because it comes way after the Bible and the theological works in the first ecumenical councils, and because they do not recognise it as the Word of God. Muslims do not cite the Bible because they are proclaiming it falsified from the true Torah and Gospel that were given to Moses and Jesus and altered by Christians. This, of course, raises the question of the link between *tawḥīd* and *taḥrīf*, which seem to be at the heart of Muslim *kalām*. Indeed, why bother citing the Christian scriptures if they are false? Perhaps because their falsity has not been understood the same way over time.

All in all, *taḥrīf* can be understood from different points of view. First, the tampering of the text itself: all the text is wrong and has been changed by the disciples of Jesus. Secondly, the tampering of the meaning of the text, which is to say the way the text was received and transmitted included errors, but the text itself bears truth, or elements of truth that can give it authority. Al-Rassī in his *al-Radd* cites much Christian scripture, especially the Sermon of the Mount in the Gospel of Matthew, and uses it to refute the Christian faith and to prove some points of the Muslim faith. This way, the link between *tawḥīd* and *taḥrīf* is strong because, from both sides, it is at the heart of demonstration, even though each interlocutor does not deny the scripture of the other, but more accu-

48 Ibid., 44.

rately, the meaning the other gave to their scriptures.

## 10. Conclusion

In the upsurge of a new religious paradigm in the seventh century, there is a need from Christians and Muslims to advocate for their doctrine in the research of truth. Christian and Muslim scholars develop a methodology for a theology of controversy, which means confronting the ideas of the other. This methodology is based on analogy or apophatic theology and, with the help of the scriptures, develops a new kind of theological reality to prove the unicity of God or *tawḥīd*. By doing so, the first theologians to write in Arabic took a position about the scripture of the other. In the case of al-Rassī, by using the Bible intentionally and intensively, he shows us that the Christian scripture had a meaning, or at least some kind of authority, that led him to use it as his proof, not by way of negating it but using its meaning to help his proof. He then shows that the unicity of God for a Muslim can be understood by a true comprehension of the Bible and the tampering of the meaning of the text. Thus, *tawḥīd* and *taḥrīf* are linked in this theological will to prove the Muslim doctrine, but are also linked to another *tawḥīd* and *taḥrīf*, one from the Christian point of view.

## Bibliography

Abū Rā'iṭa. *Die Schriften des Jacobiten Ḥabīb Ibn Ḫidma Abū Rā'iṭa*. Edited by Georg Graf. Corpus Scriptorum Christianorum Orientalum 130. Leuven: Imprimerie Orientaliste, 1951.

'Alī, Jawād. 'Yuḥanna al-Dimashqī'. *al-Risāla* 610 (12 March 1945).

Anawati, Georges C. 'Polémique, apologie et dialogue Islamo-Chrétiens Positions classiques médiévales et positions contemporaines'. In *Miscellanea in honorem Card Greg P Agagianian*, edited by Gregorio Petrowicz, Krikor Bedros Agadzhanian, and Paolo Marella, 375–451. Rome: Pontificia Universitas Urbaniana, 1969.

Caspar, Robert. 'Bibliographie du Dialogue Islamo-Chrétien (VIIe-XIIe siècle)'. *Islamochristiana* 1 (1975): 125–81.

Di Matteo, Ignazio. 'Confutazione contro i cristiani dello Zaydita al-Qāsim b. Ibrāhīm'. *Rivista degli Studi Orientali* 9, no. 3 (1922): 301–64.

Eagle, A. B. D. R. 'Al-Hādī Yaḥyā b. al-Ḥusayn b. al-Qāsim (245–98/859–911): A Biographical Introduction and the Background and Significance of the Imamate'. *New Arabian Studies* 2 (1994): 103–22.

Eutychius of Alexandria. *The Book of Demonstration (Kitāb al-Burhān)*. Vol. 1. Edited by Pierre Cachia. Corpus Scriptorum Christianorum Orientalum 192. Leuven:

Peeters, 1960.
Gallo, Maria. *Palestinese anonimo, omelia arabo-cristiana dell'VIII secolo*. Collana di testi patristici 116. Rome: Città Nuova Editrice, 1994.
Gardet, Louis. "Ilm al-kalām'. *Encyclopaedia of Islam*, 3:1141–50. Leiden: Brill, 1971.
———. *L'islam: religion et communauté*. 3rd edition. Paris: Desclée de Brouwer, 1982.
Gibson, Margaret Dunlop, ed. *An Arabic Version of the Acts of the Apostles and the Seven Catholic Epistles: From an Eighth or Ninth Century Ms. in the Convent of St. Catherine on Mount Sinai*. Cambridge Library Collection. Cambridge: Cambridge University Press, 1899.
Gilliot, Claude. 'Christians and Christianity in Islamic Exegesis'. In *Christian–Muslim Relations: A Bibliographical History: Volume 1 (600–900)*, edited by David Thomas and Barbara Roggema, 31–56. The History of Christian–Muslim Relations 11. Leiden: Brill, 2009.
———. 'Exégèse et sémantique institutionnelle dans le commentaire de Tabari'. *Studia Islamica* 77 (1993): 41–94.
Griffith, Sidney H. 'Answers for the Shaykh: A "Melkite" Arabic Text from Sinai and the Doctrines of the Trinity and the Incarnation in "Arab Orthodox" Apologetics'. In *The Encounter of Eastern Christianity with Early Islam*, edited by Emmanouela Grypeou and Mark N. Swanson, 277–310. The History of Christian–Muslim Relations 5. Leiden: Brill, 2006.
———. *Arabic Christianity in the Monasteries of Ninth-Century Palestine*. Variorum Collected Studies 380. Aldershot: Ashgate, 1992.
———. 'Faith and Reason in Christian *Kalām*: Theodore Abū Qurrah on Discerning the True Religion'. In *Christian Arabic Apologetics during the Abbasid Period (750–1258)*, edited by Samir Khalil Samir and Jorgen Nielsen, 1–43. Leiden: Brill, 1994.
———. 'The Qur'an in Christian Arabic Literature: A Cursory Overview'. In *Arab Christians and the Qur'an from the Origins of Islam to the Medieval Period*, edited by Mark Beaumont, 1–19. The History of Christian–Muslim Relations 35. Leiden: Brill, 2018.
Haddad, Rachid. *La Trinité divine chez les théologiens arabes: 750–1050*. Paris: Beauchesne, 1985.
Harris, J. Rendel. 'A Tract on the Triune Nature of God'. *The American Journal of Theology* 5, no. 1 (1901): 75–86.
Jean Damascène. *Chapitres philosophiques*. Paris, n.d.
———. *Ecrits sur l'Islam*. Sources Chrétiennes 383. Paris: Cerf, 2019.
———. *La Foi Orthodoxe 1–44*. Sources Chrétiennes 535. Paris: Cerf, 2010.
———. *La Foi Orthodoxe 45–100*. Sources Chrétiennes 540. Paris: Cerf, 2011.
Khalil Samir, Samir. 'The Earliest Arab Apology for Christianity (c. 750)'. In *Christian Arabic Apologetics during the Abbasid Period (750–1258)*, edited by Samir Khalil Samir and Jorgen Nielsen, 57–114. Leiden: Brill, 1994.

———. 'Une apologie arabe du christianisme d'époque umayyade?'. *Parole de l'Orient* 16 (1988): 85–106.

Khalil Samir, Samir, and Jorgen Nielsen, eds. *Christian Arabic Apologetics during the Abbasid Period (750–1258)*. Leiden: Brill, 2004.

Khoury, Adel-Théodore. *Apologétique Byzantine contre l'Islam (VIIIe-XIIIe s.)*. Verlag für Christlich-Islamisches Schrifttum 1. Altenberge, 1982.

Madelung, Wilferd. 'Al-Qāsim ibn Ibrāhīm and Christian Theology'. *Aram* 3 (1991): 35–44.

———. 'Imāma'. *Encyclopaedia of Islam*, 3:1163–69. Leiden: Brill, 1986.

———. 'Zaydiyya'. *Encyclopaedia of Islam*, 11:477–81. Leiden: Brill, 2002.

Micheau, Françoise. *Le début de l'Islam. Jalons pour une nouvelle histoire*. L'islam en débats. Paris: Téraèdre, 2012.

Monferrer-Sala, Juan Pedro. 'Once Again on the Earliest Christian Arabic Apology: Remarks on a Palaeographic Singularity'. *Journal of Near Eastern Studies* 69 (2010): 195–97.

Montgomery Watt, William. 'al-Ash'arī, Abu'l-Ḥasan'. *Encyclopaedia of Islam*, 1:695–96. Leiden: Brill, 1960.

Prémare, Alfred-Louis de. *Aux Origines du Coran. Questions d'hier, approches d'aujourd'hui*. L'islam en débats. Paris: Téraèdre, 2011.

Qāsim, Ibn-Ibrāhīm ar-Rassī. *La lotta tra l'islām e il manicheismo: un libro di Ibn al-Muqaffa' contro il Corano*. Translated by Michelangelo Guidi. Rome: Roma Accademia Nazioale dei Lincei, 1927.

'al-Rassi'. *Encyclopaedia of Islam*, 8:453–54. Leiden: Brill, 1995.

al-Rassī, al-Qāsim. *al-Radd ʿalā al-Naṣārā*. Edited by Imām Ḥanafī ʿAbd Allāh. Cairo: Dār al-Āfāq al-ʿArabiyya, 2000.

Reynolds, Gabriel Said. *A Muslim Theologian in the Sectarian Milieu: 'Abd al-Jabbār and the* Critique of Christian Origins. Leiden: Brill, 2004.

———. 'On the Qur'anic Accusation of Scriptural Falsification (*Taḥrīf*) and Christian Anti-Jewish Polemic'. *Journal of the American Oriental Society* 130, no. 2 (2010): 189–202.

Schadler, Peter. *John of Damascus and Islam: Christian Heresiology and the Intellectual Background to Earliest Christian–Muslim Relations*. The History of Christian–Muslim Relations 34. Leiden: Brill, 2018.

Shahîd, Irfan. *Byzantium and the Arabs in the Sixth Century*. Washington, DC: Dumbarton Oaks Research Library and Collection, 1995.

———. *Rome and the Arabs: A Prolegomenon to the Study of Byzantium and the Arabs*. Washington, DC: Dumbarton Oaks Research Library and Collection, 1984.

Swanson, Marc N. 'An Apology for the Christian Faith'. In *The Orthodox Church in the Arab World 700–1700: An Anthology of Sources*, edited by Samuel Noble and Alexander Treiger, 40–59. DeKalb: Northern Illinois University Press, 2014.

———. 'Apologetics, Catechesis and the Question of Audience in "On the Triune Nature of God" (Sinai Arabic 154) and Three Treatises of Theodore Abū Qurrah'. *Beiruter*

*Texte Und Studien* 117 (2007): 113–34.

———. 'Beyond Prooftexting: Approaches to the Qur'an in Some Early Arabic Christian Apologies'. *The Muslim World* 88, no. 3–4 (1998): 297–319.

———. 'Beyond Prooftexting (2): The Use of the Bible in Some Early Arabic Christian Apologies'. In *The Bible in Arab Christianity*, edited by David Thomas, 91–112. The History of Christian–Muslim Relations 6. Leiden: Brill, 2007.

Swanson, Mark N. 'Some Considerations for the Dating of *Fī taṯlīṯ Allāh al-wāḥid* (Sinai Ar. 154) and *al-Ǧāmiʿ wuǧūh al-īmān* (London, British Library or. 4950)'. *Parole de l'Orient* 18 (1993): 115–41.

Thomas, David. 'The Bible in Early Muslim Anti-Christian Polemic'. *Islam and Christian–Muslim Relations* 7, no. 1 (1996): 29–38.

# On Religion: Ṣadrian Metaphysics as 'Islam's Argument' (*Ḥujjat al-Islām*) against Henry Martyn

*Sajjad H. Rizvi*

How do we talk about religion and what role does philosophical argumentation have in theology? Can philosophy provide the tools for an adequate analysis of religion? Is religion even an analytical category conducive to such inquiry, a reality and actuality beyond scholarly constructions that seek to universalise and generalise rather disparate phenomena (often with a fixed, normative gaze upon Protestant Christianity)?[1] At least since the time of David Hume (1711–76), the modern study of religion has floundered on these questions, animated by the desire for naturalistic and sceptical approaches to 'religion'.[2] Hume famously critiqued existing distinctions between monotheism and polytheism and questioned the very possibility of conceiving of God in terms of the infinite, the noumenal, the supernatural, and the transcendent that lay at the heart of traditional notions of sanctity and the divine in Christian and Islamic traditions.[3]

While all these terms need unpacking and disaggregating in our contemporary study of the humanities, not least after the 'decolonial turn' (following and complementing the linguistic turn and the ontological turn), what I propose in this paper is to locate finding our understanding, even construction of 'religion', in the polemical encounter that seeks to provide an alternative approach to a philosophy and theology of religion that is not beholden to the current, colonial practice rooted in consideration of Protestant Christianity. Polemics are not merely rhetorical arguments for the apologetic defence or

---

1 One thinks, for example, of Jonathan Z. Smith's famous articulation of this idea in *Imagining Religion: From Babylon to Jonestown* (Chicago: University of Chicago Press, 1982), xi: 'Religion ... is solely the creation of the scholar's study. It is created for the scholar's analytic purposes by his imaginative acts of comparison and generalization. Religion has no independent existence apart from the academy.' Often the construction of religion divides on 'faith-based' and agnostic lines: Wilfred Cantwell Smith famously argued that the notion of religion should be dropped because in its systematisation and generalisation it fails to capture religious feelings and substitutes the dynamic of faith with a reified system. See Wilfred Cantwell Smith, *The Meaning and End of Religion: A New Approach to the Religious Traditions of Mankind* (Minneapolis: Fortress, 1963), 51.

2 The scepticism and naturalism are already clear in his *Treatise on Human Nature* completed by 1740 and applied to religion in his posthumous *Dialogues concerning Natural Religion*.

3 Broadly speaking, there is a singular concept of God across the Abrahamic religions, though there are numerous notions of God even within religious traditions. See Graham Oppy, *Arguing about Gods* (Cambridge: Cambridge University Press, 2009), 1–48. There are, of course, many types of response to Hume. One traditional (dare one say Neoplatonic?) defence of religious and even mystical experience of the divine that he considers foundational for religion is the Orthodox theologian and philosopher David Bentley Hart's *The Experience of God: Being, Consciousness, Bliss* (New Haven: Yale University Press, 2013). A more 'postmodern' set of sometimes 'anatheistic' approaches (nourished by the continental philosophy of religion) is Richard Kearney and Jens Zimmermann's edited volume *Reimagining the Sacred* (New York: Columbia University Press, 2016).

doctrine or the performative dismantling of opposing truth claims and the belittling of beliefs and practices; rather, they are often the primary vehicle for the articulation of one's own beliefs, the systematisation of the religious tradition (in appeal to fellow believers and practitioners often more than the opponents), and the postulation of the principles, hermeneutics, as well as the ontology and epistemology that underpin the tradition.[4]

While Muslim–Christian polemics have a venerable history debating the nature of beliefs, doctrines, and practices that go back to the period of the initial challenges of the message of Muḥammad and Islam, one of the interesting aspects of that history relates to the responses to missionary activity in the Qajar period, and especially the reactions to the work of Anglican missionary Henry Martyn (1781–1812), not least because they speak to our understanding of the culmination of traditional, 'rational' modes of theological presentation in Islam and its engagement with newer notions of religion arising from the European encounter.[5] Martyn, a chaplain to the military of the East India Company, having served as a missionary in India from 1806 to 1810 and translated the New Testament into Urdu, turned his attention to a Persian New Testament and visited Iran in 1811, seeking to present copies to the Shah.[6] His work perpetuated Orientalist notions of debating scripture and engaging sovereignty through appeals to political and social elites. In Shiraz, he became embroiled in disputations with Mīrzā Muḥammad Ibrāhīm Ḥusaynī Fasavī (d. 1839), and wrote two responses to his Arabic critique of Christianity.[7] He also debated Sufis like the Nūrbakhshī Mīrzā Abū al-Qāsim 'Sukūt' Shīrāzī (d. 1823), which may account for a Sufi response from his contemporary Niʿmatullāhī Ḥusayn

4 The colonial contexts of these shifts in taxonomy and polemical encounter are particularly clear in South Asian and elsewhere in British imperial realms. See Tomoko Masuzawa, *The Invention of World Religions, or How European Universalism Was Preserved in the Language of Pluralism* (Chicago: University of Chicago Press, 2005), 64ff.; SherAli Tareen, *Perilous Intimacies: Debating Hindu–Muslim Friendship after Empire* (New York: Columbia University Press, 2023). For studies on how polemical encounters shaped the construction of classical Sunnī 'orthodoxy' and heretication of difference, see Aaron W. Hughes, *An Anxious Inheritance: Religious Others and the Shaping of Sunni Orthodoxy* (Oxford: Oxford University Press, 2022); and more radically, Patricia Crone and Michael Cook, *Hagarism: The Making of the Islamic World* (Cambridge: Cambridge University Press, 1977).

5 See the series *The History of Muslim–Christian Relations*, which began under the general editorship of David Thomas and is now curated by Jon Hoover, published by Brill. For a good survey of the early Christian encounters, see Michael Philip Penn, *When Christians First Met Muslims: A Sourcebook on the Earliest Syriac Writings on Islam* (Berkeley: University of California Press, 2015).

6 John R. C. Martyn, *Henry Martyn (1781–1812), Scholar and Missionary to India and Persia: A Biography* (Lewiston, NY: E. Mellen Press, 1999), 95–128, for a useful if uncritical narrative; Avril Powell, *Muslims and Missionaries in Pre-mutiny India* (Richmond: Curzon Press, 1993), 89–102, 107–14. For a discussion of these polemics and Persian responses, see ʿAbd al-Hādī Ḥāʾirī, *Nukhustīn rūyārūyī-hā-yi andīshagarān-i Īrān bā dū rūya-yi tamaddun-i būrzhūvazī-yi gharb* (Tehran: Amīr Kabīr, 1988); for the Safavid background to the polemics, see Rasūl Jaʿfarīyān, *Siyāsat va farhang-i rūzgār-i ṣafavī* (Tehran: Nashr-i ʿilm, 2009), 965–98.

7 A manuscript that contains Fasavī's Arabic text and Martyn's two Persian responses is Bodleian Or. 765. These texts were translated in the missionary Reverend Samuel Lee's *Controversial Tracts in Christianity and Mohammadanism by the Late Rev. Henry Martyn and Some of the Most Eminent Writers of Persia* (Cambridge: J. Smith, 1824). Lee's work included the response of Mullā Muḥammad Riżā Hamadānī (d. 1822) entitled *Irshād al-muḍillīn fī ithbāt khātam al-nabiyyīn.*

ʿAlī-Shāh Iṣfahānī (d. 1818).[8] Most Shīʿī responses to Martyn in Iran and India followed the 'argument from reason' by providing philosophical objections to Christianity, as well as rational defences of the Islamic notion of prophecy and revelation.[9] After a brief contextualisation of Muslim–Christian polemics on the nature of monotheism in this period and the development of the study of metaphysics in Safavid Iran, I examine one text that deploys the thought of the Safavid sage Mullā Ṣadrā Shīrāzī (d. 1046/1636) and his hermeneutical and ontological principles to provide rational responses to Martyn: *Ḥujjat al-Islām yā burhān al-milla*, the work of the philosopher and occultist ʿAlī Nūrī (d. 1831), the thinker who did most to establish the hegemony of Mullā Ṣadrā in the imaginary and curriculum of the modern Shīʿī seminary.

## 1. Preliminaries

But before we venture on that path two preliminary discussions are required. The first relates to the nature of religion and the challenges that comparative language poses for us in describing 'religion', 'monotheism', 'theology', and so forth, extending my brief opening remarks, and the second relates on the very term *dīn* and its cognates and how we might make sense of those discussions in the later period that furthers the critique of religion but also engages with some of the recent debates on the nature of the study of Islam.

### 1.1 Religion

To argue that religion is a modern concept—very much a commonplace nowadays—is not to say that notions that proximate how we understand religion or even the term did not exist in premodern times. Immanuel Kant (1724–1804) himself in his reconceptualisation acknowledges this while orienting religion away from questions of metaphysics to those of morality and what it is that is reasonable for us to postulate that we owe each other.[10] The modernity of religion is to postulate that the notion has a history and is not merely the opposite of modern secularity with which in a sense it is born.[11] Friedrich Schleiermacher (1786–1834), cleric and Romantic, responded to the new Kantian hegem-

8 Ḥusayn ʿAlī-Shāh Iṣfahānī, *Risāla-yi radd-i pādrī*, ed. Maḥmūd Riżā Isfandyār (Tehran: Intishārāt-i ḥaqīqat, 2008), esp. 44, on the request of ʿAbbās Mīrzā. Shīrāzī was sometimes claimed as a Niʿmatullāhī but seems to have been Nūrbakhshī—see ʿAbd al-Ḥusayn Zarrīnkūb, *Dunbāla-yi justajū dar taṣavvuf-i Īrān* (Tehran: Amīr Kabīr, 1990), 317. On Ḥusayn ʿAlī-Shāh, see Zayn al-ʿĀbidīn Shīrvānī, *Bustān al-siyāḥa* (Tehran: Sanāʾī, 1895), 82–83; Maʿṣūm ʿAlī-Shāh Shīrāzī, *Ṭarāʾiq al-ḥaqāʾiq*, ed. M. J. Maḥjūb (Tehran: Intishārāt-i Sanāʾī, 1966), 3:221.

9 Compare Powell, *Muslims and Missionaries*, 170–79.

10 Immanuel Kant, *Religion within the Boundaries of Mere Reason*, trans. and ed. Allen Wood and George di Giovanni (Cambridge: Cambridge University Press, 2018), 39–49.

11 Brent Nongbri, *Before Religion: A History of a Modern Concept* (New Haven: Yale University Press, 2013), 154–59.

ony by lamenting that not only did reasonable and cultivated people in his time consider religion to be an 'evil' but that it is almost impossible to speak coherently and sensibly about religion because of the prevalent misconceptions.[12] The question of the nature of religion and of (revealed) morality seemed alien in those times and as such threatened the individual liberties of those who wished to see religion differently.

Talal Asad and his followers argue that our modern notion of religion is constructed in the Enlightenment through notions of piety and faith as morality, religion designated in terms of what is reasonable and as a private state of affairs that entails believing assent to truth claims, and that evacuates the public sphere for the 'secular'.[13] Religion is therefore rethought by him as a 'discursive tradition' in Islam (and indeed for Christianity as well). Perhaps the most salutary point that he wishes to make is that our modern conception of the opposition of religion and secularity (which, of course, is mistaken) finds its articulation in other binaries in which one side is deemed positive and the other negative such as reason versus charisma or critique versus advice and so forth.

The decolonial turn allows us to understand the coloniality of the construction of both religion and secularity, complicating their boundaries and allowing for differential and pluriversal ways of considering the phenomena of religions. The coloniality of the concept of religion (and indeed of the humanities) is predicated on the ontological and epistemic dominance of Eurocentric modernity, matrices of power, racial hierarchies, conceptions of the human, and of gender and of violence.[14] Universalising such a category of religion therefore privileges and universalises that coloniality. Decolonising the concept meanwhile involves stripping away its normativity and the binary oppositions that come with it such as the sacred and the profane, the religious and the secular, and indeed the material and the noetic. An Yountae's recent work shows how the modern concepts of religion, secularity, race, and coloniality are intertwined and force the concept of religion into colonial power structures.[15] A rethinking of this concept of religion in line with the desire for liberation from coloniality is essential to recover the sacred and the spiritual, in a critical idiom because what Yountae does not always acknowledge is how some of the decolonial thinkers on whom he relies such as Fanon were themselves fixed in the colonial paradigm of seeing Islam as a force for liberation which more often was a motivation for reactionary acquiescence to colonialism. Much of the field of the study of

---

12 Friedrich Schleiermacher, *On Religion*, trans. and ed. Richard Crouter (Cambridge: Cambridge University Press, 1996), esp. 18–54.

13 Talal Asad, *Genealogies of Religion: Discipline and Reasons of Power in Christianity and Islam* (Baltimore: Johns Hopkins University Press, 1993); Talal Asad, *Formations of the Secular: Islam, Christianity, Modernity* (Stanford: Stanford University Press, 2003); David Scott and Charles Hirschkind, eds., *Powers of the Secular Modern: Talal Asad and His Interlocutors* (Stanford: Stanford University Press, 2006).

14 Eleanor Craig and An Yountae, 'Introduction', in *Beyond Man: Race, Coloniality, and Philosophy of Religion*, ed. An Yountae and Eleanor Craig (Durham, NC: Duke University Press, 2021), 1–31.

15 An Yountae, *The Coloniality of the Secular: Race, Religion, and the Poetics of World-Making* (Durham, NC: Duke University Press, 2024).

religion seems oblivious to such problems of spirituality, coloniality, and liberation, not least because it is still invested in the problem of defining a category that is analytically used in a comparative sense broadly within a 'secular' context.[16]

More recently, Rushain Abbasi has taken issue with the modern construction of religion and secularity to argue that such concepts and distinctions did exist in premodern Islam and that in fact to argue that Islam does not allow for a secular space or that all epistemological and ontological possibilities are exhausted by religion (often reduced to a legalistic tradition) is in itself somewhat colonial.[17] Further, Sherman Jackson has outlined the possibility of contextualising the religious in Islam through the secular in his argument for an 'Islamic secular' sphere that is characterised by rational considerations, customary actions and practice, and other considerations beyond the Sharīʿa.[18] However, what these considerations do permit is a more careful analysis of how we use terms such as religion and secularity and that perhaps we are better suited to consider the use of more emic terms.

### 1.2 *Dīn*

At one level, decoloniality demands of us forsaking the term religion in favour of *dīn* (and other cognates such as *dharma*, *dao*, and so forth), a term with various resonances including the transactional, the legal, the traditional. Three critical Qurʾanic loci of the term are important as they tell us something about exegetical engagements on *dīn* in an oppositional and polemical context to which we will turn. The first is a related pairing from Sūrat Āl ʿImrān: 'Indeed, with God *dīn* is Islam and those who were given the scriptures did not differ except after knowledge had come to them, out of envy among themselves' (Q. 3:19), and 'Should anyone follow a *dīn* other than Islam, it shall never be accepted from him, and he will be among the losers in the hereafter' (Q. 3:85). And then we have the famous phrase that has become a mainstay of modern liberal Muslim discourse on liberty from Sūrat al-Baqara: 'there is no compulsion in *dīn*; rectitude has become distinct from error' (Q. 2:256).

Most exegeses on these verses focus on what is meant by *dīn* and whether it is a singular reality (and subsequently whether 'religions' are products of false consciousness or mistaken acts of wilful heresy). To take one example from the modern period influenced by the same philosophical tendencies as Nūrī, ʿAllāma Ṭabāṭabāʾī (d. 1981) in his exegesis on these verses argues that *dīn* is a singular reality identical to *islām* as the act of submission

16 A good summary of the field is Aaron W. Hughes and Russell T. McCutcheon, eds., *What Is Religion? Debating the Academic Study of Religion* (New York: Oxford University Press, 2021).

17 Rushain Abbasi, 'Did Premodern Muslims Distinguish the Religious and the Secular?', *Journal of Islamic Studies* 31, no. 2 (2020): 185–225; Rushain Abbasi, 'Islam and the Invention of Religion', *Studia Islamica* 116 (2021): 1–106.

18 Sherman A. Jackson, *The Islamic Secular* (Oxford: Oxford University Press, 2024).

to the truth (*taslīm al-ḥaqq*) and consequent beliefs and practices.[19] *Dīn* is what conforms to sound human nature (*fiṭra*) and as such is singular; the multiplicity of *dīn* in history insofar as it reflects the results of different contexts of prophecy and revelation stands not in contradiction to each of its forms but exists on a continuum separated by degrees of perfection and lack thereof.[20] As a human reality, *dīn* is an internal matter, a series of cognitive states leading to actions and beliefs that are expressions of the inclination of the heart that cannot be compelled nor inauthentic expressions of the self.[21] Thus, *dīn* is singular but modulated (to invoke Mullā Ṣadrā's concept of *tashkīk*) and an 'esoteric' matter, a theme to which we will return later.[22] Earlier another exegete influenced by Mullā Ṣadra, Sulṭān ʿAlī Shāh (d. 1911), takes the similar position that *dīn* is singular but has multiple historical manifestations and that it is a path to the afterlife that takes one from the true realisation of *islām* to internal states that motivate the person to faith (*īmān*). In that sense, he argues that *dīn* in its essence is an ontological status and a disposition as it is identical to *walāya*, the term central to the Shīʿī tradition denoting the status of the Imāms as well as what we owe to the Imām and to one another as fellow travellers on the path to God.[23]

In modern Qur'anic studies, Haddad has focused on the development of the notion of *dīn* from a set of transactions that leads to accountability at judgement into the afterlife to a focus on *tawḥīd* and the quality of one's commitment to it.[24] She rejects the idea that the singularity of *dīn* suggests an opening for religious pluralism. More recently, Friedmann's study of the juristic discussions on compulsion in *dīn* similarly does not suggest religious freedom or pluralism but the primacy of obligation.[25] Goudarzi takes *dīn* away from cognates of religion and internal states and insists that the Qur'anic usage pertains to the transactional and to acts of worship.[26]

---

19 Sayyid Muḥammad Ḥusayn Ṭabāṭabāʾī, *al-Mīzān fī tafsīr al-Qurʾān* (Qom: Manshūrāt al-ḥawza al-ʿilmiyya, n.d.), 3:120.

20 Ibid., 335–36.

21 Ibid., 2:342.

22 Other Shīʿī exegetes in the modern period take different positions. Sayyid ʿAbdullāh Shubbar (d. 1827) insists that *dīn* is singular and other claims are false; he defines *dīn* in terms of the juristic categories of commands and prohibitions, hence making *dīn* a set of transactional relationships of obedience to God. See Sayyid ʿAbdullāh Shubbar, *Tafsīr al-Qurʾān al-karīm* (Beirut: Dār Iḥyāʾ al-Turāth al-ʿArabī, 2008), 101, 110. Sayyid Muḥammad Ḥusayn Faḍlallāh (d. 2010) similarly argues that *dīn* is a singular reality connected to obedience seeking reward but also that *dīn* and its identification with *islām* suggests the privilege of the expression of divine singularity (*tawḥīd*), which for him is the central theme of the Qur'an. See Sayyid Muḥammad Ḥusayn Faḍlallāh, *Min waḥy al-Qurʾān* (Beirut: Dār al-Malāk, 1998), 5:270–71. Sayyid ʿAlī Naqī Naqavī (d. 1988) in his Urdu exegesis also insists that dīn is singular but he is less concerned with supersessionism (which he accepts) and more with the simple cognition that *dīn* applies primarily to assent to divine unity and theodicy. See Sayyid ʿAlī Naqī Naqavī, *Tafsīr Faṣl al-khiṭāb* (Lahore: Miṣbāḥ al-Qurʾān Trust, 2011), 1:454, 503.

23 Sulṭān ʿAlī Shāh, *Bayān al-saʿāda fī maqāmāt al-ʿibāda* (Tehran: Tehran University Press, 1965), 1:222, 252.

24 Yvonne Y. Haddad, 'The Conception of the Term *Dīn* in the Qurʾān', The Muslim World 64, no. 2 (1974): 114–23.

25 Yohanan Friedmann, *Tolerance and Coercion in Islam: Interfaith Relations in the Muslim Tradition* (Cambridge: Cambridge University Press, 2003).

26 Mohsen Goudarzi, 'Worship (*Dīn*), Monotheism (*Islām*), and the Qurʾān Cultic Decalogue', *Journal of*

A different approach is taken by Chittick in unifying but also pluralising *dīn* based on his reading of the work of the Sufi Ibn al-ʿArabī (d. 638/1240) and the notion of primordial traditions.[27] Based on the metaphysics of the unity of existence and the notion that everything has a singular origin and unity which then morphed into diversity due to the different agencies of the divine names, he argues that *dīn* as a path and tradition is both singular and plural: the plurality of paths into the afterlife and in the reversion to God and the very plurality of humans as expressions of the divine names entails that there are qualitative differences between people and their destinations. *Dīn* is therefore ontological mandate, eschatological reality, and psychologically differentiated states.

One example of a thinker who considered *dīn* to be a primordial tradition and hence singular and universal as well as multiple in its historical manifestations was the Mughal prince Dārā Shukoh (1615–59). His interest in Vedic traditions was prompted by the desire to find confluences of tradition, patronising various translations including a third version of the *Jog-Vasisht* (a rendition of the *Laghu-Yoga-Vāsiṣṭhā*) on the Yoga-Vedanta doctrine of metaphysics and of a selection of the Upanishads as the *Sirr-i akbar*.[28] Dārā took the position, extending a rather standard understanding of the universality of prophecy and revelation, that the Upanishads were the 'hidden scripture' (*kitāb maknūn*) and a 'revelation' (*tanzīl*) mentioned in Q. 56:77–80, and in his preface he explains the nature of the confluence.[29] These confluences—culminating in his work *Majmaʿ al-baḥrayn*, a study of the homologies between the terminology and ontological systems of the school of Ibn al-ʿArabī, especially the doctrine of the singularity and unity of existence (*waḥdat al-wujūd*), and that of the non-dualist mode of Vedanta (although he also uses the *kufr* meaning 'unbelief')—were predicated on a vision of unity of metaphysics, ethics, and of religious dispensations.[30] Non-dualism therefore was the ground of that primordial tradition and *dīn*.[31] In his time, Dārā's antipathy to differentiation—his notions of 'Islam' and 'Vedanta' were rather stylised and abstracted from historical actuality—was criticised for forgoing the particularity of Islam as *dīn*.

---

*the International Qurʾanic Studies Association* 8, no. 1 (2023): 30–71.

27 William C. Chittick, *Imaginal Worlds: Ibn al-ʿArabī and the Problem of Religious Diversity* (Albany: State University of New York Press, 1994).

28 Shankar Nair, *Translating Wisdom: Hindu–Muslim Intellectual Interactions in Early Modern South Asia* (Berkeley: University of California Press, 2020), 43–44; Supriya Gandhi, *The Emperor Who Never Was: Dara Shukoh in Mughal India* (Cambridge, MA: The Belknap Press of Harvard University Press, 2020), 195–201.

29 Dārā Shukoh, *Sirr-i akbar*, trans. Āzarmī Dukht Ṣafavī (Delhi: National Council for the Promotion of Urdu, 2022), li–liv; Gandhi, *The Emperor Who Never Was*, 203–13.

30 Gandhi, *The Emperor Who Never Was*, 186–93.

31 Nair, *Translating Wisdom*, 93–94.

### 1.2.1 *Dīn as an Esoteric Matter*

The final example of emic approaches to the question of *dīn* is Mullā Ṣadrā's position on esotericism. My starting point on Mullā Ṣadrā comes from Christian Jambet. Towards the end of the section on salvation or the return to the One in his magisterial *L'acte d'être*, Jambet discusses the nature of the divine theophany in the form of the Throne and the perfect human, culminating with a short discussion of 'no compulsion in *dīn*' that forms the logical conclusion.[32] The perfect human (*al-insān al-kāmil*) is the goal of creation moving towards God; the microcosmic homology (*ʿālam ṣaghīr*) of God, he manifests the totality of the names and always has existed and always will. In fact, the return of the cosmos to the One is mediated through the person and reality of the perfect human. Becoming such a person requires sincerity and pureness of the heart, which is the organ and reality that is the seat of the divine in the human, the homology of the divine throne.

Jambet argues that this requires, following Mullā Ṣadrā, complete obedience to the divine order. Insofar as *dīn* is an 'esoteric matter' relating to the states of the soul, it is unaffected by exoteric matters. This extinction cannot be achieved without complete obedience—in response to the desire of the divine and love, referring to the famous *ḥadīth qudsī* of the hidden treasure that desired to be known. True liberty—and this recalls a number of critical *ḥadīth* in *al-Kāfī* of al-Kulaynī—recognises the complementarity of the exoteric and the esoteric. The soul is existence—and existence self-subsists and is unconstrained. This is the point where the absence of compulsion intervenes or rather in which constraints cannot possibly apply. The harmonious movement of the heart and soul of the person towards God—what we call religion—cannot be compelled in real terms.[33]

What I am therefore proposing is a consideration of esotericism as an alternative hermeneutics of the text in the present that sets aside the existing dominant liberal, conservative, and modernist readings. This is esotericism as both a primordial tradition—and adherents of Shīʿī Islam certainly including, of course, Mullā Ṣadrā see themselves as belonging to the original faith promulgated by the first friends of God—and as a 'discipline of the arcane', a hidden or 'difficult' doctrine, access to which is required through a process of initiation. In *Baṣāʾir al-darajāt*, one of the earliest Shīʿī *ḥadīth* collections compiled by Abū Jaʿfar al-Ṣaffār al-Qummī (d. 290/903), there is a chapter of narrations on the difficult and arduous nature of the cause of the Imāms and their *walāya* (nearmost friendship and status with God); for example, Imām Abū Jaʿfar Muḥammad al-Bāqir (d. 114/733) is reported to have said: 'our matter is difficult and arduous (*ṣaʿb mustaṣʿab*) and can only be borne by one of the cherubim, a messenger prophet, and a person whose

32 Christian Jambet, *L'acte d'être: La philosophie de la révélation chez Mollā Ṣadrā* (Paris: Fayard, 2002), 411–23 (420–23 for the section on 'no compulsion').

33 Jambet says that his analysis is a brief version of a longer piece: 'Pas de contrainte en religion. Une approche de la question de la liberté en Islam', *Histoire du libéralisme en Europe*, brochure no. 15, Centre de Recherches en Épistémologie Appliquée (École polytechnique), Centre de recherches en philosophie économique (ESCP-EAP), Paris, 2004. Unfortunately, I have yet to get hold of a copy.

heart has been tested for his faith by God.'[34] This makes it clear that the Shīʿī cause is an elite whose inner states are turned towards the Imām by God and hence towards God. Esotericism is thus at the heart of Shīʿī Islam.

In a *ḥadīth* narrated from the fifth Imām, al-Bāqir, it is reported that each verse of the Qur'an has an apparent (*ẓāhir*) and a hidden (*bāṭin*) aspect, and that even the hidden aspect has further aspects, which suggests a hierarchy or multiplicity of esoteric meanings.[35] In his exegesis of Q. 32:2, Mullā Ṣadrā draws upon this famous *ḥadīth* on the exoteric and esoteric aspects of the Qur'an and relates it to the nature of the human and the cosmos. All three realities—or books, since Mullā Ṣadrā says that a book is whatever is inscribed and 'pictures' a reality[36]—the cosmos, the human, and the Qur'an, have levels and depths that do not violate their unity as a reality. It is the role of the esoteric minded, those gnostically attuned whereby their souls are attached to the divine pen and tablet and the higher divine realm, and they can discern the real meanings that underlie the phenomena that are experienced.[37] The esoteric approach allows one to see how phenomenal entities can be symbols and icons of what is not materially present to us; thus the world is a mirror of the afterlife in which the earth stands in for the hellfire from which the intercession of the Prophet will extract even one who has but a mustard seed worth of faith in his heart.[38]

The esoteric is often considered to map onto the notion of *taʾwīl* that takes the term back to the origins of its meaning. But as is clear here, the esoteric as a hermeneutics opens out with acts of grace and through the initiatic training of someone who has achieved the position of being rooted in knowledge directly from God. At one level for Mullā Ṣadrā, *taʾwīl* is merely about interpretation and possesses an exoteric aspect. However, it is also about discerning and discovering the inner depths and meanings of the word of God. It is not about the rational explaining away of the letters and the surface text as he accuses the Muʿtazila of doing, which renders the word of God inert and constitutes an agnosticism.[39] Those who have grasped the true meaning of the Qur'an do not go against the exoteric sense of it but rather supplement that with an uncovering or revealing of layers of meaning inspired by divine grace.[40] *Taʾwīl* in this sense is a *mukāshafa*.

---

34 al-Ṣaffār al-Qummī, *Baṣāʾir al-darajāt*, ed. Sayyid Muḥammad Abṭaḥī (Qom: Muʾassasat al-Imām al-Mahdī, 2010), 1:66–67.

35 Ibid., 365; Abū Naḍr al-Samarqandī al-ʿAyyāshī, *Tafsīr*, ed. Muḥammad al-Kāẓim (Beirut: Dār al-Hādī, 1991), 1:12; only the Imāms know the totality of the Qur'an, its exoteric and esoteric aspects—see Abū Jaʿfar al-Kulaynī, *al-Kāfī* (Qom: Dār al-Ḥadīth, 2005), *ḥadīth* no. 611, *kitāb al-ḥujja*, ch. 25, no. 2, 2:566–67.

36 Mullā Ṣadrā Shīrāzī, *Tafsīr al-Qurʾān al-karīm*, ed. Muḥammad Khwājawī (Tehran: SIPRIn, 2010), 6:33–34.

37 Ibid., 30–32.

38 Ibid., 33.

39 Mullā Ṣadrā Shīrāzī, *Mafātīḥ al-ghayb*, ed. Najafqulī Ḥabībī (Tehran: Sadra Islamic Philosophy Research Institute, 2007), 1:126–35.

40 Ibid., 136–37.

Let us turn to the exegesis of Mullā Ṣadrā on the phrase in the Throne Verse and consider it in more detail.[41] He divides the discussion of the phrase into five sections (*aṭwār*) that follows the classic structure of many major exegesis: a discussion of the utterance, of its meaning, a deeper delving into the meaning, the implications of the meaning for humans, and then finally a consideration of previous exegetical views.[42] In terms of the first point about the utterance (*al-lafẓ*), he argues that *dīn* here stands for the *dīn* of God that is a transaction between the believer and God and is a universal matter. The second level goes further into detail on the meaning (*al-maʿnā*) of the nature of *dīn*. Since *dīn* is a matter of 'submission and contentment that is only realised through warrants pertaining to intellectual beliefs that God causes to enter the hearts of those who are contented in their faith', and that faith is also entreated through acts of submission that invite the inner revelation and certainty, then it is clear that there can be neither compulsion nor oppression in this matter. One cannot force something on the inner states of a person:

> This is because *dīn* is an esoteric matter (*amr bāṭinī*). It is only the true One—and none other—who can have dominion over the esoteric aspect of the human and his heart through what is appropriate to it, through spiritual intimacies, ecstatic experiences, inner revelations that are desired, and divine self-disclosures. In a narration it is reported: 'When God discloses Himself upon something, He subjugates both its exoteric and esoteric aspect.' In the Prophetic *ḥadīth*, the most excellent blessings and peace be with him and his progeny: 'Religion is not mere wish.'[43]
>
> Wish is a type of will, so how is it to be obtained through force—which is coercion? *Dīn* is the submitting of oneself to the commands of the law exoterically and submission to the qualities of the Truth esoterically without any esoteric harm (*min ghayr ḥaraj fī al-bāṭin*).[44]

The third level draws upon the mystical trope of the ascent to God as well as the Muʿtazilī theological theme of facilitating grace. Once God has elaborated on the beauties of true monotheism, it would be improper for Him not to provide the ways for the seeker to achieve it. The phrase indicates this status of being pleased (*maqām al-riḍāʾ*) and contented with God, which is the status of the truly sincere gnostics (*al-ʿārifīn al-ṣiddīqīn*). This is the means by which God facilitates the ability of the morally obliged to fulfil their obligations. Of course, not everyone attains this status immediately (or even ever). Many follow their whims and desire—worship their desires in the language of

41 Shīrāzī, *Tafsīr*, 5:213–21.

42 I do not discuss the last section on other exegetical positions.

43 Abū ʿAbd al-Raḥmān al-Sulamī, *Kitāb al-arbaʿīn fī al-taṣawwuf* (Hyderabad: Dāʾirat al-Maʿārif al-ʿUthmāniyya, 1981), 4.

44 Shīrāzī, *Tafsīr*, 5:215.

Mullā Ṣadrā—and fail to recognise the true nature of reality that God has produced and informed us about. Therefore, the hate or reluctance to submit to God is a failure to recognise what God has proposed to us as well as an inability to see the nature of the reality of things as they truly are. However, if humans are willing to attain the status of pleasure and contentment, they need to hold hope (*rajāʾ*), be prepared for trials (*jafāʾ*), seek shelter in patience (*ṣabr*), and fulfil their requirement to thank the benefactor (*niʿam al-shukr*). The rational theological context here is clear—the moral obligation that faith entails is precisely an expression of the need to reciprocate God for the gift of being. Once one is attracted towards God, then one attains 'true Islam' (*al-islām al-ḥaqīqī*) that lies in setting aside any annoyance and reluctance (*al-adhā wa-l-ikrāh*): this entails being pleased with what happens and accepting it without any force.[45]

He continues:

> What is meant concerning *dīn* is not that it is coercion from God, glorified is He, but rather that the servant is given free will in it. Religion in reality is the actions of the heart when he acts in a particular manner, and if one is coerced to express the two testimonies of faith (*iẓhār al-shahādatayn*), then it is not religion in reality. Just as one who is coerced to express unbelief while his heart is contented with faith, then he is not an unbeliever (*kāfir*). What is intended is the known *dīn* that is Islam and the *dīn* of God with which he is pleased. And this aspect is close to what we have discussed.[46]

In a short section glossing the phrase 'indeed righteousness has become manifestly clear from error', he reverts to his main interpretation, contrasting true *dīn* and true disbelief and considering *dīn* to be the link and the path that is traversed towards God:

> Since it has been mentioned that *dīn* cannot obtain through coercion, this establishes a norm that glosses its reality. And he says: 'indeed righteousness has become manifestly clear from error', that is, he has made clear and revealed what was mentioned before from examples of what is known, that true *dīn* (*al-dīn al-ḥaqīqī*) is traversing the path to God and passing through stations and stages that come between the servant and his Lord that are called righteousness and guidance, away from true error (*al-ḍalāl al-ḥaqīqī*), which is traversing the path of Satan and one's caprice, known as error and misguidance.[47]

The last element of Mullā Ṣadrā's commentary on this critical section of the verse relates

45 Ibid., 216.
46 Ibid., 220.
47 Ibid., 221.

to a turn towards how the rejection of coercion and the clear nature of guidance and error privileges the human over all others that revert to God. We shall later come to how this notion of *dīn* as an esoteric matter that cannot be exoterically compelled arises in the work of Nūrī.

## 2. Polemics

The broader context of Nūrī's work lies in the Christian–Muslim polemics starting in the Mughal–Safavid period. Jerome Xavier (1549–1617), the Spanish Jesuit missionary to the Mughal court, wrote *Fuente de Vida* in 1600, translated into Persian in 1609 as *Āyīna-yi ḥaqq-numā*, on the nature of God and the Trinity, and contributed to *Mirʾāt al-quds*, a life of Jesus, which led to controversies at the Mughal court and then through the Carmelite mission established in Isfahan in 1608 made it into the Safavid court.[48] The philosopher and co-student with Mullā Ṣadrā of Mīr Dāmād, Sayyid Aḥmad ʿAlavī (d. ca. 1650), penned a refutation, *Miṣqal-i ṣafā*, in late 1622, divided into three sections on the nature of God, on Jesus, and on the Gospels. The same philosopher wrote two further refutations: the first was a refutation of the *Risāla* of Pietro Della Valle (1586–1652), composed in late 1621 entitled *Lavāmiʿ-yi rabbānī dar radd-i shubha-yi Naṣrānī* on prophecy, revelation, and images, and especially how the Trinity was incompatible with divine simplicity alongside accusations of *taḥrīf* in the biblical and Judaeo-Christian scriptures; the second was *Lamaʿāt-i malakūtiyya*, completed in 1625, which draws on Avicenna and Ibn al-ʿArabī.[49] This latter work may have been the model for later philosophical responses. ʿAlavī was a prominent Avicennian who wrote a number of commentaries on the works of the philosopher as well as his own treatises on philosophical theology, and his refutations of Christianity were the work of an established court scholar in Isfahan.

The more proximate context as we saw was the work of Martyn in India and Iran as a missionary and his disputations on the nature of prophecy, revelation, and miracles with a rational context, and especially the conception of Triune God and how that can be reconciled with the dominant Catholic notion of divine simplicity.

## 3. Nūrī

Originally from Mazandaran, ʿAlī b. Jamshīd Nūrī was an established teacher of phi-

48 Hugues Didier, 'Jerome Xavier', in *Christian–Muslim Relations: A Bibliographical History, vol. 11, South and East Asia, Africa and the Americas (1600–1700)*, ed. David Thomas and John Chesworth (Leiden: Brill, 2017), 84–91; Pedro Moura Carvalho, ed., *Mirʾāt al-quds (Mirror of Holiness): A Life of Christ for Emperor Akbar*, trans. Wheeler M. Thackston (Leiden: Brill, 2012).

49 The best study of these works, their motivation, and the role of ʿAlavī is Dennis Halft, 'The Arabic Vulgate in Safavid Persia: Arabic Printing of the Gospels, Catholic Missionaries, and the Rise of Shīʿī Anti-Christian Polemics' (PhD diss., Freie Universität Berlin, 2016), esp. 98–142.

losophy in Isfahan and renowned as a major 'philosopher concerned with theology' (*ḥukamāʾ-yi ilāhīyīn*).[50] After his elementary studies in Mazandaran and in Qazvin, he studied in Isfahan with Āqā Muḥammad Bīdābādī (d. 1197/1783) and Mīrzā Abū al-Qāsim Mudarris-i Khātūnābādī (d. 1212/1797), a scion of the Majlisī family and a teacher of the works of Avicenna. Through the former, he associated himself with a significant group of his fellow countrymen engaged in the study of philosophy and mysticism. Bīdābādī's father, Mullā Muḥammad Rafīʿ Gīlānī, was a well-known scholar, and he moved to Isfahan settling in the suburb of Bīdābād.[51] Bīdābādī himself was a philosopher inclining to theosis (*ḥakīm-i mutaʾallih*), which meant that he believed philosophy was a practice and way of life by which one requires a resemblance to the divine (*al-tashabbuh bi-l-bārīʾ*), as a mystic (*ahl-i sayr u sulūk*), and as someone known for his piety and even miracles (*ṣāḥib al-maqāmāt va karāmāt*).[52] A contemporary witness, the Niʿmatullāhī Sufi Muḥammad Jaʿfar Kabūdarāhangī, known as Majẕūb ʿAlī Shāh (d. 1823), claims that the Bīdābādī circle was renowned for their mystical and spiritual practices (*riyāżat va mujāhada-yi nafsānī*) alongside their *ʿirfān* (mystical) orientation in their study of metaphysics.[53]

If one wished to trace a lineage of teachers and disciples linking Nūrī back to Mullā Ṣadrā—and this is not identical to a chain of transmission of his works since most were still using Avicenna's *Metaphysics* of *al-Shifāʾ* and *al-Ishārāt wa-l-tanbīhāt* as the key texts in philosophy (the evidence of the biographical dictionaries and the licences authorising transmission, the *ijāzāt*, suggests as much)—then it would look something like this: Bīdābādī → Quṭb al-Dīn Nayrīzī and Mullā Ismāʿīl Khājūʾī and Muḥammad Taqī Almāsī → Ṣādiq Ardistānī → Ḥusayn Tunikābunī → Mullā Ṣadrā. However, one ought to exercise some caution with such constructed genealogies—thinkers usually did not see themselves as constituting a link in a chain, but it was much later when an individual wished to make sense of his lineage that he would articulate such a chain, using its authority to make claims for himself and for his qualification to transmit to the next generation.

---

50 Mīrzā Muḥammad ʿAlī Muʿallim-i Ḥabībābādī, *Makārim al-āsār dar aḥvāl-i rijāl-i dawra-yi Qājār* (Isfahan: Maṭbaʿ-yi Muḥammadī, 1958), 4:1264–67, §668; Muḥammad ʿAlī Khiyābānī Mudarris-i Tabrīzī, *Rayḥānat al-adab fī tarājim al-maʿrūfīn bi-l-kunya aw al-laqab* ([Tehran:] Chāpkhāna-yi Saʿdī, 1947–53), 4:249–50; Sayyid Muḥammad Bāqir Khwānsārī, *Rawḍāt al-jannāt* (Beirut: al-Dār al-Islāmiyya, 1991), 4:391–93; Manūchihr Ṣadūqī 'Suhā', *Ḥukamāʾ va ʿurafāʾ-yi mutaʾakhkhirīn-i Ṣadr al-mutaʾallihīn* (Tehran: Anjuman-i islāmī-yi ḥikmat va falsafa-yi Īrān, 1980), 33–40. For a brief discussion of the philosophers in this period, see Seyyed Hossein Nasr, *Islamic Philosophy from Its Origin to the Present* (Albany: State University of New York Press, 2006), 235–39.

51 ʿAbd al-Nabī Qazvīnī, *Tatmīm Amal al-āmil*, ed. Sayyid Maḥmud Marʿashī and Sayyid Aḥmad Ḥusayni (Qom: Maktabat Āyatullāh Marʿashī, 1987), 162.

52 Muʿallim-i Ḥabībābādī, *Makārim al-āsār*, 1:66–70; Mudarris-i Tabrīzī, *Rayḥānat al-adab*, 1:187–88; Maʿṣūm ʿAlī-Shāh, *Ṭarāʾiq al-ḥaqāʾiq*, 3:98, 214–15; ʿAlī Karbāsī-zāda, *Ḥakīm-i mutaʾallih Bīdābādī: iḥyāgarā-yi ḥikmat-i shīʿī dar qarn-i davāzdahum-i hijrī* (Tehran: Pazhūhishgāh-i ʿulūm-i insānī va muṭālaʿāt-i farhangī, 2002); ʿAbd al-Raḥmān Ḥāṭim, *Rāʾid al-ʿirfān al-Āqā Muḥammad Bīdābādī* (Beirut: Dār al-Hādī, 2002), 7–24.

53 Muḥammad Jaʿfar Kabūdarāhangī Majẕūb ʿAlī Shāh, *Mirʾāt al-ḥaqq*, ed. Ḥāmid Nājī Iṣfahānī (Tehran: Intishārāt-i ḥaqīqat, 2004), 69–70.

Later in life, Nūrī wrote a number of works in response to notables at the Qajar court and even the Shah—and perhaps that political relationship extended to networks established in his hometown as the first 'capital' of the Qajars before they moved to Tehran in 1778 was Sarī in Mazandaran. In matters of *fiqh*, he was a close student of first Mīrzā-yi Qummī, the prominent jurist and friend of Bīdābādī, then Shaykh Ibrāhīm Karbāsī and Sayyid Muḥammad Bāqir Shaftī (d. 1844). Although he was not known for his expertise in jurisprudence, Nūrī was closely associated with the leading jurists of his time both in Iran (Qummī in Qom, Shaftī and Karbāsī in Isfahan) and in Iraq (Sayyid ʿAlī Ṭabāṭabāʾī and Shaykh Jaʿfar and his son ʿAlī Kāshif al-Ghiṭāʾ). These friendships attest to his prominence and fame in the seminary and demonstrate that his scholarly reputation extended from Isfahan to other seminary centres in Iran and in the shrine cities, although we cannot necessarily deduce from his role the significance of *ḥikmat* and *ʿirfān* in this period.

Once established in Isfahan, he began teaching at the Madrasa-yi Shamsiyya, which, because it was in the neighbourhood of that name, was known as Madrasa-yi Kāse-girān. His students included Sufis such as Mīrzā Abū al-Qāsim Rāz-i Shīrāzī (d. 1869), a renowned Ẕahabī shaykh, as well as members of his circle such as his own son Mīrzā Ḥasan (d. 1888), who wrote a short treatise on mysticism entitled *Asfār-i arbaʿa* (and, in fact, the famous gloss by Nūrī on this element of the opening of Mullā Ṣadrā's work is transmitted by him) as well as glosses on the *Asfār* and Lāhījī's *Shawāriq al-ilhām*. His most famous students for the transmission of philosophy included Mullā Hādī Sabzavārī (d. 1873), the most prominent philosopher of the Qajar period as well as the author of the *Sharḥ ghurar al-farāʾid*, which became a school-text; Mullā Muḥammad Jaʿfar b. Muḥammad Ṣādiq Lāhījānī Langarūdī (d. 1844), who was a commentator on *al-Ḥikma al-ʿarshiyya* and *al-Mashāʿir*, the latter heavily influenced by Nūrī;[54] Mullā ʿAbdullāh Zunūzī (d. 1841), who was a prolific glossator on the works of Mullā Ṣadrā including *al-Shawāhid*, *Asfār*, *al-Mabdaʾ wa-l-maʿād*, and *Asrār al-āyāt*, all of which had been of interest to his teacher, and of his independent works, two in Persian stand out: *Lamaʿāt-i ilāhiyya va maʿārif-i rubūbiyya*, on the nature of God, dedicated to Fatḥ ʿAlī Shāh and completed on 29 October 1824, and *Anvār-i jaliyya*, glossing (on the request of Fatḥ ʿAlī Shāh when on procession in Fars and completed two years later in 1832) the famous narrative of Kumayl on the nature of reality (*mā al-ḥaqīqa*) reported from ʿAlī b. Abī Ṭālib. And it was Zunūzī who was sent to Tehran to teach at the Madrasa-yi Khān Marvī—on the request of the court and the patronage of Fatḥ ʿAlī Shāh—and thus he was central to the establishment of the philosophical curriculum, and especially the works of Mullā Ṣadrā there, perpetuated by his students who included his son ʿAlī as well as Mīrzā Ḥasan Ṭāliqānī and other figures.[55]

54 Muṣṭafā Dirāyatī, ed., *Fihristagān-i nuskha-hā-yi khaṭṭī-yi Īrān* (Tehran: Sāzmān-i asnād va kitābkhāna-yi millī-yi jumhūrī-yi islāmī, 2012), 20:687–88; Raḥīm Qāsimī, *Gulzār-i muqaddas* (Isfahan: Sāzmān-i farhangī u tafrīḥī-yi shahrdārī-yi Iṣfahān, 2011), 1:249–50.

55 Mudarris-i Tabrīzī, *Rayḥānat al-adab*, 2:390; Muʿallim-i Ḥabībābādī, Makārim al-āsār, 5:1551.

In that sense, Nūrī was a pivotal figure who taught subsequent generations of teachers of philosophy in Isfahan, Tehran, and beyond.

In 1829, when the Shah was on procession, he passed by Isfahan and held court in Jazz, a village near the city, and various notables came to meet him including Nūrī.[56] When he died in Isfahan on 6 January 1831, his body was taken to Najaf. Shaykh ʿAlī b. Jaʿfar Kāshif al-Ghiṭāʾ (d. 1837) received the body and led the prayer, and he was buried at the shrine in a grave at Bāb al-Ṭūsī. His surviving son, Mīrzā Ḥasan, was a philosopher, as was his grandson ʿAbd al-Ḥusayn.

### 3.1 Nūrī's Intellectual Contribution

In metaphysics, his concern was to defend and establish the positions of Mullā Ṣadrā not least because they were contested and far from uniformly accepted in the eighteenth century. This relates to the primacy and unity of existence (*aṣālat, waḥdat al-wujūd*), the graded nature of existence defined through intensity in opposition to Avicenna (*tashkīk al-wujūd bi-l-shidda wa-l-ḍuʿf*), and the dynamic of reality mediated by motion in substance (*ḥaraka jawhariyya*). Much of this is clear in his glosses on the work of Mullā Ṣadrā, especially the *Asfār*, but also critically in his *al-Raqīma al-nūriyya*. He stresses repeatedly that in our experience of phenomenal reality it is not things with their properties that are but rather they are just aspects of existence.[57] Existence is ontologically prior even if it might seem epistemologically posterior—although through mystically attuned contemplation a person can have a non-discursive vision of the fact that existence is primary and that essences are illusory.[58] Existence is identical to the being of God and is named and annexed to Him and exists because it is contingent and reliant upon Him; in themselves contingent entities do not exist.[59] God's everlasting countenance is existence and, just like existence, is hidden but also manifest in a paradoxical manner.[60]

This is further emphasised in his approach to the graded and modulated nature of existence as being the arranged manifestations of the divine; it is God's being and mercy that spreads out and is deployed to manifest the existents that we experience.[61] Hierarchy in existence is defined through the process of intensity—the higher in the pyramid the more intense, and the lower the more debilitated—and in affirming that, he agrees with Mullā Ṣadrā, on good Neoplatonic bases, criticising Avicenna who, on good Aristotelian

56 Riżā-Qulī Khān 'Hidāyat', *Fihris al-tavārīkh*, ed. ʿAbd al-Ḥusayn Nawāʾī and Mīr Hāshim Muḥaddith (Tehran: Pazhūhishgāh-i ʿulūm-i insānī va muṭālaʿāt-i farhangī, 1994), 417, 421.

57 Mullā Ṣadrā Shīrāzī, *al-Ḥikma al-mutaʿāliya fī al-asfār al-ʿaqliyya al-arbaʿa*, ed. Sayyid Muḥammad Khāminihī (Tehran: Sadra Islamic Philosophy Research Institute, 2001–4), 1:40, 45.

58 Ibid., 248.

59 Ibid., 128, 210.

60 Ibid., 118.

61 Ibid., 68, 113.

grounds, rejected the possibility of existence permitting of more or less by intensity.[62] In his treatise (or perhaps it is by a student based on his teachings) on the Simple One as the totality of what exists (*basīṭ al-ḥaqīqa*), he argues similarly that God is identical to the totality and perfection of existence, but also the most noble and highest degree of being; He is both the entirety of the pyramid of existence as well as its pinnacle and that pyramid is arranged hierarchically differentiated by intensity—this is argued alongside the proof for the primary and unity of existence.[63]

A corollary of the doctrine of existence is Mullā Ṣadrā's insistence that the dynamic of existence, and what ultimately determines that the cosmos is created anew in time constantly and also what determines the path of perfection that beings have towards their reversion to the One, is the notion of a changing self or substance in motion.[64] It is through the renewal and changing of the self that the person or the existent persists in the flowing now (*al-ān al-sayyāl*).

Ultimately, even his exposition of Mullā Ṣadrā is tinged with a mystical, monistic emphasis. In a gloss on the nature of the differentia in the *Asfār*, he comments:

> True differentia is nothing but true being and is neither a substance nor an accident as has been shown. All things are perishing, fleeting, fading into being (*wujūd*), which is singularly true insofar as it is the True One. It is what it is and there is nothing but it, just as God bears witness that there is no god but He. The entifications are a level emanated from the reality of being and its manifestations figuratively. He is the first and the last and the apparent and the hidden and they are mirrors of His manifestation. The mirror qua mirror extinguishes into the disclosure of the divine. There is no veil between Him and you except your being. So raise up your attention until it is manifest to you that He is the goal of all attention.[65]

In *ʿirfān*, we know that Nūrī upheld the monism of the school of Ibn al-ʿArabī and continued the Shīʿī expression of it through glossing significant narrations through its lens. His glosses on the *Sharḥ Fuṣūṣ al-ḥikam* of Ibn Turka are the obvious source to consider here. There is only the One—and it is not that we participate in the True One—and all else is a sign and manifestation of the One. The relationship of God and the cosmos is primarily presented through the famous formulation of ʿAlī in *Nahj al-balāgha*: God is neither

62 Ibid., 253.

63 ʿAlī Nūrī, *Rasāʾil-i falsafī: basīṭ al-ḥaqīqa wa-waḥdat al-wujūd*, ed. Sayyid Jalāl al-Dīn Āshtiyānī (Tehran: Anjuman-i ḥikmat u falsafa-yi Īrān, 1978), 9–10.

64 Shīrāzī, *al-Ḥikma*, 1:395.

65 Ibid., 2:41. See ʿAlī Nūrī, *al-Raqīma al-nūriyya fī qāʿidat basīṭ al-ḥaqīqa*, ed. Ḥāmid Nājī Iṣfahānī, in *Mīrāth-i ḥawza-yi Iṣfahān*, ed. Muḥammad Javād Nūr-Muḥammadī (Isfahan: Ḥawza-yi ʿilmiyya-yi Iṣfahān, 2010), 6:159: 'Existence in reality and in essence is naught but He; what exists in actuality is merely His essence, His acts, His creation, and His mercy that encompasses all things.'

identical nor distinct to the creation, He is 'inside' everything but not in the sense of one thing or substance being in another, and He is 'outside' everything but not in the sense in which a thing or substance is outside another in the sense of physical contiguity—God is with you wherever you are (Q. 4:57) and this is not what 'the ignorant unbelieving Sufis' (*juhhāl malāḥidat al-ṣūfiyya*) think.[66] Similarly to gloss the quotation of Ibn al-ʿArabī that the essences that determine things in the cosmos—the 'permanent archetypes' (*al-aʿyān al-thābita*)—have never been existent as independent entities (*mā shammat rāʾiḥat al-wujūd*) he cites a version of a famous narration from Imām al-Kāẓim: 'God was and there was nothing with Him, and He is as He was.'[67] He relates this to the principle of existence as the ground of everything as opposed to essence. Multiplicity arises through the desire of God—insofar as He 'was' a hidden treasure—to be known and hence He creates, and in the first instance manifests Himself through the Muḥammadan reality.[68] By citing here a supplication of the month of ʿAlī, Rajab, he insists that the person of the Imām (and the Prophet before) mediates the mystical unfolding of nature, and its return to the One.[69]

Consistent with the Shīʿī school of Ibn al-ʿArabī on the famous issue of the seal of saints, he follows the tradition of ʿAbd al-Razzāq Kāshānī and Sayyid Ḥaydar Āmulī on insisting that it was ʿAlī who constitutes the absolute seal, citing the famous saying in which he claimed to be the 'dot under the *bā*'', not least because that dot is the totality of the cosmos and the 'secret' of God (*sirr Allāh*).[70] The Imām is the simple manifestation that expresses the totality of the divine. On the question of the seal of sainthood in the Islamic dispensation, he follows again the Shīʿī school that identifies it with the Mahdī (*al-ḥaḍra al-mahdawiyya al-fāṭimiyya*), criticising what seems to be Ibn al-ʿArabī's position—but also with a nod to those later in the tradition who saw him as crypto-Shīʿī, he says that he did see an 'old' copy of a text in which the Andalusian Sufi identifies the seal with the Mahdī and not himself.[71] Another aspect of this polemic on *walāya* is to criticise as Ismāʿīlī (*malāḥidat al-bāṭiniyya*) the position that the seal is superior to the Prophet in whose dispensation his function arises.[72]

The Imām is the perfect human, the eternal Adam, the calamus, and the intellect, the first level of manifestation from the One.[73] The Imām's Adamic nature is the comprehensive reality and presence of the divine (*ḥaqīqa jāmiʿa*) as well as the comprehensive

66 Ibn Turka, *Sharḥ Fuṣūṣ al-ḥikam*, ed. Muḥsin Bīdārfar (Qom: Intishārāt-i Bīdār, 1999), 1:10, 219; see also Sayyid Ṣādiq al-Mūsawī, ed., *Tamām Nahj al-balāgha* (Beirut: al-Dār al-Islāmiyya, 2005), 39 (sermon no. 1).

67 Ibn Turka, *Sharḥ Fuṣūṣ al-ḥikam*, 1:63, 123, 2:701 (citing the same narration from Imām Ṣādiq).

68 Ibid., 1:18, 135.

69 Ibid., 138, 143–44.

70 Ibid., 107; Shīrāzī, *Mafātīḥ al-ghayb*, 703; Muḥammad Bāqir Majlisī, *Biḥār al-anwār* (Beirut: Dār al-Aḍwāʾ, 1983), xl, 165.

71 Ibn Turka, *Sharḥ Fuṣūṣ al-ḥikam*, 1:200; see also Sayyid Muḥammad Ḥusayn Ḥusaynī-yi Ṭihrānī, *Rūḥ-i mujarrad* (Mashhad: Intishārāt-i ʿAllāma-yi Ṭabāṭabāʾī, 2000), 313–71.

72 Ibn Turka, *Sharḥ Fuṣūṣ al-ḥikam*, 1:203.

73 Ibid., 24.

divine name because of Adam being the 'totality of the names' (*jawāmiʿ al-kalim*), and citing a narration of Imām al-Ḥasan al-ʿAskarī because it is the Imāms alone who truly manifest God and through whom His secret is revealed.[74] It is because of this that Adam was created in God's image so that he might reveal God, as the breath of the merciful, and then as the microcosm reverting back to God.[75] This status—of *walāya* ultimately—is the trust (*amāna*) of Q. 72:33, the vicegerency of God, through which humans revert back to God and transfer their annihilation (*fanāʾ*) into everlasting subsistence (*baqāʾ*) with the divine.[76] The Imāms are the symbols of the divine—and hence they speak in the language of symbols to facilitate through their concrete examples what God wishes to convey and manifest; Nūrī draws upon the famous metaphor of the Imām as the sun hidden in the clouds whose effulgence of existence sustains the cosmos as an expression of the light of God.[77]

Knowledge of the realities of things is difficult because one cannot access them without one who reveals their realities and knows them through divine inspiration.[78] It is the person of the Prophet and the Imāms as both the veil of God and the everlasting face of God (*wajh Allāh al-bāqī*) who can guide people. This requires that first humans recognise the luminous nature of the Imām (*maʿrifa bi-l-nūrāniyya*).[79] Proper training leads people to recognise themselves as followers of the Imāms who can then see the realities of things.[80] But that is not easy since bearing the *walāya* of the Imāms is difficult and arduous (*ṣaʿb mustaṣaʿb*), in the words of the narrations.[81] The one who is initiated and recognises himself and his Imām begins to see his own exigency and realises God, and through seeing his own ephemerality, understands that God is everlasting.[82] This is true piety (*taqwā*)—to refrain from ascribing existence to what is utterly indigent and contingent.[83] Once he understands the basic monist truth, he realises that everything in extra-mental reality is actually the product of imagination and what the universal imagination and our imagination projects; as imagination and this world is graded in intensity, imagination emanates from the universal imagination (associated with the Imāms al-Ḥasan and al-Ḥusayn as we shall see shortly) to the imagination in the imaginal realm and down to imagination in this cosmos.[84] The next step is then the path back to God, and drawing upon the Kubrawī schema of subtleties (*laṭāʾif*), Nūrī says that this

74 Ibid., 25, 206–7, 2:600–1.
75 Ibid., 1:74, 89, 242, 2:736–37.
76 Ibid., 1:117.
77 Nūrī, *al-Raqīma al-nūriyya*, 46.
78 Ibn Turka, *Sharḥ Fuṣūṣ al-ḥikam*, 1:190.
79 Ibid., 258.
80 Ibid., 272.
81 Ibid., 125.
82 Ibid., 323.
83 Ibid., 153.
84 Ibid., 305, 360.

involves seven successive stages: (1) raw nature, (2) the soul (*nafs*) that has passions, (3) the moonlike heart (*al-qalb al-qamarī*) that is manipulated by the imagination, (4) the theoretical intellect (*al-ʿaql al-naẓarī*) that enquires into reality, (5) the *rūḥ* which is the intellect assisted by God that acquires certainty, (6) the secret (*al-sirr*) through which one sees the subtle lights and acquires the rank of the saints and the ability to doff the body and experience the higher ecstasy of the beatific vision, and finally (7) the hidden (*al-khafī*) being in the world of reality and abode of prophets.[85]

Nūrī's main intellectual contribution was to establish the school of Mullā Ṣadrā with its focus on the metaphysics of existence and its particular approach to philosophy and mysticism as a singular holistic intellectual endeavour rooted in spiritual practice and received as grace of Prophetic inheritance. There is little that he adds beyond defending, reformulating, and refuting detractors; he rarely adds perspectives and approaches not found in the work of Mullā Ṣadrā. But in addition to that—retaining the Neoplatonic taste of his masters and their use of the revived Hellenic tradition of late antiquity—he had a strong commitment to the occult, especially lettrism, which demonstrates the influence of Mīr Dāmād. In that sense, he was a unique figure—there are barely any thinkers in whose work one finds the confluence of the rather different thought of Mīr Dāmād and his student Mullā Ṣadrā.

### 3.2 Proof of Islam

Nūrī's most extensive independent treatise was *Ḥujjat al-Islām yā burhān al-milla* (also known as *Radd-i pādrī*), an anti-Christian polemical response to Henry Martyn, whose completion date is 23 Rabīʿ I 1232/1817 and which was dedicated to Fatḥ ʿAlī Shāh Qājār.[86] It is the longest piece that Nūrī wrote in Persian—although similar to other Qajar-era works, it contains considerable passages in Arabic and hence was written for a scholarly audience. Another response was *Ithbāt al-nubuwwa* of Mīrzā ʿĪsā Khān Qāʾim-maqām Farahānī, known as Mīrzā-yi Buzurg (d. 1824), which was published by his son Mīrzā Abū al-Qāsim (d. 1835); he passed on the request from the court, in particular from the Qajar prince ʿAbbās Mīrzā (d. 1835), for Nūrī to write the refutation.[87] The request was partly due to the weakness of Fasavī's response and the need for a more robust defence that Nūrī himself recognised. A further impetus for Nūrī's work could have been another

85 Ibid., 279.

86 ʿAlī Nūrī, *Ḥujjat al-Islām yā burhān al-milla* [*Kitābī dar naqd-i guftār-i Henry Martyn*], ed. Ḥāmid Nājī Iṣfahānī (Tehran: Mīrās-i maktūb, 2012), 297. See Dirāyatī, *Fihristagān*, 4:498, 5:580. There are numerous manuscripts (eighteen) of this text, sometimes under the title *Radd-i pādrī* (which denotes the genre). For a brief entry on him and the text, see Dennis Halft, "ʿAlī Nūrī", in *Christian–Muslim Relations: A Bibliographical History, vol. 20, Iran, Afghanistan, and the Caucasus (1800–1914)*, ed. David Thomas and John Chesworth (Leiden: Brill, 2023), 143–49.

87 See ʿAlī-Qulī Mīrzā Iʿtiżād al-Salṭana, *Iksīr al-tavārīkh*, ed. Jamshīd Kiyānfar (Tehran: Intishārāt-i Vīsmān, 1991), 539–40.

refutation by the famous jurist Mīrzā-yi Qummī (d. 1816), a close friend of his teacher Bīdābādī as we have seen above and an acquaintance of his own; this incomplete work, entitled *Iʿjāz al-Qurʾān*, focused on Martyn's attack on the divine origins of the scripture.[88] His ambivalence to Sufi leaders and disdain for their work could also signal a need for a response as he felt that previous works like that of Ḥusayn ʿAlī-Shāh were inadequate.[89] Nūrī's work was written at roughly the same time as another philosophical refutation by Mullā Aḥmad Narāqī (d. 1829), entitled *Sayf al-umma*, commissioned by the same Qajar prince, ʿAbbās Mīrzā, and completed in 1817. Nūrī states that he wrote the work at the request of his scholarly friends and dedicated it to Fatḥ ʿAlī Shāh Qājār, the same ruler to whom Martyn sent his works, adding the need was great because of the increasing lack of intellectual skill among the scholars of his age.[90] Significantly, all the major responses to Martyn were commissions from the court, not least because he had dedicated his Persian translation of the New Testament and his vindication of Christianity to the Shah; it demonstrates the role of the court, as in the Safavid period before it, in defending the faith again missionaries.

Nūrī's method was a mix of reason and revelation, insisting upon using only rational arguments and drawing upon his training in *ḥikmat*. Nūrī's approach was threefold: begin with a rational approach to inquiry and rational premises (affirming repeatedly the superiority of intellectual proofs over scriptural and reported ones), invalidation of the opponent's position, and vindication of Islam in his own philosophical terms, designating refutations as *rajm-i shayṭān* (stoning of Satan).[91] The text itself is divided into two preliminary principles followed by a series of arguments. The preliminaries concern the nature of being and its division into perfect and imperfect, followed by a discussion of the dual nature of the human as one inclined to the good and to heaven, and as one inclined to the bad and to hell. He then moves onto the nature of prophecy and compares Jesus, critiquing the notion of his divinity and the doctrine of the Trinity as well as the doctrine of sacrifice and redemption, against Muḥammad, as a more rational exemplar. The proof in favour of Muḥammad then progresses to a discussion of the privileged nature of the Qurʾan and of miracles. Along the way there is an important discussion of *walāya* from the perspective of *ḥikmat*, the cosmological status and authority that the prophets and the Shīʿī Imāms have, citing by way of example ʿAlī's presence at the time of Dhū al-Qarnayn.[92] This in fact is the major theme of the text, an exordium on *walāya* that fits within the Qajar interest in the issue across the growing divide between Sufis and *ḥukamāʾ*.

Before examining three examples of how Nūrī engages in a polemical defence of Islam

88 Mīrzā-yi Qummī, 'Iʿjāz al-Qurʾān', ed. Sayyid Ḥusayn Mudarrissī Ṭabāṭabāʾī, *Vaḥīd* 10 (1972): 115–18.

89 Nūrī, *Ḥujjat al-Islām*, 27, 73, describes Sufis as a satanic group of heretics who in their ignorance and ability to misguide are like Christian missionaries.

90 Ibid., 4–7.

91 Ibid., 10–11.

92 Ibid., 266–73, 292–93.

through the use of his philosophical training, it is worth returning to the theme of how one understands *dīn* as an esoteric matter already found in the work of Mullā Ṣadrā. He postulates that the true human—and especially the perfect human (*insān kāmil*) who is to be followed and emulated and in an exemplary manner is Muḥammad—bears an intimacy with the divine and that path of intimacy is called *dīn*.[93] That is an affair of the heart and the way of the heart that entails true salvation from material attachment to all save God and to ignorance that arises from base matter. Drawing on the distinction between the exoteric law (*sharīʿat*) and the esoteric path (*ṭarīqat*), he argues that this is precisely why the revelation can mandate military struggle (*jihād-i aṣghar*) to defend oneself and even to spread the message of monotheism while insisting that there can be no compulsion of the heart in matters of *dīn*.[94] Free will is an expression of the grace of God that counters the polemics of force and conversion because it allows for the choice of the heart and it refutes any forced exoteric action.[95] True *dīn* is singular and indicated by verifying miracles that appeal to the heart; the presence of false *dīn* (he cites the examples of Zoroastrianism and idolatry) does not entail the falsity of all traditions and paths.[96] The truth of Islam as *dīn* thus lies in its metaphysics and the veracity of Muḥammad as the perfect human.[97]

### 3.2.1 *Example I: Miracles*

Much of the polemics revolve around the possibility and even necessity of miracles as divine interventions in nature that verify the claims of a prophet. In his section on miracles, he focused on the famous splitting of the moon in two. The problem posed by the miracle is how to bridge the gap between the human subject and the celestial object, which is somewhat similar to how we can make sense of an immaterial and intelligible angel descending and engaging with a material human person and how one can traverse dimensions. Nūrī cites the Ṣadrian idea of motion in substance (*ḥaraka jawhariyya*) to prove its possibility.[98] Divine providence entailed that all entities undergo motion in their substance and hence the moon bore within itself the possibility to split and then to re-join and thus was not a stable entity.[99] All beings for Mullā Ṣadrā are under motion as being itself is a dynamic of intensification, proceeding from perfection and reverting to it.

Nūrī's proof is prefaced by his critique of the position of ʿAbd al-Razzāq Lāhījī (d. 1070/1660), the famous theologian and son-in-law of Mullā Ṣadrā who resolved the problem of miracles by appealing to Avicennian noetics and the psychological theory

93 Ibid., 20–21.
94 Ibid., 47–49.
95 Ibid., 149–51.
96 Ibid., 152–53.
97 Ibid., 85–86.
98 Ibid., 184–86.
99 Ibid., 187–88.

of prophecy whereby miracles are the product of the heightened faculty of imagination (*khayāl*) in a prophet.[100] Lāhījī's solution was about what people perceived in this world and hence he did not argue whether the moon itself was split. While the ability of a prophet's imagination to make the world and the perception of even his opponents is impressively miraculous, for Nūrī it did not entail compliance with the truth of the teachings of the *dīn*, which in this case included exoteric actualities. For him, Lāhījī's solution did not allow for a full realisation and verification of the claims of a prophet. Nūrī was clearly defending Mullā Ṣadrā against his Avicennian disciple and in that sense using the polemical form to establish his confessional attachment to a particular philosophical tradition. By invoking the principle of motion in substance he was defending both the actual splitting of the moon as well as Muḥammad's ascension to heaven in a bodily manner (*miʿrāj jismānī*) because they both pertained to the possibility of humans connecting with and encountering the heavenly bodies, which were denied by the opponent as humanly impossible.[101]

### 3.2.2 *Example II: Muḥammad's Cosmic Walāya*

Nūrī's understanding of the cosmic role of Muḥammad provides another opportunity to deploy his philosophical training in the cosmology of Mullā Ṣadrā and the school of Ibn al-ʿArabī. Muḥammad's *walāya*, his authority and control, over the cosmos and the manipulation of the dynamic of being (*wujūd*) whose intensity he represented as the 'perfect human' function within a dynamic and graded hierarchical modulation of being (*tashkīk al-wujūd*).[102] The totality of being is modulated between perfection and imperfection; humans by nature are a mixture of the animalistic and angelic but God tips the balance for His friends towards perfection of being and perfection of human nature as its manifestation. This is also an aspect of the miraculous divine intervention in cosmology that is a feature of Muḥammad being characterised as the 'seal of prophets'.[103] It is the role of the seal that he must perform miracles and do what is beyond the natural to establish his role in the cosmos and in that sense guide and constitute the survival of the human species.[104] What is important here is to emphasise that, like Avicenna before him, Mullā Ṣadrā's ethics and politics and philosophical account of prophecy and *walāya* are deeply implicated in his metaphysics.

---

100 Ibid., 179–84.
101 Ibid., 178–79.
102 Ibid., 33–34.
103 Ibid., 12–13.
104 A classic explanation of Avicenna is Meryem Sebti, *Avicenne: Prophétie et gouvernement du monde* (Paris: Cerf, 2021); and for Mullā Ṣadrā, see Christian Jambet, *Le gouvernement divin: Islam et conception politique du monde* (Paris: CNRS, 2016), esp. 279–370.

### 3.2.3 *Example III: Dhū al-Qarnayn and the Cosmic Walāya of ʿAlī*

The final example is more specific to the Shīʿī element of Nūrī's metaphysics. He relates the example of Dhū al-Qarnayn—the two-horned one whom he associates with the hero of the (Syriac and Eastern) Alexander Romance and not the 'idolatrous' Greek Alexander—whose victories and miracles arise from his *walāya* over the cosmos, space, and time, associated with that of ʿAlī.[105] The authority of ʿAlī over space and time follows his role as the seal of 'absolute *walāya*' (*khātam al-walāya al-muṭlaqa*) to use the term of the school of Ibn al-ʿArabī.[106] The various miraculous stories associated with the ancients such as the sleepers of the cave or the two-horned one are ciphers, for Nūrī, of the cosmic role of ʿAlī across space and time. Again, we have the twin pillars of Nūrī's approach in the work: the cosmic role of prophets, especially the seal of the prophets, and saints, especially the seal of saints, alongside the need for those individuals to manifest their cosmic authority and power through the veracious and verifying performance of miracles and rending asunder the bounds of the natural.

## 4. Conclusion

*Dīn* is a complicated category that in the Shīʿī intellectual tradition, especially that associated with Mullā Ṣadrā, is inextricably linked and founded upon metaphysics and the hermeneutics of being and its dynamic. The primacy, actuality, and modulation of being as the central metaphysical doctrine postulates that being is a source of commonality and difference that is dynamic (through the notion of motion in the category of substance that is ontological and hermeneutical above and beyond a facet of Mullā Ṣadrā's category theory). For the Ṣadrian tradition inherited by Nūrī, there are three types of being: characterised by perfection (*the higher intelligibilia*); characterised as beyond perfection, which is the abode of the divine and the Real; and characterised as imperfect, which is everything on the path of perfection—every conscious being on that path across different creeds and confessions makes their own choices towards the perfect guided by divine grace in the form of the perfect human. These sorts of triads are common in the tradition. This also entails that there are metaphysical foundations for ethics, politics, aesthetics, theology, and even for our concept-formation of notions such as God, religion, secularity, and so forth. By taking the example of Nūrī's anti-Christian polemic, we have seen how a philosopher deals with the category of 'religion' and some of its fundamental notions such as God, revelation, prophecy, and miracles, and the notion of the friends of God, and how one interfaces between the spiritual and the material. In that sense, we should read Nūrī's work not just as an example of a narrow Shīʿī understanding of sacred history and an enchanted world but as a resource for problematising some of the core

105 Nūrī, *Ḥujjat al-Islām*, 55, 291–94.
106 Ibid., 267.

elements of our reading of the humanities. The emic, the spiritual, and the esoteric in his work allow us to liberate our ways of making sense of the religious and the philosophical.

## Bibliography

Abbasi, Rushain. 'Did Premodern Muslims Distinguish the Religious and the Secular?'. *Journal of Islamic Studies* 31, no. 2 (2020): 185–225.

———. 'Islam and the Invention of Religion'. *Studia Islamica* 116 (2021): 1–106.

Asad, Talal. *Formations of the Secular: Islam, Christianity, Modernity*. Stanford: Stanford University Press, 2003.

———. *Genealogies of Religion: Discipline and Reasons of Power in Christianity and Islam*. Baltimore: Johns Hopkins University Press, 1993.

al-ʿAyyāshī, Abū Naḍr al-Samarqandī. *Tafsīr*. Edited by Muḥammad al-Kāẓim. Beirut: Dār al-Hādī, 1991.

Carvalho, Pedro Moura, ed. *Mirʾāt al-quds (Mirror of Holiness): A Life of Christ for Emperor Akbar*. Translated by Wheeler M. Thackston. Leiden: Brill, 2012.

Chittick, William C. *Imaginal Worlds: Ibn al-ʿArabī and the Problem of Religious Diversity*. Albany: State University of New York Press, 1994.

Craig, Eleanor, and An Yountae. 'Introduction'. In *Beyond Man: Race, Coloniality, and Philosophy of Religion*, edited by An Yountae and Eleanor Craig, 1–31. Durham, NC: Duke University Press, 2021.

Crone, Patricia, and Michael Cook. *Hagarism: The Making of the Islamic World*. Cambridge: Cambridge University Press, 1977.

Dārā Shukoh. *Sirr-i akbar*. Translated by Āzarmī Dukht Ṣafavī. Delhi: National Council for the Promotion of Urdu, 2022.

Didier, Hugues. 'Jerome Xavier'. In *Christian–Muslim Relations: A Bibliographical History*. Vol. 11, *South and East Asia, Africa and the Americas (1600–1700)*, edited by David Thomas and John Chesworth, 84–91. Leiden: Brill, 2017.

Dirāyatī, Muṣṭafā, ed. *Fihristagān-i nuskha-hā-yi khaṭṭī-yi Īrān*. Tehran: Sāzmān-i asnād va kitābkhāna-yi millī-yi jumhūrī-yi islāmī, 2012.

Faḍlallāh, Sayyid Muḥammad Ḥusayn. *Min waḥy al-Qurʾān*. 24 vols. Beirut: Dār al-Malāk, 1998.

Friedmann, Yohanan. *Tolerance and Coercion in Islam: Interfaith Relations in the Muslim Tradition*. Cambridge: Cambridge University Press, 2003.

Gandhi, Supriya. *The Emperor Who Never Was: Dara Shuloh in Mughal India*. Cambridge, MA: The Belknap Press of Harvard University Press, 2020.

Goudarzi, Mohsen. 'Worship (*Dīn*), Monotheism (*Islām*), and the Qurʾān Cultic Decalogue'. *Journal of the International Qurʾanic Studies Association* 8, no. 1 (2023): 30–71.

Haddad, Yvonne Y. 'The Conception of the Term *Dīn* in the Qurʾān'. *The Muslim World* 64, no. 2 (1974): 114–23.

Ḥāʾirī, ʿAbd al-Hādī. *Nukhustīn rūyārūyī-hā-yi andīshagarān-i Īrān bā dū rūya-yi tamaddun-i būrzhūvazī-yi gharb*. Tehran: Amīr Kabīr, 1988.

Halft, Dennis. 'ʿAlī Nūrī'. In *Christian–Muslim Relations: A Bibliographical History*. Vol. 20, *Iran, Afghanistan, and the Caucasus (1800–1914)*, edited by David Thomas and John Chesworth, 143–49. Leiden: Brill, 2023.

———. 'The Arabic Vulgate in Safavid Persia: Arabic Printing of the Gospels, Catholic Missionaries, and the Rise of Shīʿī Anti-Christian Polemics'. PhD diss., Freie Universität Berlin, 2016.

Hart, David Bentley. *The Experience of God: Being, Consciousness, Bliss*. New Haven: Yale University Press, 2013.

Ḥāṭim, ʿAbd al-Raḥmān. *Rāʾid al-ʿirfān al-Āqā Muḥammad Bīdābādī*. Beirut: Dār al-Hādī, 2002.

Hughes, Aaron W. *An Anxious Inheritance: Religious Others and the Shaping of Sunni Orthodoxy*. Oxford: Oxford University Press, 2022.

Hughes, Aaron W., and Russell T. McCutcheon, eds. *What Is Religion? Debating the Academic Study of Religion*. New York: Oxford University Press, 2021.

Ḥusaynī-yi Ṭihrānī, Sayyid Muḥammad Ḥusayn. *Rūḥ-i mujarrad*. Mashhad: Intishārāt-i ʿAllāma-yi Ṭabāṭabāʾī, 2000.

Ibn Turka. *Sharḥ Fuṣūṣ al-ḥikam*. Edited by Muḥsin Bīdārfar. 2 vols. Qom: Intishārāt-i Bīdār, 1999.

Iṣfahānī, Ḥusayn ʿAlī-Shāh. *Risāla-yi radd-i pādrī*. Edited by Maḥmūd Riżā Isfandyār. Tehran: Intishārāt-i ḥaqīqat, 2008.

Iʿtiżād al-Salṭana, ʿAlī-Qulī Mīrzā. *Iksīr al-tavārīkh*. Edited by Jamshīd Kiyānfar. Tehran: Intishārāt-i Vīsmān, 1991.

Jackson, Sherman A. *The Islamic Secular*. Oxford: Oxford University Press, 2024.

Jaʿfarīyān, Rasūl. *Siyāsat va farhang-i rūzgār-i ṣafavī*. 2. vols. Tehran: Nashr-i ʿilm, 2009.

Jambet, Christian. *L'acte d'être: La philosophie de la révélation chez Mollā Ṣadrā*. Paris: Fayard, 2002.

———. *Le gouvernement divin: Islam et conception politique du monde*. Paris: CNRS, 2016.

Kant, Immanuel. *Religion within the Boundaries of Mere Reason*. Translated and edited by Allen Wood and George di Giovanni. Cambridge: Cambridge University Press, 2018.

Karbāsī-zāda, ʿAlī. *Ḥakīm-i mutaʾallih Bīdābādī: iḥyāgarā-yi ḥikmat-i shīʿī dar qarn-i davāzdahum-i hijrī*. Tehran: Pazhūhishgāh-i ʿulūm-i insānī va muṭālaʿāt-i farhangī, 2002.

Kearney, Richard, and Jens Zimmermann, eds. *Reimagining the Sacred*. New York: Columbia University Press, 2016.

Khān 'Hidāyat', Riżā-Qulī. *Fihris al-tavārīkh*. Edited by ʿAbd al-Ḥusayn Nawāʾī and Mīr Hāshim Muḥaddith. Tehran: Pazhūhishgāh-i ʿulūm-i insānī va muṭālaʿāt-i farhangī, 1994.

Khwānsārī, Sayyid Muḥammad Bāqir. *Rawḍāt al-jannāt*. 9 vols. Beirut: al-Dār al-Islāmiyya, 1991.

al-Kulaynī, Abū Jaʿfar. *al-Kāfī*. Qom: Dār al-Ḥadīth, 2005.

Lee, Samuel. *Controversial Tracts in Christianity and Mohammadanism by the Late Rev. Henry Martyn and Some of the Most Eminent Writers of Persia*. Cambridge: J. Smith, 1824.

Majlisī, Muḥammad Bāqir. *Biḥār al-anwār*. Beirut: Dār al-Aḍwāʾ, 1983.

Majẕūb ʿAlī Shāh, Muḥammad Jaʿfar Kabūdarāhangī. *Mirʾāt al-ḥaqq*. Edited by Ḥāmid Nājī Iṣfahānī. Tehran: Intishārāt-i ḥaqīqat, 2004.

Martyn, John R. C. *Henry Martyn (1781–1812), Scholar and Missionary to India and Persia: A Biography*. Lewiston, NY: E. Mellen Press, 1999.

Masuzawa, Tomoko. *The Invention of World Religions, or How European Universalism Was Preserved in the Language of Pluralism*. Chicago: University of Chicago Press, 2005.

Mīrzā-yi Qummī. 'Iʿjāz al-Qurʾān'. Edited by Sayyid Ḥusayn Mudarrissī Ṭabāṭabāʾī. *Vaḥīd* 10 (1972): 115–18.

Muʿallim-i Ḥabībābādī, Mīrzā Muḥammad ʿAlī. *Makārim al-ās̱ār dar aḥvāl-i rijāl-i dawra-yi Qājār*. 4 vols. Isfahan: Maṭbaʿ-yi Muḥammadī, 1958.

Mudarris-i Tabrīzī, Muḥammad ʿAlī Khiyābānī. *Rayḥānat al-adab fī tarājim al-maʿrūfīn bi-l-kunya aw al-laqab*. 6 vols. [Tehran:] Chāpkhāna-yi Saʿdī, 1947–53.

al-Mūsawī, Sayyid Ṣādiq, ed. *Tamām Nahj al-balāgha*. Beirut: al-Dār al-Islāmiyya, 2005.

Nair, Shankar. *Translating Wisdom: Hindu–Muslim Intellectual Interactions in Early Modern South Asia*. Berkeley: University of California Press, 2020.

Naqavī, Sayyid ʿAlī Naqī. *Tafsīr Faṣl al-khiṭāb*. 3 vols. Lahore: Miṣbāḥ al-Qurʾān Trust, 2011.

Nasr, Seyyed Hossein. *Islamic Philosophy from Its Origin to the Present*. Albany: State University of New York Press, 2006.

Nongbri, Brent. *Before Religion: A History of a Modern Concept*. New Haven: Yale University Press, 2013.

Nūrī, ʿAlī. *Ḥujjat al-Islām yā burhān al-milla [Kitābī dar naqd-i guftār-i Henry Martyn]*. Edited by Ḥāmid Nājī Iṣfahānī. Tehran: Mīrās̱-i maktūb, 2012.

———. *al-Raqīma al-nūriyya fī qāʿidat basīṭ al-ḥaqīqa*. Edited by Ḥāmid Nājī Iṣfahānī. In *Mīrāth-i ḥawza-yi Iṣfahān*, edited by Muḥammad Javād Nūr-Muḥammadī, 6:35–175. Isfahan: Ḥawza-yi ʿilmiyya-yi Iṣfahān, 2010.

———. *Rasāʾil-i falsafī: basīṭ al-ḥaqīqa wa-waḥdat al-wujūd*. Edited by Sayyid Jalāl al-Dīn Āshtiyānī. Tehran: Anjuman-i ḥikmat u falsafa-yi Īrān, 1978.

Oppy, Graham. *Arguing about Gods*. Cambridge: Cambridge University Press, 2009.

Penn, Michael Philip. *When Christians First Met Muslims: A Sourcebook on the Earliest Syriac Writings on Islam*. Berkeley: University of California Press, 2015.

Powell, Averil. *Muslims and Missionaries in Pre-mutiny India*. Richmond: Curzon Press, 1993.

Qāsimī, Raḥīm. *Gulzār-i muqaddas*. 2 vols. Isfahan: Sāzmān-i farhangī u tafrīḥī-yi shahrdārī-yi Iṣfahān, 2011.

Qazvīnī, ʿAbd al-Nabī. *Tatmīm Amal al-āmil*. Edited by Sayyid Maḥmud Marʿashī and Sayyid Aḥmad Ḥusaynī. Qom: Maktabat Āyatullāh Marʿashī, 1987.

al-Ṣaffār al-Qummī. *Baṣā'ir al-darajāt*. Edited by Sayyid Muḥammad Abṭaḥī. 2 vols. Qom: Mu'assasat al-Imām al-Mahdī, 2010.

Schleiermacher, Friedrich. *On Religion*. Translated and edited by Richard Crouter. Cambridge: Cambridge University Press, 1996.

Scott, David, and Charles Hirschkind, eds. *Powers of the Secular Modern: Talal Asad and His Interlocutors*. Stanford: Stanford University Press, 2006.

Sebti, Meryem. *Avicenne: Prophétie et gouvernement du monde*. Paris: Cerf, 2021.

Shīrāzī, Maʿṣūm ʿAlī Shāh Nā'ib al-Ṣadr. *Ṭarā'iq al-ḥaqā'iq*. Edited by M. J. Maḥjūb. 3 vols. Tehran: Kitābkhāna-yi Bārānī, 1960.

Shīrāzī, Mullā Ṣadrā. *al-Ḥikma al-mutaʿāliya fī al-asfār al-ʿaqliyya al-arbaʿa*. Edited by Sayyid Muḥammad Khāminihī. 9 vols. Tehran: Sadra Islamic Philosophy Research Institute, 2001–4.

———. *Mafātīḥ al-ghayb*. Edited by Najafqulī Ḥabībī. 2 vols. Tehran: Sadra Islamic Philosophy Research Institute, 2007.

———. *Sharḥ Uṣūl al-Kāfī*. Edited by Riḍā Ustādī et al. 5 vols. Tehran: Sadra Islamic Philosophy Research Institute, 2006.

———. *Tafsīr al-Qur'ān al-karīm*. Edited by Muḥammad Khwājawī. 8 vols. Tehran: SIPRIn, 2010.

Shīrvānī, Zayn al-ʿĀbidīn. *Bustān al-siyāḥa*. Tehran: Sanā'ī, 1895.

Shubbar, Sayyid ʿAbdullāh. *Tafsīr al-Qur'ān al-karīm*. Beirut: Dār Iḥyā' al-Turāth al-ʿArabī, 2008.

Smith, Jonathan Z. *Imagining Religion: From Babylon to Jonestown*. Chicago: University of Chicago Press, 1982.

Smith, Wilfred Cantwell. *The Meaning and End of Religion: A New Approach to the Religious Traditions of Mankind*. Minneapolis: Fortress, 1963.

'Suhā', Manūchihr Ṣadūqī. *Ḥukamā' va ʿurafā'-yi muta'akhkhirīn-i Ṣadr al-muta'allihīn*. Tehran: Anjuman-i islāmī-yi ḥikmat va falsafa-yi Īrān, 1980.

al-Sulamī, Abū ʿAbd al-Raḥmān. *Kitāb al-arbaʿīn fī al-taṣawwuf*. Hyderabad: Dā'irat al-Maʿārif al-ʿUthmāniyya, 1981.

Sulṭān ʿAlī Shāh. *Bayān al-saʿāda fī maqāmāt al-ʿibāda*. 4 vols. Tehran: Tehran University Press, 1965.

Ṭabāṭabā'ī, Sayyid Muḥammad Ḥusayn. *al-Mīzān fī tafsīr al-Qur'ān*. 20 vols. Qom: Manshūrāt al-ḥawza al-ʿilmiyya, n.d.

Tareen, SherAli. *Perilous Intimacies: Debating Hindu–Muslim Friendship after Empire*. New York: Columbia University Press, 2023.

Yountae, An. *The Coloniality of the Secular: Race, Religion, and the Poetics of World-Making*. Durham, NC: Duke University Press, 2024.

Zarrīnkūb, ʿAbd al-Ḥusayn. *Dunbāla-yi justajū dar taṣavvuf-i Īrān*. Tehran: Amīr Kabīr, 1990.

# PART 2

## *Sunnī Theological Perspectives on God and Monotheism*

# The *Tawḥīd*s of Ibn Taymiyya

*Jon Hoover*

## 1. Introduction

The contemporary Salafī movement typically divides divine unicity (*tawḥīd*) into three kinds. The first is *tawḥīd al-rubūbiyya*, which is confessing the exclusivity of God's lordship (*rubūbiyya*) by affirming that God is the sole creator of all things. Second is *tawḥīḍ al-ulūhiyya*. The term *ulūhiyya* refers to God's divinity in the sense of God's right to be worshipped as a god, and *tawḥīḍ al-ulūhiyya* means demonstrating God's exclusive divinity by worshipping God alone. The third *tawḥīd* is *tawḥīd al-asmāʾ wa-l-ṣifāt*, which affirms the uniqueness and incomparability of God's names and attributes.[1] The terms *tawḥīd al-ulūhiyya* and *tawḥīd al-rubūbiyya* are readily traced back to the fourteenth-century Ḥanbalī theologian Ibn Taymiyya (d. 728/1328) who develops them in his writings.[2] However, scholars of contemporary Salafism have been reticent to credit Ibn Taymiyya with the third kind of *tawḥīd, tawḥīd al-asmāʾ wa-l-ṣifāt*. For example, Bernard Haykel in his 2009 study, 'On the Nature of Salafi Thought and Action', writes, 'The terms *tawhid al-rububiyya* and *tawhid al-uluhiyya* appear to have been coined in Ibn Taymiyya's time,'[3] but he does not speculate about the origin of *tawḥīd al-asmāʾ wa-l-ṣifāt*. Similarly, Henri Lauzière in his 2016 monograph, *The Making of Salafism*, states that Ibn Taymiyya elaborated the first two types of *tawḥīd* and then credits the eighteenth-century Arabian reformer Ibn ʿAbd al-Wahhāb (d. 1206/1792) with the third.[4] There is good reason for this reticence. To the best of my knowledge, the expression *tawḥīd al-asmāʾ wa-l-ṣifāt* does not occur in Ibn Taymiyya's writings, and the threefold division of *tawḥīd* common among Salafīs today is rare.[5] Nevertheless, Ibn Taymiyya does have a lot to say about God's names and

---

1 Joas Wagemakers, *Salafism in Jordan: Political Islam in a Quietist Community* (Cambridge: Cambridge University Press, 2016), 40–42; Bernard Haykel, 'On the Nature of Salafi Thought and Action', in *Global Salafism: Islam's New Religious Movement*, ed. Roel Meijer (London: Hurst, 2009), 38–40. On the contemporary Salafī doctrine of *tawḥīd al-asmāʾ wa-l-ṣifāt* specifically, see Mohammad Gharaibeh, *Zur Attributenlehre der Wahhābīya unter besonderer Berücksichtigung der Schriften Ibn ʿUṯaimīns (1929–2001)* (Berlin: EB-Verlag, 2012).

2 Cole M. Bunzel, *Wahhābism: The History of a Militant Islamic Movement* (Princeton, NJ: Princeton University Press, 2023), 128–38; Jon Hoover, *Ibn Taymiyya's Theodicy of Perpetual Optimism* (Leiden: Brill, 2007), 27–29, 121–22, 195; Jon Hoover, *Ibn Taymiyya* (London: Oneworld, 2019), 42–43, 48–49; Henri Laoust, *La profession de foi d'Ibn Taymiyya: Texte, traduction et commentaire de La Wāsiṭiyya* (Paris: Librairie orientaliste Paul Geuthner, 1986), 37; Henri Laoust, *Essai sur les doctrines sociales et politiques de Taḳī-d-Dīn Aḥmad b. Taimīya, canoniste ḥanbalite né à Ḥarrān en 661/1262, mort à Damas en 728/1328* (Cairo: Imprimerie de l'institut français d'archéologie orientale, 1939), 472–73.

3 Haykel, 'Salafi Thought and Action', 39.

4 Henri Lauzière, *The Making of Salafism: Islamic Reform in the Twentieth Century* (New York: Columbia University Press, 2016), 210.

5 Gharaibeh, *Zur Attributenlehre*, 1, states that Ibn ʿAbd al-Wahhāb adopts the threefold scheme of *tawḥīd*

attributes,[6] and it has been shown that contemporary Salafīs draw from his works to articulate their views on this aspect of their theology, especially from his *Wāsiṭiyya* creed, his anti-Ashʿarī *Ḥamawiyya*, and his *Tadmuriyya*, an overview of theological doctrine.[7] This then raises the question of how Ibn Taymiyya conceptualises *tawḥīd* if not according to the three kinds of contemporary Salafism.

In this study I will show that Ibn Taymiyya gives theological primacy to a division of *tawḥīd* into two kinds that is linked to a distinction in Arabic linguistics between informative speech (*khabar*) and performative speech (*inshāʾ*).[8] These two kinds of *tawḥīd* do not correspond to Ibn Taymiyya's well-known *tawḥīd al-ulūhiyya* (or *ilāhiyya*) and *tawḥīd al-rubūbiyya*. Instead, the kind of *tawḥīd* linked to performative speech encompasses both of those *tawḥīd*s, while the kind linked to informative speech corresponds to what eventually becomes known as *tawḥīd al-asmāʾ wa-l-ṣifāt*. Ibn Taymiyya's twofold *tawḥīd* and its linkage to informative and performative types of speech are readily evident in his *Tadmuriyya* and a few other works. Using *Tadmuriyya* as my basis for analysis, I will explore Ibn Taymiyya's two primary *tawḥīd*s and then add some notes on the evolution of *tawḥīd* terminology up through Ibn ʿAbd al-Wahhāb to show how Ibn Taymiyya's scheme was de-emphasised to make way for the threefold division better known today.

---

from Ibn Taymiyya, but he does not provide explicit evidence for this regarding *tawḥīd al-asmāʾ wa-l-ṣifāt*. Likewise, Laoust, *La profession*, 37, says that Ibn Taymiyya sometimes uses this expression, but he does not provide any evidence. Ibrahim Kalin, 'Will, Necessity and Creation as Monistic Theophany in the Islamic Philosophical Tradition', in *Creation and the God of Abraham*, ed. David B. Burrell, Carlo Cogliati, Janet M. Soskice, and William R. Stoeger (Cambridge: Cambridge University Press, 2010), 111, reports that Ibn Taymiyya adds *tawḥīd al-asmāʾ wa-l-ṣifāt* to the other two *tawḥīd*s in his refutation of Shīʿism, *Minhāj al-sunna*; however, Kalin does not provide a reference, and I was not able to locate it. The only instance that I have found of Ibn Taymiyya outlining three types of *tawḥīd* in modern Salafī fashion is in *Sharḥ al-iṣbahāniyya*, ed. Muḥammad b. ʿAwda al-Saʿawī (Riyadh: Maktabat Dār al-Minhāj, 2009–10), 107: 'Discussion of *tawḥīd* includes three kinds. The first of them is discussion of the attributes. The second is *tawḥīd al-rubūbiyya* and clarification that God is creator of everything. The third is *tawḥīd al-ilāhiyya*, which is worshipping God alone without associate.'

6 See Farid Suleiman, *Ibn Taymiyya und die Attribute Gottes* (Berlin: de Gruyter, 2019); for an English translation, see *Ibn Taymiyya and the Attributes of God*, trans. Carl Sharif El-Tobgui (Leiden: Brill, 2024).

7 See the index entry 'Ibn Taimīya', in Gharaibeh, *Zur Attributenlehre*. See also Michael Farquhar, *Circuits of Faith: Migration, Education, and the Wahhabi Mission* (Stanford: Stanford University Press, 2017), 137–43; Alexander Thurston, *Salafism in Nigeria: Islam, Preaching, and Politics* (Cambridge: Cambridge University Press, 2016), 40–43, 61.

8 In translating *khabar* as 'informative speech' and *inshāʾ* as 'performative speech' I follow David Vishanoff, 'Informative and Performative Theories of Divine Speech in Classical Islamic Legal Theory', in *Philosophy and Language in the Islamic World*, ed. Nadja Germann and Mostafa Najafi (Berlin: de Gruyter, 2021), 183–208. Modern scholars of Arabic linguistics observe that the term *inshāʾ* maps onto the notion of performative utterances in J. L. Austin's speech act theory. Performative utterances are words that perform actions by their very pronouncement. They do not just provide information. A man who says to his wife 'I divorce you', for example, is not merely providing information about the status of his wife. He is enacting a divorce. See further J. L. Austin, *How to Do Things with Words*, ed. J. O. Urmson and Marina Sbisá, 2nd ed. (Cambridge, MA: Harvard University Press, 1962); Daniela Rodica Firanescu, 'Speech Acts', in *The Encyclopedia of Arabic Language and Linguistics*, ed. Kees Versteegh, Mushira Eid, Alaa Elgibali, Manfred Woidich, and Andrzej Zaborski, 5 vols. (Leiden: Brill, 2006–9); 4:328–34; Pierre Larcher, '*Inšāʾ*', in ibid., 2:358–61.

## 2. Informative Speech (*Khabar*) and Performative Speech (*Inshāʾ*)

*Tadmuriyya* takes up just over 140 pages in *Majmūʿ fatāwā*, the modern thirty-seven-volume compilation of Ibn Taymiyya's short- and medium-length writings.[9] The title *Tadmuriyya* derives from name of the Syrian city Palmyra (*Tadmur*). It is not known why the treatise was given this title, but Ibn Taymiyya does explain that he wrote it in response to a request for the contents of one of his teaching sessions on two principles. The first principle is God's 'unicity and attributes' (*al-tawḥīd wa-l-ṣifāt*), and the second is God's 'legislation and determination' (*al-sharʿ wa-l-qadar*). Ibn Taymiyya then seeks in *Tadmuriyya* to provide a comprehensive hermeneutical framework for interpreting the theological content of divine revelation by elaborating the two principles in terms of two kinds of speech and then two fundamental types of *tawḥīd*. He begins elucidating the two principles with the following linguistic analysis in the introduction to the treatise.

> Discussion of the category of unicity and the attributes comes under the category of informative speech (*khabar*), which has to do with negation and affirmation, and discussion of the category of legislation and determination comes under the category of request and will (*al-ṭalab wa-l-irāda*), which has to do with desire and love [on the one hand] and loathing and hate [on the other], negatively and affirmatively. A human being knows instinctively (*fī nafsihi*) the difference between negation and affirmation or deeming someone truthful and deeming someone a liar [on the one hand] and love and hate and prompting and preventing [on the other]. The difference between the one kind and the other kind is even known by the commoners and the elite (*al-ʿāmma wa-l-khāṣṣa*), as well as by different types of scholars. The jurists mention this when discussing oaths, and linguists—students of theory, grammar, and rhetoric—also mention it; they mention that speech is of two kinds: informative (*khabar*) and performative (*inshāʾ*). Informative speech has to do with negation and affirmation, and performative speech with command or prohibition or permission.[10]

---

9 Ibn Taymiyya, *Tadmuriyya*, in *Majmūʿ fatāwā Shaykh al-Islām Aḥmad Ibn Taymiyya* [hereafter: MF], ed. ʿAbd al-Raḥmān b. Muḥammad b. Qāsim and Muḥammad b. ʿAbd al-Raḥmān b. Muḥammad, 37 vols. (Riyadh: Maṭābiʿ al-Riyāḍ, 1961–67), 3:1–128 (including 15 pages paginated *alif–sīn* inserted between pp. 88 and 89; references will follow the pagination of this edition); Ibn Taymiyya, *al-Tadmuriyya: taḥqīq al-ithbāt li-asmāʾ wa-l-ṣifāt wa-ḥaqīqat al-jamʿ bayna al-qadar wa-l-sharʿ*, ed. Muḥammad b. ʿAwda al-Saʿawī (Riyadh, 1985); French translation: Ibn Taymiyya, *La lettre palmyrienne* (*Tadmuriyya*), trans. Abu Soleiman Al-Kaabi ([Paris]: Nawa, 2014). The date of *Tadmuriyya* is unknown. Laoust, *La profession*, 32, suggests that Ibn Taymiyya wrote *Tadmuriyya* sometime after his release from prison in Cairo in 1307, but he gives no evidence for this conjecture. The text probably does not come from the very latest period of Ibn Taymiyya's life because he mentions it in another treatise, *Tafsīr sūrat al-ʿalaq*, MF 16:430 (reference to *al-Masāʾil al-Tadmuriyya*). However, the date of *Tafsīr sūrat al-ʿalaq* itself is not known. Henri Laoust, 'Le Hanbalisme sous les mamlouks bahrides (658–784/1260–1382)', *Revue des études islamiques* 28 (1960): 23, also suggests that Ibn Taymiyya may have written *Tadmuriyya* for the Bedouin *amīr* Muhannā b. ʿĪsā (d. 736/1335–36), but Laoust provides no evidence for this.

10 Ibn Taymiyya, *Tadmuriyya*, MF 3:2.

In this passage, Ibn Taymiyya links the principle of God's unicity and attributes to the linguistic category of informative speech, which signifies statements that are affirmed or negated, and the principle of legislation and determination to request and will, that is, utterances that turn on love and hate and prompting and preventing. Furthermore, he adds, linguists speak of the two types as informative speech (*khabar*) and performative speech (*inshāʾ*).[11] The terminological pair *khabar* and *inshāʾ* had only come into use among Arabic linguists in the 1200s, but they had been discussed among legal theorists since the tenth century.[12]

Ibn Taymiyya says in the text above that *inshāʾ* has to do with command, prohibition, or permission. This could be understood to refer to God's legislative rulings for human beings only. However, this does not exhaust his understanding of *inshāʾ*. Ibn Taymiyya invokes a fuller meaning of *inshāʾ* outside *Tadmuriyya*. He writes, for example, 'Informative sentences conform to what is informed about. Performative speech necessitates the origination of what has not yet been.'[13] Likewise, he says, '[Informative speech] is the manifestation of knowledge, and performative speech is the manifestation of deeds.'[14] Ibn Taymiyya also includes both what God commands to exist ontologically and what God commands human beings to do legislatively within the realm of the performative: 'Speech is either performative or informative. Informative speech is true, not a lie. Performative speech—the command of ontological origination (*amr al-takwīn*) and the command of legislation (*amr al-tashrīʿ*)—is just and not unjust.'[15]

Back in the introduction to *Tadmuriyya*, Ibn Taymiyya implies both aspects of God's performative activity by linking *inshāʾ* to his second principle of legislation and determination. 'Determination' here refers to God's determination and creation of everything that exists, and it is functionally equivalent to God's command of ontological origination mentioned just above. God's performative speech then encompasses both God's legislative command and God's creation of all things.

11 Similar discussions of *khabar* and *inshāʾ* are found in Ibn Taymiyya, *Tafsīr sūrat al-ikhlāṣ*, MF 17:368–69; Ibn Taymiyya, MF 6:523 (references to MF without treatise names are to short unnamed texts); Ibn Taymiyya, *Darʾ taʿāruḍ al-ʿaql wa-l-naql*, ed. Muḥammad Rashād Sālim, 11 vols. (n.p.: n.d), 5:205, 10:215. In other texts, Ibn Taymiyya extends the scope of *khabar* beyond God's unicity and attributes to include Qurʾanic narratives about human salvation history; see Ibn Taymiyya, MF 17:207; Ibn Taymiyya, *Darʾ taʿāruḍ*, 7:273; Ibn Taymiyya, *al-Amr bi-l-maʿrūf*, MF 28:121; Ibn Taymiyya, *Minhāj al-sunna al-nabawiyya fī naqḍ kalām al-Shīʿa al-Qadariyya*, ed. Muḥammad Rashād Sālim, 9 vols. (Riyadh: Jāmiʿat al-Imām Muḥammad b. Suʿūd al-Islāmiyya, 1986), 3:290.

12 Pierre Larcher, 'Les arabisants et la catégorie de "*inšâ*": histoire d'une "occultation"', *Historiographia Linguistica* 20, no. 2–3 (1993): 259–60; Vishanoff, 'Informative and Performative Theories'.

13 Ibn Taymiyya, *Tafsīr sūrat al-kāfirūn*, MF 16:560.

14 Ibn Taymiyya, MF 20:74.

15 Ibn Taymiyya, *Tafsīr sūrat al-shams*, MF 16:245.

### 3. The *Tawḥīd* in Knowledge and Statement and the *Tawḥīd* in Intention, Will, and Deed

Continuing in *Tadmuriyya*, Ibn Taymiyya builds on the distinction between informative and performative speech to link his two principles to two types of *tawḥīd*:

> This being the case [that informative speech has to do with affirmation and negation and performative speech has to do with command, prohibition, and permission], the servant must affirm of God the attributes of perfection that must be affirmed of Him and negate of God what opposes this state [of perfection]. Regarding His judgements (*aḥkām*) [the servant] must affirm His creation (*khalq*) and His command (*amr*). He [must] believe in His creation, which includes the perfection of His power and the universality of His will, and affirm His command, which includes the explication of what He loves and what He is well pleased with in both speech and deed. He [must] believe in His legislation and His determination with a belief devoid of error. This [latter affirmation] involves exclusivity in worshipping [God] (*al-tawḥīd fī ʿibādatihi*) alone, without associate. It is exclusivity in intention, will, and deed (*al-tawḥīd fī al-qaṣd wa-l-irāda wa-l-ʿamal*). The first [affirmation] involves uniqueness in knowledge and statement (*al-tawḥīd fī al-ʿilm wa-l-qawl*), as the *sūra* 'Say! He is God, One' (Q. 112) indicates. The *sūra* 'Say! O, you unbelievers' (Q. 109) indicates [exclusivity in intention, will, and deed]. These are the two *sūras* of sincerity (*ikhlāṣ*).[16]

Ibn Taymiyya here links informative speech and his first principle concerning God's attributes to the *tawḥīd* in 'knowledge and statement', and he ties performative speech and his second principle concerning legislation and determination to the *tawḥīd* in 'intention, will, and deed'. Ibn Taymiyya outlines these two *tawḥīd*s in similar fashion in two of his large works of theology, *Bayān talbīs al-Jahmiyya* and *Minhāj al-sunna*. In both tomes, he connects God's uniqueness in knowledge and statement (*al-tawḥīd fī al-ʿilm wa-l-qawl*) to God's oneness and the uniqueness of God's attributes, and he motivates this *tawḥīd* with both the Qur'anic verse 'Say! He is God, One' (Q. 112:1) and the linguistic category of informative speech (*khabar*). Then, he explains that exclusivity in will and deed (*al-tawḥīd fī al-irāda wa-l-ʿamal*) is about worshipping God alone without associate, and he associates this *tawḥīd* with both the Qur'anic text 'Say! O, you unbelievers, I do not worship what you worship' (Q. 109:1–2) and the linguistic category of performative speech (*inshāʾ*).[17]

---

16 Ibn Taymiyya, *Tadmuriyya*, MF 3:2–3.

17 Ibn Taymiyya, *Bayān talbīs al-Jahmiyya fī taʾsīs bidaʿihim al-kalāmiyya*, ed. Yaḥyā b. Muḥammad al-Hunaydī et al., 10 vols. (Medina: Majmaʿ al-Malik Fahd, 2005), 3:140–42; Ibn Taymiyya, *Minhāj al-sunna*, 3:290–91. Ibn Taymiyya speaks similarly of two kinds of *tawḥīd* in *Iqtiḍāʾ al-ṣirāṭ al-mustaqīm mukhālafat aṣḥāb al-jaḥīm*, ed. Nāṣir b. ʿAbd al-Karīm al-ʿAql, 2 vols., 2nd printing (Riyadh: Dār Ishbīliyyā, 1998), 2:394; *al-*

Ibn Taymiyya structures the whole of *Tadmuriyya* around the two types of *tawḥīd* that correspond to his two principles 'unicity and attributes' and 'legislation and determination', which are in turn rooted in the distinction between informative and performative speech.[18] In what follows, I will examine the basics of how Ibn Taymiyya explains his two categories of *tawḥīd* in *Tadmuriyya* before turning to how they changed into the three distinct *tawḥīds* for which Wahhābism and Salafism are well known.

The first and longest part of *Tadmuriyya* treats the *tawḥīd* in knowledge and statement, which, at the very beginning of this part, Ibn Taymiyya also calls 'uniqueness in the attributes' (*al-tawḥīd fī al-ṣifāt*).[19] I have not found the expression *al-tawḥīd fī al-ṣifāt* elsewhere in Ibn Taymiyya's corpus, but it is evidently a forerunner to the later expression *tawḥīd al-asmāʾ wa-l-ṣifāt* (the uniqueness of the names and attributes). Ibn Taymiyya structures his treatment of the *tawḥīd* of knowledge and statement into an introductory discussion, two principles, two examples, and a long conclusion (*khātima*) consisting of seven rules. I limit my examination below to the introductory discussion and the two principles. The examples and rules simply elaborate Ibn Taymiyya's basic ideas, and it would take us too far from this study's focus on types of *tawḥīd* to analyse them.[20]

The second part of *Tadmuriyya* on the principle of legislation and determination deals with the *tawḥīd* in intention, will, and deed which, in the passage translated above, Ibn Taymiyya calls more briefly the *tawḥīd* 'in worshipping [God]'. Ibn Taymiyya also speaks of the *tawḥīd* 'in acts of worship' (*ʿibādāt*) at the beginning of the second part of *Tadmuriyya*,[21] and it is within this part that he discusses the better-known terms *tawḥīd al-ilāhiyya* and *tawḥīd al-rubūbiyya*, although not with the sophistication found elsewhere in his writings.[22]

---

*ʿUqūd* [*Naẓariyyat al-ʿaqd*], ed. Muḥammad Ḥāmid al-Fiqī (Cairo: Maktaba al-Sunna al-Muḥammadiyya, 1949), 10; *Jawāb ahl al-ʿilm wa-l-īmān anna 'qul huwa Allāh aḥad' taʿdilu thulth al-Qurʾān*, MF 17:107, which reads, '[Divine unicity] is of two kinds: knowledge- and statement-based (*ʿilmī qawlī*) and deed- and intention-based (*ʿamalī qaṣdī*).'

18 Ibn Taymiyya, *Tadmuriyya*, MF 3:3–88 and *alif–sīn* (first part), 3:89–128 (second part).

19 Ibid., 3.

20 See Suleiman, *Ibn Taymiyya und die Attribute Gottes*, 215–27, for a full discussion of the principles, examples, and rules. Hoover, *Ibn Taymiyya's Theodicy*, 49–52, 64–66, also discusses aspects of this material.

21 Ibn Taymiyya, *Tadmuriyya*, MF 3:89.

22 Ibrāhīm b. Muḥammad b. ʿAbd Allāh Buraykān, *Manhaj Shaykh al-Islām Ibn Taymīyya fī taqrīr ʿaqīdat al-tawḥīd* (Riyadh: Dār Ibn al-Qayyim; Cairo: Dār Ibn ʿAffān, 2004), 173–74, states that Ibn Taymiyya's *al-tawḥīd al-qawlī al-ʿilmī* includes both the *tawḥīd* of God's lordship (*rubūbiyya*) and the *tawḥīd* of affirming God's names and attributes (*al-asmāʾ wa-l-ṣifāt*) and that Ibn Taymiyya's *al-tawḥīd al-qaṣdī al-ʿamalī* involves worship and God's divinity (*ulūhiyya*). However, no persuasive evidence from Ibn Taymiyya's writings is provided for subsuming the *tawḥīds* of both God's lordship and attributes under *al-tawḥīd al-qawlī al-ʿilmī*.

## 4. The *Tawḥīd* in Knowledge and Statement: God's Attributes

In the first part of *Tadmuriyya*, Ibn Taymiyya defines the first type of *tawḥīd*, the *tawḥīd* in knowledge and statement or in God's attributes, as adherence to the traditionalist creedal conviction that revealed language about God is to be affirmed as it is. God is to be spoken of exactly as God speaks of Himself in revelation, and no distortion or stripping God of His attributes is permitted. At the same time, likeness and similarity between the attributes of God and the attributes of creatures are negated, and inquiry into the condition or modality (*kayfiyya*) of God's attributes must be avoided.

> As for the first [category of *tawḥīd*], which is uniqueness in the attributes (*al-tawḥīd fī al-ṣifāt*), the principle in this category is that God is qualified by that which He has qualified Himself and by that which His messengers have qualified Him, negatively and affirmatively. What God has affirmed for Himself is affirmed, and what He has negated of Himself is negated. It is known that the way of the Salaf of the Community and its Imāms is affirming the attributes that He affirms without modalising [them] (*takyīf*) or likening [them to something else] (*tamthīl*) and without distorting [them] (*taḥrīf*) or stripping [them] away (*taʿṭīl*) .... Their way involves affirming His names and attributes while negating likeness (*mumāthala*) with creatures—affirming without assimilating [Him to creatures] (*tashbīh*) and declaring [Him] incomparable (*tanzīh*) without stripping away [His attributes]. As He—Exalted is He—said, 'There is nothing like Him, and He is all-Hearing, all-Seeing' (Q. 42:11). In His statement 'There is nothing like Him' is a rejection of assimilation and likening, and in His statement 'He is all-Hearing, all-Seeing' is a rejection of heresy (*ilḥād*) and stripping away.[23]

Ibn Taymiyya then quotes numerous Qur'anic verses denying that God has partners or a son and affirming that God has names and attributes such as living, one, knowing, merciful, coming, sitting, and speaking.[24] After this, he accuses various groups of stripping God of His attributes, on the one hand, and likening God to what is impossible, non-existent, and inanimate, on the other. These groups include Aristotelian philosophers (*falāsifa*), Jahmīs, Qarmaṭīs, and Bāṭinīs. Ibn Taymiyya applies the label Jahmī to Muʿtazilī and post-classical Ashʿarī *kalām* theologians who reinterpret God's names and attributes non-literally when their literal meanings suggest corporeality or temporality. The Qarmaṭīs and Bāṭinīs refer to Ismāʿīlī Shīʿīs whom Ibn Taymiyya pillories for saying that God is 'neither existent nor non-existent, neither living nor dead, neither knowing nor ignorant'.[25] He argues that the first negation in each pair is meant to avoid assimilating

---

23 Ibn Taymiyya, *Tadmuriyya*, MF 3:3–4; translation adapted from Hoover, *Ibn Taymiyya's Theodicy*, 49.
24 Ibid., 4–7.
25 Ibid., 7.

God to created things and the second to avoid assimilating God to things that do not exist. He rejects this double negation as irrational and a distortion of God's revelation, and he claims that it assimilates God to things that are impossible because negating contradictories is just as impossible as combining them.[26] Ibn Taymiyya then turns to the philosophers, by whom he typically means Ibn Sīnā (d. 428/1037) and his followers. He criticises the philosophers for reducing God's attributes to nothing more than God Himself. For example, they identify God's knowledge with God and fail to distinguish God's knowledge from God's power and will. Ibn Taymiyya also faults the philosophers for describing God as an existent that in fact exists nowhere but in the mind.[27]

Ibn Taymiyya's charge that the philosophers' God exists only in the mind may appear gratuitous and unwarranted. It is comprehensible, however, from within his own frame of reference. Ibn Taymiyya adheres to a materialist ontology that denies the existence of an intelligible realm outside the mind, and he affirms that all existents are perceptible by the human senses.[28] As I have shown elsewhere, Ibn Taymiyya's God is a concrete empirical entity that is spatially extended. This God is capable of being seen but is shielded from human view in this life.[29] It then follows for Ibn Taymiyya that theologians and philosophers who position God beyond space and time in an intelligible world effectively confine God to the human mind.

In *Tadmuriyya*, Ibn Taymiyya's rejection of an extramental intelligible world manifests itself most clearly in his denial of extramental universals. His explanation is worth quoting in full, as it well illustrates his 'nominalist' or perhaps better 'conceptualist' approach to universals: universals for Ibn Taymiyya have no real existence except as concepts in the mind.[30] This passage also raises the question of whether humans can speak meaningfully about God when terms applied to God and creatures share no common extramental

26 For a more charitable interpretation of Ismāʿīlī double negation, see Khalil Andani's paper, 'Apophatic *Tawḥīd*: A Philosophical Account of Shīʿī Ismāʿīlī Theology', in the present volume.

27 Ibn Taymiyya, *Tadmuriyya*, MF 3:7–8. A little later, Ibn Taymiyya writes, 'Whoever says, "God does not have knowledge, strength, mercy, and speech, and does not love, is not well pleased, does not call, does not speak intimately (*nājā*), and does not sit" is stripping and denying [God's attributes] and likening God to non-existents and inanimate objects' (16).

28 Carl Sharif El-Tobgui, *Ibn Taymiyya on Reason and Revelation: A Study of* Darʾ taʿāruḍ al-ʿaql wa-l-naql (Leiden, Brill, 2020), 229–35. I owe the apt term 'materialist' to Mohammad Abu Shareea.

29 Jon Hoover, 'God Spatially Above and Spatially Extended: The Rationality of Ibn Taymiyya's Refutation of Faḫr al-Dīn al-Rāzī's Ašʿarī Incorporealism', *Arabica* 69 (2022): 626–74 (esp. 645–50); Jon Hoover, 'God as an Empirical Entity: The Expanded Scope of Sense Perception in Traditionalist Spatialism', in *Analytic Islamic Epistemology: Critical Debates*, ed. Ramon Harvey and Safaruk Chowdhury (Edinburgh: Edinburgh University Press, forthcoming).

30 Wael B. Hallaq, *Ibn Taymiyya against the Greek Logicians* (Oxford: Clarendon Press, 1993), xvi–xxiv, calls Ibn Taymiyya's rejection of real universals nominalism. Suleiman, *Ibn Taymiyya und die Attribute Gottes*, 106–19, argues that conceptualism is a better label for Ibn Taymiyya's approach to universals than nominalism on the grounds that nominalism rejects even mental universals. See also Anke von Kügelgen, 'The Poison of Philosophy: Ibn Taymiyya's Struggle for and against Reason', in *Islamic Theology, Philosophy and Law: Debating Ibn Taymiyya and Ibn Qayyim al-Jawziyya*, ed. Birgit Krawietz and Georges Tamer (Berlin: de Gruyter, 2013), 291–97.

reference. This leads Ibn Taymiyya to reflect on the character of theological language.

> When it is known by necessity that in existence is the Eternal and Necessary in Itself and the temporally originated, possible, and susceptible to existence and non-existence, it is known that each one is an existent (*mawjūd*). It does not follow necessarily from their coincidence in the designation 'existence' (*musammā al-wujūd*) that the existence of the one is like the existence of the other. Instead, the existence of the one is particular to it and the existence of the other is particular to it. Their coincidence in a general name does not require their mutual likeness in the designation of that term upon attribution (*iḍāfa*), particularisation (*takhṣīṣ*), qualification (*taqyīd*), and so forth.
>
> No rational person says, 'When it is said that the Throne is an existent and a gnat is an existent, the one is like the other due to the coincidence of the designations "thing" and "existence".' This is because there is no existent thing in extramental reality apart from these two in which both participate (*yashtarikān fīhi*). Instead, the mind apprehends a shared universal meaning (*maʿnā mushtarak kullī*), which is the designation of the unqualified term (*al-ism al-muṭlaq*). When it is said that two things are existents, the existence of each one of them is particular to it, and nothing else participates in it with it, even though the term ['existence'] is a reality (*ḥaqīqa*) in each one of them.
>
> Therefore, God designated Himself with names, and He designated His attributes by His names. Those names are particular to Him. If they are attributed to Him, nothing else participates in them with Him. He [also] designated His creatures with names particular to them and attributed to them. These names coincide when sundered from attribution and particularisation. It does not follow necessarily from the coincidence of two names, the mutual likeness of their designations, and their identity when unqualified and abstracted from attribution and particularisation that the two [existents] coincide. The designation is not alike upon attribution and particularisation, not to mention that the two objects of designation do not become identical upon attribution and particularisation.
>
> God called Himself 'Living'. He said, 'There is no God but He, the Living, the Self-Subsisting' (Q. 2:255). He also called some of His servants 'living'. He said, 'He brought forth the living from the dead, and He brought forth the dead from the living' (Q. 30:19). The 'Living' is not like the 'living' because His statement 'Living' is a name for God particular to Him, and His statement 'He brought forth the living from the dead' is a name for the living creature particular to it. The two [names] coincide only when unqualified and abstracted from particularisation. However, what is unqualified has no existent object of designation in the extramental world. Even so, the intellect grasps from what is unqualified a sense (*qadr*) that is shared

> between the two names. Upon particularisation, that [sense] is qualified by that which the Creator is distinguished from the creature and the creature from the Creator.
>
> This applies necessarily to all of God's names and attributes. They are understood through what the name indicates by way of univocity (*muwāṭaʾa*) and coincidence (*ittifāq*) and what it indicates by way of the attribution and particularisation that prevent the creature from participating with the Creator in any of His particularities—Glory be to Him, Exalted is He.[31]

Again, for Ibn Taymiyya, only particulars exist in extramental reality. So, while he allows attribution of terms like 'existence' and 'living' to both God and creatures in this text, he denies the existence of extramental universals called 'existence' and 'living' in which both God and creatures participate. So, at first glance, Ibn Taymiyya appears to regard theological language as equivocal; God's 'Living' has nothing in common with a human being's 'living' except the name. Yet, he also affirms that human minds grasp a certain univocal and shared sense (*qadr*) or a universal meaning (*maʿnā kullī*) in terms such as 'existence' and 'living' when unqualified and unparticularised. These meanings are universal only in the mind, and when attributed to God and particular creatures, the universality of the meaning in the human mind gives way to the particularity of the extramental world such that the 'existence' of God is unlike the 'existence' of the creature and God's 'Living' is particular to God and the 'living' of creatures particular to them. Elsewhere in his writings, Ibn Taymiyya explains that terms like 'existence' are univocal in the sense of having a universal meaning in the mind but subject to modulation (*tashkīk*) according to precedence and worthiness when ascribed to extramental particulars. For example, that which is necessary is all the worthier of 'existence' than that which is possible, and so God, who is necessary, is all the worthier of 'existence' than creatures, who are merely possible.[32] The notion of the modulation of existence goes back to the

---

31 Ibn Taymiyya, *Tadmuriyya*, MF 3:9–11.

32 For elaboration, see Hoover, 'God Spatially Above', 648–49; and the section 'Theological Language' in Jon Hoover, 'Ibn Taymiyya', in *The Stanford Encyclopedia of Philosophy*, 2024, https://plato.stanford.edu/entries/ibn-taymiyya/. My analysis of Ibn Taymiyya on the referentiality of theological language has changed since my 2007 monograph, *Ibn Taymiyya's Theodicy*. In that work, I gave great weight to Ibn Taymiyya's assertions that God's names and attributes are completely unlike the attributes of creatures and so drew the conclusion that Ibn Taymiyya's theological discourse 'does not correspond to anything humans experience in concrete reality' (53). That is, theological language is equivocal. The role of theology then is merely practical, that is, to nurture religious belief and piety, not to provide meaningful knowledge of God. It has now become clear to me with the publication of my 2022 article, 'God Spatially Above', that the meanings of God's attributes in Ibn Taymiyya's theological discourse do connect to the concrete reality of human experience in some fashion. God's overness (*ʿulūw*), for example, most definitely means that God is an empirical existent located outside the universe spatially. God is not found inside the universe or in some dimension outside space and time. However, the meanings of terms applied to God and creatures are modulated according to the particularities of each, and this introduces a degree of ambiguity into the theological project that to Ibn Taymiyya's mind respects the unlikeness of God.

philosopher Ibn Sīnā, and it is found in post-classical Muslim theologians and philosophers working in his wake.[33]

Back in *Tadmuriyya*, Ibn Taymiyya consolidates his explanation of the *tawḥīd* of knowledge and statement into two principles: (1) the equivalent reality of all God's attributes and (2) the uniqueness and distinctness of the attributes. The first principle states, 'What is said about one of the attributes is likewise said about another.'[34] This principle opposes the *kalām* practice of rejecting the plain senses of some divine attributes mentioned in revelation to avert assimilationism (*tashbīh*) and corporealism (*tajsīm*) while accepting others. Ibn Taymiyya provides the following example. Some *kalām* theologians affirm that God's attributes of life, knowledge, and power are literal or real (*ḥaqīqatan*), but they regard attributes like love and hate as non-literal or non-real (*majāzan*) to avoid assimilating God to creatures and then reinterpret them as God's 'will'.[35] Ibn Taymiyya counters that love, hate, will, knowledge, and power are all equally attributes of creatures and attributes of God. It is not acceptable to affirm will, knowledge, and power of God literally while reinterpreting God's love and hate as God's will. If it is objected that God's will is uniquely befitting of Him, then it is said that all of God's other attributes are also uniquely befitting of Him. For Ibn Taymiyya, all of God's attributes are equally real; there is no distinction between the literal and the non-literal.[36]

The second principle underlines the uniqueness of God by negating likeness with creatures in God's essence, attributes, and acts. Ibn Taymiyya writes, 'What is said about the attributes is likewise said about the essence. There is nothing like God, neither in His essence nor in His attributes, nor in His acts. Since He has a real essence (*dhāt ḥaqīqa*) that is not like [other] essences, the essence is qualified with real attributes that are not like other attributes.'[37] Similarly, the modality (*kayfiyya*) of God's attributes and the modality of God Himself are equally unknown.[38]

---

33 Damien Janos, 'Avicenna on Equivocity and Modulation: A Reconsideration of the *Asmāʾ Mushakkika* (and *Tashkīk al-Wujūd*)', *Oriens* 50, no. 1–2 (2022): 1–62; Peter Adamson and Fedor Benevich, *The Heirs of Avicenna: Philosophy in the Islamic East, 12–13th Centuries: Metaphysics and Theology* (Leiden: Brill, 2023), 109–37.

34 Ibn Taymiyya, *Tadmuriyya*, MF 3:17.

35 Ibid.

36 Ibid., 17–18, 23. Ibn Taymiyya rejects literalism as a theory of meaning, that is, he does not accept the notion that words were coined with an original meaning (e.g. 'lion' as a large cat) and then deployed with other non-literal meanings as well (e.g. 'lion' as a brave warrior). He instead adopts a pragmatic or contextual theory of meaning in which the meanings of words depend on their contexts (e.g. the word 'lion' has no meaning outside a particular context). From this perspective, Ibn Taymiyya's affirmation that all of God's attributes are equally 'literal' means that they are all equally real, not that they carry identical meanings when applied to God and humans. See further Mohamed M. Yunis Ali, *Medieval Islamic Pragmatics: Sunni Theorists' Models of Textual Communication* (Richmond: Curzon, 2000), 87–140; Suleiman, *Ibn Taymiyya und die Attribute Gottes*, 197–217.

37 Ibn Taymiyya, *Tadmuriyya*, MF 3:25.

38 Ibid.

As this second principle makes clear, Ibn Taymiyya is keen to deny all likeness between God and creatures, no doubt under pressure from Ashʿarī *kalām* theologians who harangued him for assimilating God to creatures (*tashbīh*).[39] Yet, he also observes that maintaining the utter uniqueness of God's attributes risks depriving theological discourse of its meaning in human language, and he explains that some meaning needs to be shared across the divine and human attributes for understanding to occur. He writes: 'Every name and attribute that you affirm must indicate a sense (*qadr*) that is univocal across the things named. Otherwise, the discourse would not be understood. However, we know that what is particular to God and distinguishes Him from His creation is greater than anything that occurs to the mind or the imagination.'[40] The full reality and the modality of God's names and attributes are beyond the reach of the human mind, but God's names and attributes do mean something in human language. However, Ibn Taymiyya devotes little effort in the rest of the first part of *Tadmuriyya* to explaining what that meaning might be.[41] Instead, he simply refines the rules, that is, the grammar, of his theological discourse in dialogue with opposing currents.

## 5. The *Tawḥīd* in Intention, Will, and Deed: Acts of Worship

The second of the two major parts of *Tadmuriyya* explores the *tawḥīd* 'in acts of worship' (*fī al-ʿibādāt*) which Ibn Taymiyya called the *tawḥīd* 'in intention, will, and deed' earlier in the treatise. This *tawḥīd*, he explains, includes not only believing and obeying God's revelation and command but also believing in God's creation and determination of all things: 'The second principle is the *tawḥīd* in acts of worship, which include belief in revelation (*sharʿ*) and determination (*qadar*) together.'[42] Ibn Taymiyya cites texts from the Qur'an and the *ḥadīth* to support both God's creation and determination of all things and the obligation to worship, love, and obey God alone through the religion of Islam.[43] He explains that the pinnacle of Islam is confessing that there is no god but God by worshipping God alone and not associating anything with Him in worship.[44] Ibn Taymiyya devotes comparatively little of this discussion to the exclusivity of God's creative activity because he believes that this matter is not seriously contested. He says

39 On Ashʿarī opposition to Ibn Taymiyya's approach to God's attributes, see Jon Hoover, 'Early Mamlūk Ashʿarism against Ibn Taymiyya on the Nonliteral Reinterpretation (*Taʾwīl*) of God's Attributes', in *Philosophical Theology in Islam: Later Ashʿarism East and West*, ed. Ayman Shihadeh and Jan Thiele (Leiden: Brill, 2020), 195–230.

40 Ibn Taymiyya, *Tadmuriyya*, MF 3:24.

41 For the meanings that Ibn Taymiyya gives to various attributes of God, see Hoover, 'God Spatially Above'; Suleiman, *Ibn Taymiyya und die Attribute Gottes*, 282–333; Hoover, *Ibn Taymiyya*, 107–28; Hoover, *Ibn Taymiyya's Theodicy*, esp. 53–102, 211–28.

42 Ibn Taymiyya, *Tadmuriyya*, MF 3:89.

43 Ibid., 89–94.

44 Ibid., 94–96.

that even the associators (*mushrikūn*) of the Prophet Muḥammad's day confessed that God created all things.[45] With this as background, Ibn Taymiyya shifts to a discussion of *tawḥīd* in *kalām* theology. He writes:

> The upshot of the great majority of *kalām* theologians who affirm *tawḥīd* in the books of *kalām* theology is that they deem *tawḥīd* to be of three types. They say, '[God] is one in His essence (*dhāt*) without division, one in His attributes (*ṣifāt*) without similarity, and one in His acts (*afʿāl*) without associate.' The most prominent of the three types, according to them, is the third—the unicity of acts (*tawḥīd al-afʿāl*)—which is that He alone is the creator of the world… They think that this is the desired *tawḥīd* and that this is the meaning of our statement 'There is no god but God', to the extent that they even deem the meaning of divinity (*ilāhiyya*) to be the power to originate (*al-qudra ʿalā al-ikhtirāʿ*).[46]

The tripartite theological division of essence (*dhāt*), attributes (*ṣifāt*), and acts (*afʿāl*) goes back to Ibn Sīnā who mentions it near the beginning of the metaphysics of the *Shifāʾ*. He also uses it to structure his *al-Risāla al-ʿarshiyya*.[47] Al-Ghazālī and Fakhr al-Dīn al-Rāzī then introduced this threefold division into Ashʿarī *kalām* theology, and it was well established in *kalām* by Ibn Taymiyya's day.[48] However, Ibn Taymiyya's claim that *kalām* theologians speak of three types of *tawḥīd* as such appears to be mere assertion—I am not aware that this occurs in the *kalām* literature up to his time—and the expression *tawḥīd al-afʿāl* may be of his own making. More generally, Ibn Taymiyya's propensity for forming compound expressions with *tawḥīd* may have been inspired by Ibn al-ʿArabī (d. 638/1240). Ibn Taymiyya was familiar with Ibn al-ʿArabī's writings, and he held them in positive regard before turning against the Sufi theorist at about the age of forty.[49] Ibn al-ʿArabī formulated a wide range of expressions with *tawḥīd* in the chapter on thirty-six Qurʾanic affirmations of God's unicity in his master work *al-Futūḥāt al-Makkiyya*. Among Ibn al-ʿArabī's compound *tawḥīd* expressions are *tawḥīd al-ulūhiyya* (unicity of divinity), *tawḥīd al-mashīʾa* (unicity of the will), *tawḥīd al-ittibāʿ* (unicity of following),

45 Ibid., 96–97.

46 Ibid., 97–98; for a similar analysis, see Ibn Taymiyya, *Darʾ taʿāruḍ*, 1:224–28.

47 Avicenna, *The Metaphysics of the Healing: A Parallel English–Arabic Text*, trans. Michael E. Marmura (Provo: Brigham Young University Press, 2005), 3; Ibn Sīnā, 'al-Risāla al-ʿarshiyya fī tawḥīdihi taʿālā wa-ṣifātihi', in *Majmūʿ rasāʾil al-Shaykh al-Raʾīs Abī ʿAlī al-Ḥusayn b. ʿAbd Allāh Ibn Sīnā al-Bukhārī* (Hyderabad: Maṭbaʿat Jamʿiyyat Dāʾirat al-Maʿārif al-ʿUthmāniyya, 1935).

48 Heidrun Eichner, 'The Post-Avicennian Philosophical Tradition and Islamic Orthodoxy. Philosophical and Theological Summae in Context' (Habilitationsschrift, Martin-Luther Universität Halle-Wittenberg, 2009), 14, 16, 42, 46, 60, 129, 197–98, 281, 283–84, 295, 306–7, 320, 460–64, 493.

49 On Ibn Taymiyya's regard for several of Ibn al-ʿArabī's works, see his *Fī risālatihi ilā Naṣr al-Manbijī*, MF 2:464–65; the relevant paragraph is translated in Alexander D. Knysh, *Ibn ʿArabi in the Later Islamic Tradition: The Making of a Polemical Image in Medieval Islam* (Albany: State University of New York Press, 1999), 96.

*tawḥīd al-Rabb* (unicity of the Lord), *tawḥīd al-amr bi-ʿibāda* (unicity of the command to worship), and *tawḥīd al-nuʿūt* (unicity of the [divine] characteristics).[50] The facility with which Ibn al-ʿArabī crafted such a vast array of *tawḥīd* expressions provided subsequent generations a deep reservoir from which to adapt and compound their own expressions according to need and utility.

Following the passage from *Tadmuriyya* quoted above, Ibn Taymiyya explains that the *tawḥīd*s of the *kalām* theologians contain both truth and falsehood. He agrees with the Ashʿarī *kalām* theologians' affirmation of *tawḥīd* in God's acts, which he also calls *tawḥīd al-rubūbiyya* (unicity of lordship), but he faults them for making this *tawḥīd* the primary focus of theology. To his mind, affirming God's exclusive creation of the world is unexceptional, and even the Arab associators of the Prophet's time did not dispute that. Regarding the *tawḥīd* of the attributes, Ibn Taymiyya restates views found in the first part of *Tadmuriyya*. God is unlike any created thing, but there is nevertheless a shared sense in terms like 'existence' that are attributed to both God and created things. He then criticises the Muʿtazilīs and others for stripping away the ontological reality of the multiplicity of God's attributes in the name of their erroneous *tawḥīd* of God's absolute numerical oneness. With respect to the *tawḥīd* of God's essence, Ibn Taymiyya agrees with the *kalām* theologians that God is not divisible, but he censures them for thinking that this *tawḥīd* entails denying that God is over His Throne and distinct from the world in a spatial sense.[51]

These quibbles aside, Ibn Taymiyya's primary complaint about the *kalām* theologians in *Tadmuriyya* is that their *tawḥīd* ignores worship. The words 'god' (*ilāh*) and 'divinity' (*ilāhiyya*) do not signify the power to originate, as the *kalām* theologians think, but rather the right to be worshipped as a god: 'The true God is He who has the right to be worshipped.'[52] Ibn Taymiyya insists that God's legislation, command, and prohibition should be prioritised over God's creation, lordship, and determination, and he explains that two principles derive from the Muslim confession of faith, 'There is no god but God, and Muḥammad is the Messenger of God'. The first principle is the *tawḥīd* of divinity (*tawḥīd al-ilāhiyya*), which means worshipping God alone without resort to intercessors, and the second is the Messenger Muḥammad's right to be obeyed.[53] Both principles focus on right action and not on the mere belief that God is the sole creator, that is, not just on *tawḥīd al-rubūbiyya*.

To sum up, Ibn Taymiyya outlines two fundamental *tawḥīd*s in *Tadmuriyya* with the second consisting in two further kinds. The first fundamental *tawḥīd* is in knowledge and

50 Ibn al-ʿArabī, *al-Futūḥāt al-Makkiyya*, 4 vols. (Beirut: Dār Ṣādir, n.d.), 2:405–21 (*al-faṣl al-tāsiʿ*); for a summary of this chapter, see Mohd Sani Badron, 'Ibn al-ʿArabī on Affirming the Oneness of Allah's Divinity (*al-Tawḥīd*)', *Afkar: Jurnal Akidah & Pemikiran Islam* 11, no. 1 (2010): 55–106.

51 Ibn Taymiyya, *Tadmuriyya*, MF 3:98–101.

52 Ibid., 101.

53 Ibid., 101–10; the remainder of *Tadmuriyya* outlines errors in relating God's creation and decree to God's command and legislation.

statement, and it deals with the theology of God's attributes. The second fundamental *tawḥīd* is in intention, will, and deed, and it has to do with worship. The *tawḥīd* of intention and will then encompasses the *tawḥīd* of divinity, which consists of worshiping God alone without associate, and the *tawḥīd* of lordship, which involves confessing that God is the sole creator. Ibn Taymiyya expands on his concern for the priority of worship elsewhere in his corpus using the terms *tawḥīd al-ilāḥiyya* and *tawḥīd al-rubūbiyya*. He does not, however, use the term *tawḥīd fī al-ṣifāt* or similar compounds elsewhere to denote his reflection on God's names and attributes, and the simplified threefold *tawḥīd* of contemporary Salafism is rarely to be found in his works.[54]

## 6. From Two *Tawḥīds* to Three

Ibn Taymiyya's foremost student Ibn Qayyim al-Jawziyya (d. 751/1350) follows his teacher's conceptualisation of two primary *tawḥīds*. He also introduces the idea that *tawḥīd* is of three kinds although not quite the three kinds of contemporary Salafism. The following passage from Ibn al-Qayyim's late work of moral spirituality *Madārij al-sālikīn* illustrates this:

> [Sūrat al-Fātiḥa] includes the three kinds of *tawḥīd* that the messengers agreed upon—the blessings of God and His peace be upon them. There are two kinds of *tawḥīd*: one kind in knowledge and belief (*al-ʿilm wa-l-iʿtiqād*) and another kind in will and intention (*al-irāda wa-l-qaṣd*). The first is called the knowledge-based *tawḥīd* and the second is called the intention- and will-based *tawḥīd* because the first is linked to informing and knowing (*al-ikhbār wa-l-maʿrifa*) and the second to intention and will. There are also two kinds of this second [*tawḥīd*]: a *tawḥīd* in lordship (*rubūbiyya*) and a *tawḥīd* in divinity (*ilāhiyya*). These are the three kinds. As for the *tawḥīd* of knowledge, it has to do with affirming the attributes of perfection (*ṣifāt al-kamāl*) and with negating assimilation and likening (*al-tashbīh wa-l-mithāl*) and exonerating [God] from defects and imperfections.[55]

54 See n. 5 for the one instance that I have found.

55 Ibn Qayyim al-Jawziyya, *Madārij al-sālikīn*, ed. Nāṣir b. Sulaymān al-Saʿawī, ʿAlī b. ʿAbd al-Raḥmān al-Qarʿāwī, Ṣāliḥ b. ʿAbd al-ʿAzīz al-Tuwayjirī, Khālid b. ʿAbd al-ʿAzīz al-Ghunaym, and Muḥammad b. ʿAbd Allāh al-Khuḍayrī, 6 vols. (continuous pagination) (Riyadh: Dār al-Ṣumayʿī, 2011), 1:218–19; the elaboration of these three *tawḥīds* extends to the end of the discussion of the Fātiḥa on p. 421. See also Ibn Qayyim al-Jawziyya, *Ranks of the Divine Seekers: A Parallel English–Arabic Text*, trans. Ovamir Anjum, 2 vols. (Leiden: Brill, 2020), 114–17; my translation differs somewhat from Anjum's, and Anjum has not translated the latter third of the quotation. Note also that Anjum's two volumes extend to about the midpoint of *Madārij*. For the dating of Ibn al-Qayyim's works, see Livnat Holtzman, 'Ibn Qayyim al-Jawziyyah', in *Essays in Arabic Literary Biography II, 1350–1850*, ed. Joseph E. Lowry and Devin J. Stewart (Wiesbaden: Harrassowitz Verlag, 2009), 202–23; Joseph Norment Bell, *Love Theory in Later Ḥanbalite Islam* (Albany: State University of New York Press, 1979), 95–103.

Ibn al-Qayyim's initial division of *tawḥīd* into a *tawḥīd* in knowledge and a *tawḥīd* in intention and will reflects Ibn Taymiyya's twofold *tawḥīd* grounded in the distinction between *khabar* and *inshāʾ*, and his subsequent division of the *tawḥīd* in intention and will into the two *tawḥīd*s of lordship and divinity echoes Ibn Taymiyya as well. Ibn al-Qayyim then notes that the *tawḥīd* in knowledge has to do with affirming God's attributes of perfection. He does not mention here the expression '*tawḥīd* of the names and the attributes' (*tawḥīd al-asmāʾ wa-l-ṣifāt*) used by modern-day Salafī scholars, but he does employ this expression a few pages later in *Madārij al-sālikīn*. Summing up a discussion on the praise of God as evidence for the *tawḥīd* in knowledge, Ibn al-Qayyim writes, 'This is the proof of praise for the *tawḥīd* of the names and attributes (*tawḥīd al-asmāʾ wa-l-ṣifāt*).'[56] He also uses the similar expression '*tawḥīd* of the names, attributes, and characteristics' (*tawḥīd al-asmāʾ wa-l-ṣifāt wa-l-nuʿūt*) in his earlier work *Shifāʾ al-ʿalīl*.[57] With this, Ibn al-Qayyim plants the seeds of later usage, but the expression 'names and attributes' does not displace 'informing and knowledge' as the primary way to articulate this *tawḥīd*. He remains under the sway of his teacher's two fundamental *tawḥīd*s in knowledge and intention.

This changes with the later fourteenth-century Damascene Ḥanafī Ibn Abī al-ʿIzz (d. 792/1390), who appears to be the first in the Taymiyyan theological tradition to separate out the three *tawḥīd*s of attributes, lordship, and divinity explicitly and give them primacy.[58] Ibn Abī al-ʿIzz wrote a commentary on the traditionalist Ḥanafī creed of al-Ṭaḥāwī (d. 321/933) that drew heavily on the theologies of Ibn Taymiyya and Ibn al-Qayyim. He thereby facilitated the late twentieth- and early twenty-first-century appropriation of al-Ṭaḥāwī's creed into the Salafī canon of theological texts even though the creed itself does not always support Salafī views.[59] At the beginning of his commentary on the expression *tawḥīd Allāh* in al-Ṭaḥāwī's creed, Ibn Abī al-ʿIzz writes:

> There are three kinds of *tawḥīd*. The first of them is discussion of the attributes (*al-kalām fī al-ṣifāt*). The second is the *tawḥīd* of lordship (*rubūbiyya*) and clarifying that God alone is the creator of everything. The third is the *tawḥīd* of divinity (*ilāhiyya*), which is the right of [God]—Glory be to Him, Exalted is He—to be worshipped

56 Ibn al-Qayyim, *Madārij*, 1:226; Ibn al-Qayyim, *Ranks*, 122–23. Ibn al-Qayyim also says towards the end of *Madārij*, 'There are two kinds of [*tawḥīd*]: a *tawḥīd* in knowing and affirmation (*al-maʿrifa wa-l-ithbāt*) and a *tawḥīd* in request and intention (*al-ṭalab wa-l-qaṣd*). The first is affirming the reality of the essence of the Lord (*ḥaqīqat dhāt al-Rabb*)—Exalted is He—His names, His attributes, His acts, …' (5:3827).

57 Ibn Qayyim al-Jawziyya, *Shifāʾ al-ʿalīl fī masāʾil al-qaḍāʾ wa-l-qadar wa-l-ḥikma wa-l-taʿlīl*, ed. Aḥmad b. Ṣāliḥ b. ʿAlī al-Ṣamʿānī and ʿAlī b. Muḥammad b. ʿAbd Allāh al-ʿAjlān, 3 vols., 2nd printing (Riyadh: Dār al-Ṣumayʿī, 2013), 3:1341 (at the very end of *bāb* 26). The expression *tawḥīd al-dhāt* occurs in Ibn Qayyim al-Jawziyya, *Kitāb al-ṣawāʿiq al-mursala ʿalā al-Jahmiyya wa-l-muʿaṭṭila*, ed. ʿAlī b. Muḥammad al-Dakhīl Allāh, 4 vols. (Riyadh: Dār al-ʿĀṣima, 1987–88), 3:938.

58 Bunzel, *Wahhābism*, 138.

59 Wasim Shiliwala, 'Constructing a Textual Tradition: Salafī Commentaries on *al-ʿAqīda al-Ṭaḥāwiyya*', *Die Welt Des Islams* 58, no. 4 (2018): 461–503; Farquhar, *Circuits of Faith*, 139–41.

> alone without associate.[60]

The first kind of *tawḥīd* concerns the attributes directly without mentioning its root in a *tawḥīd* of knowledge and statement. The *tawḥīds* of lordship and divinity are given separately without subsuming them under a *tawḥīd* of worship or will and intention. After elaborating these three *tawḥīds* over several pages, Ibn Abī al-ʿIzz does mention and comment upon the Taymiyyan twofold *tawḥīd* of 'a unicity in affirmation and knowing and a unicity in request and intention' (*tawḥīd fī al-ithbāt wa-l-maʿrifa wa-tawḥīd fī al-ṭalab wa-l-qaṣd*).[61] However, Ibn Taymiyya's two *tawḥīds* and the underlying distinction between informative speech (*khabar*) and performative speech (*inshāʾ*) no longer frame the overall discussion. Ibn Abī al-ʿIzz has relegated them to a subsidiary role in this thinking, probably to simplify his commentary.

This is replicated four hundred years later in the theological writings of the Arabian Ḥanbalī reformer Muḥammad b. ʿAbd al-Wahhāb (d. 1206/1792) and Muḥammad b. Aḥmad al-Saffārīnī (d. 1188/1774), an anti-Wahhābī Ḥanbalī scholar from Nablus. Al-Saffārīnī outlines three kinds of *tawḥīd* in *al-Anwār al-bahiyya*, a commentary on his own creedal poem, *al-Dhurra al-muḍiyya*, along the lines found in Ibn Abī al-ʿIzz. There is no hint of Ibn Taymiyya's two primary *tawḥīds*, but the theology is otherwise Taymiyyan:

> Know that there are three divisions of *tawḥīd*: the *tawḥīd* of lordship (*rubūbiyya*), the *tawḥīd* of divinity (*ilāhiyya*), and the *tawḥīd* of the attributes (*ṣifāt*). The *tawḥīd* of lordship is that there is no creator, provider, giver of life, giver of death, giver of existence, and giver of non-existence except God—Exalted is He. The *tawḥīd* of divinity is singling out [God]—Exalted is He—for worship, divinisation of Him, subjection, humility, love, and want [of Him], and turning towards Him—Exalted is He. The *tawḥīd* of the attributes is describing God—Exalted is He—as He describes Himself and as the Prophet—God bless him and give him peace—describes Him by way of negation and affirmation, affirming of Him what He affirmed for Himself and negating from Him what He negated from Himself. It is known that the way of the Salaf of the Community and its leaders (*aʾimma*) is affirmation of what He has affirmed of the attributes without modality (*takyīf*) or likening (*tamthīl*), and without corruption (*taḥrīf*) or stripping [the attributes] away.[62]

Ibn ʿAbd al-Wahhāb also mentions the same three-fold division of *tawḥīd* near the be-

60 ʿAlī b. ʿAlī b. Muḥammad Ibn Abī al-ʿIzz, *Sharḥ al-ʿAqīda al-Ṭaḥāwiyya*, ed. ʿAbd Allāh b. ʿAbd al-Muḥsin al-Turkī and Shuʿayb al-Arnāʾūṭ, 2nd printing (Beirut: Muʾassasat al-Risāla, 1990), 1:24 (body of the text).

61 Ibid., 42.

62 Muḥammad b. Aḥmad al-Saffārīnī, *Lawāmiʿ al-anwār al-bahiyya wa-sawāṭiʿ al-asrār al-athariyya: sharḥ al-Dhurra al-muḍiyya fī ʿaqīdat al-firqa al-marḍiyya*, 2 vols., 3rd printing (Beirut: al-Maktaba al-Islāmiyya, 1991), 128–29. I am grateful to Sarah Van Eyken for drawing this reference to my attention.

ginning of a short treatise devoted to *tawḥīd*: '*Tawḥīd* is three principles: the *tawḥīd* of lordship (*rubūbiyya*), the *tawḥīd* of divinity (*ulūhiyya*), and the *tawḥīd* of the essence, the names, and the attributes (*al-dhāt wa-l-asmāʾ wa-l-ṣifāt*).'[63] Ibn ʿAbd al-Wahhāb devotes most attention to the *tawḥīd*s of divinity and lordship and gives very little space to the *tawḥīd* of the essence, names, and attributes, but this third *tawḥīd* gained more importance in later Wahhābism alongside the first two.[64]

## 7. Conclusion

The three *tawḥīd*s of God's attributes, lordship, and divinity going back to Ibn Abī al-ʿIzz have become the dominant way of articulating the doctrine in Wahhābism and contemporary Salafism. The two *tawḥīd*s of lordship (*rubūbiyya*) and divinity (*ulūhiyya*) also go back to Ibn Taymiyya. However, Ibn Taymiyya articulates a more fundamental division of *tawḥīd* into a *tawḥīd* in knowledge and affirmation linked to the linguistic category of informative speech (*khabar*) and a *tawḥīd* in intention, will, and deed linked to performative speech (*inshāʾ*). The first fundamental *tawḥīd* concerns God's names and attributes and is largely equivalent to the contemporary Salafī *tawḥīd al-asmāʾ wa-l-ṣifāt*, even though Ibn Taymiyya did not use that very expression. Ibn Taymiyya's *tawḥīd* in intention, will, and deed concerns worship of God and includes both *tawḥīd al-ulūhiyya* and *tawḥīd al-rubūbiyya*. With Ibn Abī al-ʿIzz, al-Saffārīnī, Ibn ʿAbd al-Wahhāb, and their successors, this Taymiyyan analysis of two fundamental types, with the second having two further types, falls away in favour of the simpler threefold scheme. Ibn Taymiyya's fundamental twofold division is still known and discussed,[65] but it no longer provides the primary framing for the discussion of *tawḥīd* in Salafism.

### Bibliography

Adamson, Peter, and Fedor Benevich. *The Heirs of Avicenna: Philosophy in the Islamic East, 12–13th Centuries: Metaphysics and Theology*. Leiden: Brill, 2023.

Ali, Mohamed M. Yunis. *Medieval Islamic Pragmatics: Sunni Theorists' Models of Textual Communication*. Richmond: Curzon, 2000.

Āl al-Shaykh, Ṣāliḥ b. ʿAbd al-ʿAzīz. *Sharḥ al-ʿAqīda al-Ṭaḥāwiyya*. al-Manṣūra: Dār al-Mawadda, 2011.

63 ʿAbd al-Raḥmān b. Muḥammad b. Qāsim, ed., *al-Durar al-saniyya fī al-ajwiba al-Najdiyya: majmūʿat rasāʾil wa-masāʾil ʿulamāʾ Najd al-aʿlām min ʿaṣr al-Shaykh Muḥammad b. ʿAbd al-Wahhāb ilā ʿaṣrinā hādhā*, 16 vols., 6th printing (n.p., 1996), 2:66–73.

64 Bunzel, *Wahhābism*, 138.

65 See, for example, Ṣāliḥ b. ʿAbd al-ʿAzīz Āl al-Shaykh, *Sharḥ al-ʿAqīda al-Ṭaḥāwiyya* (al-Manṣūra: Dār al-Mawadda, 2011), 43, who mentions the twofold division within a wider discussion of the three *tawḥīds* of lordship, divinity, and names and attributes.

Austin, J. L. *How to Do Things with Words*. Edited by J. O. Urmson and Marina Sbisá. 2nd ed. Cambridge, MA: Harvard University Press, 1962.

Avicenna. *The Metaphysics of the Healing: A Parallel English–Arabic Text*. Translated by Michael E. Marmura. Provo: Brigham Young University Press, 2005.

Badron, Mohd Sani. 'Ibn al-'Arabī on Affirming the Oneness of Allah's Divinity (*al-Tawḥīd*)'. *Afkar: Jurnal Akidah & Pemikiran Islam* 11, no. 1 (2010): 55–106.

Bell, Joseph Norment. *Love Theory in Later Ḥanbalite Islam*. Albany: State University of New York Press, 1979.

Bunzel, Cole M. *Wahhābism: The History of a Militant Islamic Movement*. Princeton, NJ: Princeton University Press, 2023.

Buraykān, Ibrāhīm b. Muḥammad b. ʿAbd Allāh. *Manhaj Shaykh al-Islām Ibn Taymiyya fī taqrīr ʿaqīdat al-tawḥīd*. Riyadh: Dār Ibn al-Qayyim; Cairo: Dār Ibn ʿAffān, 2004.

Eichner, Heidrun. 'The Post-Avicennian Philosophical Tradition and Islamic Orthodoxy: Philosophical and Theological Summae in Context'. Habilitationsschrift, Martin-Luther Universität Halle-Wittenberg, 2009.

Farquhar, Michael. *Circuits of Faith: Migration, Education, and the Wahhabi Mission*. Stanford: Stanford University Press, 2017.

Firanescu, Daniela Rodica. 'Speech Acts'. In *The Encyclopedia of Arabic Language and Linguistics*, edited by Kees Versteegh, Mushira Eid, Alaa Elgibali, Manfred Woidich, and Andrzej Zaborski, 5 vols., 4:328–34. Leiden: Brill, 2006–9.

Gharaibeh, Mohammad. *Zur Attributenlehre der Wahhābīya unter besonderer Berücksichtigung der Schriften Ibn ʿUṯaimīns (1929–2001)*. Berlin: EB-Verlag, 2012.

Hallaq, Wael B. *Ibn Taymiyya against the Greek Logicians*. Oxford: Clarendon Press, 1993.

Haykel, Bernard. 'On the Nature of Salafi Thought and Action'. In *Global Salafism: Islam's New Religious Movement*, edited by Roel Meijer, 33–57. London: Hurst, 2009.

Holtzman, Livnat. 'Ibn Qayyim al-Jawziyyah'. In *Essays in Arabic Literary Biography II, 1350–1850*, edited by Joseph E. Lowry and Devin J. Stewart, 202–23. Wiesbaden: Harrassowitz Verlag, 2009.

Hoover, Jon. 'Early Mamlūk Ashʿarism against Ibn Taymiyya on the Nonliteral Reinterpretation (*Taʾwīl*) of God's Attributes'. In *Philosophical Theology in Islam: Later Ashʿarism East and West*, edited by Ayman Shihadeh and Jan Thiele, 195–230. Leiden: Brill, 2020.

———. 'God as an Empirical Entity: The Expanded Scope of Sense Perception in Traditionalist Spatialism'. In *Analytic Islamic Epistemology: Critical Debates*, edited by Ramon Harvey and Safaruk Chowdhury. Edinburgh: Edinburgh University Press, forthcoming.

———. 'God Spatially Above and Spatially Extended: The Rationality of Ibn Taymiyya's Refutation of Faḫr al-Dīn al-Rāzī's Ašʿarī Incorporealism'. *Arabica* 69 (2022): 626–74.

———. *Ibn Taymiyya*. London: Oneworld, 2019.

———. 'Ibn Taymiyya'. In *The Stanford Encyclopedia of Philosophy*, 2024. https://plato.stanford.edu/entries/ibn-taymiyya/.

———. *Ibn Taymiyya's Theodicy of Perpetual Optimism*. Leiden: Brill, 2007.

Ibn Abī al-ʿIzz, ʿAlī b. ʿAlī b. Muḥammad. *Sharḥ al-ʿAqīda al-Ṭaḥāwiyya*. Edited by ʿAbd Allāh b. ʿAbd al-Muḥsin al-Turkī and Shuʿayb al-Arnāʾūṭ. 2nd printing. Beirut: Muʾassasat al-Risāla, 1990.

Ibn al-ʿArabī. *al-Futūḥāt al-Makkiyya*. 4 vols. Beirut: Dār Ṣādir, n.d.

Ibn Qāsim, ʿAbd al-Raḥmān b. Muḥammad, ed. *al-Durar al-saniyya fī al-ajwiba al-Najdiyya: majmūʿat rasāʾil wa-masāʾil ʿulamāʾ Najd al-aʿlām min ʿaṣr al-Shaykh Muḥammad b. ʿAbd al-Wahhāb ilā ʿaṣrinā hādhā*. 16 vols. 6th printing. N.p., 1996.

Ibn Qayyim al-Jawziyya. *Kitāb al-ṣawāʿiq al-mursala ʿalā al-Jahmiyya wa-l-muʿaṭṭila*. Edited by ʿAlī b. Muḥammad al-Dakhīl Allāh. 4 vols. Riyadh: Dār al-ʿĀṣima, 1987–88.

———. *Madārij al-sālikīn*. Edited by Nāṣir b. Sulaymān al-Saʿawī, ʿAlī b. ʿAbd al-Raḥmān al-Qarʿāwī, Ṣāliḥ b. ʿAbd al-ʿAzīz al-Tuwayjirī, Khālid b. ʿAbd al-ʿAzīz al-Ghunaym, and Muḥammad b. ʿAbd Allāh al-Khuḍayrī. 6 vols. Riyadh: Dār al-Ṣumayʿī, 2011.

———. *Ranks of the Divine Seekers: A Parallel English–Arabic Text*. Translated by Ovamir Anjum. 2 vols. Leiden: Brill, 2020.

———. *Shifāʾ al-ʿalīl fī masāʾil al-qaḍāʾ wa-l-qadar wa-l-ḥikma wa-l-taʿlīl*. Edited by Aḥmad b. Ṣāliḥ b. ʿAlī al-Ṣamʿānī and ʿAlī b. Muḥammad b. ʿAbd Allāh al-ʿAjlān. 3 vols. 2nd printing. Riyadh: Dār al-Ṣumayʿī, 2013.

Ibn Sīnā. 'al-Risāla al-ʿarshiyya fī tawḥīdihi taʿālā wa-ṣifātihi'. In *Majmūʿ rasāʾil al-Shaykh al-Raʾīs Abī ʿAlī al-Ḥusayn b. ʿAbd Allāh Ibn Sīnā al-Bukhārī*. Hyderabad: Maṭbaʿat Jamʿiyyat Dāʾirat al-Maʿārif al-ʿUthmāniyya, 1935.

Ibn Taymiyya. *Bayān talbīs al-Jahmiyya fī taʾsīs bidaʿihim al-kalāmiyya*. Edited by Yaḥyā b. Muḥammad al-Hunaydī et al. 10 vols. Medina: Majmaʿ al-Malik Fahd, 2005.

———. *Darʾ taʿāruḍ al-ʿaql wa-l-naql*. Edited by Muḥammad Rashād Sālim. 11 vols. N.p., n.d.

———. *Iqtiḍāʾ al-ṣirāṭ al-mustaqīm mukhālafat aṣḥāb al-jaḥīm*. Edited by Nāṣir b. ʿAbd al-Karīm al-ʿAql. 2 vols. 2nd printing. Riyadh: Dār Ishbīliyyā, 1998.

———. *La lettre palmyrienne* (*Tadmuriyya*). Translated by Abu Soleiman Al-Kaabi. [Paris]: Nawa, 2014.

———. *Majmūʿ fatāwā Shaykh al-Islām Aḥmad Ibn Taymiyya*. Edited by ʿAbd al-Raḥmān b. Muḥammad b. Qāsim and Muḥammad b. ʿAbd al-Raḥmān b. Muḥammad. 37 vols. Riyadh: Maṭābiʿ al-Riyāḍ, 1961–67.

*al-Amr bi-l-maʿrūf*. MF 28:121–78.

*Fī risālatihi ilā Naṣr al-Manbijī*. MF 2:452–79.

*Jawāb ahl al-ʿilm wa-l-īmān anna 'qul huwa Allāh aḥad' taʿdilu thulth al-Qurʾān*. MF 17:5–205.

*Tadmuriyya*. MF 3:1–128.

*Tafsīr sūrat al-ʿalaq*. MF 16:251–476.
*Tafsīr sūrat al-ikhlāṣ*. MF 17:214–503.
*Tafsīr sūrat al-kāfirūn*. MF 16:534–601.
*Tafsīr sūrat al-shams*. MF 16:226–50.

———. *Minhāj al-sunna al-nabawiyya fī naqḍ kalām al-Shīʿa al-Qadariyya*. Edited by Muḥammad Rashād Sālim. 9 vols. Riyadh: Jāmiʿat al-Imām Muḥammad b. Suʿūd al-Islāmiyya, 1986.

———. *Sharḥ al-iṣbahāniyya*. Edited by Muḥammad b. ʿAwda al-Saʿawī. Riyadh: Maktabat Dār al-Minhāj, 2009–10.

———. *al-Tadmuriyya: taḥqīq al-ithbāt li-asmāʾ wa-l-ṣifāt wa-ḥaqīqat al-jamʿ bayna al-qadar wa-l-sharʿ*. Edited by Muḥammad b. ʿAwda al-Saʿawī. Riyadh, 1985.

———. *al-ʿUqūd* [*Naẓariyyat al-ʿaqd*]. Edited by Muḥammad Ḥāmid al-Fiqī. Cairo: Maktabat al-Sunna al-Muḥammadiyya, 1949.

Ibn ʿUthaymīn, Muḥammad b. Ṣāliḥ. *al-Qawāʿid al-muthlā fī ṣifāt Allāh wa-asmāʾihi al-ḥusnā*. 2nd printing. Cairo: Maktabat al-Sunna, 1994 [1st printing 1984].

Janos, Damien. 'Avicenna on Equivocity and Modulation: A Reconsideration of the *Asmāʾ Mushakkika* (and *Tashkīk al-Wujūd*)'. *Oriens* 50, no. 1–2 (2022): 1–62.

Kalin, Ibrahim. 'Will, Necessity and Creation as Monistic Theophany in the Islamic Philosophical Tradition'. In *Creation and the God of Abraham*, edited by David B. Burrell, Carlo Cogliati, Janet M. Soskice, and William R. Stoeger, 107–32. Cambridge: Cambridge University Press, 2010.

Knysh, Alexander D. *Ibn ʿArabi in the Later Islamic Tradition: The Making of a Polemical Image in Medieval Islam*. Albany: State University of New York Press, 1999.

von Kügelgen, Anke. 'The Poison of Philosophy: Ibn Taymiyya's Struggle for and against Reason'. In *Islamic Theology, Philosophy and Law: Debating Ibn Taymiyya and Ibn Qayyim al-Jawziyya*, edited by Birgit Krawietz and Georges Tamer, 253–328. Berlin: de Gruyter, 2013.

Laoust, Henri. *Essai sur les doctrines sociales et politiques de Taḳī-d-Dīn Aḥmad b. Taimīya, canoniste ḥanbalite né à Ḥarrān en 661/1262, mort à Damas en 728/1328*. Cairo: Imprimerie de l'institut français d'archéologie orientale, 1939.

———. *La profession de foi d'Ibn Taymiyya: Texte, traduction et commentaire de La Wāsiṭiyya*. Paris: Librairie orientaliste Paul Geuthner, 1986.

———. 'Le hanbalisme sous les mamlouks bahrides (658–784/1260–1382)'. *Revue des études islamiques* 28 (1960): 1–71.

Larcher, Pierre. '*Inšāʾ*'. In *The Encyclopedia of Arabic Language and Linguistics*, edited by Kees Versteegh, Mushira Eid, Alaa Elgibali, Manfred Woidich, and Andrzej Zaborski, 5 vols., 2:358–61. Leiden: Brill, 2006–9.

———. 'Les arabisants et la catégorie de "*inšâ*": histoire d'une "occultation"'. *Historiographia Linguistica* 20, no. 2–3 (1993): 259–82.

Lauzière, Henri. *The Making of Salafism: Islamic Reform in the Twentieth Century*. New York: Columbia University Press, 2016.

al-Saffārīnī, Muḥammad b. Aḥmad. *Lawāmiʿ al-anwār al-bahiyya wa-sawāṭiʿ al-asrār al-athariyya: sharḥ al-Dhurra al-muḍiyya fī ʿaqīdat al-firqa al-marḍiyya*. 2 vols. 3rd printing. Beirut: al-Maktaba al-Islāmiyya, 1991.

Sharif El-Tobgui, Carl. *Ibn Taymiyya on Reason and Revelation: A Study of* Darʾ taʿāruḍ al-ʿaql wa-l-naql. Leiden, Brill, 2020.

Shiliwala, Wasim. 'Constructing a Textual Tradition: Salafī Commentaries on *al-ʿAqīda al-Ṭaḥāwiyya*'. *Die Welt Des Islams* 58, no. 4 (2018): 461–503.

Suleiman, Farid. *Ibn Taymiyya und die Attributes Gottes*. Berlin: de Gruyter, 2019.

———. *Ibn Taymiyya and the Attributes of God*. Translated by Carl Sharif El-Tobgui. Leiden: Brill, 2024.

Thurston, Alexander. *Salafism in Nigeria: Islam, Preaching, and Politics*. Cambridge: Cambridge University Press, 2016.

Vishanoff, David. 'Informative and Performative Theories of Divine Speech in Classical Islamic Legal Theory'. In *Philosophy and Language in the Islamic World*, edited by Nadja Germann and Mostafa Najafi, 183–208. Berlin: de Gruyter, 2021.

Wagemakers, Joas. *Salafism in Jordan: Political Islam in a Quietist Community*. Cambridge: Cambridge University Press, 2016.

# The Qur'anic Argument for Monotheism: Controversies between al-Taftāzānī (d. 792/1390) and His Contemporaries

*Syamsuddin Arif*

## 1. Introduction

If cosmic order implies the oneness of God, does the corrosion of heaven and earth imply the plurality of gods? While most people would readily give an affirmative answer to this question, the eighth/fourteenth-century Ashʿārī theologian Saʿd al-Dīn al-Taftāzānī (d. 792/1390) did not. Touching upon the very heart of the Islamic doctrine of monotheism, al-Taftāzānī's seemingly unorthodox position drew heated responses from later theologians and continued to spark debates down to the early twentieth century. The ensuing polemic, which reached its apex in the early decades of the ninth/fifteenth century, revolved around the meaning of the Qur'anic verse "If there were other gods [in heaven and earth] besides Allah, they would both dissolve into chaos"[1] (Q. 21:22)—a statement which, according to al-Taftāzānī, is just a kind of rhetorical argument (*ḥujja iqnāʿiyya*) and, therefore, cannot be considered a conclusive proof for God's unity. While no one would doubt his commitment to the Islamic faith, al-Taftāzānī's remark has been considered a serious attack on the sacred text and the doctrine of divine unity (*tawḥīd*) so much so that the charge of unbelief was levelled against him by his contemporary ʿAbd al-Laṭīf al-Kirmānī (d. after 842/1439).

This article examines the controversy and attempts to reconsider the whole question in a somewhat new light by critically analysing al-Taftāzānī's arguments as well as those of his critics and defenders within the context of Sunnī Islam, including his disciple ʿAlā' al-Dīn al-Bukhārī (d. 840/1437) and the exegetes Maḥmūd al-Ālūsī (d. 1270/1854) of Iraq and Jamāl al-Dīn al-Qāsimī (d. 1332/1914) of Syria. It pays particular attention to the crucial points made by al-Taftāzānī in his theological work that led the detractors to reject his view and prompted others to defend his position, namely, the dispute whether the Qur'anic verse in question offers a demonstrative proof or nothing but a rhetorical argument for the oneness of God. In this study, after a brief introduction to his intellectual career, I shall identify why al-Taftāzānī's view differs from the standard opinion endorsed by his opponents with regard to the meaning of the counterfactual conditional statement used by the sacred text and how this leads him to reject the prevailing interpretation.

---

1 Translation follows *The Noble Qur'an: Arabic Text and English Translation*, trans. Thomas B. Irving (Brattleboro: Amana Books, 1992), with slight modifications to ensure readability and accuracy.

## 2. Biographical Notes on al-Taftāzānī

Saʿd al-Dīn Masʿūd b. ʿUmar b. ʿAbd Allāh was born in Ṣafar 722 (March 1322) in Taftāzān, a village near Nasā in Qushkhaneh district, Shirvan county, North Khorasan province, Iran. Although little is known about his early life,[2] it is clear that as a young man he went to study at Herat, Gijduvan, Faryūmad, Gulistan, Khwarazm, Samarqand, and Sarakhs, where he eventually settled. Notable among his teachers were ʿAḍud al-Dīn al-Ījī (d. 756/1355) and Quṭb al-Dīn Muḥammad al-Rāzī al-Taḥtānī (d. 765/1365). According to Ibn Ḥajar al-ʿAsqalānī (d. 852/1449), al-Taftāzānī was regarded as a leading scholar with whom 'science ended in the East' and 'no one could ever replace him', while Ibn al-ʿImād al-Ḥanbalī (d. 1089/1679) mentions that during his student days, when he was just sixteen years of age, al-Taftāzānī outperformed his peers by composing a commentary on ʿIzz al-Dīn al-Zanjānī's (d. 655/1257) textbook on Arabic morphology (*taṣrīf*).[3]

Al-Taftāzānī lived in a turbulent era. Both Khorasan and Khwarazm were overrun by the Turkic warlord Timur (d. 807/1405), whose rise to power and ensuing conquest are generally seen by historians as a revival of the Mongol tradition, albeit one infused with the values of a settled Islamic civilisation.[4] Timur combined his profound and sincere allegiance to Islam with the ambitious political goal that was inspired by his twofold claim to Chingizid connection, on the one hand, and ʿAlid descent, on the other. Nevertheless, like many Mongol rulers before him, Timur, who was 'much more familiar with the sword than with the pen', had high esteem for men of religion, both *ʿulamāʾ*, as well as Sufi hermits and ascetics. From his military expeditions across Eurasia, he often brought renowned scholars and poets back to his capital city Samarqand to add to the splendour of his court. Among the scholars drawn to Timur's orbit was al-Taftāzānī, who agreed to serve and work under the emperor's patronage in the years that followed.

Political upheavals notwithstanding, al-Taftāzānī managed to lead a quiet life of a scholar. At the apex of his career at Samarqand, he was able to produce a succession of treatises, many of which became quickly and permanently popular, on subjects ranging

2 Accounts of his life and works are given in Ibn Ḥajar al-ʿAsqalānī, *al-Durar al-kāmina fī aʿyān al-miʾa al-thāmina*, 2 vols. (Beirut: Dār al-Jīl, 1993), 1:214; Ibn Ḥajar al-ʿAsqalānī, *Inbāʾ al-ghumr bi-abnāʾ al-ʿumr*, 3 vols. (Cairo, 1969), 389ff.; Ibn al-ʿImād al-Ḥanbalī, *Shadharāt al-dhahab fī akhbār man dhahab*, 8 vols. (Beirut: Dār Ibn Kathīr, 1979), 6:319; Muḥammad b. ʿAlī al-Shawkānī, *al-Badr al-ṭāliʿ bi-maḥāsin man baʿd al-qarn al-sābiʿ*, 2 vols. (Cairo: Maṭbaʿat al-Saʿāda, 1929), 2:303ff.; Aḥmad b. Muṣṭafā Ṭāšköprüzādeh, *Miftāḥ al-saʿāda wa-miṣbāḥ al-siyāda fī mawḍūʿāt al-ʿulūm* (Cairo: Dār al-Kutub al-Ḥadītha, 1968), 1:205; Ghiyāth al-Dīn Khwāndamīr, *Tārīkh-i ḥabīb al-siyar*, 4 vols. (Tehran: Kitābkhāna-yi Khayyām, 1954), 3:544, trans. Wheeler M. Thackston, *Ḥabību's-siyar: The Reign of the Mongol and the Turk*, vol. 3 (Cambridge, MA: Harvard University Press, 1994), 301; Muḥammad al-Laknawī, *al-Fawāʾid al-bahiyya fī tarājim al-Ḥanafiyya* (Cairo: Maṭbaʿat al-Saʿāda, 1906), 135; C. Brockelmann, *Geschichte der arabischen Litteratur* [henceforth: *GAL*] (Leiden: Brill, 1943–49), 2:215 (648), and Supplement, 2:301; Wilferd Madelung, 'al-Taftāzānī', in *Encyclopaedia of Islam, Second Edition* [henceforth: *EI2*] (Leiden: Brill, 2000), 10:88–89.

3 See Ibn Ḥajar, *al-Durar al-kāmina*, 4:350; Ibn al-ʿImād, *Shadharāt al-dhahab*, 8:547–48.

4 On Timur and his rule, see Marshall Hodgson, *The Venture of Islam*, 3 vols. (Chicago: Chicago University Press, 1974), 2:386–436; Beatrice Forbes Manz, *The Rise and Rule of Tamerlane* (Cambridge: Cambridge University Press, 1989).

from grammar and rhetoric, law and jurisprudence, logic and metaphysics, to theology and Qur'anic exegesis. While he used Arabic for the bulk of his writing, he was well-versed in other languages; he wrote his *tafsīr* in Persian and translated a volume of Saʿdī's poetry from Persian into Turkish. Despite his numerous works, al-Taftāzānī is best known for his commentary on *The Articles of Belief* [*or Creed*] (*ʿAqāʾid*) of Najm al-Dīn al-Nasafī (d. 537/1142).[5] It is interesting to note that this creed is based on the Māturīdī school, while al-Taftāzānī is usually held to have been an Ashʿarī. As noted by Watt, 'the reason is probably that he taught in a region where Māturīdī views were dominant. He expresses himself carefully, but there are a number of points where it is clear that he disagreed with the text he was commenting on.'[6] Indeed, al-Taftāzānī's fame rests mainly on his commentaries on well-known textbooks in various field of learning, which came to be widely used in teaching at *madrasas* until modern times. Al-Taftāzānī goes through these brief texts – known as *mutūn* (sing. *matn*) – phrase by phrase, if not verbatim, explicating each point; often writing an essay on a word. Many of them received super-commentaries by later scholars.[7]

Al-Taftāzānī was upset and disappointed that Emperor Timur favoured al-Sharīf al-Jurjānī (d. 816/1413) over him. As is well-known, despite his horrific image, Timur had a penchant for theological debates, in which he used to take an active part, arguing, in Ibn Khaldūn's phrase, about what he knew and also about what he did not know.[8] The emperor's acute interest in such theological debates caused him to invite to his court prominent men of culture and learning.[9] We are told that one day a debate was held at the presence of Timur, in which the participants were al-Taftāzānī and al-Jurjānī, who was younger but equally distinguished scholar.[10] At the end of the debate, Nuʿmān al-

5 Najm al-Dīn Abū Ḥafṣ ʿUmar b. Muḥammad b. Aḥmad al-Nasafī was born in 460/1068 in Nasaf (Sogdian Nakhshab, now Qarsh/Қарши in Uzbekistan), a large city between the Oxus and Samarqand. One of the greatest jurists of the Ḥanafī school of his time, he died in Samarqand on 12 Jumādā al-Ūlā 537/4 December 1142. His creed (*al-ʿAqāʾid*) is preserved in copious manuscripts (e.g. MS Berlin 1953/4, MS Gotha 55,1, MS Tübingen 138,5) and was subject to numerous commentaries and glosses by (i) at-Taftāzānī (d. 791/1389), (ii) al-Khayālī (d. after 862/1458), (iii) Muṣliḥ al-Dīn al-Qasṭallānī (d. 907/1495), (iv) Zakariyyā al-Anṣārī (d. 926/1520), (v) Mullā ʿAlī al-Qārī al-Harawī (d. 1014/1605); it has also been versified into a didactic poem as *Ṣiyānat al-ʿAqāʾid* by Manṣūr al-Ṭablāwī (d. 1014/1605), *Naẓm al-ʿAqāʾid al-Nasafī* by Muḥammad b. Aḥmad al-Jawharī (d. 1215/1800), and *Iḍāʾat al-dujunna fī ʿaqāʾid ahl al-sunna* by Aḥmad al-Maqqarī (d. 1041/1632). See Brockelmann, *GAL*, trans. J. Lameer, 1:478–79 and Suppl. 1:787–88. For a modern edition of other commentaries, see *al-Majmūʿa al-saniyya ʿalā* [*sic*] *Sharḥ al-ʿAqāʾid al-Nasafiyya* (containing the *sharḥ* of Ramaḍān Afandī, al-Kastallī, and al-Khayālī), ed. Marʿī Ḥasan al-Rashīd (Mardin: Nūr Dār al-Ṣabāḥ, 2012) and *Shurūḥ wa-ḥawāshī al-ʿAqāʾid al-Nasafiyya*, ed. Aḥmad Farīd al-Mazīdī, 5 vols. (Beirut: Dār al-Kutub al-ʿIlmiyya, 2013).

6 William Montgomery Watt, *Islamic Philosophy and Theology* (Edinburgh: Edinburgh University Press, 1962), 154.

7 See Thomas Würtz, *Islamische Theologie im 14. Jahrhundert: Auferstehungslehre, Handlungstheorie und Schöpfungs-vorstellungen im Werk von Saʿd ad-Dīn at-Taftāzānī* (Berlin: De Gruyter, 2016), 57ff.

8 Walter J. Fischel, *Ibn Khaldun and Tamerlane: Their Historic Meeting in Damascus 1401 A.D./803 AH* (Berkeley: University of California Press, 1952), 47.

9 Edward Browne, *A Literary History of Persia*, 4 vols. (Cambridge: Cambridge University Press, 1928), 3:353.

10 A distant descendant of ʿAlī b. Abī Ṭālib, al-Sayyid al-Sharīf al-Jurjānī (d. 816/1413) was a prolific scholar whose work covers a wide range of Islamic sciences from Qur'anic exegesis and *ḥadīth*, grammar and

Dīn al-Khwārizmī al-Muʿtazilī, acting as arbitrator, while admitting that he found both scholars to be equivalent in their knowledge of Islamic theology, eventually declared al-Jurjānī the winner. Legend has it that Timur justified his unfavourable decision towards al-Taftāzānī by stating that notwithstanding their equal erudition, al-Jurjānī still had an edge over al-Taftāzānī due to the former's noble lineage – that is, being a descendant of the Prophet's family. It is said that al-Taftāzānī was so humiliated by the decision that he returned to Sarakhs and soon died of chagrin.[11]

That al-Taftāzānī's widely acclaimed commentary on al-Nasafī's creed continues to be taught in seminaries across the Muslim world until the present day is a clear testimony to his lasting impact. Already by the time of his death or very shortly afterwards al-Taftāzānī was being studied and appreciated as a scholar in Cairo, which was in those days some months distant from Samarqand or Khwarazm, where he taught and wrote. As noted by the historian Ibn Khaldūn (d. 808/1406) in his *al-Muqaddima* (Prolegomena): 'I found in Egypt numerous works on the rational sciences written by the well-known scholar Saʿd al-Dīn al-Taftāzānī, a native of Herat—a district in Khurāsān [*sic*]. Some of them are on the Kalām and the *uṣūl al-fiqh* (principles of jurisprudence), and rhetoric. They show that he had a profound knowledge (*malaka rāsikha*) of these sciences. Their contents demonstrate that he was also well versed in the philosophical sciences (*al-ʿulūm al-ḥikmiyya*) and far advanced in the rest of the rational sciences.'[12]

## 3. Moot Points

The cornerstone of the controversy was al-Taftāzānī's famous remark in his commentary on the creed of Najm al-Dīn Abū Ḥafṣ al-Nasafī (d. 537/1142) pertaining to the oneness of God.[13] In his words (Text 1):

---

morphology, jurisprudence and theology, to logic and philosophy. On his life and legacy, see Shams al-Dīn al-Sakhāwī, *al-Ḍawʾ al-lāmiʿ li-ahl al-qarn al-tāsiʿ*, 12 vols. (Cairo: Maktabat al-Quds, 1934), 5:328; al-Shawkānī, *al-Badr al-ṭāliʿ*, 1:488; A. S. Tritton, 'al-Djurdjānī', *EI2*, 2:602–3.

11 See Ibn al-ʿImād, *Shadharāt al-dhahab*, 8:547–48; Zafar I. Ansari, 'Taftāzānī's Views on *Taklīf*, *Ğabr* and *Qadar*: A Note of the Development of Islamic Theological Doctrines', *Arabica* 16, no. 1 (1969): 65–66; Madelung, 'Māturīdiyya', *EI2*, 6:847–48.

12 Ibn Khaldūn, *The Muqaddimah*, trans. Franz Rosenthal, 3 vols. (Princeton: Princeton University Press, 1958), 3:117.

13 The first Western edition of the text is in *Pillar of the Creed of the Sunnites: Being a Brief Exposition of* Their *Principal Tenets*, ed. William Cureton (London: Society for the Publication of Oriental Texts, 1843), 34–37. The text has been translated into European languages: Andreas Müllerus, *Excerpta Manuscripti cuiusdam Turcici quod de Cognitione Dei et Hominis Ipsius, a quodam Azizo Nesephaeo Tataro scriptum est Turcice et Latine* (Brandenburg: Schulzius, 1665); Joseph Schacht, 'Das Glaubensbekenntnis des an-Nasafī', in *Der Islām, mit Ausschluss des Qor'āns* (= *Religionsgeschichtliches Lesebuch in Verbindung mit fachgelehrten*), ed. Alfred Bertholet, vol. 16 (Tübingen: J. C. B. Mohr, 1931), 81–86; 'Catechism of Abu-Hafs Umar al-Nasafi', trans. A. J. Wensinck, in *The Muslim Creed: Its Genesis and Historical Development* (Cambridge: Cambridge University Press, 1932), 263–64; Duncan B. Macdonald, *Development of Muslim Theology, Jurisprudence, and Constitutional Theory* (New York: Charles Scribner's Sons, 1903), 308ff.

> The One—that is, the creator of the universe—is unique. The notion of the Necessarily Existent Being cannot be truly predicated except of one entity (i.e. God). The most well-known proof for the oneness of God among the Mutakallimūn is that of 'mutual hindrance' (*burhān al-tamānuʿ*) as stated in the word of God, 'If there were in the two of them [i.e. the heavens and the earth more] gods other than Allah, these two would have been ruined (*la-fasadatā*)' (Q. 21:22). The explanation of this [proof] is as follows:
>
> If two gods were possible, then mutual hindrance of each other would be possible, whereby one of them would will that Zayd move and the other that he should remain at rest, since each of the two things is possible in itself. In like manner the connection of the will with each of them [is possible], since there is no mutual opposition (*taḍādda*) between the two wills, but only [a mutual opposition] between the two things willed (*bayn al-murādayn*). So, in this case, either the two things would occur (*yaḥṣul al-amrāni*) and the two opposites would unite (*fa-yajtamiʿ al-ḍiddāni*) [which is impossible], or else [if only one of the two things occurs] it follows that one of the two gods is powerless. But powerlessness is an indication of being originated and being contingent, as it implies shortcoming or need of something [else], therefore, [it is concluded that] plurality necessitates the possibility of mutual hindrance which [in turn] necessitates the impossible, and so it is impossible.[14]

In this passage al-Taftāzānī adduces what is otherwise known as the argument from 'mutual exclusion', or 'proof from hypothetical mutual prevention',[15] or simply the 'argument from opposition'.[16] It consists of several premises and a conclusion, which may be arranged as follows: Either there is one god or there are many gods. If there were many gods, there would be conflict of interest, in which, for example, one god would want something to happen which another god does not will, so that they would oppose each other's preference. If all or both refuse to concede, then two contradictory things will occur. Yet if one or more is able to defeat or dominate over the other god(s), then there would be powerless god(s). Since all these consequences are absurd, the antecedent premise ('There are many gods') is invalid, and with the second disjunct (i.e. proposition *q* 'there are many gods') being negated and declared false (~*q* 'there are NOT many gods'), the first disjunct (i.e. proposition *p* 'there is only one god') is affirmed to be true. On

---

14 Saʿd al-Taftāzānī, *Sharḥ al-ʿAqāʾid al-Nasafiyya* (Beirut: Dār Iḥyāʾ al-Turāth al-ʿArabī, 2014); trans. Earl Edgar Elder, *A Commentary on the Creed of Islam: Saʿd al-Dīn al-Taftāzānī on the Creed of Najm al-Dīn al-Nasafī* (New York: Columbia University Press, 1950), 37–38.

15 See Benyamin Abrahamov, *On the Proof of God's Existence: Kitāb al-Dalīl al-Kabīr of al-Qāsim b. Ibrāhīm* (Leiden: Brill, 1990), 16.

16 See Douglas Walton, Christopher Reed, and Fabrizio Macagno, *Argumentation Schemes* (Cambridge: Cambridge University Press, 2008), 250.

closer analysis, this argument turns out to be a mixed disjunctive syllogism[17] containing a *modus tollens*,[18] which can be symbolized thus:

| | |
|---|---|
| $p \vee q$ | |
| $q \rightarrow c$ | $p$: There is only one god |
| $c \rightarrow m$ | $q$: There are many gods |
| $\sim m$ | $c$: Conflict (*yajtimuʿ al-ḍiddān*) |
| $\sim c$ | $m$: Impossible (*muḥāl*) |
| $\sim q$ | |
| $\therefore p$ | |

This argument was widely accepted by the majority of *mutakallimūn* across all schools of thought, including Abū al-Ḥasan al-Ashʿarī (d. 324/935), Abū Bakr al-Bāqillānī (d. 324/935), Abū Manṣūr al-Māturīdī (d. 333/944), the Muʿtazilī al-Qāḍī ʿAbd al-Jabbār (d. 415/1025), Abū al-Maʿālī al-Juwaynī (d. 478/1085), al-Ghazālī (d. 505/1111), and al-Shahrastānī (d. 548/1153)—to mention but a few— in their respective works.[19] Taking the existence and uniqueness of God for granted, the *mutakallimūn* spared no effort to explicate the doctrine of *tawḥīd* articulated in the Qurʾanic formula 'there is no god but Allah' (*lā ilāha illā Allāh*). Given his former theological training and affiliation to Ashʿarism, it is hardly astonishing that al-Taftāzānī would use the same argument of mutual exclusion (*dalīl al-tamānuʿ*) to establish God's oneness. What has attracted a remarkable amount of response from both supporters and detractors is his remark in the subsequent passage (Text 2):

> You should understand that God's saying [in the Qurʾān 21:22], 'Had there been in them both (heaven and earth) other gods besides Allāh, they would surely have been

17 The 'disjunctive syllogism' is one that has a disjunctive proposition (*qaḍiyya sharṭiyya munfaṣila*) in its major premise. A disjunctive proposition is one that possesses alternative predicates for the subject in which the conjunctive particle 'or' (sometimes accompanied by 'either'—in Arabic: *immā ... wa-immā...*) appears. For example, 'Swans are either white or black', 'Arguments are either valid or invalid', 'The creator is either one or many'. The different things joined together by 'or' are called alternatives or disjuncts—the term indicating that we may choose between the things, and that if one is not satisfactory, we may pick the other, or one of the others if there is more than one alternative *other*.

18 Originally called *modus tollendo tollens* (the method that denies by denying), this is a valid form of inference by negating the consequent: 'Given that $q$ is false and it is true that if $p$ then $q$, we may infer that $p$ is false'—which may be symbolised thus: 'Given that $p \rightarrow q$ and $\sim q$, we may derive $\sim p$ as conclusion'. In our case, the argument is of the form $p$ or $q$, not-$q$, so $p$. See Simon Blackburn, *The Oxford Dictionary of Philosophy*, 3rd ed. (Oxford: Oxford University Press, 2016), 311.

19 See Abū al-Ḥasan al-Ashʿarī, *Kitāb al-lumaʿ* and *Risāla fī istiḥsān al-khawḍ fī ʿilm al-kalām*, in *The Theology of al-Ashʿarī*, ed. Richard J. McCarthy (Beirut: Imprimerie Catholique, 1953), 8 and 89; Abū Bakr al-Bāqillānī, *Kitāb al-tamhīd*, ed. Richard J. McCarthy (Beirut: University of Baghdad, 1957), 25, lines 13–20; Abū Manṣūr al-Māturīdī, *Kitāb al-tawḥīd*, ed. Fathalla Kholeif (Beirut: Dar el-Machreq Éditeurs, 1970), 40ff.; al-Qāḍī ʿAbd al-Jabbār, *Sharḥ al-Uṣūl al-khamsa*, ed. ʿAbd al-Karīm ʿUthmān (Cairo, 1965), 278ff.; Abū al-Maʿālī al-Juwaynī, *Kitāb al-irshād* (Cairo, 1950), 53ff.; Abū Ḥāmid al-Ghazālī, *al-Iqtiṣād fī al-iʿtiqād*, ed. Ibrāhīm Çubuqçi and Hussein Ātā (Ankara: Nur Matbaasi, 1962), 40–44; Abū al-Fatḥ al-Shahrastānī, *Nihāyat al-iqdām*, ed. and trans. Alfred Guillaume (Oxford: Oxford University Press, 1934), 91ff.

> ruined,' is a persuasive argument (*ḥujja iqnāʿiyya*), as the implication (*mulāzama*) [between the two ideas in this context] indicates a habitual occurrence (*ʿādiya*) that is suitable for rhetorical arguments (*khiṭābiyyāt*). For it is usually the case when there are many persons exercising the office of governor, that there is mutual hindrance of one another and that one gets the upper hand, as is pointed out in the statement of Allāh, 'Some of them would impose their dominance over others' (Qur'ān 23:93). Otherwise, if actual ruin is meant—that is, the passing away from the present visible order [of the heavens and the earth]—then a mere plurality [of gods] does not necessitate that [i.e. the heavens and the earth will crumble], since it is possible that there be an agreement [between those gods] to maintain the present visible order. On the other hand, if the possibility of ruin is meant, there is nothing to indicate the denial of this, since the sacred texts bear witness to the folding up of the heavens and the removal of the present order. So, it is undoubtedly possible.[20]

There are several points in this passage which deserve more careful consideration. First, al-Taftāzānī's contention that the Qur'anic verse in question is merely expressing a persuasive argument (*ḥujja iqnāʿiyya*) seems to be correct. As a logician, al-Taftāzānī must have no interest in a sentence as a string of words or in the mental images or feelings it might call up. Having produced his own works on logic, *kalām*, and rhetoric,[21] it is not unlikely that al-Taftāzānī embraced the classical Aristotelian distinction of four forms of reasoning corresponding to the four types of audience, namely: (i) the demonstrative (*al-qiyās al-burhānī*), which is meant for the scientific-minded people; (ii) the dialectical (*al-qiyās al-jadalī*), which is specifically used for debating opponents; (iii) the rhetorical (*al-qiyās al-khiṭābī*), which is aimed at persuading or influencing the beliefs, attitudes, or behaviours of targeted individuals; and (iv) the sophistical (*al-qiyās al-mughālaṭī*), which is purposely employed in order to mislead, deceive, or confuse the audience.[22] For him, the Revelation is

---

20 al-Taftāzānī, *Sharḥ al-ʿAqāʾid al-Nasafiyya*, 49; Elder, *Commentary*, 38–39.

21 al-Taftāzānī wrote, among others, (i) *Tahdhīb al-manṭiq wa-l-kalām* on logic; (ii) *Sharḥ al-Maqāṣid* (commentary of his own *al-Maqāṣid fī ʿilm al-kalām*); and (iii) *al-Sharḥ al-muṭawwal* on rhetoric, which is a lengthy commentary on *Talkhīṣ miftāḥ al-ʿulūm* of al-Kātib al-Qazwīnī (d. 739/1338).

22 Aristotle in his logical corpus (i.e. *Topica*, VIII, 162a, and *the Art of Rhetoric* I, 1356b 4–5) enumerates no less than six types of syllogism or deductive reasoning: (i) *philosophēma* (φιλοσόφημα), which is a demonstrative or apodictic syllogism (συλλογισμὸς ἀποδεικτικός); (ii) *epicheirema* (ἐπιχείρημα), which is a dialectical syllogism (συλλογισμὸς διαλεκτικός); (iii) *sophisma* (σόφισμα), which is a disputative or eristic syllogism (συλλογισμὸς ἐριστικός); and (iv) *aphorema* (ἀπόρημα), which is a dialectical or contentious syllogism leading up to contradiction (συλλογισμὸς διαλεκτικὸς ἀντιφάσεως). The other two types of syllogism, namely, (v) *enthymeme* (ἐνθύμημα), which is a rhetorical syllogism (ρητορικὸν συλλογισμὸν), and (vi) the 'poetic syllogism' (*al-qiyās al-shiʿrī*), which is the kind of reasoning or logical inference commonly used in poetry, were appended by the medieval Arabic philosophers, who regarded Aristotle's *Rhetoric* and *Poetics* as forming integral parts of his *Organon*, following a tradition well-established by the time of Alexandrian, Neoplatonic commentators in late antiquity. For extensive discussion, see Gregor Schoeler, 'Der poetische Syllogismus: Ein Beitrag zum Verständnis der "logischen" Poetik der Araber', *Zeitschrift der deutschen morgenländischen Gesellschaft* 133, no. 1 (1983): 43–92; Deborah Black, *Logic and Aristotle's*

addressing the masses and therefore is not using a strictly scientific argument to prove its point. As al-Taftāzānī sees it, the cited Qur'anic argument belongs to the persuasive kind of reasoning—a view which is justified both on logical grounds and factual consideration.

From the logical point of view, it is important to note that the major premise used in the Qur'anic argument is a conditional proposition ($p \rightarrow q$ that is: if *p* then *q*), rather than a biconditional one ($p \leftrightarrow q$ that is: *p* if and only if *q*). This means that the logical relationship between the two statements *p* and *q* (denoted by an arrow, '$\rightarrow$') is a unidirectional or one-way implication, whereby if the antecedent (*p*) is true, then the consequent (*q*) must also be true, and yet if the antecedent is false ($\sim p$), it does not necessarily follow that the consequent is false ($\sim q$), as the truth value of the consequent is not determined by the conditional proposition. Hence, it would be fallacious to infer the denial of the consequent ($\sim q$) from the denial of the antecedent ($\sim p$) when the premise is a 'one-way' conditional proposition.

| | |
|---|---|
| Symbolically: | $p \rightarrow q$ |
| In English: | 'If *p* is true, then *q* is true.' |
| For example: | 'If it is raining (*p*), then the ground is wet (*q*).' |

It is not necessary that if it did not rain ($\sim p$), therefore the ground is not wet ($\sim q$), for it is possible that it did not rain ($\sim p$) and yet the ground is wet (*q*).

In the same vein, it may be argued, following al-Taftāzānī's reasoning, that the logical relationship between the two statements 'there were many gods' (*p*) and 'the heavens and the earth would be destroyed' (*q*), which constitute the conditional proposition ($p \rightarrow q$), being used as the major premise in the argument is a one-way implication (*luzūm*), and not a two-directional or mutual one (*talāzum*). This means that it is not necessarily true if there were *not* many gods ($\sim p$), then the universe would *not* be destroyed ($\sim q$), for it is possible that there are *not* many gods ($\sim p$) and the universe is still going to be destroyed (*q*). To corroborate his view, al-Taftāzānī cites the textual evidence from the Qur'an to the effect that the present order of the universe will be dissolved (*q*) on Doomsday which by no means implies the plurality of gods (*p*).

| | |
|---|---|
| Symbolically: | $p \rightarrow q$ |
| In English: | 'If *p* is true, then *q* is true.' |

The argument: 'If there were many gods (*p*), then the universe will be ruined (*q*).' However, it is not necessarily true that 'if there were *not* many gods ($\sim p$), the universe will *not* be ruined ($\sim q$)', for it is possible that *p* is false (i.e. there are *not* many gods ($\sim p$), that is, there is only one god) and yet the universe still be ruined (*q*)—that is, *q* is true.

---

*Rhetoric and Poetics in Medieval Arabic Philosophy* (Leiden: Brill, 1990).

From a factual point of view, al-Taftāzānī argues that even though our empirical observation attests that plurality of authorities often leads to rivalry, clash, and chaos, this is not always the case. That is to say, frequency does not imply necessity. For it is neither always nor necessarily true that whenever two or more authorities exist, there will be conflict. In this respect, one may compare al-Taftāzānī's view to al-Ghazālī's which suggests that our observation does not establish necessary connection, and that what we often take as a necessary connection between cause and effect is actually just a regular pattern of natural events occurring so frequently and repeatedly that we think they are causally related.[23] That is to say, when we observe $p$ followed by $q$, our minds become accustomed to expecting $q$ whenever $p$ occurs, even though we have no direct evidence of a necessary causal link between $p$ and $q$. Similarly, just because we sometimes or often see conflict arising when two or more individuals vie for control over the same entity, this does not warrant us to conclude that plurality always and necessarily leads to conflict or that the two are always and necessarily linked in the sense of mutually implying and entailing each other. For this reason, al-Taftāzānī maintains that the seemingly mutual implication or entailment (*mulāzama*) between the two statements ($p$ and $q$) merely represents a habitual occurrence (*ʿādiya*), rather than a perpetual, necessary connection. Consequently, one cannot rule out the possibility of there being many gods ($p$) without the cosmic system being disturbed ($\sim q$). To use his own words, 'a mere plurality [of gods] does not necessarily entail its destruction' (*fa-mujarrad al-taʿaddud lā yastalzimuhu*), as those many gods 'might possibly avoid conflict and agree to keep the cosmos intact' (*li-jawāz al-ittifāq ʿalā hādhā al-niẓām al-mushāhad*).[24]

In order to bring home this critical point, some familiarity with Aristotelian logic will be helpful. A disjunctive syllogistic argument is considered demonstrative (*burhānī*) in a strict sense only if its major premise is a biconditional proposition expressing a two-way logical implication (*talāzum*) or equivalence (*tasāwī*) between two statements of which it is made up.[25] Also known as *al-iṭṭirād wa-l-inʿikās* in *kalām* and *uṣūl al-fiqh* literature, this logical relationship is usually denoted by a double-headed arrow ($\leftrightarrow$), which signifies that the implication goes both ways: if $p$ is true, then $q$ is true, and vice versa, if $q$ is true then $p$ is true. The truth of $p$ implies the truth of $q$, and the truth of $q$ implies the truth of $p$. In other words, one statement is true if and only if the other statement is true. If one is true, the other is necessarily also true, and if one is false, the other is also necessarily

23 Al-Ghazālī's most famous treatment of causality occurs in discussion seventeen of *The Incoherence of the Philosophers: Tahāfut al-Falāsifah*, trans. Michael Marmura (Provo: Brigham Young University Press, 1997), 170. For detailed discussion, see Lenn E. Goodman, 'Did al-Ghazālī Deny Causality?', *Studia Islamica* 47 (1978): 83–120; Ilai Alon, 'Al-Ghazālī on Causality', *Journal of the American Oriental Society* 100, no. 4 (1980): 397–405; Benyamim Abrahamov, 'Al-Ghazālī's Theory of Causality', *Studia Islamica* 67 (1988): 75–98.

24 al-Taftāzānī, *Sharḥ al-ʿAqāʾid al-Nasafiyya*, 49; Elder, *Commentary*, 38–39.

25 Since a biconditional statement is made up of two conditional statements, we can derive from it two conditional statements, one in each direction, just as it is possible to break down the biconditional statement $p \leftrightarrow q$ into $(p \rightarrow q)$ and $(q \rightarrow p)$.

false. Modern logicians use the phrase 'If and only if' (often abbreviated as 'iff') to express a biconditional relationship between two statements that imply each other since they are logically equivalent, being both true or both false under the same conditions.

Symbolically: $p \leftrightarrow q$
In English: '*p* is true if and only if *q* is true.'

For example: 'A living being is human (*p*) if and only if it is rational (*q*)' such that if it is truly rational, then it is truly human, and vice versa, if it is truly human, then it must be truly rational.

Only when the major premise is a biconditional proposition ($p \leftrightarrow q$) expressing a two-way relationship, can all possible conclusions derived from it be true. That is to say, only when the major premise of the argument is a biconditional proposition indicating necessary mutual entailment, can the logical fallacy of denying the antecedent (not-*p*, therefore not-*q*) and the fallacy of affirming the consequent (*q*, therefore *p*) be avoided. Otherwise, as al-Taftāzānī suggests, the implication is not necessary (*al-mulāzama* [*ghayru*] *qaṭʿiyya*) in the sense that it would be fallacious to say that if there were *not* many gods ($\sim p$), then the universe would *not* be destroyed ($\sim q$), for it is possible that there are *not* many gods ($\sim p$) and the universe will still be ruined (*q*) as it will happen on Doomsday. Similarly, it would be fallacious to say that if the universe is dissolved (*q*), then there are many gods (*p*). Al-Taftāzānī writes:

> In no way can it be said that the implication (*mulāzama*) [between the two statements *p* and *q*] is so necessary (*qaṭʿiyya*) and that the meaning of their ruination is that they were not created, in the sense that, if two creators were assumed [to coexist], then a mutual hindering of one another in performing acts would be possible, so that one of them would not be a creator nor would anything be created.
>
> For we say that the possibility of there being mutual hindrance of one another implies nothing but the non-plurality of creator (*imkān al-tamānuʿ lā yastalzimu illā ʿadam taʿaddud al-ṣāniʿ*) [i.e. that there be but one creator only] and does not imply the denial of that which is created (*wa-lā yastalzimu intifāʾ al-maṣnūʿ*), since the necessary implication can only be denied if actual non-creation is meant, whereas the denial of the consequent can only be negated if by possible non-creation is meant.[26]

In this passage he is suggesting that the conditional proposition only represents a possible situation; it does by no means refer to the actual reality. For the fact that there is creation (*maṣnūʿ*) renders the idea of there being a conflict of interest involving two or

26 al-Taftāzānī, *Sharḥ al-ʿAqāʾid al-Nasafiyya*, 49–50; Elder, *Commentary*, 39.

more gods pointless. Since the universe is already created ($\sim s$), it can be deduced that at least one of the gods did manage to accomplish creation ($\sim r$), and hence the supposed confrontation or mutual hindrance between them becomes irrelevant ($\sim q$). Symbolically, the argument may be analysed as follows:

| | |
|---|---|
| $p \rightarrow q$ | $p$: there are two/many gods (*ṣāniʿāni/taʿaddud*) |
| $q \rightarrow r$ | $q$: there is conflict (*tamānuʿ*) |
| $r \rightarrow s$ | $r$: none of them is able to create (*lam yakun aḥaduhumā ṣāniʿan*) |
| $s$: | nothing is created at all (*lam yūjad maṣnūʿ*) |

| | |
|---|---|
| But $\sim s$ | (the universe is already created). |
| Therefore $\sim r$ | (at least one of the gods did manage to create the universe). |
| Therefore $\sim q$ | (the mutual hindrance or conflict is pointless). |
| Therefore $\sim p$ | (the assumption of there being two/more gods is false). |

Perhaps by suggesting that the conditional statement does not necessarily guarantee the falsity of the consequent, al-Taftāzānī wants his readers to think critically and consider some counter-examples that will demonstrate the erroneous reasoning—that is, by pointing out actual cases where the antecedent is false ($\sim p$) but the consequent is true ($q$) or, conversely, when the consequent is true ($q$) but the antecedent is false ($\sim p$). To sum up, according to him, it is neither true that the plurality of gods necessarily entails the destruction of the world nor is it true that destruction of the world necessarily implies the plurality of gods. In the next passage, al-Taftāzānī addresses a possible objection that might arise from a grammatical point of view. Again, it will be useful to quote him at length:

> It may be objected that [in the Qur'ān quotation above] the force of the word 'if' (*law:* ⍰⍰) is the negation of the second statement (*intifāʾ al-thānī*) in the past being due to the negation of the first (*intifāʾ al-awwal*), so it only indicates the denial of corruption in the past because of the denial of the plurality [of gods].
>
> In answer to this we reply that this is grammatically true, but 'if' (*law*) may be used to establish the negation of the apodosis (*intifāʾ al-jazāʾ*) following the negation of the protasis (*intifāʾ al-sharṭ*) irrespective of time, just as in the statement, 'If the world were eternal from the beginning it would not be subject to change'. The verse quoted above is of this kind. These two usages may seem indistinguishable from one another to some minds, and hence the confusion.[27]

27 al-Taftāzānī, *Sharḥ al-ʿAqāʾid al-Nasafiyya*, 50; Elder, *Commentary*, 39.

In this passage, al-Taftāzānī refutes the opinion that the Arabic particle '*law*' in the sentence indicates something that happened in the past, and that it cannot be used to designate future events. In other words, the conditional statement in the Qur'anic quotation 'If there were many gods in there' is taken to refer to past events and therefore signifies a real conditional (that is, if there was no corruption of the world, it is because there was only one God. If there were many gods, the world must have been corrupted). While he concedes that it may be used to denote what happened in the past, al-Taftāzānī nonetheless insists that such a conditional particle can also be used to indicate the negation of the antecedent ($\sim p$) based on the negation of the consequent ($\sim q$), which is common in counterfactual statements and statements about future events. To recall, counterfactual statements describe a hypothetical situation that is contrary to fact or contrary to what has actually occurred. These are often marked by the '"if" of impossibility' (*law al-imtināʿiyya*). Taken as a counterfactual statement, the Qur'anic verse which says, 'If there were many gods, then the universe would have been ruined,' expresses a conditional or causal relationship between two events or states of affairs, even though the events described in the antecedent ('there were many gods') did not actually happen. It merely suggests a hypothetical scenario in which the antecedent is false ('there were actually *not* many gods'), whereas the consequent ('the heavens and the earth *would have been* ruined') is imagined or supposed to be true.[28] On this account, the Qur'anic statement may be understood as implying something that would have happened if the case were different, although it means to say the contrary—that God is actually one, and the universe has always remained in order owing to the fact that God is one. A relevant explanation of the point is provided by al-Taftāzānī in his work on Arabic rhetoric, *al-Muṭawwal*:

> God's saying, 'Had there been in [the heavens and the earth] gods other than Allah, the two would have been disintegrated,' is put forward in order to argue from the impossibility of ruin to the impossibility of plurality of gods, and not vice versa.[29] For the negation of plurality of gods does not entail the negation of the ruin [of the world], as it is possible that God might ruin it for some other reason. So, the truth is that it is for [the purpose of declaring] the impossibility of the antecedent due to the impossibility of the consequent (*annahā li-imtināʿ al-awwal li-imtināʿ al-thānī*).

28 There exist, to my knowledge, at least two treatises dealing with this issue: Muḥyī al-Dīn Muḥammad b. Sulaymān al-Kāfījī, *al-Ilmāʿ bi-ifādat law li-l-imtināʿ* (Cairo: Dār al-Kutub al-Qawmiyya, n.d.), MS no. 407 coll. Tafsīr Tīmūr, fols. 31–48; Muḥammad al-Ṭayyib b. ʿAbd al-Majīd al-Fāsī, 'Risāla fī law al-sharṭiyya', ed. Ṣāliḥ b. Fahd al-Ḥantūsh, *Majallat al-Dirāsāt al-Lughawiyya* 2, no. 4 (Shawwāl–Dhū al-Ḥijja 1421/January–March 2001): 101–214.

29 There is a serious typing error in this passage, where the word *intifāʾ* before the phrase *taʿaddud al-āliha* was omitted. Cf. *Majmūʿat al-ḥawāshī al-bahiyya ʿalā Sharḥ al-ʿAqāʾid al-Nasafiyya* (Cairo: Maṭbaʿat Kurdistān al-ʿIlmiyya, 1911), 1:92. I have corrected and supplied the missing word here in translation and in Text 5 of the Appendix.

> Some seasoned scholars say that the proof is invalid, although what is claimed is true (*dalīluhu bāṭil, wa-daʿwāhu ḥaqq*). First, according to them, protasis (*sharṭ*) is too broad to signify a cause (*sabab*)—for example, [the sentence] 'If the sun shines, then the world is bright'. Nor can it denote a condition (*sharṭ*)—for instance, [the sentence] 'If I have money, I shall go for pilgrimage', or to designate something else, such as 'If there is daylight, then the sun shines'. Secondly, protasis is antecedent (*malzūm*), whereas apodosis is consequent (*lāzim*). The negation of the consequent necessarily entails the negation of the antecedent, and not vice versa. It is posited so as to render the apodosis devoid of content (*maʿdūm al-maḍmūn*), thereby disallowing the content of protasis which is the antecedent due to the impossibility of the consequent, which is the apodosis. Therefore, it is meant for denying the antecedent due to the impossibility of the consequent. In other words, it simply means that the negation of result leads to the negation of the condition. Hence, they say about exceptive syllogism: negating the consequent necessarily entails negation of the antecedent, while negating the antecedent does *not* necessarily entail negation of the consequent. For example, [it is correct] for us to say: If this is human, then it must be a living being. Yet this is not a living being, and therefore it is not human. In contrast, [it is incorrect] for us to say: [If this is human, then it must be a living being.] Yet this is not human, therefore it is not a living being.[30]

In other words, given that if *p* then *q*, to argue from the negation of the consequent (~*q*) to the negation of the antecedent (~*p*) is valid, but the other way round is invalid reasoning (if *p* then *q*, but ~*p* therefore ~*q*). Indeed, not every antecedent is a sufficient and necessary cause, for a thing or event may have multiple or more than one cause. For example, a person says, 'If I have money, I will travel.' It is possible that he will be travelling without spending a single penny. This remark is reminiscent of the distinction made by modern logicians between 'necessary' and 'sufficient' conditions. To say that '*p* is a necessary condition for *q*' means that *p* must be true in order for *q* to be true. In other words, if the necessary condition is not met, then the other statement cannot be true. However, satisfying the necessary condition alone does not guarantee the truth of the other statement. It is a requirement that must be fulfilled for the outcome to be possible, but it is not enough on its own to ensure that the outcome occurs. For example, in order to pass a class, a necessary condition might be attending all the required lectures. If a student did not attend all the lectures, it is impossible for them to pass the class. But attending all the lectures does not guarantee that the student will pass; other factors such as assignments and examinations also come into play. In contrast, to say that '*p* is a sufficient condition for *q*' means that *p*, if true, guarantees the truth of *q*. In this

30 Saʿd al-Dīn al-Taftāzānī, *al-Muṭawwal sharḥ Talkhīṣ miftāḥ al-ʿulūm* (Beirut: Dār al-Kutub al-ʿIlmiyya, 2013), 334.

case, satisfying the sufficient condition alone is enough to ensure the other statement is true. If the sufficient condition is met, the outcome is guaranteed, regardless of any other factors. For example, being a male is a necessary, but not a sufficient, condition for being a father. If manhood is a sufficient condition for fatherhood, then if someone is a male, he will definitely become a father—which is not necessarily the case. If being a male is a sufficient condition for being a father, then it does not matter whether he has a child or not; as long as he is a male, the apodosis (being a father) is true. It is clear that for al-Taftāzānī neither the plurality of gods nor the corruption of the universe is a sufficient condition for each other to be true or occur —as the case may be.

## 4. Al-Kirmānī's Critique

It comes as no surprise that al-Taftāzānī's statements concerning the nature of the Qur'anic argument for monotheism provoked intense criticism and generated responses for many centuries after his death.[31] One of the first scholars who took issue with al-Taftāzānī's views was ʿAbd al-Laṭīf al-Kirmānī (d. after 842/1439).[32] In his polemical treatise *Risālat al-tawḥīd li-radd qawl man qāla taʿaddud al-ālihah lā yastalzimu fasād al-samāwāt wa-l-arḍ* (A treatise on monotheism with the aim of refuting the opinion of him who says that the plurality of gods does not necessarily entail the corruption of the heavens and the earth),[33] al-Kirmānī categorically rejects al-Taftāzānī's logical interpretation of the Qur'anic verse about God's oneness, calling into question his assertion that religious assent and logical assent are two sides of the same coin (*anna al-taṣdīq al-sharʿī wa-l-taṣdīq al-manṭiqī kilāhumā wāḥid*).[34]

After quoting the controversial passage, al-Kirmānī commences his attack by accusing al-Taftāzānī of having renounced the doctrine of monotheism both rationally and traditionally (*ankara al-tawḥīd ʿaqlan wa-naqlan*). Rationally, he did so, according to al-Kirmānī, by allowing the existence of many gods with the possibility of their coming into agreement—that is, they may coexist without being involved in any conflict. Furthermore, al-Taftāzānī is censured for defying what al-Kirmānī believes to be a long-established scholarly consensus—that is, by claiming that the Qur'anic statement (Q. 21:22) about monotheism is a rhetorical argument (*ḥujja iqnāʿiyya*) that yields no certain knowledge. And all this was put forth according to his corrupt reason (*ʿaqlihi al-fāsid*),

31 For a listing of opposing camps in this controversy and their respective arguments, see Saʿīd ʿAbd al-Laṭīf Fūda, ed., *Bayān tawjīh al-Imām al-Taftāzānī dalālat qawlihi taʿālā law kāna fīhimā āliha illā Allāh la-fasadatā ʿalā al-waḥdāniyya wa-dhikr baʿḍ mā dāra ḥawlahu min munāqashāt bayn al-ʿulamāʾ* (Amman: Aslein Studies and Publication, 2022), 57–107.

32 For his biography, see al-Sakhāwī, *al-Ḍawʾ al-lāmiʿ*, 4:340; Taqī al-Dīn al-Tamīmī, *al-Ṭabaqāt al-saniyya* (Riyadh: Dār al-Rifāʿī, 1989), 4:385.

33 ʿAbd al-Laṭīf al-Kirmānī, *Risālat al-tawḥīd li-radd qawl man qāla taʿaddud al-ālihah lā yastalzimu fasād al-samāwāt wa-l-arḍ*, in *Bayān tawjīh al-Imām al-Taftāzānī*, 125–35.

34 Ibid., 127–28.

thereby driving him to allow the plurality and concord of many gods.[35] For al-Kirmānī, there is no difference between al-Taftāzānī's view and that of the Muʿtazilī Abū Hāshim al-Jubbāʾī (d. 321/933) who claimed that there is no rational justification for believing in one god and that monotheism is based on Revelation, since our reason does not deny the possibility of there being two or more creators of the world. Both al-Taftāzānī and Abū Hāshim shared the same rationalism by renouncing the explicit meaning of sacred texts.[36]

Al-Kirmānī tells his readers what determined him to write the treatise:

> When I was still a student, I used to hear people quote this statement [of al-Taftāzānī] which my mind repelled but could not spell out the objection. Soon I began to see some pseudo-scholars, whenever this issue was raised, became perplexed and unable to adjudicate. Meanwhile, [al-Taftāzānī's] commentary on the creed [of al-Nasafī] was already circulating in the East and the West, with the controversial issue spreading in the countries like poison in the bodies. Having visited two regions and searched in vain for someone who could discuss the matter, I came to think that I might be the only person who realized [al-Taftāzānī's] erroneous claim and therefore saw it my duty to explain its invalidity. God says in the Qur'an, 'Allah commands you to deliver things placed in your trust to those they belong' (Q. 4:85), which I believe pertains to the rights of God as well as the rights of man, and so it is incumbent upon the learned to perform [the task of removing confusion and dispelling error]. Indeed, one should not remain silent on the issue, as 'he who does not speak the truth is a dumb devil' (*al-sākit ʿan al-ḥaqq shayṭān akhras*).[37]

According to al-Kirmānī, belief in one God is unequivocally endorsed by the Qur'an and the Prophetic tradition. Therefore, by making such a controversial statement, al-Taftāzānī has not only violated the sacred texts but also defied the scholarly consensus on the matter. Al-Kirmānī marshals a number of Qur'anic verses which he believes explicitly affirm the impossibility of there being gods other than Allah, such as Q. 23:117 which declares, 'Whoever invokes, besides Allah, another god—for which they have no proof—they will surely find their penalty with their Lord. Indeed, the disbelievers will never succeed.' Al-Kirmānī refers to the famous exegete Ḥāfiẓ al-Dīn al-Nasafī (d. 710/1310) who holds that God leaves no room for reason or tradition to posit plurality of gods, so that it is logically impossible to question or doubt His unique existence (*lam yabqa li-ʿāqil shakk wa-lā shubha*). Only people with unsound or corrupt reason would entertain polytheism. Al-Kirmānī went so far as calling anyone who subscribes to al-Taftāzānī's opinion

35 Ibid., 129.

36 Ibid., 129–30. I could not find the source of al-Kirmānī's reference to Abū Hāshim al-Jubbāʾī's view.

37 Ibid., 130.

or makes a similar statement either an imbecile or infidel (*kafarū jamīʿan*).[38] In his concluding remark, al-Kirmānī writes, referring to Abū al-Muʿīn al-Nasafī as authority: 'Think about those [Qur'anic] verses. If the argument stated is rhetorical, and the correlation [between the two statements in the Qur'anic verse] is merely expressing habitual occurrence, whereby no disagreement over it is conceivable, then [it would imply as if] God has taught His messenger how to dispute with the idolaters using what is short of a good argument (*bi-mā lā yaṣluḥu dalīlan ḥaqīqatan*).' At this point, it is worth noting that al-Kirmānī's charge of unbelief against al-Taftāzānī has elicited mixed reactions from scholars who are now divided between the detractors and defenders. It was no doubt a serious accusation with serious consequences since the charge of unbelief is a legal pronouncement that involves confiscation of property, capital punishment, and the sentence to eternal punishment in hellfire.

## 5. Al-Bukhārī's Defence

Among the staunch defenders of al-Taftāzānī in the controversies was his disciple ʿAlāʾ al-Dīn al-Bukhārī (d. 840/1437).[39] His apology for his teacher is preserved by Ibn Quṭlūbughā (d. 879/1474) in his glosses (*ḥāshiya*) on *Kitāb al-musāmara* of Kamāl al-Dīn b. Abī Sharīf (d. 906/1500), which is a commentary on *Kitāb al-musayara* of Kamāl al-Dīn b. al-Humām al-Sīwāsī (d. 861/1457). Al-Bukhārī's defence, which might have been titled *al-Ifāḍa fī al-jawāb ʿalā wajh yurshid ilā al-ṣawāb* (The overflowing response in a manner that is leading to the truth), begins by citing al-Ghazālī's famous remarks concerning the use of rational arguments to prove the existence of God, which is said to be comparable to the use of medication (*tajrī majrā al-adwiya*). Just as physicians should be careful in prescribing medicine for patients according to their varying conditions, one must not use a single approach in communicating with people of various backgrounds and different levels of intelligence. For some weak minds that are stuck in blind imitation and obstinacy because they have imbibed falsehood from their childhood until old age, nothing would work on them except the whip and the sword. But there are a few who can benefit from rational proof, although the enlightenment of the mind is ultimately through the grace of God. The overwhelming majority of people, however, are of lesser intelligence and hence are incapable of understanding rational proofs, just as the eyes of bats cannot see the light of the sun. Such people would be hurt by rational arguments as a dung beetle is hurt by the smell of roses.[40]

---

38 Ibid., 133–35.

39 For his biography, see Ibn Taghrībirdī, *al-Dalīl al-shāfī ʿalā al-manhal al-ṣāfī* (Cairo: Maṭbaʿat Dār al-Kutub al-Miṣriyya, 1998), 2:698 (entry no. 2386); Muḥammad Ḥasan b. ʿAqīl Mūsā, *al-Mukhtār al-maṣūn min aʿlām al-qurūn* (Jeddah: Dār al-Andalus al-Khaḍrāʾ, 1995), 555–59.

40 Kamāl al-Dīn Ibn Abī Sharīf, *Kitāb al-musāmara fī sharḥ al-musayara* (Cairo: Maṭbaʿat al-Saʿāda, 1929), 54–55. The quoted lines are from Abū Ḥāmid al-Ghazālī, *al-Iqtiṣād fī al-iʿtiqād* (Beirut: Dār al-Kutub

Having said that, al-Bukhārī proceeds to argue that in defending one's faith there is no need to claim decisiveness for what is not decisive (*lā taḥtāj naṣrat al-dīn ilā iddiʿā' mā laysa bi-qaṭʿiyyin qaṭʿiyyan*). As a matter of fact, contrary to what al-Kirmānī wanted us to think, says al-Bukhārī, the Qur'an does contain rhetorical arguments in addition to rational, demonstrative arguments. The former type is meant for less intelligent folk, while the latter type is for those few who are not satisfied with lesser kinds of proofs. As far as the rational proof from mutual exclusion (*burhān al-tamānuʿ*) is concerned, al-Bukhārī proposes a distinction between (i) what he calls 'proof by means of allusion' (*bi-ṭarīq al-ishāra*), which he regards as demonstrative (*burhānī*) and more appealing to the educated class, and (ii) 'proof by means of articulation' (*bi-ṭarīq al-ʿibāra*), which is said to be persuasive (*khiṭābī*) in nature and more appropriate for the masses. For him, the consequent 'ruin' (*fasād*) mentioned in the Qur'anic verse may be interpreted both as the resultant failure of two or more gods to create anything, according to the demonstrative method, as well as the concomitant disintegration of the physical universe, according to the persuasive method. One should not confuse the mutual implication based on habitual occurrence (*al-istilzām al-ʿādī*) of natural events with the mutual entailment based on strict logical consideration (*al-istilzām al-ʿaqlī*).[41] In short, al-Taftāzānī's statement allowing the agreement between gods should be taken as a *prima facie* claim based on what seems to be the truth when first seen or thought because, in the final analysis, the truth is that there cannot be more than one God.

## 6. Al-Ālūsī's Rejoinder

In modern times, the Iraqi exegete Abū al-Thanā' Shihāb al-Dīn Maḥmūd b. ʿAbd Allāh al-Ālūsī (d. 1270/1854) was among the leading scholars of the day who attempted to resolve the points at issue. Once a mufti of Baghdad during the late Ottoman rule, he is best known for his *Rūḥ al-maʿānī*, a multi-volume commentary on the Qur'an, which he reportedly wrote in order to prove that he had no intellectual link with the British-supported Wahhabi movement.[42] Al-Ālūsī devoted five densely written pages to interpreting the verse and dealing with the moot point. He begins by criticising those who thought that the Arabic conditional particle *law* is used in the Qur'anic quotation for negating the consequent due to the negation of the antecedent (*li-intifā' al-thānī li-intifā' al-awwal*).

al-ʿIlmiyya, 2015), 14 (the second prologue: *al-tamhīd al-thānī*).

41 Ibn Abī Sharīf, *Kitāb al-musāmara*, 56–58.

42 See Bilal Gökkir and Necmettin Gökkir, 'Sufi or Salafi? Alusi's Struggle for His Reputation against Ottoman Bureaucracy with His *Tafsīr*, *Rūḥ al-Maʿānī*', *Usûl İslam Araştırmaları* 27 (2017): 7–18; Hala Fattah, 'Wahhabi Influences, Salafi Responses: Shaikh Maḥmūd Shukrī al-Ālūsī and the Iraqi Salafi Movement, 1745–1930', *Journal of Islamic Studies* 14, no.2 (2003): 127–48; Basheer M. Nafi, 'Abu al-Thana' al-Alusi: An Alim, Ottoman Mufti, and Exegete of the Qur'an', *International Journal of Middle East Studies* 34, no. 3 (2002): 485–86.

There is a problem (*fīhi qadḥ*), says al-Ālūsī, in al-Taftāzānī's statement that the plurality of gods does not necessarily entail 'actual' mutual hindrance (*al-tamānuʿ bi-l-fiʿl*) where each one of them wants something which the other opposes, but rather it merely implies the 'possibility' of such mutual hindrance (*imkān dhālika al-tamānuʿ*). Since being possible does not necessarily mean actually happening (*al-imkān lā yastalzim al-wuqūʿ*), the two gods might agree to cooperate in creating the world, or either one of them might just delegate the work to the other.[43] To debunk this, al-Ālūsī refers to al-Khayālī (d. after 862/1458), one of the most authoritative commentators on al-Taftāzānī's work.[44]

Contrary to al-Taftāzānī, al-Khayālī holds that if the Qur'anic verse in question is taken to mean denying the existence of many gods in the sense of occupying, controlling, and governing the universe, then the mutual entailment (*al-mulāzama*)—between two statements in the verse as a biconditional proposition—is necessary (*qaṭʿiyya*), since it would be impossible for those many gods (i) to mutually interfere (*tawārud*) and prevent each other's action, or (ii) collaborate (*ijtimāʿ*) to perform their action, or (iii) distribute (*tawzīʿ*) the job among themselves, because all of these would not only imply shortcomings and impotence that are unseemly for a god, but would also entail that nothing has come into existence at all (*inʿidām al-kull*), nor has any part of the world (which is not the case, given the fact that the world exists), supposing that one of the gods—being a partial cause (*juzʾ ʿilla*)—did not perform the act of creation. In addition, it can be argued that the mutual implication is necessary in an absolute sense (*al-mulāzama qaṭʿiyya ʿalā al-iṭlāq*). That is to say, if there were many gods, then the world would not be possible (*lam yakun al-ʿālam mumkina*), let alone come into existence. Otherwise (i.e. if the world can possibly or does exist), those gods would be involved in mutual hindrance, which is impossible, since the possibility of mutual hindrance is due to the idea of plurality and possibility of a thing. Therefore, al-Khayālī concludes, if plurality is posited, then nothing would be possible at all, including the plurality that is said to entail the impossible.[45]

---

43 Shihāb al-Dīn al-Ālūsī, *Rūḥ al-maʿānī*, 30 vols. (Beirut: Dār Iḥyāʾ al-Turāth al-ʿArabī, 1970), 4:25.

44 Aḥmad b. Mūsā al-Khayālī (d. ca. 875/1470) was a student of ʿAlāʾ al-Dīn al-Ṭūsī and Khiḍr Bey, who at that time was the professor of the Sultan Madrasa in Bursa, and through whom he traced his scientific lineage to Fakhr al-Dīn al-Rāzī, besides Mullā Yegân and Mullā Fanārī. Al-Khayālī's best known work is a gloss or super-commentary on al-Taftāzānī's commentary on al-Nasafī's creed, *Ḥāshiya ʿalā Sharḥ al-ʿAqāʾid al-Nasafiyya*, which he wrote during his stay as a teacher in Plovdiv and presented to Maḥmūd Pasha. Cf. Aḥmad b. Mūsā al-Khayālī, *Religion ou théologie des Turcs, avec la profession de foi de Mahomet fils de Pir Ali* (Brussels: Chez François Foppens, 1704).

45 al-Ālūsī, *Rūḥ al-maʿānī*, 4:25.

## 7. Al-Qāsimī's Appraisal

Another noteworthy assessment of the debate is offered by Jamāl al-Dīn al-Qāsimī (d. 1332/1914), one of the leading proponents of Islamic reformism in early twentieth-century Syria and Egypt who advocated a return to the practice of the 'pious ancestors' (*al-salaf al-ṣāliḥ*)—hence, the Salafiyya movement—and adopted a scripturalism that emphasised the authority of the textual sources of the Qur'an and the Sunna (Prophetic tradition) for determining orthodox beliefs and practices.[46] While elucidating the verse in his voluminous *tafsīr*, *Maḥāsin al-ta'wīl*, al-Qāsimī mentions a similar verse in the Qur'an which declares that 'Allah has never had any offspring, nor is there any god besides Him. Otherwise, each god would have taken away what he created, and they would have tried to dominate one another. Glorified is Allah above what they claim' (Q. 23:91). Citing the Ottoman 'Shaykh al-Islām' Abū al-Suʿūd (d. 982/1574), he asserts that when the consequent is negated, the antecedent is known to be necessarily true. The mutual implication is explained as follows: divinity or being god necessarily means being able to exercise full control of and to manage the universe totally, whether by making changes, replacement, bringing into being and eliminating, giving or taking life. From this it follows that the continuous existence of the universe is either (i) due to the collective action of each one of the gods—which is impossible, because a definite thing cannot happen or come into being through several different causes (*li-istiḥālat wuqūʿ al-maʿlūl al-muʿayyan bi-ʿilal mutaʿaddida*)—or (ii) due to the action of one of those gods, leaving the rest outside the scope of divinity. In short, according to al-Qāsimī, the argument is demonstrative enough to rule out the possibility of there being many gods at all.[47]

## 8. Concluding Remarks

It cannot be denied that controversies help scholars to gain a better understanding of the issues at stake. In the case of al-Taftāzānī's statement, even though complete agreement has not been reached and probably never will be, a re-examination of the moot points should be valuable as an attempt to separate chaff from grain that are often confused. When al-Taftāzānī claimed that the Qur'anic argument for monotheism is rhetorical and persuasive, he was repeating a contention that was already put forward three centuries earlier by al-Ghazālī regarding the need to use different approaches for different groups of people. Referring to Q. 16:25, in which God tells the Prophet, 'Call to your Lord with wisdom (*ḥikma*) and mild exhortation (*mawʿiẓa ḥasana*), and argue with them in the best manner,' al-Ghazālī suggests that we should use logic and rational arguments

46 On his life and Salafism, see Ẓāfir al-Qāsimī, *Jamāl al-Dīn al-Qāsimī wa-ʿaṣruhu* (Damascus: Maktabat Aṭlas, 1965); Nizār Abāẓā, *Jamāl al-Dīn al-Qāsimī: aḥad ʿulamā' al-iṣlāḥ al-ḥadīth fī al-Shām* (Damascus: Dār al-Qalam, 1997); Itzchak Weismann, *Taste of Modernity: Sufism, Salafiyya, and Arabism in Late Ottoman Damascus* (Leiden: Brill, 2001).

47 Jamāl al-Dīn al-Qāsimī, *Maḥāsin al-ta'wīl*, 20 vols. (Beirut: Dār al-Kutub al-ʿIlmiyya, 2004), 7:183.

when addressing the elite (*al-khawāṣṣ*) who are capable of a high level of understanding, while reserving rhetorical persuasion and dialectical approach for the masses and the opponent in a debate.[48]

In the foregoing pages I have tried to examine closely the contribution of both sides to the controversy, unravelled the complex arguments, and reveal the underlying convictions which spurred each participant's attempt to defend their views and rebut that of their adversaries. It becomes clear that while al-Taftāzānī shared the orthodox Muslim scholars' views on the Islamic doctrine monotheism, he seems to supersede them with the intent to better explain the nature of Qur'anic argument from a logical point of view. With regard to the charge of unbelief, suffice it to recall the Prophet's admonition that accusing a fellow Muslim of unbelief could render the one who levels the charge a non-believer. Finally, if this study amounts to anything, it helps us to see the intellectual dynamics which the issue of philosophical interpretation of sacred texts had triggered among successive generations of Muslim scholars together with the theological and eschatological implications embedded in what was initially a logical question.

## Bibliography

Abāzā, Nizār. *Jamāl al-Dīn al-Qāsimī: aḥad ʿulamāʾ al-iṣlāḥ al-ḥadīth fī al-Shām*. Damascus: Dār al-Qalam, 1997.

ʿAbd al-Jabbār, al-Qāḍī. *Sharḥ al-Uṣūl al-khamsa*. Edited by ʿAbd al-Karīm ʿUthmān. Cairo: n.p., 1965.

Abrahamov, Benyamim. 'Al-Ghazālī's Theory of Causality'. *Studia Islamica* 67 (1988): 75–98.

———. *On the Proof of God's Existence: Kitāb al-Dalīl al-Kabīr of al-Qāsim b. Ibrāhīm*. Leiden: Brill, 1990.

Alon, Ilai. 'Al-Ghazālī on Causality'. *Journal of the American Oriental Society* 100, no. 4 (1980): 397–405.

al-Ālūsī, Shihāb al-Dīn Maḥmūd. *Rūḥ al-maʿānī*. 30 vols. Beirut: Dār Iḥyāʾ al-Turāth al-ʿArabī, 1970.

Ansari, Zafar I. 'Taftāzānī's Views on *Taklīf*, *Ǧabr* and Qadar: A Note of the Development of Islamic Theological Doctrines'. *Arabica* 16, no. 1 (1969): 65–78.

al-Bāqillānī, Abū Bakr. *Kitāb al-tamhīd*. Edited by Richard J. McCarthy. Beirut: University of Baghdad, 1957.

Black, Deborah. *Logic and Aristotle's Rhetoric and Poetics in Medieval Arabic Philosophy*.

48 See al-Ghazālī, *al-Iqtiṣād fī al-iʿtiqād*, 14–15; Abū Ḥāmid al-Ghazālī, *Iljām al-ʿawāmm ʿan ʿilm al-kalām* (Beirut: Dār al-Kutub al-ʿIlmiyya, 2016), 115; Abū Ḥāmid al-Ghazālī, *al-Qisṭās al-mustaqīm*, in *Majmūʿat rasāʾil al-Imām al-Ghazālī* (Beirut: Dār al-Kutub al-ʿIlmiyya, 2016), pt. 3, 3–4; Abū Ḥāmid al-Ghazālī, *Iḥyāʾ ʿulūm al-dīn*, 4 vols. (Cairo: Dār Iḥyāʾ al-Kutub al-ʿArabiyya, 1957), 1:32–33.

Leiden: Brill, 1990.

Blackburn, Simon. *The Oxford Dictionary of Philosophy*. 3rd ed. Oxford: Oxford University Press, 2016.

Brockelmann, Carl. *Geschichte der arabischen Litteratur.* Leiden: Brill, 1943–49.

Browne, Edward. *A Literary History of Persia*. 4 vols. Cambridge: Cambridge University Press, 1928.

Elder, Earl Edgar, trans. *A Commentary on the Creed of Islam: Saʿd al-Dīn al-Taftāzānī on the Creed of Najm al-Dīn al-Nasafī.* New York: Columbia University Press, 1950.

al-Fāsī, Muḥammad al-Ṭayyib b. ʿAbd al-Majīd. 'Risāla fī law al-sharṭiyya'. Edited by Ṣāliḥ b. Fahd al-Ḥantūsh. *Majallat al-Dirāsāt al-Lughawiyya* 2, no. 4 (Shawwāl–Dhū al-Ḥijja 1421/January–March 2001): 101–214.

Fattah, Hala. 'Wahhabi Influences, Salafī Responses: Shaikh Maḥmūd Shukrī al-Ālūsī and the Iraqi Salafi Movement, 1745–1930'. *Journal of Islamic Studies* 14, no.2 (2003): 127–48.

Fischel, Walter J. *Ibn Khaldun and Tamerlane: Their Historic Meeting in Damascus 1401 A.D./803 AH.* Berkeley: University of California Press, 1952.

Fūda, Saʿīd ʿAbd al-Laṭīf, ed. *Bayān tawjīh al-Imām al-Taftāzānī dalālat qawlihi taʿālā law kāna fīhimā āliha illā Allāh la-fasadatā ʿalā al-waḥdāniyya wa-dhikr baʿḍ mā dāra ḥawlahu min munāqashāt bayn al-ʿulamā?* Amman: Aslein Studies and Publication, 2022.

al-Ghazālī, Abū Ḥāmid. *Iḥyāʾ ʿulūm al-dīn*. Edited with an introduction by Badawī Aḥmad Ṭabāna. 4 vols. Cairo: Dār Iḥyāʾ al-Kutub al-ʿArabiyya, 1957.

———. *Iljām al-ʿawāmm ʿan ʿilm al-kalām*. Edited by Mashhad al-ʿAllāf. Beirut: Dār al-Kutub al-ʿIlmiyya, 2016.

———. *The Incoherence of the Philosophers: Tahāfut al-Falāsifah*. Translated by Michael Marmura. Provo: Brigham Young University Press, 1997.

———. *al-Iqtiṣād fī al-iʿtiqād*. Edited by Ibrāhīm Çubuqçi and Hussein Ātā. Ankara: Nur Matbaasi, 1962.

———. *al-Iqtiṣād fī al-iʿtiqād*. Edited by ʿAbd Allāh M. al-Khalīlī. Beirut: Dār al-Kutub al-ʿIlmiyya, 2015.

———. *al-Qisṭās al-mustaqīm*. In *Majmūʿat rasāʾil al-Imām al-Ghazālī*. Beirut: Dār al-Kutub al-ʿIlmiyya, 2016.

Gökkir, Bilal, and Necmettin Gökkir. 'Sufi or Salafi? Alusi's Struggle for His Reputation against Ottoman Bureaucracy with His *Tafsīr, Rūḥ al-Maʿānī*'. *Usûl İslam Araştırmaları* 27 (2017): 7–18.

Goodman, Lenn E. 'Did al-Ghazālī Deny Causality?'. *Studia Islamica* 47 (1978): 83–120.

Hodgson, Marshall. *The Venture of Islam*. 3 vols. Chicago: Chicago University Press, 1974.

Ibn Abī Sharīf, Kamāl al-Dīn. *Kitāb al-musāmara fī sharḥ al-musayara.* Cairo: Maṭbaʿat al-Saʿāda, 1929.

Ibn al-ʿImād. *Shadharāt al-dhahab fī akhbār man dhahab*. Edited by ʿAbd al-Qādir al-Arnāʾūṭ and Maḥmūd al-Arnāʾūṭ. 8 vols. Beirut: Dār Ibn Kathīr, 1979.

Ibn Ḥajar al-ʿAsqalānī. *Inbāʾ al-ghumr bi-abnāʾ al-ʿumr*. Edited by Ḥasan Ḥabashī. 4 vols. Cairo: n.p., 1969.

———. *al-Durar al-kāmina fī aʿyān al-miʾa al-thāmina*. 4 vols. Beirut: Dār al-Jīl, 1993.

Ibn Khaldūn. *The Muqaddimah*. Translated by Franz Rosenthal. 3 vols. Princeton: Princeton University Press, 1958.

Ibn Taghrībirdī. *al-Dalīl al-shāfī ʿalā al-manhal al-ṣāfī*. Edited by Fahīm M. Shaltūt. Cairo: Maṭbaʿat Dār al-Kutub al-Miṣriyya, 1998.

al-Juwaynī, Abū al-Maʿālī. *Kitāb al-irshād*. Cairo: n.p., 1950.

al-Kāfījī, Muḥyī al-Dīn Muḥammad b. Sulaymān. *al-Ilmāʿ bi-ifādat law li-l-imtināʿ*. Cairo: Dār al-Kutub al-Qawmiyya, n.d.

al-Khayālī, Aḥmad b. Mūsā. *Ḥāshiya ʿalā Sharḥ al-ʿAqāʾid al-Nasafiyya*. In *al-Majmūʿa al-saniyya ʿalā* [*sic*] *Sharḥ al-ʿAqāʾid al-Nasafiyya*. Edited by Marʿī Ḥasan al-Rashīd. Mardin: Nūr Dār al-Ṣabāḥ, 2012.

———. *Religion ou théologie des Turcs, avec la profession de foi de Mahomet fils de Pir Ali*. Brussels: Chez François Foppens, 1704.

Khwāndamīr, Ghiyāth al-Dīn. *Tārīkh-i ḥabīb al-siyar*. Edited by Jalāl al-Dīn Humāʾī. 4 vols. Tehran: Kitābkhāna-yi Khayyām, 1954.

al-Kirmānī, ʿAbd al-Laṭīf. *Risālat al-tawḥīd li-radd qawl man qāla taʿaddud al-ālihah lā yastalzimu fasād al-samāwāt wa-l-arḍ*. In *Bayān tawjīh al-Imām al-Taftāzānī dalālat qawlihi taʿālā law kāna fīhimā āliha illā Allāh la-fasadatā ʿalā al-waḥdāniyya wa-dhikr baʿḍ mā dāra ḥawlahu min munāqashāt bayn al-ʿulamāʾ*, edited by Saʿīd ʿAbd al-Laṭīf Fūda, 125–35. Amman: Aslein Studies and Publication, 2022.

al-Laknawī, Muḥammad ʿAbd al-Ḥayy. *al-Fawāʾid al-bahiyya fī tarājim al-Ḥanafiyya*. Cairo: Maṭbaʿat al-Saʿāda, 1906.

Macdonald, Duncan B. *Development of Muslim Theology, Jurisprudence, and Constitutional Theory*. New York: Charles Scribner's Sons, 1903.

*Majmūʿat al-ḥawāshī al-bahiyya ʿalā Sharḥ al-ʿAqāʾid al-Nasafiyya*. Edited by Faraj Zakī al-Kurdī. Cairo: Maṭbaʿat Kurdistān al-ʿIlmiyya, 1911.

Manz, Beatrice Forbes. *The Rise and Rule of Tamerlane*. Cambridge: Cambridge University Press, 1989.

al-Māturīdī, Abū Manṣūr. *Kitāb al-tawḥīd*. Edited by Fathalla Kholeif. Beirut: Dar el-Machreq Éditeurs, 1970.

McCarthy, Richard J., ed. *The Theology of al-Ashʿarī*. Beirut: Imprimerie Catholique, 1953.

Müllerus, Andreas, trans. *Excerpta Manuscripti cuiusdam Turcici quod de Cognitione Dei et Hominis Ipsius, a quodam Azizo Nesephaeo Tataro scriptum est Turcice et Latine*. Brandenburg: Schulzius, 1665.

Mūsā, Muḥammad Ḥasan b. ʿAqīl. *al-Mukhtār al-maṣūn min aʿlām al-qurūn*. Jeddah: Dār al-Andalus al-Khaḍrā', 1995.

Nafi, Basheer M. 'Abu al-Thana' al-Alusi: An Alim, Ottoman Mufti, and Exegete of the Qur'an'. *International Journal of Middle East Studies* 34, no. 3 (2002): 465–94.

al-Nasafī, Najm al-Dīn Abū Ḥafṣ ʿUmar b. Muḥammad. *al-ʿAqāʾid*. In *Pillar of the Creed of the Sunnites: Being a Brief Exposition of Their Principal Tenets*, edited by William Cureton, 34–37. London: Society for the Publication of Oriental Texts, 1843.

al-Qāsimī, Jamāl al-Dīn. *Maḥāsin al-taʾwīl*. 20 vols. Beirut: Dār al-Kutub al-ʿIlmiyya, 2004.

al-Qāsimī, Ẓāfir. *Jamāl al-Dīn al-Qāsimī wa-ʿaṣruhu*. Damascus: Maktabat Aṭlas, 1965.

al-Sakhāwī, Shams al-Din. *al-Ḍawʾ al-lāmiʿ li-ahl al-qarn al-tāsiʿ*. 12 vols. Cairo: Maktabat al-Quds, 1934.

Schacht, Joseph, trans. 'Das Glaubensbekenntnis des an-Nasafi'. In *Der Islām, mit Ausschluss des Qor'āns* (= *Religionsgeschichtliches Lesebuch in Verbindung mit fachgelehrten*), edited by Alfred Bertholet, 16:81–86. Tübingen: J. C. B. Mohr, 1931.

Schoeler, Gregor. 'Der poetische Syllogismus: Ein Beitrag zum Verständnis der "logischen" Poetik der Araber'. *Zeitschrift der deutschen morgenländischen Gesellschaft* 133, no. 1 (1983): 43–92.

al-Shahrastānī, Abū al-Fatḥ. *Nihāyat al-iqdām*. Edited and translated by Alfred Guillaume. Oxford: Oxford University Press, 1934.

al-Shawkānī, Muḥammad b. ʿAlī. *al-Badr al-ṭāliʿ bi-maḥāsin man baʿd al-qarn al-sābiʿ*. 2 vols. Cairo: Maṭbaʿat al-Saʿāda, 1929.

*Shurūḥ wa-ḥawāshī al-ʿAqāʾid al-Nasafiyya*. Edited by Aḥmad Farīd al-Mazīdī. 5 vols. Beirut: Dār al-Kutub al-ʿIlmiyya, 2013.

al-Tamīmī, Taqī al-Dīn. *al-Ṭabaqāt al-saniyya*. Riyadh: Dār al-Rifāʿī, 1989.

al-Taftāzānī, Saʿd al-Dīn. *al-Muṭawwal sharḥ Talkhīṣ miftāḥ al-ʿulūm*. Edited by ʿAbd al-Ḥamīd Hindāwī. Beirut: Dār al-Kutub al-ʿIlmiyya, 2013.

———. *Sharḥ al-ʿAqāʾid al-Nasafiyya* [with the *Farāʾid al-qalāʾid* of Mullā ʿAlī al-Qārī]. Edited by ʿAlī Kamāl. Beirut: Dār Iḥyāʾ al-Turāth al-ʿArabī, 2014.

Ṭāšköprüzādeh, Aḥmad b. Muṣṭafā. *Miftāḥ al-saʿāda wa-miṣbāḥ al-siyāda fī mawḍūʿāt al-ʿulūm*. Edited by Kāmil Kāmil Bakrī and ʿAbd al-Wahhāb Abū al-Nūr. Cairo: Dār al-Kutub al-Ḥadītha, 1968.

Thackston, Wheeler M. *Ḥabību's-siyar: The Reign of the Mongol and the Turk*. Vol. 3. Cambridge, MA: Harvard University Press, 1994.

Walton, Douglas, Christopher Reed, and Fabrizio Macagno. *Argumentation Schemes*. Cambridge: Cambridge University Press, 2008.

Watt, William Montgomery. *Islamic Philosophy and Theology*. Edinburgh: Edinburgh University Press, 1962.

Weismann, Itzchak. *Taste of Modernity: Sufism, Salafiyya, and Arabism in Late Ottoman Damascus*. Leiden: Brill, 2001.

Wensinck, A. J., trans. 'Catechism of Abu-Hafs Umar al-Nasafi'. In *The Muslim Creed: Its*

*Genesis and Historical Development*, 263–64. Cambridge: Cambridge University Press, 1932.

Würtz, Thomas. *Islamische Theologie im 14. Jahrhundert: Auferstehungslehre, Handlungstheorie und Schöpfungs-vorstellungen im Werk von Saʿd ad-Dīn at-Taftāzānī*. Berlin: De Gruyter, 2016.

# PART 3

## *Shīʿī Theological Perspectives on God and Monotheism*

# Visions of *Tawḥīd*: Reconciling a Statement in the Twenty-Eighth Supplication of *al-Ṣaḥīfa al-Sajjādiyya*

*Zoheir Esmail*

## 1. Introduction

A child brought up in a traditional Shīʿī household would typically start to interact with theological doctrines in terms of numbers. One God, 14,000 prophets, 5 prophets to whom a divine book or scroll was revealed (the *ulū l-ʿazm* prophets), 14 infallibles (the Prophet, his daughter Fāṭima, and the Imāms), and 12 Imāms. Islam's central and foundational thesis concerning the very nature of God is often explained with reference to arithmetic understandings of polytheism and the Trinity as opposed to more philosophically challenging explanations. While others may believe in many gods, Muslims believe in the numerically one true God and as such the *shahāda* states that there is no god but God, understood in arithmetic terms. The very foundation of Islam and one of its defining statements is therefore interpreted as a stance on number. A typical argument against belief in the Trinity would be that three cannot be tantamount to one numerically, rendering the Trinity arithmetically nonsensical. Or, using this particular framing, one cannot equal not one, as that violates the law of non-contradiction, making the Trinity fundamentally illogical. Such reasoning often occurs in a vacuum without investigation into the intricacies of the Trinity propounded by the Christian scholastic tradition.[1] But the problematic argument from arithmetic in debating the Trinity also applies to the use of numbers to explain *tawḥīd*, according to plentiful statements from the Imāms which negate the meaning of numerical oneness when conceiving of how God is One.[2] Statements such as 'The One not meaning numerically' (*al-Wāhid bi-lā taʾwīl ʿadad*),[3] or 'One not numerically' (*Wāḥid lā bi-ʿadad*)[4] are clear in their rejection of an arithmetic understanding of *tawḥīd*. The clarity of these statements, on the one hand, and the rational conceptions of God as an unlimited Being, on the other, resulted in a framing of *tawḥīd* that found numerical oneness problematic. As such, the statement 'You have, O my God, numerical oneness' narrated in a supplication attributed to the fourth Shīʿī Imām, ʿAlī b. Ḥusayn (also re-

1 For an overview of some important discussions concerning the Trinity, as well as contributions of Trinitarian conceptions beyond the European context, see Peter C. Phan, ed., *The Cambridge Companion to the Trinity* (Cambridge: Cambridge University Press, 2011).

2 ʿAlī Khān al-Madanī, *Riyāḍ al-sālikīn fī sharḥ Ṣaḥīfat Sayyid al-Sājidīn*, 7 vols. (Qom: Jāmiʿat al-Mudarrisīn, 2006), 4:294.

3 Muḥammad b. Yaʿqūb al-Kulaynī, *al-Kāfī*, 15 vols. (Qom: Dār al-Ḥadīth, 2008), 1:341.

4 Muḥammad b. Ḥusayn al-Raḍī, *Nahj al-balāgha* (Qom: al-Hijra, 1993), 269.

ferred to by his epithets Zayn al-ʿĀbidīn and al-Sajjād), needed an interpretation other than an attestation to numerical oneness. At the same time, traditional commentators were hesitant to draw attention to any weakness in the attribution of such a statement to Imām al-Sajjād and opted to work with it rather than reject its attribution outright.[5]

In this paper I will begin by explaining the problem with an arithmetic understanding of *tawḥīd* and its tension with clear conceptions about the nature of God in scriptural sources, such as God not having a partner, limitation, or similitude. Numerical oneness in some cases simply allows for a possibility of one of these unacceptable conceptions (like in the case of classifying God in one of the five universals such as a genus in relation to a species, where divinity is one in genus, indirectly allowing for more than one species of god) and in other cases directly implies it (like the limited nature of anything within the realm of numbers). I will then explain the views presented by Sayyid Shubbar (1188–1242/1774–1826) in his *Maṣābīḥ al-anwār* with reference to some of the commentaries that preceded his work. A more intricate reconciliation in Sayyid Muḥammad Bāqir al-Mūsawī al-Ḥusaynī's *Lawāmiʿ al-anwār* is considered thereafter, showing the development of the exegetical literature and its reliance on the theoretical mysticism of the school of Ibn al-ʿArabī and the transcendental philosophy of Mullā Ṣadrā in coherently reconciling visions of *tawḥīd* beyond numerical oneness and the arguments directly understood from certain scriptural sources. Whilst Shubbar's *Maṣābīḥ* usefully summarises, interprets, and evaluates the existing opinions in a work tackling enigmatic *ḥadīth*, al-Ḥusaynī's *Lawāmiʿ* is perhaps the most important, seminal, and detailed extant commentary of *al-Ṣaḥīfa al-Sajjādiyya* and so understanding the development of its content indicates the progression in the acceptance and incorporation of certain mystical visions of *tawḥīd* among mainstream Shīʿī scholars.

## 2. The Problem with Numerical Oneness

In a detailed *ḥadīth* attributed to Imām ʿAlī, he explains the conceptions of *tawḥīd* that can be applicable to God and those that cannot. It is narrated in the *Book of Tawḥīd* by Shaykh al-Ṣadūq that on the day of the Battle of the Camel a Bedouin approached Imām ʿAlī and asked him if he believed that God was One. On hearing this question those who were there reproached the Bedouin for asking such a seemingly basic question at such a difficult time. However, Imām ʿAlī told them to leave the Bedouin alone, as what he wanted is what the Imām wanted from the people they were fighting. This statement attributed to the Imām, if considered authentic, may show that the concept of *tawḥīd*

5 This can be contrasted to other reconciliations where a problematic statement could be set aside on the basis of chain criticism; see, for example, al-Sharīf al-Murtaḍā's reconciliation of the problem of truly seeing the Prophet in a dream with historical figures that are disparaged in the Shīʿī worldview as a sign of their spiritual station. ʿAlī b. Ḥusayn al-Sharīf al-Murtaḍā, *Rasāʾil al-Sharīf al-Murtaḍā*, 4 vols. (Qom: Manshūrāt Dār al-Qurʾān al-Karīm, 1984), 2:12–13.

was perhaps elusive even to early Muslims as the Battle of the Camel was the first major civil war among Muslims. If the attribution is not considered authentic it shows a vision of how Shīʿī protagonists may have conceived of some of the sources of fundamental tension among the early community. The narration continues with the Imām proceeding to answer the Bedouin's question with the following response:

> O Bedouin! There are four ways of saying that God is One, two of which are not attributable to God, and two that are established. The two that are not permitted concerning Him are if someone says '[He is] one', meaning numerically. This is not applicable, as what does not have a second is not included in the category of numbers. Do you not see how God considers someone who says He is 'the third of three'[6] an unbeliever?
>
> [Secondly,] for someone to say that 'He is one [like one] human', meaning a species from a genus, this is not permitted as it is attributing a likeness [to Him] and our Lord is too majestic and exalted above that.
>
> As for the two aspects that are affirmed for Him, [the first] is for one to say, 'He is Singular, and there is nothing similar to Him,' such is our Lord, Mighty and Majestic.
>
> And [secondly] if one says, 'He, the Mighty and Majestic, is unique,' meaning He is not divisible in His existence, or by the intellect or in our imagination, such is our Lord, Mighty and Majestic.[7]

This tradition has particularly rich philosophical import. While some may argue that the technical terms used such as genus and species may reduce the likelihood of a sound attribution to the Imām,[8] this tradition was used throughout the commentaries investigated dealing with the statement in supplication twenty-eight entitled 'His supplication in fleeing to God' in which the statement "You have, O my God, numerical oneness" occurs. Its importance in forming arguments for the nature of *tawḥīd* in this context is therefore indicated by its widespread use. Interestingly, the argument provided for God not being numerically one from the Qur'an as not being 'the third of three' may be traced to an argument against a conception of the Trinity according to Monophysites.[9]

6 Q. 5:73.

7 Muḥammad b. ʿAlī Ibn Bābawayh, *al-Tawḥīd* (Qom: Jāmiʿat al-Mudarrisīn, 1977), 83.

8 See Muḥammad Āṣif Muḥsinī, *Mashraʿat Biḥār al-anwār*, 3 vols. (Beirut: Muʿassasat al-ʿĀrif li-l-Maṭbūʿāt, 2005), 1:108. While arguments can be made for the non-technical use of the terms or the transmission of the contents with technical terms from a later period in line with the permission to transmit *ḥadīth* by meaning rather than letter, such arguments are unlikely to satisfy critics of the occurrence of complex philosophical explanations in public discourse before the translation movement.

9 See C. Jonn Block, 'Philoponian Monophysitism in South Arabia at the Advent of Islam with Implications for the English Translation of "*Thalātha*"', *Journal of Islamic Studies* 23, no. 1 (2012): 50–75. Monophysite belief resulted in the worship of three distinct entities. See also Mun'im Sirry, *Scriptural Polemics: The*

But the reference to a certain conception of the Trinity expressed in the tradition does not directly address a perceived numerical inconsistency of one nature and three persons or the tritheism attributed to Monophysites. Rather, it is the inclusion of God in *any* discussion of numbers at all. He is not one numerically as there is no possibility of a second. A second what? A second god? A second independent existent? The use of the word 'second' without an indication of what that second is may indicate the impossibility of any real independent existent other than Him.

What exactly does such an idea entail? Central to the discussion of *tawḥīd* is the reconciliation of sheer unity with the multiplicity we intuitively experience. Objects instinctively seem separate, differentiated, and independent from each other. A glass seems separate, different, and independent from a stone, car, or pen and we do not require any complex argumentation to establish this as our intuitive grasp of the relationship between these objects. Without dismissing the intuitive experience of multiplicity as an illusion of the uninitiated or affirming real multiplicity at the expense of rejecting real unity, understanding how unity and multiplicity can be conceived together is a question at the heart of mystical and philosophical discussions.[10] In his exegetical work *Bayān al-saʿāda*, Sulṭān ʿAlī Shāh when explaining the verse of 'the third of three' draws on the mystical tradition to explain that the conception of numerical oneness as it pertains to God stems from not being able to think past the realm of multiplicity and the physical to a more refined conception of God being a single reality by which all contingent beings are self-disclosed in their loci of manifestation. Hidden yet manifest in every locus of manifestation. He further goes onto explain that the reason for rejecting the claim of numerical oneness as a conception of *tawḥīd* is that it entails limitation (*taḥdīd*) and similitude (*tamaththul*).[11] Both of these are unacceptable outcomes which contradict the vision of *tawḥid* in the scriptural sources in general, and the tradition above specifically.

Limitation is a key dilemma when subscribing to numerical oneness. In order for something to fall into the realm of numbers it must be limited, as before that, there is no number that can be determined for that thing. Something unbounded cannot be said to be arithmetically one as that itself would entail a boundary by which other than it can also be differentiated from it. An unlimited reality cannot be limited such that a numerical status can be given to it as that would involve an essential contradiction

*Qur'ān and Other Religions* (Oxford: Oxford University Press, 2014), 154–65. While reconciling positive references in Q. 5:73, al-Dimashqī recognises the plurality of Christian belief and practice; see Rifaat Y. Ebied and David Thomas, eds., *Muslim–Christian Polemic during the Crusades: A Letter from the People of Cypris and Ibn Abī Ṭālib al-Dimashqī's Response* (Leiden: Brill, 2005), 285–87.

10 This question is addressed in transcendental philosophy in the discussion of the modulation of existence; see Sajjad H. Rizvi, *Mullā Ṣadrā and Metaphysics: Modulation of Being* (London: Routledge, 2009); Abd al-Rassul Obudiyyat, *An Introduction to Islamic Philosophy Based on the Works of Murtada Mutahhari*, trans. Hussein Valeh (London: MIU Press, 2012) 43–51.

11 Sulṭān Muḥammad b. Ḥaydar Sulṭān ʿAlī Shāh, *Bayān al-saʿāda fī maqāmāt al-ʿibāda*, 4 vols. (Beirut: Muʾassasat al-Aʿlamī li-l-Maṭbūʿāt, 1988), 2:105.

(limiting the essentially unlimited); similar to the concept of infinity, which is denoted by a symbol rather than a number, as there is no single number that can be attributed to an unlimited value. To say infinity plus one is nonsensical as in order for infinity to enter the realm of numbers we must first limit it and then designate a number for it and by that process it is no longer infinite. Once something is limited it is similar to other limited beings at least in terms of the fact that it has limits. But this is also problematic in relation to the vision of God in the scriptural sources as 'There is nothing like unto Him' (*laysa ka-mithlihi shayʾ*)[12] and also what is meant by a numerical understanding of *tawḥīd* resulting in similitude.

The issue of similitude is alluded to as the other unattributable conception of God in Imām ʿAlī's answer to the Bedouin's question in the tradition above. The reasoning provided in the tradition is from the perspective of genus and species, meaning that God cannot be one from among a genus of gods such that it entails the possibility of a similar being under the same genus, even if that other god does not actually exist at all. God is not one existent god from a genus of hypothetically possible gods. His existence is unlike a unique Rolex watch, which falls under a genus of unique watches, but allows for the possibility of other unique watches, even if they haven't been made yet. Rather, He doesn't fall under even a hypothetical genus as this would entail the possibility of similitude. This is why He is beyond a partner, as nothing falls under the same genus as Him. This notion is different to Him not actually having a partner despite the possibility. He *cannot* have a partner as nothing is conceived as sharing a genus with Him. A vision of God that allows for this possibility is inconsistent with the vision of *tawḥīd* explained in this tradition.

The conception of God as not having any similitude, then, constitutes one of the acceptable visions of *tawḥīd* in the *ḥadīth* above without any further explanation, as it is the inverse outcome from the dilemma of similitude already explained in the tradition. The second conception that is acceptable refers to simplicity (*basāṭa*) as opposed to composition (*tarkīb*). Most physical phenomena can be further reduced into constituent parts. Humans, giraffes, trees, and stones can all be split into smaller parts. When we cannot physically reduce something beyond its constituent parts, we can continue imaginatively, and when we cannot continue imaginatively, we can invoke an intellectual principle that anything that has dimensions can be split into something with smaller dimensions. No matter how small those dimensions become, there is still a theoretical possibility of splitting it further as number allows us to conceive of a number between two numbers. It is corporealisation in a body that allows for infinite splitting and composition. Some sensory phenomena such as prime colours are traditionally thought to be simple, meaning that they are not split into parts, although they may be graded on a spectrum. However, defined light particles would not be subject to the same simplicity.

12 Q. 42:11.

God is a Being beyond any limitation and that includes being limited by matter or having a body. This means that He cannot have the limitations of matter and so cannot be composite or be split physically, imaginatively, or conceptually as all of these methods require defined boundaries. Since He cannot be limited, He also cannot be divided in any way. In the same way that it is impossible to actually, imaginatively, or conceptually divide infinity, God, the only unlimited Being, cannot be split into parts in any way at all.

The arguments for both acceptable and unacceptable visions of *tawḥīd* revolve around limiting God in any way. When something constitutes a limitation, that results in a vision of *tawḥīd* which is unacceptable. Conversely, the implications of an unlimited God, such as His having no similitude or the impossibility of division, are deemed acceptable visions. Limited and unlimited are contradictories and so as the law of non-contradiction dictates something cannot be limited and unlimited at the same time from the same perspective, nor can that being be neither limited or unlimited at the same time from the same perspective. How, then, can we reconcile the outward meaning of the expression found in the twenty-eighth supplication of *al-Ṣaḥīfa al-*Sajjādiyya, 'You have, O my God, numerical oneness' (*laka yā ilāhī waḥdāniyyat al-ʿadad*)? The statement's outward commitment to numerical oneness would contradict the vision of an unlimited, indivisible, unique God. It is to this question that Sayyid ʿAbdullāh Shubbar devotes a section in his *Maṣābīḥ al-anwār fī ḥall mushkilāt al-akhbār*.

## 3. Reconciliations in *Maṣābīḥ al-anwār*

Sayyid ʿAbdullāh b. Muḥammad Riḍā Shubbar (1188–1242/1774–1826) was a prolific polymath from a family of scholars who traced their lineage back to the fourth Imām of the Twelver Shīʿīs, Imām ʿAlī b. al-Ḥusayn Zayn al-ʿĀbidīn.[13] Sayyid Muḥammad Maʿṣūm wrote a biography of Sayyid ʿAbdullāh Shubbar in which he narrates that he was known as 'the son of an answered prayer' due to the divine response to the prayer of his father for rain during a period of drought.[14] Born in Najaf, Sayyid ʿAbdullāh accompanied his father to Kāẓimiyya where he began his studies in the introductory sciences, continuing until he received his licence of *ijtihād* from Shaykh Kāshif al-Ghiṭāʾ.[15] He spent the rest of his life teaching and wrote around seventy books on a variety of topics in the fields of jurisprudence, Qurʾanic exegesis, theology, ethics, and *ḥadīth*.[16] In his time he was known as the second Majlisī due to the impressive extent of his writings.[17] He is buried

13 Jaʿfar al-Muhājir, *Aʿlām al-shīʿa*, 3 vols. (Beirut: Dār al-Muʿarrikh al-ʿArabī, 2010), 2:868.

14 ʿAbdullāh Shubbar, *Maṣābīḥ al-anwār fī ḥall mushkilāt al-akhbār*, 2 vols. (Qom: Dār al-Ḥadīth, 2010), 1:17. There is a categorised list of Sayyid ʿAbdullāh's known works on pages 12–15.

15 al-Muhājir, *Aʿlām*, 2:869.

16 Ibid.

17 The first Majlisī in this context presumably being Muḥammad Bāqir al-Majlisī, the author of *Biḥār al-anwār*; see Muḥsin al-Amīn, *Aʿyān al-shīʿa*, 11 vols. (Beirut: Dār al-Taʿāruf li-l-Maṭbūʿāt, 1985), 8:82.

in the shrine of Imām al-Kāẓim and Imām al-Taqī in Kāẓimiyya.[18]

In his *Maṣābīḥ al-anwār* Sayyid Shubbar begins by elucidating the problem of numerical oneness and its unacceptability according to the scriptural sources and thereafter presents eight views on how the apparent inconsistency found in the expression of Imām Zayn al-ʿĀbidīn in the twenty-eighth supplication of *al-Ṣaḥīfa al-Sajjādiyya* can be reconciled. These views are garnered from a selection of commentaries on the *Ṣaḥīfa*, which predate the *Maṣābīḥ* but attempted to explain the statement with a view to reconciling the issue in some way. Other commentators such as Muḥammad Jawād Mughniyya (d. 1400/1979) do not tackle the apparent contradiction directly when explaining this phrase, but rather use the mention of oneness as an opportunity to explain an accepted vision of *tawḥīd*. In his *Fī ẓilāl al-Ṣaḥīfa al-Sajjādiyya* he quotes a meaning of oneness from Mullā Ṣadrā's *Asfār* which continues to explain that attributing oneness to God is a form of aggrandisement whereas oneness in relation to creation is reduction.[19] Table 1 summarises the views collected by Sayyid Shubbar and elucidates what seem to be the key reconciliations available to him at the time he wrote his work.

TABLE 1: *A summary of the views found in Maṣābīḥ al-anwār on how to reconcile the statement 'You have, O my God, numerical oneness' with non-numerical oneness*

| View number | Purport of the view | Restatement of the phrase |
|---|---|---|
| 1 | God is not within the realm of numbers but is rather described by uniqueness and the mention of numbers in the phrase is to deflect any imagination that *tawḥīd* is numerical. Rather, the word oneness has a meaning which is numerical and another completely different meaning as it pertains to God.[20] | You have, O my God, nothing numerical except uniqueness! |
| 2 | Uniqueness (*waḥdāniyya*) is not singularity (*wāḥidiyya*) and only God is described with uniqueness while created beings can be described with singularity.[21] | You have, O my God, uniqueness as a separate category from number in creation! |
| 3 | God has no partner or second.[22] | From the genus of numbers, You, O my God, are one! |

18 Ibid.

19 Muḥammad Jawād Mughniyya, *Fī ẓilāl al-Ṣaḥīfa al-Sajjādiyya* (Qom: Mu'assasat Dār al-Kitāb al-Islāmī, 2007), 371.

20 Shubbar, *Maṣābīḥ*, 1:246–47. This is the first part of view 2 in Sayyid Shubbar's discussion. View 2 is split into two different views, and view 1 I have included with view 4 due to its similar purport.

21 Ibid., 247.

22 Ibid.

| | | |
|---|---|---|
| 4 | He has created numbers, which exist because of Him. Since He created them, they are not Him and so the statement denies numerical oneness as an attribute of God.[23] This can also be explained by saying that numerical oneness is the shadow of true Oneness and so the *lām* in *laka* is similar to its possessive use in a verse like Q. 2:255.[24] | You have, O my God, created numerical oneness and so it belongs to You! |
| 5 | The *yāʾ* in *waḥdāniyya* is *yāʾ al-nisba*[25] meaning that the type of oneness used here is specifically for Him and not applicable to anything else as everything has a second except for Him.[26] | You have, O my God, a specific type of oneness only applicable to You! |
| 6 | The reality of numerical oneness is only applicable to God as He is the only one who can really be called One. When we call anything else one it is metaphorical.[27] | You have, O my God, real numerical oneness! |
| 7 | An intertextual analysis by Sayyid ʿAlī Khān (the only author Sayyid Shubbar mentions in this section). This phrase, as well as the rest of the paragraph in which it occurs, are explained by statements that appear in the next part of the supplication. The phrase that specifically relates to 'You have, O my God, numerical oneness' is 'Everyone other than Thee is ... diverse in states, constantly changing in attributes'. The meaning of the statement is therefore in opposition to changing states and attributes in the establishment of unity that is among His Attributes which themselves are considered multiple not in their reality but conceptually. The Names therefore do not entail multiplicity or differential aspects, but rather they are all unified in His Essence.[28] | You have, O my God, oneness not associated with changing states and diverse attributes! |
| 8 | The Arabic meaning of *ʿadad* can also be essence.[29] | You have, O my God, oneness of Essence! |

Sayyid Shubbar is silent on most of the views allowing the reader to reconcile the statement to any one or number of the views presented. The only view he comments on is view 8, which he identifies as a weak argument. This is probably due to the tenuous linguistic

23 Ibid., 246. This is the first view presented by Sayyid Shubbar but I have included it in the fourth view as both explanations present the case of numerical oneness being something created.
24 Ibid., 247. The part of Q. 2:255 which is referred to in this view reads: 'to Him belongs whatever is in the heavens and whatever is on the earth'; the use of the *lām* in *lahu* indicating possession.
25 Like the *yāʾ* in the word Qurashī indicating an attribution to the tribe of Quraysh.
26 Shubbar, *Maṣābīḥ*, 1:247.
27 Ibid.
28 Ibid., 248–49.
29 Ibid., 249.

connection made to essence in the context of the statement. View 3 is another weaker argument as it does not address the dilemma of attributing numerical oneness to God nor discuss any way the attribution could be reconciled. Rather, as a simple restatement of accepted concepts within scripture it avoids rationalisation. Commentators generally used a mix of the remaining views in their reconciliations. Of these views, 4, 5, and 6 were the most common. View 1 proposes that the reason for the word 'numerical' in the statement is to draw attention to the Oneness of God not being numerical and while it is not identified as a weak argument by Sayyid Shubbar it does seem to be counterintuitive. It would suggest that the outward expression does not mean what it says but rather the opposite—a convenient solution for whenever it needs to be drawn upon! However, such an interpretation conflicts with the accepted conventions of traditional interpretation in not departing from the apparent meaning to its opposite.[30]

View 2 focuses on the word 'oneness' and the difference between the words that could have been used to express oneness. While 'singularity' (*wāḥidiyya*) is applicable to creation as it indicates numerical oneness, the word used in the supplication is 'uniqueness' (*waḥdāniyya*). This is the same word used in the tradition attributed to Imām ʿAlī when he says: 'And [secondly] if one says He, Mighty and Majestic, is unique, meaning He is not divisible in His existence, or by the intellect or in our imagination, such is our Lord, Mighty and Majestic.'[31] Such a distinction, then, serves as a springboard for the elucidation of what is meant by the Oneness of God outside the realm of number as it distinguishes another way of looking at the meaning of oneness as uniqueness, where being unique does not mean being numerically one. However, a question that then arises concerns the role of the genitive *ʿadad* (number) in the statement with this distinction between singularity and uniqueness, as opposed to the genitive *maʿnā* (meaning) used in the tradition attributed to Imām ʿAlī. Since views 5 and 6 also have the function of distinguishing the oneness of creation from the Oneness of God, it seems as though these two views sat better with the commentators than view 2 as a linguistic basis to depart from the outward attestation to numerical oneness.

While some of the other views are more commonly found in the commentaries, Sayyid Shubbar specifically traces view 7 to Sayyid ʿAlī Khān al-Madanī, whose full name was Ṣadr al-Dīn ʿAlī b. Aḥmad b. Muḥammad Maʿsum al-Ḥusaynī al-Dashtakī al-Shīrāzī (1052–1118/1642–1706–7 or 1120/1708–9). He wrote an important commentary on the *Ṣaḥīfa* called *Riyāḍ al-sālikīn fī sharḥ Ṣaḥīfat Sayyid al-Sājidīn*. His intertextual reflection is unique in drawing attention to the rhetorical construct of the supplication. Al-Madanī specifically relates the statement 'diverse in states, constantly changing in attributes' to 'You have, O my God, numerical oneness' positing an opposing relationship

30 See al-Madanī, *Riyāḍ al-sālikīn*, 4:295, where al-Madanī rejects this opinion on the basis that it is not apparent.

31 Ibn Bābawayh, *al-Tawḥīd*, 83.

between them.[32] The first statement occurs as part of a paragraph which affirms that which is attributable to God, while the second statement occurs in the next paragraph that speaks of attributes for those other than God. The meaning of the first statement must be opposed to the meaning of the second statement as each line of the paragraph corresponds to a line in the following paragraph in an opposing way. This is similar to the structure of the other related statements such as '[You have] the property of eternal power', which is related to the statement 'overcome in his affair' in the next paragraph.[33] The full paragraphs have been translated by William C. Chittick as follows:

> 10- To Thee, my God, belongs the Unity of number,
> the property of eternal power,
> the excellence of force and strength,
> the degree of sublimity and elevation.
>
> 11- Everyone other than Thee is the object of compassion in his lifetime,
> overcome in his affair,
> overwhelmed in his situation,
> diverse in states,
> constantly changing in attributes.[34]

Al-Madanī considers the statements in paragraphs 10 and 11 related as what is attributable to God, on the one hand, is opposed to what is attributable to everyone other than Him. The meaning of 'You have, O my God, numerical oneness' is opposite to 'Everyone other than Thee is … diverse in states, constantly changing in attributes'. This means that different attributes and states when speaking about God refer to different concepts and expressions, not in real changes in attribute or state as the Attributes of God are at one with His Essence. There is no multiplicity as God's Essence is simple and One.[35] Al-Madanī continues to elucidate the link between God's Attributes and Essence in the rest of his explanation.[36] Perhaps another intertextual argument can be found in the last statement of the supplication in which God is extolled above any similitude or likeness.[37] Al-Madanī contributes to conceiving the need to interpret an outward commitment to numerical oneness differently through an intertextual discussion, and uses the impossibility of change to show that numerical oneness is not intended.

---

32 al-Madanī, *Riyāḍ al-sālikīn*, 4:295.
33 Ibid., 295–96.
34 Imām Zayn al-ʿĀbidīn, *The Psalms of Islam: al-Saḥīfa al-Sajjādiyya*, trans. William C. Chittick (London: The Muhammadi Trust of Great Britain and Northern Ireland, 1988), 101–2.
35 al-Madanī, *Riyāḍ al-sālikīn*, 4:296.
36 Ibid., 296–97.
37 Zayn al-ʿĀbidīn, *The Psalms of Islam*, 102.

But does the argument follow? How is change related to numerical oneness? For an object to experience a change in state it must have potential for the next potentially active state. Drawing on philosophical interpretations on the nature of God, it is clear that God is not subject to change because there is no potential perfection that He can achieve. He is necessary from every perspective (*wājib min jamīʿ al-jihāt*). His perfection is superabundant and beyond limit, in a state of action, not potential. Any state of potential would limit a current state of action as it is from the limit of a particular state of action that a potential for something beyond emerges. This is the link between change and numerical oneness. For God to change He needs to be limited, and for God's oneness to be numerical He needs to be limited. Beings other than God change and may be numerically one as they are limited. But God is unlimited and so cannot change or be numerically one.

Of the commentaries that predate Sayyid Shubbar's analysis, Mīr Damād's (d. 1041/1631) explanation has the same purport as views 5 and 6 in that he establishes numerical oneness for God but in a different way to creation. At the same time he uses the concept of numerical oneness being the shadow of true oneness expressed in view 4.[38] The grandson of al-Shahīd al-Thānī, ʿAlī b. Zayn al-Dīn b. Muḥammad al-ʿĀmilī (d. twelfth/eighteenth century), in his commentary explains that numerical oneness cannot apply to God; rather, it is from His Oneness that numerical oneness can be conceived even if not actualised. The Oneness that is attributable to God is that He is One in every aspect, which is an attribute not found in anyone other than Him.[39] Sayyid Niʿmatullāh al-Jazāʾirī (d. 1112/1700) uses views 1, 4, 5, and 6. He also quotes a tradition from Imām al-Riḍā in which the Imām is questioned about the premise that God has no likeness. If we can have a single human and a single God, isn't this a type of likeness? The Imām replies with the following:

> O Fatḥ, you are mistaken! May God make you steadfast! Similitude is in meaning, not in words. Singularity is an indication to that which is being spoken of. If you say that a human is one, you are speaking of one body which doesn't have a[n exact] likeness, but humans in themselves are not one. They have different muscles and colours. The different colours are variant. He has unequal parts that are divisible. His blood is not his flesh, and his flesh is not his blood. His nerves are not his sweat glands, and his sweat glands are not his nerves. His hair is not his skin, his whiteness is not his blackness, and similarly for the rest of creation. So a human is one in name, not one in meaning.
>
> God—His Majesty be majestic—is One and there is no other one other than Him. There is no change or difference, increase or decrease in Him.

38 Muḥammad Bāqir Dāmād, *Sharḥ al-Ṣaḥīfa al-Sajjādiyya al-kāmila* (Isfahan: Bahār-i qulūb, 2001), 273.

39 ʿAlī b. Zayn al-Dīn b. Muḥammad al-ʿĀmilī, *Sharḥ al-Ṣaḥīfa al-Sajjādiyya* (Tehran: Sāzamān tablīghāt-i Islāmī, 2017), 441.

> As for the human, he is created, fashioned, made up of different parts and substances even if he is brought together in one being.[40]

It seems as though the origin of Fatḥ's confusion is that the word 'one' is applied both to God and to other than God. The use of the same words led Fatḥ to assume that the same meaning was implied. The Imām draws Fatḥ's attention to the fact that the same word can be used for entirely different meanings. The context of the use of the word is important in deciphering the intended meaning. 'Singularity is an indication to that which is being spoken of.' God is not similar to His creation and so the words used for Him don't have the exact meaning as intended when referring to His creation. Mirroring the second valid conception of God as being simple, elucidated in the tradition attributed to Imām ʿAlī in his answer to the Bedouin, Imām al-Riḍā then explains that a created being is not one in the same sense that God is one, as physical beings are made of parts; but God is not and He does not experience change like His creation. The argument from lack of change was also found in al-Madanī's argument in view 7 discussed above.

Perhaps Sayyid Shubbar untangled the various trains of thought within such explanations such that he managed to extract three views from Mīr Damād's two-paragraph elucidation. Indeed, most of these views are also summarised and some are elucidated further in Sayyid Muḥammad Bāqir al-Mūsawī al-Ḥusaynī's (d. 1240/1824)[41] seminal commentary on the *Ṣaḥīfa*: *Lawāmiʿ al-anwār*. Sayyid Muḥammad Bāqir was a contemporary of Sayyid Shubbar.[42] He opts for view 5,[43] and his reasoning, beyond the grammatical use of the *yāʾ al-nisba*, is that both unveiling and reasoning suggest that both existence and oneness are essentially unified. The singularity of each thing is due to its specific instance of existence. Therefore, since God's existence is the reality of pure existence, which is neither general nor specific, universal, or particular, nor is it essential to anything else, without limit, and expansive of all that exists, it is *completely* unknown while being the most manifest and close. His Oneness, in the same way as His Existence, is also completely

40 al-Kulaynī, *al-Kāfī*, 1:293–94.

41 Unfortunately, it seems that not much is known about Sayyid Muḥammad Bāqir, also known as Mullā Bāshī, despite the seven works attributed to him. See Muḥammad Bāqir al-Mūsawī al-Shīrāzī, *Lawāmiʿ al-anwār al-ʿarshiyya fī sharḥ al-Ṣaḥīfa al-Sajjādīya*, 6 vols. (Isfahan: al-Zahrāʾ, 2004), 6:14–27.

42 Prior to these authors, commentaries were written by al-Kafʿamī (d. 905/1499), who was probably the earliest recorded commentator on the *Ṣaḥīfa*, with only the gloss of Abū Jaʿfar Muḥammad b. Manṣūr al-Ḥillī (d. 598/1201) predating al-Kafʿamī's efforts; a gloss by Muḥammad Taqī al-Majlisī (d. 1070/1659); Mīr Dāmād (d. 1041/1631); Ḥasan b. ʿAbbās al-Balāghī al-Najafī, who started his commentary in 1105/1693; a partial commentary by Muḥammad Bāqir al-Majlisī (d. 1110/1698); Sayyid Ṣadr al-Dīn ʿAlī b. Niẓām al-Dīn Aḥmad al-Dashtakī al-Shīrāzī (d. 1120/1708); Ḥusayn al-Jīlānī al-Iṣfahānī (d. 1129/1716); Abū al-Ḥasan b. Muḥammad Ṭāhir b. ʿAbd al-Ḥamīd al-Fatūnī al-Nabāṭī al-ʿĀmilī al-Iṣfahānī al-Gharawī (d. 1140/1727); a partial commentary by Mirzā Ibrāḥīm b. Mīr Muḥammad Maʿṣūm al-Ḥusaynī al-Tabrīzī al-Qazwīnī (d. 1149/1736); among many more. See Muḥammad Muḥsin b. ʿAlī Tihrānī, *al-Dharīʿa ilā taṣānīf al-shīʿa*, 25 vols. (Qom: Ismāʿīlīyān-i Qum va kitābkhānah-i islāmīya-i Tihrān, 1987), 13:345–59.

43 al-Shīrāzī, *Lawāmiʿ al-anwār*, 4:82–98.

unknown, meaning that God is the only being that possesses *tawḥīd*. It is therefore impossible to imagine a second, as the Oneness of God cannot be imagined in the first place.[44]

## 4. Oneness and Existence

Sayyid Muḥammad Bāqir continues his analysis to discuss the incoherency of numerical oneness for a being that is unlimited but pervades limited beings, not by being mixed with them, and transcends limited beings, without being detached from them.[45] Rather, 'there is nothing in existence except for His Essence, His Attributes, and His Actions. This is something which is not known except to the perfect from among the *ʿurafāʾ* (knowers).'[46] Since there is nothing that is without Him, all existential perfection is attributable to Him, as everything in existence is a manifestation of His perfections. Saying God has every type of oneness is like saying God has every type of existence. So, if another sentence, perhaps even more problematic than the one found in the *Ṣaḥīfa* is hypothesised, such as 'You have, O my God, contingent existence', it would not be an expression of God's existence being contingent, as that is impossible. Rather, it should be interpreted to mean that His existence encompasses all contingent existents. Contingent existence can be attributed to Him from this perspective. In the same way, since numerical oneness is attributable to creation, yet remains comprised by real oneness, it can be attributed to God.

In a separate treatise at the end of his commentary on this part of the supplication, Sayyid Muḥammad Bāqir draws heavily on the theory and language of the theoretical mysticism of the school of Ibn al-ʿArabī and the transcendental philosophy of Mullā Ṣadrā. He continues to clarify what is meant by this phrase by identifying three meanings for oneness based on three ways of looking at *wujūd*:

(1) Pure Unity that is not connected to anything nor is it limited by any limitation. This is specifically applicable to His Essence, which has no Name, no trace, no limit, and no proof [because of its exaltation above the intellect].
(2) Unity that is limited by permanent archetypes and quiddity.
(3) Unity that is unlimited and dispersed. Its generality and encompassment is not such that it is universal or shared like intellectual concepts; rather, in another complex way, which only the people of insight understand, which is the oneness that encompasses everything not through mixing or by separation. This applies to all of the Attributes such as Power and Knowledge. It is this last type that is referred to in the phrase in the supplication.

---

44 Ibid., 87–88.

45 This classic paradox is taken from a report in which Imām ʿAlī is reported to have said: '[He] is with everything not accompanying it, other than everything not by separation' (*maʿa kulli shayʾ lā bi-muqārana wa-ghayr kulli shayʾ lā bi-muzāyala*). See al-Raḍī, *Nahj al-balāgha*, 40.

46 al-Shīrāzī, *Lawāmiʿ al-anwār*, 88.

These ways of looking at *tawḥīd* draw from the Breath of the All-Merciful (*al-nafas al-raḥmānī*) elucidated in Akbarian Sufism.[47] The stage of Pure Unity identified as the first way of looking at existence corresponds to the first degree of the *nafas* called the Degree of Non-dualistic Unity (*al-martaba al-aḥadiyya*), which is also sometimes referred to as the Unseen of the Unseen (*ghayb al-ghuyūb*). The degrees in the schema of the *nafas* are degrees of manifestation and limitation, moving from the stage where nothing is manifest to the material world, in which the Names of God are the most manifest. The flip side of manifestation is that something manifest hides what is behind it and so the realms of the inner or unseen are in relation to the state of consciousness of the locus of manifestation. The first degree in the *nafas* signifies the rule of Pure Unity, which precedes the process of manifestation and limitation. It dissolves any conception of multiplicity, such that even the Names are not distinguished from one another as they are all unlimited modes of the superabundant Essence. The simple distinction of one Name from another would involve an intellectual limitation which is not acceptable at this level of unity. This Pure Unity is the unity that can be attributed to God as it necessitates no partner, division, or composition.

The second type of oneness focuses on multiplicity. Drawing from Ṣadrā's philosophy, an existent's quiddity signifies the limitations of its existence. The discussion of the relationship between quiddity and the permanent archetypes is contentious.[48] The permanent archetypes signify a stage in the knowledge of God, where the specifics of the Names which constitute each individual manifestation are known to God, but are yet to exist in the extramental as external archetypes (*al-aʿyān al-khārijiyya*). It is the permanent archetypes that give the external archetypes their specification. The permanent archetypes are the Names as they face creation and so never enter the realm of creation, similar to quiddity which does not exist or not exist in and of itself. They are permanent as the knowledge of God is not subject to change. The stage of the permanent archetypes is after a stage in which the Names are distinguished from one another in the Degree of Dualistic Unity (*al-martaba al-wāḥidiyya*). Created beings manifest perfections and hide others as the only way for an Attribute to manifest is if the other Attributes are hidden. While this way of looking at existence emphasises multiplicity, the concepts of quiddity and the permanent archetypes fall under theories which already specify the true oneness of that which they limit. It is through the lens of oneness that multiplicity is reconciled in both transcendental philosophy and Akbarian theoretical mysticism.

47 See Toshihiko Izutsu, *Sufism and Taoism: A Comparative Study of Key Philosophical Concepts* (Berkeley: University of California Press, 1983), 7–282; Sajjad H. Rizvi, 'The Existential Breath of al-Raḥmān and the Munificent Grace of al-Raḥīm: The *Tafsīr Sūrat al-Fātiḥa* of Jāmī and the School of Ibn ʿArabī', *Journal of Qur'anic Studies* 8, no. 1 (2006): 58–87.

48 See Zoheir Esmail, 'Between Philosophy and ʿIrfān: Interpreting Mullā Ṣadrā from the Qajars to Post-revolutionary Iran' (PhD diss., University of Exeter, 2015), 216–18.

The third type elucidates a balance between unity and multiplicity, not preferring one aspect over the other, yet affirming both through discussing unity as encompassing multiplicity. The idea of encompassing avoids attachment or detachment of the unifying aspect such that it does not sharply contradict or affirm multiplicity. As with all of the other Attributes, unity encompasses limitation as it transcends it. God's knowledge, while being presential is not limited by the limitations of corporeal presence. His power accounts for all that occurs within every realm, but at the same time it is not confined to any realm. His knowledge, power, unity, and all of His Attributes are transcendent as they are unlimited, but not detached entirely as every realm manifests these Attributes. They account for all perfection as there is no other source of perfection other than God, yet they are not confined to any locus of manifestation.

## 4. Concluding Remarks

Interpreting texts as a process to reconcile apparent inconsistencies is an important function of an intellectual tradition. The views presented in Sayyid Shubbar's *Maṣābīḥ al-anwār* provide us with a vista unto the visions of *tawḥīd* discussed by commentators on *al-Ṣaḥīfa al-Sajjādiyya* and the reconciliation of an outward attestation to numerical oneness with the wider scriptural and intellectual traditions which contest such a notion. It seems that the commentators were empowered in their reconciliations by the development of the mystical and philosophical traditions. This is reflected in the general increase in literature commenting on texts like the *Ṣaḥīfa* and *Uṣūl al-Kāfī* from the eleventh/seventeenth century and the refinement and clarity of thought in later commentaries like *Lawāmiʿ al-anwār* of Sayyid Muḥammad Bāqir al-Mūsawī al-Ḥusaynī. As such, this article and others like it, are windows into a garden of activity in which Shīʿī commentators engage with their scriptural sources through the lenses of philosophy and mysticism.

Reflections ranged from linguistics, intertextual analysis, and mystical theosophy but did not involve a critical assessment of the attribution of the supplication to Imām Zayn al-ʿĀbidīn. While different reconciliations were offered, through the course of critical engagement the coherency of certain interpretations ensured them a preferred position among commentators. This is one of the key advantages of intellectual frameworks that demonstrate their prowess in their ability to coherently explain dilemmas in a consistent manner, reflecting the intellectual indebtedness of commentators to their philosophical and mystical heritage. The endeavours of scriptural commentators in providing more substantial analysis using these frameworks has provided grounding for modern research which aims to retrace the roots of philosophical and mystical frameworks to scripture.[49]

49 Muḥammad Javād Rūdgar, *Mabānī-yi ʿirfān-i waḥyānī* (Tehran: Sāzmān-i intishārāt-i pajūheshgāh-yi farhang va andīshah-yi Islāmī, 2017).

## Bibliography

al-ʿĀmilī, ʿAlī b. Zayn al-Dīn b. Muḥammad. *Sharḥ al-Ṣaḥīfa al-Sajjādiyya*. Tehran: Sāzamān tablīghāt-i Islāmī, 2017.

al-Amīn, Muḥsin. *Aʿyān al-shīʿa*. 11 vols. Beirut: Dār al-Taʿāruf li-l-Maṭbūʿāt, 1985.

Dāmād, Muḥammad Bāqir. *Sharḥ al-Ṣaḥīfa al-Sajjādiyya al-kāmila*. Isfahan: Bahār-i qulūb, 2001.

Ebied, Rifaat Y., and David Thomas, eds. *Muslim–Christian Polemic during the Crusades: A Letter from the People of Cypris and Ibn Abī Ṭālib al-Dimashqī's Response*. Leiden: Brill, 2005.

Esmail, Zoheir. 'Between Philosophy and *ʿIrfān*: Interpreting Mullā Ṣadrā from the Qajars to Post-revolutionary Iran'. PhD diss., University of Exeter, 2015.

Ibn Bābawayh, Muḥammad b. ʿAlī. *al-Tawḥīd*. Qom: Jāmiʿat al-Mudarrisīn, 1977.

Izutsu, Toshihiko. *Sufism and Taoism: A Comparative Study of Key Philosophical Concepts*. Berkeley: University of California Press, 1983.

Jonn Block, C. 'Philoponian Monophysitism in South Arabia at the Advent of Islam with Implications for the English Translation of "*Thalātha*"'. *Journal of Islamic Studies* 23, no. 1 (2012): 50–75.

al-Kulaynī, Muḥammad b. Yaʿqūb. *al-Kāfī*. 15 vols. Qom: Dār al-Ḥadīth, 2008.

al-Madanī, ʿAlī Khān. *Riyāḍ al-sālikīn fī sharḥ Ṣaḥīfat Sayyid al-Sājidīn*. 7 vols. Qom: Jāmiʿat al-Mudarrisīn, 2006.

Mughniyya, Muḥammad Jawād. *Fī ẓilāl al-Ṣaḥīfa al-Sajjādiyya*. Qom: Muʾassasat Dār al-Kitāb al-Islāmī, 2007.

al-Muhājir, Jaʿfar. *Aʿlām al-shīʿa*. 3 vols. Beirut: Dār al-Muʿarrikh al-ʿArabī, 2010.

Muḥsinī, Muḥammad Āṣif. *Mashraʿat Biḥār al-anwār*. 3 vols. Beirut: Muʿassasat al-ʿĀrif li-l-Maṭbūʿāt, 2005.

Obudiyyat, Abd al-Rassul. *An Introduction to Islamic Philosophy Based on the Works of Murtada Mutahhari*. Translated by Hussein Valeh. London: MIU Press, 2012.

Phan, Peter C., ed. *The Cambridge Companion to the Trinity*. Cambridge: Cambridge University Press, 2011.

al-Raḍī, Muḥammad b. Ḥusayn. *Nahj al-balāgha*. Qom: al-Hijra, 1993.

Rizvi, Sajjad. H. 'The Existential Breath of al-Raḥmān and the Munificent Grace of al-Raḥīm: The *Tafsīr Sūrat al-Fātiḥa* of Jāmī and the School of Ibn ʿArabī'. *Journal of Qur'anic Studies* 8, no. 1 (2006): 58–87.

Rizvi, Sajjad. H. *Mullā Ṣadrā and Metaphysics: Modulation of Being*. London: Routledge, 2009.

Rūdgar, Muḥammad Javād. *Mabānī-yi ʿirfān-i waḥyānī*. Tehran: Sāzmān-i intishārāt-i pajūheshgāh-yi farhang va andīshah-yi Islāmī, 2017.

al-Sharīf al-Murtaḍā, ʿAlī b. Ḥusayn. *Rasāʾil al-Sharīf al-Murtaḍā*. 4 vols. Qom: Manshūrāt Dār al-Qurʾān al-Karīm, 1984.

al-Shīrāzī, Muḥammad Bāqir al-Mūsawī. *Lawāmiʿ al-anwār al-ʿarshiyya fī sharḥ al-Ṣaḥīfa al-Sajjādiyya*. 6 vols. Isfahan: al-Zahrāʾ, 2004.

Shubbar, ʿAbdullāh. *Maṣābīḥ al-anwār fī ḥall mushkilāt al-akhbār*. 2 vols. Qom: Dār al-Ḥadīth, 2010.

Sirry, Mun'im. *Scriptural Polemics: The Qur'ān and Other Religions*. Oxford: Oxford University Press, 2014.

Sulṭān ʿAlī Shāh, Sulṭān Muḥammad b. Ḥaydar. *Bayān al-saʿāda fī maqāmāt al-ʿibāda*. 4 vols. Beirut: Muʾassasat al-Aʿlamī li-l-Maṭbūʿāt, 1988.

Tihrānī, Muḥammad Muḥsin b. ʿAlī. *al-Dharīʿa ilā taṣānīf al-shīʿa*. 25 vols. Qom: Ismāʿīlīyān-i Qum va kitābkhānah-i islāmīya-i Tihrān, 1987.

Zayn al-ʿĀbidīn, Imām. *The Psalms of Islam: al-Ṣaḥīfa al-Sajjādiyya*. Translated by William C. Chittick. London: The Muhammadi Trust of Great Britain and Northern Ireland, 1988.

# Apophatic *Tawḥīd*: A Philosophical Account of Shīʿī Ismāʿīlī Theology

*Khalil Andani*

## 1. Introduction

The Ismāʿīlī Muslims are a minority branch of Shīʿī Islam, who recognise the religious authority of a line of hereditary Imāms from the *Ahl al-Bayt* of the Prophet Muḥammad. Unlike the majority Twelver Shīʿa, the Ismāʿīlīs trace the line of Imāms through the descendants of Ismāʿīl b. Jaʿfar al-Ṣādiq (d. after 138/755). Today the two largest Ismāʿīlī communities are the Nizārī Ismāʿīlīs, who recognise the present Aga Khan (Shāh Karīm al-Ḥusaynī) as their forty-ninth Imām, and the Dāʾūdī Bohras, who recognise a line of *dāʿīs* as the representatives of a hidden line of Imāms. Over the centuries, Ismāʿīlī Muslims under the guidance of their Imāms have developed distinctive legal, theological, and spiritual understandings of Islam that differ from Sunnīs and Twelver Shīʿa on key issues. The Ismāʿīlīs are famous for advocating an apophatic theology concerning the nature of God in which they negate all names, descriptions, and real predications from God. They also affirm a Neoplatonic understanding of divine cosmology in which God originates and sustains a vast hierarchy of cosmological realms comprising the intellectual, the spiritual, the subtle (imaginal), and physical worlds. In the Ismāʿīlī worldview, God issues a single eternal creative act—called the Command of God—which constitutes the first creation, known as the Universal Intellect—the eternal and most perfect creation of God. The Universal Intellect eternally emanates or generates the second creation, called the Universal Soul. The Soul is a spiritual substance in a perpetual state of spiritual motion as it strives to perfect itself; its spiritual movement produces the spiritual and physical worlds. The Universal Soul emanates numerous individual souls, including human souls, who are microcosms of the Universal Soul. The human souls who embody the spiritual perfections that reflect the Universal Intellect are the prophets and the Imāms, who have a cosmic mandate to guide other human beings to ontological perfection. Human souls may achieve perfection by submitting to the infallible guidance of the Imām of the time, whose pure soul receives continuous emanation and light from the Universal Intellect. In ascending towards perfection through following the guidance of the Imāms, human souls come to resemble and imitate the Universal Soul and Universal Intellect in spiritual virtues and perfections. This process of 'integration', by which the human soul is assimilated into its spiritual origin (*aṣl*), involves the act of *tawḥīḍ*, where the soul must divest and isolate every rank of God's creation from divinity and thereby recognise the absolute unity of God.

All Muslim schools of thought were concerned about the best way to uphold the absolute unity of God, *tawḥīd*, in both speech and practice. Most Sunnī theologians in the *kalām* tradition describe God through various divine names. They also affirm real-distinct entitative attributes (*ṣifāt maʿnawiyya*) for God—meaning that God has uncreated attributes that subsist in God's Essence, such as His life, knowledge, power, speech, will, hearing, and seeing—all of which are mutually distinct. Ḥanbalīs even affirmed a face, two hands, two eyes, a sitting (*istiwāʾ*), and a descending (*nuzūl*) for God while claiming ignorance about the ontological modality (*kayfiyya*) of these attributes. Meanwhile, Muʿtazilī and Twelver theologians negated entitative attributes from God. Instead, they identified God's attributes with His singular essence; thus, God's life, knowledge, and power are identical to Himself. Many Islamic philosophers in the *falsafa* tradition followed a similar approach as the Muʿtazila on the matter of divine attributes, but they argued for a negative theology of the Divine Essence.[1]

While Ismāʿīlī thought has had a variety of manifestations over history across different regions, upholding *tawḥīd* was always an ultimate concern for Ismāʿīlī thinkers. Ismāʿīlī theology is a careful attempt to speak about God in the most appropriate manner possible within the confines of human language. Ismāʿīlī philosophers, both past and present, are infamous for taking a radically apophatic approach to the theology of *tawḥīd* and criticising other approaches for falling short in this regard. Unlike many other Muslim groups, the Ismāʿīlīs prefer to *negate* all positive attributes (such as life, knowledge, or power) and all privative attributes (such as death, ignorance, or incapacity) from God. God in His absolute unity transcends all creaturely categories, both material and spiritual, such that He cannot even be called a 'thing' or an 'existent'. This approach results in the Ismāʿīlīs asserting that God is neither existent nor non-existent since He transcends the ontological scope of created things which partake in both existence and non-existence. This type of apophatic or negative theology is admittedly shocking at first glance and seems to run counter to everyday conceptions of God. However, Ismāʿīlī teaching is based on a rigorous commitment to language and logic, which Ismāʿīlī aspirants were gradually guided through.

Islamic theological schools often engaged in mutual polemics with each group undermining the theology of the other by using rational and scriptural arguments. Accordingly, many Muslim thinkers attacked Ismāʿīlī theology by portraying it in the worst possible light. They often accused Ismāʿīlī articulations of *tawḥīd* as being logically incoherent, violating linguistic conventions, or amounting to nothing more than atheism under a Muslim garb. Such attacks came from all quarters including traditionalist and rationalist Muslim schools. The Ashʿarī theologian known as the 'Imām of the Two Holy Places', al-Juwaynī (d. 478/1085), accused the Ismāʿīlī teaching of being logically incoherent be-

1 For a survey of these views, see Aydogan Kars, *Unsaying God: Negative Theology in Medieval Islam* (New York: Oxford University Press, 2019).

cause he interprets the Ismāʿīlī belief that God transcends existence and non-existence as a sort of agnosticism. Al-Juwaynī believes the Ismāʿīlīs can neither deny nor affirm God's reality and existence.[2] The Zaydī Imām al-Mu'ayyad bi-Llāh (d. 411/1020) accused the Ismāʿīlīs of denying God entirely and affirming contradictions: 'For their ignorance (*li-jahlihim*) and excessive stupidity (*farṭ ghabāwatihim*) they do not know that the negation of the negation necessitates the affirmation (*nafī al-nafī yaqtaḍī al-ithbāt*) according to the linguists (*ahl al-lisān*) ... and thus they denied what they had just affirmed and they revoked what they had said. And this is nothing of what is unknown. But their aim in this is arriving at denying of God all attributes (*taʿṭīl*) and denying the creator (*nafī al-ṣāniʿ*).'[3] The Muʿtazilī scholar al-Bustī (d. 420/1029) levelled similar charges and accused the Ismāʿīlīs of 'leaving the realm of reason' (*kharajū ʿan qismat al-ʿaql*).[4] Other Muʿtazila like al-Jishumī (d. 494/1101) referred to Ismāʿīlī theology as 'nonsense' (*fāsid*) and an atheistic denial of God (*nafī al-ṣāniʿ*) while Ibn al-Malāḥimī (d. 536/1141) critiqued their dual negation discourse as 'irrational' (*wa-dhālika lā yaʿqil aṣlan*). Even the Ḥanbalī scholar Ibn Taymiyya (d. 728/1328), who himself was subject to much criticism, concluded that the Ismāʿīlīs on account of their negative theology were the most extreme of all groups: 'They are the extremists of the extremists (*ghulāt al-ghulāt*). They negate from Him all contradictories (*al-naqīḍayn*), and say, "[He is] neither existent nor non-existent, neither living nor dead, neither knowing nor ignorant."'[5] Accordingly, Ibn Taymiyya accused the Ismāʿīlīs of negating mutually contradictory propositions (*al-naqīḍayn*) about God and violating the rules of logic.

If an outside observer took these Sunnī polemical appraisals of Ismāʿīlī theology at face value, they would conclude that such positions on *tawḥīd* were sectarian at best, heterodox and incoherent at worst, and belong to the margins of Islamic intellectual history. In fact, modern scholars sometimes endorsed such a judgement. Joseph van Ess flatly stated that Ismāʿīlīs had a 'radical position' on *tawḥīd* and that 'according to the view of the Islamic majority, such ideas were sectarian'.[6] Wilfred Madelung classified Ismāʿīlī theology as a 'suprarational theology' whose core claims cannot be argued or validated by human reason. In the contemporary tradition of analytic philosophy and theology, apophatic theology in general remains a contentious project and is opposed by major Christian analytic theologians. Alvin Plantinga, famous for his dismissal of apophaticism, contends that apophatic theology is self-defeating in stating that 'God

2 Imām al-Ḥaramayn al-Juwaynī, *A Guide to Conclusive Proofs for the Principles of Belief*, trans. Paul E. Walker (Reading: Garnet Publishing, 2000), 24.

3 al-Mu'ayyad bi-Llāh, quoted in Eva-Maria Lika, *Proofs of Prophecy and the Refutation of the Ismāʿīliyya: The* Kitāb Ithbāt Nubuwwat al-Nabī *by the Zaydī al-Mu'ayyad bi-Llāh al-Hārūnī (d. 411/1020)* (Berlin: De Gruyter, 2017), 70.

4 Ibid., 72.

5 Ibn Taymiyya, quoted in Kars, *Unsaying God*, 25, translation modified.

6 Josef van Ess, quoted in Mohammad Amin Mansouri, 'Sayyid Ḥaydar Āmulī (d. ca. 787/1385) and Ismailism', *Studia Islamica* 117 (2022): 218.

is indescribable' or 'God is ineffable'—since the person who makes such a claim is also violating his own claim by making a statement about God. Proponents of this critique further argue that apophatic theologies interpret away all religious language about God, which undermines their own Christian commitments.[7]

The few analyses of Ismāʿīlī theology and metaphysics in modern scholarship are from the standpoint of descriptive intellectual history and emphasise the wide currency of Ismāʿīlī ideas: 'In the tenth century Isma'ilism had become a powerhouse of ideas no longer limited to Isma'ilis, but circulated among scholars of diverse orientations under their intellectual and political sway, and beyond.'[8] However, these purely descriptive studies do not *philosophically assess* Ismāʿīlī theological ideas. This paper fills this gap by presenting a logically rigorous and textually rooted exposition of Ismāʿīlī apophatic theology based on the philosophical thought of the most prominent Ismāʿīlī Muslim Neoplatonic philosopher-*dāʿīs*—Abū Yaʿqūb al-Sijistānī (d. ca. 361/971), Ḥamīd al-Dīn al-Kirmānī (d. ca. 412/1021), al-Mu'ayyad al-Shīrāzī (d. 470/1077), Nāṣir-i Khusraw (d. 462/1070), ʿAbd al-Karīm al-Shahrastānī (d. 548/1153), and Naṣīr al-Dīn Ṭūsī (d. 672/1274). My primary purpose is to demonstrate the logical coherence and metaphysical merits of Ismāʿīlī apophasis both as a viable Islamic expression of *tawḥīd* and as an intellectually compelling formulation of classical theism (also called divine simplicity) in the contemporary philosophy of religion.

The first section of this study will demonstrate that Ismāʿīlīs employed natural theology to prove the existence of God and that their belief in God was rooted in rational argument. The second section focuses on how Ismāʿīlīs articulate the transcendence of God above the physical and spiritual realms through a dual negation that is consistent with the rules of logic. The third section focuses on how Ismāʿīlīs articulate divine simplicity or the absolute oneness of God by negating all attributes from Him through another type of dual negation, which is based on the Neoplatonic semantics of scalar predication. The fourth section deals with the controversial Ismāʿīlī idea that God is beyond existence and non-existence. The fifth and final section shows how Ismāʿīlī apophatic theology still accommodates positive predications about God when they are understood as metonymic descriptions as opposed to literal ones.

## 2. From Cosmos to Creator: Ismāʿīlī Natural Theologies

Madelung and Walker have claimed that Ismāʿīlī thinkers never attempted to prove the existence of God: 'Characteristically, Ismaili theology did not attempt to offer a proof of

7 His argument is well summarised in Joshua Matthan Brown, 'What We Can and Cannot Say: An Apophatic Response to Atheism', in *Eastern Christian Approaches to Philosophy*, ed. James Siemens and Joshua Matthan Brown (Cham: Springer, 2022), 88–90.

8 Karis, *Unsaying God*, 44.

God, that first concern of any rational theology. A rational proof of what is beyond reason and being was evidently futile.' Both scholars cited al-Sijistānī's statement, which they rendered as 'God is more certain than everything certain' (*athbatu min kulli thābit*).[9] However, this is a misreading. Al-Sijistānī's teaching *Allāhu athbatu min kulli thābitin* (God is more subsistent than everything that subsists) is not an epistemic claim about God being 'certain' to human intellects; it is an ontological claim about God's 'subsistence', 'permanence', or ontological stability (*thabāt, thubūt, ithbāt*) in contrast to everything other than Him. Al-Sijistānī argues this position by way of a cosmological analysis in which he considers the ontological status of every level in creation, including spatially bounded (*maḥdūd*) corporeal substances and spatially unbounded (*ghayr maḥdūd*) spiritual substances.[10] He observes that both bounded and unbounded existents suffer from 'pairedness' (*izdiwāj*) or metaphysical composition, which renders their existence dependent or contingent.

Al-Sijistānī substantiates his argument by documenting how corporeal physical things (the bounded existents) lack true subsistence because they have parts and undergo transformation and corruption. Spiritual substances (the unbounded existents) like the Universal Soul—the direct cause of material composites (*al-tarākib*) and corporeal motions (*ḥarakāt*)—are in a state of spiritual motion and do not subsist in one state. The Universal Soul is perpetually ascending towards perfection as it attains closer to the actuality of the Universal Intellect and receives benefit from it. Finally, the Universal Intellect—the treasury of all corporeal and spiritual treasures—is beyond all change and comes closest to God's real-true subsistence. However, the Intellect only subsists through what God eternally manifested (*mabrūz*) within it through His creative act. Therefore, everything other than God suffers from some aspect of ontological weakness and dependence upon another.[11] God alone is truly independent of all things: 'The subsistence (*ithbāt*) of God, may He be exalted, is beyond all relations (*al-iḍāfāt*), neither due to the existence of anything nor due to the non-existence of something else. Since His subsistence is beyond what is bounded (*al-maḥdūd*) and beyond what is unbounded (*ghayr al-maḥdūd*), it is confirmed that God is more subsistent than everything that subsists (*athbatu min kulli thābitin*).'[12]

---

9 Wilferd Madelung, 'Aspects of Ismaili Theology: The Prophetic Chain and the God Beyond Being', in *Ismāʿīlī Contributions to Islamic Culture*, ed. Seyyed Hossein Nasr (Tehran: Imperial Iranian Academy of Philosophy, 1977), 52–65; Paul E. Walker, *Early Philosophical Shiism: The Ismaili Neoplatonism of Abū Yaʿqūb al-Sijistānī* (Cambridge: Cambridge University Press, 1993), 79.

10 Abū Yaʿqūb al-Sijistānī, *Kitāb al-maqālīd al-malakūtiyya*, ed. Ismail K. Poonawala (Beirut: Dār al-Gharb al-Islāmī, 2011), 95.

11 Ibid., 95–96. Walker and Madelung take *maḥdūd* and *ghayr maḥdūd* to mean 'having a definition' and 'not having a definition', respectively, as if al-Sijistānī is trying to make epistemic claims about God lacking definitions. This reading, in the context of al-Sijistānī's *al-Maqālīd*, is incorrect. The correct meaning is bounded and unbounded existents—referring to the corporeal and spiritual things, respectively.

12 Ibid., 97.

In one passage, al-Sijistānī presents a kind of ontological argument to argue from the existence of dependent things to the absolute subsistence of God as the originator of dependent things:

> Since it is possible that in the intellectual estimation (*al-wahm*), there are things subsisting that do not subsist by their own essences (*bi-dhātihā*), it is also possible that there exists external (*khārija*) to intellectual estimation, thought, and vision, that which is nobler than everything that subsists. That which exceeds the mind is not bounded, but rather, it is He who originated the bounded and unbounded [things], He whose subsistence (*thabātuhu*) is beyond the bounded and unbounded [things]. Thus, it is confirmed that God is more subsistent than everything that subsists.[13]

While al-Sijistānī does not offer any formal cosmological argument for God's existence in this chapter, he provides all the key premises for such an argument. God alone is the 'real-true subsistence' (*al-ithbāt al-ḥaqīqī*) whereas the subsistence of everything other than God is merely a 'virtual subsistence' (*al-ithbāt al-majāzī*).

One generation after al-Sijistānī, Ḥamīd al-Dīn al-Kirmānī—one of the most learned Ismāʿīlī philosophers—offered a formal cosmological argument for the affirmation of God by building upon the teachings of the former. In one of his exoteric treatises dedicated to proving the Ismāʿīlī Imāmate, al-Kirmānī affirms that God *must* be proven first: 'it behoves us to put in first position the argument that proves the Maker, who is the Sender, on whose existence depends the existence of all.' Al-Kirmānī then explains that although God (the Maker) transcends all intellectual limits, He can be proven using a demonstrative arguments based on human knowledge of His creatures: 'Because the Maker has no quality that renders Him perceptible to sensation, nor does He have a trait that allows Him to be apprehended by the intellect, the way to prove Him follows the setting up of demonstrations consisting of both sensation and intellection as applied to the product of His making.'[14] Al-Kirmānī presents his preferred argument for God in his magnum opus titled *Rāḥat al-ʿaql* as follows:

> Among the principles is that there is no existence for the effect except by what necessitates its existence among its cause to whom its existence is connected and upon whom its existence depends. If it [the cause] did not exist then it [the effect] would not exist ... Since it is the case that some of the existents are dependent upon others and if some of those [existents] upon which others depend and whose existence

13 Ibid., 98.

14 Ḥamīd al-Dīn al-Kirmānī, *Master of the Age*, ed. and trans. Paul E. Walker (London: I.B. Tauris, 2007), 43–44.

> is connected to were not established in existence and were non-existent, then the existence of these latter is impossible. When it is confirmed that there is no existence for this one [existent] except through that one [existent], it becomes known from this that He with whom the existents terminate, through whom they exist, upon whom they depend, and from whom they obtain existence is God, there is no god except Him, whose non-existence (*laysiyya*) is impossible and whose non-ipseity is false, since if He were non-existent (*lays*), it would entail that the existents are also non-existent. But since the existents exist, His non-existence is false.[15]

The argument of al-Kirmānī is similar to Ibn Sīnā's contingency argument for God as Necessary Existence through Itself (*wājib al-wujūd bi-dhātihi*), which he was formulating around the same time. Al-Kirmānī deductively argues that the existence of dependent realities logically necessitates an absolutely independent reality—namely, God—who is the ultimate ground, source, or originator for all dependent realities. This is because dependent existents, at any and all moment that they exist, are in need and/or depend upon other existents. The latter, if they are dependent existents, also dependent upon other things. This chain of dependence cannot continue in an infinite regress of dependent existents—otherwise, nothing would exist. Therefore, al-Kirmānī concludes that there must logically be an independent or self-sufficient reality, namely, God, who cannot be non-existent. In contrast to all created things, God 'with respect to what He is in Himself is not in need of anything other than Himself and [is not in need of] anything upon which He depends ... He transcends being in need of anything other than Himself to which [His Ipseity] is connected.'[16] Al-Kirmānī's arguments show that Ismāʿīlī philosophers upheld a radically apophatic theology of God's Essence while also constructing cosmological arguments to demonstrate the reality and uniqueness of God. In subsequent sections, al-Kirmānī argues for the existence of the First Intellect and secondary Intellects using deductive arguments.

Al-Kirmānī's approach of using natural theology to prove the reality of God continued in the next generation of Ismāʿīlī philosophers. Nāṣir-i Khusraw employed various cosmological arguments to prove the existence of the entire Neoplatonic cosmic hierarchy. He first argued for the existence of the Maker of the corporeal world (*ṣāniʿ-yi ʿālam-i jism*) by providing ten arguments, each of which builds upon certain features of the physical hylomorphic Cosmos.[17] He then identified this 'world-maker' with the Universal Soul (*nafs-i kull*) responsible for causing the goal-directed motions in the physical Cosmos and inscribing intelligible forms upon Prime Matter.[18] Next, Khusraw argued for the existence

---

15 Ḥamīd al-Dīn al-Kirmānī, *Rāḥat al-ʿaql*, ed. Muṣṭafā Ghālib (Beirut: Dār al-Andalūs, 1983), 129–30.

16 Ibid., 131.

17 Nāṣir-i Khusraw, *Zād al-musāfir*, ed. Muḥammad ʿImādī Ḥāʾirī and Ismāʿīl ʿImādī Ḥāʾirī (Tehran: Mīrāth-i maktūb, 2005), 136–50 (ch. 14).

18 Ibid., 151–66.

of the Universal Intellect as the efficient cause of the Universal Soul and the final cause of its goal-directed activity.[19] Having established the Neoplatonic hierarchy of efficient causes and effects, Khusraw then presents two arguments for affirmation (*ithbāt*) of God as the True Originator (*mubdiʿ-yi ḥaqq*) of the chain of causes and effects. His first argument points to the fact that both causes and effects exist: the corporeal world (*ʿālam-i jismānī*) is the effect of an eternal cause (*ʿillat-i qadīm*). He then reasons that efficient causes and effects are essentially conjoined (*payvasta*) and therefore inseparable. Any two realities which are conjoined and inseparable are 'paired' (*juft-karda*). The existence of 'paired' things necessarily entails the existence of a 'Pairer' (*juft-kunanda*)—He who pairs together composite beings including causes and effects. Khusraw identifies this 'Pairer' with God—whom he calls the 'Causer' (*ʿāll*), absolute simple (*fard*), one (*aḥad*), and independent (*ṣamad*). Unlike causes and effects, God's origination is only a trace (*athar*) from Him and a trace is not conjoined to the tracer (*muʾaththir*).[20] Khusraw's second argument for God also argues cosmologically from the existence of causes and effects. He begins by observing that every cause is conjoined to its respective effect and that the action of each cause comes to be within its effect. He then observes that every cause is *specifically directed* towards producing its particular effect due to the existence of a specification (*khāṣiyyat*) within each cause; this specification is what bestows existence (*hast-kunanda*) upon the effect. Thus, he concludes, every cause is specified (*makhṣūṣ*) towards producing a specific effect. From this cosmological fact, Khusraw concludes that the existence of specification (*khāṣiyyat*) and the specified (*makhṣūṣ*) logically entails the existence of a 'Specifier' (*mukhaṣṣiṣ*), a 'Causer' (*ʿillat-kunanda, ʿāll*), or 'Causer-Maker' (*sāzanda-yi ʿillat, dahanda-yi ʿillat*), who bestows causal powers upon causes and directs them towards their effects; this is God, the true Originator (*mubdiʿ-yi ḥaqq*), who originates all the causes and effects. In this way, Khusraw cosmologically and rationally argues for the reality of God as the originator of causes and effects.

Regardless of how one views the merits of these Ismāʿīlī cosmological arguments, it cannot be ignored that Ismāʿīlī philosophers clearly *did* present rational arguments for the affirmation (*ithbāt*) of God. The polemical charge from Sunnī opponents that Ismāʿīlīs neither affirm nor deny the Creator and end up in agnosticism or that they simply deny God has no real basis. Likewise, the scholarly narrative that Ismāʿīlīs did not attempt to prove God and discouraged such proofs is outdated and requires revisions based on the evidence presented above.

## 3. Divine Simplicity: God as Absolute Unity

The Ismāʿīlīs uphold a strong version of what contemporary philosophers of religion

19 Ibid., 160–74.
20 Ibid., 168.

call 'divine simplicity'. This is the thesis that God has neither physical nor metaphysical parts of any kind. God's ontological unity or simplicity excludes any kind of distinction within Him—such as form/matter, essence/existence, substance/accident, essence/attribute. Al-Sijistānī, Khusraw, and al-Shahrastānī argue that the unity or oneness of God is not merely the numerical oneness of the number 'one'; nor is God's unity merely the opposite of compound numbers such as two, three, four; nor is the oneness of God that of a unitive totality of various parts; nor is it a merely abstract unity like the unity of a genus or species. These various types of unity each embed some degree of multiplicity. Numerical oneness can be divided into multiple components or compounded into further quantities. Multiplicity of any kind signifies an ontological weakness and dependence within God, since a whole may depend upon its parts or parts may depend upon a whole.[21] Divine aseity requires that the oneness or unity of God be an 'absolute oneness' (*al-fardāniyya al-khāliṣa*) totally removed from any and all multiplicity.[22]

Let us consider: if God possesses any positive ontological feature—an aspect, attribute, quality, accident—that is intrinsic to and numerically distinct from Himself, then it must be that (a) God depends upon that feature for His ipseity, thus rendering God into a dependent reality lacking aseity; (b) that positive ontological feature itself depends upon God's ipseity, thus rendering that feature into a creation; (c) both God and His positive ontological feature are independent, thus resulting in two gods each possessing aseity; or (d) God and His positive ontological feature are either co-dependent or both dependent upon some higher reality that causes them to be joined.[23] Therefore, God's unity admits of no distinctions. His is an absolute unity incomparable to anything else in existence: 'His unity (*wāḥidiyya*) exceeds numbers because He is not divisible through the duality of what He has created and originated ... thus, He is "the One" (*al-wāḥid*) beyond every "numerical one", both natural and spiritual; and [He is] "the Unique" (*al-aḥad*), who is not perceived except by the negation of everything expressions affirm and negate.'[24] God's absolute simplicity also accounts for why there cannot be two or more gods; if this were the case, then each 'god' would be ontologically complex in possessing a 'common property' shared by both and a 'specific property' differentiating one from the other. But since ontologically complexity entails dependence, God must be one without a second.[25]

One necessary consequence of God's unity transcending any form of multiplicity is that the Ismāʿīlī philosophers identify the root-principle of both numerical oneness

21 See al-Sijistānī, *al-Maqālīd*, 86–88; Nāṣir-i Khusraw, *Between Reason and Revelation: Twin Wisdoms Reconciled*, trans. Eric Ormsby (London: I.B. Tauris, 2012), 135–38; ʿAbd al-Karīm al-Shahrastānī, *Struggling with the Philosopher: A Refutation of Avicenna's* Metaphysics, trans. Wilferd Madelung and Toby Mayer (London: I.B. Tauris, 2001), 37–38, 46–47, 55–57.

22 al-Sijistānī, *al-Maqālīd*, 65.

23 al-Kirmānī, *Rāḥat al-ʿaql*, 152–53.

24 al-Sijistānī, *al-Maqālīd*, 87.

25 al-Kirmānī, *Rāḥat al-ʿaql*, 142.

and multiplicity with the first creation of God—the Universal Intellect—as opposed to God Himself. The Universal Intellect is 'the one who is the root-source (*aṣl*) and cause of the numbers, called the *pure one*'.[26] However, this originated Intellect is ontologically composite; it is not an 'absolute one' but rather a 'multiple one' (*al-wāḥid al-mutakath-thir*) because its own being is constituted by the union of two distinct aspects: the first aspect is a pure oneness (*fardāniyya, waḥda*) identical to God's creative act known as 'God's Command'; the second aspect is its own 'essence' or quiddity.[27] Furthermore, God's absolute unity beyond all multiplicity entails that He cannot directly create or originate multiple creations; this is because multiple products issuing directly from God necessitate multiple aspects within His Essence. Rather, the direct, unmediated creation of God must necessarily be a numerically single entity—the Universal Intellect. The Intellect—being externally single and internally complex—then functions as the direct source of numerical unity and multiplicity through its emanation of the Universal Soul.

## 4. Divine Dual Negation: God Transcends His Creation

Affirming a strong account of divine simplicity brings forth the age-old challenge of correctly and adequately talking about God. In contemporary philosophy of religion, divine simplicity is heavily criticised by Christian theologians like Alvin Plantinga and William Lane Craig. They charge divine simplicity with being incoherent and unintelligible, leading to modal collapse, and rendering God ineffable such that one cannot know or say anything about God at all. The Ismāʿīlī method of upholding absolute divine simplicity is to present a radical but internally consistent negative theology or apophasis. Modern analytic theologians like Plantinga and Mullins have strongly objected to apophasis, arguing that whoever claims that 'God is ineffable' or 'God is indescribable' as a doctrine is contradicting himself in making any statement about God. But this modern objection is a strawman of what most apophatic theologians are saying. The Ismāʿīlī position is that God cannot be qualified, described, or attributed with any attribute that is found among created beings. In common with other Shīʿī Muslims, the Ismāʿīlīs draw inspiration from the below sermon of Imām ʿAlī, who taught the necessity of *negating all attributes* from God:

> Foremost in religion is knowledge of Him, and the perfection of this knowledge is believing in Him, and the perfection of this belief is affirming His oneness, and the perfection of this affirmation is to purify one's devotion to Him, and the perfection of this purification is to divest Him of all attributes—because of the testimony of every attribute that it is other than the object of attribution, and because of the

26 al-Sijistānī, *al-Maqālīd*, 65.

27 Ibid., 65–67; al-Kirmānī, *Rāḥat al-ʿaql*, 176–80; Nāṣir-i Khusraw, *Between Reason and Revelation*, 136–38.

> testimony of every such object that it is other than the attribute. So whoever ascribes an attribute to God—glorified be He!—has conjoined Him [with something else], and whoever so conjoins Him has made Him twofold, and whoever makes Him twofold has fragmented Him, and whoever thus fragments Him is ignorant of Him.[28]

In the words of al-Kirmānī: 'When we say according to the affirmation of the method of negation [of attributes] that He is not *this*, and *not that*, and *not that*, and *not that*, all that we negate is from what exists within His creation. By means of this, He for whom attributes do not apply is affirmed.'[29] Stated in more analytic terms, this means that God cannot be the subject of any real predications that also apply to His creatures. This principle logically follows from God's aseity and absolute oneness. If there is a real predicate or attribute that applies to God and applies to a created being, it follows that this common predication refers to an attribute that is shared (*amr mushtarak*) between God and the creature. This entails that God is ontologically complex, as His ipseity would be dependent upon and composed of the conjunction of His Essence and the shared attribute referred to by the common predication. Thus, Ismāʿīlī apophasis is firmly rooted in a logical and rational analysis of God's aseity and simplicity. For Ismāʿīlīs and like-minded apophatic theologians, the very fact that God is unlike anything in His creation is a rationally defensible position and not based on some fideistic appeal to mystery.

One of the unique features of Ismāʿīlī theological discourse is the precise way that Ismāʿīlīs employ their apophasis to articulate God's transcendence or dissimilarity (*tanzīh*) over created things. To be sure, almost every theological school among Hindus, Jews, Christians, and Muslims employs some negative theology to talk about God. In classical Islam, most Muslim thinkers including the Muʿtazila, Ashʿarīs, Māturīdīs, and the Muslim Peripatetics negate all physical characteristics from God: God is immaterial, incorporeal, atemporal, spaceless, placeless, directionless, colourless, shapeless, odourless, motionless, non-composite, and so forth.[30] For many monotheists, negating physical attributes from God is hardly controversial and logically necessary. Ismāʿīlī philosophers agreed with these negations. But most *kalām* theologians held to a cosmology where God alone is the sole eternal and incorporeal existent while everything other than God is both temporal and material. Therefore, they found it sufficient to negate corporeal and temporal attributes from God. However, in Ismāʿīlī cosmology, God's creation consists of 'two worlds' (*ʿālamayn*): a corporeal world of 'bounded' (*maḥdūd*) material entities consisting of matter, space, time, bodies, and motions subject to corporeal limits (*ḥudūd*), and an 'unbounded' (*ghayr maḥdūd*) spiritual world of intellects, souls, angels, and spirits without

28 ʿAlī b. Abī Ṭālib, *Nahj al-balāgha*, sermon 1, quoted in Reza Shah-Kazemi, *Justice and Remembrance: Introducing the Spirituality of Imam ʿAlī* (London: I.B. Tauris, 2006), 208.
29 al-Kirmānī, *Rāḥat al-ʿaql*, 138.
30 See al-Juwaynī, *Guide*, 24–30.

corporeal limits. Therefore, for Ismāʿīlī thinkers, negating corporeal attributes from God does not go far enough in establishing God's absolute transcendence and dissimilarity in contrast to His creation. As al-Sijistānī argues, merely negating physical qualities from God still affirms that God is similar to various spiritual entities that are also within His creation: 'What does not have [corporeal] attributes, limits, or descriptions is not God in His Essence but rather, it is the Soul, the Intellect, and all of the simple substances among the angels and others.'[31] In fact, many modern analytic theologians fall into this trap. Richard Swinburne defines God as 'a person without a body (i.e. a spirit) who is eternal, free, able to do anything, knows everything.'[32] Likewise, William Lane Craig holds that 'God is very much like an unembodied soul; indeed, as a mental substance God just seems to be a soul.'[33] For Ismāʿīlīs, however, construing God as a unembodied spirit, mind, mental substance, soul, or immaterial person is a category error that renders God similar to some of His creations. Al-Sijistānī condemns what many *kalām* theologians and modern thinkers like Craig and Swinburne uphold as a 'hidden anthropomorphism' (*tashbīh khafī*) that confounds God with spiritual creations as opposed to an 'overt anthropomorphism' (*tashbīh jalī*) that invests God with physical properties.[34]

Based on their 'two-worlds' cosmology, Ismāʿīlī philosophers see it necessary to negate both *corporeal* and *spiritual* attributes from God to truly articulate God's unity and transcendence. It is correct that God is not material, not corporeal, not temporal, not coloured, not shaped, not in motion, and not in a place because He transcends the attributes of the physical world; and further, God is also not immaterial, not incorporeal, not atemporal, not colourless, not shapeless, not motionless, and not placeless in the manner of spiritual creatures because He transcends the qualities of the spiritual world. Rather, God's unity transcends both categories of things. God is not bounded (*maḥdūd*) in the manner of corporeal substances, nor is He unbounded (*ghayr maḥdūd*) in the manner of spiritual substances.

Unfortunately, certain polemicists have misconstrued the Ismāʿīlī 'dual negation' (*salibatayn*) as a 'double negation' consisting of two contradictory statements.[35] Others take the Ismāʿīlīs to be committing *taʿṭīl*, a denial or agnosticism concerning God. However, if one reads this Ismāʿīlī apophasis very closely and within its own cosmological context, these objections miss the mark. Take the dual negation that 'God is not corporeal (*jismānī*) and not incorporeal (*rūḥānī*)'—which Ismāʿīlīs also render as 'God is not bounded (*lā maḥdūd*) and God is not unbounded (*lā ghayr maḥdūd*)' and 'God is not corporeally attributed (*lā mawṣūf*) and not corporeally non-attributed (*lā lā mawṣūf*)'. Firstly, one must

31 al-Sijistānī, *al-Maqālīd*, 80.
32 Richard Swinburne, *The Coherence of Theism*, rev. ed. (Oxford: Clarendon Press, 1993), 1–2.
33 James Porter Moreland and William Lane Craig, *Philosophical Foundations for a Christian Worldview* (Downers Grove, IL: InterVarsity Press, 2003), 594.
34 al-Sijistānī, *al-Maqālīd*, 81.
35 Ibid., 80.

be clear about what the predicates *jismānī/rūḥānī*, *maḥdūd/ghayr maḥdūd*, and *mawṣūf/lā mawṣūf* are supposed to mean. The first predicate—*jismānī/maḥdūd/mawṣūf*—rigidly designates all physical and material substances; the second—*rūḥānī/ghayr maḥdūd/lā mawṣūf*—rigidly designates all spiritual and immaterial substances like intellects, souls, angels, and other simple substances. These binary predicates are contraries (*ḍiddayn*) but they are not contradictories (*naqīḍayn*) because God, as the creator of the physical and spiritual realms, is not a member of either one of them. The charge of *taʿṭīl* does not hold, as al-Kirmānī argues, because the negative particle *lā* in both negations (e.g. *innahu lā mawṣūf wa-lā huwa lā mawṣūf*) is not directed towards God's ipseity (*huwiyya*) but rather, to specific predications like *mawṣūf/maḥdūd*; meanwhile, the 'thatness' (*inniyya*) of God is maintained by the term *innahu* that begins each negative proposition. Therefore, God's ipseity is always affirmed even in negative statements that deny specific attributes to Him.[36]

The first negation—'God is not corporeal/bounded/attributed'—is an *external negation of a positive predicate*, rendered as 'it is *not* the case that God is corporeal/bounded/attributed'.[37] The contradictory of this statement is the affirmation that 'God *is* corporeal/bounded/attributed' or 'it is the case that God is corporeal/bounded/attributed'. The second negation—'God is not incorporeal/unbounded/non-attributed' is the *external negation of a negative predicate*. First, there is an *internal negation* with the term—'incorporeal/unbounded/non-attributed'—which forms a new predicate with the same syntactic range as the old predicate (corporeal/bounded/attributed) but with the reverse meaning; in this context, it refers to all spiritual or immaterial existents. This internal negation—'God is incorporeal/unbounded/non-attributed'—is then subject to an external negation with God as the subject, rendered as 'it is not the case that God is incorporeal/unbounded/non-attributed'. Putting the first and second negations together, one arrives at: 'It is not the case that God is corporeal/bounded/attributed, nor is it the case that God is incorporeal/unbounded/non-attributed.' As argued by al-Sijistānī, the two statements are both *external negations* and they are not contradictories (*naqīḍayn*) because each statement is the negation of a real predicate whose signification covers a *positive ontological range*: 'As for when there are two negative statements—one of them negating the attributes affixed to corporeal beings (*al-jismāniyyīn*) and the other negating the attributes affixed to spiritual beings (*al-rūḥāniyyīn*)—this leads to isolating (*tajrīd*) the Creator from the attributes and qualities of created beings.'[38]

The Ismāʿīlī method of negating both corporeal and spiritual attributes from God stands out among other forms of classical Muslim theology championed by the *kalām*

36 al-Kirmānī, *Rāḥat al-ʿaql*, 148–49.

37 On external vs internal negations, see John N. Martin, 'Existence, Negation, and Abstraction in the Neoplatonic Hierarchy', *History and Philosophy of Logic* 16, no. 2 (1995): 171–72.

38 al-Sijistānī, *al-Maqālīd*, 81.

theologians and the Muslim Peripatetics. However, the Sufi Akbarī metaphysical tradition associated with Ibn al-ʿArabī (d. 638/1240) would adopt the same apophatic approach taken by the Ismāʿīlīs. ʿAbd al-Razzāq al-Kāshānī (d. 730–36/1329–35), in a passage highly reminiscent of al-Sijistānī, states that 'he who "purifies" God purifies Him from all bodily attributes, but by that very act he is (unconsciously) "assimilating" (*tashbīh*) Him with non-material, spiritual beings.'[39] Al-Kāshānī is in full agreement with al-Sijistānī in criticising what he calls a 'delimiting and speculative transcendence' (*al-tanzīh al-taqyīdī al-fikrī*), which only divests God of the attributes of bodies but still makes Him similar to the spirits (*arwāḥ*).[40] Al-Kāshānī's solution is identical to that of the Ismāʿīlīs: one must perform a 'dual negation', such as the following: 'The truth of the matter is that the Absolute transcends both being in a direction and not being in a direction, having a position and not having a position; it transcends also all determinations originating from the senses, reason, imagination, representation, and thinking.'[41] Thus, the Ismāʿīlī dual negation discourse of purifying God of both corporeal and spiritual attributes has both logical structure and endorsement in Akbarī Sufi metaphysics.

The upshot of Ismāʿīlī apophasis is that God transcends all ontological, metaphysical, and physical categories. God is beyond both being a cause or an effect; rather, He is the 'causer' (*muʿill*, *ʿāll*: 'the maker of causes').[42] He transcends being a substance or an accident, for He originates both spiritual and bodily substances. He is neither a body, nor a soul, nor an intellect. God transcends the temporality (*zamān*) of physical things, the perpetuity (*daymūmiyya*) of the souls, and the eternity (*azaliyya*) of the intellects; rather, He is the 'eternaliser' (*azal*) who causes the existence of what is eternal (*azalī*).[43] These negative propositions are all logical as they negate several category errors with respect to God. Most monothetic theologians would agree that God, since He is not physical, falls outside various predicate categories whose scope applies to the natural world. These category errors take the form of dual negations that echo Ismāʿīlī discourses. For example: God is neither healthy nor sick; God is neither inside the universe nor outside the universe; God is neither bearded nor beardless; God is neither dry nor wet; God is neither even nor odd; God is nether healthy nor unhealthy; God is not in motion nor at rest. To be sure, these statements *would only be contradictory* if the subject in each statement was a physical spatio-temporal entity. But since God transcends being physical in any way, the negated predicates are merely contraries as opposed to contradictories.

---

39 al-Kāshānī, quoted in Toshihiko Izutsu, *Sufism and Taoism: A Comparative Study of Key Philosophical Concepts* (Berkeley and Los Angeles: University of California Press, 1983), 50.
40 Mansouri, 'Sayyid Ḥaydar Āmulī', 212.
41 al-Kāshānī, quoted in Izutsu, *Sufism and Taoism*, 51.
42 al-Sijistānī, *al-Maqālīd*, 70.
43 Ibid., 117, 164–65.

## 5. Divine Ultimacy: God Transcends Attributes

All Muslim theologians must account for the scriptural descriptions of God found in the Qur'an, Sunna, and ritual practices of Islam, such as the ninety-nine names of God or various statements ascribing a face, hands, eyes, sitting, and descent to God. Ḥanbalī scholars interpreted many descriptions of God as referring to real-distinct attributes of God, including God's face, hands, and so on, while insisting that these attributes are 'without modality' (*bi-lā kayf*). The Ashʿarī and Māturīdī theologians interpret some divine names as referring to uncreated 'entitative attributes' (*ṣifāt maʿnawiyya*) that subsist in God's Essence: God is knowing (*ʿālim*) through His uncreated knowledge (*ʿilm*); God is powerful (*qādir*) through His uncreated power (*qudra*); and so on.[44] These theologians held that 'God's attributes are not identical to God's Essence and they are not other (*ghayr*) than God's Essence.'[45] Meanwhile the Muʿtazila accept the divine names and attributes as real predications about God, but they interpret them by saying that every divine attribute (*ṣifa*) is ontologically identical to God's Essence.[46]

The Ismāʿīlī philosophers, in presenting their unique position, refuted the views of the above Muslim theological camps. First, they dismissed the Ḥanbalī literalism as crass anthropomorphism amounting to polytheistic pantheon of ninety-nine uncreated entities that comprise God. As Khusraw argued: 'They state that God has ninety-nine names, each of which has its own distinct meaning. But any rational person knows that anyone who has ninety-nine names cannot be a single person, for each one of the ninety-nine names must have its own essence. Polytheism, not monotheism, underlies this group's teachings.'[47] As for the Ashʿarī-Māturīdī theologies of God possessing several entitative attributes that eternally subsist in His Essence, the Ismāʿīlīs argued against the coherence of this view. Al-Kirmānī argues that affirming entitative attributes for God leads to two outcomes: (1) it either entails that God is dependent upon the attribute for His subsistence; or (2) the attribute depends upon God who necessitates it. If God depends upon the attribute for His subsistence, then God is contingent: 'He upon whom the existents depend for their existence would be in need of another (*al-ghayr mustaghniyyan*) insofar as He is He to subsist.'[48] The phrasing in some Sunnī *kalām* texts like 'God is knowing through knowledge' or 'living through life' implies that God's ipseity depends upon the attributes

44 On this ontology of the divine attributes, see Abū Ḥāmid al-Ghazālī, *Al-Ghazālī's Moderation in Belief*, trans. Aladdin M. Yaqub (Chicago: University of Chicago Press, 2013), 129–55.

45 For a defence of this formula, see Abdurrahman Mihirig, 'Classical *Kalām* and the Laws of Logic', Maydan, 23 April 2021, https://themaydan.com/2021/04/classical-kalam-and-the-laws-of-logic/. Al-Ghazālī writes in *Moderation in Belief*: 'The seven attributes, which we established, are not the [divine] essence. Rather, they are additional to the essence' (129).

46 See Abū al-Hudhayl, quoted in Kifayat Ullah, *Al-Kashshāf: Al-Zamakhshari's Mu'tazilite Exegesis of the Qur'an* (Berlin: De Gruyter, 2017), 105.

47 Nāṣir-i Khusraw, *Between Reason and Revelation*, 51.

48 al-Kirmānī, *Rāḥat al-ʿaql*, 151.

themselves.[49] Furthermore, this divine attribute itself must depend on something else for its own subsistence. This either entails an infinite regress of dependent realities or the series must terminate at a self-subsistent, independent, and absolutely simple reality that does not have any entitative attributes—which is exactly what Ismāʿīlīs claim about God. On the other hand, if one says that God's attribute depends upon God's Essence—as some Sunnīs like al-Taftāzānī and certain modern analytic philosophers (Wolterstorff, Fowler, Baddorf) propose—then this is an admission that God in His absolute unity, considered without any attribute, is independent or sufficient in Himself and has no need for the attribute; whereas the attribute is dependent upon God. Therefore, the divine attributes register as dependent created beings.[50] Al-Kirmānī thereby concludes: 'He [God] transcends and is sanctified from the attributes that fall under His creation while He, the Exalted, is the maker (*fāʿil*) of them and all other things.'[51]

The Ismāʿīlī critique of the Muʿtazilī doctrine of God's attributes being identical to His Essence is far more measured. The Muʿtazilī position appealed to many adjacent Muslim thinkers including the Twelver Shīʿa, Zaydī Shīʿa, early Muslim Peripatetics like al-Kindī and al-Fārābī, and the school of Ibn Sīnā. Muʿtazilī divine simplicity is likewise upheld by medieval and contemporary Christian classical theists, including Augustine, Aquinas, James Dolezal, Edward Feser, and Robert Koons. The Ismāʿīlī philosophers credited the Muʿtazila for being correct in denying 'entitative attributes' in God, but they find the *positive claim* that 'God's attributes are identical to His Essence' to be incoherent. The formula that God's attributes are identical to Himself or His Essence equivocates on the term 'attribute' (*ṣifa*); within the discourse of Islamic metaphysics generally, an attribute (*ṣifa*) is always distinct from its subject of attribution (*mawṣūf*), namely, a subject (*jawhar*) or essence (*dhāt*), in which the attribute subsists. However, when the Muʿtazila and other classical theists speak of God's attributes being identical to Himself, they are *not* referring to 'attributes' in the ordinary sense of the word. The phrase 'God's attributes are identical to Himself' translates into a tautology that 'God is identical to God', in which no real-distinct attribute is being affirmed of God after all. Second, those who identify every divine attribute—like God's power, life, mercy, or knowledge—with God's Essence are susceptible to this common objection: this belief implies that power, life, and knowledge are one and the same, yet this is clearly not the case for created beings. In response, the Muʿtazilī classical theist will further argue that power, life, and knowledge are only *distinct for creatures*, but for God, they are absolutely identical. Ontologically speaking this is perfectly acceptable for Ismāʿīlīs; however, it leads to linguistic and semantic ambiguities. Given the ontological gap between God's Essence and creaturely life/power/knowledge, it no longer makes any sense to use the

49 For such statements, see al-Ghazālī, *Moderation in Belief*, 129.
50 al-Kirmānī, *Rāḥat al-ʿaql*, 151–53.
51 Ibid., 153.

*same predicates* to describe God and describe creaturely attributes within the same discourse. To do so is to commit a category error, at least verbally.

This conclusion leads directly to the Ismāʿīlī position—that God in His absolute transcendent unity transcends possessing any real attributes or ontic predicates. In reality, God is neither living nor dead, neither knowing nor ignorant, neither powerful nor impotent, and likewise for all real predications because His Essence transcends all descriptions that apply to His creation. Khusraw emphatically argues this point as follows:

> Just as you call it wrong to say that He is ignorant, so too is it wrong to say that He is knowing, and for this reason: Knowing and not-knowing are both of them human traits. You term God 'knowing' because it is not fitting to say 'ignorant' of Him; you suppose that one ought not call God 'ignorant' because this is an ugly name, while it is fine to call Him 'knowing' since this is a good name. You imagine that it is wrong to call God 'ignorant' because this name is bad, and you are of the opinion too that since names which are ugly and repellent ought not to be applied to God, it is appropriate to use fine and upstanding names; and yet, this notion of yours is wrong.
>
> And just as you ought not ascribe to God a human attribute such as ignorance, so too you ought not ascribe knowledge, which is also a human attribute, to Him—glory be to Him—inasmuch as knowledge is a trait which is proper to ascribe to man, and so too is ignorance a trait properly belonging to him.
>
> Now we have shown clearly on what grounds it is wrong to describe God by such attributes as 'ignorance' and 'powerlessness'—not because they are unseemly but because they are attributes of creatures—as well as that it is also wrong to ascribe the opposites of such attributes, such as 'knowledge' and 'power', to Him—glory be to Him, He is exalted—on the grounds that these too are creaturely qualities. The so-called theologians of this community have plunged into a grievous error in their inquiry, in ascribing their own fine qualities to God and in declaring Him devoid of their bad qualities. And for this very reason, they have fallen into polytheism. They fail to grasp that whoever worships a thing whose attribute is of a creaturely nature in effect worships a creature, not its Creator.[52]

Khusraw and other Ismāʿīlī philosophers advocate for a 'dual negation' of all real predications with respect to God. This form of dual negation, where one negates a positive predicate and its opposite from God, is distinct from the dual negation seen earlier—where one negates both corporeal and spiritual qualities from God. However, both types of dual negation are rooted in the same goal—to purify the concept of God from all creaturely

52 Nāṣir-i Khusraw, *Between Reason and Revelation*, 54–55.

and contingent attributes. As seen earlier, Muslims from other theological camps often accused Ismāʿīlīs of logical incoherence and/or agnosticism when they negated both positive and negative predications from God. However, Ismāʿīlī apophasis turns out to be quite logical and internally consistent in light of recent philosophical studies on the logic of negation. The Ismāʿīlī apophatic position that 'God is not living/powerful/knowing and God is not dead/impotent/ignorant' must be understood with reference to Neoplatonic scalar predication and negation as documented by John N. Martin.[53]

In Neoplatonic thought, positive and negative predications are all *scalar* and presuppose a hierarchy of ontological value behind every real predication. Take, for example, the scalar predicates that describe the temperature of water in descending order in Table 1.

TABLE 1: *Example of Neoplatonic scalar predications*

| Scalar predicates of water temperature (various adjectives) | Scalar predicates of water temperature (indexed to 'warm') |
|---|---|
| Boiling | Boiling: hyper-warm |
| Hot | Hot: hyper-warm |
| Warm | Warm |
| Tepid | Sub-warm |
| Cold | Sub-warm |

In Table 1, the left-hand column lists various adjectives that hierarchically describe the temperature of water from boiling down to cold. The right-hand column describes the same hierarchy but uses 'warm' as the point of reference; 'hyper-' refers to all temperature levels hotter than warm while 'sub-' refers to temperatures cooler than warm. Within this scalar framework, a positive or negative predication by itself is semantically ambiguous. 'The water is not warm' is a simple negation, but it can mean one of two things: either the water is 'hyper-warm' (boiling or hot); or the water is 'sub-warm' (tepid or cold). The first meaning is a 'hyper-negation' where the scalar predicate (warm) along with every level below it is negated; this means that the water is boiling or hot (hyper-warm). Hyper-negation points to a *higher* level of the scalar hierarchy. The second meaning is a 'privative negation' in which the scalar predicate 'warm' and everything higher than warm on the scale is being negated; this means that the water is tepid or cold (sub-warm). Private negations are diminutive. The main point is that *negation in and of itself* within the Neoplatonic scalar predication framework is not necessarily a deprivation or diminution of a subject. It depends on the context in which negations occur.[54]

53 Martin, 'Existence', 173–77.
54 Ibid., 172–74.

Ismāʿīlī apophasis must be understood through the logic of this Neoplatonic scalar framework. Consider the apophatic statement 'God is not knowing and God is not ignorant'. This statement is the conjunction of two negations, each of which on its own may be semantically ambiguous. But when combined, the resultant dual negation is clearly a *hyper-negation* within Neoplatonic scalar semantics. When one maps out the scalar hierarchy of the predicate 'knowing' based on Ismāʿīlī Neoplatonic cosmology (see Table 2), the meaning of the phrase 'God is not knowing and God is not ignorant' is a *hyper-negation* that exalts God as the source of all knowledge, who transcends the hierarchy of 'knowing' beings.

TABLE 2: *Neoplatonic scalar predication applied to God*

| Scalar predicates of 'knowing' | Scalar predicates of 'knowing' |
|---|---|
| Bestower of knowledge (God) | Beyond knowing and ignorant: hyper-knowing |
| Essentially knowing (intellect) | Knowing |
| Accidentally knowing (soul) | Knowing |
| Accidentally ignorant (soul) | Ignorant: sub-knowing |
| Essentially ignorant (bodies) | Ignorant: sub-knowing |

The phrase 'God is not knowing' excludes God from the predicate range of entities that possess the attribute of knowledge either essentially (like the Universal Intellect) or accidentally (like the Universal Soul/souls). 'God is ignorant' is a simple private negation. 'God is *not ignorant*' is the *negation of a privative negation.* This negation *excludes God* from the predicate range of all entities who are *deprived of knowledge*—either because they failed to actualise knowledge (like a soul) or they are essentially unable to bear knowledge (bodies). Overall, to say that 'God is neither knowing nor ignorant' is *not* taking away anything from God; rather, it is a hyper-negation that establishes God's status above the entire scalar hierarchy of the 'knowing'/'ignorant' predicate range. One can colloquially translate this Ismāʿīlī hyper-negation as: 'God is not *merely* knowing and not *merely* ignorant.'

When Ismāʿīlī philosophers negate both life and death, knowledge and ignorance, or power and incapacity from God, they are negating two contrary pairs (*ḍiddayn*) but not two contradictories (*naqīḍayn*) from God. As Michael Scott and Gabriel Citron observe: 'Contrary statements, however, are governed by the law of contradiction but not by the law of excluded middle. So while they cannot be jointly true, it is possible for both of them to be false.'[55] This vindicates Ismāʿīlī apophasis against those Sunnī polemicists who accused them of affirming two contradictories. Scott and Citron further conclude:

55 Michael Scott and Gabriel Citron, 'What Is Apophaticism? Ways of Talking about an Ineffable God', *European Journal for Philosophy of Religion* 8, no. 4 (2016): 31.

'Apophatics, therefore, do not in general appear to be affirming contradictory sentences about God. Instead, they are presenting contrary or subcontrary sentences.'[56]

This Ismāʿīlī apophasis concerning God, even if one judges it to be rather radical, may be found in some format among important post-classical Muslim thinkers. In the Akbarī Sufi tradition, various commentators of Ibn al-ʿArabī present a wholly apophatic theology of the Divine Essence that closely resembles Ismāʿīlī *tawḥīd*. Dāwūd al-Qayṣarī (d. 751/1350) speaks of God's Essence, known as the Presence of Singularity (*aḥadiyya*), as transcending all names and attributes: 'If the reality of Being is "conditioned by nothing accompanying it", the Group calls it the Degree of Singularity (*al-aḥadiyya*) which effaces all the attributes and names.'[57] In another place, al-Qayṣarī says, 'Being at the degree of Singularity (*al-aḥadiyya*) negates all individuation. There remains neither attribute (*lā ṣifa*), nor possessor of attributes (*lā mawṣūf*), nor name (*lā ism*), nor named (*lā musammā*), but only the Essence (*al-dhāt*).'[58]

## 6. Divine Ontology: God Is Beyond Being

The most enigmatic element of Ismāʿīlī apophatic theology is the infamous claim that God is 'beyond being', that is, God is not existent (*ays, mawjūd, hast*) and God is non-existent (*lays, maʿdūm, nīst*). This distinctive Ismāʿīlī position appears to be the low-hanging fruit for Muslims of competing theological schools to refute as incoherent. But a proper assessment of the Ismāʿīlī claim must account for the semantics of the word 'being/existence' within Ismāʿīlī discourse, Neoplatonic thought, and Islamic thought more generally. In fact, the nature of 'being' and its relation to concrete 'beings' was a highly disputed and nuanced issue in Islamic intellectual history. ʿAbd al-Raḥmān al-Jāmī (d. 886/1492) in his *Precious Pearl* outlines several positions taken by Islamic theologians, philosophers, and mystics. One group, identified with some of the *kalām* theologians, said that every entity—including God and creatures—has its own specific existence unique unto itself and that the term 'existence' is applied to various entities in name only (*lafẓan*). Another group of theologians, the majority, conceives existence as a single concept or idea (*mafhūm wāḥid*) in the mind, which is then mentally subdivided into similar concepts and attributed to various things. The view of the philosophers is that there is a single mental concept of existence but in external reality, each existing thing has its own specific existence (*wujūd khāṣṣa*)—entailing multiple existences of dissimilar realities (*al-wujūdāt al-mukhtalifāt al-ḥaqāʾiq*) in extra-mental reality—each of which is a 'concomitant accident' (*ʿāriḍ lāzim lahā*) attached to an essence/quiddity. The Sufis,

56 Ibid., 33.
57 Dāwūd al-Qayṣarī, *The Horizons of Being: The Metaphysics of Ibn al-ʿArabī in the* Muqaddimat al-Qayṣarī, trans. Mukhtar H. Ali (Leiden: Brill, 2020), 53.
58 Ibid., 61.

however, affirm that there is One Absolutely Single Existent Reality (*ḥaqīqa wāḥida muṭlaqa mawjūda*), namely, God Himself, who is without any multiplicity, division, or entitative attributes; everything other than God, namely, creation, is the locus of a particularised manifestation (*ẓuhūr*) of God qua Absolute Existence.[59] What the Ismāʿīlīs present concerning existence/being and its relationship to God should be situated within this broader intra-Muslim debate about ontology.

For Plotinus and his followers, the One transcends both being (*enai*) and substance (*ousia*); these notions do not apply to God. Does this mean that Plotinus denies the existence of the One? Recently scholars of Neoplatonic studies have attended to this issue and there is an emerging interpretation of Plotinus holding that he does not deny the 'existence' of the One according to our modern understandings of 'exists'. Rather, in the Greek semantics assumed by Plotinus, the verb 'to be' has the primary function of predication, with the meaning of 'to be something or another'; the same verb only takes on an existential value (with the meaning 'to exist') in very specific secondary contexts.[60] Based on this finding of Kahn, Wiitala and DiRado clarify that 'in claiming the One is beyond being (*to, enai*), Plotinus does not mean that the One does not exist, since the existence of the One is the foundation for the existence of everything else. Instead, Kahn argues that Plotinus' denial of being to the One only entails that the One cannot be a subject of true predication.'[61] Therefore, when Neoplatonists say that God is beyond existence, they only mean to say that God cannot be the subject of any real predicates: 'The One exists, has *hypostasis*, as the principle underlying the things that it causes (unity, goodness, being, etc.) while nevertheless remaining beyond all real predication.'[62]

Given how closely the Ismāʿīlīs follow Plotinus's worldview, the above clarification suffices to rebut the charge that Ismāʿīlī philosophers, in exalting God beyond being and non-being, are agnostic or atheistic with respect to God. However, it is worth examining how the Ismāʿīlīs understand the semantics of existence/being when they deny that God 'exists' or that He is 'a being'.

The Ismāʿīlī thinkers al-Sijistānī and al-Kirmānī mostly use terms like *ays* (existent, being), *aysiyya* (existence), *lays* (non-existent, not-being), and *laysiyya* (non-existence), which come from the circle of al-Kindī. For al-Sijistānī, God is not an *ays* (existent, being), but rather, He is the *mu'ayyis*, meaning He is 'the giver of existence' (*aysiyya*) through His eternal creative act of command (*amr*)—which is the 'existentiation (*ta'yīs*) of the

59 ʿAbd al-Raḥmān al-Jāmī, *The Precious Pearl*, trans. Nicholas L. Heer (New York: State University of New York Press, 1979), 34–35.

60 This is argued at length in Charles H. Kahn, *Essays on Being* (Oxford: Oxford University Press, 2012).

61 Michael Wiitala and Paul DiRado, 'In What Sense Does the One Exist? Existence and Hypostasis in Plotinus', in *Platonic Pathways: Selected Papers from the Fourteenth Annual Conference of the International Society for Neoplatonic Studies*, ed. John F. Finamore and Danielle A. Layne (Gloucester: Prometheus Trust, 2018), 81.

62 Ibid., 90.

existents (*aysāt*) from the non-existent (*lays*)'.[63] Al-Kirmānī writes that 'the existent (*al-ays*) in its being an existent (*fī kawnihi aysan*) is in need of what it depends upon in existence'.[64] For Khusraw, writing in Persian, the terms *hast* (existent) and *hastī* (existence) carry the meaning of *contingent* existent—that which considered in itself may or may not exist: 'Whatever has existence (*harcha hastī dārad*) may also be non-existent (*nīst*) as a contrary (*ḍidd*). That to which "existent" (*hast*) does not apply, it is also not appropriate to call it non-existent. This is because both of them [existence and non-existence] are mutual contraries and whatever has a contrary cannot be God.'[65] For al-Sijistānī, al-Kirmānī, and Khusraw the term 'existent' (*ays, hast*) always has the meaning of *contingent, dependent, and originated* beings. Thus, when they say that God is neither existent (*ays, mawjūd, hast*) nor non-existent (*lays, maʿdūm, nīst*), these Ismāʿīlī philosophers are only stating that God is not dependent on anything and not limited; whereas every 'existent' depends upon God.

Furthermore, many Ismāʿīlīs conceive 'existence' (*aysiyya, hastī*) as a super-genus that subsumes the various types of things such as substances and accidents, bodies and spirits, form and matter, and so forth. Thus, whatever belongs to the category of existence must either be a substance or an accident. Since God transcends being a substance or an accident (both of which entail finitude), it is inappropriate to say God is an existent. Even if one wanted to say God is an existent in a unique manner other than substances and accidents, this would require that God is a species of existence composed of the existence genus and a differentia; this entails ontological composition in God, violates divine simplicity, and renders God dependent upon the conjunction of the existence genus and a differentia.[66] On this reading of 'existence', the Ismāʿīlīs are in complete agreement with Plotinus, for whom the term 'exists' entails the limits of form and substance: 'Plotinus is denying that the One has the sort of metaphysical structure that all beings or substances (*ousiai*) have .... This mutual entailment between *being* and *being something* is what leads Plotinus to say that the One is beyond being.'[67]

Al-Sijistānī and al-Kirmānī refuse to classify God as a *mawjūd* (a being) or what possesses *wujūd* (being) for similar reasons. Al-Sijistānī understands the terms *wujūd*/*mawjūd* in the literal sense of 'finding'/'what is found'. From this meaning, he argues that it is inappropriate for God to be a *mawjūd* (something found) because this requires that there

63 Walker, *Early Philosophical Shiism*, 53, 82.
64 al-Kirmānī, *Rāḥat al-ʿaql*, 131.
65 Nāṣir-i Khusraw, *Shish faṣl or Rawshanā'ī-nāma: Six Chapters or The Book of Enlightenment*, trans. Wladimir Ivanow (Leiden: E. J. Brill for The Ismaili Society, 1949), 34 (English), 6 (Persian), translation modified.
66 For existence as a kind of genus, which Khusraw interprets as a causal rank of the ontological hierarchy in accordance with Proclus's understanding of genus–species relations, see al-Kirmānī, *Rāḥat al-ʿaql*, 131–33; al-Shahrastānī, *Struggling*, 36–42; Nāṣir-i Khusraw, *Knowledge and Liberation: A Treatise on Philosophical Theology*, ed. and trans. Faquir Muhammad Hunzai (London: I.B. Tauris, 1998), 42.
67 Caleb M. Cohoe, 'Why the One Cannot Have Parts: Plotinus on Divine Simplicity, Ontological Independence and Perfect Being Theology', *The Philosophical Quarterly* 67, no. 269 (2017): 751–71.

be an eternal 'finder' (*wājid*) whose object of action is God; this is absurd because God cannot be the patient or direct objection of the act of any agent. If one maintains that the 'finder' is some temporal being who 'finds' God as its *mawjūd*, this entails that prior to this act of 'finding' (*wujūd*), God was a *mawjūd* and therefore, *wujūd* does not apply to God regardless.[68] For al-Kirmānī, *wujūd* is an attribute and the general argument for negating any entitative attribute from God applies to *wujūd* as well. It is either the case that the attribute of *wujūd* depends upon God, such that God is self-subsistent and independent of the attribute of *wujūd*, which is a creation, and has no need for it—which means God is not really a *wujūd* or *mawjūd*; or God Himself depends upon the attribute of *wujūd* for His subsistence, which makes God dependent like creatures and leads to an infinite regress of dependency, which is impossible.

The Ismāʿīlīs' outright refusal to speak of God as an existent within the category of existence or a being among other beings is to drive home the ontological incommensurability between God and created beings: 'He, the Exalted, is beyond being an existent (*aysan*) due to the need of the existent, in being existent, of that which precedes it who makes it exist; thus, it is absurd that He, the Exalted, should be an existent (*aysan*) when He has no need of another to be Himself and does not depend upon another.'[69] This surely cannot be interpreted as a profession of agnosticism or atheism, except by an intentional misreading of their words. In fact, given the difficulty of dispensing with 'existence' language to talk about God, Ismāʿīlīs employed alternative terminologies to speak of God's reality or actuality. Al-Sijistānī, Khusraw, and al-Shahrastānī, after denying the applicability of 'existence' (*aysiyya, hastī, wujūd*) and non-existence (*laysiyya, nīstī, ʿadam*) to God, refer to God as the 'existentiator of existence' (*muʾayyis, hast-kunanda, hast-karda, hast-āwaranda, mūjid al-wujūd*) using active agentive participles.[70] As for 'absolute existence/being' (*wujūd muṭlaq, hast-i muṭlaq*), this is still inapplicable to God because every existent gradationally participates in 'absolute existence'. Therefore, absolute existence is God's eternal creative act, His Command or Word, which is both the source of all originated existents and reflected within them in various degrees: 'Every particle of the Creation has a share of the Command of God because every creature shares a part of the Command of God through which it has come to be there and by virtue of which it remains in being (*pāyanda buwad*), and the light of the Command of God shines in it.'[71] Absolute existence, which is God's creative act of Command, is not God Himself;

---

68 al-Sijistānī, *al-Maqālīd*, 154.

69 al-Kirmānī, *Rāḥat al-ʿaql*, 131.

70 al-Sijistānī, *Kashf al-maḥjūb*, trans. Herman Landolt in Seyyed Hossein Nasr and Mehdi Aminrazavi, eds., *An Anthology of Philosophy in Persia*, vol. 2, *Ismaili Thought in the Classical Age* (London: I.B. Tauris, 2008), 88–89; Nāṣir-i Khusraw, *Shish faṣl*, 6–7 (Persian text); al-Shahrastānī, *Struggling*, 10, 48, 49, 51, 76, 86, 87, 89, 90.

71 Abū Yaʿqūb al-Sijistānī, *Kashf al-maḥjūb*, ed. Henry Corbin (Paris: Iranian Academy of Philosophy, 1949), 19; trans. Landolt in Nasr and Aminrazavi, *An Anthology of Philosophy in Persia*, 93.

rather, it is only the trace or effect (*athar*) of God and it is ontologically united with the Universal Intellect. Nevertheless, God's Command qua absolute existence subsumes and encompasses all existents in a state of oneness (*waḥda*).[72]

Al-Sijistānī and al-Kirmānī prefer to speak of God in terms of His 'subsistence' (*thubūt, thabāt, thābit, ithbāt*) instead of His 'existence'. Al-Sijistānī argues that God is the 'most subsistent' (*athbat*) of everything that subsists. He speaks of God's 'subsistence' (*thubūt, ithbāt*) as the 'real-true subsistence' (*al-ithbāt al-ḥaqīqī*) and created beings as having only 'virtual subsistence' (*al-ithbāt al-majāzī*). Likewise, al-Kirmānī speaks of God as 'subsistent' (*thubūt*) and a 'self-subsistent ipseity' (*huwiyya thābita*).[73] Thus, the Ismāʿīlīs seem to use *thubūt* for God and creatures in an equivocal manner. It is worth noting that the Ismāʿīlī preference to speak of 'subsistence' (*thubūt, thabāt, ithbāt*; meaning 'standing', 'stability') for God's reality and creaturely subsistence parallels Plotinus's use of the word 'hypostasis' (meaning 'standing under') in an equivocal manner to refer to the One, the Intellect, and other levels of being.[74] Medieval and modern scholarship on Ismāʿīlī theology has thus far failed to register the fact that Ismāʿīlī thinkers regularly affirm God's subsistence (*thubūt, thabāt, thābit, ithbāt*)—a finding that also rebuts the polemical charge that Ismāʿīlīs professed agnostic or atheist views.

Al-Kirmānī and al-Shahrastānī *do* permit one to use terms like *wujūd* (existence) to speak of God out of verbal necessity to express oneself. But they warned that 'existence' may only be used equivocally such that one is *not* making a real predication concerning God—that He *has existence, belongs to* the genus of existence, or (as modern analytics love to say) He *instantiates* the divine nature.[75] Therefore, Ismāʿīlīs *can* say 'God exists' or speak of God as the 'Necessary Existence through Himself' (*wājib al-wujūd bi-dhātihi*) in colloquial or even specialised contexts but this proposition is not a univocal predication about God; rather, it is the affirmation that God is the existentiator (*mūjid*) of existents as explained by al-Shahrastānī: 'He is "existent" (*mawjūd*) in the sense that He existentialises every existence (*mūjid kulli wujūd*), is "Necessary of Existence" in the sense that He necessitates every existent (*mūjib kulli mawjūd*); there is no existentialiser (*mūjid*) for beings other than God (Exalted is He!), the Necessary of Existence in Himself.'[76] Technically speaking, the Ismāʿīlīs use 'existence' (*wujūd*) for God as an equivocal term (*ism mushtarak*). However, 'existence' is not a 'pure equivocal' term—where one word has two wholly unrelated meanings (like the 'bark' of a tree and the 'bark' of a dog). Rather, 'existence' as used by Ismāʿīlīs for God is a special kind of equivocal term known to others as an 'impure equivocal', 'paradigmatic equivocal', or 'relative analogical

72 Nāṣir-i Khusraw, *Knowledge and Liberation*, 27, 84–85.
73 al-Kirmānī, *Rāḥat al-ʿaql*, 152.
74 Wiitala and DiRado, 'Sense'.
75 al-Kirmānī, *Rāḥat al-ʿaql*, 153; al-Shahrastānī, *Struggling*, 43, 48, 55.
76 al-Shahrastānī, *Struggling*, 48, 51.

term'.[77] Accordingly, the statements 'God exists' and 'trees exist' have different meanings but the meanings are related in some way. In this case, as used by Ismāʿīlīs, 'trees exist' means 'trees subsist dependently upon another' while 'God exists' means 'God subsists independently and in reality (*ḥaqīqī*) and He makes everything else subsist dependently and virtually (*majāzī*)'.

The Ismāʿīlīs are not the only Muslim philosophical school to deny or at least heavily qualify the applicability of the concept of 'existence' to God. Ibn Sīnā is famous for teaching that God is the Necessary Existence in Himself (*wājib al-wujūd bi-dhātihi*) whereas all created beings are contingent existence (*mumkin al-wujūd bi-dhātihi*) in itself or necessary existence due to another (*wājib al-wujūd li-ghayrihi*) because they depend upon God. For Ibn Sīnā, existence (*wujūd*) is not a univocal term, but rather, it is a modulated term (*ism mushakkak*). God, who is existent by virtue of Himself, is 'more deserving' of existence while created beings, who exist by virtue of another, are less worthy of existence. One interpretation of Ibn Sīnā's view of 'existence' is that it is a 'modulated' or 'analogical' term, whose meaning is closer to the univocal predication.[78] However, recent scholarship by Janos convincingly argues that Ibn Sīnā treats existence as an equivocal term (*ism mushtarak*).[79] The importance of this finding is that Ibn Sīnā's view of God as the Necessary Existence in Himself and the Ismāʿīlī view that God is beyond existence/non-existence do not necessarily conflict and may only differ because of their divergent semantic frameworks. The following is a quote from *al-Taʿlīqāt* of Ibn Sīnā (later reproduced by Ṣadr al-Dīn al-Qūnawī in his correspondence with Naṣīr al-Dīn Ṭūsī), where he admits that God in His reality (*ḥaqīqa*) is not the same as 'existence' (*wujūd*) in general and that the formal definition (*ḥadd*) of God as the Necessary Existence in Himself does not strictly correspond to God's reality (*ḥaqīqa*):

> Likewise, we do not know the reality of the First (*ḥaqīqat al-awwal*). We know of Him that existence is necessary for Him or it is not. *This,* [*however,*] *is His concomitant not His reality ... His reality is not the same as existence* (*laysa ḥaqīqatuhu nafs al-wujūd*), nor is it a quiddity since the existence with the quiddities is external to their realities while *He in His Essence is the cause of existence* (*ʿillat al-wujūd*). It is therefore the case that existence enters into defining Him (*taḥdīdihi*) as the genus and differentia enter into the definition of simple substances because of what the intellect requires for them; [*in this case*], *existence is a part of His formal definition*

77 Alexander Treiger, 'Modulation of Existence (*Taškīk al-Wuǧūd, Analogia Entis*) and Its Greek and Arabic Sources', in *Islamic Philosophy, Science, Culture, and Religion*, ed. Felicitas Opwis and David Reisman (Leiden: Brill, 2012), 332–33.

78 Daniel D. De Haan, 'The Doctrine of the Analogy of Being in Avicenna's *Metaphysics of the Healing*', *The Review of Metaphysics* 69, no. 2 (2015): 276.

79 Damien Janos, 'Avicenna on Equivocity and Modulation: A Reconsideration of the Asmā' Mushakkika (and Tashkīk al-Wujūd)', Oriens 50 (2022): 1–62.

> (*ḥadd*) *but not His reality*, just as genus and differentia are parts of the formal definitions of simple substances but not their essences. *Truly for Him, His reality* (*ḥaqīqa*) *is beyond existence* (*fawq al-wujūd*) and existence is among its concomitants.[80]

In the above quotation, Ibn Sīnā offers several important concessions with respect to his use of the term *wujūd* for God—concessions that bring Ibn Sīnā's views in closer alignment with the Ismāʿīlī position that God transcends existence. These remarks suggest that Ibn Sīnā only uses the term 'existence' for God as in Necessary Existence in an equivocal manner: God in His *ḥaqīqa* is not an existent, does not possess existence, and actually transcends existence (*fawq al-wujūd*) since He is the source or cause of existence (*ʿillat al-wujūd*). This appears to vindicate al-Shahrastānī's claims that existence can only be used equivocally for God and that God is truly the source of existence (*mūjid*) rather than its possessor.[81]

## 7. Ismāʿīlī Apophasis and Religious Language: Metonymic Predication

A common concern raised against Ismāʿīlī theology and similar views is how the idea of an absolutely simple, wholly transcendent, timeless, and immutable God squares with the religious language about God found in scriptural texts, prayer, and everyday God-talk among Muslims. How does Ismāʿīlī apophasis cohere with scriptural and ritual invocations like *bismillāh al-raḥmān al-raḥīm* (in the name of God, the infinitely compassionate, the most merciful)? How do predicative statements about God found in scripture and prayers—asserting that God is knowing (*ʿālim, ʿalīm*), powerful (*qādir, qadīr*), most high (*ʿalī*), exalted (*aʿlā*), the peace (*al-salām*), the sublime (*ʿaẓīm*), the sustainer of the worlds (*rabb al-ʿālamīn*), the king (*malik*), or the ever-living subsistent (*al-ḥayy al-qayyūm*)—reconcile with a theology of God transcending all attributes?

First, when approaching religious language about God, one must acknowledge the difference between 'real predication' and 'syntactic predication'. 'Real predication' occurs when a proposition refers to an entitative attribute (an ontological predicate) that the subject (God) possesses. A 'syntactic predication' is only a matter of grammar—where God is the grammatical subject (*mubtadaʾ*) of a sentence that contains a grammatical predicate (*khabar*)—but without the predicate necessarily referring to an entitative or real-distinct ontological feature within God.[82] As far as the Ismāʿīlīs are concerned, positive predications about God are all acceptable so long as they are framed as *syntactic* predications and not as *real* predications. This then raises the question of what these syntactic

80 Ibn Sīnā, *al-Taʿlīqāt*, ed. ʿAbd al-Raḥmān Badawī (Cairo: al-Hayʾa al-Miṣriyya al-ʿĀmma, 1973; repr., Beirut: Dār al-Islāmiyya, n.d.), 35 (emphasis added).

81 al-Shahrastānī, *Struggling*, 45, 48, 55, 57, 64.

82 Wiitala and DiRado, 'Sense', 82–83.

predications truly mean and what they are *really* saying about God. Before presenting the Ismāʿīlī interpretation, it is necessary to survey how Muslims of other theological schools interpret the predicative statements found in scripture. For example, take the following statements: 'God is one' (*Allāhu aḥad*), 'God is eternal' (*Allāhu azalun*), 'God is knowing' (*Allāhu ʿālimun*), 'God is merciful' (*Allāhu raḥīmun*), and 'God is a creator' (*Allāhu khāliqun*). The general principle that Islamic theologians and philosophers adhere to is that the truth value of any syntactic predication (*ḥukm*) about God must be grounded by an underlying reality (*ʿilla*).[83]

Sunnī theologians, including al-Juwaynī, al-Ghazālī, and Ibn al-Jawzī, do not read every divine name or *syntactic* predication about God as an affirmation of a *real* divine attribute. Al-Juwaynī says: 'All of the names of the Sanctified Lord are divided according to whether they signify the Essence or the eternal attributes and what signifies actions or the negation of anything the Sanctified Creator is hallowed above.'[84] For example, 'God is eternal' simply means that God is not temporal; it does not denote an ontological attribute.[85] 'God is a creator' refers to a divine action—the act of creating the world—and does not refer to an entitative divine attribute.[86] However, 'God is knowing' is taken by most Sunnī theologians to mean that 'God possesses knowledge' (*Allāhu lahu ʿilmun*) and affirms an uncreated divine attribute. Meanwhile, Sunnī theologians understand God's mercy (*raḥma*), anger (*ghaḍab*), love (*maḥabba*), guardianship (*wilāya*), and intention (*qaṣd*) as all referring to God's single attribute of will.[87] In other words, the Arabic language does not necessitate any particular ontological entailment from a mere syntactic predication: not every syntactic predication about God in Arabic is necessarily a *real* predication about God, nor must it refer to a real-distinct attribute within God.

For their part, Ismāʿīlīs interpret all syntactic predications about God—such as the ninety-nine names of God—either as the negation of creaturely qualities from God or as *metonymic predications*. The latter present God as the source, ground, and bestower of the positive attributes existing within His creation.[88] Metonymy is a broad category of non-literal speech found across multiple languages including English, Greek, and Arabic. The type of metonymy that Ismāʿīlīs understand in positive divine predications is known in academic literature as 'meaning transfer': 'the process that allows us to use an expression that denotes one property as the name of another property, provided there

---

83 Richard M. Frank, *Classical Islamic Theology: The Ashʿarites*, ed. Dimitri Gutas (London and New York: Routledge, 2016), 768–71.

84 al-Juwaynī, *Guide*, 80.

85 Ibid., 79–80.

86 Ibid.

87 Ibid., 80; Frank, *Classical Islamic Theology*, 763–64; Ibn Ḥamdān, *Nihāyat al-mubtadiʾīn fī uṣūl al-dīn* (Riyadh: Maktabat al-Rushd, 2003), 25.

88 For example, divine names such as the sanctified (*al-quddūs*), the transcendent (*al-mutaʿālī*), the mighty (*al-ʿazīz*), and the one (*al-wāḥid, al-aḥad*) are easily interpreted as the negation of attributes from God.

is a salient functional relation between the two'.[89] Accordingly, Ismāʿīlīs interpret all positive divine names and predications as instances of what Rosenthal calls 'productive metonymy'. 'Productive metonymy' is when the statement 'X is F' means 'X is productive of F-things' or 'X produces F-things' instead of meaning 'X has the property of being F' or 'X is an F-thing'.[90] Plato uses metonymic predication throughout his writings, especially when he discusses the predicates 'healthy' and 'just'; this type of metonymy endures to the present day. People refer to an action or a punishment as 'justice' because it *produces justice* in society or *contributes justice* to a particular situation. Ismāʿīlīs interpret all positive divine names in this manner: 'God is X' really means 'God originates X'.

Accordingly, al-Sijistānī interprets the phrase 'God is powerful' (*Allāhu qādirun*) as follows: 'The Creator in His surpassing glory transcends that which can be said to have power; rather it is He Who is the provider of creation's splendid and noble powers.'[91] Thus, 'God is powerful' means God is the bestower of all power upon His creation. Khusraw offers the same interpretation of 'God is powerful' and 'God is the creator': 'They call Him powerful (*qādir*) because all the power (*qudrat*) of the powerful (*qādirūn*) is from Him; likewise, it is He who has given creative power (*khalqat*) to the creators (*khāliqān*).'[92] Ismāʿīlī philosophers apply a productive metonymic reading to most positive divine names found in scripture and in theology. In the below passages, al-Shahrastānī interprets various divine names from both scripture and positive theology as metonymic predications:

> [God] is truth (*ḥaqq*) in the sense that He makes the truth true (*yuḥiqqu al-ḥaqq*) and He makes the false false (*yubṭilu al-bāṭil*), and He is necessary in His existence (*wājib wujūdihi*) in the sense that He necessitates the existence of other than Him (*yūjibu wujūd ghayrihi*), and annihilates (*yuʿdimu*), and He is living (*ḥayy*) in the sense that He gives life (*yuḥyī*) and death.[93]

> Majestic is our Lord and He is exalted above being described by perfection (*al-tamām*), exceeding being described by deficiency. Thus, He makes complete whatever is deficient (*mukammil kulli nāqiṣ*). If by 'perfection', it is meant that He makes perfect whatever is perfect (*mutammim kulli tāmm*), this is sound .... He is 'existent' (*mawjūd*) in the sense that He existentialises every existence (*mūjid kulli wujūd*), [He] is 'Necessary of Existence' (*wājib al-wujūd*) in the sense that He necessitates

89 G. Nunberg, quoted in Saul Rosenthal, 'Self-Predication and Productive Metonymy', *Apeiron* 51, no. 1 (2008): 21.
90 Ibid., 22–23.
91 Abū Yaʿqūb al-Sijistānī, *The Wellsprings of Wisdom: A Study of Abū Yaʿqūb al-Sijistānī's* Kitāb al-Yanābīʿ *Including a Complete English Translation with Commentary and Notes on the Arabic Text*, trans. Paul E. Walker (Salt Lake City: University of Utah Press, 1994), 57.
92 Nāṣir-i Khusraw, *Between Reason and Revelation*, 218, translation modified.
93 al-Shahrastānī, *Struggling*, 43 (English), 41 (Arabic), transliteration added and translation modified.

> every existent (*mūjib kulli mawjūd*), [He] is 'knowing' in the sense that He causes whatever is knowing to know (*muʿallim kulli ʿālim*), and [He] is 'powerful' (*qādir*) in the sense that He empowers whatever is powerful (*muqaddir kulli qādir*).[94]

> Instead, 'unity' is applied to Him (Exalted is He!) and to existents purely equivocally. He is 'one' (*wāḥidun*) unlike the 'ones' (units) mentioned, [He is] the one (*wāḥidun*) from Whom proceeds [both] the unity (*al-waḥda*) and the multiplicity (*al-kathra*) that are opposites. [He is] one (*wāḥidun*) with the meaning that He existentiates (*yūjidu*) the 'ones' (*al-aḥād*). He singularizes the oneness (*bi-l-waḥdāniyya*), then He makes it emanate upon His creation.[95]

In the above statements, al-Shahrastānī glosses all *predicative names* of God with the *productive active participles* derived from those predicates: God is the truth (*al-ḥaqq*) insofar that He is the one who makes the truth true (*muḥiqq*); God being called existent (*mawjūd*) and Necessary Existence (*wājib al-wujūd bi-dhātihi*) means God is the existentiator (*mūjid*) of every existence and existent and the necessitator (*mūjib*) of every contingent; God is living (*al-ḥayy*) insofar as He is the one who gives life (*muḥyī*) to the living; God is powerful (*al-qādir*) in the sense that He empowers (*muqaddir*) the powerful; He is the knowing (*ʿālim*, *ʿalīm*) insofar as He bestows knowledge (*muʿallim*) to the knowers; God is the one (*al-wāḥid*) in the sense that He gives existence to various units. God is named the perfect (*al-tāmm*) in the sense that God is the perfector (*mutammim*, *mutimm*) of whatever is perfect (*al-tāmm*); God is called the complete (*al-kāmil*) only insofar as He is the completer (*mukammil*) of whatever is complete (*kāmil*). This interpretation allows the Ismāʿīlī philosophers to *accept syntactic predications* about God while also denying all *real predications* about God. God is exalted above all real predications and is identified as the bestower of all real predicates and powers that He is verbally attributed with.

Ultimately, the truth-maker or underlying ground (*ʿilla*) for God being attributed with numerous positive predicates in scripture is the fact that God is the bestower, originator, and creator all of the powers and attributes that these predicates refer to. This means that all positive divine names and predicates are ultimately reducible to God's eternal act of originating and sustaining His creation. The Ismāʿīlīs refer to God's singular creative act of eternal creation as God's Command (*amr Allāh*). Accordingly, al-Sijistānī explains that all positive predications about God found in scripture refer to God's Command: 'The predication (*al-inniyya*) that is ascribed to God, may He be praised, is the pure origination (*al-ibdāʿ al-maḥḍ*) that is His Command (*amruhu*) and His goodness (*jūduhu*).'[96] In other words, various divine predications found in the Qurʾan, which often begin with the *inna*

94 Ibid., 48 (English), 50–51 (Arabic), transliteration added and translation modified.

95 Ibid., 56 (English), 62 (Arabic), transliteration added and translation modified.

96 al-Sijistānī, *al-Maqālīd*, 56.

particle, are only true in virtue of God's creative act of Command from which various attributes flow into His creation: 'The attribution of predication (*iḍāfat al-inniyya*) to Him means that it is He who originated the substances which are the secondary causes of the manifestation of God's blessings and favours.'[97] Likewise, Ṭūsī explains that the positive predicates that people attribute to God are grounded by His creative command: 'The fact that in relation to Him [God] people speak of Necessity, Unity, Simplicity, Will, Knowledge and Power, and likewise of [His] other attributes, is all because His exalted Command is one pure light, one uncontaminated emanation, one bounty and one generosity.'[98]

When God, who transcends all positive and negative attributes, is the originator of the various perfections that the divine names and predicates describe, it follows that within God's creation, there must also exist concrete originated beings who *literally* possess perfect created attributes described by *real predications*. In the Ismāʿīlī Neoplatonic worldview—which the Ismāʿīlī philosophers established through cosmological arguments—the first and highest creation of God is the Universal Intellect (First Intellect), and the second creation is the Universal Soul. When God is understood as the ground, source, and bestower of the various perfections (life, power, knowledge, etc.)—which are inapplicable to Him as real predications—it logically follows that the First Intellect and Universal Soul are the locus of these perfect attributes and various *real predications* apply to them. Ismāʿīlī philosophers consistently describe the First Intellect as the subject of positive divine names insofar as the divine names are predicative and descriptive. According to al-Kirmānī, the First Intellect is 'entirely living, entirely powerful, entirely knowing, entirely eternal, entirely all-encompassing, entirely perfect, complete, and singular. He is the first existent, the real, and the originated being … He is a singular essence to which these attributes are connected—some of which are due to his essence and some of which are due to his relationships with other things.'[99] In Ismāʿīlī writings, the First Intellect is predicated with various divine names and predicates: the living (*al-ḥayy*), the knowing (*al-ʿālim, al-ʿalīm*), the powerful (*al-qādir*), the perfect (*al-kāmil*), the one (*al-wāḥid*), the lord of lords (*rabb al-arbāb*), the first, the last, the manifest, the hidden (*al-awwal, al-ākhir, al-ẓāhir, al-bāṭin*), and so on.[100] Likewise, the Universal Soul as the second creation is also described by certain divine names: the lord-sustainer (*rabb, parwardigār, khudāwand*) of human souls, the sublime (*al-ʿ*aẓīm), the creator (*al-khāliq*) and the maker (*al-ṣāniʿ*) of the physical world, the enduring (*al-bāqī*), and the generous

97 Ibid., 58.

98 Naṣīr al-Dīn Ṭūsī, *Paradise of Submission: A Medieval Treatise on Ismaili Thought*, trans. S. J. Badakhchani (London: I.B. Tauris, 2005), 19.

99 al-Kirmānī, *Rāḥat al-ʿaql*, 188–89.

100 See, for example, Nāṣir-i Khusraw, *Shish faṣl*, 39, 43, 46. See also Khalil Andani, 'Neoplatonic Prayer: The Isma*ʿili Hermeneutics of Ṣalāt* according to al-Sijistānī and Nāṣir-i Khusraw', in *Islamic Thought and the Art of Translation: Texts and Studies in Honor of William C. Chittick and Sachiko Murata*, ed. Mohammed Rustom (Leiden: Brill, 2023), 277–97.

(*al-ikrām*).[101] Al-Sijistānī explains that the First Intellect and Universal Soul may be called 'lord' (*rabb*) in the virtual sense (*bi-majāz*) because they provide spiritual nourishment to the spiritual and physical creatures below them.[102]

Even the name *Allāh*, insofar as this divine name is taken as descriptive attribute or real predication, properly refers to and describes the First Intellect and, in certain contexts, refers to the Universal Soul. According to al-Kirmānī, the name *Allāh* derives from *waliha* (to bewilder); the First Intellect, as the first created being, cannot encompass God and is in a state of bewilderment (*ḥayra*) in the face of God's absolute transcendence.[103] This is why the name *Allāh* describes the First Intellect. However, it should be noted that Ismāʿīlīs commonly use *Allāh* as a nominal name for God Himself. The various invocations of *Allāh* in scripture and prayer are assumed to refer to God, but everything positively predicated of God is understood metonymically. The linguistic and scriptural basis for attributing various divine names to the First Intellect and Universal Soul is a form of metonymic speech known to Arabic grammarians as 'cognitive transference' (*majāz ʿaqlī*). *Majāz ʿaqlī* is a kind of non-literal speech in which a predicate (action or attribute) is syntactically assigned to an entity who is not the real doer of it but who is contiguously related to its real doer. For example, when a king commands a palace to be built, people will say that 'the king built the palace'. However, the king did not literally build the palace; his servants built the palace under king's command. The phrase 'the king built the palace' is a metonymic predication involving *majāz ʿaqlī* because the attribute of 'building' is transferred from the servants of the king to the king himself.[104] Examples of *majāz ʿaqlī* are found throughout the Qurʾan: one verse says God takes souls at death (Q. 39:42) but another verse says the Angel of Death takes souls at death (Q. 32:11); one verse says that God split the sea for the people of Moses (Q. 2:50) but two other verses say that Moses split the sea (Q. 20:77, 26:63); when the Prophet receives the people's offerings (Q. 9:103), it is immediately stated that God receives their offerings (Q. 9:104). Some Sunnīs interpret the *ḥadīth* about God's descent to the lowest heaven as describing His angels' descent.[105] In these examples (among many others), the Qurʾan ascribes acts or attributes to God which are concretely executed or manifested by His creatures.

Al-Kirmānī employs *majāz ʿaqlī* to articulate why God is called one (*al-wāḥid*), knowing (*al-ʿālim*), or powerful (*al-qādir*) even though these attributes properly belong to His creatures:

101 See, for example, Nāṣir-i Khusraw, *Shish faṣl*, 31–32; Nāṣir-i Khusraw, *Knowledge and Liberation*, 27, 108.
102 al-Sijistānī, *al-Maqālīd*, 63.
103 al-Kirmānī, *Rāḥat al-ʿaql*, 194, as explained in Mansouri, 'Sayyid Ḥaydar Āmulī', 205–6.
104 Abdul Gabbar Mohammed Al-Sharafi, *Textual Metonymy: A Semiotic Approach* (New York: Palgrave Macmillan, 2004), 28–31, 177–78.
105 al-Juwaynī, *Guide*, 89.

> When it is said that God is one (*wāḥid*), knowing (*ʿālim*), powerful (*qādir*), etc., it does not mean that He possesses oneness (*waḥda*), knowledge (*ʿilm*), power (*qudra*) and life (*ḥayāt*) with which He has been attributed. Rather, it means that He is the agent (*fāʿil*) of the one, knowing, living, powerful, etc., just as a king who has built a certain city, or has struck the neck of a certain person is called a 'builder' and a 'striker'. But these are not his personal attributes in the sense that he [the king] personally executed these (actions). Rather, these are the attributes of the one whom he commanded and enabled to do so—he [who] personally built and dealt the blow and by his [the king's] command became a builder and striker. But everything is ascribed to the king—for it is due to his command that the building and the striking took place.[106]

In the view of al-Kirmānī and other Ismāʿīlī philosophers, the divine names 'one', 'knowing', 'powerful', and 'living' understood as *real predications* describe the First Intellect—the first and greatest creation of God. However, Muslim scriptural texts and prayers still refer to God by these names because God is the originator of the First Intellect; the First Intellect depends entirely upon God and it acts only according to God's command. Therefore, the attributes of the First Intellect—its life, knowledge, power, perfections, etc.—are metonymically predicated to God in colloquial and scriptural speech. In the same vein, Khusraw holds that the divine names of the 'creator' (*khāliq*, *āfarīda*) and 'sovereign' (*malik*, *pādshāh*) apply to the Universal Soul and the Universal Intellect, respectively. However, Khusraw observes that God is still called the creator and the sovereign in scriptural and colloquial contexts:

> Thus, the Sovereign in a true sense is the First, that is, the First Originated Being (*mubdaʿ-i awwal*) with which the Divine Command immediately became one, and that is the First Intellect (*ʿaql-i awwal*), which is complete in both actuality and potentiality. The Creator and agent [of creation] in reality is the Universal Soul (*nafs-i kull*) which, in relation to the Universal Intellect (*ʿaql-i kull*), namely the First Intellect, is like a thought of the rational soul. Thus, the Creator and creation, the Sovereign and sovereignty, are all in the Divine Command which has no connection with God's ipseity.[107]
>
> The attribution of creatorship and sovereignty made to God is not because He is the Creator and Sovereign, but in the sense that the existence of the Creator and Sovereign is from His Command, and all existents are attributed to Him in order to

106 al-Kirmānī, quoted in Faquir Muhammad Hunzai, 'The Concept of *Tawḥīd* in the Thought of Ḥamīd al-Dīn al-Kirmānī' (PhD diss., McGill University, 1986), 139.

107 Nāṣir-i Khusraw, *Knowledge and Liberation*, 27.

> glorify Him—just as when a man commands others to build a mansion, it is built by carpenters and other workmen, yet it is not said that they made it but that this mansion was built by so-and-so, whereas he did no work except to command.[108]

The remarks of al-Kirmānī and Khusraw allow Ismāʿīlīs to affirm and even use positive divine predications about God while continuing to understand them as metonymic predications. Both authors read divine predications found in scripture as 'cognitive transference' (*majāz ʿaqlī*) and evoke the example of a king being attributed with actions that he commanded his servants to perform. This interpretative strategy effectively allows Ismāʿīlī philosophers to uphold their radical apophatic theology of God transcending all real predications; affirming the Universal Intellect and Soul as the bearers of any real predications signified by the divine names; and affirm the syntactic predications about God found in scripture and other religious contexts through interpreting them as metonymic predications.

Ismāʿīlī thinkers employ similar methods to account for the anthropomorphic scriptural descriptions of God—such as God's face, two hands, two eyes, and so on. While rejecting a literalist interpretation of these attributes, Ismāʿīlī thinkers take seriously the argument that the 'face of God' (*wajh Allāh*) and 'hand of God' (*yad Allāh*) must refer to extramental realities (*ḥaqāʾiq*) and cannot be explained away as mere allegories. Al-Sijistānī observes that God's creation consists of hierarchical ranks (*ḥudūd*) through which God's creative action flows according to a cosmic arrangement (*tartīb*) and the so-called organs of God mentioned in revelatory scripture refer to these ranks. The 'face of God' (*wajh Allāh*) signifies the First Intellect because 'he is the face of whatever the Originator manifested within him among the forms of all things and by which one distinguishes between each of the forms, and to which one turns for the recognition of the Originator'.[109] Likewise, the 'two eyes' (*ʿaynān*) of God refer to the Universal Soul. The role of the physical eyes in perceiving shapes and distinguishing corporeal forms indicates the fact that the Universal Soul perceives spiritual forms and distinguishes between spiritual and corporeal shapes. The 'twoness' of the eyes alludes to the role of the Universal Soul as the spiritual intermediary between two levels—the Intellect and Nature—since the Soul directs 'one eye' towards the Intellect and directs 'one eye' towards the physical world.[110] The 'two hands' (*al-yadān*) of God that are 'spread out' refer to the Prophet and his Legatee (the Imām), known as the 'two founders' (*al-asāsān*), because they spread forth the divine law and expound its spiritual interpretation (*taʾwīl*) on behalf of God.[111] Al-Sijistānī also refers to famous anthropomorphic *ḥadīth*s circulating among

108 Ibid., 29.

109 al-Sijistānī, *al-Maqālīd*, 104.

110 Ibid., 105.

111 Ibid., 106.

the Ḥanbalīs—such as the tradition in which the Prophet says, 'I saw my Lord in the form of a young man, beardless with short, curly hair.' This tradition was authenticated by Aḥmad b. Ḥanbal (d. 241/855) and his followers, including Ibn Taymiyya, who affirm its contents according to its apparent meaning.[112] However, al-Sijistānī argues that the Prophet's 'lord' (*rabb*) mentioned here cannot refer to God, who transcends all physical and spiritual attributes. Rather, the 'lord' whom Muḥammad saw in the form of a young man was a divinely guided human being who served as the spiritual instructor (*murabbī*) of the Prophet: 'The [person] who undertook the spiritual training (*tarbiya*) of Muḥammad, peace be upon him and his progeny, until he promoted him to the elevated ranks, was his "lord" to whom he referred and from whom he learned.'[113] In Ismāʿīlī thought, the Prophet's spiritual initiator and 'lord' was none other than Imām Abū Ṭālib, who was the last divinely appointed Imām in the cycle of Jesus.[114]

## 8. Conclusion: The Rational and Scriptural Coherence of Ismāʿīlī *Tawḥīd*

This paper has attempted to offer a philosophical exposition of the Ismāʿīlī Muslim concept of *tawḥīd* and illuminate its logical structure against certain distorted portrayals in medieval polemic and modern scholarship. While the examples cited were drawn from medieval Ismāʿīlī philosophy, the general apophatic and Neoplatonic tenor of Ismāʿīlī theology prevails well into modern times. The contemporary Nizārī Ismāʿīlī Imāmate, as seen in the teachings of Imām Ḥasan ʿAlī Shāh Aga Khan I (d. 1881), Shihāb al-Dīn Shāh (d. 1884), and Imām Shāh Karīm al-Ḥusaynī Aga Khan IV, continues to promote an apophatic theology of *tawḥīd* and Neoplatonic structure of creation.[115]

## Bibliography

Andani, Khalil. 'Metaphysics of Muhammad'. *Journal of Sufi Studies* 8 (2019): 99–175.

———. 'Neoplatonic Prayer: The Ismaʿ*ili Hermeneutics of Ṣalāt* according to al-Sijistānī and Nāṣir-i Khusraw'. In *Islamic Thought and the Art of Translation: Texts and Studies in Honor of William C. Chittick and Sachiko Murata*, edited by Mohammed Rustom,

112 On this *ḥadīth* and its reception in Ḥanbalī circles, see Wesley Williams, 'Aspects of the Creed of Imam Aḥmad ibn Ḥanbal: A Study of Anthropomorphism in Early Islamic Discourse', *International Journal of Middle East Studies* 34, no. 3 (2002): 441–63.

113 al-Sijistānī, *al-Maqālīd*, 64.

114 On the status of Abū Ṭālib as an Imām in Ismāʿīlī thought, see Khalil Andani, 'Metaphysics of Muhammad', *Journal of Sufi Studies* 8 (2019): 115–16n29.

115 See Muhammad Hasan al-Husayni, *The First Aga Khan* (London: I.B. Tauris in association with The Institute of Ismaili Studies, 2018); Shihab al-Din ibn ʿAli Shah (Khalil Allah), *Kitab-i khitabat-i ʿAliyyah: dar masa'il akhlaq vaʿqa'id-i Ismaʿiliyah* (Bombay: Ismaili Society, 1963; Aga Khan IV, unpublished *firmans* made in 1983 Silver Jubilee Visits and *Bayt al-Khayal firmans*.

277–97. Leiden: Brill, 2023.

Brown, Joshua Matthan. 'What We Can and Cannot Say: An Apophatic Response to Atheism'. In *Eastern Christian Approaches to Philosophy*, edited James Siemens and Joshua Matthan Brown, 66–94. Cham: Springer, 2022.

Cohoe, Caleb M. 'Why the One Cannot Have Parts: Plotinus on Divine Simplicity, Ontological Independence and Perfect Being Theology'. *The Philosophical Quarterly* 67, no. 269 (2017): 751–71.

De Haan, Daniel D. 'The Doctrine of the Analogy of Being in Avicenna's *Metaphysics of the Healing*'. *The Review of Metaphysics* 69, no. 2 (2015): 261–86.

Frank, Richard M. *Beings and Their Attributes: The Teaching of the Basrian School of the Mu'tazila in the Classical Period.* Albany: State University of New York Press, 1978.

———. *Classical Islamic Theology: The Ashʿarites*. Edited by Dimitri Gutas. London and New York: Routledge, 2016.

al-Ghazālī, Abū Ḥāmid. *Al-Ghazālī's Moderation in Belief.* Translated by Aladdin M. Yaqub. Chicago: University of Chicago Press, 2013.

Heer, Nicholas L. 'Al-Abharī and al-Maybudī on God's Existence: A Translation of a Part of al-Maybudī's Commentary on al-Abharī's *Hidāyat al-Ḥikmah*'. https://digital.lib.washington.edu/researchworks/bitstream/handle/1773/4887/abhari-sep.pdf?sequence=1&isAllowed=y.

Hunzai, Faquir Muhammad. 'The Concept of *Tawḥīd* in the Thought of Ḥamīd al-Dīn al-Kirmānī'. PhD diss., McGill University, 1986.

Ibn Ḥamdān. *Nihāyat al-mubtadiʾīn fī uṣūl al-dīn.* Riyadh: Maktabat al-Rushd, 2003.

Ibn Sīnā. *al-Taʿlīqāt*. Edited by ʿAbd al-Raḥmān Badawī. Cairo: al-Hayʾa al-Miṣriyya al-ʿĀmma, 1973. Reprint, Beirut: Dār al-Islāmiyya, n.d.

Izutsu, Toshihiko. *Sufism and Taoism: A Comparative Study of Key Philosophical Concepts.* Berkeley and Los Angeles: University of California Press, 1983.

al-Jāmī, ʿAbd al-Raḥmān. *The Precious Pearl.* Translated by Nicholas L. Heer. New York: State University of New York Press, 1979.

Janos, Damien. 'Avicenna on Equivocity and Modulation: A Reconsideration of the *Asmā' Mushakkika* (and *Tashkīk al-Wujūd*)'. *Oriens* 50 (2022): 1–62.

al-Juwaynī, Imām al-Ḥaramayn. *A Guide to Conclusive Proofs for the Principles of Belief.* Translated by Paul E. Walker. Reading: Garnet Publishing, 2000.

Kahn, Charles H. *Essays on Being*. Oxford: Oxford University Press, 2012.

Kars, Aydogan. *Unsaying God: Negative Theology in Medieval Islam.* New York: Oxford University Press, 2019.

Kifayat Ullah. *Al-Kashshāf: Al-Zamakhshari's Muʿtazilite Exegesis of the Qur'an.* Berlin: De Gruyter, 2017.

al-Kirmānī, Ḥamīd al-Dīn. *Master of the Age*. Edited and translated by Paul E. Walker. London: I.B. Tauris, 2007.

———. *Rāḥat al-ʿaql*. Edited by Muṣṭafā Ghālib. Beirut: Dār al-Andalūs, 1983.

Lika, Eva-Maria. *Proofs of Prophecy and the Refutation of the Ismāʿīliyya: The* Kitāb Ithbāt Nubuwwat al-Nabī *by the Zaydī al-Muʾayyad bi-Llāh al-Hārūnī (d. 411/1020)*. Berlin: De Gruyter, 2017.

Madelung, Wilferd. 'Aspects of Ismaili Theology: The Prophetic Chain and the God Beyond Being'. In *Ismāʿīlī Contributions to Islamic Culture*, edited by Seyyed Hossein Nasr, 52–65. Tehran: Imperial Iranian Academy of Philosophy, 1977.

Mansouri, Mohammad Amin. 'Sayyid Ḥaydar Āmulī (d. ca. 787/1385) and Ismailism'. *Studia Islamica* 117 (2022): 171–229.

Martin, John N. 'Existence, Negation, and Abstraction in the Neoplatonic Hierarchy'. *History and Philosophy of Logic* 16, no. 2 (1995): 169–96.

Melchert, Christopher. 'The Early Controversy Over Whether the Prophet Saw God'. *Arabica* 62, no. 4 (2015): 459–76.

Mihirig, Abdurrahman. 'Classical *Kalām* and the Laws of Logic'. *Maydan*, 23 April 2021. https://themaydan.com/2021/04/classical-kalam-and-the-laws-of-logic/.

Mohammed Al-Sharafi, Abdul Gabbar. *Textual Metonymy: A Semiotic Approach*. New York: Palgrave Macmillan, 2004.

Moreland, James Porter, and William Lane Craig. *Philosophical Foundations for a Christian Worldview*. Downers Grove, IL: InterVarsity Press, 2003.

Nahouza, Namira. *Wahhabism and the Rise of the New Salafists: Theology, Power and Sunni Islam*. London: I.B. Tauris, 2018.

Nāṣir-i Khusraw. *Between Reason and Revelation: Twin Wisdoms Reconciled*. Translated by Eric Ormsby. London: I.B. Tauris, 2012.

———. *Knowledge and Liberation: A Treatise on Philosophical Theology*. Edited and translated by Faquir Muhammad Hunzai. London: I.B. Tauris, 1998.

———. *Shish faṣl or Rawshanāʾi-nāma: Six Chapters or The Book of Enlightenment*. Translated by Wladimir Ivanow. Leiden: E. J. Brill for The Ismaili Society, 1949.

———. *Zād al-musāfir*. Edited by Muḥammad ʿImādī Ḥāʾirī and Ismāʿīl ʿImādī Ḥāʾirī. Tehran: Mīrāth-i maktūb, 2005.

Nasr, Seyyed Hossein, and Mehdi Aminrazavi, eds. *An Anthology of Philosophy in Persia*. Vol. 2, *Ismaili Thought in the Classical Age*. London: I.B. Tauris, 2008.

al-Qayṣarī, Dāwūd. *The Horizons of Being: The Metaphysics of Ibn al-ʿArabī in the* Muqaddimat al-Qayṣarī. Translated by Mukhtar H. Ali. Leiden: Brill, 2020.

Rosenthal, Saul. 'Self-Predication and Productive Metonymy'. *Apeiron* 51, no. 1 (2008): 1–36.

Scott, Michael, and Gabriel Citron. 'What Is Apophaticism? Ways of Talking about an Ineffable God'. *European Journal for Philosophy of Religion* 8, no. 4 (2016): 23–49.

Shah-Kazemi, Reza. *Justice and Remembrance: Introducing the Spirituality of Imam ʿAlī*. London: I.B. Tauris, 2006.

al-Shahrastānī, ʿAbd al-Karīm. *Struggling with the Philosopher: A Refutation of Avicenna's*

Metaphysics. Translated by Wilferd Madelung and Toby Mayer. London: I.B. Tauris, 2001.

al-Sijistānī, Abū Yaʿqūb. *Kashf al-maḥjūb*. Edited by Henry Corbin. Paris: Iranian Academy of Philosophy, 1949.

———. *Kitāb al-maqālīd al-malakūtiyya*. Edited by Ismail K. Poonawala. Beirut: Dār al-Gharb al-Islāmī, 2011.

———. *The Wellsprings of Wisdom: A Study of Abū Yaʿqūb al-Sijistānī's* Kitāb al-Yanābīʿ *Including a Complete English Translation with Commentary and Notes on the Arabic Text*. Translated by Paul E. Walker. Salt Lake City: University of Utah Press, 1994.

Swinburne, Richard. *The Coherence of Theism*. Revised edition. Oxford: Clarendon Press, 1993.

Treiger, Alexander. 'Modulation of Existence (*Taškīk al-Wuǧūd, Analogia Entis*) and Its Greek and Arabic Sources'. In *Islamic Philosophy, Science, Culture, and Religion*, edited by Felicitas Opwis and David Reisman, 327–63. Leiden: Brill, 2012.

Ṭūsī, Naṣīr al-Dīn. *Paradise of Submission: A Medieval Treatise on Ismaili Thought*. Translated by S. J. Badakhchani. London: I.B. Tauris, 2005.

Walker, Paul E. *Early Philosophical Shiism: The Ismaili Neoplatonism of Abū Yaʿqūb al-Sijistānī*. Cambridge: Cambridge University Press, 1993.

Wiitala, Michael, and Paul DiRado. 'In What Sense Does the One Exist? Existence and Hypostasis in Plotinus'. In *Platonic Pathways: Selected Papers from the Fourteenth Annual Conference of the International Society for Neoplatonic Studies*, edited by John F. Finamore and Danielle A. Layne, 77–92. Gloucester: Prometheus Trust, 2018.

Williams, Wesley. 'A Body unlike Bodies: Transcendent Anthropomorphism in Ancient Semitic Tradition and Early Islam'. *Journal of the American Oriental Society* 129, no. 1 (2009): 19–44.

———. 'Aspects of the Creed of Imam Aḥmad ibn Ḥanbal: A Study of Anthropomorphism in Early Islamic Discourse'. *International Journal of Middle East Studies* 34, no. 3 (2002): 441–63.

# PART 4

# *Philosophical Perspectives on God and Monotheism*

# Mullā Ṣadrā and His Commentators on Ibn Kammūnā's Argument Against Divine Unity

*Wahid M. Amin*

This paper examines the proofs of divine unity (*tawḥīd*) in the writings of Avicenna (Ibn Sīnā, d. 428/1037) and their reception in post-Avicennian Islamic philosophy. While Avicenna's demonstration of divine unity became widely accepted among later Muslim thinkers, it was not without its critics. One of the most significant challenges to Avicenna's argument came from the 13th-century Jewish philosopher Ibn Kammūna (d. 683/1284), who questioned whether the necessity of existence (*wujūb al-wujūd*) logically entails God's uniqueness. His counterargument, which later scholars referred to as the '*shubha* of Ibn Kammūna,' challenged a fundamental assumption in Avicenna's proof by raising the possibility of multiple Necessary Beings. This critique generated extensive debate among later Islamic philosophers, particularly within the Ṣadrian tradition.

This paper seeks to address the following key question: Does Ibn Kammūna's critique successfully undermine Avicenna's proof of divine unity, particularly when analysed through the lens of Mullā Ṣadrā's metaphysical system? To answer this, the paper first examines Avicenna's proofs of divine unity, paying particular attention to his reliance on the doctrines of divine simplicity and divine aseity. It then analyses Ibn Kammūna's objection, explaining the logical structure of his critique and its implications. Finally, the paper explores the responses of Mullā Ṣadrā (d. 1050/1640) and his commentators, demonstrating how their commitment to the primacy and modulation of existence (*aṣālat al-wujūd* and *tashkīk al-wujūd*, respectively) provides a more robust framework for defending divine unity against Ibn Kammūna's critique. By situating Ibn Kammūna's argument within the broader trajectory of Islamic metaphysics, this study aims to show that his objection does not hold in the Ṣadrian framework.

## 1. Avicenna's Proof(s) of Divine Unity

Avicenna's attempts to demonstrate the unity of the Necessary Being can be categorised into two distinct yet closely related approaches.[1] In certain arguments, he presupposes

1 There are surprisingly few studies in the English language devoted to Avicenna's doctrine of divine unity and his ideas about henology in his metaphysics more generally. Two noteworthy examples are Mohammed Saleh Zarepour's *Necessary Existence and Monotheism: An Avicennian Account of the Islamic Conception of Divine Unity* (Cambridge: Cambridge University Press, 2022) which contains a brief account of Avicenna's docrine of divine unity, and Damien Janos' *Oneness, Essence, and Self-Identity: A New Interpretation of Avicenna's Henology* (Berlin: De Gruyter, 2024) which provides a thorough analysis

the doctrine of divine simplicity (DDS) to show that divine simplicity is incompatible with the assertion that there are multiple divine entities each having the necessity of existence due to themselves. Such an approach typically takes the form of a hypothetical syllogism: If there are two Necessary Beings then they are both necessarily composed in essence. But no Necessary Being is composed in essence (DDS). Therefore, there is only one Necessary Being. What is evident in arguments of this kind is that the simplicity of the Necessary Being is taken as a premise in the argument for divine unity itself.[2] A proof that every Necessary Being must be a simple being is therefore also counted as a proof of Its uniqueness, and likewise a demonstration to the effect that there is at least one Necessary Being that is simple must also be considered a proof that It is the only possible Necessary Being.[3] Avicenna tried to demonstrate this on several occasions.[4]

However, in other arguments, Avicenna leaves out the assumption that every Necessary Being must be a simple entity and instead highlights the significance of divine aseity as the central idea with which to comprehend the nature of the Necessary Being. Such an approach emphasises the principle of sufficient reason above any other consideration. Indeed, as we shall note shortly, DDS is itself a consequence of the doctrine of divine aseity. This doctrine posits that the divine being is a self-sufficient and independent entity that lacks any requirement beyond itself for its existence or its attributes, one of which is its unity. By shifting the focus to divine aseity, Avicenna is making a conscious attempt in my view to demonstrate the external unity (*wāḥidiyya*) of the Necessary Being without assuming DDS (*aḥadiyya*), which it could be argued is a superior method of proving God's uniqueness given that it avoids taking for granted something that is in need of direct proof itself.[5] Avicenna shows that it is therefore possible to demonstrate the Necessary

---

of Avicenna's henology. On the conception of divine unity in al-Fārābī, see Olga L. Lizzini, 'L'unité et l'unicité de Dieu: Le double sens de l'être chez al-Fārābī et Avicenne', *Revue Philosophique de la France et de l'étranger*, 149, no. 1 (2024): 17–31. See also Aladdin M. Yaqub, 'Al-Ġhazālī's Philosophers on the Divine Unity,' *Arabic Sciences and Philosophy*, 20 (2010): 281–306.

2 As noted by Mayer, composition-based arguments for the uniqueness of the Necessary Being stretch back *via* al-Kindī to Plotinus's *Enneads*. For Plotinus, any kind of composition in the essence of a being—even if such compositions are purely analytical and mental in nature—precludes it being one in the absolute sense. Rather, such beings are 'one-many' and thus require a higher principle for their existence. See Toby Mayer, 'Faḫr ad-Dīn ar-Rāzī's Critique of Avicenna's Argument for the Unity of God in the *Išārāt*, and Naṣīr ad-Dīn Ṭūsī's Defence,' in *Before and Avicenna: Proceedings of the First Conference of the Avicenna Study Group*, ed. David C. Reisman (Leiden: Brill, 2003), 199–218. See also Mohammad Saleh Zarepour, *Necessary Existence and Monotheism*, 3.

3 In this paper I do not consider Avicenna's arguments for the existence of the Necessary Being. Needless to say, scholarship on this aspect of Avicenna's metaphysics is considerably vast.

4 For example, see Avicenna, *al-Taʿlīqāt*, ed. Sayyid Ḥusayn Mūsawiyān (Tehran: Mu'assasah-i Pazhūhashī Ḥikmat u Falsafah-i Īrān, 1401/[2022–2023]), 183–84.

5 It is this feature of Avicenna's proof of divine unity that makes it markedly different from the one offered by his predecessor Abū Naṣr al-Fārābī. On the Farābian proof, see al-Fārābī, *On the Perfect State* (*Kitāb Ārā ahl al-madīna al-fāḍila*), edited and translated by Richard Walzer (Oxford: Clarendon Press, 1985), 60–61: 'The First Existent is different in its substance from everything else, and it is impossible for anything else to have the existence it has. For between the First and whatever were to have the same existence as the

Being's uniqueness with or without DDS. These approaches are distinct: the first kind of argument relies on the idea that a multitude of Necessary Beings undermines their simplicity, a problem in its own right—whereas the second shows that a multiplicity of divine beings undermines their self-sufficiency. This is quite an audacious move by Avicenna and one that deliberately emphasises the role of modality in his metaphysics, and for this reason represents a significant departure in the proofs offered by earlier *falāsifa* for the Necessary Being's uniqueness because whereas the simplicity of the Necessary Being requires proof, Its self-sufficiency does not. A Necessary Being just is a self-sufficient being. Whilst it can therefore be doubted whether or not the Necessary Being is a simple being, its being necessary is impervious to doubt; Its existing necessarily is precisely what it is; and doubting this would be as illogical as doubting whether a square is a square. Moreover, it is because of divine aseity that divine simplicity itself becomes an inevitable requirement. Because a Necessary Being cannot depend on anything other than itself for Its subsistence, It cannot *ipso facto* have any proper parts which combine to make It necessarily existent.[6] Therefore, according to Avicenna, divine aseity entails divine simplicity, and it seems that necessity for him—that is, being self-sufficient—is what grounds the metaphysical notion of simplicity and not the other way round.

A key question that arises in connection with these claims is whether or not there is a logical or necessary relation between the internal unity (or simplicity) of the Necessary Being on the one hand and Its external unity (or unicity) on the other. Does committing to the doctrine of divine simplicity also commit one to believing that there is only one divine being? Avicenna believes it does. Ibn Kammūna, a thirteenth-century Jewish philosopher, believed that it doesn't. Why can't there be two Necessary Beings that are both simple and uncaused? To appreciate what is at stake in these arguments, this paper will begin with an analysis and explication of Avicenna's proofs of divine unity before turning to the debates that ensued after him in the writings of his commentators.

---

First, there could be no difference and no distinction at all. Thus there would not be two things but one essence only, because, if there were a difference between the two, that in which they differed would not be the same as that which they shared, and thus that point of difference between the two would be a part of that which sustains the existence of both, and that which they have in common the other part. Thus each of them would be divisible in thought, and each of the two parts of the First would be a cause for the subsistence of its essence; and it would not be the First but there would be another existent prior to it and a cause for its existence—and that is impossible.' (Translation by Walzer) As for the Qur'anic description of God as *aḥad* referring to the Necessary Being's simplicity in Avicenna's thought, see Daniel De Smet and Meryem Sebti, 'Avicenna's Philosophical Approach to the Qur'an in the Light of His *Tafsīr Sūrat al-Ikhlāṣ*,' *Journal of Qur'anic Studies* 11, no. 2 (2009), 137–38.

6 Avicenna, *Kitāb al-Najāt*, ed. Muḥammad Taqī Dānishpazhūh (Tehran: Intishārāt-i Dānishghāh-i Ṭihrān, 1985), 551–53; idem, *al-Ishārāt wa-l-tanbīhāt*, ed. Mujtabā al-Zāriʿī (Qom: Būstān-i Kitāb, 1423/[2002–2003]), 272.

### 1.1 Argument(s) from Aseity

An argument from aseity is one that aspires to demonstrate God's uniqueness by resorting to nothing other than God's self-sufficiency. It argues that a belief in the proposition 'God is self-sufficient' warrants the belief that 'God is one' (or, equivalently, 'That there is only one God'). In the context of Avicenna's metaphysics in which modality plays a crucial role, the argument seeks to arrive at the following conclusion: 'If the Necessary Being is self-sufficient, then there is only one Necessary Being.' The argument therefore begins with a claim about divine aseity and attempts to derive a conclusion that asserts divine unity. Avicenna provides a variety of arguments to demonstrate the truth of this conditional statement by considering the implications of denying the consequent. By assuming—for the sake of argument—that there are two or more Necessary Beings, Avicenna shows that there is a logical entailment between the affirmation of divine plurality, on the one hand, and the negation of divine self-sufficiency, on the other. If it can be shown that the existence of more than one Necessary Being undermines each individual Necessary Being's self-sufficiency, then that is a sufficient proof that there cannot be more than one Necessary Being. This is because a Necessary Being that depends on something other than Itself for Its existence (or one of Its perfections) cannot be *necessarily* what It is *due to Itself*. Avicenna utilises arguments of this kind to demonstrate that there cannot be a plurality of Necessary Beings: either there are no Necessary Beings at all or there is just one. Crucially, it is his conception of God as a being that is necessarily existent due to itself that determines this impossibility, since according to Avicenna the notion of being self-sufficient is a concept interwoven in the concept of 'existing necessarily' (*wājib al-wujūd*).[7] It is here that we can ask the question pertinent to this paper: How does Avicenna demonstrate a violation of the doctrine of divine self-sufficiency in that hypothetical scenario in which there are multiple Necessary Beings? To answer this, let us review some of Avicenna's arguments for divine unity through the principle of divine self-sufficiency.

7 Avicenna usually expresses the concept of divine self-sufficiency with the expression 'necessary of existence in all respects' (*wājib al-wujūd min jamīʿ al-wujūh* or *jamīʿ al-jihāt*). For example, see Avicenna, *al-Shifāʾ*, *al-Ilahiyyāt*, eds. G. C. Anawati, S. Zayed, M. Musa and S. Dunya (Cairo: al-Hayʾa al-ʿĀmma Li-Shuʾūn al-Maṭābiʿ al-Amīriyya, 1960), I.6, p. 37; English translation by Michael E. Marmura, *The Metaphysics of the Healing* (Provo, Utah: Brigham Young University Press, 2005), 30. A Necessary Being is not just necessary in one or some respects only; It is necessary in all respects (I will refer to this as the principle of absolute necessity). If this were not the case, then there would be at least one respect in which It is not necessary, which implies that there is an aspect or respect within the divine being in which it is contingent. As such, the presence of just a single aspect or respect in which something is contingent, whether this aspect is in relation to its existence or one of its other perfections, is sufficient to make it a contingent being and not a Necessary Being. To be necessary in all respects and perspectives, therefore, means that the Necessary Being is not just necessarily existent (*wājib al-wujūd*), but also necessarily knowing, necessarily powerful, necessarily living etc. If, for example, the Necessary Being's knowledge were not necessary for It, then Its being a knower would be contingent on something other than It's own essence. This renders God's knowledge contingent, and hence God is imperfect. On the proof of the principle of absolute necessity, see Avicenna, *al-Najāt*, 553.

Avicenna begins arguments in this vein by assuming that there are two (or more) Necessary Beings each defined as having the necessity of existence due to themselves (*wujūb al-wujūd bi-l-dhāt*). The qualifier 'due to themselves' ensures that such beings are self-sufficient and independent of any causes whatsoever. If we imagine there are two Necessary Beings, then each of these must have something by virtue of which they are different from the other. In other words, there has to be something that differentiates them from every other existence including other Necessary Beings. Otherwise, there is no difference between them, and their being indiscernible implies that they are identical. Customarily, this is known as the principle of individuation,[8] and let us therefore call that thing by virtue of which they are different the 'individuation' or 'individuating principle'. In that scenario, then, in which there are two Necessary Beings, each possesses an individuation that is lacking in the other. Depending on whether or not we assume DDS, these individuating factors will be either essential or non-essential properties of each Necessary Being. For example, when considering the hypothetical scenario in which there are two Necessary Beings at *Ilāhiyyāt* I.7 of the *Shifāʾ*, Avicenna identifies each Necessary Being's individation as an accident (sing. *ʿaraḍ* and *lāhiq*).[9] Although he does not explain in explicit terms why each Necessary Being's individuation cannot be something intrinsic or essential to them, this is presumably because he has already explained in the preceding sections that whatever has the necessity of existence due to itself cannot have a *māhiyya*, a quiddity distinct from its *inniyya*, its individual existence. Hence, given the surrounding context, it is reasonable to assume that whatever distinguishes and individuates each Necessary Being it must be something extraneous to their individual natures as beings that are comprised of existence (*inniyya*) only. In doing so, the argument appears to factor DDS into consideration. But it could be argued that the individual existences of each Necessary Being suffices as a principle of their individuation(s) and hence there is no further need beyond the very existence that each Necessary Being possesses to account for their individuations. Avicenna appears to have this objection in mind when he explains that each Necessary Being's individuation cannot simply be due to the fact that each Necessary Being has necessary existence as this would imply that the individuation in question is a concomitant of necessary existence, which entails that each Necessary Being has the *same* individuation.[10] But if each

8 Everything that exists must have an individuation that particularises its existence. This is a principle of metaphysics in Islamic philosophy referred to by the dictum '*al-shayʾ mā lam yatashakhkhaṣ lam yūjad*'. See Ghulām-Ḥusayn Ibrāhīmī Dīnānī, *Qawāʿid-i kullī-yi falsafī dar falsafah-i Islāmī* (Tehran: Pazhūhashghāh-i ʿUlūm-i Insānī u Muṭālaʿāt-i Farhanghī, 1389Sh/2011), 1:240–46. For a more general discussion of the problem, see Fedor Benevich, 'Individuation and identity in Islamic philosophy after Avicenna: Bahmanyār and Suhrawardī', *British Journal for the History of Philosophy* 28, no. 1 (2020): 4–28.

9 Avicenna, *al-Shifāʾ*, *al-Ilāhiyyāt*, I.7, pp. 43–4 (=Avicenna, *The Metaphysics of the Healing*, 35). Unless otherwise noted, all translations of Avicenna are mine.

10 Avicenna, *al-Shifā*, *al-Ilāhiyyāt*, I.7, p. 44. It is crucial to note that there is no real—i.e. ontological—difference between the existence of the Necessary Being and Its necessity. This was a bone of major contention

Necessary Being is the same *vis-à-vis* its essence (viz. the necessity of existence) and the concomitant by virtue of which they are each individuated, then every Necessary Being is just the same in reality as every other and thus indiscernible in actuality. What one Necessary Being has is also possessed by every other Necessary Being. In that case, there would be only one Necessary Being and not many. For this reason, the necessity of existence that two Necessary Beings have becomes a point of their convergence, not a point of divergence, which means that their individual existences alone are not sufficient to differentiate them from each other, and hence the mere fact that they are necesssarily existent cannot be regarded as the principle of their individuation. An explanation for why they are different is still required, therefore, and the metaphysics here—assuming that it takes DDS into consideration—requires that the difference betweem them lies outside of their individual essences, hence the reason why the difference (or individuation) is identified as an accident.

What Avicenna seems to want to emphasise therefore is that the individuations belonging to each Necessary Being cannot be due to their being necessary existents only, but neither can they be a concomitant of this shared meaning since that does not differentiate them either. In other words, that by which two Necessary Beings are the same (i.e. necessary existence) cannot itself be the reason why they are different, and this according to Avicenna appears to be an intuitive claim. Rather, the individuation that accounts for each Necessary Being's specific existence must lie entirely beyond the essence of each

among Avicenna's commentators. In some of his works, Fakhr al-Dīn al-Rāzī devoted considerable time and energy to the question of how necessity and existence are related to each other. But he assumes, in these particular works at least, that the two are really distinct. Although the question was never dealt with by Avicenna in the same detail as subsequent thinkers, he nevertheless appears to indicate that by the necessity of existence (*wujūb al-wujūd*) he means not that there is a separate attribute or property that is added to the essence or existence of a Necessary Being but rather just that It has the strongest possible mode of existence. The phrase he uses is *taʾakkud al-wujūd*. This means that whatever has the necessity of existence due to itself has existence necessarily, not that it has necessity in addition to its existence. Therefore, a Necessary Being is one the existence of which is so strong that existence is fixed (*taʾakkud*) for it—both conceptually and in existence. A Necessary Being can never not have existence, therefore, unlike a contingent being whose existence is not fixed for it but could potentially be removed from it. In the Metaphysics of *Kitāb al-Hidāya*, the expression used by Avicenna is *tawkīd al-wujūd*. See Avicenna, *Kitāb al-Hidāya*, ed. Muḥammad ʿAbdu (Cairo: Maktabat al-Qāhira al-Ḥadītha, 1974), 261 (para 157). Note, that Avicenna makes it clear that the necessity of existence and existence are not two things; rather, the former expresses a qualification of the latter as the strongest and most assured form of existence: '*idh wujūb al-wujūd tawkīd al-wujūd lā amr yaʿriḍ lahu l-wujūd bi-sabab wa-huwa ghayruh*'. Cf. Ibn Kammūna, *al-Kāshif (al-Jadīd) fī l-ḥikma*, ed. Ḥāmid Nājī Iṣfahānī (Tehran: Muʾassasah-i Pazhūhashī Ḥikmat u Falsafah-i Īrān, 1387Sh/[2008]), 428 (*wa-wujūb al-wujūd lā yaqtaḍī tarakkubuhu min wujūdin wa-wujūbin fa-inna l-wujūb huwa taʾakkud al-wujūd wa-kamāliyyatuhu wa-l-kamāliyya laysat bi-zāʾidatin ʿalā l-shayʾ fī l-aʿyān*). For our discussion later in this paper it is important to note Ibn Kammūna's association of the notion of necessity (*wujūb*) with perfection (*kamāl*), which he again highlights in his commentary on Suhrawardī's *al-Tawīḥāt*; see Ibn Kammūna, *Sharḥ al-Talwīḥāt al-lawḥiyya wa-l-ʿarshiyya*, ed. Najafqulī Ḥabībī (Tehran: Mīrāṣ-i Maktūb, 1387Sh/[2008]), 3:175 (*wa-hāhunā laṭīfa wa-hiya annaka idhā qulta «wājib al-wujūd» yanbaghī an lā yufham min «al-wujūd» maʿnan wa-min «al-wujūb»* [*maʿnan*] *ākhar fa-yalzam al-tarkīb wa-l-munāqaḍa li-mā qurrira min wujūb ʿadam al-takaththur bal wujūbuhu huwa kamāliyyatu wujūdihi wa-huwa basīṭ fa-lā ism lahu*).

Necessary Being and beyond the concommitant properties that ensue from the necessity of existence. But this leads to an infelicitous consequence. If the individuation that each Necessary Being possesses is an accident, then each Necessary Being would be *caused*. Since every Necessary Being in this scenario cannot exist without first being something individuated, it follows by the transitivity of causation that whatever causes the individuation of each Necessary Being also causes each of their individual existences.[11] This implies that the existence of each Necessary Being is an effect of something other than itself, and this in turn implies that every Necessary Being is dependent on something other than itself for Its existence.[12] However, given that anything that depends on something other than itself for its existence is not self-sufficient, it follows that each of the beings that was initially hypothesised as a Necessary Being is in actual fact just a contingent being. It is clear, then, that both DDS and the doctrine of divine self-sufficiency (a specific instance of the principle of sufficient reason) are factored into Avicenna's reasoning for divine unity. What this argument appears to demonstrate is that the presence of a multitude of Necessary Beings undermines the aseity of each Necessary Being such that none of the entities in question suffices as an independent cause or explanation of its own existence, which is precisely what they must be if they are to be considered Necessary Beings.[13]

Avicenna considers a slightly modified approach for demonstrating the external unity of the Necessary Being from aseity in his discussion immediately following the argument just explained. In this argument (*Ilāhiyyāt* I.7.5–13) he begins by supposing that the necessity of existence belonging individually to each Necessary Being is either a genus or a species. Considered in this way, the necessity of existence is treated as an essential predicate of each Necessary Being. Let us assume, then, that the necessity of existence is a universal predicable of a multitude of Necessary Beings. Now, on the one hand, if 'being necessary' is a genus then its division and distribution among multiple Necessary Beings requires a corresponding number of specific differences, since without this added consideration all of the Necessary Beings in question would be indiscernible. On the other hand, if 'being necessary' is a species then its division among a multitude of Necessary Beings requires accidents of a sufficiently great number to differentiate each instance of that species from other instances of the same. Notice that Avicenna abandons the doctrine of divine simplicity here. The argument he is developing does not

11 By the transitivity of causation I mean the following: if it is true that A causes B and B causes C, then A causes C is also true. In the context of our discussion this means that if something (*w*) causes the individuation (*a*) of a certain Necessary Being, and if that individuation is necessary for the individual existence of that Necessary Being, then it follows by the transitivity of causation that *w* is also a cause that Necessary Being's individual existence.

12 Avicenna rejects the irreflexivity of causation; i.e., nothing can be the cause of its own existence. See Avicenna, *al-Ishārāt wa-l-tanbīhāt*, IV.17, p. 270.

13 The Qur'an emphasises the sheer independence of God in numerous verses, but it is perhaps most eloquently expressed in the verse 'It is you who stand in need of God—God needs nothing and is worthy of all praise' (Q. 35:15).

assume the internal unity of the Necessary Being but instead begins with the seemingly unproblematic assumption that each Necessary Being is a composite.[14] The reason for this, I argue, is because he wishes to focus on divine aseity as the primary attribute of the Necessary Being in order to show that it is possible to demonstrate the external unity of the Necessary Being without DDS. In other words, he wants to prove the *wāḥidiyya* of God without appealing to His *aḥadiyya*.

Therefore, we have two possibilities. Either the necessity of existence is a genus divided across multiple instances through individual specific differences or it is a species whose instances are individuated by a sufficient number of accidents. However, according to Avicenna, both of these are impossible scenarios. As for the first, he starts by explaining that specific differences do not constitute a part of a genus' definition: 'rational'—for example—is not included in the definition of 'animal'; for it is possible that something is an animal without it necessarily being rational. Therefore, as Avicenna explains, a specific difference 'does not give a genus its essence', but rather 'gives it its subsistence in actuality'.[15] To put this differently, the specific difference confers actual existence (*al-wujūd bi-l-fiʿl*) upon the genus and not its reality or essence (*ḥaqīqa*). We need 'rationality' to give existence to the genus 'animal' in extramental reality, namely in the form of a human being, but we do not need it to give 'animal' its essence. This being the case, Avicenna begins his explanation of why the necessity of existence, in particular, cannot be a genus that is dependent on a specific difference for its actual existence. This is because existence cannot be given to that which is characterised as being necessary of existence, for the necessity *of* existence is nothing but existence of the strongest and most assured kind.[16] As Avicenna explains, 'The reality of the necessity of existence is nothing but the assuredness of existence [...] which is why giving existence to the necessity of existence is [tantamount to] fulfilling a condition of its reality'.[17] This remark requires a pause, for it is not immediately clear what Avicenna means by the clause 'fulfilling a condition of its reality' (*ifādatu sharṭin min ḥaqīqatihi*). To understand this, we must connect what

14 If necessity is a genus then each Necessary Being would have necessity as one part of its essence, the other part being their individual specific differences. If it is a species, then every Necessary Being would comprise a genus and specific difference that are different from *wujūb al-wujūd* just as man is different from animal and rational. In both cases the Necessary Beings that possess the necessity of existence are composite entities.

15 Avicenna, *al-Shifāʾ*: *al-Ilāhiyyāt* I.7, p. 45 (=Avicenna, *The Metaphysics of the Healing*, 36; Marmura modified).

16 To speak of an existence that is stronger and more assured than others implies that existence *per se* is a modulated reality with degrees of intensity. Avicenna does not mention *tashkīk al-wujūd* in his discussion of the unity of the Necessary Being, but it is crucial in my view to acknowledge its importance in the background in order to make sense of his discussions of the necessity of existence as *taʾakkud al-wujūd*. Indeed, this is precisely the way, as we shall see, that Mullā Ṣadrā interprets Avicenna.

17 Avicenna, *al-Shifa*: *al-Ilahiyyat* I.7, p. 45 (=Avicenna, *The Metaphysics of the Healing*, 36; Marmura's translation here is problematic). In short, conferring existence upon the necessity of existence is akin to giving something what it already has (*taḥṣīl al-ḥāṣil*).

Avicenna says here with what he has said at the beginning of his discussion at *Ilāhiyyāt* I.7. Recall, that according to Avicenna the function of a specific difference is to give the genus to which it is related its subsistence (or existence) in actuality (*al-qiwām bi-l-fiʿl*) but not its subsistence as an essence *qua* essence. If therefore the necessity of existence were a genus in need of a specific difference, then that specific difference would only serve the purpose of giving it a subsistence in actual reality and not making it subsistent in being *what it is*, viz. 'necessary of existence'.

However, there is a problem with this idea when the genus in question is *wujūb al-wujūd* itself. To explain, let us take *wujūb al-wujūd* as a genus and give it a specific difference. When that specific difference qualifies *wujūb al-wujūd* it gives it its actual existence, its *qiwām bi-l-fiʿl*, given that this is the function of a specific difference, ontologically speaking. However, by giving it actual existence (*al-wujūd bi-l-fiʿl*) the specific difference gives to the necessity of existence the very thing that constitutes its essence, namely, existence itself.[18] For there is no necessity *of existence* if there is no existence. So, by taking the necessity of existence as a genus that is made subsistent due to a specific difference, the specific difference acts in a manner such that it is now 'fulfilling a condition of its reality', meaning that the specific difference gives to the necessity of existence something that constitutes its reality, which no specific difference can do.[19] Hence, the necessity of existence (*wujūb al-wujūd*) cannot be a genus.

Whereas the argument above provides a sound reason to dismiss the characterisation of necessity as a genus, Avicenna's second justification is more explicit in noting the consequences this would have on the aseity of the Necessary Being if necessity were a genus. The argument is a quite simple one: Since the genus, which in our case is the necessity of existence, does not subsist in actuality until and unless it has been modified by a specific difference, it follows that the specific difference is what makes the necessity of existence an *actual* necessity in extramental reality. In that case, every actual instance of the necessity of existence would not be necessary of existence *due to itself* but instead necessary of existence *due to another*, viz. the specific difference. Necessity would therefore always be necessary by another if the necessity of existence were a genus. There would thus be nothing in that case to instantiate the concept of a

18 One could reply to this by arguing that *al-wujūd bi-l-fiʿl* does not constitute the reality or nature of the necessity of existence (*wujūb al-wujūd*). But this hardly makes any sense, however, for that which is necessary of existence has *actual existence* as a necessary property of its very essence. A Necessary Being is precisely just that which exists necessarily in actual reality due to itself. Otherwise, one either demarcates the *wujūd* in *wujūb al-wujūd* as existence in potentiality (*al-wujūd bi-l-quwwa*) or lacking existence altogether. But the first would make whatever has the necessity of existence a contingent being given that whatever has existence in potentiality is *mumkin al-wujūd*. As for the second alternative, it is a plain contradiction: whatever exists necessarily cannot lack existence altogether.

19 As later sections of this paper will focus on the views of Ibn Kammūna, it is worth bearing in mind that Ibn Kammūna considers this to be one of six arguments for the uniqueness of the Necessary Being. See Ibn Kammūna, *al-Kāshif (al-Jadīd fī l-ḥikma)*, 413–14.

being that is necessary of existence due to itself. But we know from Avicenna's *burhān al-ṣiddiqīn* that the set of all existent things cannot be confined to just contingent beings and that a Necessary Being must exist. According to Avicenna, then, if the necessity of existence were a genus, it would not be self-sufficient for its actual subsistence, rendering it merely contingent in reality, which contradicts the very notion of what it means to be 'necessary of existence' which is just that a Necessary Being is self-sufficient. By emphasising the modal qualifiers 'due to itself' and 'due to another', Avicenna shows why the necessity of existence that characterises Necessary Beings cannot be a genus, as this ultimately renders every putative instance of 'Necessary Being' necessary *due to another* and therefore merely contingent in themselves.[20]

Avicenna's discussion so far has shown that the distribution and division of the term 'necessary of existence' cannot be akin to a genus divided by differentiae nor a genus divided by accidents. The only option that remains is that it is a species, but he discounts this by arguing that the only plausible way for necessity to be individuated as a species among multiple yet discernible instances would be if it were individuated through individuating accidents, but this has already been shown to be problematic.[21] Each of these arguments seeks to establish the unity of the Necessary Being by first considering necessity as either a genus or a species and then showing that in either scenario any hypothesised Necessary Being would not be a self-sufficient being but would rather depend for its existence on a cause beyond itself for its own actualisation. At no point does Avicenna invoke the doctrine of divine simplicity, but rather hones in on what is to be regarded as the most salient property of necessary existsence, namely, the doctrine of divine aseity. This paves the way for a more general argument in Avicenna's thinking that avoids any specific considerations of necessity as either a genus or species. For Avicenna, since the individuation of multiple Necessary Beings through a consideration of the necessity of existence as either a genus or species and their attendant accidental properties undermines each so-called Necessary Being's intrinsic necessity, the only option that preserves the condition of self-sufficiency on the one hand hand, yet sufficiently accounts for It being individuated on the other, is the option which regards the necessity of existence itself as the individuating principle of the Necessary Being. This eliminates the need

20 Any scenario in which the necessity of existence is actualised by something other than itself contradicts the very notion of what it means to be a necessarily existent thing. Regardless then of whether the necessity of existence is a part-essential predicate or an accidental predicate of each Necessary Being, the conclusion will always be the same: what is necessary of existence by itself is necessary of existence by another, and that is absurd. As Avicenna states, 'The necessity of existence that belongs to each of them individually would be derived from something else, and yet it has been stated that whatever exists necessarily by another does not exist necessarily by itself. Rather it is in and of itself merely contingent. In this case, each and every one of these [Necessary Beings], despite being necessarily existent in itself, would also be possibly existent in and of itself, and that is a contradiction.' Avicenna, *al-Shifāʾ: al-Ilāhiyyāt* I.7, p. 44 (=Avicenna, *The Metaphysics of the Healing*, 35).

21 Avicenna, *al-Shifāʾ: al-Ilahiyyat* I.7, pp. 45–6 (=Avicenna, *The Metaphysics of the Healing*, 36).

to consider the necessity of existence as either a genus or a species capable of being instantiated in multiple instances, but at the same time requires that whatever has the necessity of existence as an individuating principle is the only instance of a being that is necessarily existent due to itself. When this is the case, the argument cannot begin with the assumption that there are two or more Necessary Beings.

Avicenna presents this generalised form of the argument toward the end of *Ilāhiyyāt* I.7 and in *Ilāhiyyāt* 8.5 of the *Shifāʾ*, and offers a much-condensed version of the same argument in *Ishārāt* IV.18, which reads as follows:

> The individuated Necessary Being, if Its individuation is due to its being necessarily existent then there is no other Necessary Being besides It. But if Its individuation is not due to that but due to something else, then It is caused. This is because if necessary existence is [(a)] an inseparable accident (*lāzim*) of Its individuation, then existence would either be an inseparable accident of an essence other than it [i.e. other than the necessity of existence] or of an attribute, both of which are impossible. And if it were [(b)] a separable accident (*ʿāriḍ*), then that is more deserving of a cause [than if it were an inseparable accident].[22]

The argument put forward in this passage is by far Avicenna's most important *textual* source for his argument for the Necessary Being's uniqueness (*tawḥīd wājib al-wujūd*) insofar as its historical reception is concerned. Indeed it is this passage and its argument that became the subject of a much-heated debate in the later traditions of Islamic philosophy and thus requires careful examination before turning to the criticisms that were made of it by later figures such as Ibn Kammūna.

The first thing to note is the significance of the surrounding context in which this remark occurs. Immediately before this passage, Avicenna presents a long discussion through *faṣl*s 8–15 in which he establishes the existence of at least one Necessary Being. The existence of *at least one* Necessary Being must therefore be taken for granted, and the question then is whether or not there are any other Necessary Beings. There are then two *faṣl*s that each provide one of two crucial premises in *faṣl*s 16 and 17, respectively, for the completeness of Avicenna's proof of divine unity, after which comes the passage cited above (*faṣl* 18). The reason why it is important to stress the significance of the surrounding context is so that we can understand exactly what Avicenna means when he begins *faṣl* 18 with the subject-term, 'The individuated Necessary Being' (*wājib al-wujūd al-mutaʿayyan*). In my view, these passages are connected and constitute a single train of thought. Avicenna begins *faṣl* 18 by referring to the very same Necessary Being that his discussion up to this point has established as a real being in extramental reality. His

22 Avicenna, *al-Ishārāt wa-l-tanbīhāt*, IV.18, p. 270. Cf. Ibn Kammūna, *al-Kāshif al-jadīd fī l-ḥikma*, 414.

remarks are therefore directly connected to what has already been said in the previous sections and are a continuation of his discussion of that Necessary Being which has been demonstrated to exist in reality. It is for this reason that the word *mutaʿayyan* enters into Avicenna's thinking and why it is now taken up as a topic for discussion; for whatever exists (and the previous sections have shown that at least one Necessary Being exists) must be individuated (i.e. It must be a *mutaʿayyan*). Unlike the previous discussions in the *Ilāhiyyāt* of the *Shifāʾ* which were based on hypothetical scenarios in which there are a multitude of Necessary Beings that each instantiate the univeresal concept or meaning of *wujūb al-wujūd*, the argument presented in *faṣl* 18 of the *Ishārāt* focusses on a non-hypothetical instance of *wujūb al-wujūd*, namely, 'the individuated Necessary Being' the existence of which has been demonstrated in the previous *faṣls*. Avicenna therefore does not begin his argument for divine unity in the *Ishārāt* with hypothetical instances of the necessity of existence, but with the fact that there is at least one Necessary Being—thus implying that there is at least one individuated being that instantiates the necessity of existence due to itself. Assuming then that there is at least one Necessary Being—and given that whatever exists must be individuated (*mā lam yatashakhkhaṣ lam yūjad*)—it makes sense for Avicenna to ask what it is that has caused this Necessary Being to be individuated. However, before answering this question, Avicenna provides two important premises in *faṣls* 16 and 17 that are needed for his proof of divine unity.

The first of these premises (*faṣl* 16) is the following:

> All things differing with respect to their extensions but agreeing with respect to something constituting [their essence] (*muqawwim*) are such that either: [(1)] What they share in common (*mā tattafiqu fīhi*) is a *lāzim* of what they do not share, such that things that are disparate [in nature] have a single *lāzim*—and this is something that cannot be denied. Or they are such that [(2)] What they do not share is a *lāzim* of what they share in common, such that the things which give rise to a single *lāzim* are themselves disparate and [even] opposed to one another in nature—and this is to be denied. Or they are such that [(3)] What they share in common is an *ʿāriḍ* of what they do not share—and the possibility of this cannot be denied. Or they are such that [(4)] What they do not share in common is an *ʿāriḍ* of what they agree on—and the possibility of this also cannot be denied.[23]

This densely packed remark contains some important considerations that are necessary for Avicenna's proof of divine unity. It begins by considering a multitude of things all of which are different from each other extensionally speaking but which have at least one part of their essences in common. Avicenna argues that in situations like this it must be

23 Avicenna, *al-Ishārāt wa-l-tanbīhāt*, IV.16, p. 269.

the case that each distinct reality that is similar in some respects but dissimilar in others is a combination of things they have in common and things they do not have in common. For example, two human beings must not only have the meaning 'humanity' in common but also other things they do not share; otherwise, as instances of humanity, they would be indiscernible and would not be two human beings but just one. Given that there is always a combination of something common and something unique, Avicenna focuses on the relationship (*nisba*) between these factors, which he calls 'that by which it is the same' (*mā tattafiqu bihi*) and 'that by which it is different' (*mā takhtalifu bihi*). Since the latter of these is the cause of the individuation (*taʿayyun*) of every existent reality, it is this particular notion that is philosophically interesting.

Avicenna argues that there are four possible ways for the converging and diverging aspects of a thing's existence to be related: (1) 'What they share in common' is a *lāzim* of 'what they do not share in common'; (2) 'What they do not share in common' is a *lāzim* of 'what they share in common'; (3) 'What they share in common' is an *ʿāriḍ* of 'what they do not share in common'; and (4) 'What they do not share in common' is an *ʿāriḍ* of 'what they do share in common'. To make sense of these combinations, we must start by clarifying the difference between two types of accidents known as *lawāzim* (sing. *lāzim*) and *ʿawāriḍ* (sing. *āriḍ*) on the one hand, and the term *muqawwim* on the other.[24] The difference between them is explained by Avicenna himself in his *Manṭiq al-mashriqiyyīn*:

> Every predicate that predicates a thing without complete correspondence is either a *muqawwim*, a *lāzim* or an *ʿāriḍ*. The *muqawwim* [of a thing] is whatever is in the essence itself of a thing such that its essence is comprised of it and something else. The *lāzim* is whatever must be predicated of a thing after its essence has been actualised in reality. The *ʿāriḍ* is whatever has been predicated of a thing but it is not necessary for that thing to be predicated with it all the time. What the *muqawwim* and the *lāzim* share in common is that neither of them can be separated from the thing [they predicate]. What the *lāzim* and *ʿāriḍ* share in common is that each of them is extraneous to the essence of the thing [they predicate] but attaches to it after [it has been completed as an essence].[25]

Every predicate is either constitutive of its subject's essence or not. If it is constitutive, then it is a *muqawwim*. If it is a non-constitutive predicate, then it is either impossible to separate it from the essence that it predicates or not. If it is the former then it is a

24 The terms *lāzim* and *muqawwim* are both mentioned in *faṣl* 16, whereas the terms *lawāzim* and *ʿawāriḍ* are both mentioned in *faṣl* 18 which contains the formal proof of divine unity.

25 Avicenna, *Manṭiq al-mashriqiyyīn*, eds. M. al-Khaṭīb and ʿA. al-Qatlā (Cairo: al-Maktaba al-Salafiyya, 1328/1910), 13–14. For a detailed breakdown of Avicenna's theory of constitutive and non-constitutive properties and their types, see Riccardo Strobino, *Avicenna's Theory of Science: Logic, Metaphysics, Epistemology* (California: University of California Press, 2021), 183–192.

*lāzim*, but otherwise it is an *ʿāriḍ*. By identifying constitutive predicates as essential predicates and non-constitutive predicates as non-essential predicates, we can summarise Avicenna's description of *lawāzim* and *ʿawāriḍ* by defining a *lāzim* as 'any non-essential but inseparable predicate of a thing' and an *ʿāriḍ* as 'any non-essential but separable predicate of a thing'.[26] A *muqawwim*, by contrast, is an essential part of the essence it predicates and thus forms a part of its definition, its 'whatness' or quiddity (*māhiyya*). By distinguishing two kinds of accidents as being either capable of being separated from their subjects or not, Avicenna distinguishes between a 'strong relation' of accidentality known as *luzūm* and a 'weak relation' of accidentality known as *ʿurūḍ*. Whereas the subject (*maʿrūḍ*) which is predicated by a certain *ʿāriḍ* is capable of having or not having that predicate, the subject (*malzūm*) and predicate (*lāzim*) of a *luzūm* relationship can never be separated from each other, even though the predicate in question does not constitute the essence of the subject.

Now, according to *faṣl* 16, Avicenna maintains that the *lawāzim* of a single essence are always the same. For example, if the essence of humanity produces a certain *lāzim* in one instance then it must produce the same *lāzim* in *every* instance of that essence. Moreover, he maintains that it is impossible for one essence to have certain *lawāzim* or concomitant properties in some instances but entirely different *lawāzim* in other instances of the same meaning—all things being equal. For example, it is impossible that 'animal' has the *lāzim* 'rationality' in some animals and 'the absence of rationality' in others. This is because the *lawāzim* of an essence are inseparable from it.[27] In our example, this would mean that both 'rationality' and the 'absence of rationality' are inseparable from 'animal', itself a contradiction since no animal is both rational and non-rational at the same time in the same way. What this example demonstrates is that if two things have something in common, their *lawāzim* cannot be different insofar as that common meaning is concerned. The key point therefore is that their *lawāzim* cannot be the cause of their individuations (*taʿyyunāt*). This is what Avicenna means when he states that what discernible things do not share in common (*mā takhtalifu bihi*)—namely, the *taʿayyun* that causes each thing's individuation—cannot be a *lāzim* of what they do share in common (*mā tattafiqu fīhi*)—namely, whatever shared meaning they have in common. In other words, a thing's individuating properties cannot be shared in any respect whatsoever. Therefore, the individuations that cause things to be different cannot be grounded in

26 Avicenna provides examples for each of these terms in the passage immediately following the one quoted above: 'An example of a *muqawwim* is "being a shape" for a triangle or "being a body" for a human. An example of a *lāzim* is a triangle being equal to two right angles [...] An example of an *ʿāriḍ* is a human being old or young or any of the other states that to occur to human.' (Ibid., 14)

27 Because such predicates are inseparable from their subjects, they are necessarily true of their subjects. For example, it is necessarily true that four is an even number, even though even number is not part of the essence of four.

the inseparable accidents (*lāzim*) of their shared meaning.[28] As a result, option 2 in the list above cannot be true.

As for the possibility that discernible things have a shared *lāzim* in common but are in and of themselves essentially different (option 1), Avicenna does not regard this as being impossible. An example of this is 'animal' and its association (or *nisba*) to 'rational' and 'non-rational' in two distinct beings such as Zayd and this particular dog called Lassie. What Zayd and Lassie have in common is that they are both animals; 'animal' here is the converging factor or that respect in which they are the same ('*mā tattafiqu fīhi*'). However, in Zayd's case, 'animality' is inseparable from rationality given that Zayd cannot be a human otherwise, and likewise for Lassie in whom 'animality' is inseparable from her being non-rational. This demonstrates that in the case of two distinct essences such as Zayd (a human) and Lassie (a dog), one of which has rationality and the other non-rationality, the meaning 'animal' is an inseparable accident of the very things by which each is differentiated from the other.[29] In Zayd's case, what differentiates him *qua* human from Lassie *qua* dog is his rational faculty, yet the meaning 'animal' is inseparable from 'rationality'. The same is true in Lassie's case. What differentiates her *qua* dog from Zayd is her lacking a rational faculty, albeit that whatever makes inchoate sounds by volition must be an animal. 'Animal' therefore is also an inseparable predicate of Lassie's 'non-rationality'.

Having considered the 'strong' relationship of *luzūm*, we are left with the 'weak' relationship of *ʿurūḍ*. However, unlike the case of *luzūm* Avicenna does not consider either of the possibilities (options 3 and 4) connected with *ʿurūḍ* as problematic. Two distinct realities may have something in common but can nevertheless be differentiated through different *ʿawāriḍ*,[30] or they may have a certain *ʿāriḍ* in common and still be individuated through essences that are different.[31] This means that out of the four possible combina-

28 In the context of our discussion, then, we can formulate the following line of reasoning. If there were two (or more) Necessary Beings, each Necessary Being would share the meaning necessary of existence due to itself with every other Necessary Being. However, in order for each Necessary Being to be an individuated being there has to be a unique individuation for each Necessary Being. Now, if what individuates and differentiates each Necessary Being is a *lāzim* of necessary of existence due to itself, then every instance of necessary of existence due to itself would have that *lāzim*. In this case, the *lāzim* of each Necessary Being is no longer its *taʿayyun* since every Necessary Being shares the same *lāzim*. Hence, the *lawāzim* of necessary of existence due to itself cannot be what individuates each Necessary Being.

29 That is, if Zayd is referred to as a 'rational being' and Lassie as a 'non-rational being', then 'animal' is an inseparable accident of both.

30 In this case, the *ʿawāriḍ* are what cause their individuations. The example given by Naṣīr al-Dīn al-Ṭūsī (d. 672/1274) is humanity and whatever its accidents are in two different human beings; for 'this human' and 'that human' are the same in virtue of their humanity, but different individuals insofar as one is a 'this' and the other is a 'that' as a result of their different accidents. See Naṣīr al-Dīn al-Ṭūsī, *Ḥall mushkilāt al-Ishārāt*, 3:30.

31 The example given by al-Ṭūsī is 'existence', which is a separable accident of 'this substance' and 'this accident'—as in the statements, 'This substance exists' and 'This accident exists' where two distinct essences have the predicate 'exists' in common. See Naṣīr al-Dīn al-Ṭūsī, *Sharḥ al-Ishārāt*, ed. Ḥasanzādah al-Āmulī (Qom: Būstān-i Kitāb, 1386Sh/[2007–2008]), 1:570.

tions between the converging and diverging factors of a being that is individuated, only option 1 is impossible. Hence, no being is ever indivduated such that its common factor is an inseparable accident (*lāzim*) of its individuation.

The second premise, offered in *faṣl* 17, draws out the aetiological implications of what has been stated in *faṣl* 16. Accidents by their nature require a subject to exist. In some cases, the subject itself is what causes the existence of the accident, and this is what characterises the strong relation of *luzūm*. In other cases, the accidents in question have their existence grounded in a subject but are caused by something other than the subject itself. For example, a particular human being's 'blackness' has the accident 'black' caused by something other than humanity *per se*. In other words, 'black' is grounded in Zayd but is not caused by his humanity *qua* humanity. Accidents like this are what Avicenna refers to as *ʿawāriḍ*. The *lawāzim*, by contrast, are not only grounded in a subject but are caused by the very essence of that subject, which is the reason why they have a 'strong relationship' of accidentality. Avicenna discusses the aetiological properties of accidents and their relation to their subjects in *faṣl* 17, focusing in particular on the accident 'existence'.

> It is sometimes admissible that the quiddity of a thing is a cause of one of its properties [i.e. one of its *lawāzim*], or that one of its properties is a cause for another property [i.e. one of its first-order *lawāzim* is a cause of a second-order property]—as in the case, for example, of the specific difference [i.e. a *muqawwim*] being a cause of a proprium [i.e. a *lāzim*]. However, it is not admissible for existence to be a property belonging to a thing and for that property to be caused by that thing's quiddity when its quiddity is not existence, or, for that matter, for it to be caused by another property. The reason for that is because the cause is always prior in existence [to the effect]; and there is nothing prior in existence before existence.[32]

Avicenna identifies two kinds of properties (accidents) in this remark. Some properties, he says, are caused by the very essence (or a part thereof) of the subjects they predicate. For example, as Naṣīr al-Dīn al-Ṭūsī explains in his commentary on the *Ishārāt*, the essence of twoness is what gives rise to and causes the meaning of evenness.[33] In this case, evenness is a *lāzim* of twoness. As for a part of a thing's essence being the cause of some of its accidental properties, the example that Ṭūsī provides is that of the specific difference 'rational' causing the proprium 'astonishment', which in turn causes the property 'laugther', all of which are grounded in the specific difference which forms a part of the very essence of humanity. However, as Ṭūsī explains, the difference between existence and all other properties is that 'all of the other properties only exist by virtue

32 Avicenna, *al-Ishārāt wa-l-tanbīhāt*, IV.17, p. 270.

33 al-Ṭūsī, *Sharḥ al-Ishārāt*, 1:570.

of the quiddity, whereas the quiddity [itself] exists [only] by virtue of existence.'[34] This means that existence has an ontological priority over everything else, implying that essence cannot precede existence. Existence cannot be the effect of something other than existence, namely, quiddity, and the existence of one thing can only be caused by the *existence* of something else. A quiddity such as humanity that does not have existence as part of its essence, therefore, cannot be the cause of existence, whether this be its own existence or the existence of something else, as this would imply that something other than existence is the cause of existence.[35]

The two premises which Avicenna discusses and which he will use to formulate his argument for divine unity can therefore be summarised as follows. In *faṣl* 16, he explains that whenever two things share some meaning in common there must also be something which they do not share in order for them to be two discernible entities. The relationship between these elements is either one of 'strong concomitance' (*luzūm*) or 'weak accidentally' (*ʿurūḍ*).[36] However, as accidents, both must be due to a cause.[37] Then in *faṣl* 17, Avicenna explains that *wujūd* cannot be a *lāzim* of *māhiyya*. Since the entire discussion appears in the context of an investigation into the Necessary Being, the conclusion that ought to be drawn from all of this is that divine existence (*wujūd*) is either a *muqawwim* of the Necessary Being or an *ʿāriḍ*, but never a *lāzim* of Its quiddity.[38] The argument for divine unity is then fleshed out as follows:

(1) There is at least one Necessary Being.[39]
(2) Every existent is something individuated.[40]
(3) Therefore, this Necessary Being is an individuated existent.
(4) The cause of this Necessary Being's individuation is either (4a) due to Its being

34 al-Ṭūsī, *Sharḥ al-Ishārāt*, 1:570–71 (*wa-l-farq bayn al-wujūd wa-sāʾir al-ṣifāt hāhunā anna sāʾir al-ṣifāt innamā yūjad bi-sabab al-māhiyya wa-l-māhiyya tūjad bi-sabab al-wujūd*).

35 This itself being an instance of the general philosophical principle that 'whatever lacks something, cannot give it to something else' (*fāqid al-shayʾ lā yuʿṭīhi*).

36 I borrow these translations from Mayer, 'Faḫr Ad-Dīn ar-Rāzī's Critique of Avicenna's Argument for the Unity of God in the *Išārāt*, and Naṣīr ad-Dīn Ṭūsī's Defence', 202.

37 In Islamic philosophy, the principle that all non-essential predicates of a thing are caused is stated in the Arabic expression '*kullu ʿaraḍī maʿlūl*'. The word *ʿaraḍī* here (as opposed to *ʿaraḍ*) denotes any non-essential—and therefore accidental—predicate of a thing and encompasses both separable (*ʿawāriḍ*) and non-separable (*lawāzim*) accidents of an essence.

38 This is not because the Necessary Being has no quiddity besides existence itself, but because of the fact that no quiddity *qua* itself precedes existence in being and cannot therefore be the cause of its own existence. It is important for this to be highlighted because Avicenna has not yet proven the simplicity of the Necessary Being, the argument for which is fleshed in the course of *faṣls* 20–22. In other words, this particular version of Avicenna's proof of divine unity does not rely on the premise that the Necessary Being is a simple being, even though, as Avicenna duly demonstrates, no Necessary Being can be a composite reality.

39 This is the conclusion of the argument Avicenna provides for the existence of a Necessary Being in *faṣls* 8–15.

40 Based on the principle '*al-shayʾ mā lam yatashakhkhaṣ lam yūjad*'.

necessarily existent or (4b) because of something else.

(5) If (4a), then nothing else can have this meaning.[41] (Hence, there is only one Necessary Being. QED.)

(6) However, if (4b), then this Necessary Being needs something else to individuate It.

(7) In that case, the relationship between Its shared meaning ('necessarily existent') and Its individuation is such that either: (7a) Its being necessarily existent is a *lāzim* of Its quiddity; or (7b) Its being necessarily existent is an *ʿāriḍ* of Its quiddity; or (7c) Its individuation is an *ʿāriḍ* of Its being necessarily existent; or (7d) Its individuation is a *lāzim* of Its being necessarily existent.

(8) However, 7a–d all imply that the Necessary Being is caused (*kullū ʿaraḍī maʿlūl*).

(9) The Necessary Being cannot be caused.

(10) Therefore, the Necessary Being cannot be individuated in any of the ways mentioned in 7a–d.

(11) Therefore, this Necessary Being's individuation is due to Its being necessarily existent.[42]

(12) Therefore, there is only *one* Necessary Being—*this* individuated Necessary Being (QED).

This remarkable argument for the unity of the Necessary Being (*tawḥīd wājib al-wujūd*) relies on nothing else apart from the notion of existence and its being necessarily existent. It emphasises the definition of what it means to exist necessarily by underscoring the importance of such a being's independence and self-sufficiency, and in doing so gives special importance to divine aseity. For this reason, the argument turns on statement 9: the aseity of a being that exists necessarily means just that the Necessary Being has within itself the ground and sufficient reason for its own existence. In other words, the Necessary Being cannot be caused by anything other than itself. But all of the possible ways of It being individuated by something other than itself mentioned in 7a–d imply that It is caused.[43] The argument thus demonstrates that this individuated Necessary

41 This is because being 'necessarily existent' is the individuation of this Necessary Being; and the individuations of each and every individuated being cannot be shared with other beings given that this would otherwise imply that 'what they share in common' (*mā tattafiqu fīhi*) is identical to 'what they do not share in common' (*mā taftariqu bihi*).

42 According to Naṣīr al-Dīn al-Ṭūsī this means that the particular existence (*al-wujūd al-khāṣṣ*) that belongs to the Necessary Being is sufficient for Its own individuation. This is important as it deflects the historical misunderstanding of some of Avicenna's commentators that necessity is extentionally different to the existence of the Necessary Being.

43 For the sake of comprehensiveness, it may be useful to explain exactly why each of the possibilities in 7a–d are impossible. The suggestion in 7a is that the essence (*māhiyya*) of the Necessary Being is the cause of Its individuation, and that 'being necessarily existent' is an inseparable accident of that essence. This means that the divine essence is the ontological cause of the Necessary Being's 'necessary existence'; the essence of the Necessary Being is the *malzūm lahu* and Its 'necessary existence' is the *lāzim*. However, Avicenna rejects this suggestion in *faṣl* 17 where he explains that no essence can be the

Being is individuated by nothing else apart from the sheer fact that it exists necessarily, and because of this there can be only one Necessary Being. It seems, therefore, that according to Avicenna, divine aseity is what grounds a proof of divine unity. Any being that exists necessarily is individuated by its necessary existence to be the only being of its kind. This is because the property of existing necessarily must itself be the individuating principle of a Necessary Being and thus cannot be shared with any other being. Hence, there are no beings other than this being that has this property, and thus there is only one being that has the property of existing necessarily due to Itself.

## 2. The *Shubha* of Ibn Kammūna

Although the historicity of the so-called 'doubt' (*shubha*) of Ibn Kammūna is not the main focus of this study, it is worth stressing that Ibn Kammūna was not the first thinker to criticise Avicenna's proof of divine unity. The Ashʿarī theologian Fakhr al-Dīn al-Rāzī had already questioned the possibility of the predicate 'necessary of existence due to itself' being predicable of more than one Necessary Being in his *Kitāb al-Muḥaṣṣal*.[44] Notwithstanding such criticisms, however, it was the 'doubt' raised by Ibn Kammūna

---

cause of Its own existence since nothing precedes existence in being. Hence 7a is false. The suggestion in 7b is that 'being necessarily existent' is a separable accident of the Necessary Being's essence. In this case, the divine essence is the *maʿrūḍ lahu* and 'being necessarily existent' is the *ʿāriḍ*. However, this is impossible because not only does every *ʿāriḍ* require a cause separate from the essence it predicates, but also because the essence itself (which is not necessary of existence due to itself) needs a cause for its existence. Hence 7b is also false. The suggestion in 7c is that the Necessary Being's individuation is a separable accident of Its 'being necessarily existent'. In this case, 'being necessarily existent' is the *maʿrūḍ lahu* and the individuation of the Necessary Being is the *ʿāriḍ*. However, this too is clearly impossible because it makes the Necessary Being's existence dependent on the very same cause that causes Its individuation to occur to It. In other words, since every *ʿāriḍ* is ontologically dependent on a separate cause different to the essence it predicates, and since that separate cause is what causes the Necessary Being's individuation, it follows by transitivity of causation that this separate cause also causes the existence of the Necessary Being. Hence 7c is also false. Finally, the suggestion in 7d is that the individuation of the Necessary Being is an inseparable accident of Its 'being necessarily existent'. This means that the individuation is the lāzim and 'being necessarily existent' is the *malzūm lahu*. But this too is false since in order for 'necessary existence' to be a cause of that individuation (as would be necessary in the case of every *lāzim*) it would first need to exist; for nothing is a cause of anything unless it is first an actual existent. But in order for it to exist it must be individuated, which therefore implies that it is both individuated and not inviduated before causing its own individuation, and that is clearly absurd. Therefore, all of the options are false. For a detailed explication of these categories and their ensuing impossibility, see al-Ṭūsī, *Sharḥ al-Ishārāt*, 1:580–84. Notice that in all of these arguments there is only one Necessary Being being considered alongside the various metaphysical configurations between Its essence, existence and inviduation.

44 Fakhr al-Dīn al-Rāzī, *Kitāb al-Muḥaṣṣal: wa-huwa Muḥaṣṣal afkār al-mutaqaddimīn wa-l-mutaʾakhkhirīn min al-ḥukamāʾ wa-l-mutakallimīn*, ed. Ḥusayn Atāʾī (Qom: Intishārāt al-Sharīf al-Raḍī, 1999), 182–83. Rāzī's suggestion is based on an equivocal understanding of the term 'necessary existence'. It is worth bearing in mind that Ibn Kammūna was familiar with the *Muḥaṣṣal* of Rāzī and Ṭūsī's rebuttal of it. See Reza Pourjavady and Sabine Schmidtke, *A Jewish Philosopher of Baghdad: ʿIzz al-Dawla Ibn Kammūna (d. 683/1248) and His Writings* (Leiden: Brill, 2006), 79–83.

that gained widespread noteriety and scholarly engagement in the eastern lands of Islam from the late fifteenth century. The Shiraz-based philosopher Jalāl al-Dīn al-Dawānī (d. 908/1502) seems to have played an important role in this regard, for not only did he draw attention to Ibn Kammūna's criticisms but reinforced them even further in his commentary on Suhrawardī's *Hayākil al-nūr* titled *Shawākil al-ḥūr fī sharḥ Hayākil al-nūr*.[45] The subsequent reception of Dawānī's writings in the early Safavid period popularised the so-called '*shubhat al-tawḥīd*' (as it was later known) among a host of thinkers, many of whom wrote independent treatises responding to the *shubha*.[46]

Ibn Kammūna discusses proofs for the uniqueness of the Necessary Being across a range of texts, but his criticisms of Avicenna's proof in the *Ishārāt* are first mentioned in a relatively short work titled *al-Maṭālib al-muhimma min ʿilm al-ḥikma*, which he completed in Shaʿbān 657/July–August 1259.[47] In the section concerning God's uniqueness, Ibn Kammūna begins by first outlining the general Avicennian argument for the Necessary Being's oneness. Though he paraphrases Avicenna's argument with slightly different philosophical terminology, the argument remains Avicennian at its core. The discussion centres on the claim that the species 'existing necessarily' (*wājib al-wujūd*) must be confined to a single individual (*shakhṣ wāḥid*). To demonstrate this, Ibn Kammūna imagines a scenario in which there are two Necessary Beings sharing the same essence but with different ipseities, which is necessary if they are to exist as two distinct realities. This leads to a disjunctive proposition: either the ipseity (*huwiyya*) of each Necessary Being is identical to its essence, which in this case happens to be 'existing necessarily', or it is something additional (and therefore different) to it. Since the *huwiyya* of each Necessary Being is what makes it an individual it is obvious that Ibn Kammūna has the principle of individuation in mind and that it is the same in meaning as Avicenna's notion of *taʿayyun*.

Now, if the individuation (*huwiyya*) of each Necessary Being is identical to its essence, then the conclusion would lead to the desired outcome that there can be only one individual that instatiates the species (or essence) 'existing necessarily'. However, if the individuation of each Necessary Being is additional to its essence then this implies that each Necessary Being's individuation is an accidental property, which Ibn Kammūna argues results in two impossibilities. Of these, the first impossibility is the one that is most pertitent: every accident requires a cause, and the cause of each Necessary Being's individuation in this case would either be the divine essence itself or something else

45 Jalāl al-Dīn al-Dawānī, *Shawāwil al-ḥūr fī sharḥ Hayākil al-nūr*, ed. Muḥammad Rajab ʿAlī Ḥasan (Amman: Dār al-Fatḥ Li-l-Dirāsāt wa-l-Nashr, 2023), 292–317.

46 See Reza Pourjavady and Sabine Schmidtke, *A Jewish Philosopher of Baghdad: ʿIzz al-Dawla Ibn Kammūna (d. 683/1248) and His Writings* (Leiden: Brill, 2006), 49–51. The list of scholars mentioned include ʿAlī b. Faḍl Allāh al-Jīlānī (Gīlānī) al-Fūmānī, Shams al-Dīn Muḥammad b. Niʿmat Allāh al-Jīlānī ('Mullā Shamsā Gīlānī', d. 1064/1654), ʿAbd al-Razzāq al-Lāhijī (d. 1072/1661), Āqā Ḥusayn b. Jamāl al-Dīn al-Khwānsārī (d. 1098/1687), and Muḥammad b. ʿAbd al-Fattāḥ Sarāb Tunikābūnī (d. 1124/1712).

47 Ibn Kammūna, 'al-Maṭālib al-muhimma min ʿilm al-ḥikma,' *Khiradnāmah-i Ṣadrā* 8, no. 32 (2003): 64–86. For more on this work, see Pourjavady and Schmidtke, *A Jewish Philosopher of Baghdad*, 92–3.

entirely. If the divine essence itself causes the accident, then the accident is a *lāzim* (Ibn Kammūna does not use this term) and as such cannot serve as an individuating principle of two Necessary Beings having the same essence, as shown by Avicenna. If, however, the accident is caused by something else entirely, then this leads to the absurd conclusion that the Necessary Being is dependent on something other than itself for its existence.[48]

Ibn Kammūna's reasoning here captures Avicenna's own individuation-based argument for divine unity albeit for one crucial difference. According to Ibn Kammūna, the argument does not go as far Avicenna intended because although it demonstrates that there cannot be two Necessary Beings having *the same essence*, it does not take into consideration how the situation might change *if they had different essences*. Indeed, the argument began with the assumption that there are two Necessary Beings having the species/essence 'existing necessarily' in common and from there proceeded to show why this is impossible. However, according to Ibn Kammūna, this does not prove *tawḥīd* absolutely, since it does not rule out the possibility of there being two (or more) Necessary Beings that share nothing in common insofar as their essences are concerned. As he writes after presenting Avicenna's argument,

> [F]rom this it becomes clear that the existence of two Necessary Beings sharing the *same* essence is impossible, but this demonstration does not yield the conclusion that it is impossible for two Necessary Beings to exist absolutely; for it is conceivable—rationally speaking—that there are two beings in existence whose species are confined to a single individual and which share the necessity of existence, since, as you are aware, necessity is something non-existential. If this is something impossible, then its impossibility must be proven by a demonstration other than this one, but I have yet to come across it other than through the methods that are mixed [with a consideration of] how the efficient cause [causes the existence] of the world.[49]

As Pourjavady and Schmidtke observe, this passage was included by Jalāl al-Dīn al-Dawānī in his *Shawākil al-ḥūr* and explicitly attributed to Ibn Kammūna.[50] Furthermore, Dawānī explains that his predecessor considered the plurality of Necessary Beings to be categorically impossible in his *al-Kāshif*, suggesting that Ibn Kammūna had found a solution to his own doubt after all.[51] Indeed a significant portion of the *Kāshif* seems to address the very problem that had been raised by Ibn Kammūna in his earlier work *al-Maṭālib al-muhimma*. Ibn Kammūna here writes that regardless of whether two Necessary Beings belong to the same species *or not* a plurality of Necessary Beings is impossible.

48 Ibn Kammūna, 'al-Maṭālib al-muhimma', 77.
49 Ibn Kammūna, 'al-Maṭālib al-muhimma', 78; cf. Ibn Kammūna, *Sharḥ al-Talwīḥāt*, 3:177.
50 See al-Dawānī, *Shawākil al-ḥūr*, 166.
51 al-Dawānī, *Shawākil al-ḥūr*, 166.

If they have the same essence, then Avicenna's proof of divine unity suffices. If they have different essences, then the necessity of existence would be neither identical to each of their essences (since this entails they have the same essence) nor a constituent part of their essences either (since this entails their being composite).[52] Therefore, two Necessary Beings, each one being the sole instance of its own unique species, would be such that they share the necessity of existence not as a single species or essence but as a concomitant property (*ʿaraḍī lāzim*) of two distinct essences.[53] This means that the necessity they have in common is something that lies outside of their essences, and that their essences, being entirely different from each other, serve as the principle by which they are individuated as unique Necessary Beings. This is precisely what later scholars refered to as 'the *shubha* of Ibn Kammūna' even though Ibn Kammūna himself rejects it in his work *al-Kāshif al-jadīd.*

> If the existence of two Necessary Beings each belonging to a different species were possible, then the property 'necessity of existence' would have been an inseparable accident for both Necessary Beings, each having the necessity of existence in common but being entirely distinct from it nevertheless by virtue of its essence. In this case, the essence (*maʿrūḍ*) that is predicated with the necessity of existence would not be necessarily existent in itself, but not in the sense that it is incapable of existing necessarily but rather in the sense that it is possible for the intellect to consider that essence by itself without considering that existence [which is predicated of it as an accidental concomitant]. Hence, the essence of the subject being predicated [i.e. the essence of each Necessary Being] cannot be the cause [of this accident], for nothing is a cause unless it exists extramentally. Otherwise, this entails that its existence precedes its own existence [and that is impossible]. Furthermore, the accident [that two Necessary Beings share, i.e. 'necessity of existence'] is not in itself necessary because it does not exist outside of the mind without first being specified [for each Necessary Being] so as to remove its community [i.e. its being a universal]. Therefore, if it is not itself necessary, it has to be contingent, which means that it requires a cause beyond that which it predicates. As a result, each Necessary Being requires a cause beyond itself for its existence, thus leading to the conclusion that each Necessary Being is not something that exists necessarily, and that is absurd.[54]

---

52 Ibn Kammūna, *al-Kāshif (al-jadīd fī l-ḥikma)*, 416.

53 Ibn Kammūna is here following Shihāb al-Dīn al-Suhrawardī in characterising the necessity of each Necessary Being as a concomitant accidental (*ʿaraḍī lāzim*).

54 Ibn Kammūna, *al-Kāshif (al-Jadīd fī l-ḥikma)*, 417. For a useful study of Ibn Kammūna's arguments for God's uniqueness, see Ahmed Alwishah, 'Suhrawardī and Ibn Kammūna on the Impossibility of Having Two Necessary Existents,' in *Illuminationist Texts and Textual Studies: Studies in Memory of Hossein Ziai*, eds. Ali Gheissari, John Walbridge and Ahmed Alwishah (Leiden: Brill, 2018): 115–134.

While he appears to have resolved any personal doubts about the proofs concerned with demonstrating the Necessary Being's uniqueness, Ibn Kammūna's 'doubt' took on a life of its own in the centuries after his death. Later scholars took the original argument seriously, and from the early Safavid period onwards the problem of proving the Necessary Being's uniqueness gained increasing notoreity. The problem persisted in the works of numerous scholars who not only grappled with its implications but who, over time, reinforced it, signaling that it could not simply be ignored. By refining and modifying Ibn Kammūna's original *shubha*, later scholars underscored that his doubt was not as easily dismissed as he himself had suggested in the *Kāshif*. Though transformed and refined, the doubt endured. Ironically, it was Jalāl al-Dīn al-Dawānī who, for dialectical reasons, refuted Ibn Kammūna's own attempt to disprove his earlier doubts—ultimately, what later became known as the '*shubha* of Ibn Kammūna' was, in reality, Dawānī's rebuttal.[55]

By the late sixteenth century, the so-called *shubha* of Ibn Kammūna had developed into one of the key *problemata* within the Shiraz and Isfahan schools of philosophy. In some scholars minds it demonstrated the rational plausibility of there being more than one Necessary Being without this leading to any of the undesirable consequences outlined by Avicenna in his individuation-based argument for divine unity.[56] To appreciate why this was so, we need to remind ourselves of some of the key steps in Avicenna's reasoning. The first and most important of these is that Avicenna basis his argument on the principle of individuation and the various ways that something can be individuated. For Avicenna, if there are two or more Necessary Beings then the principle of their individuation is either something that comprises the very essence of each Necessary Being or something accidental. The first implies compositionality, the second that whatever exists necessarily is necessary of existence due to another and not due to itself, both of which entail that each Necessary Being is caused. Hence, there is only one Necessary Being.

Ibn Kammūna accepts that these are two ways in which things may be individuated, but crucially he does not accept that these are the only ways. This is because, according to Ibn Kammūna, Avicenna ignores the possibility that two Necessary Beings are individuated by their very essences as a whole and not due to constituent parts. This being the case, argues Ibn Kammūna, it is conceivable that there are two Necessary Beings that have no parts whatsoever (thereby preserving DDS) but which nonetheless possess essences that are wholly distinct from each other, this being the sufficient cause of their individuations. They are, as eloquently expressed in the original Arabic, *mutabāyina bi-tamām al-dhāt*—entirely distinct from each other and not merely partially so.[57] Ibn

55 See al-Dawānī, *Shawākil al-ḥūr*, 293–94.

56 For example, the Safavid philosopher Āqā Ḥusayn Khwānsārī, *al-Ḥāshiya ʿalā l-Shifāʾ* (*al-Ilāhiyyāt*), ed. Ḥāmid Nājī Iṣfahānī (Qom: Dabīrkhānah-i Kangarah Āqā Ḥusayn Khwānsārī, 1378Sh/[1999–2000]), 296–97.

57 As many later thinkers have noted, the ten Aristotelian categories (*maqūlāt*) are essences that are entirely distinct from one another *bi-tamām al-dhāt*—that is, they are distinct *per se* and in their entirety,

Kammūna therefore avoids the first of Avicenna's anticipated problems, namely, the problem of composition in the Necessary Being.

The second reason why the *shubha* could not be so easily dismissed was because it brought into sharper focus the ontological status of necessity itself. If each of the two hypothesised Necessary Beings is a simple reality with no internal relations among parts and entirely distinct in nature from every other essence, then the necessity that characterises them cannot be identical to their essences, as this either requires the need for another essential part (but this is barred since each Necessary Being is assumed to be a simple reality) or the existence of an accidental property that individuates each Necessary Being (but this is also barred since each Necessary Being is *ex hypothesi* individuated by its very essence). Ibn Kammūna argues that it is still justified to apply the term 'necessarily existent' for each Necessary Being by stating that even though the expression does not refer to an actual property outside the mind it is nonetheless an accurate description of each Necessary Being upon consideration. In other words, he considers the notion of a thing being necessarily existent to be *iʿtibārī* and does not think it is necessary for all meanings to have a one-to-one correspondence with things in extramental reality.[58] Such notions are conjured in the mind upon the intellect's consideration of them but do not as such pick out actual properties within things themselves. It is crucial to note that considerations of this kind are not mere fictions conjured out of nowhere. Rather, the object upon which the intellectual act of consideration is performed is something which itself possesses actual existence in extramental reality. Whatever intellectual operations are performed on it are therefore operations grounded in the objective reality of that very thing itself.[59] The language of Islamic philosophers is highly significant in this regard: *iʿtibārī*-terms like 'possibility' and 'necessity' are thought of as being 'extrapolated' or 'extracted' from something else, implying that their existence—albeit of a purely mental character—is derived from something more primitive than the *iʿtibāri* concepts themselves. Those things from which the mind extracts *iʿtibārī* concepts are referred to as the ground, or, more literally, 'the source from which *iʿtibārī* concepts are extrapolated' (*mabdaʾ al-intizāʿ*), the language of which intimates that *iʿtibārī* concepts

---

rather than due to any shared constituent. If they were differentiated by only a part of their essence, they would necessarily share a common element, which would, in turn, imply the existence of a higher genus encompassing them. This would contradict their status as the highest genera of being, as they would then be subsumed under a more fundamental category.

58 For example, the proposition 'The chair is contingent' does not entail that the predicate 'contingent' has an existence of its own apart from the existence of the chair. In other words, the terms within the proposition 'The chair is contingent' pick out one item of existence—namely, the chair's existence. The word 'contingent' is therefore *iʿtibārī* in the sense that when the intellect considers the quiddity of the subject-term 'chair' in relation to its extramental existence it contrives the notion of it being a contingent being. This is in contrast to a more direct realist conception of language in which each of the proposition's terms picks out a separate item of existence.

59 This of course assumes that the intellect is not sullied or influenced by the non-intellectual powers of the soul.

are not mere subjective notions but ideas grounded in the objective reality of things themselves.[60] For our purposes, it suffices that for Ibn Kammūna the characterisation of each divine ipseity as being something that is necessarily existent due to itself is an *iʿtibārī* characterisation of their extramental essences which in themselves are unknown (*majhūl al-kunh*).[61] The name 'Necessary Being' does not pick out a corresponding attribute or property called *wujūb al-wujūd* in extramental existence, but nonetheless is a valid way of speaking and referring to those simple divine ipseities. The implications of this are far-reaching and have significant metaphysical consequences, particularly insofar as they help Ibn Kammūna avoid some of the pitfalls identified by Avicenna in his arguments against divine multiplicity.

Firstly, like Avicenna, Ibn Kammūna preserves the ontological requirement that all existent things must be individuated by maintaining that what causes each Necessary Being's individuation is none other than their unique essences, a consideration ignored by Avicenna. However, this means that the necessity of each Necessary Being is not to be regarded *pace* Avicenna as the essence of each Necessary Being nor a part thereof. Rather, according to Ibn Kammūna, each Necessary Being's necessity is an *iʿtibārī* (as opposed to *ḥaqīqī*) concept extracted by the mind's contemplation of those extramental ipseities. This in turn has two important consequences. The first is that each Necessary Being shares a non-essential property known as its necessity, which is important because we would not otherwise be able to speak of more than one Necessary Being. This necessity is *iʿtibārī*, meaning that it is an accident of those ipseities *in the mind* as opposed to a real accident of theirs in extramental existence.

This leads to the second outcome which is that the standard philosophical view which asserts that all accidental properties are caused (*kullu ʿaraḍī maʿlūl*) is now restricted in scope to exclude properties that are *iʿtibārī*. Later philosophers in the Shīʿī tradition such as Mullā Hādī Sabzawārī (d. 1289/1873) and al-ʿAllāma al-Ṭabāṭabāʾī (d. 1402/1981) explain the basis for this exclusion by first distinguishing between two kinds of predicates known as *al-maḥmūl bi-l-ḍamīma* and *al-khārij al-maḥmūl* (also known as *al-maḥmūl min ṣamīmihi*).[62] For the sake of simplicity, we can loosely translate these as 'predicates added to their subjects' and 'predicates extracted from their subjects', respectively. Let us

---

60 For more on the history and importance of *iʿtibārī* concepts, see Jari Kaukua, '*Iʿtibārī* Concepts in Suhrawardī: The Case of Substance', *Oriens* 48 (2020): 40–66.

61 The epistemic point about their essences being unknown was added and highlighted by Jalāl al-Dīn al-Dawānī.

62 See al-ʿAllāma al-Ṭabāṭabāʾī, *Nihāyat al-ḥikma*, ed. ʿAbbās ʿAlī Zurāʿī Sabzawārī (Qom: Muʾassasat al-Nashr al-Islāmī al-Tābiʿa Li-Jamāʿat al-Mudarrisīn), 2:130–131; cf. Mullā Hādī Sabzawārī, *Sharḥ al-Manẓūma fī l-manṭiq wa-l-ḥikma*, ed. Muḥsin Bīdārfar (Qom: Manshūrāt-i Bīdār, 1432/[2010–2011]), 1:39; idem., *Sharḥ al-asmāʾ aw Sharḥ Duʿā al-Jawshan al-kabīr*, ed. Najafqulī Ḥabībī (Tehran: Intishārāt-i Dānishghāh-i Ṭihrān, 1385Sh/[2006–2007]), 373–74. The distinction is alluded to by Mullā Ṣadrā, *al-Mabdaʾ wa-l-maʿād*, ed. Muḥammad Żabīḥī and Jaʿfar Shāh-Naẓarī (Tehran: Bunyād-i Ḥikmat-i Islāmī-yi Ṣadrā, 1381Sh/[2002–2003]), 1:17, 20.

consider the propositions 'The body is blue' and 'The body is contingent' to explain the difference between them. In the first proposition, the predicate-term 'blue' is something that is added to the referent of the subject-term in extramental reality; thinking of the subject-term on its own (i.e. body *qua* body) will not give the mind the concept of blueness. 'Blue' is thus an added property or predicate of 'body', without the addition of which the proposition 'The body is blue' would be false. By contrast, if we consider the statement 'The body is contingent', the predicate-term 'contingent' does not refer to a property or quality that is *added* to the referent of the subject-term. Rather, by contemplating the nature of the subject-term the mind itself extrapolates the notion of contingency from it without anything being added to the subject in actual reality. The difference between these predicates can therefore be explained in terms of whether or not the rational faculty can extrapolate the notion of the predicate from the subject itself without recourse to any non-rational processes such as perception or experimentation. For example, in the case of bodies, the rational faculty can itself deduce that whatever is a body must have extension, and whatever has extension must have parts, and whatever has parts must be composed, and whatever is composed must be contingent, and hence the contingency of bodies can be known *a priori*. For Islamic philosophers, this implies that no quality or property has been added to bodies extramentally in order for them to be contingent: one can know that bodies are contingent by simply 'considering' (*iʿtibār*) the concept of a body on its own. By contrast one cannot derive the notion of blueness from the mere thought or conceptualisation of body *qua* body. One verifies the statement 'The body is blue' through experience, which implies that something must have been added to a body extramentally in order for it to be blue. Since blueness cannot be deduced from body itself, and given that a predicate like 'blue' is a real as opposed to *iʿtibārī* predicate, it must be an accident that requires a cause for its predication. We can therefore conclude that the principle 'All accidental predicates must be caused' (*kullu ʿaraḍī maʿlūl*) only applies to those predicates that have been added to a subject extramentally but not to *iʿtibārī* predicates extracted from their subjects in the mind. The principle '*kullu ʿaraḍī maʿlūl*' thus applies to accidentals that are *al-maḥmūl bi-l-ḍamīma* but not to those that are *al-khārij al-maḥmūl*.

In the context of Ibn Kammūna's argument against divine unity, then, the implications of this are as follows. Since the notion of each divine ipseity being 'necessarily existent' is *iʿtibārī*, the accidental nature of this necessity does not mean that necessity is an accident in the same way that a real predicate like 'blue' is an accident in the extramental world. The reason is that necessity is now taken to be a predicate extrapolated from—as opposed to a predicate added to—the very essence of each divine ipseity. Necessity is an accidental predicate that is *al-khārij al-maḥmūl* and not *al-maḥmūl bi-l-ḍamīma*, and therefore not subject to the principle that 'all accidentals are caused'.[63] This implies that even though the necessity of each divine ipseity is something accidental, it is not caused in the robust metaphysical sense of efficient causation outside the mind. Ibn Kammūna thus appears to have found a workaround for each of the potential pitfalls of Avicenna's argument against divine multiplicity by showing that there can be two or more Necessary Beings that have nothing in common other than the mere label 'being necessarily existent' which is extrapolated from their simple essences by an act of intellectual appraisal. As such, two or more Necessary Beings could potentially coexist alongside each other without either of them being composed or their individuations being caused. Avicenna's so-called *burhān* for the unity of the Necessary Being is therefore shown to be inconclusive.

## 3. Mullā Ṣadrā and His Commentators on the *Shubha* of Ibn Kammūna

In the remaining sections of this paper, I examine the ideas of the 17th-century Safavid philosopher Ṣadr al-Dīn al-Shīrāzī (d. 1045 or 1050/1635 or 1640), commonly known as Mullā Ṣadrā, as well as the philosophers who carried forward his school of thought from the Qajar period to the present day. I discuss Ṣadrā's engagement with the *shubha* of Ibn Kammūna and examine the ways in which he sought to resuscitate Avicenna's proof of the unity of the Necessary Being. I then explore what I consider to be the 'missing gap' in Avicenna's argument for divine unity, at least from a Ṣadrian perspective—namely, the doctrine of divine perfection (DDP) and its importance as a crucial device in understanding the concept of necessary existence. Finally, I analyse some of Ṣadrā's own proofs for the unity of the Necessary Being which are grounded in the principles of perfect being theology to highlight the depth and originality of his contributions to Islamic debates surrounding God's uniqueness.

Mullā Ṣadrā's responses to Ibn Kammūna's *shubha* appear across a wide range of texts, each offering a different perspective on the problem.[64] Some of these responses

63 Mullā Hādī Sabzawārī, *Sharḥ al-Manẓūma*, 1:447.

64 Mullā Ṣadrā, *al-Ḥikmat al-mutaʿāliyya fī l-asfār al-arbaʿa*, ed. Aḥmad Aḥmadī (Tehran: Bunyād-i Ḥikmat-i Islāmī-yi Ṣadrā, 1380Sh/[2001]), 6:52–58; cf. idem., *al-Shawāhid al-rubūbiyya fī l-manāhij al-sulūkiyya*, ed. Sayyid Muṣṭafā Muḥaqqiq Dāmād (Tehran: Bunyād-i Ḥikmat-i Islāmī-yi Ṣadrā, 1382Sh/[2003]), 50-1; idem., *al-Mabdaʾ wa-l-maʿād fī l-ḥikmat al-mutaʿāliyya*, 1:85–91; idem., *Sharḥ u taʿlīqah-i Ṣadr al-Mutaʾallihīn bar Ilāhiyyāt-i Shifāʾ*, ed. Najafqulī Ḥabībī (Tehran: Intishārāt-i Bunyād-i Ḥikmat-i Islāmī-yi Ṣadrā, 1382Sh/[2003]), 1:159–180; idem., *Asrār al-āyāt wa-anwār al-bayyināt*, edited by Muḥammad ʿAlī Jāwidān (Tehran: Intishārāt-i Bunyād-i Ḥikmat-i Islāmī-yi Ṣadrā, 1389Sh/[2010]), 57–60; idem., *al-Maẓāhir al-ilāhiyya fī l-ʿulūm al-kamāliyya*, ed. Sayyid Muḥammad Khāmanāʾī (Tehran: Intishārāt-i Bunyād-i Ḥikmat-i Islāmī-yi Ṣadrā, 1391Sh/[2012]), 28–34; idem, *Sharḥ al-Hidāya al-Athīriyya*, ed. Maqṣūd Muḥammadī (Tehran: Intishārāt-i Bunyād-i Ḥikmat-i Islāmī-yi Ṣadrā, 1393Sh/[2014]), 2:150–56; idem., *al-Ḥikmat al-ʿarshiyya*, ed. Aṣghar Dādbih, in *Majmūʿah-i rasāʾil-i falsafī*, 4:50–1 (Tehran: Bunyād-i Ḥikmat-i Islāmī-yi Ṣadrā, 1391Sh/[2012]); idem., *al-Masāʾil al-qudsiyya*, ed. Manūchahr Ṣadūqī Sahā, in *Majmūʿah-i rasāʾil-i falsafī* (Tehran: Bunyād-i Ḥikmat-i Islāmī-yi Ṣadrā, 1391Sh/[2012]), 4: 246–48; idem., *al-Mashāʿir*, ed. Maqṣūd Muḥammadī, in *Majmūʿah-i rasāʾil-i falsafī* (Tehran: Bunyād-i Ḥikmat-i Islāmī-yi Ṣadrā, 1391Sh/[2012]), 4:385–6.

are rooted in Ṣadrā's own metaphysical commitments, while others draw from more conventional Avicennian foundations. The *Asfār* addresses the problem using the former approach, which explains why Ṣadrā is quick to identify the primary reason why thinkers in the post-Avicennian tradition struggled to provide an adequate refutation of Ibn Kammūna's counterargument. He begins his response by asserting that the problem is particularly acute because of the fact that many of Avicenna's later followers characterise existence (*wujūd*) as a kind of empty concept devoid of extramental reference. As Ṣadrā explains,

> This doubt presents itself with great difficulty for those later scholars who say that existence is a term that lacks reference [in extramental reality] and is just a mental consideration. This is because, in their view, the only thing that existent things [*qua* existent things] share in common is this generic extrapolated notion. This shared existence does not, in their view, have a real instantiation, neither in God the Necessary Being nor in anything contingent. Their use of the expression 'individual existence' for the Necessary Being is just technical jargon since by using this phrase they refer to something unknown.[65]

Ṣadrā begins his engagement with Ibn Kammūna's argument against *tawḥīd* by admitting that it presents a significant and genuine problem for those holding the view that existence is *iʿtibārī*. But the problem doesn't stop just there. Indeed, according to Ṣadrā, assigning an *iʿtibārī* status to existence (and as a corollary to necessity) not only impacts philosophical arguments that aspire to prove the unity of the Necessary Being but also their ability to demonstrate that such a being even exists. This is explained in Ṣadrā's *al-Mabdaʾ wa-l-maʿād* in which the discussion focusses on the very notion of what it means to be necessarily existent (*wājib al-wujūd*). The idea that there is something 'necessarily existent' can be interpreted in one of two ways: (1) that there is something that *has* the necessity of existence, but which in and of itself is something else, or (2) that something *is* the necessity of existence *per se*.[66] An analogy helps clarify what is meant here. 'Being white', for example, can either be a property of something which in itself is not white (such as a piece of cloth), or it can be a semantic description or label of the colour white itself. In other words, according to Ṣadrā, the ascription 'necessarily existent' can either be used as a description of the very essence of that which it names or as a description of something whose essence is something other than 'necessary existence' but which nevertheless has the necessity of existence, the latter of these being the

65 Mullā Ṣadrā, *al-Ḥikmat al-mutaʿāliyya*, 6:54.

66 Mullā Ṣadrā, *al-Mabdaʾ wa-l-maʿād*, 1:83. In other words, there are two kinds of necessary being: (1) necessary due to itself (*al-wājib bi-l-dhāt*) and (2) necessary due to another (*al-wājib bi-l-ghayr*). A necessary being in the former sense *is* the necessity of existence, while a being in the latter sense *has* the necessity of existence. Cf. Mullā Ṣadrā, *Sharḥ al-Hidāya*, 2:152.

view of Ibn Kammūna.[67] From a metaphysical point of view, then, the expression 'being necessarily existent' used for beings of the former kind does not require any cause or qualification just as the predicate 'white' used for the colour white itself does not need anything beyond the subject itself, being as it were a kind of tautology.[68] However, its application to beings of the second kind does, implying that the validity of the predicate 'necessarily existent' for such beings is grounded in the fact that some property has been added to or extrapolated from them.[69] For this reason, Ṣadrā explains that

> Any necessary existent that is not identical to necessary existence itself, but is something that possesses a reality or essence [other than necessary existence] and that this essence is what is then attributed with being necessarily existent, such a thing requires for its being attributed with necessary existence the accidental occurrence of this meaning (*amr*) and therefore a *cause* to make it be this way or to make it *per se*, so that it then may be attributed with this property, depending on which of the two opinions one takes on this issue.[70] Regardless, the thing itself is merely contingent, and it is only on account of that property that it becomes something necessarily existent. Whatever is like this cannot be necessarily existent due to itself.

67 Recall that according to Ibn Kammūna, the essence of each Necessary Being is unknown (*majhūl al-kunh*). Hence, each so-called 'Necessary Being' has an essence to which the necessity of existence is asribed, but which in itself is not the necessity of existence. As for what that 'Necessary Being' might be in itself, this is unknown.

68 In such cases, if *a*'s F-ness is because of *a* itself, then F is an essential property of *a*. Therefore, the statement '*a* is F' is essentially true. Hence, if N is a necessary being and its necessary existence is due to it being N, then N is a necessary being due to itself. But if N's necessary existence is not due to N itself, then N's necessary existence is due to something else. In this case, N is not necessary existence *per se*, but rather has the necessity of existence.

69 There exists, in other words, a *ḥaythiyya taʿlīliyya* —an intermediary causal explanation—for the notion of 'necessary existence' which makes it a predicate of beings in the second category, but no such *ḥaythiyya* for beings in the first category. To explain what is meant here consider a proposition of the kind 'S is P'. If P is true of S *insofar as S is S and only S*, then there is no further cause or justification needed for the predication of P for S. An example would be 'X is a human, and X is rational', for the rationality of human beings is true by definition and not because of something else besides being a human. By contrast, when S *qua* S is not sufficient for it having the predicate P, then there must be some cause or justification for the predication of the predicate term of the subject term. The statement, 'X is a human being, and X is a philosopher' can only be true if there is a cause or good reason for X's being a philosopher, for the mere fact that X is a human being does not suffice for X to be a philosopher. In this case, there has to be a *ḥaythiyya taʿlīliyya*, 'an aspect of causation', that justifies X's being a philosopher. In the context of our discussion, the predicate 'necessarily existent' in 'X is necessarily existent' can be interpreted in two ways, either as a predicate of X that requires a *ḥaythiyya taʿlīliyya* or not. In the former case, X cannot be necessarily existent due to itself, for its being necessarily existent is *due to a cause*. In the latter case, X's being necessarily existent has no cause, and the reason why this is so is because X is 'the necessity of existence' *per se* in the same manner, loosely speaking, that white *per se* is white.

70 The controversy that Mullā Ṣadrā is referring to is the problem of instauration (*jaʿl*) which asks whether it is the existence of things or their quiddities that is made when things are caused to be. For Ṣadrā, the existence of things is what is instaurated *per se* (*majʿūl bi-l-dhāt*) by the efficient cause, not their quiddities. The efficient cause of a human being in other words does not make a human a human, but rather it makes it an existent human.

> Hence, every necessarily existent thing due to itself is necessarily existent in itself.[71]

However, both existence and its necessity are *iʿtibārī* according to Ibn Kammūna and other so-called 'Illuminationist' philosophers. The implication from a Ṣadrian perspective is that each so-called 'Necessary Being' is therefore just some unknown essence that *has* the necessity of existence but which in and of itself is neither existence nor necessity. But if the necessity of existence is not itself the essence of the Necessary Being then its being necessarily existent requires a cause, and that entails that what is initially presumed to be a Necessary Being is in fact just a contingent being. Hence, there are no beings that are truly necessary of existence due to themselves if existence and necessity are *iʿtibārī*.

For these reasons, Ṣadrā believed that any attempts to refute Ibn Kammūna's counterargument based on similar metaphysical presumptions about the nature of *wujūd* were bound to fail, and it is not suprising that his discussion immediately turns on the assumption that existence is *iʿtibārī*.

> As for the truth of the matter verified by us, namely, that this extrapolated notion [i.e. existence] has real instances [outside the mind] and that its relation to them is akin to the relation the general accident has to its individuals and species, then the objection is not so strong. Rather, it can be deflected with the least amount of reflection since this notion, notwithstanding the fact that it is something extrapolated from quiddity due to an accidental cause, is nonetheless a meaning extrapolated from a real instance of every individual existence *qua* its essence due to itself. Therefore, its relation to the particular existence possessed by each individual being is the same as the relation that infinitive nouns have to their quiddities—such as the meaning 'humanity' which is extropolated from each human being or 'animality' extrapolated from every animal. All of these are shared as meanings which are subsequent to the fact that they have something in common [in extramental reality] from which their meanings can be expolated.[72]

Ṣadrā's emphasis here is that the concept of being (*mafhūm al-wujūd*) is in some sense grounded in the extramental things that instantiate it just as the concepts 'humanity' and 'animality' are gounded in the essence of individual humans and animals. Being has a reality (*ḥaqīqa*) outside the mind and is not just some concept our minds conjure up without anything running parallel to it in extramental reality. One proof of this is that the concept of being cannot be derived from quiddities *qua* quiddities: the idea of a horse, for example, cannot give to the mind the concept of being *per se* since no quiddity has the meaning of *wujūd* included within itself. Rather it is the *existence* of the horse that

71 Mullā Ṣadrā, *al-Mabdaʾ wa-l-maʿād*, 1:85–86; cf. idem., *Sharḥ al-Hidāya*, 2:152.
72 Mullā Ṣadrā, *al-Ḥikmat al-mutaʿāliyya*, 6:54.

allows the mind to abstract and formulate a general concept of *wujūd*, but this is only possible if individual existences are real.

Therefore, if Ṣadrā's claim is true and the reason why Ibn Kammūna's *shubha* poses a genuine threat to Avicenna's argument for divine unity is because it assumes that being (*wujūd*) is merely an abstract concept that has no real ontological status in extramental reality, then it is because of this very assumption that subsequent thinkers too have failed to adequately respond to the challenge of Ibn Kammūna's counterargument. For Ṣadrā, there is no adequate way of responding to the *shubha* of Ibn Kammūna without first denying the very premise on which it is built. What this means in effect is that the only way of proving the *tawḥīd* of the Necessary Being is by first commiting to the doctrine that being itself is something real (*ʿayniyyat al-wujūd*) and that this reality is what grounds the perfections of all existent things (i.e. *aṣālat al-wujūd*). Therefore, whatever perfections an existent thing has, it derives these from its *wujūd* and not from its *māhiyya*.

Ṣadrā's proof of divine unity in the *Asfār* therefore begins with him first affirming the reality of *wujūd* itself *pace* Illuminationist thinkers like Ibn Kammūna. By doing this he removes the basic premise on which Ibn Kammūna's argument against divine unity is constructed: *wujūd* has a *ḥaqīqa* and is not merely *iʿtibārī*. From Ṣadrā's perspective, the *shubha* of Ibn Kammūna is a basic non-starter. It begins with a false premise (i.e. *iʿtibāriyyat al-wujūd* and *aṣālat al-māhiyya*) and therefore ends in a false conclusion (i.e. multiplicity of Necessary Beings, *taʿaddud wājib al-wujūd*). Avicenna's argument for divine unity thus remains intact and immune from Ibn Kammūna's counterargument on the proviso that one reads into it the Ṣadrian notion of being's ontological primacy (*aṣālat al-wujūd*). This understanding about the nature and existence of *wujūd* is thus incorporated by Ṣadrā as an explicit premise within formal argument of the Necessary Being's unity:

> Therefore, if in existence there are two Necessary Beings whose necessity is due to themselves, then [the notion of] existence that is extrapolated from them would be a shared meaning as admitted by the opponent also. But this implies that the real existence that runs parallel to this notion and which happens to be the principle for the extrapolation of [each being's] existence-status is also shared in some respect. Hence, each Necessary Being's distinction from the other must be due to something essential, for whenever the aspect from which two things happen to agree is something essential, then the aspect from which they are different—that is, each being's individuation—must also be something essential. However, the result of this would be that the essence of neither Necessary Being is simple; and being composed—as is known—negates necessity.[73]

73 Mullā Ṣadrā, *al-Ḥikmat al-mutaʿāliyya*, 6:55.

The crucial point here is that the both the notion of existence (*mafhūm al-wujūd*) and the notion of necessity (*mafhūm al-wujūb*) are not just some mind-conjured notions that have no ontological footing in being itself. Ṣadrā's emphasis is that what the mind grasps through notions such as *wujūd* and *wujūb* are not mere fabrications of the mind, but extrapolations of meanings from things that have extramental existence. Running parallel to each person's mental conceptualisation of the meaning of existence—the existence that Ṣadrā here refers to as 'extrapolated existence' (*al-wujūd al-intizāʿī*)—is a real instantiation of existence itself (*al-wujūd al-ḥaqīqī*). Both 'existence' and 'necessity' are referring terms. Without this real instance of existence there would be no extrapolated notion of existence. In other words, as Ṣadrā explains, the real instantiations of existence are principles that give rise to the extrapolated notion of existence; they are the '*mabdaʾ intizāʿi al-mawjudiyya al-maṣdariyya*', the ontological counterparts of our notion of being as an infinitive noun. The concept of being thus follows from the fact that being itself is an actualised reality, albeit that what is conceived (*mafhūm*) differs from its extramental reality in the same way that a verbal noun or infinitive (*maṣdar*) like 'humanity' differs from the extramental instances of 'human'.[74] The concept of being as a *maṣdar* is therefore something 'extrapolated from' the external things that instantiate it just as Ibn Kammūna believed, but unlike Ibn Kammūna what it is extrapolated from is none other than the reality of each thing's *wujūd* as opposed to their *māhiyya*, since no quiddity *qua* itself is capable of purveying the notion of existence. It is for this reason that Avicenna's argument for divine unity stands according to Mullā Ṣadrā.

In that scenario, then, where there are two Necessary Beings, the mind extrapolates a single notion of existence and a single notion of necessity which it then predicates of both entities. This means that *wujūd* and *wujūb* are not equivocal notions, but have a single meaning shared by two Necessary Beings. This implies that each Necessary Being has a real instantiation of *wujūd* running parallel to our understanding of it as a concept, an extramental counterpart which must also be shared in some sense. The analogy here is similar to that of any other infinitive noun: although Zayd and ʿAmr have different instances of humanity extramentally (they are extensionally different), they are nonetheless the same essentially (they are intensionally the same). And just as each instance of humanity in Zayd and ʿAmr cannot differentiate them from each other, so too in the case of two Necessary Beings that participate in a real instantiation of necessary existence: their existences do not and cannot individuate them as particular beings and hence they cannot be differentiated from each other through existence alone. Given that in Ṣadrā's

74 Ṣadrā draws on the linguistic relationship between infinitives and their corresponding concrete nouns to illustrate how the concept of *wujūd* ought to be related to its extramental instances. For example, just as Zayd's being a human (*insān*) is due to the fact that he possesses 'humanity' (*insāniyya*), so too is this *mawjūd*'s being a *mawjūd* due to the fact that it possesses *wujūd*. Therefore, in the same way that there would be no 'humans' if 'humanity' did not exist, likewise there would be nothing *mawjūd* if *wujūd* itself did not exist.

metaphysics each Necessary Being is just being in its purest and most intense form, the 'essence' of each Necessary Being is just existence itself. Existence is thus essential to each Necessary Being. But if there are two Necessary Beings that each have existence as their essence, then there are only two possibilities: either (1) they are not really two individual beings but in fact just one and the same, or (2) they are really distinct from each other and differentiated by some other part within their essence, which implies that they are not simple beings. However, any kind of mereological distinction within the essence of either Necessary Being implies that it is composed and in fact not necessary of existence due to itself. Therefore, there can be only one Necessary Being—*tawḥīd*.

Ṣadrā's proof of divine unity undercuts the *shubha* of Ibn Kammūna and substitutes what it considers to be the false premises on which it is built with the correct premises from a Ṣadrian point of view. Ibn Kammūna assumed that two Necessary Beings could co-exist if they had unique but unknowable essences other than existence. From Ṣadrā's perspective, this is precisely where the argument fails: it prioritises essence over existence and subsequently demotes *wujūd* to a non-instantiated mind-constructed phenomenon with no actual footing in extramental reality. Ṣadrā's argument by contrast begins with *wujūd* as the primary ontic reality and from there proceeds to demonstrate that there cannot be two *wujūd*s that are both essentially necessary. It is a simple and efficient argument that avoids the initial trappings of the objections raised by Ibn Kammūna.

The above argument has the imprint of Ṣadrā's own philosophical commitments and is based on the assertion that existence is a concrete, mind-independent reality, which is a claim rejected by so-called Illuminationists. The dispute here focuses on the nature of existence itself and less on the formal structure of Ibn Kammūna's counterargument. But let us suppose, for the sake of argument, that we do not concede to Ṣadrā's belief that existence is a single modulated reality (*ḥaqīqa wāḥida mushakkika*) and argue along the lines of the Illuminationists' philosophy and demarcate existence as a purely mental notion. In that case, Ṣadrā highlights another problematic feature of Ibn Kammūna's counterargument which does not require a commitment to his own doctrine of *aṣālat al-wujūd*; and that is that while he may disagree with the Illuminationists on whether or not existence has extramental reference, both he and they agree that the notion of being (*mafhūm al-wujūd*) is a *single* concept in the mind.[75] But a single notion such as existence can only be a shared notion if the things from which it is extrapolated have something in common. However, this is explicitly not the case in the *shubha* of Ibn Kammūna, and the question arises as to how it is possible to extrapolate and predicate a single notion of existence/necessity when each Necessary Being has a unique essence that shares nothing in common with the essence of the other Necessary Beings. How can any singular notion be derived from the many *qua* many?

75 That is, the concept of being is monosemic (*mushtarak maʿnawī*).

Ṣadrā expresses this concern in several works. In the *Asfār*, he writes as follows:

> Therefore, it is self-evident that a single infinitive meaning cannot be predicated of disparate essences *qua* disparate essences without there being an aspect of unity between them. Hence it follows on the basis of the aforementioned assumption [i.e. the notion of existence being a single notion] that two Necessary Beings must agree in some intrinsic property not lying outside of their essences. However, an agreement in something essential necessitates that differentiation and multiplication are the result of an aspect within the essence also—such as a specific difference when they have a genus in common, or individuating properties when they share the same species. However, the result in each case is composition [within the divine essence] and that negates the essential necessity [of each Necessary Being].[76]

This is a criticism that Illuminationist philosophers must respond to. From Ṣadrā's perspective, it is simply impossible to derive a single unified notion from the many *qua* many, and thus a further nail in the coffin from his perspective for Ibn Kammūna's hypothetical argument against God's uniqueness.[77] Mullā Hādī Sabzawārī, the chief commentator and propagator of Ṣadrā's ideas in Qajar Iran, went a step further by arguing that it was not just the Illuminationists but other 'Peripatetics' too who are confronted with the same objection.[78] The reason, he explains, is that although *mashā'ī* philosophers like Avicenna believe in *wujūd* having real ontological presence outside the mind, they nonetheless deny the claim that existence is a single reality extramentally. The Peripatetics reject the notion of an underlying unity among ontologically subsistent existences. Sabzawārī argues that this position creates a dilemma within the Peripatetic tradition. If all extramental existences are essentially distinct—a claim he attributes to the Peripatetic school given their metaphysical stance that each instance of being (*wujūd*) is 'entirely distinct' (*ḥaqā'iq mutabāyina bi-tamām al-dhāt*) from all others[79]—then it should not be possible to conceive of a single, unified notion of *wujūd*, as the Peripatetics themselves purportedly maintain.[80] In other words, if each instance of *wujūd* has nothing in common with any other instance outside the mind, then the concept (*mafhūm*) of *wujūd* must be equivocal. This follows from the principle that when two things share nothing in common, there is

76 Mullā Ṣadrā, *al-Ḥikmat al-muta'āliyya*, 6:56; cf. idem., *Sharḥ al-Ḥidāya*, 2:153; idem., *Sharḥ u ta'līqah-i Ṣadr al-Muta'allihīn bar Ilāhiyyāt-i Shifā'*, 1:170.

77 Cf. Mullā Muḥammad Ismā'īl Iṣfahānī 'Wāḥid al-'Ayn' (d. ca. 1242/1826), *Sharḥ al-Ḥikmat al-'arshiyya*, ed. Muḥammad Mas'ūd Khudāwardī (Tehran: Mu'assasah-i Pazhūhashī Ḥikmat u Falsafah-i Īrān, 1391Sh/[2012–2013]), 440.

78 See Mullā Hādī Sabzawārī, *ta'līqa* no. 89 in Mullā Ṣadrā, *al-Ḥikmat al-muta'āliyya*, 6:472–73.

79 See Mullā Hādī Sabzawārī, *Sharḥ al-Manẓūma*, 1:207–10.

80 See Ḥasan Ḥasanzādah Āmulī, *Waḥdat az dīdghāh-i 'ārif u ḥakīm* (Qom: Alif Lām Mīm, 1383Sh/[2004–2005]), 64–5.

no justification for predicating a single notion of both.[81]

If this is indeed the case, then Ibn Kammūna's well-known objection appears to present a genuine problem: two Necessary Beings having nothing in common would each give rise to an equivocal notion of being 'necessarily existent,' which is merely a name they have in common rather than a unified concept. Consequently, if the notion of each Necessary Being's existence is equivocal then there is no *jihat al-ittifāq* (basis for agreement) between them, and thus no need for a *jihat al-iftirāq* (basis for differentiation) beyond their already distinct essences. As a result there would be no logical obstacle preventing the simultaneous existence of multiple Necessary Beings.[82] The necessity of existence is not, in the strict sense, then, a common accident (*ʿaraḍ ʿāmm*), and hence does not require a cause contrary to Avicenna's concerns. So, even within the Peripatetic framework, Sabzawārī contends that the existence of multiple Necessary Beings does not necessarily entail composition or causation. The Peripatetics therefore cannot demonstrate God's uniqueness in the face of Ibn Kammūna's counterargument.

Sabzawārī's provocation sparked outrage among later proponents of Avicenna's philosophy. For thinkers in the Ṣadrian tradition, however, there was widespread support for Sabzawārī's claim that it is impossible to extrapolate or derive a single meaning from diverse things whose realities are entirely distinct or which have no accidental properties or features in common.[83] In their view, it is simply not possible to derive a singular meaning from diverse things *qua* diverse things.[84] A uniform concept can only be derived

81 See Ḥasan Ḥasanzādah Āmulī, *Wahdat az dīdghāh-i ʿārif u ḥakīm*, 68–72.

82 As Sabzawārī states, there is a single 'label' (*ʿunwān*) called 'Necessary Being' for each so-called Necessary Being, but in reality what is being referred to by that label, i.e. the *muʿanwan*, is entirely different and distinct in each case. This is precisely the reason why in Ibn Kammūna's *shubha* each so-called 'Necessary Being' is referred to as *mahjūl al-kunh*, 'unknown in essence'. Because although they share the label 'necessary of existence due to themselves', this is not their essence; it is merely a label (*ʿunwān*) for things whose essences in actual fact are unknown and dissimilar in every instance. See Sabzawārī, *taʿlīqa* no. 89 in Mullā Ṣadrā, *al-Ḥikmat al-mutaʿāliyya*, 6:472.

83 See, for example, Muḥammad Riḍā Qumsha'ī's *Risāla fī radd jawāz intizāʿ mafhūm wāḥid min al-ḥaqā'iq al-mutabāyina*, in Ḥāmid Nājī Iṣfahānī (ed.), *Majmūʿah-i aśār-i ḥakīm-i ṣuhbā: ʿārif ilāhī Āqā Muḥammad Riḍā Qumsha'ī* (Tehran: Qānūn Pazhūhash, 1378Sh/[1999–2000]), 245–52. Abū l-Ḥasan Jilvah, who was a staunch Avicennian and opposed Ṣadrā's philosophy, tried to rebut Sabzawārī's claims in his *Risāla fī anna mahfūm al-wāḥid kayfa yuntazaʿ min al-ḥaqā'iq al-mutabāyina*, in Ḥasan Riḍā Zadah (ed.), *Majmūʿah-i āśār-i Ḥakīm Jilvah* (Tehran: Intishārāt-i Ḥikmat, 1385Sh/[2006–2007]), 605–8. The question has been discussed extensively in a variety of philosophical contexts by thinkers in the modern era; see, for example, al-ʿAllāma al-Ṭabāṭabā'ī, *Nihāyat al-ḥikma*, ed. ʿAbbās ʿAlī al-Zāriʿī al-Sabzawārī (Qom: Mu'assasat al-Nashr al-Islāmī, 1426/[2005–2006]), 1:33–34.

84 While there is an almost unanimous agreement that things insofar as they are different cannot produce a common notion predicable of them, there is a significant difference of opinion on the converse proposition as to whether or not it is possible to predicate diverse meanings of a reality whose essence is simple and has no composition or multiplicity whatsoever. On this particular aspect of the debate and its relevance to the discussion of God's attributes, see Rūḥullāh Farūghī, 'Arziyābī pāsikh-hā-yi falāsifah u ʿurafā bih ishkāl-i nāsāzghārī-yi taʿaddud-i ṣifāt-i khudāvand u waḥdat-i dhāt', *Ilāhiyāt u falsafah-i muʿāṣir*, 1, no. 1 (2021): 234–46.

when things have some degree of 'overlap'.[85] According to Sabzawārī, the only solution to the problem is to revert to the Ṣadrian intuition that existence is a single modulated reality that is, by its very essence, the cause of all unity and multiplicity, a unity-in-multiplicity and multiplicity-in-unity. 'As for the victorious *madhhab*', boasts Sabzawārī, 'in which existence is primary (*aṣīl*) and a label (*ʿunwān*) for a simple luminous reality that is modulated through an acute sense of modulation (*al-tashkīk al-khāṣṣī*),[86] whose relation to that reality is akin to the relation of the essential to its subject, or a concept (*mafhūm*) to its actual instance [outside of the mind]—and not akin to the relation that an extrapolated concept (*al-mafhūm al-intizāʿī*) has to its source—then [the objection in Ibn Kammūna's *shubha*] is easily deflected [...]'.[87]

There are other potential pitfalls and criticisms, however. All of the arguments presented so far assume that the principle of each Necessary Being's individuation is distinct from what unites them as Necessary Beings.[88] But one may question why this is so given that according to Ṣadrā's own metaphysics, existence is both the principle of unity and difference. This of course invokes an idea inherent to Ṣadrā's philosophy known as the modulation of being (*tashkīk al-wujūd*) and is something which Ṣadrā himself believed is necessary to properly grasp the relation between the one and the many. It is thus an objection made from within the Ṣadrian system itself. A possible criticism here would be that if existence itself is both what unites and distinguishes things, then is it not conceivable for there to be multiple Necessary Beings? One could argue that among them,

85 See Sabzawārī, *Sharḥ al-Manẓūma*, 1:447.

86 The expression 'acute sense of modulation' (*al-tashkīk al-khāṣṣī*) refers to the idea that the reality of being is modulated through different degrees of intensification and debilitation. This is a crucial aspect of Mullā Ṣadrā's metaphysics according to which being (*wujūd*) itself is what unites and differentiates different levels of existence just as the essence of light itself is what differentiates different intensities and hues of light. The implications of this are profound and far-reaching: there is only one true existence, which manifests itself in different orders of hierarchy, some more intense than others, yet not distinct at root from existence itself. As Sabzawārī, *Taʿlīqāt ʿalā l-Shawāhid al-rubūbiyya*, ed. Sayyid Jalāl al-Dīn Āshtiyānī (Beirut: Mu'assasat al-Ta'rīkh al-ʿArabī, n.d.), 395–96 remarks, existence being modulated in the acute sense (*al-tashkīk al-khāṣṣī*) means that 'prior and posterior levels of existence are not separated through detachment (*baynūna ʿuzliyya*)', but rather that each level of existence is just the same as the others at root except that each level has more or less existential perfections than the others. It is crucial to note the language here; the expression '*baynūna ʿizliyya*' is a direct reference to the words of ʿAlī b. Abī Ṭālib, the first Shīʿī Imam, who in some of the sermons attributed to him is reported as saying that 'declaring God's unity (*tawḥīd*) is to differentiate Him from his creation, such that His distinction from them is like that of how an attribute is separate [from what is attributed] and not that He is separated from them by detachment' (*wa-tawḥīduhu tamyīzuhu min khalqihi wa-ḥukm al-tamyīz baynūnatu ṣifatin lā baynūnatu ʿizlatin*). See Abū Manṣūr Aḥmad b. ʿAlī al-Tabrasī, *al-Iḥtijāj*, ed. Ibrāhīm al-Bahādurī and Muḥammad Hādī Bih (Qom: Intishārāt-i Uswa, 1413/[1992]), 1:475; cf. Shaykh al-Ṣadūq, *al-Tawḥīd*, ed. Sayyid Hāshim al-Ḥusaynī al-Tihrānī (Qom: Mu'assasat al-Nashr al-Islāmī, 1430/[2009]), 43 where in the course of a long sermon the Imam is reported as saying, 'He does not inhere in His creation that it may be said "He is among them," nor is He removed from it that it may be said, "He is separate [from His creation]".'

87 Mullā Hādī Sabzawārī, *taʿlīqa* no. 89 in Mullā Ṣadrā, *al-Ḥikmat al-mutaʿāliyya*, 6:473; cf. idem., *Sharḥ al-Manẓūma*, 1:446–47 fn. 3.

88 That is, they assume that the '*mā bihi al-ifitirāq*' is different from the '*mā bihi l-ishtirāk*'.

one possesses a more intense and perfect degree of existence, distinguishing it from others whose existences are comparatively weaker and less perfect. This does not raise concerns about existence being composite, since variations in intensity do not add to or subtract from existence itself. Nevertheless, a distinction remains between what is more intense and what is less intense in relation to existence. Thus, even within Ṣadrā's own metaphysical framework, the possibility of multiple Necessary Beings seems justifiable.

Ṣadrā's response and subsequent discussion of this problem brings into sharper focus some of the most salient aspects of his metaphysics. His responses shed important light on how he understood the nature of existence and its necessity as being intricately woven with the idea of perfection; how that which exists necessarily due to itself must be understood and equated with a being that is not only perfect but maximally perfect.[89] The idea of perfection thus becomes a crucial link in Ṣadrā's metaphysics. It ties together concepts such as existence, necessity and unity, and as such serves to fill a missing gap in Avicenna's arguments for God's uniqueness by giving greater prominence to an idea that seems to have less emphasis and importance in Avicenna's own metaphysics. Ṣadrā responds to the objection as follows:

> This [objection] is deflected based on what we have alluded to previously: that any kind of defeciency [in a thing] entails [that thing] being caused. This is because it is not possible for the nature of existence *qua* existence to have any deficiency without a cause, since the meaning of 'being deficient' is not the same as the meaning of 'existence'. Deficiency is a privation, and nothing can necessitate its own privation. This is not the case with perfection, since a thing's perfection is its assuredness for it.[90]

What this passage highlights is that inasmuch as existence is just existence it is absolute perfection. For this reason, the nature of existence cannot have any deficiency, because any kind of deficiency would be tantamount to a privation (*ʿadam*). But there is by definition no *ʿadam* in being *qua* being. Therefore, if an existence is deficient, then this cannot be due to an intrinsic privation since *ʿadam* is not an inherent property of *wujūd* but rather its opposite. Any limitation or curtailment of being must therefore result from an external factor imposing a restriction from without on the nature of *wujūd* itself.[91]

89 On perfect being theology, see the excellent study by Yujin Nagasawa, *Maximal God: A New Defence of Perfect Being Theism* (Oxford: Oxford University Press, 2017).

90 Mullā Ṣadrā, *al-Ḥikmat al-mutaʿāliyya*, 6:55.

91 Ṣadrā provides a useful analogy here. Imagine two lines, one of which is longer than the other. Whilst it is true that the perfection of the longer line lies in the fact that it is a line, it is not correct to say that the imperfection of the shorter line is due to its being a line only. In other words, it is not because of the nature it possesses as a line that it is deficient. Its deficiency comes from the fact that its length has been curtailed and limited, but this does not come from lineness *qua* lineness. According to Sadra, this means that if there is an infinite line, then there is nothing present other than lineness itself, whereas

This means that a 'Necessary Being' that is less than perfect (or less perfect than another) cannot be sheer existence, but a less than infinite existence that is limited by a privation caused by something other than existence itself. It would thus be a combination of being and non-being and hence a contingent being.[92] In Ṣadrā's metaphysics, pure being—existence entirely free from any association with non-being[93]—is inseparably linked to ultimate perfection. Every maximally perfect being is pure existence, and every pure existence is maximally perfect. The Necessary Being is therefore existence in its most intensified form (*muta'akkid al-wujūd*), a being that Ṣadrā himself describes as 'that greater than which nothing more perfect can be conceived' (*wa-lā yutaṣawwar mā huwa atamm minhu*).[94] In contrast, a contingent being is any entity that is not maximally perfect and therefore not pure existence, but is rather a being whose essence in tinged with non-being.[95] Its contingency arises from its inherent deficiency, and because it is contingent it must necessarily be caused. The highest intensity of existence corresponds to infinite existence, therefore, and consequently whatever is necessarily existent by itself must be entirely devoid of imperfections since it is the deprivation of being (i.e. the lack of existential perfections) that renders entities finite.[96] Therefore, if a so-called 'Necessary Being' were in any way less than absolutely perfect, it would be contingent and thus subject to causation—rendering it finite. The conclusion, then, is that there can be only one ultimately perfect being, and thus only one true Necessary Being.[97] Ṣadrā summarises these points as follows:

> Therefore, every existence of finite intensity must have a cause other than its own individual existence that limits [its intensity], and it is that cause that specifies and individuates a particular rank [for it] within the nature of existence. However, being-caused negates the necessity of existence; i.e. it negates a thing being exist-

in the case of a finite line there is not only lineness itself but something else besides lineness, namely a limit or terminus that constrains the line from being only a line—that is, an infinite line. See Mullā Ṣadrā, *al-Ḥikmat al-muta'āliyya*, 6:55.

92 In the Ṣadrian framework, possessing a quiddity is tantamount to an ontological privation, metaphysically speaking; for quiddity itself is defined as the 'limitation of being' (*ḥadd al-wujūd*), and any limit is a privation of sorts (*amr 'adamī*). Therefore, every contingent being the essence of which is not identical to its existence (*wujūd*) possesses *wujūd* in a limited sense, and thus comprises both *wujūd* and its limitation which is a privation (*'adam*). For Ṣadrā, the combination of *wujūd* and *'adam* is itself a kind of composition (*tarkīb*), therefore, and in the Ṣadrian tradition is depicted as 'the most detestable form of compositionality' (*sharr al-tarākīb*). See Mullā Hādī Sabzawārī, *ḥāshiya* no. 146 in Mullā Ṣadrā, *al-Ḥikmat al-muta'āliyya*, 1:565.

93 Whatever has no association with non-being must therefore be a Necessary Being.

94 Mullā Ṣadrā, *al-Ḥikmat al-muta'āliyya*, 6:16.

95 All contingent beings possess a quiddity. No quiddity is existence. Hence, the essence of every contingent being is characterised by non-*wujūd*.

96 For this reason, the Necessary Being cannot have a *māhiyya* because a *māhiyya* is something other than *wujūd* (e.g. 'human' is other than 'existence'), and whatever is other than *wujūd* is by definition non-*wujūd*, i.e. non-being (*'adam*).

97 See Mullā Hādī Sabzawārī, *Sharḥ al-asmā'*, 374.

> ent by eternal necessity. Therefore, it is impossible for there to be more than one Necessary Being. This explanation of *tawḥīd* in the manner presented here is not found in proofs of other scholars (*ahl al-iʿtibār*).[98]

One of the most profound metaphysical implications of this is that if God is maximally perfect and infinite in His existence then there is by definition no ontological scope for any other form of (necessary) existence. All of reality must therefore be occupied by the reality of the Necessary Being. If this were not the case, there would exist something not encompassed by the reality of the Necessary Being, implying that the existence of the Necessary Being is distinct from the existence of that other entity. However, this is inadmissible in Ṣadrā's system as it necessitates a limitation on the existence of the Necessary Being. As previously established, any limitation renders existence finite, caused, and contingent in essence. Such attributes are incompatible with that which possesses necessity of existence in and of itself. Consequently, the only coherent conclusion is that 'the Simple Reality is all things' (*basīṭ al-ḥaqīqa kullu l-ashyāʾ*).[99] For these reasons, there is both a logical and metaphysical impossibility in the idea of there being two or more Necessary Beings.

## 4. Mullā Ṣadrā on Necessity, Unity and Perfection

The notion of perfection plays a pivotal role in Ṣadrā's metaphysics.[100] I now want to consider how Ṣadrā utilises it to prove divine unity in a more principled way. More specifically, I want to show how this idea links to other crucial concepts such as necessity, simplicity and unity in Ṣadrā's thought thereby giving it an overarching importance in different parts of Ṣadrā's metaphysics.

98 Mullā Ṣadrā, *al-Ḥikmat al-mutaʿāliyya*, 6:56.

99 I discuss this principle (which I call the Simple Reality Principle) and its far-reaching implications, as well as its reception in the Qajar period, in a forthcoming article. If God is pure being and pure being is everything, then there is no 'other'; hence there is only God—and that in the Ṣadrian framework is *tawḥīd*. The fact that God's existence—or existence *per se*—encompasses the whole of reality does not imply that His existence is akin to a universal that encompasses all its particulars. Rather, His existence encapsulates being through another sense of enompassing (*shumūl*), one that Ṣadrā himself writes is 'only known to the mystics firmly rooted in knowledge' (*al-ʿurafāʾ al-rāsikhūn fī l-ʿilm*), alluding to Q. 3:7, and which in the *ʿirfānī* tradition is referred to as the Breath of the All-Merciful (*al-nafas al-raḥmānī*). See Mullā Ṣadrā, *al-Mashāʿir*, 340–41.

100 Avicenna recognises perfection as a metaphysical property of the Necessary Being but he does not give it the same degree of importance as later thinkers like Suhrawardī and Ṣadrā. The historical roots of thinking about perfection as a metaphysical concept can of course be traced back to Plotinus, who conceived of the One as ἁπλῶς τέλειον (*aplôs teleion*), the Absolutely Perfect, and to Aristotle, who in *Metaphysics* XII.6–9 described the Unmoved Mover as pure actuality (ἐνέργεια)—the highest expression of perfection in the cosmos. In Avicenna's words, 'The Necessary Being is the True-Perfect (*al-kamāl al-ḥaqq*), having within itself no contingency or potentiality. In short, the Necessary Being has no privation or evil inside It; and It is the source of every perfection' (Avicenna, *al-Hidāya*, 263).

Our discussion thus far has shown that there is a linkage in Ṣadrā's thinking between a thing existing necessarily and it being maximally perfect. The Necessary Being is by Its nature a maximally perfect being—a being devoid of contingency and impossibility. Consequently, all perfections belong to the Necessary Being by necessity, without any deficiency or limitation. Since privation signifies an absence of being and the lack of a perfection, and because the Necessary Being is defined as existence in its most complete and unconditioned form (*al-wujūd al-muṭlaq*), it must be absolutely simple—pure existence (*wujūd ṣirf*), wholly unassociated with non-being in any respect. The Necessary Being cannot therefore have any 'aspect' or 'perspective' under which it might be said to be contingent or that its relation to some perfection may be said to be impossible.[101] It is for this reason that Avicenna and later philosophers describe the Necessary Being as a being that is 'necessary in all respects'; necessary, that is, in relation to every *perfection* conceivable for It and hence a maximally perfect being.[102] Avicenna argued for this principle, which I term the 'principle of absolute necessity', by examining the alternative hypothesis and considering its implications for a Necessary Being that is not necessary in all respects. He demonstrates that if the Necessary Being had just a single aspect in which its relation to a certain perfection is merely contingent then it would fail to be self-sufficient in that regard, and anything that is not self-sufficient is by definition a contingent being. Mullā Ṣadrā advanced this line of reasoning by explaining how contingency itself is grounded in essential non-being: an entity is contingent precisely because its essence *qua* itself fails to provide sufficient grounds for its own perfections.[103] A being that is not necessary in all respects is thus a composite of being and non-being from different aspects given that a single aspect cannot account for both being and its privation.[104]

Building on these premises, Ṣadrā articulated a novel argument for divine unity grounded exclusively in the concept of maximal perfection (i.e. being absolutely necessary). He begins by positing the existence of two distinct Necessary Beings, A and B. By defi-

101 The terms 'aspect' and 'perspective' translate the Arabic word *jiha*, which is used to denote those attributes of the Necessary Being that are considered perfections for It (i.e. *al-ṣifāt al-kamāliyya*), such as knowledge, life and power. Therefore, the assertion that 'the Necessary Being is necessary in all aspects' just means that 'the Necessary Being is necessary with respect to every perfection that is conceivable for It'. See al-ʿAllāma al-Ṭabāṭabāʾī, *Nihāyat al-ḥikma*, 2:93 (fn. 1); Shihāb al-Dīn al-Suhrawardī, *al-Talwīḥāt al-lawḥiyya wa-l-ʿarshiyya*, ed. Najafqulī Ḥabībī (Tehran: Muʾassasah-i Pazhūhashī-yi Ḥikmat u Falsafah-i Īrān, 1388Sh/[2009–2010]), 211.

102 It is not sufficient for the Necessary Being to have a perfection to just some degree, but rather It must possess whatever perfections are conceivable for It to a *maximal* degree. A Necessary Being is thus a perfect being in the utmost sense of perfection.

103 If A is contingent with respect to *x*, then this means that A *qua* itself is not *x* and that *x* may or may not exist for A. However, this cannot be the case with respect to the Necessary Being as it woud imply that the perfection in question has no necessary or essential relation to the Necessary Being. This means that the Necessary Being *qua* itself does not have that perfection, and hence there is a privation at the level of the Necessary Being's essence. Such a being cannot be a maximally perfect being according to Ṣadrā.

104 For Mullā Ṣadrā's discussion of the principle of absolute necessity, see his *al-Ḥikmat al-mutaʿāliyya*, 1:142–149; idem., *Sharḥ al-Hidāya*, 2:157–164; cf. al-ʿAllāma al-Ṭabāṭabāʾī, *Nihāyat al-ḥikma*, 1:93–7.

nition, a Necessary Being is maximally perfect, beyond which no greater perfection can be imagined or realised. Such a being possesses all perfections to their utmost degree. However, if A and B are distinct, they must be discernible realities, and since a being that is necessary of existence by itself cannot be individuated by accidental properties, their differentiation must be due to their essential properties. Yet, this leads to insurmountable contradictions. If A possesses a perfection that B lacks, then A is by definition more perfect than B, negating B's status as a maximally perfect being. Conversely, if B possesses a perfection that A lacks, then B would be superior to A, contradicting A's supposed maximal perfection. If both A and B possess perfections which the other lacks, then neither can be truly maximally perfect. In each scenario, then, Ṣadrā observes that what is purported to be a maximally perfect being is in reality less than maximally perfect, and each so-called 'Necessary Being' turns out to be comprised of both being and non-being given that each lacks a perfection which the other possesses.[105] This inherent deficiency renders the entity composite, possessing some perfections while being deprived of others. Ṣadrā terms this the composition of being and non-being (*tarkīb al-wujūd wa-l-ʿadam*), which followers of Ṣadrā's philosophy regard as the most problematic or 'evil' form of composition (*sharr al-tarākīb*). The reason is because it implies that non-being (*ʿadam*) has infiltrated into the very essence of existence (*wujūd*) itself, an impossibility for the Necessary Being whose nature must be pure undivided being (*al-wujūd al-ṣirf*). By showing that any supposed plurality of Necessary Beings results in at least one aspect of essential non-being, Ṣadrā concludes that there can be only one maximally perfect being—one Necessary Being.

> If besides the Necessary Being there existed another Necessary Being, then it would necessarily be distinct from it. [...] This implies that each of them has a rank of perfection in existence that does not belong to the other, which is neither an effect nor an emanation of the other, therefore implying that each of them lacks an existential perfection and is deprived of a second-order actualisation. Hence, the essence of each cannot be sheer actuality and necessity, but instead a thing whose essence is a referent of one thing's presence and another thing's absence, both belonging to the nature of existence *qua* existence. Its essence is not a pure existence nor a real one, therefore, and being a composite negates being essentially necessary. What is necessary of existence due to itself must therefore be of utmost actuality and perfect actualisation and something that combines all existential planes. There can be no equal to it in existence, nor can it have an opposite or likeness. Instead, its

105 For example, if A has the perfection $x$ but lacks the perfection $y$, and B has the perfection $y$ but lacks the perfection $x$, then each would be perfect in one sense and deficient in another. In A's case, therefore, 'A *qua* itself is $x$, but not $y$' would be true, and this clearly is impossible given that there is a combination of being and non-being.

> essence is not only the most perfect essence there is but also the ground of all other perfections, and this is the meaning of it being perfect and beyond perfection.[106]

The conclusion is that there can never be more than one instance of sheer existence.

There is something intriguing in these arguments. The same could be said of anything that is merely itself. For example, the concept of *sheer* humanity—that is, human *qua* human—cannot have more than one instance either. In fact, anything that is mutliplied or replicated across multiple instances cannot be just itself *extensionally* speaking. There can be multiple instances of humanity, for example, but only if humanity is conjoined with things besides humanity itself (e.g. particular spatial positions). The difference then is that whereas other concepts can be conceivably multiplied through multiple instances, the concept of a Necessary Being cannot. All instances of multiplication imply a combination of being and non-being. 'Human' is conceivably multiple because humanity can be conjoined to things apart from humanity, hence resulting in a combination of being (i.e. 'human') and non-being (i.e. 'not-human') in each instance. Zayd is a combination of his being a human, on the one hand, and his being not a human (e.g. a particular height, a particular weight), on the other. But this is impossible for the necessity of existence, because that which is necessary in all respects cannot be contingent in any respect whatsoever, and hence cannot be conjoined with anything that is not itself—namely, necessary of existence. Rather than attempting to explain how multiple Necessary Beings would be individuated, therefore, the inquiry is more fundamentally concerned with whether it is even logically conceivable for *wujūd*—existence in its purest form—to be subject to multiplication or replication.

This shift in perspective provides an independent proof for divine unity, one that has been formally recognised within the post-Ṣadrian philosophical tradition as *burhān al-ṣarāfa*, or 'the proof from sheer simplicity'.[107] The core principle of this argument states that something which is purely and exclusively itself cannot be duplicated or repeated (*ṣirf al-shayʾ lā yatathannā wa-lā yatakarrar*).[108] To illustrate this, consider the quiddity 'human'. When we reflect on *ṣirf al-insān*—humanity in its most unadulterated sense—we are contemplating the very notion of human *qua* itself, stripped of all accidental attributes.[109]

106 Mullā Ṣadrā, *al-Shawāhid al-rububiyya*, 1:51; cf. idem, *al-Ḥikmat al-mutaʿāliyya*, 1:156–57; idem., *Sharḥ al-Hidāya*, 2:155–6; idem., *Asrār al-āyāt*, 63; idem., *al-Mashāʿir*, 385–86; idem., *al-Masāʾil al-qudsiyya*, 246–48.

107 The term *simplicity* in this context is open to equivocation. Here, it refers not to the standard metaphysical notion of a thing lacking compositionality but to something being unmixed with anything other than itself. For example, human in its pure and simple form is just human, even though it can be analysed in terms of animality and rationality. To consider *human* in its simplicity, then, is to regard it solely as rational animal—nothing more, nothing less.

108 The Arabic word *ṣirf* is difficult to translate into English, but its semantic meaning conveys the sense of something being unmixed, pure, and unattached to anything apart from itself.

109 It may be argued that a thing considered in this way is to be understood analytically as it being considered with the condition of nothing else alongside it (*bi-sharṭ lā*). In the context of our discussion, *ṣirf*

In this purely undifferentiated state there is no logical possibility of duplication, for there is nothing extrinsic to mark one instance as distinct from another. Hence, two instances of *ṣirf al-insān* would be identical. To speak of multiple instances of *ṣirf al-insān* would therefore be incoherent, for in every attempt to identify a second occurrence we would be left with the same undifferentiated notion without any criterion to individuate them. This stands in stark contrast to the case of two particular human beings such as Zayd and ʿAmr. While both are instances of 'human,' they are not instantiations of *ṣirf al-insān*.[110] Rather, they are accompanied by individuating characteristics—physical, temporal, and spatial distinctions—that allow for their differentiation. It is these additional attributes that permit multiplicity among particular instances of a general concept. However, sheer existence (*al-wujūd al-ṣirf*) does not admit of any such individuating attributes, for it is not conditioned by any limiting factor. It is existence in its most fundamental and unqualified form, devoid of all admixture with non-being. Since individuation requires some principle of distinction, and since *al-wujūd al-ṣirf* is an absolute reality untainted by negation or limitation, the very notion of a second instance becomes unintelligible. The principle *ṣirf al-shayʾ lā yatathannā wa-lā yatakarrar* thus serves as a philosophical corollary to the principle of indiscernibility, and affirms that there can be no multiplicity of concepts *qua* themselves.

This line of thinking provides a powerful demonstration of the Necessary Being's uniqueness which does not merely reject the possibility of multiple deities on metaphysical grounds but establishes through pure logical reasoning that the very structure of existence itself precludes any form of multiplicity within necessary existence. In doing so, it upholds the doctrine of *tawḥīd* as an inescapable conclusion derived from the nature of being itself.[111] This is one reason why 'God witnesses that there is no god but He' (Q. 3:18), because if God, the Necessary Being, is pure existence, then pure existence itself is what precludes there being another like it.[112] This is because had it been possible for the necessity of existence to be duplicated or repeated it would no longer be just sheer existence, for in order for there to be multiple instances there would also have had to be something else besides just sheer existence that makes each Necessary Being a discernible reality distinct from others. The very idea of there being something that is just 'sheer existence' is therefore defeated from the outset. The argument therefore demonstrates that if there is a Necessary Being that is just sheer existence then there can only be one instance of it.[113]

---

*al-wujūd* is the same analytically speaking as *al-wujūd bi-sharṭ lā*, 'existence with the condition that it is not accompanied by anything apart from existence'. This is explicitly noted by Ṣadrā's commentators; see for example Mullā Hādī Sabzawārī, *Sharḥ al-Manẓūma*, 1:445.

110 Based on what I have said in the previous footnote, Zayd instantiates 'human without any conditions' (*al-insān lā bi-sharṭ*) but not 'human with the condition of nothing else' (*al-insān bi-sharṭ lā*).

111 For Ṣadrā's presentation of this argument, see his *al-Mabdaʾ wa-l-maʿād*, 1: 87, 90; idem., *Asrār al-āyāt*, 57–8. See also Mullā Ismāʿīl al-Iṣfāhānī, *Sharḥ al-Ḥikmat al-ʿarshiyya*, 433.

112 Mullā Ṣadrā, *al-Ḥikmat al-mutaʿāliyya*, 6:23, 129; idem., *Sharḥ al-Hidāya*, 2:154.

113 For Ṣadrā's presentation of this argument, see his *al-Mabdaʾ wa-l-maʿād*, 1: 87, 90. See also Mullā Ismāʿīl

By his own admission Ṣadra's use of this argument is directly sourced from the insights of the twelfth-century Illuminationist philosopher Shihāb al-Dīn al-Suhrawardī. In his *Talwīḥāt*, Suhrawardī remarks that:

> Being in the purest sense (*ṣirf al-wujūd*), besides which there is nothing more perfect, whenever [and wherever] a second [instance of it] is supposed [to exist] is upon reflection merely just itself. For there can be no distinctions within a thing in its purest sense. Whatever, then, is mixed with being cannot be the aforementioned Necessary Being. Since whatever the mind separates into a quiddity and existence is not incapable of having an accidental predicate nor is it something [whose meaning] cannot be shared [among many things]. How can this be otherwise when it must, by necessity, be something that belongs to one of the categories. Take note! For these are indeed inspirations from the Divine Throne! And take heed, therefore, that whatever exists necessarily cannot, as a matter of principle, be multiplied through multiple instances, so there can never be two Necessary Beings in existence.[114]

In his marginal comments on Ṣadrā's *Asfār*, Sabzawārī presents the argument from *ṣarāfa* in its proper logical form. The argument begins with the assertion that pure being represents existence in its most fundamental and unqualified state devoid of any determinations or limitations. All conditions—positive or negative—have been removed. This premise establishes the conceptual foundation for what follows. The crucial move in Sabzawārī's reasoning emerges in his second premise, where he demonstrates that the very nature of what exists in its purest sense precludes the possibility of distinction or differentiation. This follows from the recognition that distinction requires some basis of difference, yet pure being—by definition—admits of no such qualifying features that could serve as grounds for differentiation. The logic here is that if something exists in absolute purity (*ṣirf al-shayʾ*), there can be no features or characteristics that would allow us to distinguish one instance from another, as any such distinguishing marks would constitute a departure from pure unqualified being. From these premises, he draws the desired conclusion that pure being must be unique and irreplicable. This conclusion leads to other important observations, one being that multiplicity or duplication at the level of pure being is not merely contingently absent but logically impossible. This conclusion carries significant implications for understanding the relationship between unity and multiplicity in existence. Any apparent multiplicity must be understood as occurring at a derivative level, where pure being has already undergone some form of determination or qualification. Manyness is thus a hallmark of qualifed existence, not

---

al-Iṣfāhānī, *Sharḥ al-Ḥikmat al-ʿarshiyya*, 433.

114 Shihāb al-Dīn al-Suhrawardī, *al-Talwīḥāt*, 206; cf. Ibn Kammūna, *al-Kāshif* (*al-Jadīd fī l-ḥikma*); Mullā Ṣadrā, *al-Ḥikmat al-mutaʿāliyya*, 1:155–56.

existence *per se*. As Ṣadrā explains in his *Asrār al-āyāt*, the very notion of there being a duality or twoness in the concept of sheer existence is impossible, nevermind the question of whether there are two instances of it or not in reality. In other words, there is a logical impossibility, never mind an ontological one, in the very notion of there being two pure existences that are necessarily existent.[115]

## 5. *Tawḥīd* and Numerical Oneness

This brings us to the final section of this study: the concept of 'oneness' itself. As we have seen, the term 'one' can be understood in at least two different senses. The oneness of pure being—singular and irreplicable—stands in stark contrast to the oneness of ordinary entities such as human beings which can exist in multiple instances.[116] Given this complexity, Shīʿī *mutakallimūn*, philosophers, and mystics have been meticulous in ensuring that God's uniqueness is correctly articulated, a concern that arises from the necessity of distinguishing between the different senses in which 'oneness' can be predicated. Notably, the recorded statements of the Shīʿī Imams suggest that they too were acutely aware of this distinction. Imam ʿAlī, regarded as the preeminent source of wisdom (*ḥikma*) in Shīʿī Islam, articulated four distinct perspectives on divine oneness, asserting that only two accurately capture its true nature.[117]

The concept of 'oneness' (*waḥda*) signifies that a thing is indivisible from the perspective in which it is said to be 'one.' Broadly, this can be categorised into two types: (1) essential oneness (*al-wāḥid al-ḥaqīqī*) and (2) non-essential oneness (*al-wāḥid ghayr al-ḥaqīqī*). Essential oneness is further divided into (1a) true essential oneness (*al-waḥda al-ḥaqqa al-ḥaqīqiyya*) and (1b) nominal essential oneness, the latter often referred to as 'numerical oneness' (*al-waḥda al-ʿadadiyya*). Given these distinctions, we must ask: when the Qur'an declares, 'Your God is one God; there is no god besides Him' (Q. 2:163), in what specific sense is divine oneness being affirmed? Addressing this question requires first clarifying the meaning of these various types of oneness—particularly, the distinction between true essential oneness and numerical oneness.

Numerical oneness is a familiar concept—one that we typically have in mind when we speak of something being 'one.' However, an entity is described as numerically one when the thing itself and the oneness attributed to it are not identical. For example, in the statement, 'There is one pen on the table,' the subject is qualified by numerical oneness, but the concept of pen *qua* pen is distinct from the concept of one *qua* one.

---

115 Mullā Ṣadrā, *Asrār al-āyāt*, 57 where Ṣadrā explains that the existence of two pure existences is *muḥāl al-farḍ*, i.e. impossible to conceive.

116 As Avicenna and other philosophers point out, 'one', like 'being', is predicated with ambiguity (*maqūl bi-l-tashkīk*).

117 al-Shaykh al-Ṣadūq, *Kitāb al-Tawḥīd*, ed. Sayyid Hāshim al-Ḥussaynī al-Ṭihrānī (Qom: Mu'assasat al-Nashr al-Islāmī, 1430/[2008–2009]), 81 *hadith* no. 3.

In this case, oneness functions as a extrinsic rather than an intrinsic part of the pen's essence. This distinction explains why the number of pens can be one or many. If 'being one' were identical to 'being a pen' or a part thereof, then the number of pens could never exceed one.

Numerical oneness is thus defined by the possibility of repeated instantiation. If I am holding one pen, and then pick up another, I now have 'two pens.' The addition of a second pen is neither logically incoherent nor metaphysically problematic, nor would be the addition of a third or a fourth. This is because numerical oneness presupposes a certain finitude, a limitation in existence. A single pen is one, but not infinite; therefore, it allows for the possibility of other pens existing alongside it. In contrast, if a pen were infinite—an 'infinite pen', so to speak—there would be no logical space for a second pen. What this shows is that in order for something to be countable, it must possess a finite existence. There is thus a fundamental link between countability and ontological limitation. If countability and finitude characterise numerical oneness, then 'true essential oneness' refers to that which is 'one' in a way that excludes the very possibility of multiplicity. Such an entity is not only unique but necessarily so, because its infinitude precludes the existence of anything else like it.[118] In the context of our discussion this means that just as God is necessarily existent He is also necessarily one, and, more importantly, that 'there is nothing like Him' (*laysa ka-mithlihi shayʾ*).

When the Qurʾan states, 'Your God is one God,' therefore, this statement can be interpreted in two ways. The first interpretation is that 'one' refers to numerical oneness, meaning that while it is a fact that there is only one God, there is no logical impossibility in the idea of there being more than one. By contrast, the second interpretation understands the predicate 'one' as referring to true essential oneness, and on that basis affirms the subject's infinity whilst also eliminating the possibility of there being further instances of the same. Therefore, while both readings affirm the unity of God, they have starkly different implications for the possibility of plurality. The first affirms unity but does not deny the logical possibility of plurality, whereas the second affirms unity but also denies the logical possibility of its instances being multiplied.

The modern Shīʿī philosopher al-ʿAllāma al-Ṭabāṭabāʾī draws upon the philosophical notion of true essential oneness in his commentary on those Qurʾanic verses that explicitly affirm God's unity. In particular, he observes that whenever the Qurʾan describes God as

118 As al-ʿAllāma al-Ṭabāṭabāʾī explains, true essential oneness is 'a kind of unity with which the presumption of any kind of multiplicity is impossible' (*al-waḥda allatī yastaḥīlu maʿahā farḍ al-takaththur*); see al-ʿAllāma al-Ṭabāṭabāʾī, *Bidāyat al-ḥikma*, 157; cf. idem, *Nihāyat al-ḥikma*, 1:241, 2:225. Given that things predicated with true essential oneness cannot be multiplied, they are often referred to as 'one in the non-numerical sense' (*al-wāḥid bi-lā ʿadad*), unlike things that are one but capable of being multiplied, in which case their unity or oneness is referred to as numerical oneness (*al-wāḥid bi-l-ʿadad*). In the Shīʿī tradition, the Imams described God as one in the non-numerical sense. For more on this aspect of Shīʿī scholarship, see Zoheir Esmail's contribution in this volume.

being 'one', it frequently qualifies this oneness with the attribute *al-qahhār*.[119] This term has been rendered in various ways in modern English translations, but regardless of the specific word chosen, the Qur'an undeniably associates God's oneness with *qāhiriyya*, prompting the question: why? For Ṭabāṭabā'ī, this linguistic detail provides an important hermeneutical opportunity to explore the philosophical implications of divine unity. From a grammatical perspective, *al-qahhār* is the intensified active participle of the root *q-h-r* (to overpower, subjugate). By ascribing this quality to God's oneness, the Qur'an implicitly rejects any notion of divine unity being characterised by the passive participle *maqhūr* (overpowered or subdued). Ṭabāṭabā'ī argues that this distinction is significant: the Qur'an not only affirms God's unity but also emphasises His absolute dominance, thereby rejecting in his view a purely numerical understanding of oneness.

For Ṭabāṭabā'ī, then, whenever the Qur'an declares God's oneness, it does more than simply assert that there is only one God—it also *negates* the very possibility of any other divine or quasi-divine entities. This is not a weak metaphysical claim, but a strong one. Such an assertion is particularly important within the historical context of the Qur'an's revelation. According to Ṭabāṭabā'ī, the *mushrikūn* of seventh-century Arabia did not practice outright polytheism but rather adhered to a form of henotheism. While the Qur'an condemns their beliefs as *shirk*, their theology suggests that they acknowledged Allah as the supreme deity while also venerating lesser deities for intercession or worldly benefits.[120] Thus, the primary mission of the Qur'an was not merely to affirm belief in Allah but to categorically reject the existence of any other divine or quasi-divine beings. One way the Qur'an accomplishes this, according to Ṭabāṭabā'ī, is by describing God as *al-Wāḥid al-Qahhār*—a formulation that decisively refutes the notion of numerical oneness and underscores His absolute and unparalleled supremacy.

> The Qur'an in its highest teachings denies numerical oneness (*al-waḥdat al-ʿadadiyya*) of God. This kind of oneness exists only by virtue of this 'one thing' being distinguished from this other 'one thing' due to the finitude [of their being] that rules over them and the measurability [of their quantities] that overpowers them. An example of this is the water in a river. When this water is divided into different containers, then the water contained inside each of them is 'one water', but it is not the same as the other waters in the other containers, which are also 'one water' in

119 See Qur'an 12:39, 14:48, 38:65, 39:4, 40:16.

120 See al-ʿAllāma al-Ṭabāṭabā'ī, *al-Mīzān fī tafsīr al-Qur'ān* (Qom: Mu'ssasah-i Maṭbūʿātī-yi Ismāʿīliyyān, 1973), 16:148, commentary on Q. 29:61 (also 31:25, 39:38). Elsewhere in the Qur'an the *mushrikūn* are reported as saying, 'We only worship them so they may bring us closer to Allah in position' (Q. 39:3), an attitude which suggests a belief in a hierarchy where Allah was supreme, but the intercessors were necessary for gaining divine favour. The *mushrikūn*'s error, Ṭabāṭabā'ī argues, was not that they denied the existence of Allah, but rather that they failed to worship Him alone by admitting the existence of other lesser deities. Cf. Patricia Crone, 'The Religion of the Qur'ānic Pagans: God and the Lesser Deities', *Arabica* 57 (2010): 151–200.

> their own right. The only reason each of them is 'one water' and distinguishable from the others is because what is contained in the other containers is negated from it; they do not all exist together in one container, but are separated [...] If God is affirmed to be the overpowerer and not the one overpowered, the one who subjugates and not who is subjugated by anything whatsoever, then there is no way of conceiving a numerical oneness or numerical plurality for Him.[121]

At the core of these claims is the metaphysical assertion that a thing's distinction and separability—qualities that coexist with its unity and oneness—stem from the finitude of its existence. The implication is that God's existence, being infinite, cannot logically permit the simultaneous existence of other beings, whether divine or contingent, alongside Him. For Ṭabāṭabāʾī, a holistic reading of Qurʾanic verses pertaining to God, His existence, and His attributes affirms the philosophical and mystical view that all perfections belong exclusively to God. He is the Perfect Being and by virtue of His perfection He bestows all other beings with whatever perfections they possess. Nothing possesses any perfection except insofar as it is already present in God.[122]

Like Ṣadrā, Ṭabāṭabāʾī therefore also identifies the Necessary Being as a maximally perfect being. God possesses all perfections to greatest extent possible and He is the source of these perfections in other beings. This is supported by numerous verses of the Qurʾan on the one hand and a robust metaphysics on the other. If the Necessary Being lacks a certain perfection then His being is characterised by privation. This means two things: (1) that it is a combination of being and non-being and (2) that it is finite, both of which entail its being contingent. Its finitude results from the fact that it is limited by privation: when something lacks a perfection, it is limited with respect to that thing. But a Necessary Being is sheer existence and therefore does not have any privations, and hence it cannot be limited—metaphysically speaking—in any sense whatsoever. In the context of divine unity, this means that because God's existence is sheer existence, and because whatever is sheer existence has to be infinite, the unity that is predicated of Him can only be true essential oneness (*al-waḥdat al-ḥaqīqiyya al-ḥaqqa*). This unity overpowers and subjugates the possibility of reproduction, replication or duplication, and thus negates the possibility of any other Necessary Being. In essence, there is a complete ontological overlap between the concepts of unity and (necessary) being: pure being is truly one, and whatever is truly one can only be sheer existence. This is the Necessary Being.

In light of the foregoing analysis, it is evident that Ibn Kammūna's counterargument against divine unity does not stand when examined through the lens of the Ṣadrian tradition. While Ibn Kammūna challenges Avicenna's proof by arguing that multiple Necessary Beings could exist with distinct yet unknowable essences, this critique is

121 al-ʿAllāma al-Ṭabāṭabāʾī, *al-Mīzān fī tafsīr al-Qurʿān*, 6:88.
122 Ibid., 89.

tantamount to an equivocal understanding of existence that Ṣadrā explicitly rejects. Central to Ṣadrā's metaphysics is the doctrine of the modulation of existence (*tashkīk al-wujūd*), which posits that existence is a single graded reality rather than a collection of disparate, unrelated essences (and/or existences). This perspective allows Ṣadrā and those who followed his philosophical scheme to dissolve Ibn Kammūna's objection by demonstrating that any putative second Necessary Being would be either (1) a manifestation of the same reality of necessary existence, in which case it would not be truly distinct, or (2) a being whose necessity of existence is qualified by limitation, thereby rendering it contingent rather than necessary. Furthermore, Ṣadrā's commitment to the principle that pure being (*wujūd ṣirf*) is necessarily one and indivisible reinforces the impossibility of multiple Necessary Beings. If God is maximally perfect and infinite in His existence, as the Ṣadrian framework asserts, then any other putative Necessary Being would either partake in this perfection—rendering it identical to God—or fall short of it, making it contingent. The notion of a second Necessary Being thus collapses into incoherence, as it would either be redundant or lack the very attributes that define necessary existence.

## Bibliography

Aliwshah, Ahmed. 'Suhrawardī and Ibn Kammūna on the Impossibility of Having Two Necessary Existents.' In *Illuminationist Texts and Textual Studies: Essays in Memory of Hossein Ziai*, edited by Ali Geissari, John Walbridge and Ahmed Alwishah, 115–134. Leiden: Brill, 2018.

Āmulī, Ḥasan Ḥasanzādah. *Waḥdat az dīdghāh-i ʿārif u ḥakīm*. Qom: Alif Lām Mīm, 1383Sh/[2004–2005].

al-Āshtiyānī, Mīrzā Mahdī al-Mudarris. *Taʿlīqāt al-Āshtiyānī ʿalā Sharḥ al-Manẓūma*. 2 vols. Beirut: Mu'assasat al-Tārīkh al-ʿArabī, 2012/1433.

Avicenna (=Ibn Sīnā). *al-Ishārāt wa-l-tanbīhāt*. Edited by Mujtabā al-Zāriʿī. Qom: Būstān-i Kitāb, 1423/[2002–2003].

———. *Kitāb al-Hidāya*. 2nd Edition. Edited by Muḥammad ʿAbdu. Cairo: Maktabat al-Qāhira al-Ḥadītha, 1974.

———. *Kitāb al-Najāt*. Edited by Muḥammad Taqī Dānishpazhūh. Tehran: Intishārāt-i Dānishghāh-i Ṭihrān, 1985.

———. *Manṭiq al-mashriqiyyīn*. Edited by Muḥibb al-Dīn al-Khaṭīb and ʿAbd al-Fattāḥ al-Qatlān. Cairo: al-Maktaba al-Salafiyya, 1328/1910.

———. *al-Risālat al-ʿArshiyya fī tawḥīdihī wa-ṣifātih*. Edited by al-Sayyid ʿAbdullāh b. Aḥmad al-ʿAlawī. Hyderabad: Dā'irat al-Maʿārif al-ʿUthmāniyya, 1353/1934.

———. *al-Shifā, al-Ilāhiyyāt*. Edited by G. C. Anawati, S. Zayed, M. Musa and S. Duna. 2 vols. Cairo: al-Hay'a al-ʿĀmma Li-Shu'ūn al-Maṭābiʿ al-Amīriyya, 1960.

———. *al-Taʿlīqāt*. Second Edition. Edited by Sayyid Ḥusayn Mūsawiyān. Tehran: Mu'assasah-i Pazhūhashī Ḥikmat u Falsafah-i Īrān, 1401Sh/[2022–2023].

Benevich, Fedor. 'Individuation and identity in Islamic philosophy after Avicenna: Bahmanyār and Suhrawardī', *British Journal for the History of Philosophy* 28, no. 1 (2020): 4–28.

Crone, Patricia. 'The Religion of the Qurʾānic Pagans: God and the Lesser Deities', *Arabica* 57 (2010): 151–200.

al-Dawānī, Jalāl al-Dīn. *Shawāwil al-ḥūr fī sharḥ Hayākil al-nūr*. Edited by Muḥammad Rajab ʿAlī Ḥasan. Amman: Dār al-Fatḥ Li-l-Dirāsāt wa-l-Nashr, 2023.

De Smet, Daniel and Meryem Sebti. 'Avicenna's Philosophical Approach to the Qur'an in the Light of His *Tafsīr Sūrat al-Ikhlāṣ*,' *Journal of Qur'anic Studies* 11, no. 2 (2009), 134–148.

Dīnānī, Ghulām-Ḥusayn Ibrāhīmī. *Qawāʿid-i kullī-yi falsafī dar falsafah-i Islāmī*. 2 vols. Tehran: Pazhūhashghāh-i ʿUlūm-i Insānī u Muṭālaʿāt-i Farhanghī, 1389Sh/2011.

al-Fārābī, Abū Naṣr. *On the Perfect State* (*Kitāb Ārā ahl al-madīna al-fāḍila*). Edited and translated by Richard Walzer. Oxford: Clarendon Press, 1985.

Farūghī, Rūḥullāh. 'Arziyābī pāsikh-hā-yi falāsifa u ʿurafā bih ishkāl-i nāsāzgharī-yi taʿaddud-i ṣifāt-i khudāvand u waḥdat-i dhāt,' *Ilāhiyāt u falsafah-i muʿāṣir* 1, no. 1 (2021): 234–246.

Ibn Kammūna. *al-Kāshif* (*al-Jadīd fī l-ḥikma*). Edited by Ḥāmid Nājī Iṣfahānī. Tehran: Mu'assasah-i Pazhūhashī Ḥikmat u Falsafah-i Īrān, 1387Sh/[2008].

———. 'al-Maṭālib al-muhimma min ʿilm al-ḥikma.' Edited by Sayyid Ḥusayn Sayyid Mūsawī, *Khiradnāmah-i Ṣadrā* 8, no. 32 (2003): 64–86.

———. *Sharḥ al-Talwīḥāt al-lawḥiyya wa-l-ʿarshiyya*. Edited by Najafqulī Ḥabībī. 3 volumes. Tehran: Mīrāṡ-i Maktūb, 1387Sh/[2008].

Iṣfahānī, Mullā Muḥammad Ismāʿīl. *Sharḥ al-Ḥikmat al-ʿarshiyya*. Edited by Muḥammad Masʿūd Khudāwardī. Tehran: Mu'assasah-i Pazhūhashī Ḥikmat u Falsafah-i Īrān, 1391Sh/[2013–2014].

Janos, Damien. *Oneness, Essence, and Self-Identity: A New Interpretation of Avicenna's Henology*. Berlin: De Gruyter, 2024.

Kaukua, Jari. '*Iʿtibārī* Concepts in Suhrawardī: The Case of Substance', *Oriens* 48 (2020): 40–66.

Khwānsārī, Āqā Ḥusayn. *al-Ḥāshiya ʿalā l-Shifāʾ* (*Ilāhiyyāt*). Edited by Ḥāmid Nājī Iṣfahānī. Qom: Dabīrkhānah-i Kangarah Āqā Ḥusayn Khwānsārī, 1378Sh/[1999–2000].

Jilvah, Abū l-Ḥasan. *Risāla fī anna mafhūm al-wāḥid kayfa yuntazaʿ min al-ḥaqāʾiq al-mutabāyina*. In *Majmūʿah-i āṡār-i Ḥakīm Jilvah*, edited by Ḥasan Riḍā, 605–608. Tehran: Intishārāt-i Ḥikmat, 1385Sh/[2006–2007].

Lizzini, Olga L. 'L'unité et l'unicité de Dieu: Le double sens de l'être chez al-Fārābī et Avicenne', *Revue Philosophique de la France et de l'étranger* 149, no. 1 (2024): 17–31.

Mayer, Toby. "Faḫr ad-Dīn ar-Rāzī's Critique of Avicenna's Argument for the Unity of God in the *Išārāt*, and Naṣīr ad-Dīn Ṭūsī's Defence." In *Before and Avicenna: Proceedings of the First Conference of the Avicenna Study Group*, edited by David C. Reisman, 199–218. Leiden: Brill, 2003.

Morvarid, Mahmoud. 'Varieties of Avicennian arguments for the existence of God,' *Religious Studies* 58 (2002): 576–596.

Mullā Ṣadrā, *Asrār al-āyāt wa-anwār al-bayyināt*. Edited by Muḥammad ʿAlī Jāvidān. Tehran: Bunyād-i Ḥikmat-i Islāmī-yi Ṣadrā, 1389Sh/[2010–2011].

———. *al-Ḥikmat al-ʿarshiyya*. Edited by Aṣghar Dādbih. In *Majmūʿah-i rasāʾil-i falsafī*, vol. 4, pp. 307–426. Tehran: Bunyād-i Ḥikmat-i Islāmī-yi Ṣadrā, 1391Sh/[2012–2013].

———. *al-Ḥikmat al-mutaʿāliyya fī l-asfār arbaʿa*. Edited by Aḥmad Aḥmadī. 9 vols. Tehran: Intishārāt-i Bunyād-i Ḥikmat-i Islāmī-yi Ṣadrā, 1381Sh/[2002–2003].

———. *al-Mabdaʾ wa-l-maʿād fī l-ḥikmat al-mutaʿāliyya*. Edited by Muḥammad Żabīḥī and Jaʿfar Shāh-Naẓarī. 2 vols. Tehran: Intishārāt-i Bunyād-i Ḥikmat-i Islāmī-yi Ṣadrā, 1381Sh/[2002–2003].

———. *al-Masāʾil al-qudsiyya*. Edited by Manūchahr Ṣadūqī Sahā. In *Majmūʿah-i rasāʾil-falsafī*, vol. 4, pp. 195–306. Tehran: Bunyād-i Ḥikmat-i Islāmī-yi Ṣadrā, 1391Sh/[2012–2013].

———. *Al-Mashāʿir*. Edited by Maqṣūd Muḥammadī. In *Majmūʿah-i rasāʾil-i falsafī*, vol. 4, pp. 307–426. Tehran: Bunyād-i Ḥikmat-i Islāmī-yi Ṣadrā, 1391Sh/[2012–2013].

———. *Sharḥ u taʿlīqah-i Ṣadra l-Mutaʾallihīn bar Ilāhiyyāt-i Shifāʾ*. Edited by Najafqulī Ḥabībī. 2 volumes. Tehran: Intishārāt-i Bunyād-i Ḥikmat-i Islāmī-yi Ṣadrā, 1382Sh/[2003–2004].

Nasgasawa, Yujin. *Maximal God: A New Defence of Perfect Being Theism*. Oxford: Oxford University Press, 2017.

Pourjavady, Reza and Sabine Schmidtke. *A Jewish Philosopher of Baghdad: ʿIzz al-Dawla Ibn Kammūna (d. 683/1284) and His Writings*. Leiden: Brill, 2006.

Qumsha'ī, Muḥammad Riḍā. *Risāla fī radd jawāz intizāʿ mafhūm wāḥid min al-ḥaqāʾiq al-mutabāyina*. In *Majmūʿah-i aśār-i ḥakīm-i ṣuhbā: ʿārif ilāhī Āqā Muḥammad Riḍā Qumshaʾī*, edited by Ḥāmid Nājī Iṣfahānī, 245–252. Tehran: Qānūn Pazhūhashī, 1388Sh/[1999–2000].

al-Rāzī, Fakhr al-Dīn. *Kitāb al-Muḥaṣṣal: wa-huwa Muḥaṣṣal afkār al-mutaqaddimīn wa-l-mutaʾakhkhirīn min al-ḥukamāʾ wa-l-mutakallimīn*, ed. Ḥusayn Atāʾī. Qom: Intishārāt al-Sharīf al-Raḍī, 1999.

Sabzawārī, Mullā Hādī. *Sharḥ al-asmāʾ aw Sharḥ Duʿā al-Jawshan al-kabīr*. Edited by Najafqulī Ḥabībī. Tehran: Intishārāt-i Dānishghāh-i Ṭihrān, 1385Sh/[2006–2007].

———. *Sharḥ al-Manẓūma fī l-manṭiq wa-l-ḥikma*. Edited by Muḥsin Bīdārfar. 2 vols. Qom: Muntasharāt-i Bīdār, 1432/[2010].

———. *Taʿlīqāt ʿalā l-Shawāhid al-rubūbiyya*. Edited by Sayyid Jalāl al-Dīn Āshtiyānī.

Beirut: Mu'assasat al-Ta'rīkh al-ʿArabī, n.d.

al-Shaykh al-Ṣadūq, Abū Jaʿfar Muḥammad b. ʿAlī b. al-Ḥusayn Ibn Bābawayh al-Qummī. *al-Tawḥīd*. Edited by al-Sayyid Hāshim al-Ḥusaynī al-Ṭihrānī. Qom: Mu'assasat al-Nashr al-Islāmī, 1430/[2008–2009].

Strobino, Riccardo. *Avicenna's Theory of Science: Logic, Metaphysics, Epistemology*. California: University of California Press, 2021.

Suhrawardī, Shihāb al-Dīn al-. *al-Talwīḥāt al-lawḥiyya wa-l-ʿarshiyya*. Edited by Najafqulī Ḥabībī. Tehran: Mu'assasah-i Pazhūhashī-yi Ḥikmat u Falsafah-i Īrān, 1388Sh/[2009–2010].

Tabrasī, Abū Manṣūr Aḥmad b. ʿAlī al-. *al-Iḥtijāj*. Edited by Ibrāhīm al-Bahādurī and Muḥammad Hādī Bih. Qom: Intishārāt-i Uswa, 1413/[1992].

al-Ṭabāṭabā'ī, al-ʿAllāma al-Sayyid Muḥammad Ḥusayn. *Bidāyat al-ḥikma*. Edited by ʿAbbās ʿAlī al-Zāriʿī al-Sabzawārī. Qom: Mu'assasat al-Nashr al-Islāmī, 1426/[2005–2006].

———. *al-Mīzān fī tafsīr al-Qur'ān*. 20 vols. Qom: Mu'ssasah-i Maṭbūʿātī-yi Ismāʿīliyyān, 1973.

———. *Nihāyat al-ḥikma*. Edited by ʿAbbās ʿAlī al-Zāriʿī al-Sabzawārī. 2 volumes. Qom: Mu'assasat al-Nashr al-Islāmī, 1427/[2006–2007].

al-Ṭūsī, Naṣīr al-Dīn. *Sharḥ al-Ishārāt*. Edited by Ḥasanzādah al-Āmulī. 2 vols. Qom: Būstān-i Kitāb, 1386Sh/[2007–2008].

Yaqub, Aladdin M. 'Al-Ġhazālī's Philosophers on the Divine Unity,' *Arabic Sciences and Philosophy*, 20 (2010): 281–306.

Zarepour, Mohammed Saleh. *Necessary Existence and Monotheism: An Avicennian Account of the Islamic Conception of Divine Unity*. Cambridge: Cambridge University Press, 2022.

# Logico-linguistic Analysis of the *Kalimat al-Tawḥīd*: al-Rāzī vs al-Kūrānī

*Yusuf Daşdemir*[1]

The first part of the *Kalima* is blasphemy while the last is belief ... Do not be stuck in the first station but move to the second!

Majd al-Dīn Aḥmad al-Ghazālī[2]

The succinct and striking formulation of Islamic monotheism, the Word of Unification (*kalimat al-tawḥīd*), 'there is no deity but God' (*Lā ilāha illā All*āh), lies at the very centre of Islam, and its heartfelt articulation has been viewed as the basic manifestation of Muslim identity. Commensurate with this importance, the *Kalimat al-tawḥīd* (hereafter: *Kalima*) has been subject to great scrutiny from multiple disciplinary perspectives, resulting in a plethora of literature on the topic. Scholars of the Arabic linguistic sciences, for example, paid great attention to aspects of the *Kalima* relevant to their studies.[3]

With Fakhr al-Dīn al-Rāzī (d. 606/1210), one of the founding figures of the post-classical period of Islamic thought, discussions about the *Kalima* took on a new dimension. Al-Rāzī introduced a range of logical and philosophical considerations to the discussion, such as the denial of essence itself (*nafy al-māhiyya*), which involves the question of whether it is conceivable to deny an essence independently, without reference to its connection to any predicate. When one asserts, for example, 'No deity!' in the *Kalima*, would the denial pertain to the essence of deity (*ulūhiyya*) in and of itself, or rather to its relation to existence? This move caused the discussion to be carried out in the more general context of philosophical problems, such as the reality of essence in itself and its relation to existence and whether essences are made (*majʿūla*), the central topics of Islamic philosophy and theology after Avicenna (Ibn Sīnā, d. 428/1037).

1 I am thankful to Wahid M. Amin for his helpful comments and suggestions and to my colleagues at the University of Jyväskylä, Jari Kaukua, Francesco O. Zamboni, and Hassan Rezakhany, for their invaluable comments on an earlier draft of this paper. I am also grateful to Wihuri Foundation for generously funding my research on Ottoman logic.

2 Majd al-Dīn Aḥmad al-Ghazālī, *al-Tajrīd fī kalimat al-tawḥīd* (MS Ankara: National Library, Collection of Manuscripts A 1263), fols. 23a7–9.

3 Despite this relatively intense interest in the *Kalima* in classical sources, to the best of my knowledge, there is a notable absence of studies on the *Kalima* and particularly on its linguistic, logical, and philosophical features in the secondary literature.

The fifteenth-century Persian scholar Jalāl al-Dīn al-Dawānī (d. 908/1502) added yet another dimension to the issue when he authored two treatises on the *Kalima*,[4] one in Persian and one in Arabic, and in his preface to the Arabic treatise, promised to point out how such features relate to issues of purely rational investigation and of revealed theology. More significantly, he dedicated, for the first time as far as I am aware, one of the five parts of his treatise to the logical analysis of the *Kalima* so as to determine what kind of proposition it is. Rather short and based on only one grammatical interpretation of the *Kalima*, this analysis would be later both criticised and expanded by Ibrāhīm al-Kūrānī (d. 1101/1690).[5]

A Sufi of the Akbarian tradition as well as a prolific author with more than a hundred works on controversial issues of his time, al-Kūrānī authored two works devoted to the *Kalima*: *Inbāh al-anbāh ʿalā iʿrāb Lā ilāha illā Allāh* and *ʿUjālat dhawī al-intibāh fī taḥqīq iʿrāb Lā ilāha illā Allāh.*[6] In the *Inbāh*, very probably the most comprehensive work ever written on the subject, he discusses in depth not only syntactical, but also philosophical, theological, and jurisprudential problems that originate from the *Kalima* by frequently citing and quoting numerous scholars. The two names above, al-Rāzī and al-Dawānī, however, bear the brunt of al-Kūrānī's dialectical attacks.

This paper will examine the philosophical, logical, and linguistic treatment of the *Kalima* by al-Rāzī and al-Kūrānī,[7] who represent to a large extent two main strands of philosophy in the post-classical era, namely, philosophical *kalām* and Akbarian Sufism, respectively. It will show that these discussions revolve around two main problems:

(1) Is the *Kalima* a complete (*tāmm*) sentence as it is?
(2) How many and what propositions does the *Kalima* contain?

The first syntactical question brings us to the philosophical problem of whether the denial of an essence in itself is conceivable. As will be seen shortly, while al-Rāzī argues that one could deny an essence itself with no reference to its relation to any predicate and therefore the *Kalima* is a complete sentence, al-Kūrānī contends that denial pertains only to a relation between an essence and a predicate, which is why the *Kalima* is not

4 Jalāl al-Dīn al-Dawānī, 'Fī kalimat al-tawḥīd', in *Khams rasāʾil li-l-ʿAllāma Jalāl al-Dīn al-Dawānī*, ed. Anwar F. ʿUlwānī al-Zuʿayrī (Cairo: Dār al-Imām al-Rāzī, 2021), 131–41; Jalāl al-Dīn al-Dawānī, *Tahlīliyya sharḥ lā ilāha illā Allāh*, ed. F. Farīdūnī Firūzanda (Tehran: Intishārāt-i Gayhān, 1953), 27–74. In the latter, which is in Persian, al-Dawānī does not devote notable attention to the logical aspects of the *Kalima*.

5 On al-Kūrānī's milieu, life, and works, see Naser Dumairieh, *Intellectual Life in the Ḥijāz before Wahhabism: Ibrāhīm al-Kūrānī's (d. 1101/1690) Theology of Sufism* (Leiden: Brill, 2022); Ömer Yılmaz, *İbrahim Kûrânî Hayatı, Eserleri ve Tasavvuf Anlayışı* (Istanbul: Insan Yay., 2005).

6 The latter is a rather brief summary of the former, which was edited by Ahmet Gemi in *Kelime-i Tevhidin İ'râbı* (Ankara: İlâhiyât, 2019), 65–412. The latter was also edited in Muṣṭafā S. al-Māziq, "Ujālat dhawī al-intibāh fī taḥqīq iʿrāb lā ilāha illā Allāh li-Ibrāhīm al-Kūrānī', *Majallat Shimāl Janūb*, no. 12 (2018): 21–45.

7 Al-Dawānī will only be occasionally cited because his treatise has little that we could not find in al-Rāzī.

complete as it is. The second question, on the other hand, is logical in nature, which yields a very significant theological quandary, namely, whether the *Kalima* signifies the existence of God. The two questions are also interconnected because if the *Kalima* is a complete sentence, then it contains only one proposition, but if it is not—that is, if it has some implicit elements—then there must be more than one proposition. The former position will be defended by al-Rāzī while the latter by al-Kūrānī.

This study consists of two sections, which address the two questions above, respectively. It aims to substantiate by this specific example the view that there are many concepts and discussions in the works of linguistic and Islamic sciences of post-classical Islam that are clearly of a logical and philosophical nature.

## 1. The Completeness of the *Kalima*

To begin, some basic Arabic grammar necessary to understand the debate is in order. In Arabic, there are mainly two types of sentence: nominal (*ismiyya*) and verbal (*fiʿliyya*). A sentence is nominal if it begins with a noun and verbal if it begins with a verb. In either case, the sentence is complete (*mufīd*) with at least two elements, the subject (*musnad ilayh*) and the predicate (*musnad*). The subject of a nominal sentence is called the 'topic' (*mubtadaʾ*) and its predicate is called the 'report' (*khabar*). In the verbal structure, the predicate comes as a 'verb' (*fiʿl*) at the beginning of the sentence while the subject following it functions as its 'agent' (*fāʿil*).[8] These two elements, nonetheless, might not always be available, but may be elided, in the utterance of the sentence. This linguistic phenomenon, which is called *iḍmār*, 'indicates the suppression of an element that may be reconstructed from the context' and that is 'necessary for the explanation of the surface structure'.[9] In such a case of suppression, 'it is the grammarian's task to reconstruct these hidden elements in order to explain the surface structure of the sentence'[10] and this procedure of reconstruction or restitution is called *taqdīr*.

In the context of this paper, therefore, if the *Kalima* is thought of as a verbal sentence, it will need a verb and an agent, explicit or implicit, to be complete, but if it is a nominal sentence, then it will need a topic and a report. In order to prove that the sentence is

8 For the earliest sources of these classifications, see ʿAmr b. ʿUthmān Sībawayhi, *al-Kitāb*, ed. ʿAbd al-Salām M. Hārūn, 3rd ed. (Cairo: Maktabat al-Khānjī, 1988), 1:23; Abū Bakr Ibn al-Sarrāj, *al-Uṣūl fī al-naḥw*, ed. ʿAbd al-Ḥusayn al-Fatlī (Beirut: Muʾassasat al-Risāla, 1996), 58–59. For modern explications of the issue, see William Wright, *A Grammar of the Arabic Language* (Cambridge: Cambridge University Press, 1898), 250–51; Kees Versteegh, 'Isnād', in *Encyclopedia of Arabic Language and Linguistics*, gen. ed. Kees Versteegh (Leiden: Brill, 2006), 2:434–37.

9 Michael C. Carter and Kees Versteegh, 'Iḍmār', in *Encyclopedia of Arabic Language and Linguistics*, 2:301. For a comprehensive account of the conditions and types of *iḍmār*, see Ibn Hishām al-Anṣārī, *Mughnī al-labīb ʿan kutub al-aʿārīb*, ed. Muḥammad M. ʿAbd al-Ḥamīd (Beirut: al-Maktaba al-ʿAṣriyya, 1991), 2:692–749.

10 Kees Versteegh, 'Taqdīr', in *Encyclopedia of Arabic Language and Linguistics*, 4:446.

complete, one has to show, in the latter case, that its topic and report are explicit, and if they are not, one must reconstruct the elided elements. Al-Rāzī takes the first option by interpreting the *Kalima* as a verbal sentence, arguing that both its verb and agent are explicit in the surface structure, whereas al-Kūrānī takes it as a nominal sentence to argue that, although its topic is explicit, its report is implicit. As a sentence with the necessary elements, al-Rāzī claims, the *Kalima* is complete and capable of conveying its intended meaning without any additions.[11] I will call this view *the completionist reading* of the *Kalima*. According to the majority, including al-Kūrānī, however, it is necessary on linguistic and logical grounds to reconstruct the *Kalima* with some implied elements, which I will call *the restitutionist reading*.

## 1.1 The Completionist Reading

Both in his *Tafsīr* and *Lawāmiʿ al-bayyināt*, al-Rāzī opens the discussion by questioning the opposite position, that is, the restitutionist reading. He first explains that most grammarians suggest that the *Kalima* needs to be reconstructed with certain additional phrases, among which 'for us' (*la-nā*) and 'in existence' (*fī al-wujūd*) often prevail.[12] However, neither could satisfy al-Rāzī: the first signifies only the unity of *our* god, but not any god in the absolute sense. This is evidently far from the perfect sense of 'God's being one'. The latter, though free from this deficiency, is also questionable in that the sentence 'There is no deity *in existence* save God' denies only the existence of a second god, but the *Kalima* as it is denies the essence (*māhiyya*) of a second god, and represents a more robust assertion of God's uniqueness than merely denying a second deity's existence. Consequently, al-Rāzī deems it more appropriate (*awlā*) to read the *Kalima* without any implied additions.[13]

Regarding the question of why denying the essence of a second deity would be a more emphatic way of conveying *tawḥīd*, al-Rāzī raises the following argument:

> [t1] This is because our statement 'No man' (*Lā rajul*) [for example] implies the denial (*nafy*) of this essence and once this essence is denied (*intafat*), all its individuals (*afrāduhā*) would be denied as well on account of the fact that if one of

11 Before al-Rāzī, such prominent grammarians as Jār Allāh al-Zamakhsharī argued for the completeness of the *Kalima*, but on a different reading. To him, '*Lā ilāha*' was the foregrounded report (*al-khabar al-muqaddam*) and '*illā Allāh*' the backgrounded topic (*al-mubtadaʾ al-muʾakhkhar*): 'Masʾala fī kalimat al-shahāda', ed. Muḥammad A. al-Dāllī, *Majallat Majmaʿ al-Lugha al-ʿArabiyya bi-Dimashq*, no. 68 (1993): 86.

12 The *Kalima* would accordingly be reconstituted as either *Lā ilāha la-nā illa Allāh* ('There is no deity for us save God') or *Lā ilāha fī al-wujūd illa Allāh* ('There is no deity in existence save God').

13 Fakhr al-Dīn al-Rāzī, *al-Tafsīr al-kabīr aw Mafātīḥ al-ghayb*, ed. Sayyid ʿAmrān (Cairo: Dār al-Ḥadīth, 2012), 2:469–70; Fakhr al-Dīn al-Rāzī, *Lawāmiʿ al-bayyināt sharḥ asmāʾ Allāh taʿālā wa-l-ṣifāt*, ed. Muḥammad Badr al-Dīn al-Niʿsānī (Cairo: al-Maṭbaʿa al-Sharafiyya, 1905), 93.

> the individuals of this essence were to obtain (*ḥaṣala*), then when that individual obtains, the essence would obtain too, which would contradict what the utterance signifies, namely, that the essence is denied. It is established then that our expression 'No man' implies a general, comprehensive negation. If one adds after that 'but Zayd' (*illā Zayd*), this will convey perfect, definite unity.[14]

Here we are given significant clues about how al-Rāzī identifies the necessary elements, the subject and predicate, of the *Kalima*. First, he seems to have viewed it as a verbal sentence, in which *lā* functions as the predicate by standing for the verb 'is denied' (*intafā*) while the noun following *lā* functions as the subject of the sentence, that is, the agent of the verb. If this is the case, then the *Kalima*, as a verbal sentence with a verb and its agent, will be a complete sentence. Yet this account seems vulnerable to the objection al-Kūrānī would later raise that, grammatically speaking, it is not possible to argue that *lā* stands for a verb in this way.[15]

The text also reveals al-Rāzī's rationale for his claim that denying the essence of a second deity would express a stronger form of divine unity: once the essence is denied, there would be no way for its individuals to exist at all. However, does not 'denying an essence' sound somewhat strange? Might he have meant by this that the essence did not have any extramentally existent instances? In that case, however, his interpretation would be no different from the *Kalima*'s second interpretation above together with 'in existence', that is, 'There is no deity *in existence* save God.' Hence, al-Rāzī must have been talking about a reading of the *Kalima* with no reference to existence, a reading that negates the essence in itself without considering its relation to anything else. To do so, he would first have to prove the possibility of such a negation.

Before moving on to his argument, let us consider his analysis of the syntactical status of the *Kalima*'s last part, *illā Allāh*. If Lā *ilāha* is a complete sentence, signifying that the essence of deity is denied, then what is the syntactical function of the last part of the *Kalima*? For al-Rāzī, the expression of *illā* in the *Kalima* has the same meaning or function as *ghayr*, 'other than',[16] and therefore *illā Allāh* is a complementary part of the agent in the sentence;[17] the agent in the *Kalima* as a verbal sentence is not *ilāh* alone, but rather *ilāh* along with its descriptive complement, *illā Allāh*. It is this combination, *ilāha illā Allāh*, 'any deity other than God'—that is, a second god, or a counterpart of God—that the *Kalima* denies in a conclusive way, according to al-Rāzī. Therefore, the *Kalima* is a complete verbal sentence with *Lā* as its predicate and *ilāha illā Allāh* as its subject, meaning that the essence of any deity other than God is denied.

---

14 al-Rāzī, *Tafsīr*, 2:269; al-Rāzī, *Lawāmiʿ*, 97.

15 Ibrāhīm al-Kūrānī, 'Inbāh al-anbāh ʿalā iʿrāb lā ilāha illā Allāh', in *Kelime-i Tevhidin İʿrâbı*, 279–80.

16 On *ghayr*, see Abdurrahman Ali Mihirig, 'On the Linguistic and Technical Meanings of *Ghayr* and Their Consequences for Understanding the Divine Attributes in Classical Kalām', *Kader* 20, no. 3 (2022): 894–921.

17 al-Rāzī, *Lawāmiʿ*, 94–95.

Let us now turn to al-Rāzī's argument for the possibility of the denial of an essence:

> [t2] If one says: How could one conceive the denial of essences? When you say, 'Black is not black,' it becomes a judgement that blackness is not blackness, which is not conceivable.[18] But if you say, 'Blackness does not exist,' that would be reasonable, regular, and proper. We would respond: The denial of an essence is inevitable because when you say, 'Blackness does not exist,' you deny the existence, and existence qua existence is an essence. This means that when you deny it [i.e. existence], you deny the essence that is called existence. If the denial of this essence qua essence is conceivable, why would it be inconceivable to deny that essence as well?[19]

Appealing to common sense, al-Rāzī's dialectical opponent questions the very possibility of denying essences. For her, this is nothing but to say that the essence is not itself, for example, blackness is not blackness, which is inconceivable. Therefore, she concludes, al-Rāzī should insert existence in the negation and say that blackness is not existent, that is, there is nothing in existence that is black. However, as noted above, if al-Rāzī were to accept this move, then it would commit him to the reading of the *Kalima* with the addition of 'in existence', which would imply that the *Kalima* is not complete in its surface structure. He counters this objection with a new argument that yields a conclusion contradictory to the opponent's: denying an essence is inevitable, that is, necessary. This is because, he insists, by saying 'Blackness does not exist', one denies nothing but the essence that is called 'existence' due to the fact that existence is also an essence in itself. And if the denial of existence qua essence in itself is conceivable, then it necessarily follows that denying an essence is perfectly possible.

Al-Rāzī's opponent, however, takes the floor again to correct al-Rāzī's misunderstanding or distortion: in the sentence 'Blackness does not exist' it is neither existence (*wujūd*) nor the essence (*māhiyya*), that is, blackness, that is denied but the essence's being attributed existence (*mawṣūfiyyat al-māhiyya bi-l-wujūd*). In other words, this sentence denies the relation that the essence stands in to existence, which I call 'attributedness'. This time al-Rāzī puts forward his second argument to show that denying an essence is still inevitable:

> [t3] The essence's being attributed existence is either separate from both the essence and existence or not. If it is separate from both, then denying it would amount to denying an essence. [This means] that denying an essence qua essence is possi-

18 The *Lawāmiʿ* version of the argument explains why this is not conceivable: because this amounts to something's changing into its contradictory, and the change of essences (*qalb al-ḥaqāʾiq*) is impossible (ibid., 93).

19 al-Rāzī, *Tafsīr*, 2:470.

> ble. … If the attributedness is not something separate from both, then the denial of it means nothing but a denial of an essence or a denial of existence. In this case, the explanation given above holds again. Therefore, it is established that our statement *Lā ilāha illā Allāh* is true and correct with no need at all to presume anything implicit.[20]

Here al-Rāzī's purpose seems to show that it would make no difference even if the denial is taken as targetting the essence's being attributed existence. This relational property of attributedness, he claims, is either something different from its *relata* or something identical to either. In the former case, the denial is directed to the attributedness alone, but if the attributedness considered in itself is also an essence, then denying an essence in itself should be possible. In the latter case, that is, if the attributedness is identical either to the essence or existence, the denial then attaches to either essence or existence, but in both cases, it relates to an essence, as al-Rāzī showed in t2. That is, whatever the case, the denial of essence qua essence is not only possible but also inevitable, because every attempt to negate something ultimately culminates in the denial of an essence in itself. If this is the case, then the *Kalima* is complete as a verbal sentence that denies the essence of any god other than God. Notice here that al-Rāzī does not categorically deny the denial of existence but reduces it to the denial of an essence itself.

That being said, a significant question still remains regarding what al-Rāzī really meant by the denial of an essence in itself. Now I will try to answer this based on two premises. I will not, however, delve into their justification but merely clarify how I understand them:

(1) Al-Rāzī represents a realist interpretation of Avicenna's distinction between essence and existence.
(2) Al-Rāzī is of the view that essences are made (*majʿūla*).

To begin with the first premise, al-Rāzī is known to have embraced a realist reception of the Avicennian essence–existence distinction, arguing against the conceptualist camp that essence and existence are extramentally distinct. As a rejector of mental existence, especially in his *Mulakhkhaṣ*,[21] he seems to embrace the view that 'there are in the extramental world essences *qua* essences in a neutral ontological state, which have their own identity and are primary to existence'.[22] He also hesitantly suggests that

20 Ibid.; al-Rāzī, *Lawāmiʿ*, 94. For a parallel argument, see al-Dawānī, 'Fī kalimat al-tawḥīd', 138.

21 Fakhr al-Dīn al-Rāzī, *al-Mulakhkhaṣ fī al-manṭiq wa-l-ḥikma*, ed. Ismail Hanoğlu (Amman: al-Aṣlayn li-l-Dirāsāt wa-l-Nashr, 2021), 1:297–98; Heidrun Eichner, 'Essence and Existence: Thirteenth-Century Perspectives in Arabic-Islamic Philosophy and Theology', in *The Arabic, Hebrew and Latin Reception of Avicenna's Metaphysics*, ed. Dag Nikolaus Hasse and Amos Bertolacci (Berlin: De Gruyter, 2012), 119–22.

22 Fedor Benevich, 'The Essence-Existence Distinction: Four Elements of the Post-Avicennian Metaphysical Dispute (11–13th Centuries)', *Oriens* 45, no. 3–4 (2017): 249.

these extramentally real essences may subsist by themselves or inhere in a hidden body as a Platonic form.[23] Although this does not necessarily mean that he subscribed to the doctrine of Platonic forms, as Benevich rightly warns,[24] it suffices for our purposes to say that he seems to ascribe essences a kind of reality.

The second premise brings us to another long-running debate of post-classical Islamic philosophy, that is, the problem of the making of essences (*jaʿl al-māhiyyāt*). I will start with the semantics of the verb *j-ʿ-l*. Al-Rāghib al-Iṣfahānī (*fl.* the first quarter of the eleventh century) enumerates five distinct senses of the verb, of which the second and fourth matter most to us. According to the second, the verb has the same meaning as *awjada*, that is, '[He] created' or 'brought into existence'. Used this way, the verb is transitive and needs one object. In the fourth form, however, it means 'to change something from one state to another', and takes two objects.[25] *Jaʿl* seems to have been usually taken by scholars, including al-Kūrānī himself as will be seen below, in the fourth sense, but I argue that al-Rāzī was using it in the second sense to mean the creation of essences,[26] not in the sense of bestowing them existence. Such a distinction was possible for al-Rāzī as a proponent of the realist reading of the essence–existence distinction. This is because if it is the case that essences have a certain kind of extramental reality and identity before they exist, then they are subject to creation; they are created as essences before being made existent:[27] 'The Omnipotent, just as He makes the essence existent, makes also the essence an essence.'[28] That is to say, if an essence has not been made by the Omnipotent in the first place, it is not possible yet to talk about whether it is existent or instantiated in the external world.[29]

Also relevant is al-Rāzī's treatment of impossible essences, which pose some peculiar problems to his realism about essences due to the fact that they cannot subsist in themselves or inhere in hidden bodies, as Athīr al-Dīn al-Abharī (d. ca. 663/1265) reminds

23 al-Rāzī, *Mulakhkhaṣ*, 298.

24 Fedor Benevich, 'The Reality of the Non-Existent Object of Thought', *Oxford Studies in Medieval Philosophy* 6 (2018): 45.

25 al-Rāghib al-Iṣfahānī, '*J-ʿ-l*', in *al-Mufradāt fī gharīb al-Qurʾān*, ed. Ṣafwān ʿA. al-Dāwūdī (Damascus: Dār al-Qalam, 1991).

26 This clarification is made by the sixteenth-century Ottoman scholar Kamālpashazāda, who himself held the position that essences are made in the second sense of the verb *j-ʿ-l*: 'Risāla fī bayān maʿnā al-jaʿl wa-taḥqīq anna al-māhiyya majʿūla', in *Majmūʿ rasāʾil al-ʿAllāma Ibn Kamāl Bāshā*, ed. Ḥamza Bakrī et al., vol. 6 (Istanbul: Dār al-Lubāb, 2018), esp. 290.

27 Indeed, this interpretation of the Rāzīan position is supported by Naṣīr al-Dīn al-Ṭūsī's objection against him. See Naṣīr al-Dīn al-Ṭūsī, *Sharḥ al-Ishārāt wa-l-tanbīhāt*, ed. Sulaymān Dunyā (Beirut: Muʾassasat al-Nuʿmān, 1992), 3:34. For the translation and discussion of the related passage, see Benevich, 'The Essence-Existence Distinction', 246–47.

28 Fakhr al-Dīn al-Rāzī, *al-Arbaʿīn fī uṣūl al-dīn*, ed. Aḥmad Ḥijāzī al-Saqqā (Cairo: Maktabat al-Kulliyyāt al-Azhariyya, 1986), 1:99.

29 *Pace* Ibrahim, who says '*jaʿl* is introduced independently of the question of God as the Creator of essences and independently of the temporal origination of essences'. Bilal Ibrahim, 'Causing an Essence: Notes on the Concept of *Jaʿl al-Māhiyya*, from Fakhr al-Dīn al-Rāzī to Mullā Ṣadrā', in *Philosophical Theology in Islam: Later Ashʿarism East and West*, ed. Ayman Shihadeh and Jan Thiele (Leiden: Brill, 2020), 156.

us.[30] For al-Rāzī, impossible objects of thought, such as a second god (*sharīk al-bārīʾ*), cannot be said to be objects (*dhawāt*), realities (*ḥaqāʾiq*), or essences (*māhiyyāt*).[31] This is where we find the key to understanding what he meant by the negation of essences. If an essence has not been created by God, it is said to be nothing at all, and in this sense it is denied. In the case of the alleged essence of a second god, it is not possible to talk about such an essence (except as being a combination of some real essences) because it is impossible. Therefore, al-Rāzī seems to mean above that the *Kalima* as it is signifies that there is no such essence as the second deity because it is not created by God due to its being impossible. Notably, in this interpretation, just like *jaʿl*, the term 'to deny' (*nafy*) is construed as a transitive verb with a singular object, specifically 'to deny something', rather than a dual-object structure such as 'to negate something of something'.[32]

### 1.2 The Restitutionist Reading

When we turn to the other, restitutionist, reading of the *Kalima*, we see al-Kūrānī strive both to show the accuracy of his own reading and to respond to al-Rāzī's arguments, countering them first on the linguistic level. He introduces his deep disagreement with al-Rāzī by asserting that the original form of the *Kalima* was a nominal sentence, that is, 'God is a deity' (*Allāhu ilāhun*), but as a result of a series of operations carried out for the sake of restricting (*qaṣr*) divinity to God alone, it evolved into its current form, namely, an exceptive sentence (*istithnāʾ*). Its predicate meanwhile has been brought forward and its subject has been pushed back: *ilāhun Allāhu*. Afterwards, the *lā* of general denial has been attached to the very beginning of the sentence to govern the initial predicate while the subject has been put in the scope of the *illā* of exception, called the 'excepted' (*al-mustathnā*). Thus we obtain *Lā ilāha illā Allāh*.[33] Notice, however, in the new structure of the *Kalima*, the word *ilāha* seems to occupy the place of the subject, which is called now the noun of the *lā*, but there is a missing essential element in the sentence, namely, the predicate of the *lā*. According to al-Kūrānī, the predicate of the *lā* must be implied if it does not occur in the literal structure; an exceptive sentence with the *lā* must be a complete sentence either explicitly or implicitly.

In proving this, he resorts to two grammatical arguments, the first based on the linguistic convention that Arabic speakers use the particle *lā* with a noun and a predicate,

30 See Benevich, 'The Reality of the Non-Existent Object of Thought', 50.

31 al-Rāzī, *al-Arbaʿīn*, 1:95. For more on his treatment of such objects of thought, see Benevich, 'The Reality of the Non-Existent Object of Thought', 50ff.

32 On different meanings and usages of the verb *n-f-y*, see Muḥammad Jamāl al-Dīn Ibn Manẓūr, '*n-f-y*', in *Lisān al-ʿArab* (Beirut: Dār Ṣādir, 1993).

33 For details of these complicated grammatical operations, see al-Kūrānī, 'Inbāh', 165–75. The part of the exceptive sentence before *illā* is called the 'antecedent' (*al-mustathnā minh*) and the part after it the 'excepted' (*al-mustathnā*). See Elsaid Badawi, Michael G. Carter, and Adrian Gully, *Modern Written Arabic: A Comprehensive Grammar*, 2nd ed. (London: Routledge, 2016), chap. 9.

which shows that it only attaches to complete nominal sentences. The predicate might be implicit, if ordinarily understood from the context, but it is still there.[34] For al-Kūrānī, such a convention is decisive due to the fact that the usage of Arabic speakers is the final authority in linguistic conflicts.[35]

The second argument is that particles (*ḥurūf*) have no independent meaning of their own: they have meaning only by means of the nouns and verbs they are related to. If a particle is such that it can only have a complete meaning by means of two things, such as the *lā* of general denial, then these two things must be present either explicitly in the sentence's surface structure or implicitly in its underlying form. Otherwise, the meaning of the particle could not be realised.[36] In other words, the negation expressed by the *lā* always requires two elements: a negated meaning (*manfī*) and that of which it is denied (*manfī ʿanh*), the non-existence of either drastically harming the meaning of the *Kalima*'s negation.[37]

Alongside these grammatical and semantical arguments, al-Kūrānī has also logical and philosophical ones against the Rāzīan view that denial can concern only one element, namely, the essence signified by the noun after the *lā*. In this context, he refers to one of the most prominent figures in post-classical Islamic thought, al-Sayyid al-Sharīf al-Jurjānī (d. 816/1413), quoting at length al-Jurjānī's comments on Abū Yaʿqūb al-Sakkākī's (d. 626/1229) statement that 'The denial of essences themselves (*anfus al-dhawāt*) is impossible; only their attributes can be denied. The proof for this is sought in other sciences.'[38] After expositing different meanings of *dhāt*, al-Jurjānī proceeds to the most probable one in this context, according to which *dhāt* is that which is independent in terms of conceivability (*mafhūmiyya*), that is, capable of being conceived and considered on its own. Defining *dhāt*, al-Jurjānī adds, as 'that which can be known' points to the same meaning. In this case, the term 'attribute' (*ṣifa*) will mean 'that which is not independent in terms of conception', that is, something which can only be a mirror (*mirʾā*) for the consideration of another concept, as al-Jurjānī puts it. The relation of judgement (*al-nisba al-ḥukmiyya*) between the subject and predicate is also an attribute in this sense. That is, it is not a *dhāt* and it is this relation that is subjected to negation and affirmation. Al-Jurjānī explicates the distinction at stake between an essence[39] and attribute as follows:

> [t4] [a] When you conceive of, for example, 'Zayd', 'man', or 'blackness', but do not

34 al-Kūrānī, 'Inbāh', 93.
35 Ibid., 157.
36 Ibid., 77.
37 Ibid., 233.
38 Abū Yaʿqūb al-Sakkākī, *Miftāḥ al-ʿulūm*, ed. Nuʿaym Zarzūr (Beirut: Dār al-Kutub al-ʿIlmiyya, 1987), 290, see also 309.
39 In al-Sakkākī and al-Jurjānī, we are faced with somewhat different terminology in that they use *dhāt* instead of *māhiyya*, which we saw above used by al-Rāzī, but considering the definition of *dhāt* by al-Jurjānī, I can sense no substantial difference between these terms. Hence, I use 'essence' for both.

conceive of anything else alongside it, you will be able to carry out neither negation nor affirmation. Even if you conceive of 'existence' or 'subsistence in the other', but do not attend to a relation between these two [sets of concepts], no negation or affirmation will be possible, either. [b] When you attend to this [relation], you [b1] either consider it for itself (*bi-l-dhāt*) insofar as it is a relation of existence or subsistence to one of them; even then you do not deny or affirm it. Granted, you could then posit it as a subject or predicate so as to say 'The relation of existence to Zayd obtains' or 'This relation is the relation of existence to Zayd'. Or [b2] you consider it as a means (*ālatan*) to consider these two parts [i.e. the subject and predicate], regarding it as being posited between them. It is only then that it becomes possible for you to deny or affirm it. Thus, it is evident that the judgement of negation or affirmation cannot attach to essences. Rather, these [judgements] can only attach to attributes that are relations of judgements [in this context] insofar as they are regarded as being between the parts of those [relations] and as a means to find out their properties.[40]

Al-Jurjānī here meticulously differentiates between three possible cases to identify the real object of affirmation and negation. In the first case (a), one considers different concepts, which are potentially either subjects or predicates, but one has not yet established any relation of judgement between them; they stand, as it were, apart from each other in one's mind. In the second case (b1), one makes a relation of judgement between the terms and considers, for example, Zayd's being existent, provided that one considers this relation, however, as an independent entity in itself, a *dhāt* in al-Jurjānī's terminology. In these two cases, however, there is still no affirmation or negation. Finally, in the case of b2, there occurs affirmation or negation because it is in this case that one relates the predicate to the subject, but this time conceiving of the relation not as something in itself but as something *about* other things. The relation of judgement, in this case, appears to belong to a meta-level or to be a second-order concept, which is *about* its two *relata* belonging to the first order. Al-Jurjānī expresses the relation's being a second-order concept by his famous metaphor of the mirror, according to which a mirror can be seen from two different perspectives: as something in itself or as a means of assessing other things reflected in it. Someone who looks at a mirror, al-Jurjānī says, can take it as a means and focus his attention on the form reflected in the mirror to make judgements about it or learn more about its properties. In this case, no judgement will be made about the mirror itself. But if one instead focuses on the mirror itself, considering it on its own, then one can learn about it and its properties, such as its substance and brightness.[41] Thus, I conclude, in the

---

40 al-Sayyid al-Sharīf al-Jurjānī, *Ḥāshiya ʿalā al-Muṭawwal* (Istanbul: Ṣaḥāfiya-i ʿUthmāniya, 1891), 231. For al-Kūrānī's quotation, see 'Inbāh', 73–75.

41 al-Sayyid al-Sharīf al-Jurjānī, *Ḥāshiya ʿalā Tasdīd al-qawāʿid fī sharḥ Tajrīd al-aqāʾid*, ed. Eşref Altaş et

case of b2, the relation of judgement is only taken for the sake of its *relata*, not in itself at all, which makes it a second-order concept, or an attribute according to al-Jurjānī. As such, the relation can serve as the only object of affirmation and negation.

Based on these statements by al-Jurjānī, al-Kūrānī reaches the following conclusion: the negation signified by the *lā* does not relate to the noun it attaches to, but to the relation between the subject and the predicate, and given that a single concept could not be sufficient on its own to make a relation, there must be at least two *relata* to sensibly talk about a relation. In the absence of either *relatum*, the relation—and therefore both affirmation and negation—will also fail to obtain. Therefore, according to al-Kūrānī, it is obvious that when negation is bound to the subject, it is in fact bound to a relation that a predicate stands in to the subject, and when it is bound to the predicate, it is in fact bound to a relation that a subject bears to the predicate. In either case, if the predicate is not explicit, it must be assumed as implicit.[42]

Al-Kūrānī is also aware that the discussion bears heavily on the problem of *jaʿl al-māhiyyāt* and resumes the discussion where al-Rāzī left off, namely, where he argued in t3 that every attempt of denial, even if it seems to deny a relation, ends up affecting an essence in itself. Al-Kūrānī seems to grant that but does not concede what al-Rāzī's argument appears to presuppose according to my interpretation above, that is, that essences are created by God in the first place (*ibtidāʾan*) qua essences ready to be given existence, and an essence is said to be denied if not created by God. In other words, the crux of his disagreement with al-Rāzī is whether the essence qua essence is created or not. For al-Kūrānī, it is not in itself an object of temporal origination or negation; its *jaʿl* amounts to nothing but its being given existence whereas its *nafy* amounts to its being shorn of it.[43]

Al-Kūrānī raises several arguments for the uncreatedness of essences, but I will limit my treatment here to one that reflects his Akbarian tendencies:[44]

> [t5] Verification [provides the conclusion] that the essences of all possible things in terms of their presence in God's eternal self-knowledge are definitely eternal and uncreated because everything created must be known to the creator before creation, and everything known must have some sort of presence in the knowledge of the knower due to that knowledge's being the relation between the known and its knower. This relation can obtain only with two *relata*, which are necessarily distinct from each other in some way, and there can only be distinctness if each *relatum*

al. (Istanbul: Türkiye Diyanet Vakfı Yayınları, 2020), 2:217–18. Al-Jurjānī has also a treatise on knowledge based on this metaphor, for the text of which, see ibid., 218n1.

42 al-Kūrānī, 'Inbāh', 75–76, 79.

43 Ibid., 79–80.

44 For al-Kūrānī's Akbarianism, see Alexander Knysh, 'Ibrāhīm al-Kūrānī (d. 1101/1690), an Apologist for Waḥdat al-Wujūd', *Journal of the Royal Asiatic Society* 5, no. 1 (1995): 39–47; Dumairieh, *Intellectual Life in the Ḥijāz*, chap. 5.

> has some sort of presence... Therefore, everything known has a kind of presence in God's eternal self-knowledge and this presence is eternal and uncreated.[45]

In the dense argument here, we find significant hints of an Akbarian background for his adamant rejection of the *jaʿl* theory. Above all, al-Kūrānī's recognition of possible essences as eternal objects of God's eternal self-knowledge reveals its unmistakably Akbarian roots.[46] However, he afterwards adopts a more orthodox approach to prove this view, more orthodox because it is based on the view of knowledge as relation that is also embraced by al-Rāzī.[47] If knowledge is the relation between the knower and the known, then every object of knowledge must have a kind of distinctness and therefore some sort of presence, given that there can be no distinction among pure non-existents. From these premises, al-Kūrānī deduces that non-existent essences of possible things are eternally present (*thābita*) in God's self-knowledge. If they are eternal, he reaches the conclusion he seeks: they are not subject to *jaʿl* or *nafy*, to being created or not being created.[48]

Now that we have seen the arguments from both sides, a brief assessment is in order. The bone of contention here is logico-philosophical rather than linguistic. This is because al-Rāzī, on the one hand, seems to have argued that denial, *nafy*, is first and foremost, so to speak, a one-place predicate, that is, 'S is denied', but he never rejects its usage as a two-place predicate, 'P is negated of S'. Particularly, in his *Nihāyat al-ījāz*, he is unmistakably clear that both affirmation and negation require two elements to be meaningful.[49] However, his point is that its usage as a one-place predicate is primary while the other is reducible to it; in 'S is not P', what is denied is the relation R between them.

Al-Kūrānī, on the other hand, emphasises *nafy* as a two-place predicate, but he seems somewhat unable to satisfactorily refute al-Rāzī's arguments showing its reducibility and therefore appears to have finally granted it, even if grudgingly. Yet his main concern was not grammatical or logical, but theological; he was resisting the theological consequences of al-Rāzī's argument, that is, the createdness of essences. Although he agrees with al-Rāzī in principle that there are non-existent essences, he differs with him in details; for al-Rāzī, these essences are created by God as essences ready to be brought into existence,

45 al-Kūrānī, 'Inbāh', 80–81.

46 On Ibn al-ʿArabī's own view that the objects of God's knowledge are synonymous with non-existent essences of possible things, that is, on the so-called theory of immutable entities (*al-aʿyān al-thābita*), see e.g. William C. Chittick, *The Sufi Path of Knowledge: Ibn al-ʿArabi's Metaphysics of Imagination* (Albany: State University of New York Press, 1989), 11–12, 83–85.

47 On this, see Fakhr al-Dīn al-Rāzī, *al-Maṭālib al-ʿāliya min al-ʿilm al-ilāhī*, ed. Aḥmad Ḥijāzī al-Saqqā (Beirut: Dār al-Kitāb al-ʿArabī, 1987), 3:103–4.

48 al-Kūrānī, 'Inbāh', 87–88. Al-Kūrānī also has a treatise devoted to the explication of his view that non-existent essences are present in God's knowledge, which was edited in M. Bilal Gültekin, 'İbrahim Kûrânî'nin "Cilâu'l-Fuhûm fi Tahkiki's-Sübût ve Ru'yeti'l-Madûm" Adlı Risalesinin Tahkikli Neşri', *Tahkik İslami İlimler Araştırma ve Neşir Dergisi* 4, no. 2 (2021): 55–147.

49 Fakhr al-Dīn al-Rāzī, *Nihāyat al-ījāz fī dirāyat al-iʿjāz*, ed. Nasrullah Hacımüftüoğlu (Beirut: Dār Ṣādir, 2004), 75.

but for al-Kūrānī, they are eternally present in God's eternal self-knowledge. Al-Kūrānī rejects the creation of essences as this would lead to the unacceptable outcome, in his view, that the content of God's eternal knowledge is not eternal but created.

In sum, al-Rāzī maintains that the *Kalima* is a complete verbal sentence that perfectly signifies the negation of a second deity, but for al-Kūrānī, it is a nominal sentence in need of an additional predicate because negating the essence signified by the noun after the *lā* is impossible for logical as well as grammatical reasons; it is only the relation between the subject and predicate that is negated or affirmed. What predicate is implied in the *Kalima* according to al-Kūrānī? As I explained above, the original form of the *Kalima* is *Allāhu ilāhun*, but in order to restrict the predicate to the subject, it was changed to *Lā ilāha illā Allāh*, in which *ilāh* becomes the new subject. In Arabic, there are two kinds of subject: nominal or adjectival.[50] Therefore, we can take the subject (*ilāh*) of the current structure of the *Kalima* either as a noun or as an adjective in the sense of 'worshipped' (*maʾlūh*). In the former case, that which is excepted by the *illā*, that is, *Allāhu*, is in the nominative case (*marfūʿ*) because it is in apposition to the subject, *ilāh*, when it is not yet under the governance of the *lā*, and the implied predicate is 'in existence' or the like. In the latter case, on the other hand, when the subject is an adjective, that which is excepted becomes the agent of the verb, which is implicit in *ilāh*, and renders any predicate redundant. On the former reading, the *Kalima* means that 'No deity exists save God', but on the latter, 'No one is a deity save God'. Although the former is the prevalent position, al-Kūrānī prefers the latter due to several advantages it enjoys over the former.[51] Below, we will examine the propositions he deduces from the *Kalima* according to this reading.

## 2. The Proposition(s) in the *Kalima*

The question of the nature and number of propositions the *Kalima* contains is closely related to discussions about the principle that the exception to negation is tantamount to an affirmation and vice versa (*al-istithnāʾ min al-nafy ithbātun wa-bi-l-ʿaks*). For there is an obvious negation in the *Kalima*, signified by the *lā*, but whether it also contains an affirmation is a matter of controversy. Those who see the negation alone, but no affirmation alongside, maintain that it contains only one judgement and therefore one proposition. I will call this approach *the monadic reading* of the *Kalima*. On the other hand, those who subscribe to the principle that the exception to negation is tantamount to an affirmation defend the existence of two judgements and thus two propositions, one being negative and the other affirmative. I will call this approach *the dyadic reading*. The former is held by al-Rāzī while al-Kūrānī emphatically places himself in the opposite camp yet again.

50 On this, see e.g. Nūr al-Dīn ʿAlī al-Ushmūnī, *Manhaj al-sālik ilā Alfiyyat Ibn Mālik* (Beirut: Dār al-Kutub al-ʿIlmiyya, 1998), 1:88ff.; Fāḍil Ṣāliḥ al-Sāmarrāʾī, *Maʿānī al-naḥw* (Amman: Dār al-Fikr, 2000), 1:166–67.

51 See al-Kūrānī, 'Inbāh', 176–77, 188–89, 191ff.; al-Māziq, 'ʿUjālat dhawī al-intibāh', 29–31.

### 2.1 The Monadic Reading

The representative of this interpretation, al-Rāzī, does not directly deal with the question of how many propositions there are, but examines at length the two issues that lie at the root of the question. The first of these is whether the *Kalima* is complete or not, and as seen above, al-Rāzī opted for the former alternative. To recap, the *Kalima* read as a complete verbal sentence means for him that any deity other than God is denied because, he explains, *Lā* means 'is denied' and *illā* 'other than', and hence the *Kalima* conclusively denies the essence of 'any deity other than God'.[52]

The second relevant issue, which will occupy us in this section, is whether the exception to negation gives us an affirmation. In other words, does any sentence, like the *Kalima*, that includes both a negation and an exception to it make only one or two judgements, a negative one in the antecedent of the sentence (*Lā ilāha*) and an affirmative one in the exceptive part (*illā Allāh*)? That is, does the exceptive part make an independent judgement in the opposite quality to that in the antecedent, or does it only negate the judgement of the antecedent, making no independent judgement? We see that this problem has been intensely discussed especially in the works of Islamic legal theory (*uṣūl al-fiqh*) in such a way as to lead to the formation of two main camps: the Ḥanafī scholars of legal theory, who argue that neither does the exception to negation mean affirmation nor vice versa, and the majority, who hold the opposite position that both the exception to negation means affirmation and vice versa.[53] Let us extend the naming above to cover all exceptive sentences and call the former position the 'monadic reading of exception' and the latter the 'dyadic reading of exception'.

Al-Rāzī seems to have assumed different stances on the issue in his different works, his most extensive treatment being in his *Lawāmiʿ*.[54] There al-Rāzī states, presumably referring to Ḥanafīs, that some scholars of Islamic legal theory (*baʿḍ al-uṣūliyyīn*) claimed that the exception to negation is not an affirmation. Their argument here could be reconstructed as follows. In the *Kalima*, for example, 'There is no god save God', there are two semantical elements in the antecedent, 'There is no god': the non-existence itself of any god and the judgement of that non-existence. The second part, 'save God', therefore, either constitutes an exception to the non-existence itself or the speaker's judgement of non-existence.

52 Al-Dawānī reiterates the same idea, but he is clearer that *lā* means 'is denied': 'Fī kalimat al-tawḥīd', 138; see also al-Kūrānī, 'Inbāh', 283–84.

53 On the details of the debate, see e.g. Sayf al-Dīn ʿAlī al-Āmidī, *al-Iḥkām fī uṣūl al-aḥkām*, ed. ʿAbd al-Razzāq ʿAfīfī (Riyadh: Dār al-Ṣamīʿī, 2003), 2:378; ʿAbd al-Raḥmān al-Bannānī, *Ḥāshiyat al-ʿAllāma al-Bannānī ʿalā sharḥ al-Jalāl ʿalā Jamʿ al-jawāmiʿ* (Beirut: Dār al-Fikr, 1982), 2:13–16; ʿAlāʾ al-Dīn al-Bukhārī, *Kashf al-asrār ʿan Uṣūl Fakhr al-Islām al-Bazdawī*, ed. ʿAbd Allāh M. M. ʿUmar (Beirut: Dār al-Kutub al-ʿIlmiyya, 1997), 3:187–98; Saʿd al-Dīn al-Taftāzānī, *Sharḥ al-Talwīḥ ʿalā sharḥ al-Tawḍīḥ li-matn al-Tanqīḥ* (Cairo: Dār al-Kutub al-ʿArabiyya al-Kubrā, 1909), 2:20–28.

54 A shorter version of the argument occurs also in his *Tafsīr*, 5:435–36. However, in his work on legal theory, *Maḥṣūl*, al-Rāzī this time features a short argument in the opposite direction, that is, for the view that the exception to negation is affirmation: *al-Maḥṣūl fī ʿilm uṣūl al-fiqh*, ed. Ṭāhā J. F. al-ʿAlwānī (Beirut: Muʾassasat al-Risāla, 1992), 3:39.

The latter case would not imply that there is an affirmation in the exceptive part of the sentence because the exceptive particle removes the judgement of non-existence, without making an affirmative judgement instead. In other words, the excepted element—God in this sentence—remains unspoken of (*maskūt ʿanh*) in this case, with no judgement, whether negative or affirmative, made of it. In the latter case, however, that is, if the exception is related to the non-existence itself to remove it, then there would be an affirmative judgement of God in the excepted part because there is no intermediate value between the two contradictories, that is, between affirmation and negation.[55]

In other words, the negative antecedent of the exceptive sentence can be interpreted in two ways: it can refer to either the state of affairs in the extramental reality or the mental judgement formed by the speaker when uttering this sentence. Depending on whether the former or the latter option is chosen, the exceptive particle *illā* will exclude one of these things. If the exceptive particle denies and eliminates the former, then there obtains the affirmative judgement that God exists. This is because any judgement that negates non-existence must affirm existence, given that there is no intermediary. Nonetheless, if the particle *illā* is taken to eliminate the mental judgement of the speaker then no judgement would obtain: the elimination of judgement amounts to the non-existence of any judgement, affirmative or negative. In this case, no judgement would be passed about the excepted element, God.

Afterwards, al-Rāzī turns to elucidating his own position that the exception should relate to the judgement of non-existence rather than non-existence itself and tries to justify it with the following two arguments:

> [t6] First, expressions (*al-alfāẓ*) have been invented to signify mental judgements, not external existents, because when you say, 'The world is pre-eternal,' it does not indicate that the world is really pre-eternal in itself. Otherwise, when we say, 'The world is pre-eternal, and the world is originated,' the world would have to be both pre-eternal and originated at the same time, which is impossible. Rather, this statement indicates your judgement that the world is pre-eternal. Thus, it has become clear that the expressions have been posited to signify mental judgements, not external individuals. If this is the case, taking the exception as pertaining to the judgement of non-existence is more fitting than to the non-existence itself due to the fact that the closer referent of the expression is the mental judgement. The external being, on the other hand, is the referent of the mind. Taking the utterance according to its near referent is better than taking it according to its distant referent. Secondly, something's non-existence or existence in itself is not subject to someone else's (*al-ghayr*) agency. Rather, it is the judgement regarding this non-existence or

55 al-Rāzī, *Lawāmiʿ*, 95.

> existence that is subject to the speaker's (*al-qāʾil*) agency. Given that is the case, it has been established that relating the exception to the judgement is more appropriate than relating it to the predicate (*al-maḥkūm bih*).[56]

Presumably departing from Aristotle's well-known semiotic triangle between language and thinking, on the one hand, and thinking and reality, on the other (*De Int.* 16a4–9), which was widely embraced by Arabic logicians as well,[57] al-Rāzī seems to have reached here a mediated reference theory.[58] For him, a linguistic expression has to follow an indirect route to reach its final destination, its extramental referent; there is a significant stop on the way, which is the mental content. Such an expression first and immediately signifies the mental representation which in turn refers to the real objects. To assume otherwise, al-Rāzī argues rather controversially, would lead to the impossible consequence that the world would be pre-eternal and originated at the same time, were a sentence to say so. If this is the case, then an affirmative sentence, for example, should be thought of as standing first for its mental counterpart such that its negation also would eliminate that mental affirmative judgement. This view will have the consequence in our case that the exceptive particle in the *Kalima* affects the negative judgement in the antecedent of the sentence and indicates that it does not apply to the excepted.

Before moving on, let us briefly touch upon what I see as the Achilles heel of al-Rāzī's argument. Would the argument for direct reference of linguistic expressions to their referents necessarily amount to saying that the referent really exists or obtains? More clearly, if I say that 'Zayd is standing' makes direct reference to external reality, would this mean that necessarily Zayd is standing? According to al-Taftāzānī, no, because the relation between the sentence and its external referent is, though direct, a conventional one (*waḍʿī*), always liable to truth and falsity; it never guarantees its own truth, the referent's obtaining. In other words, upon hearing, for example, 'Zayd left the room', one understands that he left the room, but always keeps in mind the possibility that he did not, in which case the sentence would be false.[59]

---

56 Ibid., 95–96. The words *al-ghayr* and *al-qāʾil* in the text read *al-ʿayn* and *al-qābil*, respectively, in the published edition of the work, but as such, they hardly make any sense. In my research through the manuscript copies, I have found that my reading above is more faithful to these copies. See e.g. Fakhr al-Dīn al-Rāzī, *Lawāmiʿ al-bayyināt fī sharḥ al-asmāʾ wa-l-ṣifāt* (MS Istanbul: Süleymaniye Manuscript Library, Ragıp Paşa 664), fols. 35b6–7. This copy is significant in that it carries a colophon by the scholar and prolific author Abū al-Faraj Ibn al-Jawzī (d. 1201/1786), which makes it almost certain that it was handwritten in al-Rāzī's lifetime. On the same issue, see also Fakhr al-Dīn al-Rāzī, *Sharḥ al-Ishārāt wa-l-tanbīhāt*, ed. ʿAlī Riḍā Najafzāda (Tehran: Dānishgāh-i Tehran, 1964), 1:21.

57 See e.g. F. W. Zimmermann, *Al-Farabi's Commentary and Short Treatise on Aristotle's De Interpretatione* (London: British Academy, 1991), 10 ff.; Ibn Sīnā, *al-Shifāʾ: al-ʿIbāra*, ed. Maḥmūd al-Khuḍayrī (Cairo: al-Hayʾa al-Miṣriyya al-ʿĀmma li-l-Taʾlīf wa-l-Nashr, 1970), chap. I.1.

58 On mediated reference theory, see e.g. Robert J. Stainton, *Philosophical Perspectives on Language* (Peterborough, ON: Broadview Press, 1996), chap. 4.

59 Saʿd al-Dīn al-Taftāzānī, *al-Muṭawwal sharḥ Talkhīṣ Miftāḥ al-ʿulūm* (Beirut: Dār al-Kutub al-ʿIlmiyya,

In the second argument, al-Rāzī emphasises another difference between the judgement and its external counterpart, that is, the judgement of non-existence and non-existence itself. For him, unlike the former, the latter is independent of any agent's mental consideration. When one utters, for example, the *Kalima* to exclude God from the scope of the antecedent, his mental effort in the exception should be aimed at the judgement in the antecedent, which is open to one's agency, and not at the non-existence itself, which is not open to it. Therefore, according to al-Rāzī, the exception of the *illā* governs the judgement that any deity is denied, instead of the negation, which is the predicate of this judgement. And if the exception attaches to the judgement of negation, then the *Kalima* includes only one proposition. In a nutshell, in forming a sentence, the speaker is the agent of the judgement in her mind, having power over it alone, and not over external reality, as is also pointed out by al-Rāzī's younger contemporary, al-Sakkākī, when he describes the utterer of a declarative sentence (*khabar*) as 'the agent of the judgement'.[60]

Incidentally, al-Rāzī resorts in his *Maḥṣūl* to a similar argument for the same conclusion, but here he argues that otherwise, that is, if the signification of a sentence was not the mental judgement, then 'the false [sentence] would not be declarative',[61] which is nonsense. This is because if what is meant by a declarative sentence was extramental reality, then false sentences could not count as declarative, the reason being that they do not have any external correspondence. I will return to this point when I discuss al-Kūrānī's position on the issue.

Setting aside the question of whether these arguments are strong enough to prove al-Rāzī's monadic position, I would like to note here his apparent inconsistency. As discussed above, al-Rāzī was of the view that the *illā* in the *Kalima* has the same meaning as *ghayr*, that is, an adjective meaning 'otherness'. Moreover, he argues that the *illā* should not be taken to denote exception.[62] That is to say, the combination of this *illā* and the noun after it constitutes a part of the subject of the *Kalima*, which is 'any deity other than God' as a whole. Taken this way, there would be no exception in the *Kalima* and no need at all to discuss what element it affects. Hence, there seems to be an apparent inconsistency between the two interpretations of the *illā* by al-Rāzī. However, another option might be that these arguments are only hypothetical, that is, if the *illā* were to be taken as exceptive, and he makes them only in order to show that even if this were the case, there would be a defensible way to maintain the dyadic reading. Even if the *illā* denoted exception, there would be no second judgement after it due to the fact that the exception affects the judgement of negation itself, which is to say, the *Kalima* includes only a single proposition. This seems to me a promising way to explain away al-Rāzī's apparent inconsistency.

2013), 181.

60 al-Sakkākī, *Miftāḥ al-ʿulūm*, 166.

61 al-Rāzī, *Maḥṣūl*, 4:223–24.

62 al-Rāzī, *Lawāmiʿ*, 95.

Nevertheless, if there is only one negative proposition in the *Kalima* to the effect that any other god besides God is denied, will the *Kalima* still express God's existence? This question brings us to one of the most intriguing aspects of al-Rāzī's discussion of the *Kalima* because for him it has nothing to say about God's existence: 'Our statement *Lā ilāha illā Allāh* is a declaration (*taṣrīḥ*) of the denial of other deities, but it is not the recognition of the existence of God.'[63] Al-Rāzī is, of course, aware of the potential objection that the articulation of the *Kalima* does not suffice to make one Muslim because negating other deities would not commit one to God's existence. He seems to acknowledge this objection to be right but tries to diminish the severity of the situation. For one thing, what is at stake in the *Kalima* is not God's existence because everyone around the Prophet already believed in His existence. The issue was that they recognised some other deities alongside Him, and the *Kalima* is a rejection of this polytheistic approach. Second, although it does not signify God's existence in terms of linguistic convention (*al-waḍʿ al-lughawī*), it does so in terms of religious convention (*al-waḍʿ al-sharʿī*).[64] That is to say, Muslims came to the consensus that its meaning includes affirming God's existence.

It seems, therefore, that ironically enough, on his way to prove that the *Kalima* expresses a complete unification of God, al-Rāzī has at the end of the day reduced it to a statement that rejects only polytheism and that is devoid of even signifying the existence of God. Understandably, this would be a position that al-Kūrānī could not be content with. Let us now turn to al-Kūrānī's dyadic reading of the *Kalima*.

## 2.2 The Dyadic Reading

To resume the discussion from where al-Rāzī left off, I would like to state that al-Kūrānī rejects, at some length and without mentioning his name, al-Rāzī's view that the *Kalima* signifies God's existence only due to religious convention. However, I will not linger on the details of his counter-arguments as they are mostly based on religious and historical traditions,[65] which are beyond the scope of the paper. I will therefore move to discuss al-Kūrānī's position on the debate between the monadic and dyadic readings of exceptive sentences.

Al-Kūrānī devotes the fourth chapter of his *Inbāh* to the debate, implying his position with the very title of the chapter: 'on the fact that the exception to negation means an affirmation and vice versa'. He begins the chapter with the arguments for the two sides of the debate, first giving those of the monadic reading. He emphasises two arguments in this context, the first being that the leading Arab philologists (*aʾimmat al-lugha*) have

63 Ibid., 96.
64 Ibid., 97.
65 al-Kūrānī, 'Inbāh', 127–28. Al-Kūrānī's account seems to have heavily depended on Ibn al-Ḥājib and ʿAḍud al-Din al-Ījī. See ʿAḍud al-Din al-Ījī, *Sharḥ Mukhtaṣar al-Muntahā al-uṣūlī* (Beirut: Dār al-Kutub al-ʿIlmiyya, 2004), 3:50.

reached the consensus that the exception to negation is affirmation and vice versa, and their views are authoritative in the discussions about the signification of linguistic expressions. The second argument refers to the meaning of the *Kalima*, positing that if the monadic reading of exception were granted, then the *Kalima* would only mean the negation of other deities without affirming God's existence. According to the supporters of the dyadic reading, the consequent of this hypothetical proposition is false, and therefore so is the antecedent. Thereafter al-Kūrānī proceeds to the counter-arguments. They answer the first argument by saying that the philologists' view of the subject builds on a metaphor: they are expressing the non-existence of the judgement of affirmation by the judgement of non-existence (on which more below). Against the second argument above, they state that the *Kalima* affirms God's existence, but this is only in terms of religious, not linguistic, convention.[66]

From the previous section above, we are familiar with the part of the arguments and answers thereto that are related to the *Kalima*'s signification. So, I would like to focus, before dealing with al-Kūrānī's own treatment of the problem, on the ascription of metaphorical expression to the philologists by the exponents of the monadic reading, according to whom a sentence like the *Kalima* makes a negative judgement in the antecedent but does not assert anything about the excepted, God; He is not spoken of at all. That is, no judgement is passed on the exceptive part of the sentence, which is what they mean by 'the non-existence of judgement'. However, for them, philologists express this non-existence of judgement by the judgement of non-existence, or more clearly, the judgement that the predicate is non-existent for the subject of the exceptive part, God.[67]

When he commences voicing his own perspective, al-Kūrānī reiterates the paradigm argument of the dyadic camp: affirmation and negation are contradictory judgements, and therefore they cannot both be true or false of the same subject at the same time. Otherwise, something excluded from, or prevented to enter in,[68] either of the two judgements would necessarily be included in the scope of the other, and two contradictories would be both false (*irtifāʿ al-naqīḍayn*), which is impossible.[69] However, as we saw in t6, this argument is far from persuasive to the monadic reader because arguably there would be no contradiction if there were no judgement.

Indeed, he concedes such a third option, that is, the subject's being completely neglected with no judgement about it at all, which would not count as a violation of the

66 al-Kūrānī, 'Inbāh', 116.

67 Al-Taftāzānī seems to have given some credit to this interpretation of the monadic reading in the case where the antecedent of the exceptive sentence is affirmative, but he regards it as rejecting necessary knowledge in the case of negative antecedents: 'Ḥāshiya ʿalā sharḥ Mukhtaṣar al-Muntahā al-uṣūlī', in *Sharḥ Mukhtaṣar al-Muntahā al-uṣūlī*, 3:50–51.

68 These two alternatives are due to different definitions of exception, the first as 'exclusion' (*al-ikhrāj*) by most scholars, e.g. Ibn al-Ḥājib, *al-Kāfiya* (Karachi: Maktabat al-Bushrā, 2008), 76, and the second as 'prevention' (*al-manʿ*) exclusively by Ṣadr al-Sharīʿa al-Maḥbūbī. For the latter, see al-Taftāzānī, *Talwīḥ*, 2:20.

69 al-Kūrānī, 'Inbāh', 116–17.

principle of excluded middle. However, once the speaker has mentioned the name of the excepted element, for instance, God in the *Kalima*, this option will not be available anymore. By uttering the *illā* of exception, one makes the judgement that the excepted is excluded from, or prevented from being included in, the judgement in the antecedent, which means one has passed a judgement of it. Al-Kūrānī deduces therefrom that the excepted could no longer be unspoken of or have a neutral status vis-à-vis negation or affirmation.[70]

Al-Kūrānī comes up with a somewhat different formulation of the exceptive sentence, presumably as a counter-case against al-Rāzī's mediated reference theory. For al-Kūrānī, who seems to have embraced a kind of direct theory of reference or referentialism,[71] when one says, for example, 'I negate existence of gods, except of God,' the excepted part of this sentence could be thought of as devoid of any judgement because in this case the judgement would be realised between the speaker and the verb 'negate', the speaker being the agent of the verb. In that case, exception would mean the elimination of the speaker's judgement regarding the excepted part.[72] In this way, al-Kūrānī seems to argue that unless there is some clear indication in a sentence, such as the pronoun 'I', its signification cannot be limited to the mental judgement of the speaker, and it should rather be taken as an expression of external facts. Therefore, the utterer of the last sentence begins with the pronoun to point out that she is expressing her inner speculation. Nonetheless, this is not possible in, for example, 'There is no god save God', in which case the sentence is about the external situation, not the subjective judgement of the speaker.

To conclude this section, al-Rāzī's case for the monadic reading of exceptive sentences in general and of the *Kalima* in particular seems relatively more persuasive. Above all, he seems to have made an effective point when he averred that linguistic expressions primarily signify mental judgements and hence the exception made by the particle *illā* should be related to the judgement. Moreover, as al-Jurjānī also notes,[73] he was also right to claim that it is this judgement that is open to the agency of the speaker; one passes a judgement in the antecedent of the exceptive sentence and, purposing to make an exception, one should, or rather could only, turn to the judgement one has already made, not things in themselves, which are beyond the agency of the speaker. On the other hand, al-Kūrānī's counter-argument based on the law of the excluded middle seems to have failed to hit the mark because if there is no judgement concerning the subject of the exceptive part, there is no possibility for talking about a contradiction between the affirmative and negative judgements.

70 Ibid., 117.
71 On this, see Stainton, *Philosophical Perspectives*, chap. 3.
72 al-Kūrānī, 'Inbāh', 119–20.
73 al-Sayyid al-Sharīf al-Jurjānī, *Sharḥ al-Miftāḥ* (MS Istanbul: Süleymaniye Manuscript Library, Ragıp Paşa 1277), fols. 13b15–17.

I would like now to discuss as a final section the propositions that al-Kūrānī claims to be involved in the *Kalima*.

## 2.3 Al-Kūrānī's Propositions

As should be clear by this point, al-Kūrānī argues that two propositions are contained in the *Kalima*. According to his preferred reading—outlined above ('No one is a god, but God [is]')—one of them is a universal negative and the other a singular affirmative, but both are necessary. The first, that is, the universal negative, is 'Necessarily, no one is a god' while the singular affirmative is 'God is necessarily a god'. However, according to the prevalent interpretation, which reads the *Kalima* as 'No deity exists, but God', there would also be two necessary propositions: 'Necessarily, no deity exists' and 'God necessarily exists'. The excepted on this reading, God, is in apposition to 'deity', which is taken as the subject of the sentence after the elements were swapped but before the subject comes under the governance of the *lā*.[74] Notice here that the additional element on this reading ('exists') functions as the predicate of the *lā* and therefore of both propositions, but al-Kūrānī's interpretation supplies 'one' to serve as the subject of the universal proposition. Let us examine now his two propositions, beginning with the universal one.

### 2.3.1 *Necessarily, No One Is a God*

The subject of this proposition is 'one' after the sentence is made an exceptive sentence, and its predicate is the negative meaning in *ilāh* (*ḥiṣṣat al-nafy min ilāh*). Al-Kūrānī means here that the noun of the *lā*, which is *ilāh*, refers to an essence qua essence, which is not affirmative or negative in itself but liable to become affirmative in an affirmative judgement and negative in a negative one. In other words, there is an affirmative, as well as a negative, meaning in the concept of *ilāh* because just as there are subjects or individuals that fall under the universal term *ilāh* such that it could be affirmed of them, there are others too, of which it could only be negated. Here in this negative proposition, the term *ilāh* is negated of any individuals that would not belong to its extension, namely, anything other than God.[75] This explanation includes some hints as to how al-Kūrānī will ward off the doubt that there could be a contradiction between the universal and singular propositions of the *Kalima*, as will become clear shortly.

To explain the universality of the proposition, al-Kūrānī makes reference to the possibilities of Arabic grammar, according to which the *lā* of general denial expresses that the genus of the noun following it, if indefinite (*nakira*), includes all the individuals falling under it. Therefore, a sentence with *lā* clearly states that the noun that follows it is negated of all individuals because there is an agreement among Arab philologists that

74 al-Kūrānī, 'Inbāh', 282–83.

75 Ibid., 271.

it has the meaning of the *min* of generality (*istighrāq*).[76] It seems, therefore, that the *lā* of general denial and the genus name following it together are sufficient to form a universal negative proposition without the need for any additional universal-negative quantifiers.

It seems prima facie somewhat strange that al-Kūrānī deduced two necessary propositions from the *Kalima*, even though it contains no hint, let alone explicit mention, of necessity. Al-Kūrānī views the necessity of the unity of God as an evident fact in the light of rational as well as religious evidence. As for the necessity of these propositions, he accounts for it on linguistic grounds, stating that its explanation should be sought primarily in the character of nominal sentences. In this context, he refers again to al-Jurjanī, for whom the nominal sentence with a nominal predicate indicates the continuity (*al-istimrār*) of affirmation if it is affirmative and of negation if it is negative.[77] For al-Kūrānī, continuity is used in this context in a general sense to cover the impossibility, as well as the possibility, of the separation of the predicate from the subject. Therefore, it can mean that it is impossible for the predicate to be negated of the subject if the proposition is affirmative, and this is nothing, al-Kūrānī concludes, but what logicians (*ahl al-mīzān*) call necessity (*al-ḍarūra*).[78]

#### 2.3.2 *God Is Necessarily a God*

The subject of this singular affirmative proposition is 'God', which is in the position of the excepted under the governance of the particle *illā*. Now that we know why it is necessary, I would like to address here another problem of al-Kūrānī's account, namely, the apparent contradiction between the two propositions. The problem arises because the first proposition universally denies a predicate of a subject whereas the second confirms the same predicate of an individual falling under the same subject, given that 'God' can easily be put under the term 'one', the subject of the universal proposition. Let us now see how al-Kūrānī will overcome this alleged contradiction.

The potential of exceptive sentences to cause contradiction seems to have attracted the attention of Arabic philologists from early times. For example, in his commentary on al-Zamakhsharī's *Mufaṣṣal*, Ibn al-Ḥājib (d. 646/1249) feels the need to deal with an issue that seriously endangers the possibility of the exception made by the *illā* in general. For him, exceptive sentences first include the excepted in the scope of the element from which it is excepted (*al-mustathnā minh*) and then exclude it therefrom. In 'The people stood up, except Zayd', for example, the attribution of standing up to Zayd is necessary as he is a member of 'people', but the exceptive part denies it of him from the same respect,

76 Ibid., 270. According to al-Zamakhsharī, if the indefinite noun after the *lā* of general denial is in the accusative case, the sentence certainly expresses generality (*istighrāq*): *Tafsīr al-Kashshāf*, ed. Khalīl M. Shīḥā, 3rd ed. (Beirut: Dār al-Maʿrifa, 2009), 36. For al-Taftāzānī, on the other hand, any sentence with an overt or implicit *min* of generality necessarily signifies generality: *Talwīḥ*, 1:55.

77 al-Jurjānī, *Sharḥ al-Miftāḥ*, fols. 95a5–7.

78 al-Kūrānī, 'Inbāh', 253–54.

which might lead to the doubt that the two parts of the sentence are contradictory.

Ibn al-Ḥājib's solution to the problem is this: first, all the elements of the proposition, namely, the act of standing up, the people (of which Zayd is a member), and the exception of Zayd from these people, are fully conceivable. It is only after these elements are conceived that standing up is predicated of 'the people' from which Zayd has been excepted.[79] The commentator of Ibn al-Ḥājib's *Kāfiya*, Raḍī al-Dīn al-Astarābādī (d. after 688/1289), elaborates on this solution, saying that exception occurs entirely during the process of taking the subject-term such that the predicate is affirmatively or negatively attributed to the subject, which does not include the excepted any more. In other words, the whole of 'the people, except Zayd' constitutes the subject of the proposition. This is completely understandable because predication is a relation, and therefore, its *relata* have to be already existent before it obtains. Since one of these *relata* is the *mustathnā minh*, from which the excepted is excluded, it is inevitable that the excepted is both included in and excluded from it before the relational judgement is made. In this case, there will occur no contradiction.[80]

In his *Inbāh*, al-Kūrānī cites al-Astarābādī's solution in a long quotation from al-Dawānī and finds this solution successful in overcoming the doubt of contradiction. According to him, in this way, the doubt can also be eliminated by noting that the genus before the *illā* (i.e. *ilāh* in the *Kalima*) would not include the excepted because, given the negative judgement that comes after the exception, the genus is open to both affirmative and negative attributions before the judgement is made. However, once the negative judgement is made, it no longer includes the excepted that has a positive relationship with this genus: God *is* an *ilāh*.[81]

This would be a promising solution to the problem of contradiction if it does not otherwise cause trouble to al-Kūrānī. For when we take the subject of the universal proposition in the *Kalima* as the solution suggests, that is, as 'no god except God', and negate the predicate of it, there will remain only one proposition, making it considerably difficult to argue for the dyadic reading of the *Kalima*. This is because, as the reader may have already noticed, the subject taken so is no different at all from al-Rāzī's interpretation of it, and therefore, this is not just a matter of the number of propositions, but, more importantly, a matter of whether the *Kalima* is to signify the existence of God or not. Therefore, with this solution, al-Kūrānī may have found a satisfactory way out of the problem of contradiction, yet he seems to have risked his dyadic reading and more significantly the *Kalima*'s signification of God's existence. This is an unfortunate dilemma for him: he must either concede that the *Kalima* is self-contradictory or forfeit his dyadic

79 Ibn al-Ḥājib, *al-Īḍāḥ fī sharḥ al-Mufaṣṣal*, ed. Mūsā B. al-ʿAlīlī (Baghdad: Iḥyāʾ al-Turāth al-Islāmī, 1976), 1:359–60.

80 Raḍī al-Dīn al-Astarābādī, *Sharḥ al-Kāfiya*, ed. Yūsuf Ḥ. ʿUmar (Benghazi: Manshūrāt Jāmiʿat Qāryūnus, 1996), 2:77–78.

81 al-Kūrānī, 'Inbāh', 279.

reading. Perhaps it was this dilemma that compelled al-Rāzī to prefer the latter option considering that the former would leave us empty-handed.

## 3. Conclusion

In this paper, I have examined two interpretations of the *Kalima* held by al-Rāzī and by al-Kūrānī, respectively, which are hardly reconcilable. On the one hand, there is al-Rāzī's position that the *Kalima* is a *complete verbal* sentence that makes only one judgement, which is that the essence of any gods other than God is denied. For him, negating an essence qua essence is perfectly possible or rather inevitable. According to al-Kūrānī's interpretation, on the other hand, the *Kalima* is an *incomplete nominal* sentence having an implicit predicate that must be supplied by the reader, the reason being that negation is not possible unless there are two elements. Accordingly, the *Kalima* involves two judgements, one asserting that no one is a god while the other asserts that God is a god. Al-Kūrānī's position, however, seems to approach al-Rāzī's when the former tries to avoid the apparent problem of contradiction between these two propositions. He takes the subject-term of the universal proposition in such a way as to make the *Kalima* contain only one judgement. I conclude that al-Kūrānī seems to have faced a dilemma that would compel him either to give up his dyadic reading or to concede that the *Kalima* is self-contradictory.

More striking, however, is the way in which the propositional forms that Aristotelian logic does not recognise, such as exceptive and restrictive sentences, were treated within the body of linguistic or Islamic sciences. These discussions must be taken into account when drawing a complete picture of the tradition of 'Arabic' logic.

## Bibliography

al-Āmidī, Sayf al-Dīn ʿAlī. *al-Iḥkām fī uṣūl al-aḥkām*. Edited by ʿAbd al-Razzāq ʿAfīfī. 3 vols. Riyadh: Dār al-Ṣamīʿī, 2003.

al-Astarābādī, Raḍī al-Dīn. *Sharḥ al-Kāfiya*. Edited by Yūsuf Ḥ. ʿUmar. 4 vols. Benghazi: Manshūrāt Jāmiʿat Qāryūnus, 1996.

Badawi, Elsaid, Michael G. Carter, and Adrian Gully. *Modern Written Arabic: A Comprehensive Grammar*. 2nd ed. London: Routledge, 2016.

al-Bannānī, ʿAbd al-Raḥmān. *Ḥāshiyat al-ʿAllāma al-Bannānī ʿalā sharḥ al-Jalāl ʿalā Jamʿ al-jawāmiʿ*. 2 vols. Beirut: Dār al-Fikr, 1982.

Benevich, Fedor. 'The Essence-Existence Distinction: Four Elements of the Post-Avicennian Metaphysical Dispute (11–13th Centuries)'. *Oriens* 45, no. 3–4 (2017): 203–58.

———. 'The Reality of the Non-Existent Object of Thought'. *Oxford Studies in Medieval*

*Philosophy* 6 (2018): 31.

al-Bukhārī, ʿAlāʾ al-Dīn. *Kashf al-asrār ʿan Uṣūl Fakhr al-Islām al-Bazdawī*. Edited by ʿAbd Allāh M. M. ʿUmar. 4 vols. Beirut: Dār al-Kutub al-ʿIlmiyya, 1997.

Carter, Michael C., and Kees Versteegh. 'Iḍmār'. In *Encyclopedia of Arabic Language and Linguistics*, edited by Kees Versteegh (general editor), 2:300–302. Leiden: Brill, 2006.

Chittick, William C. *The Sufi Path of Knowledge: Ibn al-ʿArabi's Metaphysics of Imagination*. Albany: State University of New York Press, 1989.

al-Dawānī, Jalāl al-Dīn. 'Fī kalimat al-tawḥīd'. In *Khams rasāʾil li-l-ʿAllāma Jalāl al-Dīn al-Dawānī*. Edited by Anwar F. ʿUlwānī al-Zuʿayrī. Cairo: Dār al-Imām al-Rāzī, 2021.

———. *Tahlīliyya Sharḥ lā ilāh illā Allāh*. Edited by F. Farīdūnī Firūzanda. Tehran: Intishārāt-i Gayhān, 1953.

Dumairieh, Naser. *Intellectual Life in the Ḥijāz before Wahhabism: Ibrāhīm al-Kūrānī's* (*d. 1101/1690*) *Theology of Sufism*. Leiden: Brill, 2022.

Eichner, Heidrun. 'Essence and Existence: Thirteenth-Century Perspectives in Arabic-Islamic Philosophy and Theology'. In *The Arabic, Hebrew and Latin Reception of Avicenna's* Metaphysics, edited by Dag Nikolaus Hasse and Amos Bertolacci, 123–52. Berlin: De Gruyter, 2012.

Gemi, Ahmet. *Kelime-i Tevhidin İ'râbı*. Ankara: İlâhiyât, 2019.

al-Ghazālī, Majd al-Dīn Aḥmad. *al-Tajrīd fī kalimat al-tawḥīd*. MS Ankara: National Library, Collection of Manuscripts A 1263.

Gültekin, M. Bilal. 'İbrahim Kûrânî'nin "Cilâu'l-Fuhûm fi Tahkiki's-Sübût ve Ru'yeti'l-Madûm" Adlı Risalesinin Tahkikli Neşri'. *Tahkik İslami İlimler Araştırma ve Neşir Dergisi* 4, no. 2 (2021): 55–147. https://doi.org/10.5281/ZENODO.5803751.

Ibn al-Ḥājib. *al-Īḍāḥ fī sharḥ al-Mufaṣṣal*. Edited by Mūsā B. al-ʿAlīlī. 2 vols. Baghdad: Iḥyāʾ al-Turāth al-Islāmī, 1976.

———. *al-Kāfiya*. Karachi: Maktabat al-Bushrā, 2008.

Ibn Hishām al-Anṣārī. *Mughnī al-labīb ʿan kutub al-aʿārīb*. Edited by Muḥammad M. ʿAbd al-Ḥamīd. 2 vols. Beirut: al-Maktaba al-ʿAṣriyya, 1991.

Ibn Manẓūr, Muḥammad Jamāl al-Dīn. 'n-f-y'. In *Lisān al-ʿArab*, 15:337–38. Beirut: Dār Ṣādir, 1993.

Ibn al-Sarrāj, Abū Bakr. *al-Uṣūl fī al-naḥw*. Edited by ʿAbd al-Ḥusayn al-Fatlī. Beirut: Muʾassasat al-Risāla, 1996.

Ibn Sīnā. *al-Shifāʾ: al-ʿIbāra*. Edited by Maḥmūd al-Khuḍayrī. Cairo: al-Hayʾa al-Miṣriyya al-ʿĀmma li-l-Taʾlīf wa-l-Nashr, 1970.

Ibrahim, Bilal. 'Causing an Essence: Notes on the Concept of *Jaʿl al-Māhiyya*, from Fakhr al-Dīn al-Rāzī to Mullā Ṣadrā'. In *Philosophical Theology in Islam: Later Ashʿarism East and West*, edited by Ayman Shihadeh and Jan Thiele, 156–94. Leiden: Brill, 2020. https://doi.org/10.1163/9789004426610_008.

al-Ījī, ʿAḍud al-Dīn. *Sharḥ Mukhtaṣar al-Muntahā al-uṣūlī*. 3 vols. Beirut: Dār al-Kutub

al-ʿIlmiyya, 2004.
al-Iṣfahānī, al-Rāghib. 'J-ʿ-l'. In *al-Mufradāt fī gharīb al-Qurʾān*, edited by Ṣafwān ʿA. al-Dāwūdī, 197. Damascus: Dār al-Qalam, 1991.
al-Jurjānī, al-Sayyid al-Sharīf. *Ḥāshiya ʿalā al-Muṭawwal*. Istanbul: Ṣaḥāfiya-i ʿUthmāniya, 1891.
———. *Ḥāshiya ʿalā Tasdīd al-qawāʿid fī sharḥ Tajrīd al-aqāʾid*. Edited by Eşref Altaş et al. 3 vols. Istanbul: Türkiye Diyanet Vakfı Yayınları, 2020.
———. *Sharḥ al-Miftāḥ*. MS Istanbul: Süleymaniye Manuscript Library, Ragıp Paşa 1277.
Kamālpashazāda. 'Risāla fī bayān maʿnā al-jaʿl wa-taḥqīq anna al-māhiyya majʿūla'. In *Majmūʿ rasāʾil al-ʿAllāma Ibn Kamāl Bāshā*, edited by Ḥamza Bakrī et al., 6:283–342. Istanbul: Dār al-Lubāb, 2018.
Knysh, Alexander. 'Ibrāhīm al-Kūrānī (d. 1101/1690), an Apologist for *Waḥdat al-Wujūd*'. *Journal of the Royal Asiatic Society* 5, no. 1 (1995): 39–47.
al-Kūrānī, Ibrāhīm. 'Inbāh al-anbāh ʿalā iʿrāb lā ilāha illā Allāh'. In *Kelime-i Tevhidin İ'râbı*, by Ahmet Gemi, 65–412. Ankara: İlâhiyât, 2019.
al-Māziq, Muṣṭafā S. "ʿUjālat dhawī al-intibāh fī taḥqīq iʿrāb lā ilāha illā llāh li-Ibrāhīm al-Kūrānī'. *Majallat Shimāl Janūb*, no. 12 (2018): 21–45.
Mihirig, Abdurrahman Ali. 'On the Linguistic and Technical Meanings of *Ghayr* and Their Consequences for Understanding the Divine Attributes in Classical *Kalām*'. *Kader* 20, no. 3 (2022): 894–921.
al-Rāzī, Fakhr al-Dīn. *al-Arbaʿīn fī uṣūl al-dīn*. Edited by Aḥmad Ḥijāzī al-Saqqā. 2 vols. Cairo: Maktabat al-Kulliyyāt al-Azhariyya, 1986.
———. *Lawāmiʿ al-bayyināt fī sharḥ al-asmāʾ wa-l-ṣifāt*. MS Istanbul: Süleymaniye Manuscript Library, Ragıp Paşa 664.
———. *Lawāmiʿ al-bayyināt sharḥ asmāʾ Allāh taʿālā wa-l-ṣifāt*. Edited by Muḥammad Badr al-Dīn al-Niʿsānī. Cairo: al-Maṭbaʿa al-Sharafiyya, 1905.
———. *al-Maḥṣūl fī ʿilm uṣūl al-fiqh*. Edited by Ṭāhā J. F. al-ʿAlwānī. 6 vols. Beirut: Muʾassasat al-Risāla, 1992.
———. *al-Maṭālib al-ʿāliya min al-ʿilm al-ilāhī*. Edited by Aḥmad Ḥijāzī al-Saqqā. 9 vols. Beirut: Dār al-Kitāb al-ʿArabī, 1987.
———. *al-Mulakhkhaṣ fī al-manṭiq wa-l-ḥikma*. Edited by Ismail Hanoğlu. 2 vols. Amman: al-Aṣlayn li-l-Dirāsāt wa-l-Nashr, 2021.
———. *Nihāyat al-ījāz fī dirāyat al-iʿjāz*. Edited by Nasrullah Hacımüftüoğlu. Beirut: Dār Ṣādir, 2004.
———. *Sharḥ al-Ishārāt wa-l-tanbīhāt*. Edited by ʿAlī Riḍā Najafzāda. 2 vols. Tehran: Dānishgāh-i Tehran, 1964.
———. *al-Tafsīr al-kabīr aw Mafātīḥ al-ghayb*. Edited by Sayyid ʿAmrān. 16 vols. Cairo: Dār al-Ḥadīth, 2012.
al-Sakkākī, Abū Yaʿqūb. *Miftāḥ al-ʿulūm*. Edited by Nuʿaym Zarzūr. Beirut: Dār al-Kutub

al-ʿIlmiyya, 1987.
al-Sāmarrāʾī, Fāḍil Ṣāliḥ. *Maʿānī al-naḥw*. 4 vols. Amman: Dār al-Fikr, 2000.
Sībawayhi, ʿAmr b. ʿUthmān. *al-Kitāb*. Edited by ʿAbd al-Salām M. Hārūn. 3rd ed. 5 vols. Cairo: Maktabat al-Khānjī, 1988.
Stainton, Robert J. *Philosophical Perspectives on Language*. Peterborough, ON: Broadview Press, 1996.
al-Taftāzānī, Saʿd al-Dīn. 'Ḥāshiya ʿalā sharḥ Mukhtaṣar al-Muntahā al-uṣūlī'. In *Sharḥ Mukhtaṣar al-Muntahā al-uṣūlī*, by ʿAḍud al-Dīn al-Ījī. Beirut: Dār al-Kutub al-ʿIlmiyya, 2004.
———. *al-Muṭawwal sharḥ Talkhīṣ Miftāḥ al-ʿulūm*. Beirut: Dār al-Kutub al-ʿIlmiyya, 2013.
———. *Sharḥ al-Talwīḥ ʿalā sharḥ al-Tawḍīḥ li-matn al-Tanqīḥ*. 2 vols. Cairo: Dār al-Kutub al-ʿArabiyya al-Kubrā, 1909.
al-Ṭūsī, Naṣīr al-Dīn. *Sharḥ al-Ishārāt wa-l-tanbīhāt*. Edited by Sulaymān Dunyā. 4 vols. Beirut: Muʾassasat al-Nuʿmān, 1992.
al-Ushmūnī, Nūr al-Dīn ʿAlī. *Manhaj al-sālik ilā Alfiyyat Ibn Mālik*. 4 vols. Beirut: Dār al-Kutub al-ʿIlmiyya, 1998.
Versteegh, Kees. 'Isnād'. In *Encyclopedia of Arabic Language and Linguistics*, edited by Kees Versteegh (general editor), 2:434–37. Leiden: Brill, 2006.
———. 'Taqdīr'. In *Encyclopedia of Arabic Language and Linguistics*, edited by Kees Versteegh (general editor), 4:446–49. Leiden: Brill, 2006.
Wright, William. *A Grammar of the Arabic Language*. 2 vols. Cambridge: Cambridge University Press, 1898.
Yılmaz, Ömer. *İbrahim Kûrânî Hayatı, Eserleri ve Tasavvuf Anlayışı*. Istanbul: Insan Yay., 2005.
al-Zamakhsharī, Jār Allāh. 'Masʾala fī kalimat al-shahāda'. Edited by Muḥammad A. al-Dāllī. *Majallat Majmaʿ al-Lugha al-ʿArabiyya bi-Dimashq*, no. 68 (1993): 77–94.
———. *Tafsīr al-Kashshāf*. Edited by Khalīl M. Shīḥā. 3rd ed. Beirut: Dār al-Maʿrifa, 2009.
Zimmermann, F. W. *Al-Farabi's Commentary and Short Treatise on Aristotle's De Interpretatione*. London: British Academy, 1991.

# PART 5

## *Contemporary Perspectives on God and Monotheism in Islam*

# Divine Names for Interreligious Engagement

*Celene Ibrahim*

## 1. Divine Names in Islamic Thought and Practice

Foundational Islamic sources describe the divine entity by a multiplicity of attributes known as 'the most beautiful names' (*al-asmāʾ al-ḥusnā*). Given the ubiquity of these names in Muslim thought and popular devotion, the subject is ripe for consideration from an interreligious lens. Here, I suggest tradition-specific avenues for adherents of various conceptual systems to explore the cross-conceptual resonances of these divine names. I outline how particular names, and the concept of divine names more broadly, may resonate with those who seek paradigms for conceptual enrichment, moral introspection, and spiritual development across metaphysical paradigms. My comparative lens includes Abrahamic and broader Near Eastern religions, dharmic religions, West African traditions, East Asian traditions, select modern pluralistic traditions, and the 'spiritual but not religious'.[1] As an introduction for the non-specialist, I begin with a survey of the divine names in Islamic thought.

### 1.1 The Most Beautiful Names (*al-Asmāʾ al-Ḥusnā*)

In an Islamic conceptual framework, everything originates, is sustained in existence, and ceases to exist according to the divine will. The divine is the being through whom all other entities have contingent existence. The divine transcends human experiences of time, transcends the physicality of human sensory perceptions, and exists beyond all physical confines or spatial measures. Divine existence is beyond a body that can be aptly conceptualized; though gendered by language, the divine is not bound by an ontological gender. The divine is utterly unique in bringing creation from non-existence and is the originator, sustainer, and knower of everything, without partners, internal divisions, or offspring. The divine nature is self-sufficient, uninhibited by neediness, and divine attributes are intrinsic and not dependent upon the actions of created entities. Moreover, the divine entity is characterized by an uncompromising self-sufficiency that contrasts the profound intrinsic interdependency of created entities. Still, divine power and transcendence are mediated by qualities of intimacy, benevolence, and cosmos-pervading love. Witnessing and testifying to divine unicity (*tawḥīd*, lit. to deem or to declare one)

---

1 I am grateful to the Reverend Allison Read, Dr Joan Listernick, Shannon Rivers of the Akimel O'otham people, Dr Shashi Dwarakanath-ji, Fatimah Ashrif, Matine Khalighi, and Gabriel Fouasnon for their insights on this work in progress. The research was generously supported by the Dillon Fund at Groton School.

is the foundation of Islamic theology and spiritual practice.[2]

The Qur'an explicitly instructs reciters to invoke the divine by 'the most beautiful names': 'To Allah belong the most beautiful names (*al-asmāʾ al-ḥusnā*), so invoke [Allah] by them' (Q. 7:180).[3] The concept of Allah's 'most beautiful names' also appears in the Qur'an in conjunction with the credal pronouncement of Islamic monotheism (*lā ilāha illā Allāh*): 'Allah, there is no divine other than [Allah] to whom belongs the most beautiful names' (Q. 20:8). 'Allah' is the most common Qur'anic appellation, appearing in over 2,700 instances. Etymologically, the word *Allāh* could be regarded as a proper name that does not have a morphological derivation or as a composition of the definite article *al-* and the term *ilāh*, which derives from the root *ʾ-l-h*. Significances of the root *ʾ-l-h* include to serve, worship, or adore, as well as concepts related to offering refuge and deliverance.[4] The word 'names' (*asmāʾ*, sing. *ism*) in the phrase *asmāʾ Allāh al-ḥusnā* derives from the root *s-m-w*, signifying something elevated, eminent, or even sublime. In Arabic grammatical discourse, *ism* also signifies the part of speech that functions akin to nouns. The superlative adjective *al-ḥusnā*, or 'the most beautiful', derives from the root *ḥ-s-n*, which signifies intrinsic and extrinsic beauty, goodness, and related meanings. The root also produces the word *iḥsān*, a key term referring to beauty and goodness in Islamic virtue ethics.[5]

By the late Islamic second century (late eighth century CE), several lists of ninety-nine names circulated as *ḥadīth*. One widely attested listing in Sunnī sources is related by Walīd b. Muslim al-Dimashqī (d. 195/810–11, Gorgan) on the authority of the Prophet's Companion ʿAbd al-Raḥmān b. Ṣakhr (d. 59/681, Medina), best known by his moniker Abū Hurayra. Another popular listing of ninety-nine names among Shīʿa transmitters is that of Sulaymān b. Mihrān al-Aʿmash (d. ca. 147–48/765, Kufa) on the authority of ʿAlī b. Abī Ṭālib (d. 40/661, Kufa), the Prophet's first cousin, son-in-law, esteemed caliph, and first Shīʿa Imām.[6] In both chains of narration, the Prophet is reported to have stated to

2 For a concise work on Muslim conceptions of the divine, see Celene Ibrahim, *Islam and Monotheism*, Cambridge Elements in Religion and Monotheism (New York: Cambridge University Press, 2022). A survey of academic resources on Islamic theologies of other religions is beyond the scope of this work; however, for a sophisticated survey of relevant Qur'anic verses, see Mun'im Sirry, *Scriptural Polemics: The Qur'ān and Other Religions* (New York: Oxford University Press, 2014).

3 Translations of the Qur'an are numbered according to the 1924 Cairo edition and are sourced with slight modifications from *The Study Quran: A New Translation and Commentary*, ed. Seyyed Hossein Nasr, Caner K. Dagli, Maria Massi Dakake, Joseph E. B. Lumbard, and Mohammed Rustom (San Francisco: HarperOne, 2015). I have retained the word 'Allah' where it occurs in Qur'anic verses as well as in *ḥadīth* and have translated the Arabic third-person pronoun as '[Allah]' (in brackets) or as 'the divine entity'.

4 For an etymological exploration including the relation to Hebrew and Aramaic, see Umar Faruq Abd-Allah, *One God, Many Names*, Nawawi Foundation Paper (Chicago: Nawawi Foundation, 2004), 3.

5 For an explication of the implications of *iḥsān* as an aspirational moral value, see Amira Abou-Taleb, 'Iḥsān: A Mandate for Beauty and Goodness in Family Relations', in *Justice and Beauty in Muslim Marriage: Towards Egalitarian Ethics and Laws*, ed. Ziba Mir-Hosseini, Mulki Al-Sharmani, Jana Rumminger, and Sarah Marsso (London: OneWorld, 2022), 101–33.

6 For discussion of these early transmissions, see Daniel Gimaret, *Les noms divins en Islam: exégèse lexicographique et théologique* (Paris: Editions du Cerf, 1988).

the effect: 'Allah, the most high, has ninety-nine names, one hundred minus one—and whosoever enumerates them will enter into paradise.'[7] Here, 'enumerates' (*aḥṣā*) likely implies an experiential, gnostic knowledge rather than an act of mere counting.

Despite the ubiquity of the number ninety-nine, the divine epithets attested to in the Qur'an and Islamic oral tradition extend beyond this number. In one *ḥadīth* recorded in the famous *Musnad* of Aḥmad b. Ḥanbal (d. 241/855, Baghdad), the Prophet supplicates by evoking the expansiveness of the divine names: 'I [Muḥammad] ask You [Allah] by every name with which You have named Yourself, revealed in Your book, taught any of Your creation, or reserved for Yourself in the knowledge of the unseen that is with You.'[8] Other *ḥadīth* describe how the Prophet evoked specific names in regular devotional practice. A *ḥadīth* transmitted on the authority of the Prophet's wife ʿĀ'isha bt. Abī Bakr (d. 58 /678, Medina), for example, specifies that the Prophet was in the habit of concluding his ritual prayers with a supplication evoking the divine entity as 'the peace', a practice that many followers mimic when saying: 'You [divine entity] are peace (*al-salām*) and from You is peace. Blessed are You, possessor of glory and honour.'[9] In this way, a divine appellation becomes incorporated into daily ritual practice. The root *s-l-m*, which conjugates the divine epithet *al-salām*, is also the root of the words *islām* and *muslim*. It signifies willing surrender and the peaceful state that ensues. The root expresses the notion of safety, completeness, freedom from impairment, wholeness, contentment, and fulfilment. Here, as in many other instances, a divine name often expresses more of a semantic range than what a one-word English translation conveys.

## 2. Divine Appellations in Qur'anic Verses

The Qur'an emphasises the quality of divine compassion (*raḥma*) and instructs reciters to: 'Call upon Allah or call upon the all-compassionate (*al-raḥmān*), whichever you call upon, to [Allah] belong the most beautiful names' (Q. 17:110). In another oft-quoted verse, the Qur'an describes the divine entity as self-bound by this compassion (Q. 6:12). Yet another verse connects monotheism and divine compassion: 'Your divine entity (*ilāh*) is a singular entity; there is no *ilāh* other than [Allah], the all-compassionate (*al-raḥmān*), the ever-compassionate (*al-raḥīm*)' (Q. 2:163). The names *al-raḥmān* and *al-raḥīm*, as well as the noun *raḥma* (compassion), derive from the root *r-ḥ-m*. 'Womb' (*raḥim*) also

7 See the famed collection of Abū ʿAbd Allāh Muḥammad b. Ismāʿīl al-Bukhārī (d. 256/870, Samarkand), whose work *Ṣaḥīḥ al-imām al-Bukhārī al-musammā al-jāmiʿ al-musnad al-ṣaḥīḥ al-mukhtaṣar min umūr rasūl Allāh wa-sunanihi wa-ayyāmihi*, or *Ṣaḥīḥ al-Bukhārī* for short, is regarded as one of the canonical Sunnī *ḥadīth* collections (https://sunnah.com/bukhari:2736). *Ḥadīth* offered here are sourced from Sunnah.com and cited with reference to that platform's numbering system.

8 *Musnad* of Aḥmad b. Ḥanbal (https://sunnah.com/hisn:120). See also Abd-Allah, *One God, Many Names*, 4.

9 See the famed *ḥadīth* collection known as *Ṣaḥīḥ Muslim*, compiled by Muslim b. al-Ḥajjāj al-Qushayrī al-Naysāburī (d. 261/875, Nishapur) (https://sunnah.com/muslim:592a).

derives from this root. The names *Allāh*, *al-raḥmān*, and *al-raḥīm* together constitute a phrase known as the *basmala* that functions as a preface to all but one Qur'anic sūra. The phrase is challenging to adequately render but could be translated as: 'In the name of Allah, the endlessly compassionate and ever-compassionate'. For a scripture containing more than 70,000 words, several numerical equivalences between the central concepts of *raḥmān*, *raḥīm*, and *raḥma* are noteworthy: Outside of the introductory *basmala*s, the Qur'an mentions the divine name *raḥīm* 115 times; notably, the Qur'an also mentions *raḥma*, the noun signifying compassion, a nearly equivalent 114 times, a number that also corresponds with the total number of sūras. Outside the *basmala*, the name *raḥmān* is mentioned 57 times, precisely half of 114, which is precisely the number of occurrences of *raḥma*.

As in the case of *al-raḥmān* and *al-raḥīm* in the *basmala*, the Qur'an often evokes paired appellations, usually at the end of verses. For instance, close to 40 of the nearly 300 verses in the longest *sūra* of the Qur'an, Sūrat al-Baqara, conclude with pairs of divine names. Hundreds of verses end with paired appellations, often emphasising divine omniscience and clemency. A sample of such verses includes the following:

> To Allah belong the East and the West. Wheresoever you turn, there is the countenance of Allah. Truly Allah is all-encompassing, knowing. (Q. 2:115)
>
> To [Allah] belongs all that dwells in the night and the day, and [Allah] is the hearing, the knowing. (Q. 6:13)
>
> [Allah] knows what every female bears, how wombs diminish and how they increase; everything with [Allah] is according to a measure—/ knower of the unseen and the seen, the great, the exalted. (Q. 13:8–9)
>
> The seven heavens, the earth, and whoever is in them glorify [Allah]. And there is no entity, save that it hymns [Allah's] praise, though you [human beings] do not understand their praise. Truly [Allah] is clement, forgiving. (Q. 17:44)
>
> O humankind! You are needful of Allah; and [Allah] is the self-sufficient, the praised. (Q. 35:15)
>
> Allah decrees with truth, and those on whom they invoke apart from [Allah] do not decree with anything. Truly Allah is the hearer, the seer. (Q. 40:20)
>
> O humankind! We [the divine] created you from a male and female and made you peoples and tribes such that you may come to know one another. Surely, the

> most noble of you with Allah are the most reverent of you. Truly Allah is knowing, aware. (Q. 49:13)

In addition to paired attributes at the ends of verses, the Qur'an contains several lists of divine attributes. The following verses are among the many examples of this feature:

> Whatever is in the heavens and the earth glorifies [Allah], and [Allah] is the mighty, the wise. / To [Allah] belongs sovereignty over the heavens and the earth; [Allah] gives life and causes death, and [Allah] is powerful over all things. / [Allah] is the first, the last, the outward, and the inward; and [Allah] is a knower of all things. (Q. 57:1–3)

> The divine is Allah—there is no divine entity other than [Allah]—the sovereign, the holy, the peace, the faithful, the protector, the mighty, the compeller, the proud. Glory be to [Allah] above the partners they ascribe. / The divine entity is Allah, the creator, the maker, the fashioner; to [Allah] belong the most beautiful names. Whatever is in the heavens and the earth glorifies [Allah], and [Allah] is the mighty, the wise. (Q. 59:23–24)

> If you lend to Allah a goodly loan, [Allah] will multiply it for you and forgive you; and Allah is appreciative, clement, / knower of the unseen and the seen, the mighty, the wise. (Q. 64:17–18)

### 1.2 Muslim Conceptual Frameworks for the Most Beautiful Names

Hundreds of Qur'anic verses and *ḥadīth* include divine epithets or describe the divine nature, attributes, or actions; from these sources, Muslim scholars derive frameworks for conceptualising, evoking, and teaching the most beautiful names. Devotional literature on divine appellations ranges from philosophical discussions of divine nature to practical instructions for evoking the spiritual potencies of various appellations. Works on divine names abound, including those in dozens of languages composed by scholars and practitioners who draw upon written and oral traditions alongside experiential insights.

For instance, a popular litany dating from the early period, known as *Duʿāʾ al-jawshan al-kabīr* or the 'great chain armour supplication', is attributed to ʿAlī b. Abī Ṭālib and incorporates approximately a thousand divine names and attributes. From the classical period, a leading work of philosophical theology on the divine appellations is that of Abū Ḥāmid al-Ghazālī (d. 505/1111, Ṭūs), the renowned systematiser of Sunnī thought.[10] Theo-

10 [Abū Ḥāmid] al-Ghazālī, *The Ninety-Nine Beautiful Names of God: al-Maqṣad al-asnā fī sharḥ asmāʾ Allāh al-ḥusnā*, trans. David B. Burrell and Nazih Daher (Cambridge: Islamic Texts Society, 1992).

logical treatises such as al-Ghazālī's emphasise divine attributes (*ṣifāt*) and fundamental characteristics of the divine essence (*dhāt*), such as knowledge, power, life, will, hearing, sight, speech, and so forth. Such works are informed by the legacy of Greek intellectualism and offer argumentative proofs regarding various aspects of the divine nature, including discussions of themes like relational and non-relational divine attributes. A contemporary example of an esoteric, practice-geared resource for spiritual self-development is a book by Rosina-Fawzia al-Rawi (b. 1965, Baghdad), a Vienna-based spiritual teacher in the Shādhiliyya Sufi lineage whose directives for evoking divine names are accompanied by calligraphic presentations by Majed Seif, Jerusalem-born, New York-based calligrapher.[11] For its compelling artistry and focus on self-transformational love, the book has garnered wide appeal even beyond Muslim audiences and is distributed by Simon & Schuster, a prominent international publisher headquartered in New York. These three examples of works drawn from different geographies and periods of Islamic history are merely a sampling of the vast Muslim literature on divine appellations.

Muslim scholars systematise Islamic theology most immediately from the Qur'an and the teachings of the Prophet Muḥammad. Some divine attributes are specified by the Qur'an or a widely attested Prophetic teaching; other appellations derive from an action that the divine entity carries out. For instance, in the Arabic language, fate, power, and measurement share a common root (*q-d-r*); hence, the divine can be referred to as *al-qādir* and *al-muqtadir*, the all-powerful entity who measures out and ordains: 'Truly We [the divine] have created everything according to a measure' (Q. 54:49). Another oft-quoted verse conveys a quality of responsive intimacy from which a name derives:

> When My [Allah's] servants ask you [Prophet] about Me, truly I am near. I respond to the invocation of the supplicant when they invoke Me. So let them respond to Me and have faith in Me, that they may be led aright. (Q. 2:186)

Here, the description of divine action elicits the name 'the responsive one' (*al-mujīb*). Another verse describes the divine as 'prevailing in purpose' (Q. 12:21), which occasions *al-ghālib*, the one who prevails.

Listings of appellations also include phrases, such as 'knower of what is what is hidden and manifest' (*ʿālim al-ghayb wa-l-shahāda*, Q. 59:22) or 'possessor of the glorious throne' (*dhū al-ʿarsh al-majīd*, Q. 85:15). The divine entity is twice described as 'possessor of majesty and magnanimity' (*dhū/ī jalāl wa-l-ikrām*) in Sūrat al-Raḥmān (Q. 55:27 and 55:78). In multiple verses, bounty (*faḍl*) emanates from the divine, and the name 'possessor of bounty' (*dhū faḍl*) appears on more than a dozen occasions. Several names derive from the same linguistic root but occur in morphological patterns that convey subtle shades

11 Rosina-Fawzia al-Rawi, *Divine Names: The 99 Healing Names of the One Love*, trans. Monique Arav (Northampton, MA: Olive Branch Press, 2015).

of meaning. For instance, the names *al-ghaffār*, *al-ghafūr*, and *al-ghāfir* all derive from the root *gh-f-r* and relate to clemency.[12]

Divine names are often pairings of opposite qualities. For instance, the Qur'an describes the divine as the ascendant and the intimate (*al-ẓāhir wa-l-bāṭin*, Q. 57:3), evoking qualities of both transcendence and immanence. The divine entity is the one who denigrates (*al-khāfiḍ*) and who raises (*al-rāfiʿ*), the one who debases (*al-mudhill*) and who bestows honour (*al-muʿizz*), the reckoner (*al-muntaqim*) and the pardoner (*al-ʿafuww*), the bearer of harm (*al-ḍārr*) and the one who averts harm (*al-mānīʿ*), the one who brings death (*al-mumīt*) and who gives life (*al-muḥyī*), and so forth. A related way of organising the names is into those of beauty or grace (*jamāl*) and those of majesty or rigour (*jalāl*). Hence, the divine is characterised simultaneously by profound compassion and discerning justice: the divine is the avenger (*al-muntaqim*) but also the clement (*al-ḥalīm*). The divine is the withholder (*al-qābiḍ*) but is also the kind (*al-raʾūf*) and the generous (*al-karīm*).

Qur'anic verses that refer to divine might and rigour could be employed nefariously to typecast Muslims as worshipping a uniquely vengeful deity. Yet, divine might and power create a meaningful conceptual system when understood in tandem with qualities of grace and compassion. This balance of attributes is not uncommon in metaphysical systems. For instance, in dharmic, Daoist, and many native conceptual systems, constructive and destructive power are complementary; likewise, Abrahamic scriptures and traditions often depict divine retribution, punishment, wrath, and destructive power alongside creative and cajoling divine attributes. In this vein, Sa'diyya Shaikh, a South African-based Muslim feminist scholar, evokes the cosmology of the renowned Andalusian scholar and mystic Muḥyī al-Dīn Ibn al-ʿArabī (d. 638/1240, Damascus) to argue that qualities of divine majesty (the *jalālī* qualities) are mediated by the qualities of beauty (the *jamālī* qualities).[13]

## 2.2 Contemplating the Beautiful Names as a Process of Character Refinement

According to Muslim understanding, divine unicity is known by the innate human disposition (*fiṭra*) and through contemplation of various signs (āyāt) in the created world.[14] Meditation on the meanings and manifestations of the names in the physical world is a spiritual practice that fulfils a Qur'anic command, as issued in the divine first-person voice: 'Remember Me, and I will remember you' (Q. 2:152). Nearly 300 verses of the Qur'an evoke divine 'remembrance' (*dhikr*, from the root *dh-k-r*, lit. to mention or to recall). Muslims engage in various modalities of 'remembrance' including by repeating phrases with various combinations of names that can be recited individually or in communal

12 For instances of the different forms, see Q. 39:5, 2:173, and 40:3, respectively; see also al-Ghazālī, *Ninety-Nine Beautiful Names*, 25.

13 Sa'diyya Shaikh, 'In Search of al-Insān: Sufism, Islamic Law, and Gender', *Journal of the American Academy of Religion* 77, no. 4 (2009): 781–822.

14 For an extended discussion, see Celene Ibrahim, *Islam and Monotheism*, 18.

devotional settings. Gatherings dedicated to *dhikr* include litanies of divine names alongside Qur'anic supplications and formulas of praise taught by the Prophet Muḥammad, his close Companions, or saintly figures throughout the ages.

The names offer those who invoke them a source of comfort, guidance, inspiration, and metaphysical insight. For instance, Qaiser Shahzad, a Pakistani-based professor of comparative religion, explains how the names offer a means for developing human potential whereby individuals strive to 'adopt the moral quality underlying a particular Divine Name, to the extent humanly possible'.[15] Writing in the domain of spiritual psychology, Iranian American psychologist Laleh Bakhtiar (d. 2020, Chicago) offers instruction on how to achieve 'moral healing' by evoking the names.[16] William Chittick, a prolific New York-based scholar of Islamic theology, explains that the goal of this contemplation is to discern 'the reality of the Object of Worship, the Absolute *Ḥaqq* [truth], so that people can relate to it in the right and appropriate manner'.[17] Camille Helminski, scholar of the teachings of Afghani jurist and mystic Jalāl al-Dīn Rūmī (d. 672/1273, Konya), offers poetic meditations on the names to inspire contemporary readers striving to imbibe the qualities.[18] Likewise, writer A. Helwa offers guidelines for using names for introspection and spiritual revival.[19] Through such modalities, a devotee strives to psychologically, intellectually, and spiritually come to have experiential knowledge of the names.

An adept teacher may advise a student to focus on specific names to bring about a new awareness or shift a stuck behavioural pattern. In the context of spiritual development, the names of rigour provide an ego-check, a reminder of divine power and human frailty. Alternately, divine names can offer a horizon of hope and possibility for someone with weak self-esteem who may turn to a name such as *al-quddūs* (the holy) to help shift psychosomatic patterns of self-doubt, enabling that person to feel sustained through a sublime and majestic connection to a cosmic force. A person enduring a calamity and seeking forbearance may evoke *al-ṣabūr* (the patient) as a supplication to help activate patient perseverance within their psyche. Many names correspond to universal virtues, such as forbearance and wisdom. Relating to the most beautiful names in this manner provides a framework for attending to physical, social, emotional, mental, behavioural, and spiritual well-being. Individuals develop cognitive and experiential awareness through introspection and an ongoing commitment to character refinement.

---

15 See Qaiser Shahzad, 'Playing God and the Ethics of Divine Names: An Islamic Paradigm for Biomedical Ethics', *Bioethics* 21, no. 8 (2007): 414.

16 See Laleh Bakhtiar, *Moral Healing through the Most Beautiful Names: The Practice of Spiritual Chivalry, vol. 3 of God's Will Be Done* (Chicago: Kazi Publications, 1994).

17 William C. Chittick, 'Worship', in *The Cambridge Companion to Classical Islamic Theology*, ed. Tim Winter (Cambridge: Cambridge University Press, 2008), 221.

18 Camille Hamilton Adams Helminski, *Ninety-Nine Names of the Beloved: Intimations of the Beauty and Power of the Divine* (Escondido, CA: Sweet Lady Press, 2017).

19 See A. Helwa, *Secrets of Divine Love: A Spiritual Journey into the Heart of Islam* (Capistrano Beach, CA: Naulit Publishing, 2020), 73–75.

A common explanation is that the divine possesses attributes in their total manifestation, and entities in the world reflect these attributes, as the moon reflects the sun. For instance, though people can acquire some knowledge of discrete subjects, the divine entity is the knower of all the particulars (*al-ʿalīm*). People may strive to demonstrate compassion towards other sentient beings; however, human expressions can only approximate the boundless quality of divine compassion. Still, the divine can begin to be grasped through similitudes that enable people to acquire experiential awareness. On one occasion, for instance, the Prophet is said to have elucidated the quality of divine compassion by pointing to the attentiveness of a nursing mother.[20]

Ultimately, the names require experiential tasting, not just a conceptual articulation. The prolific Sri Lankan American teacher known as Bawa Muhaiyaddeen (d. 1986, Philadelphia), from the spiritual lineage of ʿAbd al-Qādir al-Jīlānī (d. 561/1166, Baghdad), describes how a person achieves an understanding of the names in accord with that person's spiritual state: 'as one's wisdom and purity develop, deeper and deeper meanings will be revealed'.[21] Tosun Bayrak (d. 2018, New York), a teacher in the Turkish al-Jerrahi-al-Halveti lineage that traces its roots to the Persian ʿUmar Khalwatī (d. 800/1347, Tabriz), emphasises the distinction between conceptual knowledge and esoteric knowledge of the divine names. Bayrak describes individuals who have conceptual knowledge but lack experiential knowledge:

> They know the Name but not the Named. They are like someone who is hungry and who tries to satisfy his [her/their] hunger by saying 'bread, bread, bread'; all the benefit such a person may hope for is that his repetition may increase his wish and effort to find bread and eat it.[22]

Taking Bayrak's insight into an interreligious context, the divine names are a poignant place of departure in part because they invite individuals into a space of epistemic humility and intimate experiential learning.

## 3. Dialogical Exchange across Metaphysical Paradigms

This work has offered a survey of the most beautiful names in the context of Muslim spirituality and metaphysics. I now identify how, using the names as a point of departure, Muslim scholars can be in generative dialogue with people whose worldviews or conceptions of divinity diverge from Islamic premises. In the notes, I survey the most

20 See al-Bukhārī (https://sunnah.com/bukhari:5999).

21 Muhammad Raheem Bawa Muhaiyaddeen, *Asma' ul-Husna: The 99 Names of Allah* (Philadelphia: The Fellowship Press, 1979), 2–3.

22 Tosun Bayrak al-Jerrahi al-Halveti, *The Name and the Named* (Louisville: Fons Vitae, 2000), 36.

recent and valuable comparative work related to the nature of the divine or ultimate reality in Muslim–Jewish, Muslim–Christian, Muslim–Hindu, Muslim–Buddhist, Muslim–Sikh, Muslim–Daoist, Muslim–Confucian thought. I also offer potential avenues of engagement with Zoroastrians, Jains, Ifá and Vodún practitioners, practitioners of Native American spiritualities and Shinto, as well as people of Bahá'í faith, Humanist, scientific materialist, Unitarian Universalists, and transcendentalist perspectives. The field of comparative theology and interreligious studies is now vast; I offer here an exploratory sampling of tradition-specific avenues for fruitful practical engagement.[23]

### 1.3 The Most Beautiful Names and Muslim–Jewish or Muslim–Christian Encounter

Resonances between Jewish and Muslim, theology, jurisprudence, and ritual practice have been the subject of multitudes of academic works, as have the interactions between Jewish and Muslim communities throughout history. Muslims can unreservedly endorse the core monotheistic impulse of Judaism as expressed in the Torah's creedal statement of the Shema (Deuteronomy 6:4). Hebrew scriptural assertions about the divine nature often have Qur'anic parallels; for instance, the prophet Isaiah conveys divine speech: 'I am God, and there is no other; I am God and there is none beside me' (Isaiah 45:5 and 46:9).[24] Due to the Semitic roots of Hebrew and Arabic, a host of divine names have precise cognates. Moreover, the divine entity creates through language in both traditions.[25] In Jewish mysticism, the concept of *ayin*, or the divine as 'no thing', offers a rich conceptual point of departure involving the inherent difficulties in describing transcendent realities.[26]

Yet, despite these broad points of understanding, subtle differences in Jewish and Muslim theological discourses invite discussion. In Jewish contexts, the divine may be portrayed as being influenced by human action in a manner that is distinct from characterisations found in mainstream Muslim discourses. Thus, the divine appellations *al-ṣamad* (the everlasting), *al-ḥayy* (the living), and *al-qayyūm* (the eternal) make for an apt place

23 I know of no other academic work with comparable scope, though recent works on Jewish–Christian–Muslim encounter include that of Irish theologian Máire Byrne, *The Names of God in Judaism, Christianity and Islam: A Basis for Interfaith Dialogue* (New York: Continuum, 2011). David B. Burrell of the University of Notre Dame has compared the divine names in the works of Muslim theologian Abū Ḥāmid al-Ghazālī (d. 505/1111, Ṭūs), Christian theologian St. Thomas Aquinas (d. 1274, Sicily), and Maimonides (d. 1204, Egypt), the famed Jewish polymath. See David B. Burrell, 'Naming the Names of God: Muslims, Jews, Christians', *Theology Today* 47, no. 1 (1990): 22–59.

24 For a helpful resource, see Safi Kaskas and David Hungerford, *The Qur'an with References to the Bible: A Contemporary Understanding* (Fairfax: Bridges of Reconciliation, 2016).

25 For a detailed exploration of various Jewish perspectives on the Tetragrammaton, the four Hebrew letters that make up the unvoiced representation of the ultimate divine name, see Michael T. Miller, *The Name of God in Jewish Thought: A Philosophical Analysis of Mystical Traditions from Apocalyptic to Kabbalah* (New York: Routledge, 2016).

26 See Or N. Rose, 'Jewish Mystical Resources for Interreligious Engagement: A Practitioner's Perspective', in *The Georgetown Companion to Interreligious Studies*, ed. Lucinda Mosher (Washington, DC: Georgetown University Press, 2022), 308–16, esp. 309–11.

to begin conversation on subtle understandings of the divine nature in relation to human qualities. For instance, in reflecting on the divine appellation *al-ṣamad*, contemporary Sufi teacher Rosina-Fawzia al-Rawi offers the following observations:

> When we lose touch with our own value, we feel empty, inferior, incomplete, and we need to fill this void from the outside in the form of praise, agreement, or recognition. We are solely aware of our own wishes and needs. 'I want this and that. I want to be successful. I want so and so to love me. I want this help and that recognition!' The ego takes the lead, and our essence fades more and more into the background, into the unconscious. Each of our hollows is filled with a psychological issue, with dogmas, specific experiences, ideas, and pictures from the past so that we end up being not *in* this world but *of* this world. The Sufis [Muslim mystics] describe those who are connected to their essence as being *in* this world but not *of* this world. … Aṣ-Ṣamad makes us knock on the gates of the subconscious and of our higher consciousness until the dams become porous and we are flooded in the waters of Unity. Aṣ-Ṣamad, the Inscrutable, makes us wide and boundless, sweeping away all fear and doubt.[27]

For Muslims, the name *al-ṣamad* points to the pure, consistent nature of the divine entity, an entity that is in no way confined to time or space. Given how tensions and ongoing territorial disputes in the Israeli–Palestinian crisis cast a shadow over many Jewish–Muslim dialogical encounters, this name instead invites contemplation on transcendent realities. Likewise, the names *al-ḥayy* (the living) and *al-qayyūm* (the eternal) invite reflection on the primal connection of human life to the divine source, a connection that transcends nationalism, notions of spiritual entitlements, or claims to exclusive divine favour. Discussion of these three names, and the lessons that they impart in the realm of spiritual psychology, can be provocative in Jewish–Muslim engagement.

Likewise, Christian–Muslim encounter also has a robust history dating back to the earliest Muslim polity.[28] As with Jewish sources, numerous commonalities can be identified between Christian and Muslim conceptions of the divine nature; however, original sin and the Trinity are central doctrines for many Christians that are refuted in the Qur'an. For Muslims, the figure of Jesus (ʿĪsā) has a prophetic status akin to that of the Prophet Muḥammad: each is an exemplar calling to monotheism and righteousness. According to Islamic teaching, there is no role for a sacrificial lamb to ameliorate the sins of the world, as is commonly held in dominant strains of Christian thought, because beings are

---

27 al-Rawi, *Divine Names*, 254.

28 For one excellent work that details early Christian perceptions of Muslims, see Michael Philip Penn, *Envisioning Islam: Syriac Christians and the Early Muslim World* (Philadelphia: University of Pennsylvania Press, 2015).

born with a pure disposition (*fiṭra*). Despite Trinitarian's claim that the divine consists of three 'persons', many Christian theologians describe the divine nature as ontologically non-divisible. The Qur'an evokes 'the holy spirit' (*rūḥ al-qudus*, Q. 16:102), an entity that emanates from the divine but is not a 'part' of the divine entity.

Divine appellations for dialogical contexts involving Christian–Muslim encounter include *al-wadūd* (the lover), *al-bāʿith* (the resurrector), as well as *al-muʾmin* and *al-muhaymin*, two appellations that evoke divine protection. The names *al-mujīb* (the one who responds), *al-ḥamīd* (the praiseworthy, the glorious), and *al-shakūr* (the appreciative) also hold resonance, considering that Christian liturgy and piety more broadly is often organised around praise, glory, thanksgiving, and supplication. Given that Christian discourses theorise the divine as a redeemer of sin, the name *al-ʿafū* (the obliterator, eraser) and other epithets related to divine forgiveness are compelling. Finally, appellations such as *al-hādī* and *al-walī* that pertain to guidance, or *al-wakīl* (the trustee) that pertains to divine support, or *al-khabīr* that pertains to omniscience, or *al-barr* (the beneficent) that pertains to kindness and goodness, will all resonate with Christian ideas about divine succour and human reliance. Divine forgiveness and compassion are emphasised even in Qur'anic sūra titles: Ghāfir (Q. 40) is named for this epithet contained within it and al-Raḥmān (Q. 55) is a sūra that contains poetic imagery of divine blessings.

In terms of experiential learning, Christians with interests in mysticism or embodied spiritualities may enjoy witnessing a Muslim gathering dedicated to divine remembrance through the divine names. For instance, Catholic theologian Lynn Cooper reflects on her embodied experience attending one such gathering led by Muslim chaplain Halimah Naila Baloch, who was Cooper's colleague in campus ministry. Cooper writes:

> As a Roman Catholic, I use the word 'mercy' all the time. We speak of the corporal acts of mercy in our work with vulnerable populations. We call out to God for mercy throughout the mass—upward of eight times, depending on some liturgical choices. But it is only in Naila's apartment on this windy November evening that I begin to feel the word 'merciful'. The reality and profundity bleeds into my bones and I am full of gratitude for the gift of this moment and for clarity, albeit fleeting. I am taken by God's infinite mercy but also our own capacity for mercy and compassion. Reciting and singing attributes of God, I am moved to tears. With each word, I feel something within me expand and an entry point widen. I have long been a believer in the meeting of breath and prayer.... I can intellectualize this experience all I want, but the embodied knowing—the practice itself—is what stirs me to a novel state in which peace and wakefulness coexist, nourishing one another.[29]

29 Lynn Cooper, 'Sacred Moments of Liminality', in *One Nation, Indivisible: Seeking Liberty and Justice from the Pulpit to the Streets*, ed. Celene Ibrahim (Eugene, OR: Wipf and Stock, 2019), 30.

Cooper's embodied experiences of a divine attribute speak to the potential for interreligious friendships to become sites of spiritual cultivation.[30]

Beyond contemplating the divine names, Muslim–Christian theological dialogue can find common ground in the shared esteem given to Jesus and his family as well as the figures shared with the Jewish biblical tradition. As a point of religious literacy, Muslims can seek to understand how early Christian doctrine on the nature of Jesus developed over many centuries in an Eastern Mediterranean context and how the Prophet and the early Muslim community built political alliances with supportive Christian polities.

### 3.2 The Most Beautiful Names and the Dharmic Traditions

I now consider fruitful points of conceptual and experiential exchange between Muslims and practitioners of the dharmic traditions of Hinduism, Buddhism, Jainism, and Sikhism. Given the core belief in the cyclical nature of the universe and human life in dharmic traditions, names such as *al-mubdiʾ* (the originator) and *al-muʿīd* (the returner) could make for provocative conversation in relation to dharmic concepts on the cyclical nature of existence.

In dialogical settings, Muslims must remember that 'Hinduism' is an umbrella term encompassing vastly different forms of practice. Muslims should resist the tendency to collapse Hindu thought into overly simplistic themes without due attention to the sophistication of ancient Hindu philosophies on the nature of the divine. Many Hindus do, in fact, regard themselves as monotheists and regard avatars of deities as different manifestations of one supreme entity, as described in ancient Vedantic thought.[31]

The emphasis in Jain monastic traditions on minimising worldly distractions to allow a devotee to concentrate on pursuing God-consciousness resonates deeply with the aim of Muslim pious practice. In terms of virtue ethics, Muslims can be inspired by the Jain dedication to the practice of doing no harm, or *ahimsa*, a Sanskrit term that is also rooted in other South Asian traditions. Thus, for Jain–Muslim exchange, epithets related to the divine as the source of peace (*al-salām*) and balance or harmony (*al-ʿadl*) would be poignant in dialogical exchanges. Additionally, for Buddhist–Muslim dialogue, the idea that self-knowledge is the root of knowledge makes the appellation *al-ḥaqq* (the truth, the reality) a powerful theme.[32]

30 For a practical guide catered to Catholics seeking interreligious competencies, see Lynn Cooper, *Embracing Our Time: The Sacrament of Interfaith Friendship* (Minneapolis: Fortress, 2024).

31 For an excellent comparative and historical work, see Shankar Nair, *Translating Wisdom: Hindu–Muslim Intellectual Interactions in Early Modern South Asia* (Oakland: University of California Press, 2020). For a study of modern Muslim understandings of Hinduism, see SherAli Tareen, *Perilous Intimacies: Debating Hindu–Muslim Friendship after Empire* (New York: Columbia University Press, 2023).

32 An indispensable work on Muslim–Buddhist dialogue is that of Reza Shah-Kazemi and Hamza Yusuf, *Common Ground between Islam and Buddhism* (Louisville: Fons Vitae, 2010). See also the body of work of Imtiyaz Yusuf, including his article 'Building Muslim–Buddhist Understanding: The Parallels of *Taqwa*/

Sikh and Muslim shared conceptions of divine oneness make names related to divine unity, such as *al-aḥad* (the singular) and *al-wāḥid* (the one), particularly poignant. Muslims could appreciate the Mul Mantra, a core creedal statement of Sikhism that evokes the qualities of the divine in terms that resonate with Muslim understanding of applications such as the first principle (*al-awwal*) and the last principle (*al-ākhir*). Sikh–Muslim exchange has been burdened by a history of regional violence in the Punjab, but the post-9/11 context in the United States and political developments in the United Kingdom have opened new forms of collaboration as both Muslims and Sikhs navigate their shared context as minority traditions. Even when targeted by misplaced anti-Muslim bigotry, many Sikhs have courageously placed themselves at the forefront of movements for religious liberty and against xenophobia and bigotry. Muslims can also be inspired by the commitment of Sikh practitioners to visible markers of religiosity, despite climates of heightened bigotry. Given the respective central values of each religion, the divine epithet *al-qisṭ* (the just) is a promising theme for dialogical exchange. Though Sikh–Muslim exchange can be complicated by histories of political conflict, centuries-long proximity has also made possible rich cultural, intellectual, and spiritual exchange.

### 3.3 The Most Beautiful Names in the Context of Confucian, Daoist, and Shinto Traditions

Muslim–Confucian encounters can be traced back to early Muslim–Chinese trade networks. In more recent centuries, a robust body of philosophical literature dating to the Qing dynasty even expresses Islamic metaphysics using Neo-Confucian concepts.[33] In Muslim–Daoist comparative thought, the leading work remains that of Japanese scholar Toshihiko Izutsu (d. 1993, Kamakura).[34] Given that Daoist philosophy finds harmony in the joining of opposites, complementary pairs of divine epithets resonate.[35] When it comes to Muslim–Shinto exchange, Naoki Yamamoto, a Japanese scholar of Islamic intellectual history, has offered preliminary analyses of classical Islamic virtue ethics in comparison with values drawn from the Samurai code of ethics known as Bushido, which includes values such as truthfulness, honour, courage, politeness, loyalty, justice, and kindness.

---

Allah Consciousness in the Qur'an and Satipatthana/Mindfulness in Anapanasati Sutta', in *Overcoming Orientalism: Essays in Honor of John L. Esposito*, ed. Tamara Sonn (New York: Oxford University Press, 2021), 173–90.

33 For a discussion of this body of literature that is referred to as the Han Kitāb, see Oludamini Ogunnaike and Mohammed Rustom, 'Islam in English', *American Journal of Islamic Social Sciences* 36, no. 2 (2016): 102–13, esp. 105–6. A starting point for Confucian–Muslim learning is Sachiko Murata, William C. Chittick, and Tu Weiming, *The Sage Learning of Liu Zhi: Islamic Thought in Confucian Terms* (Cambridge, MA: Harvard University Press, 2009).

34 See Toshihiko Izutzu, *Sufism and Taoism: A Comparative Study of Key Philosophical Concepts* (Berkeley: University of California Press, 1983).

35 See discussions in Sachiko Murata, *The Tao of Islam: A Sourcebook on Gender Relationships in Islamic Thought* (Albany: State University of New York, 1992), 6–8.

Appellations referring to purity and goodness also provide common ground, as do concepts of chivalry in Islamic and Japanese cultural traditions more broadly. Shinto–Muslim exchange could also consider ways in which the divine epithets are reflected in the natural world. Japan has a small but thriving population of Muslims, and a translation of the Qur'an into Japanese was first undertaken in the mid-twentieth century by Izutsu.[36]

### 3.4 The Most Beautiful Names in Muslim–Native Encounter

In general, indigenous traditions have value systems that are closely aligned with Islamic values relating to personal responsibility and stewardship. Names related to the divine entity as creator and fashioner of the earth could be poignant for Muslim–Native dialogical exchanges. Such names include *al-khāliq* (the creator), *al-bāriʾ* (the originator), and *al-muṣawwir* (the fashioner). Other names that resonate with the concept of a 'great spirit' include *al-ʿazīz* (the mighty), *al-kabīr* (the great), and *malīk al-mulk* (the possessor of dominion). Names related to gifting and gratitude, including *al-wahhāb* (the bestower), *al-razzāq* (the provider), *al-shakūr* (the appreciative), could also resonate. Muslims can remain curious about the wisdom contained in ancient indigenous knowledge systems, particularly teachings relating to human dispositions and to divine signs in the created world. Given the history of Native dispossession and the Native power movements that have resisted this oppression, divine names that relate to strength and might—including *al-matīn* (the resolute), *al-qawī* (the powerful), *al-qahhār* (the compeller), and *al-raqīb* (the vigilant)—could be potent sites for conceptual and experiential engagement.[37]

### 3.5 The Most Beautiful Names alongside West African Spiritual Traditions

Ifá and Vodún traditions predate Muslim traditions in West Africa. Nigerian American academic and Muslim scholar Oludamini Ogunnaike offers a detailed comparative account of the knowledge systems of Ifá and Tijānī Sufism that serves as an excellent source for building interreligious knowledge.[38] Powers of the supreme deity and orishas as metaphysical spirit-entities offer sites of interreligious learning for Muslims. Names related to divine healing and guardianship, such as *al-shāfī* (the healer) and *al-mānīʿ* (the preventer [of harm]), are sites of experiential and dialogical encounter.

36 See Naoki Yamamoto, 'Muslim Scholars in Japan: Contemplating Islam in a Non-Muslim Society', *Traversing Tradition*, 21 November 2022, https://traversingtradition.com/2022/11/21/muslim-scholars-in-japan-contemplating-islam-in-a-non-muslim-society/.

37 As Shadaab Rahemtulla points out, the dialogue between Muslims and indigenous peoples must center Native justice; see Shadaab Rahemtulla, 'Decolonising Islam: Indigenous Peoples, Muslim Communities, and the Canadian Context', *Religions* 14, no. 9 (2023): 1–19.

38 Oludamini Ogunnaike, *Deep Knowledge: Ways of Knowing in Sufism and Ifa, Two West African Intellectual Traditions* (University Park: Penn State University Press, 2020).

### 3.6 The Most Beautiful Names alongside Zoroastrian, Bahá'í, and Unitarian Universalist Traditions

Zoroastrians have experienced persecution in Muslim-majority territories, even as Muslims were influenced by Zoroastrian thought. Of the many points of overlap between the two traditions, themes related to purity and light are apt starting places for interreligious exchange. The appellations *al-quddūs* (the holy) and *al-nūr* (the light) would resonate in Zoroastrian contexts (as well as in Bahá'í and Unitarian Universalist ones). Bahá'ís too have experienced political oppression in Muslim-majority territories though the Bahá'í faith has also been shaped in fertile ways through this encounter with Islamicate cultures.[39] For instance, traditional Bahá'í supplications include dozens of divine appellations that are derived from the Islamic tradition.

Unitarianism's roots can be traced in part to Muslim–Christian contact in Ottoman-influenced regions of Eastern Europe. As a formalised religious association, Unitarian Universalism is of newer provenance, established in 1961 as a merger of Unitarian and Universalist organisations. Given that Unitarian Universalism regards direct personal experience as a central principle, Unitarian Universalists are often keen on experiencing the spiritual practices of other faith traditions, and Unitarian Universalists, like Bahá'ís, regard Muslim spirituality as a sincere path to transcendent truth. For instance, Massachusetts-based Unitarian Universalist and transcendentalist the Reverend Jim Sherblom offers a provocative account of his experiences with the devotional practices of Mevlevi Sufis in Istanbul:

> We had been whirling and meditating all night, and it was nearly four in the morning when a Sufi saint called Baba—a term of endearment [meaning father]—approached me.... Baba placed his hand on my chest. He infused my Ka'ba—the temple within my heart—with loving kindness. Energy exploded from all my extremities. I felt the incredible power of God's love. I have never before felt so thoroughly engulfed by the dynamic energy of love. My heart was broken open. The next morning, it still left a large red circle over my heart.[40]

Moreover, Unitarian Universalists, like Bahá'ís, emphasise egalitarianism among human beings. Divine appellations relating to justice, righteousness, and peacebuilding, including *al-qisṭ* (the just), *al-rashīd* (the righteous), and *al-salām* (the peace) resonate, as do ideas about divine loving compassion. Given that Unitarian Universalist and Bahá'í guiding principles emphasise interpersonal harmony, the divine qualities of beauty are

---

39 For a starting place on Muslim–Bahá'í relations, see Todd Lawson, *Being Human: Baha'i Perspectives on Islam, Modernity, and Peace, Studies in the Bábí and Bahá'í Religions* (Los Angeles: Kalimát Press, 2020).

40 Jim Sherblom, *Spiritual Pilgrim: Awakening Journeys of a Twenty-First Century Transcendentalist* (Minneapolis: Wise Ink, 2018), 78–79; provocative questions appear at the conclusion of the chapter.

particularly resonant. Epithets pertaining to divine oneness and eternality, including *al-wāḥid* (the one) and *al-ṣamad* (the everlasting), are also apt. Both Bahá'í and Unitarian Universalist traditions recognise the Qur'an as a sacred scripture, which makes for a promising starting place for interreligious engagement.

### 3.7 Humanists, Scientific Materialists, Agnostics, Nature Mystics, the Spiritual but Not Religious

Appreciation for the natural world pervades the Qur'anic discourse. As such, appellations that relate to processes in the natural world and epithets that communicate wonder and awe of cosmic occurrences may be of interest to environmentalists and nature mystics. For instance, *al-ʿalīm* (the knower) is derived from the root *ʿ-l-m*, which also produces 'science' (*ʿilm*). Other poignant epithets include *al-jāmiʿ* (the gatherer), *al-majīd* (the glorious), *al-shahīd* (the witness), *al-baṣīr* (the observer), *al-ḥafīz* (the preserver), *al-muqaddim* (the accelerator), *al-muʿakhkhir* (the delayer), *al-ẓāhir* (the apparent), *al-bāṭin* (the hidden), and *al-wāsiʿ* (the expansive). For Muslims, the divine entity has 'the keys of the unseen' and documents everything 'in a clear register' (Q. 6:59); such imagery could offer inspiration for nature enthusiasts and those passionate about scientific pursuits. In an Islamic worldview, unadulterated monotheism is not only the essential and original nature of the human being but also the primal state of all sentient and non-sentient existence. Thus, even non-sentient entities reflect divine names in their properties and capacities, and this idea makes for a compelling conversation between Muslims and other nature mystics.[41]

## 4. Conclusion

I have offered here a concise survey of Islamic conceptions of the divine names for non-specialists in Islamic theology. I then put forth concise tradition-specific suggestions to highlight the potency of the names for dialogical exchange across metaphysical paradigms. I have suggested that the divine names constitute a compelling framework for cognitive, moral, and spiritual elevation, even when not invoked in tandem with the entirety of the Islamic conceptual system. The most beautiful divine names could function akin to the yogic knowledge of Hinduism, the mindfulness practices of the dharmic traditions generally, or qigong practices rooted in Daoism. These spiritual modalities all have broader appeal as grounding practices beyond the specific communities in which the practices were refined. When expressed as vibrational frequencies, as in the context of

41 Here, the works of Muslim eco-theologian Munjed Murad are an excellent starting place; see, for instance, Munjed M. Murad, 'Inner and Outer Nature: An Islamic Perspective on the Environmental Crisis', *Journal of Islam and Science* 10, no. 2 (2013): 117–37.

*dhikr*, the names offer an embodied way for those who do not identify as Muslim to have an experiential encounter with Muslim spirituality. Given their prominent role in Islamic artistry, the names also serve as a compelling visual introduction to Islamic spirituality.[42]

In short, the most beautiful names constitute an avenue for Muslims to have generative exchanges with practitioners of traditions who espouse differing conceptions of reality. Engagement across metaphysical paradigms is not only a venue for humanising and coming to know the 'other' but also serves as a vehicle of self-knowledge for professed Muslims too. Dialogic settings ideally draw even seasoned practitioners out of the realm of rote experience and into spaces of discovery that can become the inspiration for spiritual rejuvenation. The divine nature and attributes are sufficiently rich to sustain a lifetime of such dialogic inquiry and to draw people into ever-deeper states of self-discovery, or 'unveiling' (*kashf*), a concept used in Muslim esoteric discourses to refer to a person's direct experiential encounter with cosmic Truth.

I have demonstrated here how the most beautiful names are an aspect of Muslim devotion and embodied practice that may readily resonate with the consciousness, worldviews, and outlooks of those who do not self-identify as Muslims. Towards this end, I have provided concise, tradition-specific insights regarding how engagement with different divine names could prove conceptually rich for people of various metaphysical commitments. I put forth possibilities for interpersonal engagement that can, ideally, push people beyond knee-jerk impulses towards religious supremacy or the impulse to become unduly insular in terms of philosophical exposure.

Muslim American theologian and scholar Martin Nguyen has observed that in order to articulate their faith and values in contemporary societies, Muslims 'must come to recognize the predispositions and prejudices that pervade our modern worldview and reincorporate within it those elements of our faith tradition that we have lost, overlooked, or misplaced'.[43] Much in this spirit, I have offered here insights to support just such an integration.[44] The divine names could also be a pathway for broader and better public appreciation of Islamic spirituality. In dialogue settings, Muslims often introduce Islamic piety through religious jurisprudence on matters pertaining to maintaining daily prayers, fasting Ramadan, dressing with discretion, or avoiding the consumption of alcohol. These practices allow for the development of self-control and keep the egotistical nature of the human being in check. However, for some audiences, the countercultural rigour of these

---

42 For one example of contemporary devotional artistic work, see Hafeez Shaikh, '99 Names of Allah', accessed 19 July 2023, www.arthafez.com.

43 Martin Nguyen, *Modern Muslim Theology: Engaging God and the World with Faith and Imagination* (Lanham, MD: Roman & Littlefield, 2019), 47.

44 For educators in secular classrooms, I have reflected on the value of acquiring religious and civilisation literacy and have offered some pedagogical strategies; see Celene Ibrahim, 'Simulation-Based Pedagogy for Interreligious Literacy: Critical Thinking Exercises for Teens and Young Adults', in *Georgetown Companion to Interreligious Studies*, ed. Lucinda Mosher (Washington, DC: Georgetown University Press, 2022), 396–407.

practices might constitute a barrier that prevents worthwhile deeper engagement with Islamic metaphysics and virtue ethics. Instead, exposure to the divine names and their properties could offer a poignant, accessible entry point for non-Muslims to encounter Islamic spiritual modalities.

A critic of this approach might allege that teaching about the most beautiful names beyond the confines of Islamic theology and Muslim practice could too readily encourage appropriation. Indeed, popularisation could even render the divine names from their roots—akin to how mindfulness practices have been appropriated from dharmic traditions in sometimes questionable ways.[45] A sceptic of the value of such a dialogical encounter across worldviews might also express concern that sustained exposure to other conceptual systems could induce a state of existential confusion for Muslims, or that a personal change of conviction could result from encountering other metaphysical paradigms. As someone who had opportunities to explore multiple traditions conceptually and experientially before discerning which notions personally resonated, I still hold that learning about other metaphysical paradigms is more enriching than it is destabilising.[46]

The most beautiful names are an aspect of the Qurʾan, *ḥadīth*, and wider Islamic intellectual heritage that offers people across eras, geographies, and metaphysical persuasions opportunities for intellectual, moral, and spiritual enrichment. According to Muslim understanding, scripture appeared in specific times and places; however, core messages possess universal appeal. At the most fundamental level, the conceptual systems discussed here encourage to the pursuit of character development and cosmic truth; learning about how others pursue virtue and engage in existential discernment is a generative space for dialogical cross-cultural exchange.[47] Much more could—and hopefully will—be written on this subject, but this essay highlighted leading scholarship and pathways for experiential inquiry.

---

45 For a detailed discussion of the dynamics of this spirituality industry, see Andrea R. Jain, *Peace Love Yoga: The Politics of Global Spirituality* (New York: Oxford University Press, 2020).

46 I explain how processes of exploration inspired civic and interreligious engagement in Celene Ibrahim, 'Preface', in *One Nation, Indivisible: Seeking Liberty and Justice from the Pulpit to the Streets*, ed. Celene Ibrahim (Eugene, OR: Wipf and Stock, 2019), xxxiii–xlvii.

47 For a compelling framework for self-introspection when engaging across differences, see Jennifer Howe Peace, 'Responses to Sameness and Difference', in *Deep Understanding for Divisive Times: Essays in Celebration of Ten Years of the Journal of Interreligious Studies*, ed. Mary Elizabeth Moore, Lucinda Mosher, Or Rose, and Axel Takacs (Newton Centre, MA: Interreligious Studies Press, 2020), 6–11. Peace provides a schematic for introspection and encourages readers not to collapse differences or, conversely, to create unnecessary chasms in our fundamental human interconnectedness.

## Bibliography

Abd-Allah, Umar Faruq. *One God, Many Names*. Nawawi Foundation Paper. Chicago: Nawawi Foundation, 2004.

Abou-Taleb, Amira. 'Iḥsān: A Mandate for Beauty and Goodness in Family Relations'. In *Justice and Beauty in Muslim Marriage: Towards Egalitarian Ethics and Laws*, edited by Ziba Mir-Hosseini, Mulki Al-Sharmani, Jana Rumminger, and Sarah Marsso, 101–33. London: OneWorld, 2022.

Bakhtiar, Laleh. *Moral Healing through the Most Beautiful Names: The Practice of Spiritual Chivalry*. Vol. 3 of *God's Will Be Done*. Chicago: Kazi Publications, 1994.

Burrell, David B. 'Naming the Names of God: Muslims, Jews, Christians'. *Theology Today* 47, no. 1 (1990): 22–59.

Chittick, William C. 'Worship'. In *The Cambridge Companion to Classical Islamic Theology*, edited by Tim Winter, 218–36. Cambridge: Cambridge University Press, 2008.

Cooper, Lynn. *Embracing Our Time: The Sacrament of Interfaith Friendship*. Minneapolis: Fortress, 2024.

———. 'Sacred Moments of Liminality'. In *One Nation, Indivisible: Seeking Liberty and Justice from the Pulpit to the Streets*, edited by Celene Ibrahim, 29–31. Eugene, OR: Wipf and Stock, 2019.

al-Ghazālī, [Abū Ḥāmid]. *The Ninety-Nine Beautiful Names of God: al-Maqṣad al-asnā fī sharḥ asmāʾ Allāh al-ḥusnā*. Translated with notes by David B. Burrell and Nazih Daher. Cambridge: The Islamic Texts Society, 1992.

Gimaret, Daniel. *Les noms divins en Islam: exégèse lexicographique et théologique*. Paris: Cerf, 1988.

Helminski, Camille Hamilton Adams. *Ninety-Nine Names of the Beloved: Intimations of the Beauty and Power of the Divine*. Escondido, CA: Sweet Lady Press, 2017.

Helwa, A. *Secrets of Divine Love: A Spiritual Journey into the Heart of Islam*. Capistrano Beach, CA: Naulit Publishing, 2020.

Ibrahim, Celene. *Islam and Monotheism*. Cambridge Elements in Religion and Monotheism. New York: Cambridge University Press, 2022.

———. 'Preface'. In *One Nation, Indivisible: Seeking Liberty and Justice from the Pulpit to the Streets*, edited by Celene Ibrahim, xxix–xlii. Eugene, OR: Wipf and Stock Publishers, 2019.

———. 'Simulation-Based Pedagogy for Interreligious Literacy: Critical Thinking Exercises for Teens and Young Adults'. In *Georgetown Companion to Interreligious Studies*, edited by Lucinda Mosher, 396–407. Washington, DC: Georgetown University Press, 2022.

———. '*Sūrat al-ʿAlaq* and Dispositions for Interreligious Engagement'. In *Words to Live By: Sacred Sources for Interreligious Engagement*, edited by Or Rose, Homayra Zaid, and Soren Hessler, 82–92. Maryknoll, NY: Orbis, 2018.

———. *Women and Gender in the Qur'an*. New York: Oxford University Press, 2020.

Ibrahim-Lizzio, Celene, and Teresa Soto González. 'Al-Asmā' al-Ḥusnā (Allah's Most Beautiful Names)'. In *Islam: A Worldwide Encyclopedia*, edited by Cenap Cakmak, 98–101. Santa Barbara, CA: ABC-CLIO, 2017.

Izutzu, Toshihiko. *Sufism and Taoism: A Comparative Study of Key Philosophical Concepts*. Berkeley: University of California Press, 1983.

Jain, Andrea R. *Peace Love Yoga: The Politics of Global Spirituality*. New York: Oxford University Press, 2020.

Kaskas, Safi, and David Hungerford. *The Qur'an with References to the Bible: A Contemporary Understanding*. Fairfax: Bridges of Reconciliation, 2016.

Lawson, Todd. *Being Human: Baha'i Perspectives on Islam, Modernity, and Peace*. Studies in the Bábí and Bahá'í Religions. Los Angeles: Kalimát Press, 2020.

Miller, Michael T. *The Name of God in Jewish Thought: A Philosophical Analysis of Mystical Traditions from Apocalyptic to Kabbalah*. New York: Routledge, 2016.

Mosher, Lucinda, ed. *The Georgetown Companion to Interreligious Studies*. Washington, DC: Georgetown University Press, 2022.

Murad, Munjed M. 'Inner and Outer Nature: An Islamic Perspective on the Environmental Crisis'. *Journal of Islam and Science* 10, no. 2 (2013): 117–37.

Murata, Sachiko. *The Tao of Islam: A Sourcebook on Gender Relationships in Islamic Thought*. Albany: State University of New York, 1992.

Murata, Sachiko, William C. Chittick, and Tu Weiming. *The Sage Learning of Liu Zhi: Islamic Thought in Confucian Terms*. Cambridge, MA: Harvard University Press, 2009.

Nair, Shankar. *Translating Wisdom: Hindu–Muslim Intellectual Interactions in Early Modern South Asia*. Oakland: University of California Press, 2020.

Nasr, Seyyed Hossein, Caner K. Dagli, Maria Massi Dakake, Joseph E. B. Lumbard, and Mohammed Rustom, eds. *The Study Quran: A New Translation and Commentary*. San Francisco: HarperOne, 2015.

Nguyen, Martin. *Modern Muslim Theology: Engaging God and the World with Faith and Imagination*. Lanham, MD: Roman & Littlefield, 2019.

Ogunnaike, Oludamini. *Deep Knowledge: Ways of Knowing in Sufism and Ifa, Two West African Intellectual Traditions*. University Park: Penn State University Press, 2020.

Ogunnaike, Oludamini, and Mohammed Rustom. 'Islam in English'. *American Journal of Islamic Social Sciences* 36, no. 2 (2016): 102–13.

Peace, Jennifer Howe. 'Responses to Sameness and Difference'. In *Deep Understanding for Divisive Times: Essays in Celebration of Ten Years of the Journal of Interreligious Studies*, edited by Mary Elizabeth Moore, Lucinda Mosher, Or Rose, and Axel Takacs, 6–11. Newton Centre, MA: Interreligious Studies Press, 2020.

Penn, Michael Philip. *Envisioning Islam: Syriac Christians and the Early Muslim World*. Philadelphia: University of Pennsylvania Press, 2015.

Rahemtulla, Shadaab. 'Decolonising Islam: Indigenous Peoples, Muslim Communities, and the Canadian Context'. *Religions* 14, no. 9 (2023): 1–19.

al-Rawi, Rosina-Fawzia. *Divine Names: The 99 Healing Names of the One Love.* Translated by Monique Arav. Calligraphy by Majed Seif. Northampton, MA: Olive Branch Press, 2015.

Rose, Or N. 'Jewish Mystical Resources for Interreligious Engagement: A Practitioner's Perspective'. In *The Georgetown Companion to Interreligious Studies*, edited by Lucinda Mosher, 308–16. Washington, DC: Georgetown University Press, 2022.

al-Ṣadūq, [Abū al-Ḥasan ʿAlī b. al-Ḥusayn b. Mūsā b. Bābawayh al-Qummī]. *The Book of Divine Unity* (*Kitāb al-tawḥīd*). Commentary by Ḥāshim al-Ḥusaynī al-Ṭihrānī. Translated by Ali Adam. Edited by Michal Mumisa and Mahmood Dhalla. Birmingham: Al-Mahdi Institute, 2013.

Shah-Kazemi, Reza, and Hamza Yusuf. *Common Ground between Islam and Buddhism.* Louisville: Fons Vitae, 2010.

Shahzad, Qaiser. 'Playing God and the Ethics of Divine Names: An Islamic Paradigm for Biomedical Ethics'. *Bioethics* 21, no. 8 (2007): 413–18.

Shaikh, Hafeez. '99 Names of Allah'. Accessed July 19, 2023. www.arthafez.com.

Shaikh, Sa'diyya. 'In Search of *al-Insān*: Sufism, Islamic Law, and Gender'. *Journal of the American Academy of Religion* 77, no. 4 (2009): 781–822.

Sirry, Mun'im. *Scriptural Polemics: The Qur'ān and Other Religions.* New York: Oxford University Press, 2014.

Tareen, SherAli. *Perilous Intimacies: Debating Hindu–Muslim Friendship after Empire.* Foreword by Faisal Devji. New York: Columbia University Press, 2023.

Yamamoto, Naoki. 'Muslim Scholars in Japan: Contemplating Islam in a Non-Muslim Society'. Traversing Tradition, 21 November 2022. https://traversingtradition.com/2022/11/21/muslim-scholars-in-japan-contemplating-islam-in-a-non-muslim-society/.

Yusuf, Imtiyaz. 'Building Muslim–Buddhist Understanding: The Parallels of *Taqwa*/Allah Consciousness in the Qur'an and *Satipatthana*/Mindfulness in *Anapanasati Sutta*'. In *Overcoming Orientalism: Essays in Honor of John L. Esposito*, edited by Tamara Sonn, 173–90. New York: Oxford University Press, 2021.

# God as a Moral Agent: An Inquiry into the Nature of Divine Agency

*Abolghasem Fanaei*[1]

## 1. Introduction

The question of divine nature, attributes, will, and actions is one of the most significant issues in mysticism, philosophy of religion, theology, religious ethics, and religious legal theory and jurisprudence.[2] Apart from the theoretical importance of this question for scholars, the conception that believers have of divine essence, attributes, and the foundations of divine conduct, around which they organise their individual and collective lives, profoundly impacts their way of life, and plays an important role in their religious knowledge and practice.[3] This is because practical theology is shaped by theoretical theology.[4] A believer's actual conception of God, embodied in his or her way of life, affects their character and moral development; and shapes their interaction with God, fellow people, and other creatures.

This influence upon the believer's identity and character is so profound that one can say: 'Tell me which God you worship so that I can tell you who you are.'[5] God is the supreme exemplar for believers, but each believer may have his or her own conception of God which acts as a lens through which God is known and worshipped. In adopting a particular conception of God, we are in fact choosing a role model for how to live, that is, how to think, feel, and behave. Worshipping is akin to loving, as both cultivate the attributes of the object of devotion within the devotee. Thus, in worshipping a deity, one effectively venerates the traits and qualities that motivated worship in the first place. Consequently, those attributes flow into, and manifest within, the worshipper. Furthermore, different

1 I would like to express my gratitude to the organisers of the Islamic Perspectives on God and (Other) Monotheism(s) Workshop held at Al-Mahdi Institute on 20–21 February 2023. I thank the workshop convener, Dr Wahid Amin, and the committee members for providing me the opportunity to present this research and receive valuable feedback. I am also thankful to my colleagues Wahid M. Amin and Riaz Walji for their thoughtful comments and suggestions, which have helped improve the article.

2 As we will see later, this question is deeply related to the unity of God (*tawḥīd*), which is the first principle of monotheistic religions. Divine unity is so fundamental that the validity of our understanding of other religious teachings depends on their alignment with this principle. Our conception of divine agency is no exception to this rule.

3 I will discuss the role of theology in religious jurisprudence (*ijtihād*) in more detail later. Here it suffices to note that the specific presupposition that religious jurisprudents have in the back of their minds about the nature of God influences the form and content of their legal inference.

4 Theoretical theology focuses on articulating and justifying religious beliefs about the theoretical side of religious life. It deals with abstract religious ideas and doctrines. Practical theology, in contrast, focuses on articulating and justifying religious beliefs related to religious practice. This includes areas like religious ethics, religious law, religious education, and other aspects of how religion is applied in daily life.

5 Worship should not be viewed solely as gaining theoretical knowledge about what is being worshipped. Worship is a type of practice that, if repeated often enough, can transform the personality and character of the worshipper.

conceptions of God can play a significant role in social life, having a positive or negative influence on the establishment of social justice and tolerance towards dissenters.

Theistic religions are God-centric in both theory and practice, that is, the God of theism is more than just the origin of existence. He also bestows meaning, radiance, and warmth to life,[6] and is the focal point (*qibla*) for believers in their practice.[7] Within these faiths, the ultimate concern of life is to become God-like, by cultivating divine virtues within oneself,[8] taking on the divine's colour and scent,[9] seeking His closeness,[10] reorienting to Him,[11] attaining preparedness to behold Him,[12] and ultimately reunion with Him[13] as the final destination of a life-long journey.[14] This is the goal for which humans were created.

Across cultures, people share a common, broad *concept* of God, facilitating fruitful dialogue about the nature of God and His existence, attributes, will, creation, and legislation. Yet, despite this shared foundation, particular *conceptions* of God differ markedly between groups and individuals.[15] Although monotheistic religions agree upon the unity of God, adherents of these religions diverge significantly in their conceptions of the nature of God and His unity and uniqueness, leading to a set of deep theoretical and practical differences. As we shall see later, there is a close link between theoretical and practical theology. Everyone sees and hence worships God through the lens of the attributes that are embedded in their conception of God. In fact, worshipping God is worshipping a combination of His attributes, which leads to the formation and growth

6 'Allah is the Light of the heavens and the earth' (Q. 24:35).

7 Stewart Goetz, 'The Meaning of Life', in *The Routledge Companion to Theism*, ed. Charles Taliaferro, Victoria S. Harrison, and Stewart Goetz (New York: Routledge, 2012), 720–31. 'Say, "Indeed my prayer and my worship, my life, and my death are for the sake of God, the Lord of all the worlds"' (Q. 6:162).

8 'Acquire divine virtues'. Muḥammad Bāqir Majlisī, *Biḥār al-anwār* (Beirut: Mu'assasat al-Wafā', 1982), 58:129, *ḥadīth* no. 254283.

9 '[Take on] the colour of God! And whose dye is better than God's? And we are His worshippers' (Q. 2:138).

10 'Neither your possessions nor your children will bring you close to Us, except whoever has faith and does righteous deeds, so they will have a double reward for what they did, and they will be secure in lofty chambers' (Q. 34:37).

11 'O you who have faith! Repent to God with sincere repentance' (Q. 66:8).

12 '[Some] faces on that Day will be radiant, looking at their Lord' (Q. 75:22–23).

13 'O man! You are striving toward your Lord laboriously, and you will meet Him' (Q. 84:6); 'And be conscious of God and know that you shall meet Him' (Q. 2:223); 'Those who deny meeting God have certainly lost' (Q. 6:31); 'Then We gave Moses the Book, perfect for the one who is virtuous and elaborating everything, and as a guidance and mercy, so that they may believe in the encounter with their Lord' (Q. 6:154). See also Q. 2:46, 2:249, 10:7, 10:11, 10:15, 10:45, 11:29, 13:2, 18:105, 18:110, 25:21, 29:5, 29:23, 30:8, 32:10, 32:23, 41:54.

14 'And that to your Lord is the final destiny' (Q. 53:42); 'Say, "Indeed my prayer and my worship, my life, and my death are for the sake of God, the Lord of all the worlds"' (Q. 6:162).

15 The distinction between 'brief notion' and 'detailed notion' has precedent both in classical Islamic philosophy and Western philosophy. For example, in classical Islamic logic, this distinction was used to respond to the problem of vicious circularity in real/essential definitions. See Maḥmūd Shahābī, *Rahbar-e kherad* (Tehran: Ketābkhāna-ye Khayyām, 1960), 114–17. For two similar examples of the distinction framed as the difference between 'concept' and 'conception' in Western philosophy, see John Rawls, *A Theory of Justice*, rev. ed. (Cambridge, MA: Harvard University Press, 1999); Ronald Dworkin, *Law's Empire* (Cambridge, MA: Harvard University Press, 1986), esp. 71–72, 74.

of those attributes in the worshipper.[16] Therefore, it is more accurate to speak of religious *ways* of life. In what follows I will elaborate on two competing religious ways of life, each of which has been shaped around a particular conception of God as an agent. The first conceives God as a moral agent while the second conceives Him as a non-moral agent.[17]

Each of these two perspectives on the nature of divine agency underpins associated forms of spirituality with their attendant ramifications. This study illuminates how fundamental assumptions about divine agency shape theoretical and practical theology. Examining these assumptions reveals how conceptions of God as a moral or non-moral agent yields divergent religious ways of life.

This article argues that envisioning God as a moral agent is the accurate theological conception, while the rival conception is flawed. Admittedly, literal readings of religious scripture can provide support for each of these two perspectives. Thus, irreconcilable contradictions within the texts emerge that cannot be settled by scriptural reference alone. However, by considering external evidence and arguments, the conception of God as an agent bound by moral requirements proves more plausible and compelling. While scriptural interpretation alone fails to reconcile conflicting passages, philosophical reasoning and experiential insights assist in evaluating these two conceptions of divine agency. The conception of God as a moral agent coheres better with our wider web of knowledge. A moral conception of divine agency withstands rational scrutiny through corroborating external and internal (scriptural) evidence which is otherwise unavailable.

This research investigates two central questions:

(1) Is God a moral[18] agent? That is, does God have a moral nature? Is God, like humans, subject to moral obligations? Are divine essence, attributes, will, and actions morally assessable?

(2) If so, is divine morality the same as human morality, or does it differ in some way? For example, are acts like murder and injustice as morally wrong when committed by God as they are when committed by humans? Or do they hold a different moral status or lack any moral status at all when committed by God? The issue is whether divine morality and human morality are identical or if they

16 Divine attributes are identical to God's essence. Therefore, worshipping divine attributes cannot be separated from worshipping Him. To separate divine attributes from His essence would be a form of polytheism (*shirk*). However, there seems to be conflict between divine morally neutral attributes, such as power, ownership, and sovereignty, and His moral attributes, such as justice, benevolence, mercifulness, and forgiveness, if these are viewed as absolute. Therefore, believers should reconcile this conflict by accepting that one set of His attributes overrides or limits the other. In this way, they avoid logical contradiction in their conception of divine attributes. How believers reconcile this conflict will have a major impact on what they are worshipping.

17 By 'non-moral agent', I mean an agent who is not only beyond moral evaluation but also whose will or command is the source of moral norms and values.

18 Throughout this article, I use 'morality' to refer to morality itself, and 'ethics' to refer to the branch of philosophy concerned with studying morality and its foundations.

diverge partially or completely.

This second question can also be framed as a question about the scope of morally responsible agency. Is the bearer of moral responsibility the human qua human or the rational free agent qua rational free agent? It further relates to the relationship between religion and morality, specifically God's connection to morality, and the compatibility of divine *moral* attributes like justice and benevolence with His *non-moral*[19] attributes like omnipotence, ownership, and authority.

The dispute over the nature of divine agency is closely related to the principle of divine unity (*tawḥīd*) as one of the most fundamental divine attributes in monotheistic religions. The principle of divine unity is not just a theoretical doctrine according to which there is only one God and He is the ultimate and unique origin of existence. In fact, it has many further theoretical and practical implications. Therefore, those who regard God as a moral agent are under pressure to show that their position is compatible with the unity of God. In fact, as we shall see later, some of the arguments that are presented to reject this conception of divine agency are based on the claim that this position leads to polytheism (*shirk*) and hence should be rejected for the sake of preserving the unity of God.

## 2. The Nature of Divine Creation: Personal vs Impersonal Explanation

Conceptions of God can be primarily organised under two major categories: God as an agent verses God as a mere cause. Therefore, one of the preliminary questions in this research is whether God is an agent. If so, what does it mean for God to be an agent and how is this possible? Can one provide a rational explanation of divine agency, or is attributing agency to God merely a metaphorical ascription that projects human qualities, as an anthropomorphic construction, onto a formless God? If this is the case, then the true definition of God should glorify Him by negating such an attribute (negative theology).

Many Muslim thinkers, including mystics, philosophers, and theologians, agree that God is the 'Creator' (*al-khāliq*), although they differ in explaining how divine creativity should be accounted for. The divine act of creation can be explained in at least two ways: one is in terms of a kind of 'causal' relationship between God and the creation, in which God is not an agent, similar to the relationship found in natural processes between two things. Let us call this 'impersonal explanation'.[20] Such a relationship is necessary regardless of divine will and hence seems incompatible with divine free will and divine

19 By 'non-moral attributes of God', I mean those divine attributes that are morally neutral, in the sense that they do not imply any moral meaning. God is devoid of immoral attributes, but His attributes are divided into moral and non-moral.

20 Some standard philosophical arguments made for the existence of God, such as the argument from motion or the necessity/contingency argument, assume such a model of divine creativity. Many philosophers call God the 'First Cause' or 'Prime Mover'.

agency. The second way to explain divine creativity is to elucidate it in terms of another kind of causality that is there between an agent and his or her voluntary act. One may term this 'personal explanation'. Accordingly, creation is a voluntary act stemming from a decision made by God as an agent who has free will.[21]

Personhood or personality is an essential component for agency, but attributing personhood or personality to God seems at odds with divine transcendence and absolute otherness as understood by some traditional philosophers and theologians. Resolving this tension requires re-examining metaphysical assumptions about whether divine transcendence precludes personhood and agential qualities. The mystics, however, show in a plausible way that there is no such tension, and that God can be simultaneously transcendent and immanent, impersonal and personal. The God of mysticism, therefore, can be a rational and autonomous agent, albeit at the level of divine manifestations, which is different from the level of divine essence, which is transcendent.[22]

In any case, my assumption in this article is that being a person and hence being an agent are real attributes of God Himself that are predicated of Him in the literal sense of the word. I contend that when an action is attributed to God in the scripture, the real agent is God Himself who has manifested Himself as an agent in that situation,[23] not that someone else performs an action and that action is metaphorically attributed to God. In short, manifestations of God are different from projections of the human mind onto God.

Divine personhood is a prerequisite for divine agency, which enables meaningful moral evaluation of divine character and actions and provides justification for attributing moral properties to God. Only within this framework can (1) divine moral virtues

21 The point is to distinguish two forms of causality and hence two forms of explanations. In the first form, A created B by operating under a pre-existing causal law which is necessarily imposed upon A in such a way that A has no choice in creating or not creating B. This is what I call 'impersonal explanation', in which A is not an agent who has free will. In the second form of explanation, however, A is an agent who freely decided to create B. I call this kind of explanation 'personal explanation', because for A to be an agent in this sense A should be a person or has personality. The term 'personal explanation' is borrowed from Richard Swinburne's *The Existence of God* (Oxford: Clarendon Press, 2004), and *Is There a God?*, rev. ed. (Oxford: Oxford University Press, 2010). In his explication of creation, Swinburne delineates a distinction between personal and causal explanations, positing that the former, wherein God assumes the role of agent rather than cause, constitutes the apposite elucidation of creation. However, a more nuanced approach necessitates the differentiation between two categories of causes or causality. While every agent can be classified as a cause, the converse does not hold true. Consequently, causal explanations can be bifurcated into personal and impersonal variants. With respect to the divine, it is prudent to assert that God embodies both cause and agent, signifying that His causality is fundamentally agential in nature.

22 William C. Chittick, *The Self-Disclosure of God: Principles of Ibn al-ʿArabī's Cosmology* (Albany: State University of New York Press, 1997); William C. Chittick, *The Sufi Doctrine of Rumi* (Bloomington: World Wisdom, 2005); Ismail Lala, *Knowing God: Ibn ʿArabī and ʿAbd al-Razzāq al-Qāshānī's* Metaphysics of the Divine (Leiden: Brill, 2019).

23 Divine manifestation and theophany in the form of an active person or persons, such as angels, prophets, believers, and other things, as referred to in Q. 17:8 and other verses, corresponds to the annihilation of that person or persons in God.

be substantive; (2) worshipping and obeying divine commands be morally warranted;[24] (3) supplication, prayer, and communion with God be perfectly meaningful; and (4) divine revelation become possible. If none of the attributes predicated of God are real (radical negative theology), or if His anthropomorphic attributes, including moral ones, are denied as metaphorical (moderate negative theology), then many fundamental theistic teachings, such as divine communication with humans, worship, prayer, the enlightening and heartwarming presence of God in the natural world and human life, and establishing a personal relationship with Him would become utterly meaningless and logically incoherent.

Exclusively transcendent theology strives to uphold divine otherness, but denying the realistic account of divine moral attributes deprives human beings of having a meaningful relationship with God. A choice thus emerges between a meaningful relationship with an engaging God and preserving divine absolute otherness at the expense of meaningful worship.

## 3. The Relation of God to Morality

The relation between God and morality has a long history, as shown by the rich literature from theology and philosophy on this question.[25] It has preoccupied the minds of scholars since antiquity, as illustrated in Plato's *Euthyphro* dialogue, where Socrates asks his interlocutor whether piety is loved by the gods because it is inherently pious, or whether it is pious merely because the gods happen to love it.[26] The Socratic question was later called the 'Euthyphro dilemma' and has been much discussed. The debate continues between those who ground morality in the factual/real (but non-existent) nature of things and those who ground it in divine command or sovereign will.

Both horns of the dilemma presume that God is an agent, yet they diverge on the nature of divine agency. The latter depicts God as a non-moral agent with an arbitrary, whimsical will, lacking standards, and being beyond morality as the source of moral values and obligations. The former, on the other hand, envisions God as a *moral* agent subordinate to, and bound by, objective, independent moral principles prior to His will and commands. These two conceptions vary based on whether the divine agency is non-moral, or moral in nature. In the following sections, I will expand upon each conception in turn.

---

24 Alasdair MacIntyre, 'Which God Ought We to Obey and Why?', *Faith and Philosophy* 3, no. 4 (1986): 359–71.

25 John Hare, 'Religion and Morality', *Stanford Encyclopedia of Philosophy*, 27 September 2006, rev. 8 August 2019, https://plato.stanford.edu/entries/religion-morality/.

26 Plato, *Five Dialogues*, trans. G. M. A. Grube (Indianapolis: Hackett, 1981), 10a.

## 4. God as a Non-Moral Agent

A non-moral agent is someone whose will (or command for that matter) is not constrained by any objective and independent normative criteria. Rather, his will itself constitutes the ultimate source for all values and norms, including moral values and norms.[27] In Islamic culture, the early Ashʿarīs[28] and in Western culture some prominent Christian philosophers and theologians, such as Augustine, William of Ockham, and Kierkegaard, have defended such a view.[29]

According to this view, divine will is absolute, in the sense that it is not constrained by any norms. Not only is God omnipotent with no ontological limits on His will,[30] but He is also free from any normative restrictions on His right to exercise His will. Thus, the ideas of divine moral obligations towards His creatures or His creatures' moral rights in relation to Him are absurd. God is unfettered even from the obligation to honour His own promises. His will represents an unconstrained freedom from all moral and non-moral (normative) standards.[31]

In other words, according to this conception of divine agency, God possesses only natural rights without any natural obligations. His rights stem from His non-moral attributes, that is, His absolute power and ownership, not from His moral attributes. Not even God can bind Himself by obligations. All values and norms, including moral

---

27 For a comparison of different views on the source of normativity, see Christine M. Korsgaard, *The Sources of Normativity*, ed. Onora O'Neill (Cambridge: Cambridge University Press, 1996). The non-moral conception of divine agency is the basis for the classical reading of the divine command theory in meta-ethics, which itself can be interpreted or formulated in various ways. For an examination and critique of diverse readings of the divine command theory, see Abolghasem Fanāeī, *Din dar tarāzūy-e akhlagh: paghuheshi dar bab-e nesbat-e akhlagh-e dini wa akhlagh-e secular* (Tehran: Intishārāt-e Ṣerāt, 2016); Abolghasem Fanāeī, *Akhlaq-e din shenāsi: paghūheshi dar bab-e mabāni-ye akhlaghi wa maʿrefat shenāsi-ye fiqh* (Tehran: Intishārāt-e Negāh-e Moāṣer, 2020).

28 Abū al-Ḥasan al-Ashʿarī, *al-Lumaʿ fī al-radd ʿalā ahl al-zaygh wa-l-bidaʿ* (Abu Dhabi: Majlis Ḥukamāʾ al-Muslimīn, 2022), 270–77; Abū Bakr al-Bāqillānī, *al-Inṣāf fīmā yajibu iʿtiqāduhu wa-lā yajūzu al-jahl bihi* (Cairo: al-Maktaba al-Azhariyya li-l-Turāth, 2000), 150; George F. Hourani, 'Two Theories of Value in Medieval Islam', *The Muslim World* 50, no. 4 (1960): 269–78.

29 Michael W. Austin, 'Divine Command Theory', *Internet Encyclopedia of Philosophy*, https://iep.utm.edu/divine-command-theory/; Mark Murphy, 'Theological Voluntarism', *Stanford Encyclopedia of Philosophy*, 2 July 2002, rev. 4 June 2019, https://plato.stanford.edu/entries/voluntarism-theological/; Michael J. Harris, *Divine Command Ethics: Jewish and Christian Perspectives* (London: Routledge, 2003). Wittgenstein, likewise, considers an interpretation of the nature of good according to which 'the good is good because God willed it' to be deeper and more acceptable than its rival interpretation that 'God willed the good because the good is good in itself'. Allan Janik and Stephen Toulmin, *Wittgenstein's Vienna* (New York: Simon and Schuster, 1973), 194.

30 By 'ontological limit', I mean a kind of limit that is imposed upon the will of an agent by causal laws. It does not include 'logical limits' expressed in terms of logical principles, such as the principle of non-contradiction.

31 al-Ashʿarī, *al-Lumaʿ*, 268. Regarding divine fulfilment of God's promises, see Q. 2:80, 9:111. For Muʿtazilīs' critiques of the divine command theory, see Hashem Morvarid, 'The Muʿtazila's Arguments against Divine Command Theory', *Religious Studies* 58, no. 3 (2021): 610–27; George F. Hourani, *Reason and Tradition in Islamic Ethics* (Cambridge: Cambridge University Press, 2007); Fanāeī, *Din dar tarāzūy-e akhlagh*; Fanāeī, *Akhlaq-e din shenāsi*.

ones, stem from divine legislative will. But only humans are bound by these values and norms; they do not apply to God. Hence, divine construction of values and norms does not limit God's ontological or legislative freedom or His right to revise them arbitrarily.[32]

Therefore, God can prohibit humans from lying, deceiving, or killing, yet commit these acts Himself without violating any prohibition.[33] God also has the right to command humans to lie, deceive, and kill, and issuing such commands is not morally wrong for God. Since, *metaphysically* His will or commands constitute moral standards, *epistemically* there is no independent criterion for the moral evaluation of His will or commands.

## 4.1 The Arguments for the Conception of God as a Non-Moral Agent

The conception of God as a non-moral agent can be argued for in two ways: either through rational arguments analysing the nature of God and prioritising His non-moral attributes over moral ones, or through scriptural arguments based on literal readings of sacred texts. In what follows, I will confine myself to some of the rational arguments.

### 4.1.1 *The Argument from Divine Ownership*

This argument holds that divine ownership is absolute, in the sense that God owns human beings as His possessions. Therefore, the acts or commands that are directed by God at human beings are the acts of an owner exploiting what he owns, based on the natural rights of ownership.[34] Therefore, if God sends prophets and saints to hell and Satan and criminals to heaven, or punishes an innocent child in the afterlife, or permits people to torture an innocent child just for entertainment, this would not be morally wrong, neither for God nor for people acting on His permission/command.[35]

### 4.1.2 *The Argument Based on the Right to Issue Commands*

According to this argument, an act could be morally wrong for two reasons: either for being an instance of occupying another's property without permission, or of disobeying someone who has the right to be obeyed. However, 'God is not the property of someone else, nor is He subject to the authority of another ruler. Therefore, no act [or command

---

32 al-Ashʿarī, *al-Lumaʿ*, 269; al-Bāqillānī, *al-Inṣāf*, 46–47.

33 al-Ashʿarī, *al-Lumaʿ*, 269–78, tries to omit lying from this list. In his view, God cannot be described as a liar, not because lying is morally bad, and God does not lie because it is morally bad, and therefore He has a moral reason to avoid lying, but because God is unable to lie. To him, lying is like ignorance. Just as God cannot be ignorant because knowledge is part of His essence, He cannot lie because truthfulness is part of His essence. But one may ask: first, on what criterion is truthfulness considered part of divine essential attributes while justice is not? Second, if God is unable to lie, and thus *voluntarily* tell the truth, then how can truthfulness be attributed to God as a moral virtue and a kind of perfection?

34 al-Ashʿarī, *al-Lumaʿ*, 269.

35 Ibid., 268; Hourani, *Reason and Tradition*, 145.

for that matter] issues from Him that is bad or wrong.'[36]

### 4.1.3 *The Argument from Sovereignty*

This argument holds that divine sovereignty is *absolute*, so we cannot imagine a divine command that oversteps that authority, even if it contravenes our human understanding of moral norms and values.

### 4.1.4 *The Argument from the Dependency of Norms on a Norm-Maker*

Norms require a norm-maker, in the same way in which positive laws require a lawgiver who has authority over those who are obligated to obey his commands.[37] Therefore, the existence of independent moral standards contradicts the nature of divinity itself. The *existence* of an independent norm prior to divine will or command, especially if God Himself is obliged to follow that norm, entails polytheism; that is, it entails the existence of another god superior to the God we humans are supposed to obey; and this is incompatible with divine unity.

### 4.1.5 *The Argument from the Existence of Moral Properties*

God is the sole origin of existence. Therefore, claiming that moral properties *exist* independently of divine will implies polytheism—another god beyond God. But a god surpassed by a higher god cannot truly be God.[38]

### 4.1.6 *The Argument from the Limitation of Human Practical Reason*

According to the dominant view among rationalist Muslim scholars, moral obligations are commands of practical reason, and hence they cannot encompass God as their subject. This is because human practical reason has neither the right nor capacity to obligate God. At most, human reason has authority over humans themselves, not over God. God has no duty to obey human reason.

### 4.1.7 *The Argument from the Dependency of Moral Command on Authority*

A 'command' denotes a relational concept that presupposes the existence of two persons: the one who commands and the one who obeys. For a command to be binding, the commander must have the right to command (right to be obeyed), and the addressee must have the duty to obey that command. Thus, (1) the commander and the one commanded

36 al-Ashʿarī, *al-Lumaʿ*, 269; al-Bāqillānī, *al-Inṣāf*, 47.

37 al-Ashʿarī, *al-Lumaʿ*, 269; al-Bāqillānī, *al-Inṣāf*, 46–47.

38 In other words, if moral properties exist, they are either necessary beings or contingent beings. If they are necessary beings, their existence beyond God's existence would directly imply polytheism. But if they are contingent beings, they would need a necessary being to create them, which is, by hypothesis, other than God. Therefore, in this hypothesis too, affirming the existence of moral properties independent of, and prior to, divine will indirectly implies polytheism.

cannot be identical and (2) the commander must be superior to the one commanded. Therefore, (3) humans cannot command God, (4) nor can God command Himself; (5) moral duties are divine commands to humans; (6) these commands do not apply to God, and finally, (7) God has no moral duty.

In conclusion, these arguments support the classical version of divine command theory, according to which, morality is totally subordinate to divine will/commands, and hence God is free from moral constraints.[39] Divine will/command can make any act moral or immoral, because acts lack a positive or negative moral quality in themselves or due to their consequences. In short, divine command is the unique morally good-making and bad-making, and morally right-making and wrong-making, property.

### 4.2 Critique of the Arguments Supporting the Conception of God as a Non-Moral Agent

In the previous subsection, I presented seven rational arguments in favour of conceiving God as a non-moral agent. In this subsection, I will critique these arguments in turn and demonstrate why, in my view, they are false.

#### 4.2.1 *The Argument from Divine Ownership*

'Ownership' and 'ownership rights' are not the same thing; the former can be absolute, while the latter are limited. Thus, owning something absolutely does not mean having absolute rights over it. It is true that divine ownership is absolute, meaning that God owns everything including human bodies, souls, and possessions. But His *right* of ownership is not absolute, in the sense that this right is surrounded by other moral considerations such as justice. Therefore, there are some moral principles that God would not violate when dealing with what He owns.[40] This is because ownership rights themselves are moral/natural rights; they depend not on the power to exploit, but on moral considerations. Therefore, the range and limits of ownership rights are determined by morality, not by ownership itself. An owner has not only rights but also duties towards what he owns. Like any other owner, divine interaction with what He owns is subject to moral evaluation. Of course, since

39 The literature discussing the divine command theory is very rich. Throughout its long and turbulent history, this theory has been reformed; and proponents of reformed readings have tried to reconstruct it in ways that do not entail some of the unacceptable implications of the classical reading. For some contemporary reformed readings of this theory, see Philip L. Quinn, 'The Recent Revival of Divine Command Ethics', *Philosophy and Phenomenological Research* 50 (1990): 345–651; Robert Merrihew Adams, *Finite and Infinite Goods: A Framework for Ethics* (New York: Oxford University Press, 2002).

40 This is not to beg the question. The point is to illustrate that since property rights are natural/moral rights, substantiating the scope of these rights demands more than exhibiting the extent of the power or capability of the property owner. This is because might does not make right. In other words, an owner's moral rights over his or her property are inherently circumscribed by pertinent moral principles, such as the principle of justice. Therefore, one cannot argue that the property rights of God are absolute merely because He is omnipotent and is capable of doing whatever He wants.

God has a moral nature, He will never break moral rules—that is, if He wants to exercise His rights, He will do it within the boundaries of morality. In other words, divine justice comes before divine ownership, and determines how God interacts with what He owns.[41]

#### 4.2.2 *The Argument Based on the Right to Issue Commands*

The right to issue commands does not rely on the commander owning the one who is commanded, nor does the duty to obey hinge on the one who is commanded being owned by the commander. Both commandment and obedience make perfect sense without assuming the master–slave relationship. Therefore, God does not have to be the slave of a master to have obligations. Of course, no one has the right to command God, and therefore, He is not subject to anyone else's command, but why does He, as a free, rational, and autonomous agent, not have the right to issue commands to Himself and then be subject to His own command?

#### 4.2.3 *The Argument from Sovereignty*

Divine sovereignty is not only legal and political but also moral. It gains significance within a broader framework of moral/natural rights and responsibilities. Therefore, divine sovereignty is not absolute or unbounded. It operates within certain moral limits. Importantly, though, these moral limitations are not externally imposed on God by some outside force or sovereignty. Rather, in exercising His sovereignty, God voluntarily restricts His own actions to align with moral principles. He possesses the raw power to violate moral laws, but actively chooses not to, as doing so would be incompatible with His moral integrity. While ontologically God has the power to transgress moral boundaries, He deliberately chooses not to, due to His own morally perfect nature.

#### 4.2.4 *The Argument from the Dependency of Norms on a Norm-Maker*

First, it is important to make the distinction between positive norms and natural norms, noting that only positive norms require a norm-maker. Hence, if one embraces the view that moral norms fall into the category of natural norms, one could claim that moral norms do not need a norm-maker. Second, even if one views moral laws as expressing positive norms, there is still no contradiction in the case of God, because, like any free, rational, and autonomous agent, God can serve as both the norm-maker and the one bound by the norms. Therefore, God is not bound by external restraints. Rather, He

41 It is clear that the argument from ownership and some subsequent arguments are based on moral premises concerning natural rights such as the rights of ownership or the right to be obeyed. If so, the validity of these arguments depends on presupposing that not only is morality independent from God's will and command but it is also prior to His will and command. Therefore, those who believe God is above morality can only resort to these arguments dialectically. Because if God is above morality, then moral rights, like moral duties, will originate from His will or command, and speaking of divine moral and natural right in this framework will become utterly meaningless.

chooses to abide by self-imposed moral guidelines. This means that God has the rational agency to decide to abide by certain principles, and then voluntarily constrains His own actions to align with those self-imposed principles. While God has the power to violate the moral boundaries He has decreed, He intentionally chooses not to do so. Therefore, even without an external authority imposing binding norms upon Him, God acts as His own lawgiver and upholds self-imposed moral guidelines, underscoring His moral integrity.[42]

As Kant elegantly explains, the lawgiver does not necessarily have to be separate from the subject bound by the law.[43] In fact, any rational, autonomous agent who wants to act rationally must make decisions and act according to rules they would be willing to universalise. In other words, a rational agent should only act in ways that could be made into general laws applicable to all rational beings qua rational beings. As a supremely rational and free agent, God is no exception to this higher-order principle of practical rationality. When God acts, He makes decisions based on moral laws He would be willing to universalise. Therefore, even without external imposition, God's own rational nature binds Him to moral laws, which He chooses not to transgress.[44]

#### 4.2.5 *The Argument from the Existence of Moral Properties*

For a property to have objective reality, its existence is not a necessary prerequisite. As al-Ṣadr states, 'the realm of facts extends beyond the realm of existences.'[45] Levin also notes, 'Objectivity is one thing, objects another; truths outnumber substances.'[46] For instance, contingent beings are characterised by contingency before they exist. So contingency is a real property that does not yet exist prior to the contingent being's actual existence. Whether currently existing or not, contingent things remain contingent. Therefore, their characterisation as contingent does not require their existence or the existence of contingency as a property. Similarly, mathematical facts like 'two plus two equals four' and true negative propositions like 'God's partner does not exist', pointing to a non-existent

42 In other cases, too, legislators are not exempt from the laws they establish. For example, members of parliament do not have the right to violate tax laws or traffic laws.

43 Immanuel Kant, *Groundwork of the Metaphysics of Morals*, Cambridge Texts in the History of Philosophy, ed. Mary Gregor (Cambridge: Cambridge University Press, 1998).

44 According to Kant, the subject of moral responsibility is not just the human qua human, but the rational being qua rational being. Human beings are morally responsible because they are rational. Therefore, moral responsibility revolves around rationality, not around humanity or human rationality. Of course, as we will see later, Kant believes that God does not need moral law (expressed in terms of moral principles) because His reason and will are so pure that He cannot be affected by the opposite immoral desires and inclinations, since God lacks such inclinations and desires. Unlike God, humans have such desires and inclinations, and thus moral considerations appear to them as categorical imperatives. Robert Johnson and Adam Cureton, 'Kant's Moral Philosophy', *Stanford Encyclopedia of Philosophy*, 23 February 2004, rev. 21 January 2022, https://plato.stanford.edu/entries/kant-moral/, §2.

45 Muḥammad Bāqir al-Ṣadr, *Buḥūth fī ʿilm al-uṣūl: mabāḥith al-ḥujaj wa-l-uṣūl al-ʿamaliyya*, ed. Ḥasan ʿAbd al-Sattār (Beirut: al-Dār al-Islāmiyya li-l-Ṭibāʿa wa-l-Nashr, 1996), 8:85.

46 Michael Levin, 'Understanding the Euthyphro Problem', *International Journal for Philosophy of Religion* 25, no. 2 (1989): 91.

state of affairs, describe a fact without requiring existence. These types of facts are real, but do not exist. They are beyond the domains of existence and non-existence.[47]

Now, in light of the distinction between having reality and existence, we can investigate the nature of moral attributes. But before continuing the discussion, it is necessary to pay attention to another distinction which plays an equally important role in the metaphysical explanation of moral attributes. Moral concepts are divided into *thin*—such as goodness, badness, rightness, and wrongness—and *thick*—such as justice, compassion, generosity, benevolence, and forgiveness.[48] While thick moral concepts refer to properties that have both reality and existence, thin moral concepts refer to properties that only have *reality* and do not have *existence*, neither as natural nor as supernatural qualities.[49]

On this basis, it can be said that since the attributes to which thin moral concepts refer do not have existence, they do not need a creator. The goodness of truth-telling and the badness of lying, for example, are attributes of those acts themselves, prior to their existence.[50] Therefore, they are real, but they do not exist.

However, the emergence of those moral properties signified by thick moral concepts, for example, moral virtues in people, does require a creator. Such moral properties are created by God—in fact they are manifestations of divine virtues. Nonetheless, the moral status of justice as good and virtuous does not require its existence or a creator. For justice to be considered good and a virtue, only the reality of justice, virtue, and goodness is required—not their existence. Therefore, the goodness of justice does not depend on divine (creative or legislative) will or command. 'Justice is a moral virtue' and 'justice is morally good' are akin to 'four is even'—the moral status follows directly

47 More precisely, 'non-existence' is a relational concept with two meanings: 'the negation of existence' and 'the negation of reality'. Therefore, when we say, 'everything that exists is real, but not everything real necessarily exists', we have not violated the self-evident principle of non-contradiction. According to this principle, 'A does not exist' contradicts 'A exists', not 'A is real'. The negation of 'A is real' is 'A is not real', not 'A does not exist'.

48 Simon Kirchin, 'Thick and Thin Concepts', *The International Encyclopedia of Ethics*, 29 June 2019, https://doi.org/10.1002/9781444367072.wbiee262.pub2.

49 This account of moral realism and the metaphysics of moral values has important implications. One of these implications is that, on the basis of such an account, the dispute among moral realists about whether moral facts are natural or non-natural, as well as their disagreement with moral anti-realists, is resolved appropriately. Moral properties do not exist, so one cannot meaningfully and reasonably ask whether, if these properties exist, they are natural or supernatural, and if they are natural, why they are queer, i.e. essentially different from other natural properties. J. L. Mackie, *Ethics: Inventing Right and Wrong* (London: Penguin Books, 1990). But their lack of existence does not entail a denial of their reality. Moral realism is not the claim that moral properties exist, but rather the claim that they are real. Entities are divided into natural and non-natural, but those realities that do not exist are neither natural nor non-natural.

50 The subject matter of moral judgements is not concepts existing in the human mind, but rather the instantiation of those concepts in the external world prior to their actual existence. For example, when we say, 'lying is bad', the subject matter of this judgement is the act of lying in the external world before its occurrence in that world, not the concept of lying. Therefore, the predicate of this judgement, i.e. badness, is also an attribute that is predicated of that subject matter in the external world; and since by hypothesis this judgement is true prior to the lying by moral agents, we must conclude that the universe of reality is broader than the universe of existence.

from the concept itself. Therefore, while God manifests virtues in creation, their moral goodness is inherent, not imposed by divine will or commands.

### 4.2.6 *The Argument from the Limitation of Human Practical Reason*

It is true that moral obligations represent judgements made by practical reason. However, practical reason is not exclusive to humans; it exists in any rational agent, including God. Mystically speaking, the human capacity for practical reason, which is a kind of perfection, is a manifestation of the divine practical reason, who is the source of all perfections. Therefore, when we make a statement such as 'keeping promises is obligatory for God', it is not an instance of human reason imposing duties upon God. Rather, it is an expression of God's own practical reason commanding Himself. The role of human reason here is to *discover* the judgements of divine practical reason, not to *issue* top-down commands from a position above God to God. In other words, moral obligations for God stem from His own innate practical reason, of which human practical reason is a limited manifestation. Human reason does not legislate God's duties but discerns the moral order already inherent in God's perfect rational nature.

The process of discovery unfolds as follows: first, human theoretical reason deduces the universal judgement of pure practical reason, shared by both God and human beings[51]—namely, that 'any rational, free agent who has made a promise is obligated to keep that promise'.[52] This judgement applies universally to all rational agents, not solely to humans. Next, by applying this universal judgement to God as a supremely rational, free agent, human theoretical reason concludes that God's own practical reason obligates Him to keep promises. In other words, through the use of theoretical reason, humans can recognise that divine practical reason necessarily entails certain moral judgements, including the judgement that promise-keeping is obligatory. Therefore, by way of rational examination, we *discover* that God's practical reason commands Him to abide by universal moral laws that are binding on all rational beings.

Hence, while God is not obligated to obey human reason, obeying the commands of His own practical reason raises no philosophical or theological issues and is fully compatible with His divinity. To say that divine will is subject to the commands of the divine's practical reason, or governed by His moral virtues, or that His practical reason directs His will and places normative restrictions on it, is entirely different from claiming that human reason restricts divine freedom and will. The former demonstrates God's rational self-consistency in adhering to the universal moral laws posited by His perfect

---

51 Pure practical reason has multiple instances. Its perfect instance is divine practical reason. Human practical reason is an imperfect instance of pure practical reason. In fact, practical reason in humans is a manifestation of divine practical reason, and this manifestation is limited. Therefore, human practical reason comes in degrees.

52 As Imām ʿAlī said: 'One who is asked for help is free until he promises.' Muḥammad al-Sharīf al-Raḍī, *Nahj al-balāgha* (Qom: Muʾassasat-e Anṣāriyān li-l-Ṭibāʿa wa-l-Nashr, 2006), 612 (no. 336).

practical reason. The latter, however, would improperly impose external constraints on divine agency. In summary, God choosing to obey the moral laws of His own practical reason upholds rather than diminishes His divine nature and sovereignty.[53]

### 4.2.7 *The Argument from the Dependency of Moral Command on Authority*

Both human and divine practical reason share a common rational source of normative self-legislation. The practical reason inherent in any rational, free, and autonomous agent has commanding authority over that agent. Therefore, just as human practical reason has the right to obligate humans to act in certain ways, divine practical reason also possesses authority over God Himself as a supremely rational being. Like any rational, free, and autonomous agent, God is a 'self-legislator' being and can impose moral duties on Himself, as the Qur'an affirms (see Q. 6:12, 6:54). Of course, in addition to divine authority over Himself, He also holds authority over humans—yet this authority is not absolute, since divine authority originates from His moral rights, and moral rights operate within a moral framework.[54] In other words, God freely chooses to exercise His authority over human beings in accordance with the moral laws intrinsic to His practical reason, not in an arbitrary manner.

## 5. God as a Moral Agent[55]

Simply defined, moral agents are those who *primarily* decide (and act) based on *moral* reasons for action, whether deontological or consequential.[56] Then, if morality is silent,

53 When deciding what to do, a free agent has no more than three options: (1) following the judgement of reason; (2) following their own inclinations and arbitrary will; and (3) following the will or inclination of someone else. The third option is ruled out regarding God, because it is incompatible with His very nature, or, in religious terms, it implies polytheism. Therefore, the disagreement between theists (Ashʿarīs and Muʿtazilīs) here is over the first two options. Now, if by 'judgement of reason' we mean the judgement of *human* practical reason, we cannot claim that God is obligated to obey the command of human practical reason. But if we mean the command of pure practical reason or divine practical reason, God's obeying the command of practical reason does not entail any unacceptable theological implication. On the contrary, if we do not accept this possibility, we have no choice but to accept the second option, which is incompatible with divine wisdom, justice, and moral nature. According to Kant, an agent who follows their own arbitrary inclinations or will is not autonomous. In other words, for Kant, heteronomy includes not only following the will of someone else but also following one's own inclinations. Andrews Reath, *Agency and Autonomy in Kant's Moral Theory: Selected Essays* (Oxford: Clarendon Press, 2006); Henry E. Allison, *Kant's Theory of Freedom* (Cambridge: Cambridge University Press, 1990); Kant, *Groundwork*.

54 As we shall see later, the boundedness or conditionality of divine ownership and authority is in the context of action, not essence. That is, like other divine attributes, these two attributes are absolute in themselves, but in the context of action, divine moral attributes restrict God's other attributes.

55 In Fanāeī, *Din dar tarāzūy-e akhlāq*, ch. 7, I have argued in favour of the idea that from a religious perspective, God can be seen as an ideal observer in the moral domain. Obviously, playing such a metaphysical and/or epistemic role requires God Himself to be a moral agent. In inviting others to live morally, the behaviour of the moral teacher is more effective than his speech (advice and exhortation), if not to say that the preaching of immoral advisors has an adverse effect.

56 'Deontological' refers to a type of theory in normative ethics that judges the moral status of an action

they make decisions and act based on *aesthetic* reasons or personal preferences grounded in taste or discretion. Hence, for a moral God, moral considerations constitute the fundamental framework for decision-making. Of utmost importance here is whether moral considerations are to be formulated as *moral norms* or *moral virtues*, as I will later address.

Note that the function of moral reasons as a *basis* differs from their function as a *framework*. Acting on the *basis* of moral reasons means that morality is the *source* of both justifying and motivating reasons for action, providing the entire rational justification and psychological motivation for the agent, as when I am honest just *because* it is my moral duty, not *because* honesty is the best policy.

However, sometimes morality has no clear stance on an action, granting permission through its silence. Here, moral agents have to decide based on non-moral, yet morally compatible, reasons for action, stemming from outside morality. The compatibility of the agent's decision and action with morality in these cases is not because their decision and action have *originated* from moral considerations, but because their decision and action do not *violate* moral considerations; that is, they are within the moral *framework*. These non-moral reasons could be pragmatic or personal preferences.

Therefore, a morally perfect God need not always act solely out of moral reasons, since morality sometimes lacks any action-guidance and remains silent. We term this silence 'moral permissibility'. Such a God is the agent whose actions would align with morality, contravening no moral considerations, whether originating from *moral* reasons or *morally permissible non-moral* reasons.[57]

## 6. Divine Agency and the Process of Decision-Making

Whether divine agency resembles human agency has sparked extensive theological and philosophical debate.[58] Before presenting my view, two preliminary issues warrant attention.

### 6.1 How to Reconcile Competing Approaches in Normative Ethics

Normative ethics features three dominant approaches: virtue ethics, duty-based ethics (deontology), and consequentialist ethics (utilitarianism). These are commonly deemed mutually exclusive. But personally, I am inclined to a particular combination

is not solely based on the goodness or badness of its consequences, but also, or solely, on its intrinsic morally relevant features.

57 One example that can be mentioned in this regard is divorce. A famous *ḥadīth* states: 'The most detestable of permissible things to God is divorce.' For a comprehensive analysis of the authenticity and content of this *ḥadīth*, see Mahdī Jalālī and Muḥammad Mahdī Ajiliān, 'Barresi-ye sanadi wa matni-ye ḥadīth-e abghaḍ al-ḥalāl ela Allāh al-ṭalaq', *Amouzehā-ye Ḥadithi* 1 (2017): 75–98.

58 William J. Abraham, *Divine Agency and Divine Action, Volume I: Exploring and Evaluating the Debate* (Oxford: Oxford University Press, 2018).

of these three approaches, such that in reconciling moral consequentialism and moral deontology, I subscribe to *the ethics of prima facie duties*, endorsing consequentialism within the framework of deontology. According to this theory, producing morally good consequences and preventing morally bad consequences is only one prima facie duty among other prima facie duties of moral agents.[59]

There is no scope here for a reasoned judgement in favour of this theory.[60] I have argued in detail elsewhere in its favour by appealing to ethical and meta-ethical intuitions.[61] Therefore, the common conception among Muslim thinkers that the moral rightness or wrongness of acts is solely dependent on their good (benefits) or bad (harms) consequences is untenable; and a God who acts solely based on the good or bad consequences of acts, or solely legislates laws based on assessing harms and benefits, without considering other moral factors such as the fair distribution of good consequences, would not be considered a moral agent and a virtuous lawgiver.

Then in the second step for the reconciliation, I differentiate moral agents into two groups: imperfect agents, that is, those with anti-moral inclinations, and perfect agents, that is, those lacking such inclinations. The former comprise most people early in their moral development. These agents need some normative principle(s) to guide them, while such inclinations persist, to serve epistemic and psychological functions. Moral principles inform the agent of what morality requires in each situation—what they ought and ought not to do—while also providing them with the suitable motivation to follow the principle.

However, morally perfect agents split into two subgroups: holy agents, who are inherently virtuous and innately lacking anti-moral inclinations, like God and the angels, and those who are not initially virtuous but attain moral maturity through sustained practice, gradually internalising virtues and finally becoming virtuous. The former group has no need for moral principles at all, while the latter initially requires moral principles until virtues take root.

For morally perfect agents, moral virtues substitute moral principles as the source of both moral knowledge and moral motivation. That is, moral virtues help perfect agents to discern and fulfil their moral duties. However, the fact that virtuous agents do not need moral principles does not mean that they have no moral duty, nor does it mean that their duties are different from those lacking moral virtues. Moral duties stay constant pre- and post-virtue acquisition. However, repetition transforms the principle-based processes of acquiring moral knowledge, making moral decisions, and discharging moral duties into virtue-based processes.

---

59 Anthony Skelton, 'William David Ross', *Stanford Encyclopedia of Philosophy*, 12 August 2010, rev. 2 March 2022, https://plato.stanford.edu/entries/william-david-ross/, §4.1.

60 For a classical articulation and defence of this theory, see W. D. Ross, *Foundations of Ethics* (Oxford: Clarendon Press, 1939); W. D. Ross, *The Right and the Good*, ed. Philip Stratton-Lake (Oxford: Oxford University Press, 2002).

61 Abolghasem Fanāeī, 'Che akhlāqī be che siāsatī marbūṭ ast?' (forthcoming).

More precisely, virtuous agents act upon a suitable combination of moral virtues and the knowledge of morally relevant non-moral facts of the situation. Therefore, regarding the action-guiding content of a moral theory, there is no difference between virtue ethics and the version of moral deontology mentioned earlier, though they differ in their epistemic and psychological foundations.

### 6.2 Virtue Ethics and Deontological Ethics: Contrast or Consonant?

If this reconciliation in normative ethics is plausible, two key conclusions follow. Firstly, the fact that virtuous agents do not need moral principles does not mean that moral duties are lifted from their shoulders. They still have the same moral duties and are in need of justifying and motivating reasons for action. However, the required reasons are supplied for them by moral virtues rather than moral principles. Virtues are skills[62]—those who have acquired requisite skills for driving, cooking, and so on, no longer need principle-based instruction. Similarly, moral virtues would supersede principles in moral epistemology and psychology. Nonetheless, the demands of moral virtues can be articulated in terms of universal moral principles covering both perfect and imperfect moral agents.

### 6.3 Virtue Ethics as the Proper Foundation for the Divine Agency

Secondly, one can plausibly claim that since God is a perfect moral agent, we should explain His agency in terms of virtue ethics. Moral virtues intrinsically constitute divine nature, that is, they are in fact manifestations of divine nature. However, this does not release God from moral duties, nor does it differentiate divine obligations from the obligations of imperfect moral agents. Hence, moral demands upon God can be formulated in terms of moral principles identical to the principles governing imperfect moral agents.

In this way, moral duties can be seen as the requirements of moral virtues, and since moral virtues constitute the nature of God, His moral duties can be seen as originating from His own nature. That is, God's own character requires Him to act or refrain from acting in certain ways. And that is why it can be said that God has obliged Himself to be merciful, just, loyal, honest, benevolent, and so on, just as these are duties for humans too.[63]

---

62 Julia Annas, 'Virtue as a Skill', *International Journal of Philosophical Studies* 3, no. 2 (1995): 227–43.

63 Some traditional thinkers believe that regarding God one cannot use the expression 'incumbent *upon* Him' (*wajaba ʿalayhi*) and say, 'doing something is obligatory *for* God'. Rather, one can only use the expression 'incumbent *from* Him' (*wajaba ʿanhu*) and say, 'doing something is obligatory *from* Him'. However, the above explanation shows that in this case, both expressions are true and compatible with the nature of divinity. The divine moral duties are both incumbent *from* Him and incumbent *upon* Him. They are incumbent *from* Him because these duties originate from His own essence, and it is His own rational nature that imposes these duties upon Him. They are incumbent *upon* Him because all rational and free agents can make something incumbent upon themselves. No one can compel God to do something, as

This explanation is endorsed by divine revelation. The Qur'an states that '[God] has made mercy obligatory upon Himself' (Q. 6:12), and that 'Your Lord has prescribed mercy upon Himself' (Q. 6:54). Similarly, it can be said that God has prescribed justice, keeping promises and covenants, truthfulness, forgiveness, and so forth, upon Himself.

To clarify, claiming that God has some moral (natural) duties is like claiming that He has some moral (natural) rights; it does not imply imposition of duty or bestowal of rights by an external authority, nor does it imply that imperfect human reason is binding God, or that God goes through the same process of moral deliberation that imperfect humans must go through. Rather, it means that God's own practical reason, or His perfect, virtuous nature, obligates Him. Nonetheless, the moral demands are the same. Just as injustice and negative discrimination are abhorrent for humans, they are abhorrent for God too. Therefore, even though the moral decision-making process, and how it shapes divine and human will, is not the same, these two different processes result in the same conclusion about moral duties.[64]

## 7. Conceptions of the Divine Agency in Practical Theology

The two rival perspectives on divine agency explained in previous sections hold divergent ramifications in practical theology, including religious ethics, religious jurisprudence, and political theology. I will briefly highlight some of these implications below.

### 7.1 The Role of God in Ethics and Morality[65]

The nature of divine agency plays an important role in shaping the form, content, purpose, and function of religious morality. Similarly, believers' conception of the nature of divine agency (theoretical theology) plays an important role in religious ethics, which is the most important part of practical theology. The task of religious ethics is to discover, formulate, and defend religious morality. In this subsection, I address the role of God in morality in general, and in religious morality in particular, as well as the role of theoretical theology in ethics in general and religious ethics in particular.

The role of God in morality, or the relationship between God and morality, is one of the important issues in moral philosophy, philosophy of religion, and theology. This

that would contradict His divinity, but God Himself can and has the right to do so.

64 One may say 'taking an innocent human life', if done by a human, is morally wrong, but if done by God, it is not morally wrong, and this shows that divine morality is distinct from human morality. In response, it can be said that first, 'taking life' is an exclusive act of God and no human can take another human's life. 'Killing' another human, which is the act of one who commits murder, is distinct from taking their life. Second, the moral judgement on killing another is not 'absolute' but 'context sensitive'.

65 As mentioned, I use 'morality' and its derivatives like 'moral' to refer to morality itself, and the word 'ethics' and its derivatives like 'ethical' to refer to the branch of philosophy concerned with studying morality and its foundations.

issue has extensive theoretical and practical implications for both religious and moral ways of life. Previously, I referred in passing to some points about this issue. My aim here is to further elaborate on the implications of the two conceptions discussed regarding the nature of divine agency in the realm of morality and ethics. The conclusion that can be drawn from the above discussions in this regard can be formulated in the following eight propositions:

(1) Morality consists of two parts: universal and specific. By 'universal' morality, I mean the part of morality which is independent from specific aspects of religious and non-religious worldviews. This morality neither presupposes the existence nor the non-existence of God, for example. By 'specific' morality, on the other hand, I refer to the other part of morality which is in some way dependent on the specific aspects of a particular religious or non-religious worldview.
(2) Universal morality has its own metaphysical, linguistic, epistemological, psychological, and rational foundations. However, these foundations are quite universal and therefore neutral between competing religious and non-religious worldviews. Hence it is reasonable for everyone to accept this morality and its foundations and live by it.
(3) While universal morality is unique and not plural, specific morality is relative and plural; it varies from one worldview to another.
(4) Universal morality takes precedence over specific morality, in the sense that the latter would be rationally justified insofar as it is compatible with the former. In other words, universal morality has veto power over specific moralities and can falsify them in case of conflict.
(5) Disputes between the adherents of different specific moralities can be resolved by invoking the principles of universal morality.
(6) To say that 'morality is independent from, and prior to, religion' is to say that universal morality is independent from, and prior to, the whole of religion, including religious morality as an instance of specific morality.
(7) Universal morality is independent of and takes precedence over all versions of specific moralities, whether religious or secular.
(8) The scope of universal morality is broader than that of global morality, because global morality is limited to humans, while universal morality, in the sense that I intend, includes humans, God, and any other rational, free being, if any.

As stated, by 'universal morality' I do not mean a morality that merely encompasses all humans qua humans. Rather, it also includes all other rational, autonomous, and free agents, such as God. For such a morality to be so encompassing, it must not presuppose distinctive characteristics of God or humans. In other words, it must rely solely on features shared between God, humans, and other rational, autonomous, and free agents. These features are reason, autonomy, and free will. To justify the existence of these features, I believe, requires no novel metaphysics. Rather, the metaphysics developed in the Islamic mystical tradition already provides a satisfactory account. From this mystical point of view, reason, autonomy, and free will are the real attributes of God, while human reason, autonomy, and free will are manifestations of divine reason, autonomy, and free will.

Universal morality is rooted in 'nature', but not peculiar human or divine nature. Rather, it stems from the nature that is common between all rational, autonomous, and free agents qua rational, autonomous, and free agents. Thus, wherever this nature manifests, such morality accompanies it. This common nature exists in both God and humans. Therefore, it is not created by God, nor does the morality arising from it originate from divine creative will, let alone His legislative will as a source of religious positive law (*sharīʿa*).

For this reason, such morality precedes both divine creative and legislative will as a source of religious positive law, and it can be a source of normativity for God, guiding His will in the domain of creation and legislation of *sharīʿa*. Rational nature comes in degrees, with the perfect level being instantiated in God as portrayed by theistic religions, and lower levels being its manifestations in humans and other rational, autonomous, and free beings, if any. Speaking of the moral nature of God or of God as a moral agent refers precisely to this idea. It is meaningless to claim that God is subject to a morality that is peculiar to humans or adherents of a specific religious or non-religious worldview. But it is perfectly reasonable to say that God adheres to the universal morality arising from the nature common between Him and other rational, autonomous, and free agents, such as humans.

As a simple example, the principle that 'imposing unbearable obligations is wrong', referred to in Islamic theology and jurisprudence as 'reprehensibility of obligations beyond capacity', belongs to universal morality, because this principle is so absolute that not only does it include obligations a human imposes on other humans, but also obligations God imposes on humans. As is evident, this moral judgement plays the role of a 'framework' for divine command, stemming from the nature common between God and humans, and delineates the boundaries of religious and secular positive law as well as religious and secular morality. Therefore, there is a morality which is not dependent on human nature qua human or divine nature qua divine. Hence God and humans alike fall under its dictates, and both can be evaluated by its standards.

This morality views all rational, autonomous, and free agents equally, and since its dictates apply uniformly to all such agents, it provides a reasonable and impartial basis for regulating the relationship of God with humans, humans with God, humans with each other, and humans with the natural environment. In addition to properly ordering the connection between heaven and earth, this morality creates suitable conditions for peaceful coexistence and cooperation among all people regardless of their religion, race, gender, nationality, and so on.

Religious morality, however, presupposes the theological doctrines of a specific religion, thus varying from one religion to another. Its subjects are the followers of that religion who have accepted its theological assumptions, not all people. A counterpart exists among atheists; they too, in addition to the universal morality shared by all rational, free, and autonomous agents, have another morality based on atheistic assumptions, addressing only those who accept those assumptions. Since universal morality has universal scope, it can provide a suitable space, that is, public sphere, where adherents of different religions, as well as atheists and agnostics, can follow their own specific morality without needing or having the right to impose it on others.

The difference between universal and specific morality can be explained in terms of contrasting 'reasons for action'. Reasons for action divide into 'justifying reasons' that rationally justify the act for the agent, and 'motivating reasons' that motivate them to perform it. The justifying and motivating reasons provided by universal morality are universally binding, like doing one's moral duty for the sake of duty or respecting the dignity of dignified beings simply because they have dignity. However, the justifying and motivating reasons specific morality provides for its adherents are exclusive, like seeking closeness to God and attaining His satisfaction, or achieving salvation and going to heaven rather than hell, or clear conscience or fame.

An important question that can be raised here concerns the relationship between these two parts of morality. I have defended the idea of 'the priority of meta-religious morality over religious morality', or more broadly, 'the priority of universal morality over specific morality'.[66] According to this theory, neither of these two parts of morality satisfies our need for the other. Specific morality becomes plausible within the framework of universal morality: the principles of any specific morality in fact result from combining the principles of universal morality with particular religious or non-religious beliefs and doctrines.

For example, obeying God's commands is obligatory because God is the benefactor of humans, and gratitude towards benefactors is a principle of universal morality. Therefore, religious morality does not replace universal morality, but presupposes it and operates within its framework. Specific morality cannot veto or negate universal morality or relieve its followers of duties imposed by universal morality. If lying or stealing is wrong in universal morality, then specific morality cannot say that these acts are permissible for its followers.

However, specific morality, as part of the teachings of a specific religion or non-religious ideology, can make something obligatory or prohibited for the followers of that religion or ideology in areas where univeral morality is silent and has no binding judgement. For example, modesty is a virtue in universal morality. On the other hand, Islam or a particular interpretation of Islamic morality has made hijab obligatory for Muslim women. Based on the fundamental principles of universal morality, choosing clothing is both a right and a

66 See Fanāeī, *Din dar tarāzūy-e akhlagh*; and Fanāeī, *Akhlaq-e din shenāsi.*

duty. It is a right in the sense that Muslim women have the right to choose hijab as their attire. It is a duty in the sense that gratitude towards God as their benefactor obligates them to follow the dictates of their own specific morality. At the same time, Muslims have neither the right nor the duty to impose hijab on non-Muslim women or Muslims who have different interpretations of Islam and do not consider hijab as obligatory.

Likewise, even if they are the majority, Muslims do not have the right to render this religious obligation into a secular law by criminalising not wearing hijab and imposing fines and punishments on those who do not respect this law. Such a law lacks moral validity and is therefore untenable. In fact, it is unjust and contradicts human dignity and the golden rule of universal morality. Forced hijab is morally wrong for the same reasons that forced unveiling is morally wrong. Universal morality recognises civil disobedience and equally allows opponents of forced hijab and forced unveiling to resist unjust laws through civil means.

When universal morality is endorsed by God, its nature and content do not change, but it simply gains additional justificatory and motivational support. Therefore, the moral teachings present in religious texts can be divided into two parts: the first expresses universal or meta-religious morality, while the second expresses a religious version of specific ethics. Followers of a religion, depending on their psychological make-up, may derive the required motivational reasons for following universal morality either from this morality itself or from their specific morality. The important point, however, is that the positive or negative role of religion in the moral life of human beings entirely depends on whether the followers are right or wrong in understanding and practising their religion.

The adherents' understanding of the nature of God has a direct effect on their understanding of the nature and content of both parts of morality. In this regard, two conceptions of morality can be distinguished from each other. In the first conception, arbitrary will replaces moral standards; that is, in this conception, either nothing remains of morality, or if something does remain, its survival is conditioned by, and subject to, conformity with the requirements of tyranny. But according to the second conception, the demands of universal morality constitute the framework of religion and religious morality.

Harbouring an inaccurate theory about the relationship between universal and religious morality, and about the role of God in the realm of morality, is a fundamental mistake that would undermine a worthy religious and moral life for believers. If they believe in an impersonal and formless God who cannot be an agent, as proponents of negative theology and some proponents of extremely naturalised readings of theology claim, then worshiping God and developing a meaningful relationship with Him becomes entirely impossible.[67]

67 Abolghasem Fanāeī, 'Elahiyyāte ṭabiei shodeh, metaphisike ḥadde aghalli, phizike ḥadde aksary', *Dīn va Donmāye Moāṣer* 14 (2021): 15–64.

If, on the other hand, the God of believers is a non-moral agent, as early Ashʿarī theologians state, then morality will be reduced, or constrained, to the commands of a non-moral God. The religious way of life (religious knowledge and religious practice) that takes shape around such theology turns humans into slaves who have lost their human identity and become alienated from themselves.[68]

Therefore, conceiving God as a non-moral agent not only undermines human moral agency but also negates the moral relationship between God and humans. However, if the God of believers is a moral agent, as Muʿtazilī theologians state, then the religious knowledge and practice of believers who worship such a God will have a moral framework. In such a context, the relationship of God to humans will not be the relationship of master to slave. Rather, it will be the relationship of two rational, free, and dignified agents. Regulating God–human relationships in this way cultivates the human identity of believers.[69]

### 7.2 The Role of God in Sharīʿa (Religious Positive Law)

The second implication concerns the impact that the nature of divine agency would have on the form and content of religious law (*sharīʿa*). Regarding positive law, whether religious or secular, one can distinguish two types of legislator, yielding two distinct legal systems differing in form and content:

(1) Non-moral legislators do not follow any independent, objective moral criteria. Rather, they act arbitrarily on spontaneous desires, emotions, and preferences. Although some non-moral legislators claim that their concern is to protect the public interest, since they do not rely upon an impartial scientific method of inquiry, nor do they consult public opinion, the result would be the same.

(2) Moral legislators, however, operate within moral constraints, prioritising fundamental individual rights over public interest when conflicts arise. They utilise a process governed by moral principles. Their legislation violates no moral tenets in form or content. Bear in mind that by 'moral legislators' I do not mean those who merely dress moral principles in legal garb (moralism). Morality is not the sole or even necessary source of law. The source of law may be something other than morality. Still, laws stemming from non-moral sources could be moral in another sense if legislators observe moral principles governing the process of legislation.

Positive law comes in two forms: religious and secular. The legislator of religious law is

68 The human identity, composed of theoretical and practical parts, plays a key role in moral knowledge and moral practice. Korsgaard, *Sources of Normativity*.

69 For more on the relationship between religious ethics and universal ethics, see Abolghasem Fanāeī, *Afsoone gole sourkh* (Tehran: Intishārāt-e Neghāh-e Moāṣer, 2021), ch. 5.

either God or someone like a prophet divinely authorised to legislate in the name of God. Meanwhile, secular law's legislator is a human individual or institution. The typology of moral and non-moral legislators extends to both secular and religious positive laws. The nature of divine agency determines the nature of divine legislation and the nature of resultant religious law (*sharīʿa*). Hence, God as a religious legislator, and those legislating on His authority, fall under the two types of legislator outlined previously. If divine agency is non-moral, divine legislation will not be within the boundaries of moral principles. Likewise, a moral God will legislate within moral limits.

## 7.3 The Role of God in Religious Jurisprudence (*Fiqh* and *Uṣūl al-Fiqh*)

Jurisprudence as a part of practical theology depends on theoretical theology, because jurists' understanding of the nature of divine agency directly influences their perspective on the *nature of sharīʿa*. If what was explained in the previous subsection is correct, one can conclude that there can be two types of religious jurist (*faqīh*) and, correspondingly, two types of jurisprudence (*fiqh*), each based on a specific theological assumption about the nature of divine legislation.

These two types of religious jurists are (1) those who consider God as a non-moral legislator, and (2) those who consider God as a moral legislator. The first theological conception of God is behind the idea of *sharīʿa* as an unconnected and heterogeneous heap of commandments and prohibitions lacking any kind of rational order. According to such jurists, '*Sharīʿa* rests on congregating disparities and separating similarities.'[70]

However, conceiving God as a moral agent yields a theory about the nature of *sharīʿa*, which I, inspired by Kant,[71] termed '*Sharīʿa* within the boundaries of morality'.[72] Thus, jurists who in their theoretical theology believe in a moral God will see *sharīʿa* laws as morally constrained in form and content.

These two metaphysical perspectives on the nature of *sharīʿa* lead to two rival theories in the *ethics of ijtihād*, about the epistemic and hermeneutical foundations of religious jurisprudence. Conceiving *sharīʿa* as a set of disjointed laws restricts the sources of legal

70 For a critique of this conception of the nature of Sharīʿa, see Ḥusayn Ṣāberī and Mūsā Zarqī, 'Naqdi bar nazariye-ye jamʿ beyn mufarriqat wa tafriq-e mujtamaʿat dar shariʿat', *Motaleʿāt-e Islāmi: Fiqh wa-Uṣūl* 94 (2013): 43–62.

71 Immanuel Kant, *Religion within the Boundaries of Mere Reason: And Other Writings*, Cambridge Texts in the History of Philosophy, 2nd ed., ed. Allen Wood and George di Giovanni (Cambridge: Cambridge University Press, 2018).

72 For further exposition of this theory, see Fanāeī, *Din dar tarāzūy-e akhlagh*; Fanāeī, *Akhlaq-e din shenāsi*. '*Sharīʿa* within the boundaries of morality' is different from '*Sharīʿa* based on morality' or '*Sharīʿa* corresponding to morality'. If *sharīʿa* were based on or corresponded to morality, by knowing and following one of these two normative systems, believers would not need to know and follow the other. But I believe neither morality nor *sharīʿa* is a suitable substitute for the other and does not satisfy believers' need for the other. Because, despite any partial overlap they may have, these two normative systems differ in terms of origin, aims, audience, function, and enforcement or consequences of observance and violation.

knowledge to the literal meaning of religious texts, with the valid method of interpretation limited to a literal analysis of those texts.

On the other hand, seeing *sharīʿa* as a morally bounded system of law enables moral principles to function as a defeater for the literal interpretation of the relevant texts on ethical grounds. As an a posteriori step in the process of legal inference (*ijtihād*), jurists holding this view about the nature of *sharīʿa* are required to check their understanding of the text against moral standards. One may call this theory 'moral falsificationism in jurisprudence' and its fundamental hermeneutical principle 'the moral falsification of jurisprudential verdicts'.

### 7.4 The Role of God in Political Theology

The various conceptions of divine agency in theoretical theology have different implications in political theology, playing an important role in shaping the form and content of the political system. This includes the structure of political institutions, state–citizen interactions, citizens' interactions, incorporation of religious law into secular law, and law enforcement. For instance, an absolute monarch or caliph governing a religious society may view himself as the representative of a non-moral God on earth, justifying his own despotism by invoking this conception of divine agency and by appealing to the will or command of a non-moral God. Meanwhile, citizens sharing this notion of divine agency in their theoretical theology more readily submit to such rulers.

If, on the other hand, someone embraces the *moral* conception of divine agency as theologically plausible, they must also commit themselves to the political implications associated with that conception, including how it impacts the relationship between religion and politics. The foremost implication is a political theory that could be entitled 'religious governance within the boundaries of moral governance'. Hence, the idea of God as a moral agent provides theological grounds for impartial and tolerant governance and citizenship.[73]

## 8. Conclusion

The idea of God as a moral agent is a view that, in the light of moral and religious intuitions, possesses a prima facie justification. Therefore, the opponents of this view, namely, the proponents of the rival theories about the nature of God, carry the burden of proof, and are inevitably compelled to present arguments to refute it. Hence, to accept this theory, it is sufficient to invalidate the arguments put forward or potentially raised in

73 The reasons that justify impartiality and tolerance for atheists and agnostics are solely meta-religious reasons, but believers, in addition to having the meta-religious reasons that they share with non-believers, also have religious reasons for impartiality and tolerance based on the idea of God as a moral agent.

favour of the rival theory. In this article, I have adopted such an approach and attempted to demonstrate the fallacies of these arguments.

In my view, many purportedly objectionable implications of this theory dissolve if we accept that God's moral attributes normatively constrain His morally neutral attributes. Metaphysically, all divine attributes are absolute, yet their absoluteness creates conflicting practical demands, which can be reconciled in two ways: either in favour of His moral attributes or in favour of His non-moral attributes.[74] The first method of reconciliation is intuitively appealing. According to this solution, although divine power, sovereignty, authority, and ownership are absolute in themselves, in the sense that there is no external agent who can restrict the practical requirements of these attributes, God as a rational, autonomous, and free agent has decided to exercise His power and authority to the extent that is morally permissible.[75]

The key point here is that God Himself, not an external source—such as imperfect human reason—is prioritising the demand of the divine moral attributes over the demand of His non-moral attributes, and this is the precise definition of divine moral perfection. A religion centred on such a conception of God is a 'religion within the boundaries of morality'. If the deity introduced by religion is a moral agent, exercising His will within a moral framework, then all other aspects of religion should align with that framework, since an amoral divine agent creates conflict between religion and universal morality, forcing a choice between the two. This basic principle applies to religious beliefs, individual and social religious duties, religious politics, and economics in religious societies.

In contrast, advocates of a non-moral God subordinate divine moral attributes and divine wisdom to His non-moral attributes, rendering the former meaningless platitudes. With justice restricted by power, divine acts and decrees escape moral evaluation, and worship is reduced to mere reverence of power. Prioritising divine non-moral attributes over moral ones means that humans worship God because He is powerful, not because He is just, benevolent, and forgiving, and the result of such worship is nothing but religious extremism.

## Bibliography

Abraham, William J. *Divine Agency and Divine Action, Volume I: Exploring and Evaluating the Debate*. Oxford: Oxford University Press, 2018.

Adams, Robert Merrihew. *Finite and Infinite Goods: A Framework for Ethics*. New York:

74 All those who believe in the theistic conception of God confront this dilemma and have to resolve it in one way or another.

75 One of the beautiful names attributed to God in supplications is 'O You whose mercy precedes His wrath' (Muḥammad b. al-Ḥasan al-Ṭūsī, *Miṣbāḥ al-mutahajjid wa-silāḥ al-muta'abbid* (Beirut: Mu'assasat Fiqh al-Shī'a, 1990), 2:696) and 'You whose mercy rushes ahead of His wrath' (Majlisī, *Biḥār al-anwār*, 97:408).

Oxford University Press, 2002.

Allison, Henry E. *Kant's Theory of Freedom*. Cambridge: Cambridge University Press, 1990.

Annas, Julia. 'Virtue as a Skill'. *International Journal of Philosophical Studies* 3, no. 2 (1995): 227–43.

al-Ashʿarī, Abū al-Ḥasan. *al-Lumaʿ fī al-radd ʿalā ahl al-zaygh wa-l-bidaʿ*. Abu Dhabi: Majlis Ḥukamāʾ al-Muslimīn, 2022.

Austin, Michael W. 'Divine Command Theory'. *Internet Encyclopedia of Philosophy*. https://iep.utm.edu/divine-command-theory/.

al-Bāqillānī, Abū Bakr. *al-Inṣāf fīmā yajibu iʿtiqāduhu wa-lā yajūzu al-jahl bihi*. Cairo: al-Maktaba al-Azhariyya li-l-Turāth, 2000.

Chittick, William C. *The Self-Disclosure of God: Principles of Ibn al-ʿArabī's Cosmology*. Albany: State University of New York Press, 1997.

———. *The Sufi Doctrine of Rumi*. Bloomington: World Wisdom, 2005.

Dworkin, Ronald. *Law's Empire*. Cambridge, MA: Harvard University Press, 1986.

Fanāeī, Abolghasem. *Afsoone gole sourkh*. Tehran: Intishārāt-e Neghāh-e Moāṣer, 2021.

———. *Akhlaq-e din shenāsi: paghūheshi dar bab-e mabāni-ye akhlaghi wa maʿrefat shenāsi-ye fiqh*. Tehran: Intishārāt-e Negāh-e Moāṣer, 2020. First published 2010.

———. 'Che akhlāgi be che siāsati marbūt ast?'. Forthcoming.

———. *Din dar tarāzūy-e akhlagh: paghuheshi dar bab-e nesbat-e akhlagh-e dini wa akhlagh-e secular*. Tehran: Intishārāt-e Ṣerāt, 2016. First published 2005.

———. 'Elahiyyāte ṭabiei shodeh, metaphisike ḥadde aghalli, phizike ḥadde aksary'. *Dīn va Donmāye Moāṣer* 14 (2021): 15–64.

Goetz, Stewart. 'The Meaning of Life'. In *The Routledge Companion to Theism*, edited by Charles Taliaferro, Victoria S. Harrison, and Stewart Goetz, 720–31. New York: Routledge, 2012.

Hare, John. 'Religion and Morality'. *Stanford Encyclopedia of Philosophy*. 27 September 2006. Revised 8 August 2019. https://plato.stanford.edu/entries/religion-morality/.

Harris, Michael J. *Divine Command Ethics: Jewish and Christian Perspectives*. London: Routledge, 2003.

Hourani, George F. *Reason and Tradition in Islamic Ethics*. Cambridge: Cambridge University Press, 2007.

———. 'Two Theories of Value in Medieval Islam'. *The Muslim World* 50, no. 4 (1960): 269–78.

Jalālī, Mahdī, and Muḥammad Mahdī Ajiliān. 'Barresi-ye sanadi wa matni-ye ḥadīth-e abghaḍ al-ḥalāl ela Allāh al-ṭalaq'. *Amouzehā-ye Ḥadithi* 1 (2017): 75–98.

Janik, Allan, and Stephen Toulmin. *Wittgenstein's Vienna*. New York: Simon and Schuster, 1973.

Johnson, Robert, and Adam Cureton. 'Kant's Moral Philosophy'. *Stanford Encyclopedia of Philosophy*. 23 February 2004. Revised 21 January 2022. https://plato.stanford.

edu/entries/kant-moral/.

Kant, Immanuel. *Critique of Practical Reason*. Cambridge Texts in the History of Philosophy. Revised edition. Translated by Mary Gregor. Cambridge: Cambridge University Press, 2015.

———. *Groundwork of the Metaphysics of Morals*. Cambridge Texts in the History of Philosophy. Edited by Mary Gregor. Cambridge: Cambridge University Press, 1998.

———. *Religion within the Boundaries of Mere Reason: And Other Writings*. Cambridge Texts in the History of Philosophy. 2nd edition. Edited by Allen Wood and George di Giovanni. Cambridge: Cambridge University Press, 2018.

Kirchin, Simon. 'Thick and Thin Concepts'. *The International Encyclopedia of Ethics*. 29 June 2019. https://doi.org/10.1002/9781444367072.wbiee262.pub2.

Korsgaard, Christine M. *The Sources of Normativity*. Edited by Onora O'Neill. Cambridge: Cambridge University Press, 1996.

Lala, Ismail. *Knowing God: Ibn ʿArabī and ʿAbd al-Razzāq al-Qāshānī's* Metaphysics of the Divine. Leiden: Brill, 2019.

Levin, Michael. 'Understanding the Euthyphro Problem'. *International Journal for Philosophy of Religion* 25, no. 2 (1989): 83–97.

MacIntyre, Alasdair. 'Which God Ought We to Obey and Why?'. *Faith and Philosophy* 3, no. 4 (1986): 359–71.

Mackie, J. L. *Ethics: Inventing Right and Wrong*. London: Penguin Books, 1990.

Majlisī, Muḥammad Bāqir. *Biḥār al-anwār*. Beirut: Muʾassasat al-Wafāʾ, 1982.

Morvarid, Hashem. 'The Muʿtazila's Arguments against Divine Command Theory'. *Religious Studies* 58, no. 3 (2021): 610–27.

Murphy, Mark. 'Theological Voluntarism'. *Stanford Encyclopedia of Philosophy*. 2 July 2002. Revised 4 June 2019. https://plato.stanford.edu/entries/voluntarism-theological/.

Plato. *Five Dialogues*. Translated by G. M. A. Grube. Indianapolis: Hackett, 1981.

Quinn, Philip L. 'The Recent Revival of Divine Command Ethics'. *Philosophy and Phenomenological Research* 50 (1990): 345–65.

Rawls, John. *A Theory of Justice*. Revised edition. Cambridge, MA: Harvard University Press, 1999.

Reath, Andrews. *Agency and Autonomy in Kant's Moral Theory: Selected Essays*. Oxford: Clarendon Press, 2006.

Ross, W. D. *Foundations of Ethics*. Oxford: Clarendon Press, 1939.

Ross, W. D. *The Right and the Good*. Edited by Philip Stratton-Lake. Oxford: Oxford University Press, 2002.

Ṣāberī, Ḥusayn, and Mūsā Zarqī. 'Naqdi bar nazariye-ye jamʿ beyn mufarriqat wa tafriq-e mujtamaʿat dar shariʿat'. *Motaleʿāt-e Islāmi: Fiqh wa-Uṣūl* 94 (2013): 43–62.

al-Ṣadr, Muḥammad Bāqir. *Buḥūth fī ʿilm al-uṣūl: mabāḥith al-ḥujaj wa-l-uṣūl al-ʿamaliyya*. Edited by Ḥasan ʿAbd al-Sattār. Vol. 8. Beirut: al-Dār al-Islāmiyya li-l-Ṭibāʿa wa-l-

Nashr, 1996.
Shahābī, Maḥmūd. *Rahbar-e kherad.* Tehran: Ketābkhāna-ye Khayyām, 1960.
al-Sharīf al-Raḍī, Muḥammad. *Nahj al-balāgha.* Qom: Muʾassasat-e Anṣāriyān li-l-Ṭibāʿa wa-l-Nashr, 2006.
Skelton, Anthony. 'William David Ross'. *Stanford Encyclopedia of Philosophy.* 12 August 2010. Revised 2 March 2022. https://plato.stanford.edu/entries/william-david-ross/.
Swinburne, Richard. *The Existence of God.* Oxford: Clarendon Press, 2004.
———. *Is There a God?* Revised edition. Oxford: Oxford University Press, 2010.
al-Ṭūsī, Muḥammad b. al-Ḥasan. *Miṣbāḥ al-mutahajjid wa-silāḥ al-mutaʿabbid.* Beirut: Muʾassasat Fiqh al-Shīʿa, 1990.
al-Ṭūsī, Naṣīr al-Dīn. *Sharḥ al-Ishārāt wa-l-tanbīhāt.* Qom: Nashr al-Balāgha, 1996.
al-Ṭūsī, Naṣīr al-Dīn, and al-Ḥasan b. Yūsuf b. al-Muṭahhar al-Ḥillī. *Kashf al-murād fī sharḥ Tajrīd al-iʿtiqād.* Beirut: Muʾassasat al-Aʿlamī li-l-Maṭbūʿāt, 1988.

# Friendly (A)theism: A Philosophical-Theological Defence

*S. Yaser Mirdamadi* [1]

*Recently, and perhaps more stridently than for many years, accusations of 'irrationality' have been bandied about directed at people and their views and also to their modes of reasoning or lack of them.*[2]

## 1. Introduction

In this article, I argue for a stance I refer to as 'friendly (a)theism', presenting it in contrast to its two counterparts: unfriendly atheism and unfriendly theism. Throughout, I use atheism in a broad sense, encompassing both the denial of God's existence and the suspension of theistic belief.[3] By friendliness, I mean a combination of epistemic recognition and practical tolerance, even in the presence of significant theoretical differences.

The article begins with a narrative establishing the backdrop of widespread intolerance stemming from accusations of irrationality. Subsequently, I delve into the characterisation and philosophical argumentation for friendly (a)theism. I address and counter various objections to this perspective. Moving forward, I defend friendly (a)theism from a scriptural (Qur'anic) standpoint and conclude by examining it within diverse religious epistemological models.

## 2. Accusation of Irrationality

One theoretical root cause of intolerance is arguably the accusations of irrationality. It would not be an exaggeration to say that the accusation of irrationality and its concomitant intolerance was, and still is, ubiquitous. Rooted in the Enlightenment, modern conventional wisdom stipulates that irrationality hinders human progress and must be eradicated at all costs.

---

1 I express my gratitude to Wahid M. Amin for organising the conference from which this paper has emerged. Special thanks are owed to Seyed Sadra Kashani, John Greco, Sajjad Rizvi, Mahmoud Morvarid, Mohammad Saleh Zarepour, Farhad Shafti, and Hamid Vahid for providing comments on the initial draft.

2 Rom Harré, 'Introduction', in *Beyond Rationality: Contemporary Issues*, ed. Carl Jensen and Rom Harré (Newcastle upon Tyne: Cambridge Scholars Publishing, 2012), 1.

3 However, to add further emphasis, especially in the Qur'anic part of the article, I make reference to both atheists and agnostics at times.

More recently, the new atheists accuse theists of being irrational and superstitious. For Richard Dawkins (b. 1941), a British evolutionary biologist, theology is a non-subject, and a theology degree is useless. He even wonders why there is a theology faculty at the University of Oxford, or anywhere else for that matter:

> If all the achievements of theologians were wiped out tomorrow, would anyone notice the smallest difference? Even the bad achievements of scientists, the bombs and sonar-guided whaling vessels, work. The achievements of theologians don't do anything, don't affect anything, don't achieve anything, don't even mean anything. What makes you think that 'theology' is a subject at all?[4]

According to Dawkins, if theology is systemically useless but presents itself as essential, then theology is inherently irrational. Unsurprisingly, Dawkins turns to neuroscience to elucidate the phenomenon of religious irrationality.

> Could irrational religion be a by-product of the irrationality mechanisms that were originally built into the brain by selection for falling in love? Certainly, religious faith has something of the same character as falling in love (and both have many of the attributes of being high on an addictive drug).[5]

A somewhat similar position, implicitly or otherwise, is adopted by Bertrand Russell (1872–1970),[6] Daniel Dennett (1942–2024),[7] Sam Harris (b. 1967),[8] and Christopher Hitchens (1949–2011).[9] All these figures are among *new* atheists, except for Russel, who is, one might say, an *old* atheist.

Historically, the atheistic accusation of irrationality levelled against religion as the hallmark of irrationality has not (only) been a disinterested theoretical discussion among academicians or intellectuals. It was, instead, part and parcel of, for example, the Soviet Union's harsh 'atheistic programme'. As the editorial from the August 1954 issue of *Vestnik Shkoli* (Bulletin of the School), the monthly journal of the USSR Ministry of Higher Education, puts it:

4 Richard Dawkins, 'Letter: Scientific versus Theological Knowledge', *Independent*, 20 March 1993, www.independent.co.uk/voices/letter-scientific-versus-theological-knowledge-1498837.html.

5 Richard Dawkins, *The God Delusion* (London: Bantam, 2006), 185.

6 Bertrand Russell, *Why I Am Not a Christian: And Other Essays on Religion and Related Subjects* (New York: Simon and Schuster, 1957), 44, 47.

7 Daniel Dennett and Robert Winston, 'Is Religion a Threat to Rationality and Science?', *Guardian*, 22 April 2008, www.theguardian.com/education/2008/apr/22/highereducation.uk5.

8 Sam Harris, *The End of Faith: Religion, Terror and the Future of Reason* (New York: W. W. Norton & Company, 2004), 111, 165, 223.

9 Christopher Hitchens, *God Is Not Great: How Religion Poisons Everything* (New York: Twelve, 2007).

> No toleration is possible ... of the manifestation of survivals of religion amongst students and staff. ... The communist party and the Soviet state consistently put into practice the provision in the Constitution of the USSR on freedom of conscience, but this in no sense gives anybody grounds for considering freedom of conscience only as freedom to disseminate religious views.[10]

The result of zero tolerance of the irrational (superstitious and obscurantist views of religious people) was six waves of USSR anti-religious campaigns from initial suppression (1917–29), intensification (1928–41), and following the World War II interlude (1941–53), which brought a relative relaxation, then a renewed suppression (1953–64)[11] and again after a period of relative easing up (1964–85)[12] a renewed crackdown (1985–91). Although the Soviet seventy-year 'war on religion', from the early years of the October Revolution in 1917 until the 1991 collapse of the USSR, failed to convert most Russian people to 'scientific atheism',[13] it led to harsh suppression of religious figures and institutions. This intolerance is no surprise for as John Gray (b. 1948), an English political philosopher and self-acclaimed atheist, said, 'In the past, most atheists have not been liberals.'[14]

As a reaction to atheistic accusations of irrationality, certain religious believers, particularly those with conservative views, have counter-accused atheists of being irrational:

> The fundamental irrationality of the atheist can primarily be seen in his actions, and it is here that his general lack of intellectual conviction is also exposed. Whereas Christians and the faithful of other religions have rational reasons for attempting to live by their various moral systems, the atheist does not.[15]

Accusations of irrationality between theists and atheists aside,[16] theists have also kept throwing accusations of irrationality at each other. It happens, more importantly, among theists on main theological issues such as *tawḥīd* (monotheism). Ibn Taymiyya, for example, notoriously argues that Christianity is replete with irrational and superstitious

10 J. M., 'The Anti-Religious Campaign in Higher Education', *Soviet Studies* 6, no. 3 (1955): 315.
11 N. S. Timasheff, 'The Anti-Religious Campaign in the Soviet Union', *The Review of Politics* 17, no. 3 (1955): 335.
12 Eren Tasar, *Soviet and Muslim: The Institutionalization of Islam in Central Asia* (New York: Oxford University Press, 2017), 194–241.
13 Paul Froese, 'Forced Secularization in Soviet Russia: Why an Atheistic Monopoly Failed', *Journal for the Scientific Study of Religion* 43, no. 1 (2004): 35–50.
14 John Gray, *Seven Types of Atheism* (London: Penguin, 2018), 1.
15 Vox Day, *The Irrational Atheist: Dissecting the Unholy Trinity of Dawkins, Harris, and Hitchens* (Dallas: BenBella Books, 2008), 262.
16 Some in-between positions acknowledge that both theism and atheism could be considered irrational, yet find them acceptable, recognising the inevitability of irrationality; see, for example, Crispin Sartwell, 'Irrational Atheism', *The Atlantic*, 11 October 2014, www.theatlantic.com/national/archive/2014/10/a-leap-of-atheist-faith/381353/.

doctrines, some of which, such as incarnation (*ḥulūl*) or receiving a blessing from a dead saint, reappeared among Muslims mainly in Shīʿī and Sufi Islam.[17]

Again, this was not only a disinterested theoretical discussion among theologians and jurists. It was, for example, part and parcel of Wahhabi Islam, which was—and still is—anti-Shīʿī, anti-Sufi, and, at least partially, anti-traditional-Sunnī Islam. This led to numerous suppressions of Shīʿī and Sufi Muslims. One prominent example was the sacking of the city of Karbala and the shrine of Imām Ḥusayn in 1802, which resulted in looting, partial destruction of the shrine, and the death of around 4,500 local people.[18] Heavily influenced by Ibn Taymiyya, Wahhabis take the pilgrimage to the shrine of Shīʿī Imāms and Sufi saints as tantamount to *shirk* (polytheism), and they view *shirk* as the peak of irrationality (superstition), a great sin to be eradicated at all costs.

In light of this protracted and acrimonious history stained with bloodshed, all in pursuit of eliminating irrationality,[19] is there a way to consider both sides of the theism–atheism or intra-(a)theism debate (or many other similar deep theoretical conflicts), in principle, rational even after exposure to peer disagreement, without (1) lapsing into relativism or (2) compromising one side for the other? I believe so. The result in our context would be friendly (a)theism.

Though I am a theist, I am not willing to defend theism or disprove atheism.[20] Instead, I will defend the rationally friendly model in the theism–atheism debate (see Figure 1). In other words, if you are agnostic or atheist, I am not going to convince you otherwise. Instead, I will try to convince you to adopt a rationally friendly model of atheism or agnosticism. The same is true of theism. As I shall argue, the epistemic friendliness of (a)theism lies in its anti-irrationality ascription.

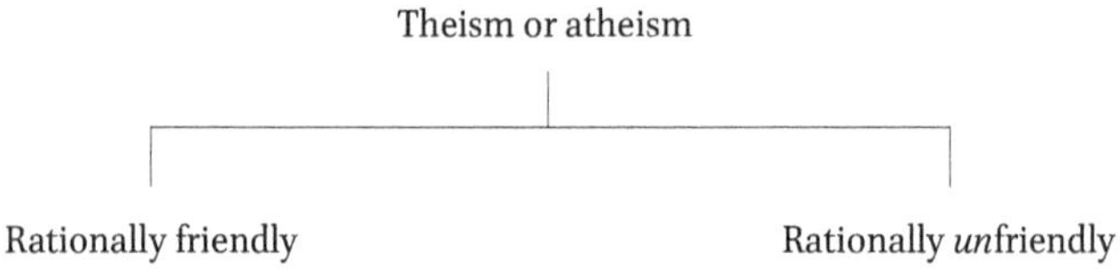


FIGURE 1: *(A)theism in terms of (un)friendliness*

17 Yahya Michot, 'Between Entertainment and Religion: Ibn Taymiyya's Views on Superstition', *The Muslim World* 99, no. 1 (2009): 6.

18 Cole M. Bunzel, *Wahhābism: The History of a Militant Islamic Movement* (Princeton, NJ: Princeton University Press, 2023), 219.

19 I am not claiming that the sole driving force behind these historical movements is the 'pursuit of eliminating irrationality'. The historical situation has been much more complex than that, even in instances where charges of irrationality are explicitly made. What I am proposing is that the accusation of irrationality, particularly in the form of criticising 'superstitious' beliefs, has also been one of many driving forces.

20 Elsewhere, however, I have defended the reasonability of Muslimness from a friendly theistic perspective; see S. Yaser Mirdamadi, 'Why I Am Muslim', in *The Rowman & Littlefield Handbook of Philosophy and Religion*, ed. Mark A. Lamport (Lanham: Rowman & Littlefield, 2022), 383–91.

## 3. Friendly (A)theism: A Philosophical Defence

'Friendly (a)theism' is drawn from and further develops 'friendly atheism'. To better understand the former term, let us first discuss the latter.

### 3.1 Rowe on Friendly Atheism

William Rowe (1931–2015), an American philosopher, coined the term 'friendly atheism'. He argued for it in a now-classic paper, 'The Problem of Evil and Some Varieties of Atheism'. Rowe presents a famous argument against theism, called the evidential argument from evil. Although he wholeheartedly defends atheism with what he adopts as a 'forceful' argument,[21] he argues against the unfriendly model of atheism. According to unfriendly atheism, 'no one is rationally justified in believing that the theistic God exists'.[22] But according to friendly atheism, 'some theists are rationally justified in believing that the theistic God exists'.[23] In general terms, unfriendly atheism is based on the following epistemological thesis:

> *Unfriendly atheism* (*initial characterisation*): no one can be rational in believing a false proposition. 'God exists' is a false proposition. Then, no one can be rational in believing this theistic proposition.

On the contrary, friendly atheism is based on the following epistemological thesis, roughly put:

> *Friendly atheism* (*initial characterisation*): Under certain conditions, one can be rational in believing a false proposition. 'God exists' is a false proposition. Then, under certain conditions, one can be rational in believing this theistic proposition.

An immediate refinement must be introduced to Rowe's characterisation. This adjustment becomes necessary as there may be false propositions that are inherently irrational to believe under any circumstances, such as 'two plus two equals five' or 'this object in front of me is literally yellow all over and yet not yellow all over at the same time'. However, it is important to note that these false propositions pertain to self-evident matters. On the other hand, the question of God does not seem to fall within the self-evident issues. Therefore, we can refine the characterisation as follows:

21 William L. Rowe, 'The Problem of Evil and Some Varieties of Atheism', *American Philosophical Quarterly* 16, no. 4 (1979): 339. See also William L. Rowe, 'Friendly Atheism Revisited', *International Journal for Philosophy of Religion* 68, no. 1–3 (2010): 7–13.

22 Rowe, 'The Problem of Evil', 340.

23 Ibid.

> *Friendly atheism* (*second characterisation*): Under certain conditions, one can be rational in believing a false proposition, if it is not about a self-evident issue. 'God exists' is a false proposition, which is not about a self-evident issue. Then, under certain conditions, one can be rational in believing this proposition.

Again, the second characterisation remains insufficiently fine-tuned. An atheist may contend that theistic beliefs might have been rational in medieval times when atheistic arguments were not yet fully advanced, but this rationale is no longer valid due to subsequent atheistic full advancements. In response, it should be noted that arguments on both theistic and atheistic sides have conspicuously evolved since almost the second half of the twentieth century and there is no consensus that one side has conclusively disproved the other.[24] With this clarification, the characterisation can be further refined:

> *Friendly atheism* (*third characterisation*): Under certain conditions, one can be rational in believing a false proposition, if it is not about a self-evident issue. 'God exists' is a false proposition that is not about a self-evident issue. Then, under certain conditions, one can be rational in believing this proposition, even in modern times.[25]

Given this third refined characterisation, let us return to Rowe, who argues that one can be rational in believing a false proposition.[26] But by asserting that someone may be rational in embracing the 'false' proposition of God's existence, a friendly atheist does not affirm the theist's belief as true. It is helpful to differentiate between 'personal' and 'doxastic' justification in this context. When you conscientiously pursue your epistemic goals, you achieve personal justification. However, this personal justification does not necessarily extend to the justification of your belief. *You* might be rational, but your *belief* might not. I term personal justification as rationality. Is friendly atheism logically consistent and epistemologically tenable? Rowe argues for logical consistency and epistemological tenability of friendly atheism through a thought experiment that can be called the 'crashed plane scenario' (CPS).

Here is my appropriation of the scenario. You accompany your friend to the plane's door. As he/she waves at you from the plane's window, you watch the plane take off. Hours later, you hear a distressing radio official announcement stating that the same plane has crashed, with no survivors found by the rescue team. Unbeknown to you or anyone else, your friend has miraculously survived the crash. Unnoticed by the rescue team, he/she is left wandering amid the debris, struggling to find his/her way to safety.

24 See in this regard Steven M. Duncan, *Analytic Philosophy of Religion: Its History since 1955* (Tirril, Penrith: Humanities-Ebooks, 2007).

25 Still, two more refinements are in order below.

26 With two provisos I added above and two more below.

In such a situation, your friend is justified to believe he/she is alive, and anyone else is wrong about his/her death. But given your reliable information, you are also justified in believing that your friend perished in a plane crash, even though, in fact, he/she did not.

It is important to note that friendly atheism, as characterised by Rowe, is a non-factive theory of justification (see Figure 2).

> *Non-factive theory of justification*: for a belief to count as a justification, it need *not* be true.

To see the point, let us return to the CPS argument. You are justified in believing that your friend died because you heard about the plane crash from a reliable radio announcement and perhaps later via the newspapers. Your justification is not based on fact, but still, it is justification. So, according to the non-factive theory of justification, false justified belief is possible. It is contrasted with a factive theory of justification.

> *Factive theory of justification*: for a belief to count as a justification, it has to be true.[27]

Given the factive theory of justification, you are not justified in believing that your friend is dead due to a plane crash because your belief, which is not based on fact, does not count as justification. Friendly atheism, as characterised by Rowe, however, does not seem compatible with the factive theory of justification. So, if the factive theory is defensible, the friendly atheism of Rowe fails.

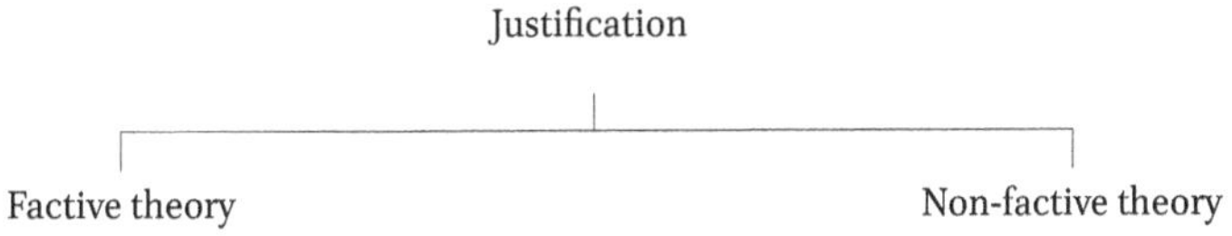


FIGURE 2: *Justification and factivity*

Since there is an ongoing debate about factivity or non-factivity of justification, Rowe's proposition remains unstable, depending on where one stands in this debate. Here, there is no need to adjudicate between factive and non-factive theories of justification. Instead, I will reformulate friendly atheism to remain neutral about the factive or non-factive debate, and still, the position's main aim (rational friendliness) remains intact. Then, I will extend this model to include friendly theism.

27 Factive theory of justification has made a marginal comeback in the last two decades or so in analytic epistemology; see this first collection of essays by factivist epistemologists: Veli Mitova, ed., *The Factive Turn in Epistemology* (Cambridge: Cambridge University Press, 2018).

My reformulation is not based on justification (factive or non-factive) but on rationality in the sense of blamelessness and excusability (personal justification). Rationality, in this sense, depends on the evidence available for the agent and also the agent's *responsible* response to the evidence, even if the response turns out to be wrong.[28] If so, then in CPS, you are excusable and blameless in believing your friend died in the plane crash.

> *Friendly atheism* (*fourth characterisation*): Under certain conditions, one can be rational (blameless and excusable) in believing a false proposition, if it is not about a self-evident issue. Since 'God exists' is a false proposition that is not about a self-evident issue, one can be rational (blameless and excusable) in believing this proposition under certain conditions, even in modern times.

But how are we to characterise a responsible response to available evidence? One promising way would be through epistemic norms:

> *Epistemic* (*deontic*) *rationality*: The responsible response of the agent to the available evidence, where responsibility requires following available epistemic norms, would render the agent blameless, excusable, and therefore rational.

Epistemic norms guide mental states such as (1) acquisition, holding, and evolution of belief and acceptance, (2) speech acts such as assertion, and (3) wilful actions (see Figure 3).[29]

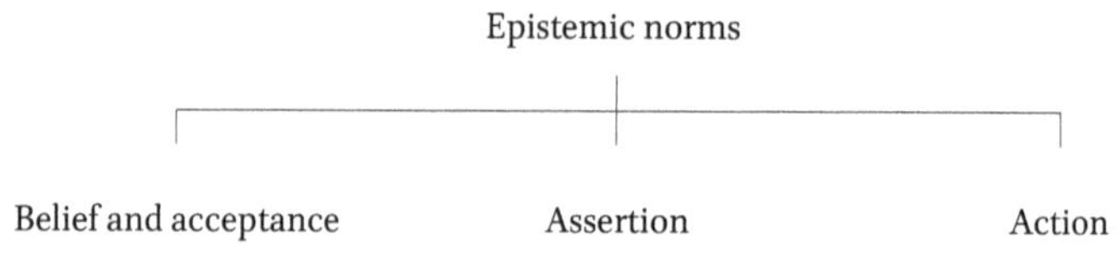


FIGURE 3: *Epistemic norm-guiding areas*

For example, everyday epistemic norms could be 'you better get your news from BBC, not Fox News' and 'do not believe in rumours'. But suppose someone lives in an epistemic community where tea leaf reading is an agreed way to decide on specific issues: could a community member be blameless and excusable if he/she decides according to the community's tea leaf reading norms?

---

28 I admit that this conceptualisation of rationality closely resembles a non-factive theory of justification. However, to sidestep the factive–non-factive debate of justification, I adhere to the normative epistemic concept of 'rationality'.

29 Matthew A. Benton, 'Knowledge Norms', *Internet Encyclopedia of Philosophy*, accessed 10 July 2023, https://iep.utm.edu/kn-norms/.

The answer seems, in principle, positive. Tea leaf reading might not be an epistemic norm in a different community or, objectively, not a minimally good epistemic norm at all. Still, as far as one is a part of an epistemic community in which it is an acceptable epistemic norm, one is, in principle, blameless and excusable if one decides according to the tea leaf reading norm of the community. However, this holds true only if the community is receptive to critiques and ultimately decides to adhere to its practice of tea leaf reading. To assume that if the community were more open to critique, it would have abandoned this practice appears overly imperialistic to me.

### 3.2 Friendly (A)theism

There is no reason to think that this rationally friendly model should only be suggested by atheists concerning theists. We can extend this model to the way theists should treat atheists, and the result is friendly theism:

> *Friendly theism*: Under certain conditions, one can be rational (blameless and excusable) in believing a false proposition, if it is not about a self-evident issue. 'God does not exist' is a false proposition that is not about a self-evident issue. Then, under certain conditions, one can be rational (blameless and excusable) in believing this proposition, even in modern times.

The combination of a friendly theism and a friendly atheism would give us friendly (a) theism:

> *Friendly (a)theism (initial characterisation)*: Under certain conditions, one can be rational (blameless and excusable) in believing a false proposition if it is not about a self-evident issue. Whether or not 'God exists' is true, which is not about a self-evident issue, one can be rational (blameless and excusable) under certain conditions in dis/believing this proposition, even in modern times.[30]

What are the conditions under which one is rational (blameless and excusable) in dis/ believing a non-self-evident false proposition? In CPS, you acquired the information from reliable sources, such as your perceptual experience that your friend boarded the plane and your information from the official radio channel or newspapers that he/she has not survived the plane crash. In the theism–atheism or intra-theism debate,[31] both

30 For a similar position, but with the focus on acceptance and not belief, see Jie Gao, 'Rational Action without Knowledge (and Vice Versa)', *Synthese* 194, no. 6 (2017): 1901–17.

31 Also, intra-atheism, as I do not assume that all atheists are friendly with each other. To explore a variety of incompatible atheistic perspectives, see Gray, *Seven Types of Atheism*.

sides have arguments that make them rational in their position. Theists have, among other things, cosmological, teleological, ontological, moral arguments and arguments from religious experience. Atheists also have, among other things, the problem of evil and divine hiddenness argument.

Friendly (a)theism makes complete sense when both sides of the debate have different evidence. One side, for example, appeals to evolution or the problem of evil to argue for atheism, and the other side appeals to religious experience or theistic arguments to argue for theism. But what about an occasion where both sides have (almost) the same evidence and similar cognitive ability but arrive at different conclusions? When, for example, both sides refer to evolution, and one side draws a theistic conclusion, and the other side draws an atheistic or agnostic conclusion, could both sides be rational? Yes, they could, as I will explain below by referring to Rowe's explanation. But even if they could not, all other things being equal, still friendly (a)theism is possible, though on a more restricted (uniqueness) ground in which rational friendliness is limited to an occasion in which both sides have different evidence for their position (see Figure 4).

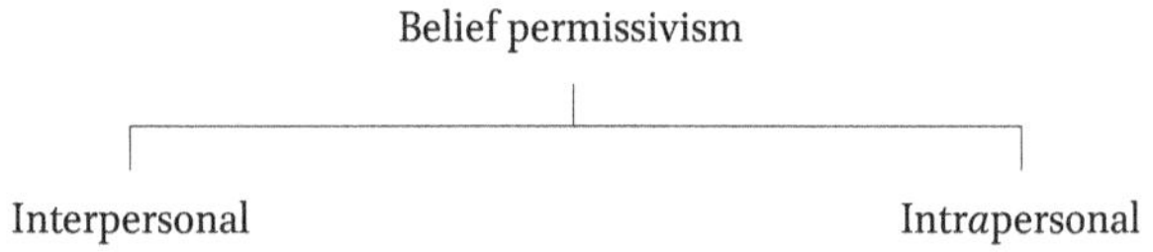


FIGURE 4 *The relation of evidence to friendliness*

> *Permissivism*: For a given body of evidence E and proposition *p*, more than one rational doxastic attitude exists that different agents with that evidence can adopt towards *p*.[32]

> *Uniqueness theory*: For a given body of evidence E and proposition *p*, only one rational doxastic attitude exists that different agents with that evidence can adopt towards *p*.

Rowe defends a permissivist version of friendly atheism. He depicts a scenario where you perform three iterations of adding an extended sum of numbers and obtain the result *x*. You share this information with your friend. Now, your friend has similar evidence to what you have. Subsequently, your friend uses his/her calculator twice and concludes

32 For a sympathetic and up-to-date characterisation of permissivism, see Elizabeth Jackson and Margaret Greta Turnbull, 'Permissivism, Underdetermination, and Evidence', in *The Routledge Handbook of the Philosophy of Evidence*, ed. Maria Lasonen-Aarnio and Clayton Littlejohn (New York: Routledge, 2024), 358–70.

that the sum of the numbers is not *x*. However, considering the damage to your friend's calculator unbeknown to him/her, it is reasonable for you to believe that the sum is *x* and that your friend is rational in holding that it is not *x*. This scenario presents a situation in which you and your friend possess almost all the evidence supporting proposition *p*. Yet, you are rational in holding *p*. You can reasonably believe that your friend is also rational in holding not-*p*.[33] Let us call this 'the calculator argument'.

Before addressing some objections, it is worth noting that what Rowe defends here is interpersonal and not intra-personal belief permissivism (see Figure 5).

> *Interpersonal belief permissivism*: For a given body of evidence E and proposition *p*, more than one rational doxastic attitude exists that *different agents* with evidence E can adopt towards *p*.

> *Interapersonal belief permissivism*: For a given body of evidence and proposition *p*, more than one rational doxastic attitude exists that *a single agent* with evidence E can adopt towards *p*.

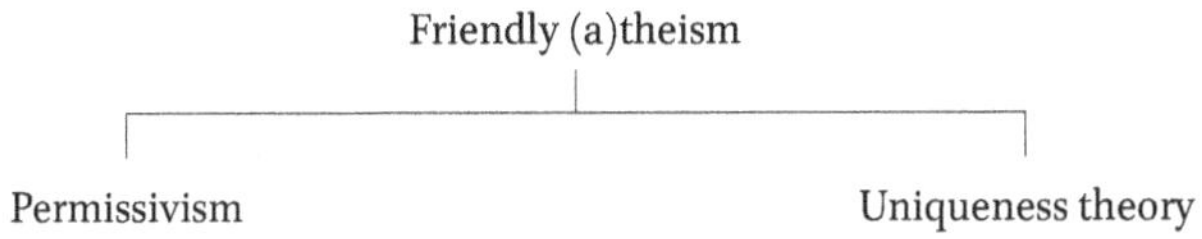


FIGURE 5: *A variety of belief permissivism*

Interpersonal belief permissivism can sometimes find justification within the framework of inter*a*personal belief permissivism itself. For instance, given my epistemic background, if evidence regarding a particular issue is so undetermined that it allows for multiple rational doxastic attitudes, I can infer that another epistemic agent with a different background might find him/herself in a similar situation. But it need not be so. Even if, given my epistemic background, evidence for a subject is determined enough to support only one rational doxastic attitude, I can still assume that another epistemic agent with a different background might be rational in adopting a different rational attitude. If so, then as far as our purpose in this article is concerned, which is to defend the friendly version of both theism and atheism, we do not need to focus on intra-personal belief permissivism.[34]

33 Rowe, 'The Problem of Evil', 340–41.
34 For a defence, see Elizabeth Jackson, 'A Defense of Intrapersonal Belief Permissivism', *Episteme* 18, no. 2 (2021): 313–27.

### 3.3 Some Objections to Friendly (A)theism

Let me address four objections to friendly (a)theism and respond to them. In light of the fourth objection, I will reformulate friendly (a)theism.

#### 3.3.1 *Relativism Objection*

One might argue that friendly (a)theism is prone to relativism:

> *Relativism objection*: If friendly (a)theism amounts to this position that both sides of a deep theoretical conflict, such as the theism–atheism debate, could be equally rationally held, then friendly (a)theism would be relativistic. Since relativism is not defensible, then what amounts to relativism is also not defensible. Because friendly (a)theism amounts to relativism, it is not defensible.

Friendly (a)theism would be relativistic because the idea of equal validity of radically conflicting ideas lies at the heart of relativism.[35]

*Response*: Alethic relativism is entailed neither by the unique (impermissivist) version of friendly (a)theism nor by its permissivist version. Both versions are about the rationality of belief and not the truth of belief. But what about relativism about rationality? The uniqueness version does not entail relativism about rationality since it does not entail equal validity. What might be the candidate for relativism about rationality is the permissivist version. The objection is that although permissivism might not amount to alethic relativism, its connection to truth is eliminated, which inevitably leads to relativism about rationality.

I depict rationality as depending on responsible responsiveness to evidence available to an epistemic agent. If so depicted, rationality's connection to truth, though weakened, is not eliminated since responsiveness to evidence is more likely truth conducive than non-responsiveness. This weak but not eliminated connection of rationality to truth seems enough for at least *prima facie* rationality of a position taken by an epistemic agent[36] and to do away with at least the everything-goes version of relativism about rationality.

#### 3.3.2 *Too Minimal Objection*

Yet, another objection can be formulated as follows:

> *Too minimal objection*: The theory of rationality upon which friendly (a)theism is based is too minimal to rule out pseudo-sciences, such as phrenology and astrology, and superstitious beliefs such as 'touch wood' or not walking under a ladder. Too minimal a theory of rationality is not defensible. Therefore, friendly (a)theism is

35 Paul Boghossian, *Fear of Knowledge: Against Relativism and Constructivism* (New York: Oxford University Press, 2006), 2–7.

36 More on this below.

not defensible too.

*Response*: Objectively, a theory of rationality based on responsible responsiveness to evidence allows for the gradual refinement of our theories. While some pseudo-sciences or superstitious beliefs may not be immediately debunked, responsible responsiveness to evidence can, over time, lead to rejecting or revising such claims. Rationality is an ongoing process, and responsible responsiveness to evidence provides a framework for refining our understanding. Objectively speaking, though pseudo-sciences, such as phrenology and astrology, and superstitious beliefs, such as 'touch wood' or not walking under a ladder, might be *prima facie* rational, over time, it turns out that they are not *ultima facie* rational.

Furthermore, minimal rationality can serve as a safeguard against dogmatism, urging one to refrain from hastily categorising a theory as pseudo-scientific or superstitious. Historically, some scientific theories have been initially labelled as pseudo-scientific, but they did withstand criticisms over time and emerged as viable scientific theories.

One such example is the theory of continental drift, proposed by Alfred Wegener in the early twentieth century. It was initially met with resistance and considered pseudo-scientific. However, continental drift became an integral part of the scientific understanding of earth's geological history with the discovery of seafloor spreading and the development of the theory of plate tectonics and methodological shifts in geology.[37]

### 3.3.3 *Redundancy Objection*

Another objection says if the primary goal of friendly (a)theism is to theoretically safeguard tolerance among different religious believers and among believers and non-believers, then there is no need to dig all the way, considering both sides of the theism–atheism debate as, in principle, rational. Instead, one can appeal to a practical rule according to which 'Everybody Has the Right to Be Wrong (At Least Once)', to borrow the title of Frank Sinatra's famous 1965 song. One can easily be friendly with an irrational person as long as one's irrationality does not lead to harming others. This objection concludes that reconsidering rationality to safeguard tolerance is not necessary but redundant.

*Response*: This objection misses three points. First, there is a higher likelihood of displaying intolerance towards someone perceived as irrational. How can one epistemically and pedagogically tolerate an individual who espouses beliefs such as the earth being flat? The fundamental objective of education as an institution is to assist people in overcoming irrational beliefs. Second, the aim of friendly (a)theism is not only theoretical safeguarding of tolerance but also reconsidering the widespread accusation of irrationality in the theism–atheism debate, one of whose problems is intolerance. My objective extends

37 Naomi Oreskes, *The Rejection of Continental Drift: Theory and Method in American Earth Science* (New York: Oxford University Press, 1999).

beyond practical considerations—beyond merely eliminating intolerance. Through a friendly analysis of the nature of rationality, I argue that accusations of irrationality are often misplaced, especially in the theism–atheism debate. Third, given the widespread allegation of irrationality, which takes all but one group as irrational, tolerance is not safeguarded, even if we consider 'the right to be wrong' principle. Typically, rational individuals perceive irrational groups as potentially harmful to society, leading in the best-case scenario to a tolerant stance without regard for them as complete epistemic agents from which rational people can glean meaningful insights. The result is 'epistemic injustice', a kind of injustice done to people in their capacity as epistemic agents.

Epistemic injustice comes in two forms: (1) testimonial injustice, which gives more epistemic credit to the groups considered 'rational' and less to the groups considered 'irrational', and (2) hermeneutical injustice, which prevents groups considered 'irrational' and marginalised from developing skills to be able to express themselves.[38]

Therefore, since the widespread accusation of irrationality in the theism–atheism context is neither theoretically defensible nor able to avoid epistemic injustice, creating an alternative and friendly theory of rationality is theoretically *and* practically a desideratum.

#### 3.3.4 *Strong Evidence Objection*

According to this objection, even a permissivist may adopt an unfriendly stance as either a theist or an atheist. Within the permissive framework, an unfriendly theist may argue that the theism–atheism debate lacks permissiveness due to compelling evidence supporting theism. The theistic arguments, including ontological, teleological, cosmological, and moral reasoning, assert that atheism is irrational. Conversely, an unfriendly atheist adopting permissivism may counter that the theism–atheism discourse is non-permissive because substantial evidence supports atheism, such as the problem of evil, incoherent divine attributes argument, or the argument from divine hiddenness, rendering theistic beliefs irrational.

*Response*: However, I contend that the theism–atheism debate is permissive for at least two reasons. Firstly, as mentioned above, interpersonal belief permissivism can sometimes find justification within the framework of intra*a*personal belief permissivism. So, within the realm of interpersonal belief permissivism, after scrutinising the arguments on both sides, some individuals, myself included, find them inconclusive.[39] The inclusiveness of theistic and atheistic arguments allows for the permissivity of both theistic and atheistic beliefs.[40]

Secondly, a survey conducted by Bourget and Chalmers reveals that approximately 70

38 Miranda Fricker, *Epistemic Injustice: Power and the Ethics of Knowing* (New York: Oxford University Press, 2007).

39 I am ultimately a theist, not due to theistic arguments, but because I have had at least two religious experiences.

40 Elizabeth Jackson, 'A Permissivist Defense of Pascal's Wager', *Erkenntnis* 88 (2021): 2319.

per cent of professional philosophers identify as atheists, with 15 per cent considering themselves theists. Notably, when focusing on philosophers of religion who specialise in questions about God's existence, around 70 per cent identify as theists.[41] This substantial disagreement among specialists demonstrates that intelligent and informed individuals exist on both sides, making the theism–atheism debate a strong candidate for permissiveness.

This objection, however, compels us once again and for the last time to refine our characterisation of friendly (a)theism:

> *Friendly (a)theism (final characterisation)*: Under certain conditions, one can be rational (blameless and excusable) in believing a false proposition if it is not about a self-evident issue and there is no conclusive reason against it. Whether or not 'God exists' is true, which is not about a self-evident issue, and there is no conclusive reason for or against it, one can be rational (blameless and excusable) under certain conditions in dis/believing this proposition, even in modern times.

Given the above, we can characterise unfriendly (a)theism as follows:

> *Unfriendly (a)theism (final characterisation)*: Either there are no certain conditions under which one can be rational (blameless and excusable) in believing a false proposition if it is not about a self-evident issue and there is no conclusive reason against it, or even if there are such conditions, 'God exists' or 'God does not exist' is not an instance of them. Then, no one can be rational (blameless and excusable) under certain conditions in dis/believing this proposition, even in modern times.</EXT>

## 4. Friendly Theism: A Scriptural Defence

Although the philosophical defence of friendly (a)theism and critique of unfriendly (a)theism might be enough to convince a (philosophically interested) atheist and theist, it might not be enough to convince a (religiously inclined) theist. A theological defence is also needed for such a person. In the analytic tradition, which was—and more or less still is—mainly Christian-based, few efforts have been made to develop a friendly theism model after Rowe's friendly atheism or one that is even friendlier than his model.[42]

---

41 David Bourget and David J. Chalmers, 'What Do Philosophers Believe?', *Philosophical Studies* 170, no. 3 (2014): 476.

42 See e.g. John Greco, 'Friendly Theism', in *Religious Tolerance through Humility*, ed. James Kraft and David Basinger (Burlington, VT: Ashgate, 2009), 51–58; Francis Jonbäck, 'How to Be a Friendly Skeptical Theist', *Forum Philosophicum* 17, no. 2 (2012): 197–210.

But, to my knowledge, there has not been any effort to develop a friendly Muslim theism, at least not in the analytic tradition of philosophy. In this article, I can only sketch such a task in the hope that others may join in further developing such a model. To begin, let us consider the Qur'an as the central text of Muslimness.

### 4.1 Friendly Theism and the Qur'an

The Qur'anic ethics of belief emphasises the importance of the *way* we acquire, hold, transmit, and assess our action-related beliefs as well as the *content* of our beliefs. Although the Qur'an condemns some doctrines, such as the Trinity[43] and Jesus being the son of God,[44] it praises pious Christians:

> You [Prophet] ... are sure to find that the closest in affection towards the believers are those who say, 'We are Christians,' for there are among them people devoted to learning and ascetics. These people are not given to arrogance, and when they listen to what has been sent down to the Messenger, you will see their eyes overflowing with tears because they recognize the Truth [in it]. They say, 'Our Lord, we believe, so count us amongst the witnesses. Why should we not believe in God and in the Truth that has come down to us, when we long for our Lord to include us in the company of the righteous?' For saying this, God has rewarded them with Gardens graced with flowing streams, and there they will stay: that is the reward of those who do good.[45]

One might conclude from this verse and similar verses[46] that although the content of belief is not without significance, the ethics of belief is more important for the Qur'an, to such a degree that from the Qur'anic perspective, despite having false doctrines, humble and truth-seeking Christians would have a chance to enjoy salvation.

The Qur'an emphasises its ethics of belief both positively (those who are humble and truth-seekers, even if false-believers, under certain circumstances, would have a chance to enjoy salvation) and negatively (those who are persistently arrogant and willingly and knowingly truth-blockers will be damned unless God forgives them):

> But when Our enlightening signs came to them, they said, 'This is clearly [just] sorcery!' They denied them, in their wickedness and their pride, *even though their souls acknowledged them as true*. See how those who spread corruption met their end![47]

43 See e.g. Q. 5:73.
44 See e.g. Q. 4:171, 5:72, 112:3.
45 Q. 5:82–85. All Qur'anic translations are from M. A. S. Abdel Haleem, *The Qur'ān: A New Translation* (Oxford: Oxford University Press, 2008).
46 Such as Q. 2:62, 5:69.
47 Q. 27:13–14 (emphasis added).

That is why the Qur'an emphatically adds in multiple verses, including the one just quoted, a proviso, namely, 'they willingly choose the wrong path', to distinguish between wilful wrongdoers/false-believers and those who, despite their truth-seeking and humble efforts, make a mistake in belief and/or act. Another example among many[48] is: 'Do not mix truth with falsehood, or hide the truth *when you know it*.'[49] And if one is a wrongdoer but not willingly and knowingly so, then one has a chance of salvation if one repents when given warning and advice:

> God loves those who do good. Those who remember God and implore forgiveness for their sins if they do something shameful or wrong themselves—who forgives sins but God?—and *who never knowingly persist in doing wrong*.[50]

One, however, might make this challenging argument. The Qur'anic ethics of belief is confined to Abrahamic religions and not comprehensive enough to include atheists and agnostics, or at least the Qur'an is silent about their ethical status and soteriological destiny. Then, although Jews and Christians, even if their monotheism might not be pure, have a chance of salvation under certain circumstances, atheists and agnostics have no chance of salvation since they do not believe in God. The objection concludes that the Qur'anic ethics of belief does not support friendly theism.

It is true that atheism, or one could say naturalism or agnosticism, has only been passingly mentioned a few times in the Qur'an,[51] but there is no verse in which mere doubt and denial have been condemned.[52] '*Kufr*' in the Qur'an is not mere doubt or denial but intimately tied with arrogance and stubbornness:

> The *kāfir* is not one who *cannot* see the signs of the divine presence and power which are understood as such by the *mu'min*, but simply one who does not see or refuses to see them … Presumably the activities of a *kāfir* can include giving the lie (*kadhdhaba*), forging a lie (*ifk*) against God, plotting, mocking (*haza'a*), and many others.[53]

48 Some other examples would be Q. 2:22, 2:75, 2:146, 2:188, 3:71, 3:75, 3:78, 8:27, 9:115, 23:117, 43:86.
49 Q. 2:42 (emphasis added).
50 Q. 3:135 (emphasis added).
51 Atheistic/naturalistic cosmology has been mentioned probably only two times in the Qur'an: (1) 'Were they created without any agent? Were they the creators? Did they create the heavens and the earth? No! They do not have faith' (Q. 52:35–36); (2) 'They say, "There is only our life in this world: we die, we live, nothing but time destroys us." They have no knowledge of this; they only follow guesswork' (Q. 45:24). To find a verse addressing agnosticism as a healthy scepticism and not as wilful suspicion is even more complex, but perhaps this verse is pertinent: 'Can there be any doubt about God, the Creator of the heavens and earth?' (Q. 14:10).
52 Verses such as 34:21, 34:54, 38:8, 41:45, and 44:9 condemn irresponsible doubt, not mere doubt.
53 Marilyn Robinson Waldman, 'The Development of the Concept of *Kufr* in the Qur'ān', *Journal of the American Oriental Society* 88, no. 3 (1968): 444–45.

So, *kufr* is intimately tied in the Qur'an with wrongdoing (hiding or covering the truth) rather than mere doubt or denial. *Kufr* is ingratitude and repudiation rather than mere non-/false belief. It is more moral than doxastic. Therefore, in the Qur'an, 'the opposite of belief does not seem to be repudiation (*kufr*) but sin .... Belief, it appears, must be understood to involve at least an anticipatory commitment to avoiding future transgressions.'[54]

Moreover, the Qur'anic ethics of belief is based on the fundamental rule that 'God does not burden any soul with more than it can bear [alternative translation: God tasks no soul beyond its capacity],[55] each gains whatever good it has done, and suffers its bad'.[56]

This oft-cited verse has been widely, though not unanimously, interpreted as denoting that people are not responsible for what is beyond their physical and/or mental capacity. Put another way, it means *taklīf bimā lā yuṭāq* (requiring individuals to do what they cannot) is inadmissible (*qabīḥ*). The Muʿtazila[57] and Shīʿa[58] consider the absence of coercion as the prerequisite of moral agency, while for the Ashʿarīs, 'there is nothing inherent in coercion itself that would make its absence a necessary condition for moral agency'.[59] So, Ashʿarīs do not consider *taklīf bimā lā yuṭāq* as inadmissible.[60] But, I am inclined towards the Muʿtazilī-Shīʿī interpretation, as the notion of 'God being merciful, just, and all-knowing'[61] implies that He does not burden individuals beyond their capacity.

Considering the specific Qur'anic ethics of belief in addition to the moral nucleus of the key term '*kufr*' in the Qur'an and given the Muʿtazilī-Shīʿī interpretation of the above verse (inadmissibility of *taklīf bimā lā yuṭāq*), one can plausibly conclude that the Qur'anic ethics of belief does not exclude truth-seeking and open-minded/hearted atheists and agnostics. Simply put, God's anger in the Qur'an was not due to belief as such but to how that belief was formed. The Qur'an, then, supports ethical and soteriological pluralism.

Again, I must emphasise that although these are presented as three concepts in the Qur'an (see Figure 6), they are interdependent. They depend on some divine attributes such as divine mercy and justice, repeated in many verses emphasising that 'God is never unjust to people'.[62] According to the Muʿtazilī-Shīʿī interpretation, this necessitates that

54 Nicolai Sinai, *Key Terms of the Qur'an: A Critical Dictionary* (Princeton, NJ: Princeton University Press, 2023), 476; see also 605–10.

55 Alternative translation taken from Seyyed Hossein Nasr, Caner K. Dagli, Maria Massi Dakake, Joseph E. B. Lumbard, and Mohammed Rustom, eds., *The Study Quran: A New Translation and Commentary* (New York: HarperCollins, 2015), 125.

56 Q. 2:286; see also 2:233, 6:152, 7:42, 23:62, 65:7.

57 See e.g. Abū al-Qāsim Maḥmūd b. ʿUmar al-Zamakhsharī, *Tafsīr al-kashshāf* (Beirut: Dār al-Maʿrifa, 2009), 159.

58 See e.g. Muḥammad Ḥusayn Ṭabāṭabāʾī, *al-Mīzān fī tafsīr al-Qurʾān* (Beirut: Muʾassasat al-Aʿlamī li-l-Maṭbūʿāt, 1997), 2:449–50.

59 Mairaj U. Syed, *Coercion and Responsibility in Islam: A Study in Ethics and Law* (New York: Oxford University Press, 2017), 67.

60 See e.g. Fakhr al-Dīn al-Rāzī, *Tafsīr al-Fakhr al-Rāzī* (Beirut: Dār al-Fikr, 1981), 7:151–53.

61 Here are only some examples containing this notion: Q. 2:134, 2:281, 3:18, 6:164, 41:46, 52:21. See also the following note.

62 In addition to the verses mentioned in the previous note, see Q. 3:182, 8:51, 22:10, 50:29.

God does not 'burden people with what is beyond their capability'. If so, then the Qur'anic ethics of belief corroborates friendly theism.[63]

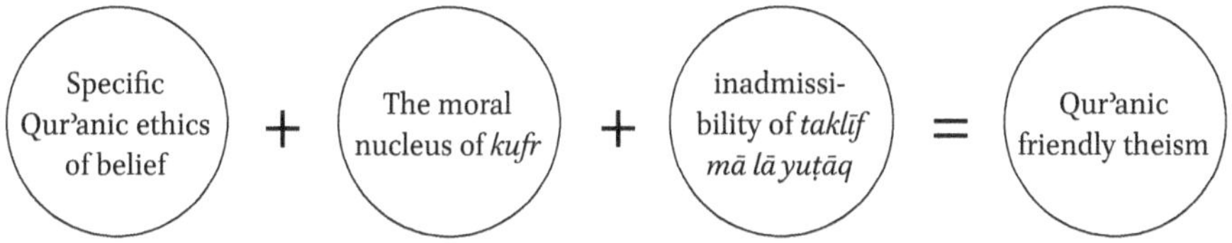


FIGURE 6: *Main elements of Qur'anic friendly theism*

In a sense, my task of laying out a Muslim theological defence of friendly theism is already done. I argued that Qur'anic friendly theism could be derived from holistic hermeneutics. This approach gathers different verses into a unified account while avoiding atomistic hermeneutics, which only relies on one or a few verses, ignoring other relevant and perhaps conflicting verses.

But one might argue that any position backed by an (even holistic) interpretation of the Qur'an without being supplemented by independent rational corroboration is like taking anthropomorphism at face value only by referring to the Qur'anic verses whose superficial (*ẓāhir*) meaning denotes God having hands, eyes, or a face. Anthropomorphic interpretation of some verses should be set aside not only by considering other apophatic verses (holistic hermeneutics) but also by extra Qur'anic arguments (holistic philosophical theology) that argue for the impossibility of God having a body.

To supplement holistic hermeneutics with a holistic natural theology (the scriptural with the rational), in the next section, I will argue for friendly theism by referring to the current debates in religious epistemology.

## 5. Friendly Theism: An Epistemological Defence

My main argument in this section is that one's religious epistemological model is usually based on either perception, testimony, argument, or faith (see Figure 7). To substantiate friendly (a)theism, I do not need to adjudicate between these religious epistemological models to judge which one is preferable or to come up with a mixed version. As far as defending friendly theism is concerned, I will show that in each of these epistemological models, an epistemic friendly version of theism is not only possible but preferable to its non-friendly version.[64]

63 I concentrated solely on the Qur'an in my scriptural defence, but only due to limited space. I do not imply a *sola scriptura* approach.

64 Except for the faith model, I drew inspiration from Greco's model: Greco, 'Friendly Theism'.

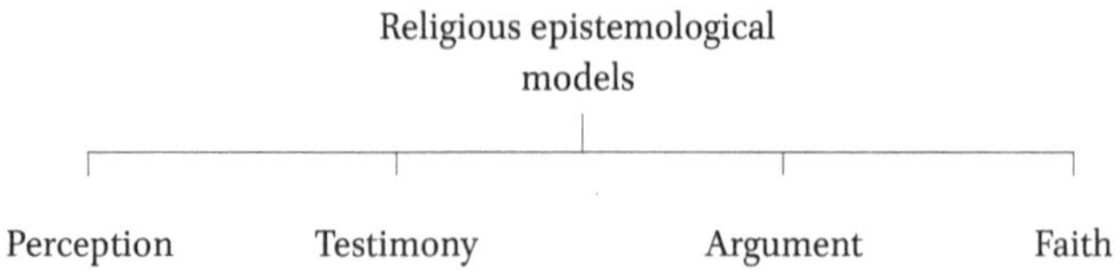


FIGURE 7: *A variety of religious epistemological models*

## 5.1 Perception Model

In the perception model, which works in those kinds of theologies in which God is depicted as personal (the dominant, but not the sole, theology of Judaism and Islam) or a person (Christianity), one gains knowledge, understanding, and justified, warranted, or rational belief of God mainly through perceiving God,[65] which works *in a proper environment* via a special cognitive faculty called *sensus divinitatis* (the sense of the divine). The result is that belief in God is properly basic and, therefore, rational.[66]

Now, let us see how the perception model corroborates friendly theism. If God is a person/personal, then in principle, the logic of interhuman perceptual encounters applies to human–God perceptual encounters. The logic of interhuman perceptual encounters is that one might be someday happy and sad another day, or soft with someone, and harsh with another. Accordingly, one might experience someone as happy when she is happy, and another might experience her as sad when she is sad. Despite their differences, both sides are correct in their perception of her.

Even if we assume that Person(al) God has no feelings,[67] divine personal attributes such as omnibenevolence might have different manifestations with different people. It might partially explain conflicting understandings of the divine, such as perplexingly various understating of monotheism within and between Abrahamic religions. If so, then the logic of the human–God perceptual encounter corroborates friendly intra-theism, formulated as follows:

> Friendly intra-theism (experiential model): Let us suppose A and B have perceived God differently, A has perceived God as so close that God is felt closer to one's jugular

65 William P. Alston, *Perceiving God: The Epistemology of Religious Experience* (Ithaca: Cornell University Press, 1991).

66 Alvin Plantinga, *Warranted Christian Belief* (New York: Oxford University Press, 2000), ch. 6.

67 Although there have been some Jewish, Christian, and Muslim theologians who have had sympathy with anthropopathism (a form of anthropomorphism that takes God to have non-physical sublime emotions and passions), the comparative study of anthropopathism in Abrahamic religions is still in its nascent stages of development, if not non-existent. For a recent study of anthropomorphism with a focus on anthropomorphism only in a part of the Old Testament, see Anne K. Knafl, *Forming God: Divine Anthropomorphism in the Pentateuch* (Winona Lake, IN: Penn State University Press, 2014).

> vein, based upon which A forms a pantheistic conception of God. In contrast, B has perceived God as totally other and beyond, based upon which B forms an apophatic conception of God. Let us further suppose that pantheism and apophaticism are not compatible. Given the experiential model, since God has different manifestations, A and B are faultlessly rational in believing in two somewhat incompatible conceptions of God.

But what about atheists? Given the perception model, could their position be rationally held? One might suspect that while theistic differences could be explained to be rationally held, in principle, by the perception model, atheism cannot be similarly explained. Because if God exists, the non-existence of God cannot be perceived.

The answer is that atheists do not perceive the non-existence of God; rather, they simply do not perceive God. It is like a situation in which you are looking for a drink. 'It's in the fridge,' your wife tells you. You open the fridge and look carefully inside, and you do not find it. If this situation makes you form the belief that 'the drink is not in the fridge', your belief is rationally held, even if the drink is somewhere hidden in the fridge. The same situation is true for a truth-seeking atheist. If the God of Abrahamic religion exists, then for whatever reason, God might not be willing to show Himself to such an atheist in this world. Then, such a truth-seeking atheist can rationally withdraw from believing in God since one does not perceive God. Some Muslim mystics like Rumi have alluded to this experiential model. He says, addressing God:

> Once You conceal Yourself from me, darkness and disbelief consume me,
> Once You reveal Yourself to me, I am a devout believer by Your soul.[68]

This model can be formulated as follows:

> Friendly (a)theism (experiential model): If God exists, God might not manifest Himself, for whatever reasons, to a truth-seeker. Given the experiential model, a truth-seeking atheist who has not experienced divine manifestation can, in principle, rationally withdraw from believing in God.

However, one might object to this model in the following way. Consider our perception of the world. Suppose that by engaging in various unhealthy activities, I knowingly damage my sense organs to such an extent that I fail to have veridical experiences and, thus, end up with mostly false beliefs. Indeed, I must admit that I have not behaved epistemically responsibly. The same analogy can be applied to the spiritual realm. After

68 Jalāl al-Dīn Muḥammad Rūmī, *Dīvān Kabīr*, ed. Badiozzaman Forouzanfar (Tehran: Amir Kabir, 1999), 5:30, ghazal no. 2162.

leading a sinful life for many years, my sensus divinitatis may be damaged to the extent that I am no longer able to perceive the presence of the deity and even lose all my moral sensibilities. In such a case, I cannot claim that my atheism is rationally grounded. Yes, there are instances where God refuses to reveal Himself despite the genuinely persistent attempts of the would-be believer. However, this is not the rule.

In response, one could argue that while the possibility of a sinful life blocking the divine sense is one option among others, if atheists lead an ethical life and are truth-seekers, then the experiential model becomes a more plausible explanation for their atheism than the sinful life.

### 5.2 Testimony Model

Before delving into the issue, some preliminaries are in order. First, many people form, hold, change, or modify and assess their beliefs based on the testimony of others. Testimony is the most social source of knowledge or justified/rational belief among all epistemic sources.[69] Second, testimony is inherently intertwined with placing trust in someone or a group as the testifier. Third, even if one takes a reductionist theory of testimony—according to which testimonial knowledge can be arguably reduced to other more fundamental sources of knowledge such as sense experience, introspection, memory, and inference—testimony seems an inevitable source of knowledge, justified, or rational belief.

Given these preliminaries, the question is: can atheists be rational in dis/non-believing in God based on the testimony of others? The answer seems, in principle, positive. Exactly like theists who may find the testimony of prophets, sacred figures, theologians, and religious communities as compelling evidence for the existence of God and divine attributes,[70] atheists, for instance, may find the testimony of atheist scientists like Dawkins, philosophers like Russel, or communities such as Atheist Alliance International (AAI) as compelling evidence for the non-existence of God.

69 Here, I do not need to take a stance on whether testimony serves as a generative or transmitted source of knowledge, justified, or rational belief. For a pro-generative treatment of this issue, see Jennifer Lackey, *Learning from Words: Testimony as a Source of Knowledge* (New York: Oxford University Press, 2008).

70 See in this regard John Greco, *Individualism and Anti-Individualism in Islamic Epistemology* (forthcoming).

## 5.3 Argument Model

When it comes to the argument model, one might say although perceptual experience and testimony do not tip the scale—once, for all, and forever—in favour of either theism or atheism, argument, in the form of mathematical 'proof', does so. However, two responses are in order. First, argument, in the form of mathematical proof, even if applicable to the theism–atheism debate, is not necessarily incompatible with (at least a version of) friendly (a)theism. To understand why, we already saw how Rowe, in his calculator argument above, depicts a scenario in which although two people are differently calculating, one might be *rationally* wrong because, unbeknown to him/her, the calculator is not working properly.

Second, in the theism–atheism, intra-theism, or intra-atheism debate, arguments in the form of mathematical proof either turned out to be highly unlikely or even categorically ruled out. Arguably, it is highly unlikely or impossible to demonstrate or disprove God's existence. The argument in the form of proof (deductive argument) is still prevalent in mathematics and logic, but taking it as a model in all spheres of knowledge, including the theism–atheism debate, is a model called classical foundationalism.

> *Classical foundationalism*: Justified beliefs must be either foundational (basic) or non-basic but deductively derived from foundational beliefs. Foundational beliefs are self-evident, indubitable, or incorrigible.

There are numerous problems with classical foundationalism. One is that classical foundationalism itself is self-inferentially incoherent. It refutes itself. Classical foundationalism is neither foundational, nor is there any prospect of deducing it from foundational beliefs. So, by its own light, it does not meet its own criterion of being justified belief.[71] Moreover, given classical foundationalism, much of our ordinary knowledge of the past is unjustified, as it is neither foundational nor derivative from basic beliefs. The unintended result of classical foundationalism, then, is scepticism.

I do not claim that these critiques are devastating. There have been attempts to defend foundationalism (classical or otherwise) against these critiques.[72] But one thing is

71 See Alvin Plantinga, 'Reason and Belief in God', in *The Analytic Theist: An Alvin Plantinga Reader*, ed. James F. Sennett (Grand Rapids, MI: W. B. Eerdmans Publishing Company, 1998), 135–38; Alvin Plantinga, *Warrant: The Current Debate* (New York: Oxford University Press, 1993), 84–86; Alvin Plantinga, *Warrant and Proper Function* (New York: Oxford University Press, 1993), 182–83.

72 See e.g. William P. Alston, 'Has Foundationalism Been Refuted?', *Philosophical Studies: An International Journal for Philosophy in the Analytic Tradition* 29, no. 5 (1976): 287–305; John Greco, 'Plantinga, Foundationalism, and the Charge of Self-Referential Incoherence', *Grazer Philosophische Studien* 31, no. 1 (1988): 187–93; Daniel Howard-Snyder and E. J. Coffman, 'Three Arguments against Foundationalism: Arbitrariness, Epistemic Regress, and Existential Support', *Canadian Journal of Philosophy* 36, no. 4 (2006): 535–64; John M DePoe, 'In Defense of Classical Foundationalism: A Critical Evaluation of Plantinga's Argument That Classical Foundationalism Is Self-Refuting', *South African Journal of Philosophy* 26, no. 3 (2007): 245–51.

beyond reasonable doubt. Since (classical) foundationalism is no longer the only viable epistemological option, alternatives are available. These include, but are not limited to, minimal foundationalism (basic beliefs are not infallible), coherentism (there are no non-propositional foundations), externalism (justification depends on factors external to the person's awareness), pragmatism (beliefs are justified when they serve our practical goals), pragmatic encroachment (pragmatic factors play a crucial role in epistemic knowledge), and critical rationalism (conjectures are corroborated, though not justified, when they withstand criticism).

It is beyond the scope of this article to adjudicate between these alternatives. Suffice it to say that if (classical) foundationalism is not the only epistemological option, then argument in the form of demonstrative proof of theism or atheism is not the only option in religious epistemology. As already mentioned, although argument in the demonstrative proof form is compatible with (at least a version of) friendly (a)theism, the fact that the demonstrative proof is not the only epistemological option further paves the way for friendly (a)theism. Argument is not exclusively reserved for classical foundationalism. All alternative epistemological options involve some form of argumentation. However, if the argument is not solely rooted in (classical) foundationalism, it is more likely conducive to friendly (a)theism than otherwise.

### 5.4 Faith Model

Fideism, which literally means faith-ism, is not another name for religious belief. Instead, it is a philosophical account of faith. Fideism is an ancient approach in theology in which one does not need to base the belief in the proposition 'God exists' on independent propositional evidence, but one can base it on 'faith', either in the lack of independent propositional evidence or even despite independent evidence against it. Fideists, whose positions date back to the early Catholic tradition, support their belief scripturally by appealing to the words of St Paul. For example: 'We walk by faith, not by sight.'[73]

Historically, fideism is closely linked with the mystical traditions of Christianity, Judaism, and Islam.[74] Although fideism is an ancient movement from early Christianity, 'fideism' is a much later French term traced back to the second half of the nineteenth century.[75] Not surprisingly, fideism denies natural theology, an ancient approach that uses independent rational tools to defend theistic belief. Tertullian, William of Ockham, Pierre Bayle, Erasmus, Montaigne, Kierkegaard, William James, Karl Barth, and some Wittgensteinians (if not Wittgenstein himself) are usually associated with fideism (of one form or another).

---

73 2 Corinthians 5:7.

74 For a study of Islamic fideism, see Aziz Al-Azmeh, 'Orthodoxy and Ḥanbalite Fideism', *Arabica* 35, no. 3 (1988): 253–66. For a study of Jewish fideism, influenced by Islamic fideism, see Ehud Krinis, *Judah Halevi's Fideistic Scepticism in the Kuzari* (Berlin: De Gruyter, 2020).

75 See Thomas D. Carroll, 'The Traditions of Fideism', *Religious Studies* 44, no. 1 (2008): 1–22.

Scepticism and fideism are historically intertwined.[76] If propositional reason (natural theology) cannot dis/prove God, or if what is dis/proven is not the God of Abraham, Isaac, and Jacob, but the (irrelevant) God of philosophers, and if religious faith is existentially vital and spiritually inevitable, then one might be rational in having faith without propositional reason or by going beyond reason or perhaps even paradoxically despite reason. But not all defenders of fideism take it to be anti-rational. For them, faith is arational (supra-rational) rather than irrational.[77]

Even if interpreted fideistically, the faith model of religious epistemology makes room for friendly theism. If faith is just either a fundamental existential decision and a wilful leap of faith or a light that God casts into the heart of whomever He wills, and it is not something that can/should be proven, then whoever finds themselves not willing to take a leap of faith or find their heart devoid of the divine light, might in principle be rational in dis/non-believing in God. Put simply, if faith is a rational choice among many other acceptable options, then other options are, in principle, equally acceptable—unless otherwise proven.

This is equally the case regarding those who do not have faith and those with different religious faiths. If so, then Christian fideism cannot prove atheism, agnosticism, Islam, or Judaism to be irrational. The same applies to Islamic or Jewish fideism concerning other (a)theistic options.

## 6. Conclusion

An accusation of irrationality in the theism–atheism debate has been a fundamental source of intolerance. I defended friendly (a)theism against its counterpart—unfriendly (a)theism. Drawing on William Rowe, I addressed various objections. Subsequently, I presented the scriptural (Qur'anic) defence of friendly theism and concluded with its epistemological defence.

## Bibliography

Abdel Haleem, M. A. S. *The Qur'ān: A New Translation*. Oxford: Oxford University Press, 2008.

Al-Azmeh, Aziz. 'Orthodoxy and Ḥanbalite Fideism'. *Arabica* 35, no. 3 (1988): 253–66.

76 For a historical and philosophical treatment of this entanglement, see T. Penelhum, *God and Skepticism: A Study in Skepticism and Fideism* (Dordrecht: Springer, 1983).

77 For two recent defences of 'supra-rational fideism', see C. Stephen Evans, *Faith beyond Reason: A Kierkegaardian Account* (Grand Rapids, MI: William B. Eerdmans Publishing Company, 1998); John Bishop, *Believing by Faith: An Essay in the Epistemology and Ethics of Religious Belief* (New York: Oxford University Press, 2007).

Alston, William P. 'Has Foundationalism Been Refuted?'. *Philosophical Studies: An International Journal for Philosophy in the Analytic Tradition* 29, no. 5 (1976): 287–305.

———. *Perceiving God: The Epistemology of Religious Experience*. Ithaca: Cornell University Press, 1991.

Benton, Matthew A. 'Knowledge Norms'. *Internet Encyclopedia of Philosophy*. Accessed 10 July 2023. https://iep.utm.edu/kn-norms/.

Bishop, John. *Believing by Faith: An Essay in the Epistemology and Ethics of Religious Belief.* New York: Oxford University Press, 2007.

Boghossian, Paul. *Fear of Knowledge: Against Relativism and Constructivism*. New York: Oxford University Press, 2006.

Bourget, David, and David J. Chalmers. 'What Do Philosophers Believe?'. *Philosophical Studies* 170, no. 3 (2014): 465–500.

Bunzel, Cole M. *Wahhābism: The History of a Militant Islamic Movement*. Princeton, NJ: Princeton University Press, 2023.

Carroll, Thomas D. 'The Traditions of Fideism'. *Religious Studies* 44, no. 1 (2008): 1–22.

Dawkins, Richard. *The God Delusion*. London: Bantam, 2006.

———. 'Letter: Scientific versus Theological Knowledge'. *Independent*, 20 March 1993. www.independent.co.uk/voices/letter-scientific-versus-theological-knowledge-1498837.html.

Day, Vox. *The Irrational Atheist: Dissecting the Unholy Trinity of Dawkins, Harris, and Hitchens*. Dallas: BenBella Books, 2008.

Dennett, Daniel, and Robert Winston. 'Is Religion a Threat to Rationality and Science?'. *Guardian*, 22 April 2008. www.theguardian.com/education/2008/apr/22/highereducation.uk5.

DePoe, John M. 'In Defense of Classical Foundationalism: A Critical Evaluation of Plantinga's Argument That Classical Foundationalism Is Self-Refuting'. *South African Journal of Philosophy* 26, no. 3 (2007): 245–51.

Duncan, Steven M. *Analytic Philosophy of Religion: Its History since 1955*. Tirril, Penrith: Humanities-Ebooks, 2007.

Evans, C. Stephen. *Faith beyond Reason: A Kierkegaardian Account*. Grand Rapids, MI: William B. Eerdmans Publishing Company, 1998.

Fricker, Miranda. *Epistemic Injustice: Power and the Ethics of Knowing*. New York: Oxford University Press, 2007.

Froese, Paul. 'Forced Secularization in Soviet Russia: Why an Atheistic Monopoly Failed'. *Journal for the Scientific Study of Religion* 43, no. 1 (2004): 35–50.

Gao, Jie. 'Rational Action without Knowledge (and Vice Versa)'. *Synthese* 194, no. 6 (2017): 1901–17.

Gray, John. *Seven Types of Atheism*. London: Penguin, 2018.

Greco, John. 'Friendly Theism'. In *Religious Tolerance through Humility*, edited by James

Kraft and David Basinger, 51–58. Burlington, VT: Ashgate, 2009.
———. *Individualism and Anti-Individualism in Islamic Epistemology*. Forthcoming.
———. 'Plantinga, Foundationalism, and the Charge of Self-Referential Incoherence'. *Grazer Philosophische Studien* 31, no. 1 (1988): 187–93.
Harré, Rom. 'Introduction'. In *Beyond Rationality: Contemporary Issues*, edited by Carl Jensen and Rom Harré, 1–7. Newcastle upon Tyne: Cambridge Scholars Publishing, 2012.
Harris, Sam. *The End of Faith: Religion, Terror and the Future of Reason*. New York: W. W. Norton & Company, 2004.
Hitchens, Christopher. *God Is Not Great: How Religion Poisons Everything*. New York: Twelve, 2007.
Howard-Snyder, Daniel, and E. J. Coffman. 'Three Arguments against Foundationalism: Arbitrariness, Epistemic Regress, and Existential Support'. *Canadian Journal of Philosophy* 36, no. 4 (2006): 535–64.
Jackson, Elizabeth. 'A Defense of Intrapersonal Belief Permissivism'. *Episteme* 18, no. 2 (2021): 313–27.
———. 'A Permissivist Defense of Pascal's Wager'. *Erkenntnis* 88 (2021): 2315–40.
Jackson, Elizabeth, and Margaret Greta Turnbull. 'Permissivism, Underdetermination, and Evidence'. In *The Routledge Handbook of the Philosophy of Evidence*, edited by Maria Lasonen-Aarnio and Clayton Littlejohn, 358–70. New York: Routledge, 2024.
Jonbäck, Francis. 'How to Be a Friendly Skeptical Theist'. *Forum Philosophicum* 17, no. 2 (2012): 197–210.
Knafl, Anne K. *Forming God: Divine Anthropomorphism in the Pentateuch*. Winona Lake, IN: Penn State University Press, 2014.
Krinis, Ehud. *Judah Halevi's Fideistic Scepticism in the Kuzari*. Berlin: De Gruyter, 2020.
Lackey, Jennifer. *Learning from Words: Testimony as a Source of Knowledge*. New York: Oxford University Press, 2008.
M., J. 'The Anti-Religious Campaign in Higher Education'. *Soviet Studies* 6, no. 3 (1955): 312–15.
Michot, Yahya. 'Between Entertainment and Religion: Ibn Taymiyya's Views on Superstition'. *The Muslim World* 99, no. 1 (2009): 1–20.
Mirdamadi, S. Yaser. 'Why I Am Muslim'. In *The Rowman & Littlefield Handbook of Philosophy and Religion*, edited by Mark A. Lamport, 383–91. Lanham: Rowman & Littlefield, 2022.
Mitova, Veli, ed. *The Factive Turn in Epistemology*. Cambridge: Cambridge University Press, 2018.
Nasr, Seyyed Hossein, Caner K. Dagli, Maria Massi Dakake, Joseph E. B. Lumbard, and Mohammed Rustom, eds. *The Study Quran: A New Translation and Commentary*. New York: HarperCollins, 2015.

Oreskes, Naomi. *The Rejection of Continental Drift: Theory and Method in American Earth Science*. New York: Oxford University Press, 1999.

Penelhum, T. *God and Skepticism: A Study in Skepticism and Fideism*. Dordrecht: Springer, 1983.

Plantinga, Alvin, 'Reason and Belief in God'. In *The Analytic Theist: An Alvin Plantinga Reader*, edited by James F. Sennett, 135–38. Grand Rapids, MI: William B. Eerdmans Publishing Company, 1998.

———. *Warrant and Proper Function*. New York: Oxford University Press, 1993.

———. *Warranted Christian Belief.* New York: Oxford University Press, 2000.

———. *Warrant: The Current Debate*. New York: Oxford University Press, 1993.

al-Rāzī, Fakhr al-Dīn. *Tafsīr al-Fakhr al-Rāzī*. Vol. 7. Beirut: Dār al-Fikr, 1981.

Rowe, William L. 'Friendly Atheism Revisited'. *International Journal for Philosophy of Religion* 68, no. 1–3 (2010): 7–13.

———. 'The Problem of Evil and Some Varieties of Atheism'. *American Philosophical Quarterly* 16, no. 4 (1979): 335–41.

Rūmī, Jalāl al-Dīn Muḥammad. *Dīvān Kabīr*. Edited by Badiozzaman Forouzanfar. 10 vols. Tehran: Amir Kabir, 1999.

Russell, Bertrand. *Why I Am Not a Christian: And Other Essays on Religion and Related Subjects*. New York: Simon and Schuster, 1957.

Sartwell, Crispin. 'Irrational Atheism'. *The Atlantic*, 11 October 2014. www.theatlantic.com/national/archive/2014/10/a-leap-of-atheist-faith/381353/.

Sinai, Nicolai. *Key Terms of the Qur'an: A Critical Dictionary*. Princeton, NJ: Princeton University Press, 2023.

Syed, Mairaj U. *Coercion and Responsibility in Islam: A Study in Ethics and Law*. New York: Oxford University Press, 2017.

Ṭabāṭabā'ī, Muḥammad Ḥusayn. *al-Mīzān fī tafsīr al-Qur'ān*. 22 vols. Beirut: Mu'assasat al-Aʿlamī li-l-Maṭbūʿāt, 1997.

Tasar, Eren. *Soviet and Muslim: The Institutionalization of Islam in Central Asia*. New York: Oxford University Press, 2017.

Timasheff, N. S. 'The Anti-Religious Campaign in the Soviet Union'. *The Review of Politics* 17, no. 3 (1955): 329–44.

Waldman, Marilyn Robinson. 'The Development of the Concept of *Kufr* in the Qur'ān'. *Journal of the American Oriental Society* 88, no. 3 (1968): 442–55.

al-Zamakhsharī, Abū al-Qāsim Maḥmūd b. ʿUmar. *Tafsīr al-kashshāf.* Beirut: Dār al-Maʿrifa, 2009.

# Towards a Grammatical Approach to Monotheism: Unpacking Ṭabāṭabā'ī's Theological Perspective

*Javad Taheri*

## 1. Preliminary Discussion

### 1.1 Comprehending *Tawḥīd*: Challenges and Issues

The concept of monotheism, a cornerstone of the Abrahamic faiths, holds a paramount position within these religious traditions. In each, the omnipotent deity's absolute sovereignty and uniqueness is acknowledged and revered. In Islam, the concept of *tawḥīd*, or 'monotheism', is the fundamental principle of the Islamic worldview. This doctrine, central to the *shahāda* or the Islamic profession of faith, is ingrained in every facet of Islamic theology, shaping its structure and underpinning its belief system. Reinforced by numerous Qur'anic verses and Prophetic teachings, *tawḥīd* transcends being merely a theological concept; it is a dynamic foundation that guides every aspect of a Muslim's faith and practice.[1]

The concept of *tawḥīd* has been comprehended and interpreted in different ways throughout Islamic intellectual history. This reflects how each generation of believers has progressively understood and wrestled with the meaning and implications of declaring God's unity. From Islamic theology, jurisprudence, and philosophy to Sufism, and even, to a certain extent, the Islamic perspective on natural sciences, various fields try to interpret the principle of *tawḥīd* and explore its foundational assertion that God is one.[2]

The broad spectrum of interpretations associated with the concept of *tawḥīd*, despite sharing numerous elements, inevitably leads to an array of contrasting perspectives and potential controversies concerning this doctrine. This scenario is what I encapsulate under the umbrella term 'problem of *tawḥīd*'. It is crucial to note that by using the term 'problem', my aim is not to suggest that the doctrine of *tawḥīd* itself is inherently problematic. Rather, it is an acknowledgement of the complexities associated with our comprehension and conceptualisation of this notion. Our understanding can oscillate between being logically coherent to logically inconsistent, or it might exhibit a combination of both—with some aspects of our comprehension being sound while others erring. The grammatical method used in this paper proposes that the most appropriate articulation of the concept of monotheism extends beyond certain conventional views on the concept, which may be deemed problematic.

1 Colin Turner, *Islam: The Basics* (London: Routledge, 2006), 75; Celene Ibrahim, *Islam and Monotheism*, Elements in Religion and Monotheism (Cambridge: Cambridge University Press, 2022).

2 Muḥammad Ḥusayn Ṭabāṭabā'ī, *A Shi'ite Anthology*, trans. William C. Chittick (London: Muhammadi Trust of Great Britain & Northern Ireland, 1981), 23.

### 1.2 Ṭabāṭabāʾī's Take on the Issue

In addition to the aforementioned potential problems, the paramount issue emerges when there is an endeavour to simultaneously acknowledge, firstly, the rendition of *tawḥīd* as it is delineated in the *kitāb* (the Book, the Qurʾan) and *sunna* (Islamic tradition) and secondly, an intellectually reasoned exposition of it. Historically, Islamic philosophical theology has grappled with this challenge, demonstrating that reason (*ʿaql*) and faith (*dīn*) can harmoniously collaborate in their elucidation of the concept of *tawḥīd*.[3]

Among contemporary Islamic thinkers, ʿAllāma Sayyid Muḥammad Ḥusayn Ṭabāṭabāʾī (1904–81) is renowned for his notable contributions to interpreting the complexities inherent in the conceptualisation of the divine and related theological considerations. Recognised as the founder of neo-Ṣadrian philosophical theology, he integrated theological, linguistic, and epistemological approaches to discuss the concept of religious language. A substantial portion of Ṭabāṭabāʾī's intellectual exertion was directed towards an exploration of ideas posited by Islamic thinkers such as Avicenna (Ibn Sīnā, 980–1037) and Mullā Ṣadrā (Ṣadr al-Dīn al-Shīrāzī, 1571/72–1635/40). Given the indelible imprint these figures have left on the annals of intellectual history of Islam, their contributions received careful examination in his scholarly investigations. While Ṭabāṭabāʾī was often cited as a staunch proponent of Mullā Ṣadrā,[4] he embraced Ṣadrian philosophy with a critical edge,[5] aiming to offer a more coherent interpretation of Islamic philosophical theology.

## 2. On the Grammatical Method

The primary objective of this article is to offer an innovative interpretation of the concept of *tawḥīd* in Ṭabāṭabāʾī's philosophical theology by means of David Burrell's grammatical-philosophical method.[6] Viewing Thomas Aquinas's theology through the lens of Wittgenstein's grammatical philosophy led to the development of grammatical Thomism. This perspective emphasises the important interaction between linguistic expression,

---

3 To explore the role of intellectual reasoning as a source of knowledge of the divine, particularly in Mullā Ṣadrā's school of thought, see Sajjad Rizvi, '"Only the Imam Knows Best": The Maktab-e Tafkīk's Attack on the Legitimacy of Philosophy in Iran', *Journal of the Royal Asiatic Society* 22, no. 3–4 (2012): 487–503, https://doi.org/10.1017/S1356186312000417. For a reference to Ṭabāṭabāʾī's notion of 'perfect compatibility of reason and revelation', see Sajjad Rizvi and Ahab Bdaiwi, 'ʿAllāma Ṭabāṭabāʾī (d. 1981), *Nihāyat al-Ḥikma*', in *The Oxford Handbook of Islamic Philosophy*, ed. Khaled El-Rouayheb and Sabine Schmidtke (Oxford: Oxford University Press, 2017), 654, https://doi.org/10.1093/oxfordhb/9780199917389.013.32.

4 For his commentary on Mullā Ṣadrā's magnum opus, see Muḥammad Ḥusayn Ṭabāṭabāʾī, 'Taʿlīqāt [scholia]', in *al-Ḥikma al-mutaʿāliya fī al-asfar al-ʿaqliyya al-arbaʿa*, by Ṣadr al-Dīn al-Shīrāzī, 9 vols. (Beirut: Dār Iḥyāʾ al-Turāth al-ʿArabī, 1981), vol. 6.

5 For more on this, see e.g. Mohammad Saeedimehr and Alireza Musadiqi Haqiqi, 'Naqd-i ʿAllāmih Ṭabāṭabāʾī bar ruykard-i furukahishi-yi ḥikmat-i mutaliyih dar mafhūm shinasi iradih-yi dhati khodavand', *Ayinih-yi Maʿrifat*, no. 15 (1387 SH/2008): 21–40.

6 The application of this method in discussing Ṭabāṭabāʾī does not aim to replace his philosophy with Burrell's but provides insights into his account of religious language and his interpretation of *tawḥīd*.

theological understanding, and grammatical analysis, leading to a re-examination of religious language.[7] It is necessary to highlight a few specificities of Burrell's approach to help the reader become acquainted with my manner of reading Ṭabāṭabā'ī's notion of *tawḥīd* through the lens of Burrell.

Burrell's grammatical Thomistic approach suggests an investigation of theological statements' depth grammar—as opposed to surface grammar[8]—allegedly the most appropriate way in specifying the meanings of certain assertions about God within our language.[9] Highlighting the role of distinction between these two kinds of grammars, influenced by Wittgenstein's thought, and Burrell's idiosyncratic way of using that in reading Aquinas sets his method apart. Burrell's grammatical Thomistic approach aims to reconcile pre-Kantian attention to metaphysics with a post-Kantian renewed conception of knowledge, religion, and language. His method stands out from both transcendental and analytic Thomists, who attempt to adapt Thomistic metaphysics to the context of twentieth-century scholarship. I cannot compare these three versions of Thomism here, which is beyond the scope of this article. However, it is perhaps helpful to note that Burrell's grammatical approach, on the one hand, seeks to sidestep a certain type of 'referentialism' often associated with the 'natural theology' of analytic Thomism. On the other hand, it seeks a kind of realism that affords more weight to metaphysical elements than transcendental Thomism does. Noteworthy examples include his discomfort with an attempt made by many analytic Thomists to explain how Aquinas has provided five arguments for God's existence.[10] Burrell argues that unaided human understanding cannot reason about God's existence in a way similar to reason about the things in the world, as God is not an entity among or alongside worldly things. Another example is his interpretation of 'substance', differing from that of Bernard Lonergan, a transcendental Thomist and his master in Rome. Burrell suggests that what he terms 'judgement'—the process of human knowledge of the world—for a more Aristotelian conception of 'substance', moves beyond viewing it simply as a nominal designation.[11]

7 For further study on grammatical Thomism, see Stephen Mulhall, *The Great Riddle: Wittgenstein and Nonsense, Theology and Philosophy* (Oxford: Oxford University Press, 2016), 1; Simon Hewitt, 'Grammatical Thomism', *Religious Studies* 57, no. 1 (2021): 30–48, https://doi.org/10.1017/S0034412518000896.

8 For an expanded exploration of the differentiation between surface and depth grammars, see Gorazd Andrejč, *Wittgenstein and Interreligious Disagreement: A Philosophical and Theological Perspective* (New York: Palgrave Macmillan, 2016), 42; David B. Burrell, *Aquinas: God and Action* (London: Routledge and Kegan Paul, 1979), 4; David B. Burrell, 'Future of Philosophical Theology as Reflective Awareness', in *The Future of Philosophical Theology*, ed. Robert A. Evans (Philadelphia: The Westminster Press, 1971), 86.

9 See David B. Burrell, *Analogy and Philosophical Language* (New Haven: Yale University Press, 1973), 2.

10 David B. Burrell, *Freedom and Creation in Three Traditions* (Notre Dame, IN: University of Notre Dame Press, 1993), 13–14.

11 Simon Hewitt, *Negative Theology and Philosophical Analysis: Only the Splendour of Light*, Palgrave Frontiers in Philosophy of Religion (Cham: Palgrave Macmillan, 2020), 72, 76, 86; John Milbank, 'Foreword', in *Stations on the Journey of Inquiry: Formative Writings of David B. Burrell, 1962–72*, ed. Mary Budde Ragan (Eugene, OR: Cascade Books, 2017), xvi–xvii.

Influenced by Wittgenstein's observation that 'grammar tells what kind of object anything is',[12] he came to realise that all human interactions, including both verbal and non-verbal behaviour, occur within the realm of language, representing a structured form of communication.[13] According to this account, the central task of theology is to demonstrate how we can speak of a transcendent creator who is fundamentally distinct from the created world.[14] While he believes that our language is not perfect for capturing the reality of God, he also asserts that using language 'appropriately' to refer to God is not only theologically correct but also useful.[15] Theology, within this scope, evolves into a grammatical and critical exploration, concentrating on 'formal features' that disclose the shape of a religious tradition.[16] In addition to its critical—or deconstructive, so to speak—task, theology also includes a correlative or constructive task that aims to reformulate the tradition, rendering it congruent with the present situation.[17] This oscillation between grammatical and constructive tasks heightens the intelligibility and progressiveness of theological investigation which refrains from subscribing to a theory-building approach taken by scientific methodology. Instead, it provides a therapeutic approach to theology, steering away from a mere theory of the divine.[18]

The quest to comprehend divine intervention as a fundamental religious belief highlights theology's dual objectives: exploring what can/cannot be expressed about the divine and understanding how this divinity relates to us.[19] On this account, perfection-terms (e.g. good, wise) and specific portion of transcendentals (e.g. one, infinite) are regarded as the most suitable candidates for charactering the divinity.[20] The transcendence of God, being impenetrable to description, indicates, in Burrell's view, the need for a more nuanced comprehension of the term. By appropriating abstract and concrete nouns in a non-standard context, a more appropriate understanding of God is facilitated. According to this, we can *concurrently* attribute to God abstract terms like 'simple', denoting Aristotle's category of 'form', and concrete terms such as 'subsistence', primarily representative of the concept of 'matter'. This permissibility of such a *concurrent* attribution is exclusive to the divine realm and does not extend to the things in the world. Any worldly entity is described as a combination of matter and form, with each element retaining its distinct

12 Ludwig Wittgenstein, *Philosophical Investigations*, trans. G. E. M. Anscombe (1958; repr., Oxford: Blackwell, 1968), sec. 373.

13 Burrell, *Analogy and Philosophical Language*, 1.

14 David B. Burrell, *Knowing the Unknowable God: Ibn-Sina, Maimonides, Aquinas* (Notre Dame, IN: University of Notre Dame Press, 1986), 3, 71.

15 David B. Burrell, 'Philosophy and Religion: Attention to Language and the Role of Reason', *International Journal for Philosophy of Religion* 38, no. 1–3 (1995): 111.

16 Burrell, 'Future of Philosophical Theology as Reflective Awareness', 86.

17 Ibid., 92–93.

18 Burrell *Aquinas*, 15.

19 Ibid., 6.

20 Burrell, *Analogy and Philosophical Language*, 22–23, 95, 145–46; Burrell, *Aquinas*, 26, 59–60.

and non-transferable characteristics within this dual structure.[21]

Finally, grammatical Thomism places special emphasis on negative theology. Acknowledging this approach, Burrell demonstrates that negative theology, which he refers to as 'agnostic theology',[22] can paradoxically offer a positive enhancement to our understanding of God. The main takeaway from this account is the assertion that a more fittingly affirmative understanding of God can be gleaned from an analogical application of perfection-terms, accompanied with logical considerations. The gist of Burrell's account, at least the way I understand it, highlights the significance of metaphysics. Metaphysics functions as a grammatical instrument to delineate the logical space of God-talk, clearing up misconceptions. Through this process, metaphysics leverages negative theology to clarify what God is not. It also engages in the analysis of significant tautologies to deepen our understanding of the divine. On another front, metaphysics utilises analogies to further develop our grasp of revealed knowledge, offering hints into the nature of a transcendent God.[23]

Burrell's application of his grammatical approach to elucidate metaphysics offers significant insights. He suggests that a meticulous study of the language employed in metaphysics can reveal that metaphysical statements often function more as negative assertions than is conventionally perceived. In addition, Burrell interprets the way of analogy differently—advocating for the positive aspects of metaphysics, yet he cautions against replicating the approaches of traditional metaphysicians like Duns Scotus or those in natural theology of neo-scholastic theologians and certain contemporary analytic Thomists whose accounts do not highlight the distinction between the creator and the creation. Additionally, he carefully differentiates his stance from certain transcendental interpretations, which could render access to metaphysics challenging. It is worth noting that Burrell's work, like that of many other thinkers, has received criticisms. While there are elements of his thought that still need more clarification and perhaps modification, I find a great portion of his methodological insights particularly beneficial in deepening my understanding of Ṭabāṭabāʾī's work.[24] In what follows, I will demonstrate how the application of these insights, which I will elaborate on in more detail, illuminates my interpretation of Ṭabāṭabāʾī's concept of monotheism.

21 Burrell, *Aquinas*, 5.

22 Burrell, *Aquinas*, 142.

23 See Burrell, *Analogy and Philosophical Language*, 207.

24 For a similar methodological approach applied to Ṭabāṭabāʾī's work, see Javad Taheri, 'Semantics of Divine Names: Tabatabai's Principle of "Focal Meaning" and Burrell's Grammar of God-Talk', *International Journal of Philosophy and Theology* 84, no. 2 (2023): 157–77, https://doi.org/10.1080/21692327.2023.2169743.

## 3. Navigating the Intricacies of *Tawḥīd*

The crux of the intellectual discourse on *tawḥīd* lies within the tension between the inherent unity of God and the manifold attributes ascribed to the divine. This dynamic engenders an apparent contradiction: God is simultaneously represented as singular and multitudinous. How, then, does the unity of God reconcile with the multiplicity of divine names and attributes? Such a query spirals outwards, echoing broader ruminations within the realm of religious language itself: how can a transcendent God—an entity beyond our knowledge and description—be expressed via language?

To answer this question, one might begin by providing definitions and characterisations for the nature of God and the nature of language. On the one hand, the divine is characterised through specific 'transcendentals': God is transcendent, simple, one, infinite, omniscient, omnipresent, omnipotent, incorporeal, limitless, and timeless. Furthermore, God possesses every existential perfection which allows characterising the divine as wise, good, and perfect—a different type of transcendentals named perfection-terms. Conversely, language is a natural construct, rooted in our everyday lives and functioning as a product of our minds. Yet, it is neither supernatural nor heavenly, that is, its words, concepts, and meanings are not divinely revealed. Its ordinary structure grapples with the task of expressing the Perfect Being, whose essence is beyond ordinary conceptualisations. Therefore, when language attempts to depict an entity as transcendent and otherworldly as God, one of two outcomes may ensue: either the language falls short of adequately capturing the divine, or the entity is represented in a manner that deviates from the ordinary use of language. In other words, the religious language may either appear to be meaningless or bear meaning that diverges from the sense we are familiar and work with.

As suggested in this paper, this intellectual dilemma should not be viewed as an insurmountable obstacle. Rather, it presents an opportunity for fruitful exploration. By gaining a deeper understanding of the issue and using grammatical tools effectively, a suitable response to the problem of religious language can be developed. This approach will further illuminate the elusive yet comprehensible concept of *tawḥīd*.

### 3.1 The Semiotics of *Iʿtibāriyyāt* and Their Influence on God-Talk

#### 3.1.1 *Innate Development of Language*

Navigating the intricacies of religious language as framed by Ṭabāṭabāʾī's philosophy of language necessitates a careful examination of the concept of *iʿtibāriyyāt* (mental constructs). Ṭabāṭabāʾī offers a crucial distinction between *iʿtibārī*, the constructs birthed and nurtured within the domain of human cognition, and *ḥaqīqī*, the realities that dwell beyond the boundaries of subjective human understanding. This delineation categorically positions language, along with the large portion of religious discourse, under the banner of *iʿtibārī*. In essence, this emphasises that words, along with their underlying connotations and the meanings they establish, are the fruits gleaned from the rich orchard of human cognitive capabilities, rather than being products of divine revelation or spiritual emanations.[25]

The theory of *iʿtibāriyyāt* serves as a central notion in Ṭabāṭabāʾī's philosophical works, exerting an influence not only in his practical philosophy but also in his metaphysical, linguistic, and cognitive discussions. He defines mental construction essentially as the process of attributing conceived (*ḥadd*) or judged (*ḥukm*) qualities of one entity to another devoid of them.[26] What is crucial here is the process itself, wherein a form of mapping transpires, both cognitively and linguistically, irrespective of the precise elements being mapped.

The realm of mental constructs, according to Ṭabāṭabāʾī, spans a variety of categories. On one level, these mentally constructed notions, being rooted in individual needs and emotions, can be classified into 'collective/universal constructs' or *iʿtibāriyyāt-i jamʿī* (e.g. universal human tendencies like 'loving' and 'hating') and 'personal constructs' or *iʿtibāriyyāt-i shakhṣī/khuṣūṣī* (e.g. personal inclinations towards a specific object or activity). Mental constructs can also be divided into (1) pre-social *iʿtibāriyyāt* (*iʿtibāriyyāt-i qabl az ijtimāʿ*), which emerge independent of social interaction and originate from the inherent characteristics of the species. 'Necessity' (*vujūb*) in its non-metaphysical, practical usage (arguably synonymous with 'requisite') is identified by Ṭabāṭabāʾī as a pre-social mental construct, despite the presence of countless socially induced necessities;[27] and (2) social *iʿtibāriyyāt* (*iʿtibāriyyāt-i baʿd az ijtimāʿ*), which are the products of interpersonal interaction within societal contexts. Constructs like 'ownership' or 'property' fall under this category, having evolved to facilitate social existence.[28]

Ṭabāṭabāʾī's proposition of the pre-social concept of 'utilisation' (*istikhdām*) sets the stage for his exploration into the genesis of language. He contends that the *iʿtibār* of *istikhdām* is grounded when humans instinctively realise that their needs cannot be

25 Among the proponents of the latter perspective, al-Ghazālī proposes that the origins of the meanings are fundamentally rooted in divine revelation, despite their widespread use in human linguistic exchange. See Abū Ḥāmid Muḥammad b. Muḥammad al-Ghazālī, *Iḥyāʾ ʿulūm al-dīn*, 2nd ed., 16 vols. (Beirut: Dār al-Kitāb al-ʿArabī, n.d.), 1:664, 12:91; Abū Ḥāmid Muḥammad b. Muḥammad al-Ghazālī, 'Iljām al-ʿawāmm ʿan ʿilm al-kalām', in *Majmūʿat rasāʾil al-Imām al-Ghazālī* (Beirut: Dār al-Fikr, 1996), 324; Abū Ḥāmid Muḥammad b. Muḥammad al-Ghazālī, *al-Maqāṣid al-asnā fī sharḥ asmāʾ Allāh al-ḥusnā* (Beirut: Dār al-Mashriq, 1986), 19.

26 See Muḥammad Ḥusayn Ṭabāṭabāʾī, 'Risālat al-iʿtibāriyyāt', in *Rasāʾil al-ʿAllāma al-Ṭabāṭabāʾī* (Qom: Maktabat Fadak li-Iḥyāʾ al-Turāth, 2007), 346–47. For relevant discussions on the concept of *iʿtibāriyyāt* and its place in Ṭabāṭabāʾī's account of religious language, see Javad Taheri, 'I'tibariat: A New Possible Theoretical Basis for Interreligious Dialogue', *Edinost in Dialog* 74, no. 2 (2019): 99–108, https://doi.org/10.34291/Edinost/74/02/Taheri; Taheri, 'Semantics of Divine Names'.

27 See Muḥammad Ḥusayn Ṭabāṭabāʾī, *Uṣūl-i falsafih va ravish-i riʾalism*, 5 vols. (Tehran: Ṣadrā, 1985), 2:197, 209.

28 Ibid., 220.

fulfilled in isolation. Utilisation, conceptualised as leveraging others for personal gain,[29] subsequently gives rise to the mental construct of 'congregation', laying the foundation for social bonds and social structures.[30] Consequently, Ṭabāṭabāʾī proposes that ordinary language (speech, *kalām*) is a product of the mental construct of congregation.[31]

According to Ṭabāṭabāʾī, language *basically* consists of representations of mental elements (which he considers as meanings), that in turn reflect extra-mental realities. The representational characteristic of language is primarily a function of mental constructs, leading to an *iʿtibārī* principle, that is, a knowledge-corresponding reality (*aṣl-i mutābiʿat-i ʿilm*).[32] Through consistent usage of specific speech forms, a strong cognitive association is established, linking certain meanings to specific words or signs.[33] Ṭabāṭabāʾī's detailed explication of the mental construction underscores how language, via cognitive extensions, transitions from primary meanings to increasingly abstract and spiritual meanings, a process inherently of an *iʿtibārī* nature. He also states that this process of meaning extension is not exclusive to ordinary use of language but also pervades the realm of religious language.[34]

### 3.1.2 *Semantic Continuity along with Linguistic Transformation*

Ṭabāṭabāʾī's principle of 'focal meaning'[35] represents a crucial phase in this mental construction, especially where language is employed to articulate attributes of the divine entity. This 'focal meaning' identifies the most prominent aspect within the wide range of a word's semantic scope, thereby making it appropriate for attributing to God. Naturally, this leads to a series of intricate enquiries: what constitutes the 'focal meaning', and through what process is it extracted from the complex array of meanings and connotations?

To fully comprehend this process, one must turn to a key concept within Ṭabāṭabāʾī's thought, '*tanzīh* alongside *tashbīh*', or dissimilation alongside assimilation.[36] This strategy

---

29 Ṭabāṭabāʾī argues that the precept of *istikhdām* is fundamentally anchored in *fiṭrat*, a particular kind of knowledge imparted through divine inspiration which is part of the divine guiding plan intended for human completion. See Muḥammad Ḥusayn Ṭabāṭabāʾī, 'Risālih-yi vaḥy yā shuʿūr-i marmūz', in *Majmūʿih-yi rasāʾil*, ed. Sayyid Hādī Khusrawshāhī, 3 vols. (Qom: Muʾassisih-yi Būstān-i Kitāb, 2008), 1:143–80.

30 Ibid. For more on the concept of 'utilisation', see Muḥammad Ḥusayn Ṭabāṭabāʾī, *al-Mīzān fī tafsīr al-Qurʾān*, 22 vols. (Qom: Daftar Intishārāt, 1997), 1:337.

31 Ṭabāṭabāʾī, 'Risālat al-iʿtibāriyyāt', 356–57.

32 See Muḥammad Ḥusayn Ṭabāṭabāʾī, *Nihāyat al-ḥikma* (Qom: Muʾassasat al-Nashr al-Islāmī al-Tābiʿa li-Jimāʿat al-Mudarresīn, 1983), 307–8; Ṭabāṭabāʾī, 'Risālat al-iʿtibāriyyāt', 346–47.

33 Muḥammad Ḥusayn Ṭabāṭabāʾī, *Ḥāshiyat al-kifāya*, vol. 1 (Qom: Bunyad-i ʿIlmi va Fikri-yi ʿAllāmih Ṭabāṭabāʾī, n.d.), 16, 30.

34 See ibid., 17–18; Ṭabāṭabāʾī, *Uṣūl-i falsafih*, 2:223–24.

35 The term 'focal meaning' is my English translation of the Persian words '*maʿnā-yi aṣlī*' or '*aṣl-i maʿnā*', frequently used by Ṭabāṭabāʾī. After studying his texts, I have chosen to use 'focal meaning' rather than 'original meaning' or 'principal meaning', which might initially appear as proper literal translations of the term in question.

36 For instances of the application of *tanzīh–tashbīh*, see Ṭabāṭabāʾī, *al-Mīzān*, 1:11, 8:57, 10:272–73.

is an integral methodological approach that Ṭabāṭabāʾī employs to sift through the myriad meanings of words to be used for extracting a 'focal meaning'—deemed to be the most appropriate meaning of a word predicated of God. This strategic approach acknowledges the semantic layers of the linguistic statements. Each word in a given language is akin to a repository of signifiers, capable of accommodating a multitude of meanings. These meanings range from the base sensory associations that arise from immediate, tangible experiences, progress through a series of less sensual connotations abstracted from those perceptual experiences, and extend, at the farthest reach, into the higher level, so to speak, echoing spiritual meanings.[37] In this context, the 'focal meaning' operates as a semantic bridge that binds these diverse layers, forging a semantic continuum that underpins the word. Arriving at the focal meaning of a term employed to speak of the divine requires the application of *tanzīh* alongside *tashbīh*, serving as a purification of meanings from their finite connotations.[38]

This strategy can be employed to elucidate the meanings of Qurʾanic *mutashābihāt* (non-explicit expressions with initially unclear meanings)—terms like 'hand' (*yad*), 'face' (*wajh*), and 'throne' (*ʿarsh*) when ascribed to God. The facility of employing these meanings becomes even more pronounced when considering words that possess fewer bodily connotations, such as *nūr*—'light'. For instance, in the Qurʾanic verse *Allāh nūr al-samāwāt wa-l-arḍ* (Q. 24:35), as Ṭabāṭabāʾī suggests, it is the focal meaning of *nūr* that is to be attributed to God. Although the process of purification theoretically enables any term to be used in the characterisation of the divine, the most befitting ones are the 'attributes of perfection' (*ṣifāt-i kamālī*), words that represent different aspects of divine perfection.[39] The appropriate ascription of attributes of perfection to God follows the processes of *iʿtibāriyyāt* and *tanzīh–tashbīh*.

After emphasising the effectiveness of the principle, it is crucial to explore its explanation further, returning to the grammatical insights outlined in the early sections of this paper. This exploration into the methodological use of grammar in theology has played a key role in sharpening my understanding of the importance and function of 'focal meaning' in discussions about God.

Exploring the concept of 'focal meaning' through Burrell's analogical framework introduces a challenging epistemological difficulty. Although this principle seems to propose that there is a single semantic kernel shared by a word's different meanings, it is precarious to assert that the connecting link between the meanings is univocally ingrained in these semantic levels. Semantic cohesion can be more clearly grasped if we accept that meanings are of 'family resemblance', an idea originally introduced by Witt-

37 Ibid., 3:64–72, 5:381–82.
38 Ibid., 1:11, 8:57, 10:272–73.
39 Ṭabāṭabāʾī, 'Taʿlīqāt [scholia]', 124; Muḥammad Ḥusayn Ṭabāṭabāʾī, *Rasāʾil-i tawḥīdī*, trans. Ali Shirvani (Qom: Muʾassisih-yi Būstān-i Kitāb, 2009), 54.

genstein.[40] This concept suggests that there is not a univocal nucleus binding meanings together; instead, meanings interweave based on an array of overlapping/criss-crossing similarities. In other words, the association of meanings is enabled by the flexible nature of semantic extension. Accordingly, the 'focal' meanings of the words retain a certain kind of intrinsic indeterminacy when applied to the divine. This intrinsic flexibility and absence of strict definition demonstrates the presence of an irreducible metaphorical core embedded within the web of meanings.[41]

## 4. Grammatical Examination of the Concept of *Wujūd*

In what follows, the emphasis is placed upon the exposition of a grammatical interpretation of Ṭabāṭabāʾī's nuanced concept of *vujūd* (Ar. *wujūd*), translated interchangeably as 'being', 'existing', and 'existence'. Initially, an examination of Ṭabāṭabāʾī's discussion of the concept of *vujūd* is provided. This is followed by an exploration into the definition of *vujūd-i vājibī* (lit. 'a necessarily existent being'). Then, the logical relation between the dual modalities of *vujūd*, namely, the necessary (*vājib*) and the contingent beings (*mumkināt*), is pursued. This further navigates the difference between the universal applicability of the concept of *vujūd* and its application when referring to the individual realisation of the existents. Finally, the usefulness of grammatical insights is highlighted, showing how they help in understanding and translating Ṭabāṭabāʾī's terminology of the divine.

In Ṭabāṭabāʾī's work, the notion of *vujūd* holds a central position, bearing a lineage that traces back to the metaphysical ideas of Mullā Ṣadrā.[42] Primarily, he posits that the concept of *vujūd* is self-evident (*bidāhat-i vujūd*) and does not necessitate complicated speculative efforts for its comprehension. Further, he accepts that it is an all-encompassing, universal concept, with applicability beyond the boundaries of specificity to extend to everything that exists. Closely linked to this idea is the principle of semantic commonality of the 'existence' (*ishtirāk-i maʿnavi-i vujūd*), which, according to Ṭabāṭabāʾī, directs the application of the concept of *vujūd* to different entities. Also, the concept of *vujūd* is universally attributed to a range of entities, regardless of their varying ontological levels. While everything can be placed within the category of existence, each specific existent can be said to possess a mode of existence distinct from others.

Following his examination of the concept of *vujūd*, Ṭabāṭabāʾī then proceeds to examine the concept of Necessary Being (*vājib al-vujūd*). This concept is central to his metaphysical framework, accompanied by a series of grammatical clarifications that establish the foundation for its understanding. A 'necessarily existent being', in his view, denotes an entity of utmost reality that possesses an inviolable way of being, thus rendering its

40 Wittgenstein, *Philosophical Investigations*, secs. 66–67; Burrell, *Analogy and Philosophical Language*, 18.
41 Burrell, *Aquinas*, 10; Burrell, *Analogy and Philosophical Language*, 9–10.
42 For Mullā Ṣadrā's elaboration on these principles, see al-Shīrāzī, *al-Ḥikma al-mutaʿāliya*, 1:35–84.

non-existence impossible. Following Burrell, I interpret Ṭabāṭabāʾī's assertion that the necessity of God's being makes divine existence inviolable as suggesting that God's way of being is not merely a mode of being but is, in fact, 'being itself'.[43] Moreover, this being is characterised by embodying all existential perfections, devoid of any imperfection. Ṭabāṭabāʾī agrees that this metaphysical concept corresponds to the concept of God, leading to the claim that the divine essence and existence are, in reality, identical.

In elucidating the intricate relationship between the inherently necessary way of being and the contingent mode of being, Ṭabāṭabāʾī appeals to the principle of causality (*ʿilliyat*)—an intellectual apparatus with huge implications for the idea of creation. Based on this principle, he puts forward a number of propositions that merit detailed examination. Firstly, he states that the Necessary Being is the primordial causative force that breathes life into all extant beings—those entities deemed as God's 'effects' within the realm of existence. In this schema, the Necessary Being assumes a position of ontological primacy, being the fountainhead of existence from which all existence originates. Secondly, Ṭabāṭabāʾī asserts that there exists no being whose existence does not hinge on the causal beneficence of the Necessary Being.[44] Lastly, he underlines an ontological dependence of beings that inhabit the realm of existence on the divine being. He asserts that God is the origin of the existence of all existents, and this originality is absolute, meaning 'there is no real existential agent other than God'.[45]

Certainly, one of the most intricate philosophical challenges Ṭabāṭabāʾī faces is unravelling the distinction between the universality and individuality—instantiation/particularisation (*tashakhkhuṣ*)[46]—of *vujūd*. On the one hand, Ṭabāṭabāʾī upholds the idea that while the universal concept of *vujūd* cannot emerge without the knowing subject (knower) experiencing the world and its entities, it is not directly rooted in perceptual experience; rather, it is conceptually abstracted from these entities.[47] Instead, he suggests, our understanding of external entities is primarily mediated through our apprehension of their *māhiyyāt* (quiddities) rather than any direct knowledge of their *vujūd*.[48] For Ṭabāṭabāʾī, it is not logical to suggest that the concept of *vujūd* directly corresponds to any specific entity or object in the external world. In other words, the universal applicability of *vujūd* precludes it from being considered a *property/quality*[49] inherent to things. Expanding this line of thought, Ṭabāṭabāʾī situates this concept within the realm of the

43 Ibid., 5, 17–18, 21; Burrell, *Analogy and Philosophical Language*, 128–29.

44 Ṭabāṭabāʾī, *Nihāyat al-ḥikma*, chs. 3, 4, 8, 12; Muḥammad Ḥusayn Ṭabāṭabāʾī, *The Elements of Islamic Metaphysics* (*Bidayat al-Hikmah*), trans. Sayyid ʿAli Quli Qaraʾi, 2nd ed. (London: ICAS Press, 2003).

45 Ṭabāṭabāʾī, *Nihāyat al-ḥikma*, 176.

46 Rizvi and Bdaiwi, '"Allāma Ṭabāṭabāʾī', 665.

47 Ṭabāṭabāʾī's viewpoint is in alignment with that of Mullā Ṣadrā in this regard: 'Mullā Ṣadrā takes pains to show that what the mind perceives of the reality of existence is only its mental representation, which is removed from the actual reality of things as they are' (ibid.).

48 Ṭabāṭabāʾī, *Elements of Islamic Metaphysics*, 86.

49 Rizvi and Bdaiwi, '"Allāma Ṭabāṭabāʾī', 666.

so-called philosophical secondary intelligibles (*maʿqūlāt-i thānī falsafī*). On the other hand, Ṭabāṭabāʾī proposes that we can also acknowledge the existence of individual entities (*afrād*) within the external world. This represents a distinct type of reference to *vujūd* compared to when we consider it as a universal concept. This affirmation suggests that what truly exists in the external world are individual entities, each bearing a unique and distinct mode of *vujūd*.

Exploring the nature and implications of individual manifestations of *vujūd* is challenging, particularly because its characterisation is not as immediately apparent as those defining the 'accidental' features (*aʿrāż*) of quiddities (*māhiyyāt*). The concept of *vujūd* prompts critical questions, particularly regarding the origin of its universal conception. If *vujūd* is extra-mentally individual in reality, how do we then conceive it universally? Is there a common trait or properties linking individual instances of *vujūd* together, making it applicable as a universal concept? If so, this appears to be at odds with the idea that *vujūd*'s only extra-mental manifestation is individuality. This consequently engenders a further line of enquiry: given that both the Necessary Being and contingent beings possess their unique, individual modes of *vujūd*, how are these modes interconnected? How do these distinct ways of being, each defined by its intrinsic individuality, relate to each other? This exploration underscores the necessity of analysing the intricate interplay between the individual and the universal within the construct of *vujūd*. Responses to these questions can be found in Ṭabāṭabāʾī's work, yet the metaphysical concepts he frequently utilises in a concise manner require further clarification through a grammatical approach.

While attempting to clarify *vujūd*, one faces a challenging dilemma. There is a temptation to directly probe into the nature of *vujūd*, aiming to define its 'type' or 'kind' linguistically. However, this approach is at odds with the essence of *vujūd* itself, which resists being categorised as a specific 'kind' of entity.[50] Instead, having an accurate understanding of the concept of *vujūd* requires the exploration of its source, thereby uncovering its nature by tracing it back to its origin. Ṭabāṭabāʾī argues that *vujūd* and *māhiyyat* (quiddity) are extra-mentally united. Quiddity, in this sense, becomes so intrinsically entwined with *vujūd* that it emerges as the hallmark of the idividuality intrinsic to this existence.

To demonstrate that this is not merely an 'accidental' conceptual association but an ontological unity, Ṭabāṭabāʾī asserts:

> The perception the [*sic*] one has of the outside realm and established that that [*sic*] which one perceives is really a compound of quiddity and existence. We established that this differentiation between existence and quiddity is really only possible in the mind, not in the outside. That is, everything we see in the outside is individually

50 '[While] the concept of existence is thus applied to the Necessary and contingents univocally ... the reality of existence ... is a different matter altogether. Since the Necessary has no essence, no other being can partake of whatever we may conceive of the Necessary's essence' (ibid., 665).

> one existence, when we conceive it then we can break it down into parts.[51]

He also adds that 'if one perceives a flower, one can divide it into flowerness and its existence within the mind, but in the outside there is only one thing rather than two'.[52] This perspective underpins the conceptualisation of *vujūd* and *māhiyyat* as a singular entity within the external world, where the inherent individuality of *vujūd* is its defining characteristic. As a consequence, beyond the mental realm, quiddities are essentially expressions of the intrinsic individuality of *vujūd*. This intimates a fundamental unity of being, wherein quiddities do not subsist independently, but rather as unique expressions or individuations of existence itself.

Moreover, it is important to note that in Ṭabāṭabā'ī's view, our language, when functioning in its most typical form, originates from our perceptual data processed by the imaginative faculty (*quvvih-yi mukhayyalih*). This language is essentially a product of mediated knowledge (*ʿilm-i ḥuṣūlī*), where 'accidental' features or *aʿrāż* form the primary basis of our concepts.[53] The ordinary operation of language, rooted in our perceptual knowledge, typically involves the conception of *aʿrāż* from perceived things (*māhiyyāt*), which are then predicated in our conceptual sphere.[54] This reflects the surface grammar at work in this level of language use.

However, when we seek to predicate the 'existence' of 'existing beings'—and even more importantly, of God—in a metaphysical language, we must venture beyond these ordinary linguistic boundaries.[55] This depth grammar of representations, which penetrates beneath the surface to unravel the underlying metaphysical structure of language—or the way metaphysical concepts are utilised to provide words predicated of God with specific meanings in certain theological contexts—requires careful attention. Only then can such a usage adequately guide those to whom this language is spoken, offering them an appropriate comprehension of what we imply when we speak of *vujūd* and *māhiyyāt*. In this respect, the language of metaphysics transcends its ordinary limitations, allowing the depth grammar to illuminate the intricate interplay between *vujūd* and *māhiyyāt*.

Revisiting the previously mentioned distinction between *vujūd* as a universal concept and *vujūd* representing individual existence, I interpret Ṭabāṭabā'ī as suggesting that this differentiation highlights that our grasp of the universal concept of *vujūd* does not completely clarify the nature of *vujūd* in its individualised form in the external world. This is mainly due to our lack of direct knowledge or comprehension of the existence of external realities. Ṭabāṭabā'ī further reinforces this notion, in line with Mullā Ṣadrā,[56]

---

51 Ṭabāṭabā'ī, *Elements of Islamic Metaphysics*, 15.
52 Ibid., 16.
53 Ṭabāṭabā'ī, *Uṣūl-i falsafih*, 2:209.
54 Ṭabāṭabā'ī, *Nihāyat al-ḥikma*, chs. 6, 11; Ṭabāṭabā'ī, *Elements of Islamic Metaphysics*, 48.
55 Ṭabāṭabā'ī, *Elements of Islamic Metaphysics*, 23.
56 Ṣadr al-Dīn al-Shīrāzī, *Kitāb al-mashāʿir*, ed. Khālid ʿAbd al-Karīm al-Ṭarzī (n.p.: Muṣawwirāt Maktabat

by proposing that a true knowledge of the effects is gained by knowing their causes. Our awareness of our own *vujūd* is founded on 'immediate knowledge' (presential knowledge, *ʿilm-i ḥużūrī*), suggesting that one's knowledge of oneself is more revealing than the knowledge of other existents. Furthermore, grasping the essence of God's existence is impossible due to our limited knowledge. Our understanding of the existence of other beings is also incomplete because without knowledge of the ultimate—first—cause (the divine), we cannot fully comprehend God's effects (entities in the world). Through rational reasoning and meticulous analysis of *māhiyyāt*, it only becomes discernible that the external reality of things does not originate from their *māhiyyāt*, but rather arises from an alternate source referred to as *vujūd*.[57]

Elucidating the differentiation between the divine and created entities within the 'gradational reality of existence' (*ḥaqīqat-i mushakkak-i vujūd*) requires further conceptual exploration. The divine stands as the creator, crafting our existence, albeit through intermediaries or *vasāʾiṭ*.[58] There exists a connecting link between us and the divine, given that the entirety of the world's reality ultimately originates from God. However, the *vujūd* conferred upon us does not originate directly from God, but instead is channelled through these *vasāʾiṭ*. These intermediaries themselves draw their *vujūd* from other *vasāʾiṭ*, creating a chain that ultimately leads back to God. This structure manifests both a relation and a differentiation between God, the creator, and the created beings. Thus, within the gradational reality of *vujūd*, the simultaneous presence of difference and connection must be affirmed between God as the originator and the created entities.[59] The distinction-within-connection in the ontological status of *vujūd*, as well as the epistemological clarification of *vujūd* (including the difference between the universal and individual treatment of the concept of *vujūd*), contributes to the elusiveness of the concept in question.

The aforementioned complexities shed light on the inherent challenge of pinpointing an ultimate focal meaning for the term *vujūd*. Given our finite nature and the associated limitations in understanding, says Ṭabāṭabāʾī, achieving complete clarity regarding the true and ultimate meanings of words referring to God proves to be difficult.[60] Consequently, in Burrell's term,[61] an irreducible nucleus of metaphoricity maintains an inherent flexibility of the meanings of the terms that intriguingly becomes extended enough to allude to both the divine and created entities. In this context, attributing *vujūd* to both

al-Ṣadūq, n.d.), para. 92.

57 Rizvi and Bdaiwi, "ʿAllāma Ṭabāṭabāʾī', 665.

58 Ṭabāṭabāʾī, 'Risālih-yi vasāʾiṭ', in *Rasāʾil-i tawḥīdī*, 155.

59 Ṭabāṭabāʾī, *Nihāyat al-ḥikma*, 17–20. For an in-depth analysis and elaboration on this matter, see Rizvi and Bdaiwi, "ʿAllāma Ṭabāṭabāʾī', 667.

60 Muḥammad Ḥusayn Ṭabāṭabāʾī, *Shiʿite Islam*, trans. Seyyed Hossein Nasr (Albany: State University of New York Press, 1975), 87.

61 Burrell, *Aquinas*, 10; Burrell, *Analogy and Philosophical Language*, 9–10.

God and created beings becomes semantically coherent. However, we should moderate our expectations, as it does not adequately represent the divine reality. It cannot even reasonably be asserted that the concept of *vujūd* and its meanings, including the focal meaning one may propose, fully capture the reality of the existence of contingent beings. Still, we require the focal meanings of words and terms predicated of God to render such predications theologically sound.

Situated at this crossroads, the *apophatic* (negating) and *cataphatic* (affirming) theological orientations within Ṭabāṭabā'ī's framework move in tandem with each other, suggesting that a distinct mode of utilising the term *vujūd* offers the most viable linguistic strategy in characterising the divine. This specific kind of utilisation ensures a correlation between the implications of *vujūd* when applied to both God and the creatures. My Burrellian reading of Ṭabāṭabā'ī suggests that the focal meaning of *vujūd* can thus be attributed to both God and creatures in an *analogous* manner. As we move forward, the defining features of focal meaning are becoming clearer, and this trend of gaining clarity is expected to persist. For instance, I employed the concept of analogy to further elucidate the concept of focal meaning grammatically. Analogical application of focal meaning does not necessarily equate a univocal, or single, core meaning across different meanings of a word. Used in this manner, the term *vujūd* can be aptly applied to both God and worldly entities, without implying that the transcendent essence of God shares the same existential basis as that of creatures. This specific understanding of the concept of *vujūd* captures both the divine's unparalleled uniqueness and its intrinsic link to the created. It strikes a delicate balance that recognises the complexity of theological language and God's supreme transcendence.

## 5. Tracing the Grammatical Map of Monotheism

In the initial section of this article, it is suggested that comprehending the concept of monotheism might be theologically problematic, as this concept shares a familial relation with the problem of religious language. My interpretation of Ṭabāṭabā'ī through the lens of Burrell proposes that the proper account of religious language leads one to treat God-talk in three distinct levels. The first level (*aḥadiyyat*)[62] positions God as a transcendent entity, rendering the divine unfathomable. Consequently, this level requires the negation of any imaginable characteristics from Him, honouring the divine otherness. Here, Ṭabāṭabā'ī underlines the need to negate all forms of constraints (*quyūd*, sing. *qayd*) from God, including the *qayd* of having no *qayd*. This statement suggests, as unveiled by my

62 Ṭabāṭabā'ī, *Rasā'il-i tawḥīdī*, 16 ('Risālih-yi tawḥīd'), 39, 42–43, 61 ('Risālih-yi asmā-i ilāhī'); Muḥammad Ḥusayn Ṭabāṭabā'ī, *The Qur'an in Islam*, trans. Asadullah Ad-Dhakir Yate (London: Zahra Publications, 1987), 32.

grammatical approach, that God should not be spoken of at this level.[63] The secondary level invites us to speak of God through the analytical examination of the concept of the Necessary Being and its attendant 'essential attributes'.[64] This venue, enveloped in logical examination, illuminates the concept of the divine within the realm of our conceptual reasoning. Ultimately, the third level suggests that we can speak of God by attributing perfections to Him, drawing upon our knowledge of how divine perfections manifest in the creation.[65] However, this attribution warrants careful navigation, ensuring that the most proper connotations of these perfection-terms are distilled and employed.[66]

Distinguishing these three levels of meanings can be seen as a grammatical tool to elucidate the linguistic framework of theological discourse on monotheism. Starting with the first level, divine unity is embraced, not as a numerical entity, but as a transcendent reality beyond the limitations of created existence. This stage necessitates the acknowledgement of the divine's mysterious, elusive nature and its incomprehensibility by finite understanding. As a result, our understanding of God converges towards the idea of an entity *existing* in a realm that surpasses worldly comprehension—an expression of *aḥadiyyat*. This initial level resonates in harmony with elements of negative theology, thereby acting as a purifying influence not only for the linguistic structure used in discussing the divine but also for the kind of knowledge we can have of that entity. This paradigm of understanding resonates with the grammatical approach we adopt here and aligns with postmodern theological trends and certain mystical orientations. Furthermore, it aligns with ground-breaking contemporary scientific methodologies aimed at exploring the recognition of an inherent 'uncertainty' in the human quest for uncovering the ultimate truth. In Ṭabāṭabāʾī's scholarly vocabulary, this particular explanation of monotheism is referred to as *tawḥīd-i iṭlāqī* (ineffable unity).[67]

Upon progressing to the second level, we speak of God as *huvīyyat*, shifting our focus towards an analytical treatment of religious language. Here, logical self-evident truths form the basis of elucidating the concept of the Necessary Being. At this juncture, certain concepts such as 'simplicity' and 'infiniteness' are utilised to shed light on the oneness of God. Thus, in an attempt to specify the 'logical space of God-talk',[68] an identity between the divine essence and divine essential attributes is imperative, as the latter are logically inferred through an in-depth examination of the former. Grammatically speaking, such a logical treatment of the notion of Necessary Being functions primarily as a mechanism to underscore what God should not be conceived as, rather than positively stipulating how God could be understood. The interpretation of Ṭabāṭabāʾī's concept of *tawḥīd*, as far as

63 Muḥammad Ḥusayn Ṭabāṭabāʾī, 'Treatise on Monotheism', in *Rasāʾil-i tawḥīdī*, 32, 39.
64 Muḥammad Ḥusayn Ṭabāṭabāʾī, 'Treatise on Divine Names', in *Rasāʾil-i tawḥīdī*.
65 Muḥammad Ḥusayn Ṭabāṭabāʾī, 'Treatise on Divine Acts', in *Rasāʾil-i tawḥīdī*.
66 Ṭabāṭabāʾī, *al-Mīzān*, 14:131–32.
67 Ṭabāṭabāʾī, 'Risālih-yi tawḥīd', in *Rasāʾil-i tawḥīdī*, 30.
68 Burrell, *Aquinas*, 8.

the second level is concerned, can also be aptly regarded as an example of his *apophatic* theological approach. However, when it is coupled with the affirmative content found in Islamic traditions (*naql*), the result would be an adjusted and appropriate affirmative understanding of the concept of *tawḥīd*.

Ultimately, the third level directs our attention towards recognising and characterising God as the cause of all creation. Given the nature of God as pure being (*vujūd-i maḥż* or *esse purus*), encapsulating an indivisible, unified 'act of existence', the concepts of 'God as the Creator' and 'God as the One' are intrinsically referring to the same entity, 'God as the Pure Act' (*actus purus*). To substantiate the sameness of divine essence and action, it becomes necessary for us to refer to the paradigmatic meaning of action. To further clarify this concept, it is important to notice Ṭabāṭabāʾī's subtle distinction between three approaches to the ascription of 'attributes of action' (*ṣifāt-i afʿāl*) to the divine essence. The first approach considers these attributes as being identical with the divine essence, thus asserting a fundamental unity. The second approach suggests that these attributes act as an additional element, enhancing our understanding of the divine essence without endangering changelessness of the divine. The third approach, in contrast, stringently negates the ascription of attributes of action to the divine essence, supporting a deep distinction. Contrary to initial impressions, further examination reveals that Ṭabāṭabāʾī's argument is that these three perspectives are not in contradiction or conflict because they feature the meaning of the act differently. Each perspective offers a unique aspect in understanding the intricate relationship between the divine essence and the attributes of action. Taken together, these perspectives provide a more complete and thorough understanding of the divine in connection with these attributes.[69]

If my grammatical understanding is correct, the first meaning, in Ṭabāṭabāʾī's work, situates God as inherently a 'pure act' based on a paradigmatic understanding of the term 'act'.[70] In this context, based on the focal meaning of 'act', an act encompasses all instances of action, including understanding or awareness. According to this perspective, an act does not necessarily demand 'accomplishment', that is, it does not require movement in the physical sense. Being intrinsically (and 'necessarily') in possession of existence or *vujūd* equates to being purely active, as *vujūd* is the foundational driver of all things' efficacy (*manshaʾ-i asar būdan*).

The second meaning of 'act' considers the emanation of intermediaries or *vasāʾiṭ* as non-material entities (*mujarradāt*). Here, God is conceived as the direct causative agent of the first intellect's (ʿaql-i avval) existence. This particular understanding of 'act' is logically attributable to God.[71] In this sense, the act does not entail any alteration in either the First Cause (God) or the First Effect (*maʿlūl-i avval*). Alteration, as Ṭabāṭabāʾī

69 Ṭabāṭabāʾī, *Elements of Islamic Metaphysics*, 294.
70 See Burrell, *Analogy and Philosophical Language*, 152.
71 Ṭabāṭabāʾī, 'Risālih-yi vasāʾiṭ', in *Rasāʾil-i tawḥīdī*, 155.

understands it, is a feature inherent to entities of a material nature. He also argues that both the First Cause and the First Effect are not material beings; rather, they are categorised as immaterial entities (*mujarradāt*).

The third meaning of 'act', which cannot be ascribed to God, involves activities that necessitate physical movement and temporal engagement. Such acts signify imperfections and the fulfilment of actions in time and space, characteristics that are decidedly unattributable to God.[72] Nonetheless, it is logically conceivable that God, as the initial causative agent of creation, is regarded as an entity to whom returns the origination of all actions. Similarly, in the third meaning of the word—where actions signify transitions from potentiality to actuality, equating to movement—all such actions are directed towards God as the final cause of creation. This concept gives rise to the idea of movement seeking completion, or teleological progression.

This expedition across the triadic levels of religious language, paralleled with a careful examination of the concept of *tawḥīd*, dovetails with a grammatical exploration of the intricate interplay between cognitive dynamics, linguistic components, and metaphysical considerations.

## 6. Conclusion

The scholarly expedition undertaken herein has ventured into the intellectual depths of the eminent Shīʿī scholar Muḥammad Ḥusayn Ṭabāṭabāʾī, with a deliberate focus on his intricate rendition of monotheism (*tawḥīd*). The cornerstone of this exploration has been the analysis of Ṭabāṭabāʾī's principle of 'focal meaning', serving as a compass guiding us through the intricate web of epistemological, linguistic, and theological enigmas. Based on my Burrellian interpretation of Ṭabāṭabāʾī, focal meaning is the most proper meaning of certain theological concepts, such as existence, Necessary Being, divine action, and divine oneness, which can be identified by understanding the depth grammar of those terms. Among these concepts, existence or *vujūd* calls for a particular attention. Therefore, in this paper, the grammatical examination of this concept, woven through various metaphysical conceptualisations, has been explored. A similar exploration was offered to Ṭabāṭabāʾī's explanation of the distinction between the universal and individual conceptions of *vujūd*. Consequently, it became evident that the appropriate meaning of *vujūd*, when considering its depth grammar, is dependent on the context in which it is used, as well as the intended purposes. In one context, the universality of the concept is emphasised, while in another, its individuality is brought to the forefront. This grammatical analysis plays a crucial role in shaping our characterisation of God and in interpreting the concept of monotheism.

---

72 Ṭabāṭabāʾī, *Elements of Islamic Metaphysics*, 294.

The methodological approach of this paper has offered an interpretation of Ṭabāṭabā'ī that was previously absent from the literature. It highlights that his examination of religious language, particularly concerning monotheism, embodies a grammatical investigation. His treatment of *tawḥīd-i iṭlāqī* or 'divine ineffable unity', along with his original idea of the distinction between divine essential attributes and divine action attributes, indicates his dedication to presenting a more pronounced *apophatic* theology. Following his grammatical examination of discourse about God, he suggests that when employing concepts such as 'existence', 'necessity', 'action', and 'perfection' in reference to God, we must pay attention to the deeper areas beneath the surface—the 'depth grammar'—of these terms; that is, their usage, the contexts in which they are applied, and the purposes they serve. This is a process of provision of the focal meanings of these concepts.

Ṭabāṭabā'ī has also illustrated that in all such instances, we must constantly remember that God is a transcendent entity whom we cannot truly comprehend or describe. Therefore, according to my grammatical interpretation of Ṭabāṭabā'ī, caution is paramount when speaking of God, suggesting that any reference to God should either be exclusively negative in tone or accompanied by a negative emphasis. In conclude that Ṭabāṭabā'ī would suggest that the true reality of *tawḥīd* is not captured by human knowledge and language, though we are theologically justified to stick to its focal meaning, which is grammatically examined. Instead, he would argue that while human knowledge and language cannot fully capture the true essence of *tawḥīd*, we are theologically justified in adhering to its grammatically examined focal meaning.

## Bibliography

Andrejč, Gorazd. *Wittgenstein and Interreligious Disagreement: A Philosophical and Theological Perspective*. New York: Palgrave Macmillan, 2016.

Burrell, David B. *Analogy and Philosophical Language*. New Haven: Yale University Press, 1973.

———. *Aquinas: God and Action*. London: Routledge and Kegan Paul, 1979.

———. *Freedom and Creation in Three Traditions*. Notre Dame, IN: University of Notre Dame Press, 1993.

———. 'Future of Philosophical Theology as Reflective Awareness'. In *The Future of Philosophical Theology*, edited by Robert A. Evans, 85–112. Philadelphia: The Westminster Press, 1971.

———. *Knowing the Unknowable God: Ibn-Sina, Maimonides, Aquinas*. Notre Dame, IN: University of Notre Dame Press, 1986.

———. 'Philosophy and Religion: Attention to Language and the Role of Reason'. *International Journal for Philosophy of Religion* 38, no. 1–3 (1995): 109–25.

al-Ghazālī, Abū Ḥāmid Muḥammad b. Muḥammad. *Iḥyāʾ ʿulūm al-dīn*. 2nd ed. 16 vols. Beirut: Dār al-Kitāb al-ʿArabī, n.d.

———. 'Iljām al-ʿawāmm ʿan ʿilm al-kalām'. In *Majmūʿat rasāʾil al-Imām al-Ghazālī*, 300–33. Beirut: Dār al-Fikr, 1996.

———. *al-Maqāṣid al-asnā fī sharḥ asmāʾ Allāh al-ḥusnā*. Beirut: Dār al-Mashriq, 1986.

Hewitt, Simon. 'Grammatical Thomism'. *Religious Studies* 57, no. 1 (2021): 30–48. https://doi.org/10.1017/S0034412518000896.

———. *Negative Theology and Philosophical Analysis: Only the Splendour of Light*. Palgrave Frontiers in Philosophy of Religion. Cham: Palgrave Macmillan, 2020.

Ibrahim, Celene. *Islam and Monotheism*. Elements in Religion and Monotheism. Cambridge: Cambridge University Press, 2022.

Milbank, John. 'Foreword'. In *Stations on the Journey of Inquiry: Formative Writings of David B. Burrell, 1962–72*, edited by Mary Budde Ragan, xvi–xvii. Eugene, OR: Cascade Books, 2017.

Mulhall, Stephen. *The Great Riddle: Wittgenstein and Nonsense, Theology and Philosophy*. Oxford: Oxford University Press, 2016.

al-Shīrāzī, Ṣadr al-Dīn. *al-Ḥikma al-mutaʿāliya fī al-asfār al-ʿaqliyya al-arbaʿa*. 9 vols. Beirut: Dār Iḥyāʾ al-Turāth al-ʿArabī, 1981.

———. *Kitāb al-mashāʿir*. Edited by Khālid ʿAbd al-Karīm al-Ṭarzī. N.p.: Muṣawwirāt Maktabat al-Ṣadūq, n.d.

Rizvi, Sajjad. '"Only the Imam Knows Best": The Maktab-e Tafkīk's Attack on the Legitimacy of Philosophy in Iran'. *Journal of the Royal Asiatic Society* 22, no. 3–4 (2012): 487–503. https://doi.org/10.1017/S1356186312000417.

Rizvi, Sajjad, and Ahab Bdaiwi. 'ʿAllāma Ṭabāṭabāʾī (d. 1981), *Nihāyat al-Ḥikma*'. In *The Oxford Handbook of Islamic Philosophy*, edited by Khaled El-Rouayheb and Sabine Schmidtke, 654–75. Oxford: Oxford University Press, 2017. https://doi.org/10.1093/oxfordhb/9780199917389.013.32.

Saeedimehr, Mohammad, and Alireza Musadiqi Haqiqi. 'Naqd-i ʿAllāmih Ṭabāṭabāʾī bar ruykard-i furukahishi-yi ḥikmat-i mutaliyih dar mafhūm shinasi iradih-yi dhati khodavand'. *Ayinih-yi Maʿrifat*, no. 15 (1387 SH/2008): 21–40.

Ṭabāṭabāʾī, Muḥammad Ḥusayn. *The Elements of Islamic Metaphysics* (*Bidayat al-Hikmah*). Translated by Sayyid ʿAli Quli Qaraʾi. 2nd edition. London: ICAS Press, 2003.

———. *Ḥāshiyat al-Kifāya*. Vol. 1. Qom: Bunyad-i ʿIlmi va Fikri-yi ʿAllāmih Ṭabāṭabāʾī, n.d.

———. *al-Mīzān fī tafsīr al-Qurʾān*. 22 vols. Qom: Daftar Intishārāt, 1997.

———. *Nihāyat al-ḥikma*. Qom: Muʾassasat al-Nashr al-Islāmī al-Tābiʿa li-Jimāʿat al-Mudarresīn, 1983.

———. *The Qurʾan in Islam*. Translated by Asadullah Ad-Dhakir Yate. London: Zahra Publications, 1987.

———. *Rasāʾil-i tawḥīdī*. Translated by Ali Shirvani. Qom: Muʾassisih-yi Būstān-i Kitāb,

2009.
———. 'Risālat al-iʿtibāriyyāt'. In *Rasāʾil al-ʿAllāma al-Ṭabāṭabāʾī*, 341–65. Qom: Maktabat Fadak li-Iḥyāʾ al-Turāth, 2007.
———. 'Risālih-yi vaḥy yā shuʿūr-i marmūz'. In *Majmūʿih-yi rasāʾil*, edited by Sayyid Hādī Khusrawshāhī, 1:141–80. 3 vols. Qom: Muʾassisih-yi Būstān-i Kitāb, 2009.
———. *A Shiʿite Anthology*. Translated by William C. Chittick. London: Muhammadi Trust of Great Britain & Northern Ireland, 1981.
———. *Shiʿite Islam*. Translated by Seyyed Hossein Nasr. Albany: State University of New York Press, 1975.
———. 'Taʿlīqāt [scholia]'. In *al-Ḥikma al-mutaʿāliya fī al-asfar al-ʿaqliyya al-arbaʿa*, by Ṣadr al-Dīn al-Shīrāzī. 9 vols. Beirut: Dār Iḥyāʾ al-Turāth al-ʿArabī, 1981.
———. 'Treatise on Divine Acts'. In *Rasāʾil-i tawḥīdī*, translated by Ali Shirvani, 83–150. Qom: Muʾassisih-yi Būstān-i Kitāb, 2009.
———. 'Treatise on Divine Names'. In *Rasāʾil-i tawḥīdī*, translated by Ali Shirvani, 39–74. Qom: Muʾassisih-yi Būstān-i Kitāb, 2009.
———. 'Treatise on Monotheism'. In *Rasāʾil-i tawḥīdī*, translated by Ali Shirvani, 15–33. Qom: Muʾassisih-yi Būstān-i Kitāb, 2009.
———. *Uṣūl-i falsafih va ravish-i riʾalism*. 5 vols. Tehran: Ṣadrā, 1985.
Taheri, Javad. 'I'tibariat: A New Possible Theoretical Basis for Interreligious Dialogue'. *Edinost in Dialog* 74, no. 2 (2019): 99–108. https://doi.org/10.34291/Edinost/74/02/Taheri.
———. 'Semantics of Divine Names: Tabatabai's Principle of "Focal Meaning" and Burrell's Grammar of God-Talk'. *International Journal of Philosophy and Theology* 84, no. 2 (2023): 157–77. https://doi.org/10.1080/21692327.2023.2169743.
Turner, Colin. *Islam: The Basics*. London: Routledge, 2006.
Wittgenstein, Ludwig. *Philosophical Investigations*. Translated by G. E. M. Anscombe. 1958. Reprint, Oxford: Blackwell, 1968.

www.ingramcontent.com/pod-product-compliance
Lightning Source LLC
Chambersburg PA
CBHW041134110526
44590CB00027B/4014
*9781915550064*